POPULATION DYNAMICS

Causes and Consequences of World Demographic Change

POPULATION DYNAMICS

Causes and Consequences

of World Demographic Change

Ralph Thomlinson

CALIFORNIA STATE COLLEGE AT LOS ANGELES

Random House   New York

TO M.W.T., E.B.T., AND W.L.T.
without whose frequent interruptions
I might never have finished this book

Acknowledgments

These tokens of intellectual arrears are offered for contributions to my thinking that cannot be adequately indicated by footnotes.

To Kingsley Davis, my demographic mentor, I owe the maximum plaudits I am able to convey.

Formative influences were also exerted by my instructors in various departments at Columbia University, Yale University, Harvard University, and Oberlin College. Additional indebtedness is due to faculty colleagues and librarians at the University of Wisconsin at Madison, Denison University, and California State College at Los Angeles, as well as to research associates in the Bureau of Applied Social Research at Columbia and the Actuarial Department of the Metropolitan Life Insurance Company. Articulate students have undoubtedly contributed more than I realize from their fertile imaginations and recondite erudition.

The writing process was greatly aided by valuable editorial advice from Gilbert Geis and Charles H. Page. The manuscript also benefited from the extensive clerical assistance of Margaret W. Thomlinson, the cartographic work of Elsa R. Shafer, and the conscientious copy-editing of the Random House staff. To all, herewith my thanks.

Despite this help, I can legitimately claim all faults of organization, content, and writing style that inhere in this book. Being an only author offers the privilege of doing pretty much as I please, but it also carries the handicap of ensuring that there is no co-author to whom to pass the buck for my inevitable blunders.

R.T.

❦ Contents

PART II: MORTALITY, FERTILITY, AND MIGRATION

PART III: ISSUES AND PROBLEMS

PART IV: COMPOSITION AND DESCRIPTION

xviii :: Contents

✕ *Tables*

✖ *Figures*

PART I

PERSPECTIVES

1 ⤬ *The Study of Population*

A recent United Nations report began by declaring that "the growth of world population during the next twenty-five years . . . is at the very heart of the problem of our existence."[1] Population problems are subjects of television shows, books, magazine articles, and newspaper stories. C. P. Snow writes of "the three menaces which stand in our way—H-bomb war, over-population, the gap between the rich and the poor."[2] In the 1960 Presidential election, candidates for major public offices were frequently required to state their views regarding the distribution by United States agencies of birth control information to other countries. Religious dignitaries give speeches and make public proclamations concerning family planning. Enthusiastic amateur demographers have written numerous articles exhorting us to conserve our natural resources or to practice birth control, with the threat of national or even world calamity impending should we ignore these suggestions. And when such prominent communication organizations as Columbia Broadcasting System, *Life* Magazine, and the *Saturday Review* devote valuable time and space to the presentation of controversial demographic issues, we may be sure that the subject is both timely and important. The mark of final public acceptance has been its adoption by the "sick" comedians: "Drive dangerously—avoid overpopulation."

Grave difficulties appear to be arising.

The revolutionary changes in population size, composition, and distribution during the modern era, and especially during the course of this century, have precipitated problems which are among the most

---

[1] United Nations, *The Future Growth of World Population*, New York, 1958, p. v.

[2] Charles Percy Snow, *The Two Cultures and the Scientific Revolution*, Cambridge University Press, London, 1959, pp. 48-49.

serious confronting the contemporary world. . . . Revolutionary population change is still under way. It is not an event which has already occurred, to which adjustment can be made in leisurely fashion. The "population explosion" is, unlike the ordinary explosion, a chain reaction which began several centuries ago and is still going on. Fortunately, man has the ability to observe the process even while being party to it. And in analyzing the facts and assaying their implications man, also fortunately, has the capacity to devise policy and program to control the process, and thereby to ameliorate or prevent its undesirable consequences.[3]

Population is different from the weather; not only does everybody talk about it, but some people *do* do something about it. In the words of Robert Louis Stevenson, "we theorize with a pistol to our head; we are confronted with a new set of conditions on which we have not only to pass judgment, but to take action, before the hour is at an end."

INFLUENCES OF DEMOGRAPHIC PHENOMENA

Ramifications of population change in both industrial and underdeveloped countries are numerous and highly significant. Social scientists and political leaders alike are faced with a need to take account of population trends in their analyses, interpretations, and policies. Similarly, professors of geography, government, economics, and history cannot teach their subjects adequately without making extensive use of demographic facts.

Consumer demand, the relation between labor supply and available jobs, dependency of children and the aged, farm production, housing needs, school construction and the supply of teachers, and a variety of other social phenomena are all influenced by the size and character of population. From the government economist dealing with national and international issues to the social welfare worker trying to help the families in his neighborhood, social science practitioners and theoreticians are continually trying to solve problems that have been generated by demographic events.

Population factors have been advanced as causes of wars, depressions, and other occasions of human distress. The pressure of unchecked population growth against natural resources has become a matter for legislative action by the governments of several Western and Asiatic nations. Other ruling bodies have been worried by the prospect of a declining population and the resulting loss of military manpower and productive labor force. Whatever the direction taken by demographic trends and

[3] Philip M. Hauser, *Population Perspectives*, Rutgers University Press, New Brunswick, 1960, Preface.

characteristics, there are serious consequences to be allowed for or avoided as well as we can.

Population Analysis

Population study involves the number and variety of people in an area and the changes in this number and variety. Population analysis consists of: 1) acquiring basic information concerning population distribution, characteristics, and changes; 2) explaining the causes of changes in these basic facts; and 3) analyzing anticipated consequences of probable future changes.

The word "demography," coined from the Greek by Guillard a century ago,[4] is used as a synonym of population study, although some experts prefer to restrict its meaning to vital statistics (births, deaths, and related statistics).

The word "population" has a Latin derivation and a longer history. Godefroy noted its use in French as early as 1335: "Et n'a oudit terrover villes ne maisons ne populacion de genz" (And he did not hear about land or cities or houses or population of people). Nicolas Oresme, tutor of Charles V and Bishop of Lisieux, is credited with writing in 1349 of "la particion de la populacion de la terre" (the distribution of the population of the earth).[5] In sixteenth-century English, the word originally meant devastation or laying waste—a definition which has come to have somber significance in a new sense today—and was then changed to a meaning akin to modern usage: "neere at hand were great populations."[6] The verb "to populate" was in use in 1578. Francis Bacon, while representing Ipswich in the ninth Parliament of Elizabeth in 1597, spoke against land inclosures and "depopulation of towns and homes of husbandry," expanding these views in "Of the True Greatness of Kingdoms and Estates" in the 1612 edition of his *Essays*. He was the first writer to make extensive use of the word "population" in its modern sense.[7]

THREE DEMOGRAPHIC VARIABLES

Population is a function of three variables: births, deaths, and migration. There are four ways in which the number of people in an area can

---

[4] Achille Guillard, *Éléments de statistique humaine ou démographie comparée*, Guillaumin, Paris, 1855.

[5] Frédéric Godefroy, "Complement," *Dictionnaire de l'ancienne langue française et de tous ses dialectes du ixe au xve siècle*, Librairie Émile Bouillon, Paris, 1880-1902, Vol. X, p. 377.

[6] Thomas Nicholas, *Cortes' Pleasant Historie of the Conquest of the West India*, translated and published in 1578.

[7] James Spedding, *The Letters and Life of Francis Bacon*, London, 1861, Vol. II, pp. 57-60.

change: 1) someone may be born in the area, 2) an inhabitant may die, 3) an outsider may move into the area, and 4) a resident may move out. Consequently, population analysis requires research methods that permit calculation of accurate rates of births, deaths, and in and out migration. These three "facts of life" are called the demographic variables. The first two are sometimes combined to form a composite variable: natural increase, or the excess (or deficit) of births over deaths.

The basic information with which demographers work includes, in addition to knowledge about these three primary variables, data concerning present and past biological characteristics of the inhabitants (age, sex, race), plus their social characteristics (marital status, occupations, literacy, and so forth).

SCOPE OF POPULATION STUDIES

The neologisms "macrodemography" and "microdemography" have been coined to differentiate between large- and small-scale units of research. Whereas macrodemography deals with aggregates of people, with whole systems, and with cultures and societies, microdemography elicits information about individuals, families, small groups, and neighborhoods. The primary units of microdemography are not only smaller than those of macrodemography, but also they are generally internal, dependent parts of the autonomous entities that form the primary units of macrodemography. Macrodemographic research operates on the level of magnitude of continents, nations, and their major areal subdivisions—regions, states, provinces, and cities. Microdemography is "the study of the growth, distribution, and redistribution of the population within a community, state economic area, or other local area. This includes both numerical and compositional aspects, and is performed by using meaningful subdivisions of the community or local area."[8]

Most demographic research is macrodemographic, though copious statistical data for small areas are sometimes published, and research on small groups offers rewarding opportunities to study motives and attitudes. That both macro- and microdemography contribute to comprehension of population behavior is indicated by six examples—two for each demographic variable. In studying deaths, macromortality research traces mass effects of vaccines and sanitation, and micromortality studies investigate personal decisions to seek medical care. Natality may be studied either by macrofertility—for instance, the influence of social

---

[8] Donald J. Bogue, "Micro-Demography," in D. J. Bogue, *Applications of Demography; The Population Situation in the U.S. in 1975*, Scripps Foundation for Research in Population Problems, Oxford, Ohio, and Population Research and Training Center, Chicago, 1957, pp. 46-52.

change and kinship on birth rate trends—or microfertility, the internalization of reproductive norms and attitudes toward voluntary childbearing. So too with research concerning migration: net flow of people from one area to another (macro-), and a family decision whether or not to move (micro-).

PURPOSES AND USES OF DEMOGRAPHY

The three demographic variables, various population characteristics, and related phenomena are used by demographers for four purposes: to ascertain the quantity and distribution of people within the area being studied; to describe past growth, decline, and dispersal as accurately as available records permit; to explore causal relations between population trends and various aspects of social organization; and finally, to attempt to predict future developments and their possible consequences.

Knowledge of population is important to private and public authorities on both national and local levels. Programs relating to education, taxation, military service, social security, farm and factory production, highways, hospitals, shopping centers, housing, and recreation are better shaped if information about the numbers and types of people is taken into consideration.

> If you wish to know how fast a nation is progressing in its economic modernization, look at the figures on occupations, at the percentage of the population engaged in agriculture, in industry, and in services. For an indication of its living standards, look at the life expectancy, because there is no better measure than the years of life a civilization gives each man. Would you know the state of national culture? Literacy figures and years of school completed will give you some idea. Race relations? Look for differences in occupation, income, schooling, and length of life by race. National power? Population size combined with income or occupation figures will provide a basis for estimation.[9]

Outline of This Book

This book is divided into four parts. Part I supplies the historical setting, a brief survey of research procedures, and a theoretical context —all useful before setting out to analyze the dynamics of population. Part II exposes the heart of demography and is organized around the three basic variables. Part III branches out to consider various ramifications of demographic phenomena: cities, food, industrial products, power politics, and instruments of population control. Part IV ab-

---

[9] Katherine Organski and A. F. K. Organski, *Population and World Power*, Alfred A. Knopf, New York, 1961, p. 5.

stracts information concerning demographic attributes of individuals and nations.

The book as a whole attempts to trace world and local changes in human population, especially during the last two centuries. Its purpose is implicit in its title: namely, to explain the changing population situation and the processes and agencies which produce demographic alterations.

2 ❧ World Population History

"Viewed in the long-run perspective, the growth of the earth's population has been a long, thin powder fuse that burns slowly and haltingly until it finally reaches the charge and then explodes."[1] Not only does this sentence emphasize the dynamic quality of recent demographic changes, vividly conveying the contrast with the past, but it also intimates the drastic penalties that may soon be imposed upon mankind unless we take adequate preventive measures.

It is an excellent thing, surely, to belong to an intelligent and dominant species that can choose its own method of becoming extinct. We never think of the dodo or the dinosaur without a feeling of quiet pride and thankfulness. Whereas they, poor ignorant brutes, could only evolve a little and then wait for a changing world to find them unfit to survive, we fortunate masters of all earthly things, including nuclear physics, can venture boldly forth and make the world unfit for ourselves. It is reassuring to learn, moreover, that if we choose, for one reason or another, to avoid annihilation by war, we may still count on an early success. For here is Dr. Heinz von Foerster, a scientist at the University of Illinois, to demonstrate that we can easily become extinct merely by continuing to thrive. Dr. von Foerster has it figured out that in just sixty-six more years, barring some catastrophe, the population of the world will approach infinity, and we all "will be squeezed to death." It is an interesting prospect. It puts us in mind of an uncomfortable quarter of an hour we once spent in a stalled subway car. As we shifted from leg to leg and sought to ease our neighbor's elbow out of our rib cage, we chanced to see, just above our nose, an institutional ad that pointed with some pleasure to the increase in the national population and cheerfully predicted that

---

[1] Kingsley Davis, *Human Society*, The Macmillan Co., New York, 1949, p. 595.

"Your Future Is Great in a Growing America." Humor is out of place in the subway.[2]

Growth of the World's Population

The population of the world today is approximately three billion. By the end of the twentieth century, it will probably *double* that size. Such a tremendous growth has never before been experienced. If this trend continues, as many people will be added to the world's population in the next three or four decades as have been added in all of mankind's previous history. Table 1 contrasts the magnitude and velocity of present and past growth.

TABLE 1. *Billion-Fold Increases in the World's Population*

NUMBER OF PEOPLE	APPROXIMATE DATE OF ACHIEVEMENT	APPROXIMATE TIME TAKEN TO ADD ANOTHER BILLION
One billion	1820	Hundreds of thousands of years
Two billion	1930	110 years
Three billion	1965	35 years
Four billion	1980	15 years
Five billion	1990	10 years

The surplus of births over deaths is adding 150,000 people to the world's population every day. The Office of Population Research at Princeton University has calculated that at our present rate of increase, the people will outweigh the earth's mass in about 1,200 years. In 6,500 years, people will form a solid sphere of live bodies having a radius expanding at the velocity of light, which prohibits removal of the surplus by migration to other planets.[3] Obviously, these *reductio ad impossibile* eventualities of growth and density will not come to pass. "In a finite space nothing, including man, can increase without limit and indeed at current rates of growth the numbers would become fantastically large in a few generations."[4] One way or another, it seems that the present growth trends must decline. And although some experts believe that new food resources could prevent widespread famine for another century, there is substantial agreement among demographers

---

[2] Notes and Comment, "The Talk of the Town," *The New Yorker*, Vol. XXXVI, No. 44, December 17, 1960, p. 29.

[3] Ansley J. Coale, "Increases in Expectation of Life and Population Growth," in International Union for the Scientific Study of Population, *International Population Conference*, Vienna, 1959, p. 36.

[4] Frank W. Notestein, "Introduction," in Thomas Malthus, Julian Huxley, and Frederick Osborn, *Three Essays on Population*, The New American Library, New York, 1960, p. viii.

that uncontrolled human fertility is a luxury the world can no longer afford.

LONG-RUN STABILITY

Homo sapiens is approximately one-half million years old, which makes us one of the younger species. Although world population growth has fluctuated considerably, even declining at times, our average rate of increase has been probably on the order of .000005 per cent per year. Our present rate of increase is approximately 2 per cent per year. From a virtually static situation we have shifted to one in which we are doubling our size in thirty-five years.

Throughout 99 per cent of man's history, population was very sparse. As long as our sustenance came from hunting, fishing, and gathering, huge areas were required to maintain small groups. The average density of Paleolithic man was probably on the order of one person per square mile in hospitable areas. In Arctic and semi-arid regions the density was more like one inhabitant for every 50 to 100 square miles. In Tasmania, the indigenous density was about one person per 100 square miles. During the Upper Paleolithic period, it is estimated that there may have been only about 250 men in what is now England. With the shift to settled agriculture and the domestication of animals some 10,000 years ago, a greater density became possible. But even then, from the Neolithic era until around three hundred years ago, the world's population continued to grow with extreme slowness.

For example, the population of India in 300 B.C., estimated at approximately 100 million, was still the same in 1600 A.D. Thus in two thousand years there was virtually no population growth. But in the last three and one-half centuries, India's population doubled, and then doubled again.

Available evidence indicates that a common condition prior to 1650 was general population stability, with frequent irregularities. During periods of peace and plenty, a slow growth took place; but not many years elapsed before a war, a crop failure, or an epidemic resulted in a sharp loss of population. The net result was a zigzag growth curve showing an extremely gradual long-term increase.

CULTURAL EVOLUTION

Three revolutionary changes in man's ability to adjust to and control his environment have had profound demographic consequences. The first of these cultural accomplishments was the acquisition of tools some million years ago. The tool-using revolution antedates man; use of tools by prehuman primates may even have been the major impetus giving rise to the initial differentiation of *Homo sapiens* from apes. By increasing primate ability to cope with his environment, tools probably increased the density of habitation.

Second came the agricultural revolution about 10,000 years ago, changing man from a hunting-gathering-scavenging nomad to a villager with domesticated animals and cultivated fields of wheat and barley. Without settled farming, congregation into cities would have been impossible. This great achievement of our species took place initially in the fertile crescent of southwest Asia and later (possibly independently) in China and (certainly independently) in the Western Hemisphere. In the million or more years intervening between these two revolutions, men and other primates must have devoted their days to the search for their next meal—and when they made a kill, they gorged on it. Not until man learned to produce his own food (and store it against hard times) instead of collecting it subject to the vicissitudes of his environs did his horizon expand. He could then look forward confidently to eating next week, and his energies and preoccupations were released for a wide spectrum of new endeavors and inventions.

The third of these technological revolutions was industrialization.

Each of these three periods is a stage in demographic history. Achievement of a new technological level was accompanied by a surge of population. Associated with every stage of culture is a usual density of habitation—an equilibrium between the opposing forces of natural increase and environmental restrictions. Each density level exceeds its predecessor. When prehominid primates handled the first crude tools, they made possible a higher density than had ever before been achievable. Attainment of the environmental control implicit in settled farming permitted a greater density, and in the relatively short time of a few thousand years the number of men increased appreciably, though not rapidly. In the scientific-industrial period, a still higher density became feasible.

Cultural evolution makes possible (though not inevitable) demographic evolution. Population expands when enabled to do so by new technological weapons in the battle against environment. For nearly the entirety of man's existence, we were forced to concede the upper hand to nonhuman forces, a balance of power reversed only by the technological skills acquired during the last quarter millennium. However, some scholars are coming to tremble at the prospect that man's present phenomenal increase may turn us to a state of subjection to natural forces—a speculation of doubtful probability.

THE DEMOGRAPHIC REVOLUTION

After 1650 the world's population began to show signs of significant increase, an acceleration which became rapid following the industrial revolution. Table 2 shows the tremendous quickening of the growth of the population of the world. Human beings have quintupled since 1650 and trebled since 1800. Currently, natural increase amounts to about 50 million people a year or 6,000 an hour.

If the 1950-60 growth rate continues, there will be 6 billion human mouths to feed at the end of this century and 17 billion within one hundred years from now. Moreover, the growth rate itself continues to

TABLE 2. *Growth of World Population**

YEAR	POPULATION	PER CENT INCREASE PER YEAR SINCE THE PREVIOUS DATE	YEARS TO DOUBLE SINCE THE PREVIOUS DATE
10,000 B.C.	100,000-10,000,000	a	b
5,000 B.C.	5,000,000-20,000,000	a	b
0	200,000,000	a	b
1300 A.D.	400,000,000	a	b
1650	.5 billion	.1	1000
1700	.6 billion	.2	300
1750	.7 billion	.3	230
1800	.9 billion	.4	180
1850	1.2 billion	.5	140
1900	1.6 billion	.6	120
1950	2.4 billion	.8	90
1960	2.8 billion	1.7	40

ª Smaller than .05 per cent.
ᵇ A very large number of years.
All figures are rounded to avoid a false impression of accuracy. Even today world population totals are not highly accurate; early figures are best described as informed guesses. However, the over-all import of the table is factually substantiated.

* United Nations, *Demographic Yearbook: 1949-50*, New York, p. 10; United Nations, press releases, 1959-62; A. M. Carr-Saunders, *World Population*, The Clarendon Press, Oxford, 1936, p. 42; and Kingsley Davis, "Future Population Trends and Their Significance," *Transactions of the Eighteenth North American Wildlife Conference*, Wildlife Management Institute, 1953, pp. 8-21.

rise, showing no sign of reaching a plateau. Since our rate of increase is increasing, these figures may be too conservative.

For many Americans, rising rates seem inherently desirable. An expanding population is part of the everyday outlook and increase is a criterion of "normality." In one city, reported by the Bureau of the Census to have had a very small decrease in population during the previous decade, City Hall was shaken, businessmen were shocked, and enraged citizens wrote letters to the editors of local papers claiming that the Census was faulty. Following an indication that the Census was accurate, the letters changed to the themes "Don't give up the ship" and "Those who desert our town(ship) are rats." Given the traditional high rate of increase in the United States, Americans, not surprisingly, are accustomed to taking for granted that population will grow in every city and state. But this history is unusual; indeed, few countries have had such a record of growth over a period of two centuries.

Twentieth-century world population changes are even more abrupt. The two hundred and fifty years before 1900 were characterized by considerable population increase, but its pace was negligible in comparison to growth in the present century. Never before has there occurred such a blossoming of births coupled with a sharp curtailment of deaths. The death rate is becoming smaller annually. In the frame of reference of a previous era, everyone is living "on borrowed time."

For every four persons on the earth in 1950, there are now five. For every five today, there will probably be ten in the year 2000. In the last minute, some 120 people died and about 190 babies were born in the world—a net gain of about 70 a minute.

Causes of the Population Explosion

At first inspection, the unparalleled rate of increase in population growth might be attributed to rising birth rates. However, no proof exists of increased fertility continuing for a century or longer during modern times in any sizeable section of the world. On the contrary, considerable evidence points to a decline in fertility. Likewise, migration obviously cannot be a factor in world population change. Therefore, the third demographic variable, mortality, must be responsible for this explosive population increase.

MORTALITY DECLINE

The cause of the rapidly mounting rate of population growth is clearly the spectacular reduction of the death rate made possible by recent medical discoveries. In earlier centuries other forces were at work to lower mortality. A rising standard of living resulted from extravagant improvements in agricultural and industrial production and also in the ability to distribute these goods quickly, widely, and inexpensively.

For nearly all of his existence Homo sapiens had to fight hard to survive. Since he was threatened by inclement climate, predatory animals, starvation, and disease, it is miraculous that man ever endured beyond those early times. Even when he achieved a settled existence founded on agricultural and domesticated animals, life remained challenging. Most people died at what would now be considered a very young age, over half before attaining adulthood. Those who survived were frequently permanently weakened or crippled by disease or malnutrition. Under such conditions, men had to do everything in their power to increase their numbers, lest they perish.

Credit for the improved mortality is commonly given to medicine, but in fact scientific medicine and sanitation did not have a potent impact on mortality until the late nineteenth century. A more important factor, long before then, was the gradual adoption of improved industrial and agricultural production techniques, whereby food and other scarce goods began to be available to most people in large and regular quantity. The more abundant, consistent, and varied food supply, coupled with such improvements as central heating and other elements in the general rise in the standard of living, resulted in a virtual doubling of life expectancy since the late seventeenth century. Famine and disease ceased to decimate populations. Old people came to be less doubtful about surviving the winter. This decline in the death rate probably began in Europe and then diffused to other continents.

FERTILITY DECLINE

Paradoxically, a reduction of fertility occurred during this period of modernization and population expansion. The tremendous population growth resulted from the lag between the decreasing death rate and the decreasing birth rate.

At the same time that men were receptive to techniques which would minimize mortality, they were attempting to maximize fertility. In the struggle against the adversities of nature, a high birth rate was essential to counterbalance the high death rate. Thus any belief or practice that would encourage people to bear and rear children was *eufunctional*, that is, had positive consequences for society. Religious and secular authorities were consistently pronatalist; the traditional institutions and other elements of the social systems were usually so ordered as to maximize the populace. Value systems encouraged people to have as many children as they could and to keep them alive as long as possible. The Biblical blessing was: "Be fruitful and multiply."

When methods became available for saving people from disease and starvation, they were adopted quickly because they conformed to existing beliefs; by contrast, lowering the birth rate was generally opposed because it contradicted the prevailing value system. And ingrained norms often linger long after they have become inappropriate. As long as the mores favor bearing as many children as possible, fertility is apt to remain high. Under such conditions, if mortality control reaches a high level of efficiency, natural increase is substantial.

In contrast, economic changes encouraged lowering the birth rate. People became aware of the financial liability of too many children in a competitive, individualistic, nonagricultural society. "He travels fastest who travels alone." The large family became a heavy burden, especially for the bourgeoisie. "He that hath wife and children hath given hostages to fortune; for they are impediments to great enterprises, either of virtue or mischief."[5] "Children are no longer 'production durables.' Children do not produce income for parents as they did in the agrarian period of history. They are now 'consumer durables' and cost money to bring into the world and rear. In fact, a United States Department of Agriculture estimate shows that it costs something over $15,000 per child to rear him to his sixteenth birthday."[6]

As a result, mores regarding childbearing were violated privately without public acknowledgement. In some countries, fertility declined to approximately the same level as mortality. But this lowering of the birth rate lagged far behind the saving of lives.

NONDEMOGRAPHIC CHANGES

A useful image in explaining the demographic revolution is the ladder of abstraction. Ground level represents the present population. The first rung of the ladder consists of a simple statement of population increase, its rate of change, and the acceleration or deceleration of that rate. The second rung or level of explanation requires examination of the three demographic variables; we conclude that mortality decline is the cause of the population increase. Ascending to the third rung involves abandoning purely demographic variables in favor of the social and economic factors that have contributed to these declining death rates. The fourth carries the causal chain one step further, into the realm of religion and the value system. Thus a complete explanation of the causal sequence underlying these demographic events depends on a thorough examination of the culture as well as of the constituent people.

One important hypothesis attempts to find the functional interrelations between rungs three and four. Economic historian Max Weber, in a work that has come to be regarded as a sociological classic,[7] analyzed the interaction between religion and economics, comparing world religions and economic systems in order to clarify the relation between religious values and the rise of capitalism. His thesis is that Protestantism supplied a congenial ethos for the set of values upon which modern capitalism is founded: hard work, acquisition, self-discipline, accumula-

---

[5] Francis Bacon, "Of Marriage and Single Life," *Essays or Counsels: Civil and Moral,* 1625, Essay VIII.

[6] Bernice Milburn Moore, *Practical Home Economics;* quoted in Consumers Union of U.S., *Consumer Reports,* Vol. XXVI, No. 1, January 1961, p. 6.

[7] Max Weber, *The Protestant Ethic and the Spirit of Capitalism* (translated by Talcott Parsons), George Allen and Unwin Ltd., London, 1930.

tion of money, rationality, competition, and individual initiative. *The Protestant Ethic* begins by quoting Benjamin Franklin: "The way to wealth . . . depends chiefly on two words, industry and frugality. . . . Make the best use of both."

It was on these cultural supports that capitalism leaned in its formative years. "In praising the virtues of thrift, sobriety, promptness and industry, Protestantism facilitated the growth of a system of economy founded on monetary accumulations and regularity in productive processes. Grass may grow and sheep may graze if the peasant lies drunk under the hedge occasionally, but the wheels of mills cannot turn steadily if boiler stokers must have frequent debauches."[8] The patron saint of this movement was John Calvin, who "made the pursuit of wealth and preservation of property a Christian duty, calling for the same arduous discipline as the warfare against the temptations of the flesh. He exalted the acquisitive virtues of enterprise, diligence, sobriety, frugality, thrift. He invented an ideal type hitherto unknown to religion and culture, a type neither humanistic nor ascetic—the God-fearing businessman."[9] Two centuries later, John Wesley struggled to justify the economic ways of Western man: "We must exhort all Christians to gain all they can and to save all they can; that is, in effect, to grow rich." The Protestant motto "God helps those that help themselves is readily twisted into the belief that one helps God by helping himself, and it has been observed that presently they began helping themselves to a lot; but at its purest, their ethical and religious program lent itself to such perversion."[10] Nowhere has this doctrine been more enthusiastically embraced than in America, where

> a profit has never been without honor. "Let your Business ingross the most of your time," Cotton Mather advised the Puritan merchants. Their successors have never wanted for similar welcome encouragement from latter-day shepherds. "The American Ministers of the Gospel do not attempt to draw or fix all the thoughts of man upon the life to come," de Tocqueville remarked, adding that "it is often difficult to ascertain from their discourses whether the principal object of religion is to procure eternal felicity in the other world or prosperity in this." The difficulty lingers on . . . [in] Dr. Norman Vincent Peale.[11]

---

[8] Charles A. Beard, "Individualism and Capitalism," in Edwin R. A. Seligman (ed.), *Encyclopaedia of the Social Sciences*, The Macmillan Co., New York, 1930, Vol. I, p. 149.

[9] Herbert J. Muller, *The Uses of the Past*, The New American Library, New York, 1952, p. 266.

[10] *Ibid.*, p. 267.

[11] John Bainbridge, "The Super-American State: VII—Prosperity in This," *The New Yorker*, Vol. XXXVII, No. 14, May 20, 1961, p. 49.

Insofar as these religious values have the latent function of supporting a higher standard of living, they contribute to lower mortality. They also indirectly encourage smaller families. Thus they encourage both elements of the transition from the old balance to the new.

Old and New Balances

A new kind of demographic stability was first reached in northwest Europe, and later elsewhere. Instead of high fertility balancing against a high level of mortality, countries like France, England, and Sweden maintained their population through low fertility and low mortality.

FIGURE 1. *The Demographic Transition*

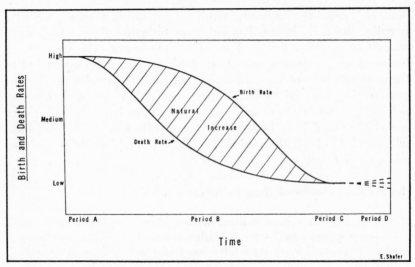

These two conditions are called "the old balance" and "the new balance," respectively.[12]

Figure 1 is a schematic diagram of the shift from the old to the new balance. Specific dates and rates are omitted so that the graph may have general applicability rather than being descriptive of only one country; different nations enter periods A, B, and C at different times. Period A represents the old balance, period C the new. The transitional period B occurs when mortality has declined or is declining rapidly and

---

[12] Kingsley Davis, "The World Demographic Transition," *The Annals of the American Academy of Political and Social Science*, Vol. CCXXXVII, January 1945, pp. 1-11.

fertility is declining slowly. The shaded area represents natural increase —the growth of population due to the surplus of births over deaths.

THE OLD BALANCE

The old balance is normal to mankind. Indeed, throughout almost all of human existence, man's control over environment was negligible. The result was a high death rate. Consequently a large supply of births was necessary if society were to balance the large number of deaths— a very inefficient way to maintain the population.

Its extreme form was animal-like. Hobbes characterized man's natural state as one of "continual fear and danger of violent death, and the life of man solitary, poor, nasty, brutish, and short."[13] The high incidence of various kinds of illnesses, debilitating and death-provoking famines, and the sometimes appalling lack of personal hygiene and public sanitation all contributed to make life both unpredictable and brief. The ravages of pain and the pangs of bereavement were familiar to both adults and children.

> Under the old regime of high fertility and high mortality women experienced the drain and danger of pregnancy often to no purpose, because a large proportion of the offspring died before reaching maturity. Too much effort was spent in trying to bring each new generation to adulthood; too much energy was lost in sickness, malnutrition, and mourning; too much time was taken for mere sustenance. The new type of demographic balance released a large part of this energy—a tremendous amount of human energy—for other things.[14]

Consider the difficulty of trying to run a complex industrialized society like ours under these conditions. How would the advance planning and careful timing of manufacturing plants, transportation systems, and business organizations fare, demanding as they do reasonable predictability of personnel as regards both attendance and vigor? Or an educational system in which half of the students died before completing their schooling? Imagine how large school taxes would be if property owners had to pay for the education of huge numbers of children who would never be economically productive.

THE NEW BALANCE

In contrast, the new balance represents an improved condition of human efficiency and health, a level of well-being never before achieved by any other species or society. And—be it good or bad—the new balance involves a larger number of people. With fewer deaths, less

---

[13] Thomas Hobbes, *Leviathan*, London, 1651, chap. XIII.
[14] Davis, *Human Society, op. cit.*, pp. 600-601.

sickness, and fewer pregnancies, considerably less effort is required to bring a generation to maturity. Production of agricultural and industrial commodities is greater because of the larger proportion of the populace in the adult ages and the smaller percentage of people who are chronically unable to do a full week's work.

This novel equilibrium is accompanied by relative freedom from health worries. "Eat, drink, and be merry, for tomorrow we may die" is no longer a tenable outlook on life. Our ancestors' extensive preoccupation with death and sickness has been replaced by an assumption of good health and long life. We take it for granted that our children will reach adulthood, and a son or daughter who is deceased before his aged parent is said to have died untimely.

This modern equipoise is not possible, however, for all types of societies. Western countries did not achieve it until after the industrial revolution, and it is unlikely that any region can reach this high standard of living without industrialization and its concomitants. No one factor is responsible for achieving the new balance: its creation is the joint accomplishment of the change from an "other world" to a "this world" outlook, of the maturation of science and the invention of manifold applications of discoveries, and of many other influences. The demographic variables are only a part of a larger nexus.

Once a society gives up the subsistence level of living (old balance) and adopts modern technology (new balance), it can support a larger number of people (because technological advances aid the food supply). Further, the society cannot retain its enhanced food supply without also retaining the advanced standard of living and high per capita consumption. It cannot regress to mere subsistence and keep the same size, because its ability to produce and distribute large quantities of food and other necessities is dependent upon other capacities which would disappear under subsistence conditions—for example, a rapid and efficient transportation system, modern agricultural techniques (including education of farmers), and mass production.

IMBALANCE

In the interval between abandonment of the old balance and achievement of the new, rapid natural increase results from the discrepancy between the still-high birth rate and the newly-lowered death rate (counterbalanced in some areas by a net outward migration). This growth is very helpful for underpopulated nations, supplying larger markets, more productive manpower, greater military potential, and enthusiastic optimism. But for countries already overcrowded, population increase impedes improvement in the standard of living and may even decrease military strength through its internal disruptiveness.

The imbalance of period B in the demographic transition has many results. Rapid increase among the peasants of Europe after 1750, for instance, promoted economic and social instability in a society that placed high value on stability. Demographic and economic changes induced heavy migration to European cities and to the new world.

> An ironic providence had, in the old days, made sure that not too many boys would reach an age to claim a man's estate. The same kind fate that kept more children alive complicated the problem of their settlement. . . . Men grew up for whom there was no longer room within the constricted acreage of the village. . . . You cannot make the land to stretch. . . . Some early gave up and joined the drift to the towns, where, as in England, they supplied the proletariat that manned the factories of the Industrial Revolution.[15]

Others swelled the ranks of émigrés to the Americas. "Europe watched them go—in less than a century and a half, well over thirty-five million of them from every part of the continent. In this common flow were gathered up people of the most diverse qualities, people whose rulers had for centuries been enemies, people who had not even known of each other's existence. Now they would share each other's future.[16]

Stages of Demographic Evolution

These world changes suggested to demographers that a typology might be constructed which would describe the historical transition already made by some countries and perhaps permit us to guess what will happen in those countries just beginning to abandon the old balance. Let us consider four possibilities: 1) high birth rate, high death rate; 2) high birth rate, low death rate; 3) low birth rate, low death rate; and 4) low birth rate, high death rate. The last type is rare and obviously could not be maintained for many generations without a large in-migration to keep the society going; it is illustrated by the period of early contact between Western culture and some primitive peoples. The first three possibilities have been grouped into a widely accepted typology known as the transition theory.[17] In the order given above,

---

[15] Oscar Handlin, *The Uprooted*, Little, Brown and Co., Boston, 1951, pp. 26-33.
[16] *Ibid.*, p. 35.
[17] Warren S. Thompson, "Recent Trends in World Population," *American Journal of Sociology*, Vol. XXXIV, No. 6, May 1929, pp. 959-975; and Frank W. Notestein and others, *The Future Population of Europe and the Soviet Union*, League of Nations, Geneva, 1944.

the types are customarily labeled: 1) high potential growth, 2) transitional growth, and 3) incipient decline. In 1950 three-fifths of the world's people were in the first category and one-fifth in each of the other two.

This tripartite scheme may be regarded from four points of view: a) as a simple historical description of what happened in the past, b) as a classification scheme, c) as a theoretical explanation of the forces impelling demographic changes, and d) as a prediction of the sequence through which countries will progress. The present focus is on the first and second viewpoints. Where a country has in fact proceeded sequentially through these three stages, the first viewpoint is legitimate in studying its history. When comparing countries at a given time, the classification scheme is valuable. Options (c) and (d) will be treated later.

HIGH POTENTIAL GROWTH

This first stage describes the old balance commonly found in agrarian cultures with traditional tribal or peasant social organizations largely unaffected by industrialization, secularization, and urbanization. Both fertility and mortality are very high. The former is rooted in well-entrenched marriage customs and reproductive norms; the latter maintained by endemic disease and chronic undernourishment. The death rate is subject to recurrent increases in response to epidemics, famines, wars, and other disasters not controllable by the skills of that culture; natural increase accelerates in times of bumper harvests, political stability, and absence of pandemics. These natural and man-made year-by-year fluctuations tend to cancel one another out in the long run, eventuating in a near-static condition of growth.

The label for stage one is derived from the high rate of growth that is latent in the old balance. The decisive reduction of the death rate customarily attendant upon a rising level of living might cause the population to enlarge rapidly. Also, the low life expectancy produces a concentration of people in the age groups having the greatest likelihood of becoming parents. Thus the age distribution favors continuing high natality.

Many people are now living under conditions of high fertility and high mortality (most of Africa and much of South America and Asia). Lowering their death rates will probably result in rapid and possibly lengthy population increase. But while some of these countries have room for such expansion, many are already crowded, thus presenting an obstacle to raising the living standard.

TRANSITIONAL GROWTH

When the potential for natural increase of the first stage is released, stage two is reached—B in Figure 1. It is this type that Kingsley Davis had in mind in the opening sentence of this chapter when he referred to the explosion that occurs when the burning powder fuse reaches the explosive. Transitional growth nations have achieved considerable control over their death rates, but their slender control over birth rates makes for erratic but high natural increase.

Constituting in mid-twentieth century about a fifth of the world's population, type two is almost certain to comprise a larger proportion by the end of the century. Countries which have attained control over death but only partly cut their fertility—Southeast Europe, many Latin American nations, India, and the Soviet Union—are now undergoing rapid growth. Transitional growth usually accompanies the first steps toward industrialization and urbanization.

European countries moved from stage one to stage two earlier than others, and most have continued on to stage three. For those countries now in the first stage it is generally assumed that they will soon reach the second level, as preventive medicine, sanitation, and improved food supply make inroads on the death rate. With modern medical discoveries open to them, these now underdeveloped areas should require far less time for the passage to the transitional stage than was necessary for the nations of northwest Europe, who pioneered this movement.

INCIPIENT DECLINE

The first stage in the transition theory can be likened to a coiled spring, the second to a forceful expansion following release of restraining pressure, and the third to a relaxed, unwound spring with its force largely expended.

Completion of the move toward modernization is ordinarily coupled with lowered fertility, bringing about the new balance. Most of Europe is in this category.

A few of the northwest European nations reached a condition of population decline in the 1930's, but the name of this type must not be taken as a prediction of population decrease. In fact, some of the areas in this class are now growing rather rapidly. At the time the transition theory was formulated and disseminated, leaders in many countries feared that population decline was imminent—and in the international depression of the 1930's, this fear was legitimate. But since then, the conditions of life and the fertility practices of the populace have changed, and few persons worry today about the prospect of an abidingly dwindling population. Present-day demographers probably would not choose the label "incipient decline." But it has achieved such universal acceptance that a change in terminology would introduce confusion.

PROSPECTS FOR THE FUTURE

Demographers expect countries now in the high potential and transitional stages to enter the third stage in the future. The rapidity with which they pass through the transitional growth period to stage three will depend heavily on their readiness and ability to limit their fertility. Davis identifies three possibilities over the next four to ten decades in underdeveloped areas: "1) Gradual industrialization and modernization which eventually will affect fertility as it has done in the now industrialized countries. 2) Decline in fertility prior to such industrialization and modernization. 3) Rise in death rate."[18] The first is usually thought most probable, but rapid growth in already dense areas impedes economic development, and in any case, the process is very slow. Although the third choice disturbs the equanimity of all but misanthropists, it is definitely possible. The second prospect has never before been achieved— but that does not demonstrate that it is impossible. A peasant-agricultural population might espouse a planned fertility program if the mores were receptive or ready for change and if the government or another agency supplied sufficient encouragement and information concerning techniques.

In Figure 1, period A corresponds to the High Potential Growth type, period B to Transitional Growth, and period C to the stage of Incipient Decline. Period D is a crude indication of three possibilities for future fertility and mortality: rising rates, stability, or falling rates. To date, not enough countries have entered this stage to permit demographers to give it a title or to use it predictively or even descriptively. Perhaps the United States is now in what demographers in a few decades will agree to call stage four, by whatever name. Other countries too are possibly entering a new phase of demographic development. However, until we acquire more evidence to this effect, we cannot yet justify the adoption of period D as a supplement to the Thompson-Notestein typology. We cannot even approximate the correct relative positions of the dotted lines representing the birth and death rates for this period.

These three stages have distinguishing economic properties. The third stage has a productive economy, high efficiency, and the world's highest level of living. The intermediate stage is characterized by a less productive economy in which machine industry is spreading and agricultural products are increasing (though not always keeping pace with population growth). Technological backwardness is being abandoned in favor

---

[18] Davis, "Future Population Trends and Their Significance," *op. cit.*, pp. 18-21.

of Western economic standards, offering anticipations of greater economic, demographic, and political stature. The earliest period is characterized by a low level of productivity, primitive energy sources, and dim immediate prospects of a rising level of living. These peoples often lack necessary surplus capital for investment in education, social welfare, and producing equipment. Many, however, have raised living standards, improved health conditions, and moved into stage two.

Conclusion

For most of man's existence, the earth's population grew at an almost infinitesimal rate. Then in the late seventeenth century, acceleration became rapid enough to inspire demographers to call the last three hundred years a time of "population explosion"—though skeptics might prefer the terms "backfire" or "population pop."

This demographic swelling is attributable to declining mortality, which in turn was brought about by a better level of living. In a tiny village near Calcutta, an old man with a gray stubble of beard, broken teeth, and tired eyes told the story of a lifetime of demographic change: "When I was a boy, they took away forty or fifty bodies after a cholera epidemic. It happened every five or ten years. Now they come and vaccinate our children. I have lived here almost seventy years. The biggest change in my time has been health. We've learned how to keep from dying."[19] In some countries, fertility has now become approximately as low as mortality, generating the new balance.

Explosions are caused not by force alone, but by force that overpowers restraint. The powder charge that set off the population explosion was excess fertility. The old restraint (high mortality) was imposed upon man by the environment over which he had feeble and insubstantial control; the new restraint (low fertility) lies in his command of his own nature through family planning. The explosion mentioned in the opening sentence of this chapter was the beginning of a chain reaction of ferocious aspect. Whether we will dampen it with fertility limitation or let it continue and try to harness the resultant manpower is a momentous issue today.

---

[19] Reported by Rowland Evans, Jr., "India Experiments with Sterilization," *Harper's Magazine*, Vol. CCXXIII, No. 1338, November 1961, pp. 79-80.

3 ✖ Data Sources and Formal Analysis

Because of the enormous expense involved, the collection of population statistics is normally confined to governmental agencies. Analysis and interpretation of these data are conducted largely at academic institutes and a few independent private foundations.

RESEARCH CENTERS

The United Nations has several agencies which deal with population, including the Population Branch of the Bureau of Social Affairs, New York; the Statistical Office of the Department of Economic and Social Affairs (which publishes the *Demographic Yearbook*), New York; the Latin American Center for Research and Teaching in Demography, Santiago, Chile; the Demographic Training and Research Center, Bombay; the Food and Agricultural Organization, Rome; the International Labour Office, Geneva; and United Nations Educational, Scientific, and Cultural Organization, Paris. They all publish reports and conduct or encourage research.

One prominent government agency is L'Institut National d'Études Démographiques (National Institute for Demographic Studies), established in 1945 in Paris. The I.N.E.D. publishes the quarterly journal *Population* and also produces a monograph series. It is dependent upon the Ministry of Public Health and Population for financial support, but maintains almost complete autonomy.

Private organizations are best represented in the United States. The Population Council in New York City was formed in 1953 to encourage research and training by awarding grants for demographic and medical studies. The oldest research institute is the Scripps Foundation for Research in Population Problems in Oxford, Ohio, founded in 1922 by E. W. Scripps, the newspaper publisher. The Milbank Memorial Fund of New York City issues a quarterly journal of demography and public health and sponsors annual conferences of experts. The Metropolitan Life Insurance Company maintains a permanent research staff analyzing data obtained from their 40 million policy-holders. The Population Reference Bureau in Washington, D.C., founded in 1929, is an autonomous institution bringing research results to the public through a small periodical.

Some universities have graduate programs in population. Two of the largest ones are the Population Research and Training Center at the University of Chicago, founded in 1954, and the Office of Population Research at Princeton University, established in 1936. Princeton publishes the quarterly bibliography *Population Index* jointly with the Population Association of America.

These governmental, private, and university organizations are all of recent origin. There are four noteworthy differences, however, between present-day demographic research and that of its formative years: 1) investigations now are frequently conducted by teams rather than by individual scholars; 2) specialists have replaced the old-fashioned generalists; 3) the often minimal research skills of the early days have yielded to careful training in methodology; and 4) practitioners, who were once amateurs, are now professionals.

The Development of Demography

Curiosity about the number and character of inhabitants arose with the first civilizations, usually in response to some practical motivation. Except for a few isolated instances, the disinterested, objective study of demographic variables dates only from the seventeenth century.

POLITICAL ARITHMETIC

Several men have been nominated for the title "Father of Demography," among them, Giovanni Botero (1533-1617), John Graunt (1620-1674), Johann Peter Sussmilch (1707-1767), and Antoine de Montyon (1733-1820). Botero's claim rests mainly on his 1589 treatise in Italian, *On the Causes of the Growth of Cities*, in which he discussed urban-rural differences in fertility and mortality. His *Wealth of Nations* (1606) anticipated Malthus by stating that while the power to produce subsistence has limits, man's reproductive powers are limitless. However, neither book was comprehensive nor analytical enough to be of paramount significance for the early history of demography.

Graunt undoubtedly deserves the greatest eminence among the demographic pioneers. His study of the causes of death (including a primitive life table), published in 1662, is the first true landmark in the history of demography. Using burial permits and parish christening records from London and environs, Graunt systematically assembled data for the years 1604 through 1661, probing for weaknesses and seeking numerical regularities. His conclusions included the following observations:

> That about one third of all that were ever quick die under five years old, and about thirty-six percentum under six.
> Abortives, and Stillborn, to those that are Christned are as one to twenty.
> The Plague Anno 1603 lasted eight years, that in 1636 twelve years, but that in 1625 continued but one single year.
> That about ⅕ part of the whole people died in the great Plague-years, so two other fifth parts fled.
> That Plagues always come in with King's Reigns is most false.
> That in London there have been twelve Burials for eleven Christenings.
> That in the Country there have been, contrary-wise, sixty-three Christenings for fifty-two Burials.
> That about 6000 per Annum come up to London out of the Country.
> Physicians have two Women Patients to one Man, and yet more Men die than Women.
> That every Wedding one with another produces four children.
> London not so healthful now as heretofore.[1]

Current worry about smog had its seventeenth-century counterpart: "I have heard that Newcastle is more unhealthful then [sic] other places, and that many People cannot endure the smoak of London, not onely for its unpleasantness, but for the suffocations which it causes."[2] Shelley was more vivid: "Hell is a city much like London—a populous and smoky city."

Several English contemporaries of Graunt also warrant citation. William Petty (1623-1687) helped Graunt in his research and did original work of his own. Stressing the fiscal and adminstrative advantages of a large population ("fewness of numbers is real poverty"), he wrote extensively on applications of demography to economic and political issues. Gregory King (1648-1712) continued Graunt's work. The astronomer and bon vivant Edmund Halley (1656-1742), whose name is immortalized by a comet, contributed a 15-page monograph

---

[1] John Graunt, *Natural and Political Observations Made Upon the Bills of Mortality*, London, 1662, reprinted by The Johns Hopkins Press, Baltimore, 1939, pp. 9-15.
[2] *Ibid.*, p. 76.

containing the first life table using both births and deaths (Graunt had used only deaths).[3] Halley also invented the term "expectation of life."

Sussmilch, a Lutheran clergyman and quondam chaplain to Frederick the Great, wrote a book that is the second major landmark in demographic history.[4] This massive work of 1,200 pages (with an appendix of 68 tables) was the first comprehensive book on population. Though motivated by a desire to demonstrate that vital events are the expressions of the divine mind, Sussmilch's assiduous data-gathering and sedulous analysis was empirical and heavily statistical. He tried to construct a mortality table of universal applicability by combining Swedish, German, and French data. His life table was founded on a larger quantity of factual evidence that anyone else had accumulated up to this time (indeed, it became the standard reference for German insurance companies for the next two hundred years). He favored early marriage as an encouragement to a growing population, but preferred a slowly declining rate of growth. Sussmilch was extensively quoted by Malthus.

Daniel Bernoulli (1700-1782) published a statistical study of the efficacy of inoculation against smallpox, using Halley's life table.[5] This was one of the first applications of the statistical method and the life table to a single disease. Bernoulli computed the risk of death and the life expectancy at various ages for both induced (variolated) and natural cases.

The last of the four possible fathers of demography is Antoine Jean Baptiste Robert Auget de Montyon, who wrote under the pseudonym Moheau.[6] His treatise on the population of France was the first non-moralistic and systematic analysis of the growth of population and the causes of population change. However, he does not measure up to the stature of Graunt and Sussmilch.

VITAL STATISTICS

Demography has been restricted in all aspects of its development by the supply of basic data. Until the mid-eighteenth century, data were insufficient to support a full-scale discipline. But with the advance of registration systems and census-type enumerations, the way was cleared

---

[3] Edmund Halley, "An Estimate of the Degrees of the Mortality of Mankind, Drawn from Curious Tables of the Births and Funerals at the City of Breslaw, with an Attempt to Ascertain the Price of Annuities upon Lives," *Philosophical Transactions of the Royal Society of London*, Vol. XVII, 1693, pp. 596-610.

[4] Johann Peter Sussmilch, *The Divine Order in the Changes of the Human Race Shown by Its Birth, Death, and Propagation*, Berlin, 1741, second edition, 2 vols., 1762.

[5] Daniel Bernoulli, "Essai d'une nouvelle analyse de la mortalité causée par la petite vérole," *Histoire de l'académie royale des sciences, année 1760*, Paris, 1766.

[6] Moheau, *Recherches et considérations sur la population de la France*, Paris, 1778.

in many countries to begin the systematic analysis of population trends.

The history of science is in large part a story of increasing quantification, and demography and sociology are no exceptions to this rule. Indeed, the development of demography is bound up with the origins of statistics. "Demography would not truly exist without statistics. . . . Statistics is not its only tool, but it is in many ways a precious instrument. Demography is indebted to the development and progress of statistics for a large part of its own development and progress."[7] The term *Statistik* was coined in 1748 by Gottfried Achenwall, a German professor, from the Italian word *statista* (statesman).

Many advances in population research have been contributed by mathematical statisticians, especially those responsible for the elaboration of probability theory. But while statistical sophistication is of considerable utility in demographic research, it is not indispensable, as some demographers are almost statistically illiterate. Aside from general descriptive statistics and inductive inference, population analysis also makes use of several special techniques for quantitative manipulation of data.

One man—Adolphe Quételet (1796-1874)—merits citation as an extreme case of successful enthusiasm for statistical studies. A Belgian mathematician and astronomer who had studied under Fourier and Laplace and was elected to the Royal Academy in Brussels at the age of twenty-four, Quételet was instrumental in the organization of the International Statistical Congress in 1853. "A visionary conception of 'social Physics' as a science of man, to include studies ranging from anthropometry through demography to psychology and 'moral statistics' was advanced by Adolphe Quételet in the mid-nineteenth century, the 'era of enthusiasm' for statistical inquiries. With boundless energy he promoted international cooperation in official statistical programs and conducted research on population, the theory of probability, anthropometry, criminology, and other topics."[8] He wrote prodigiously on the life table, causes of death, sex ratios, birth and marriage rates, criminality, unemployment, the normal curve, and psychological traits. But although Quételet was a brilliant scholar who made original contributions to intellectual history, his most important contribution was inspirational rather than ideational. He may have been the most effective catalyst that population statistics has ever known. One of his converts and ardent admirers became a pioneer in nursing and hospital administration: Florence Nightingale, "the passionate statistician."

---

[7] Adolphe Landry, *Traité de démographie*, Payot, Paris, 1945, pp. 28-29.

[8] Frank Lorimer, "The Development of Demography," in Philip H. Hauser and Otis Dudley Duncan, *The Study of Population*, University of Chicago Press, Chicago, 1959, p. 159.

MATURATION OF DEMOGRAPHY

Having outgrown the phase of amateurism (characteristic of most disciplines in their early period of development) and political arithmetic, and having acquired the trappings of quantification, demography was now ready to expand into a full-blown science. A turning point occurred in 1798 with the publication of Malthus' famous *Essay on Population*. Demography had now come of age. Here was a detailed, organized compilation of existing statistics, bound together by analyses of their causes and consequences. The *Essay* attracted considerable attention among Malthus' contemporaries, and it continues to be included in lists of most influential books.

Scores of men studied and wrote about population before the nineteenth century, but they did so as amateurs. Graunt made his living as a haberdasher; Botero and Sussmilch were clergymen; Halley an astronomer. Most of the scholars were primarily engaged in studying other subjects and only incidentally interested themselves in population. Some were poorly educated. Graunt, as a youthful draper's apprentice, was self-taught in the manner of Lincoln. Malthus was the first man to take demography as his professional specialty—though he did have other interests in the areas of political economy and Christian morality. If Graunt can be called the father of demography, Malthus was certainly its first professional.

From its origins in seventeenth-century dilettantism, eighteenth-century political economy, and nineteenth-century economics, demography shifted allegiance in the twentieth century to the newly-established field of sociology. Of the 262 members of the Population Association of America holding doctorates in 1956, the distribution into fields was: sociology, 62 per cent; biology and medicine, 10 per cent; economics, 9 per cent; statistics, 5 per cent; geography, 4 per cent; psychology and mathematics, 3 per cent each; and all others (history, government, anthropology, city planning, law, philosophy, and physics), 5 per cent.[9] The preponderance of sociologists is even stronger in teaching—about 90 per cent of all population courses offered in American colleges are given by departments of sociology; the others are in public health, medicine, economics, geography, biology, and government.

PERSONNEL

Demographers are not plentiful. The world professional organization, the International Union for the Scientific Study of Population, founded

---

[9] Philip M. Hauser and Otis Dudley Duncan, "Demography as a Profession," in Hauser and Duncan, *The Study of Population, op. cit.*, p. 107.

in 1928 and reorganized in 1947, listed 472 members from 55 principalities as of 1961.[10] Almost one-fourth of the members are residents of the United States. Hauser and Duncan estimate the world population of demographers at "two thousand, or rather less than one demographer per one million population. This estimate seems to be well on the generous side."[11] However, "there is some comfort in the thought that the number of demographers in the world is increasing faster than the population."[12]

The foremost demographers may be identified by the criterion of frequency of entries in the indexes of population books. Analysis of eleven prominent population books of general coverage published in 1953 through 1961 identifies the ten individuals most often cited (in order of frequency of mention) as P. K. Whelpton, W. S. Thompson, T. R. Malthus, K. Davis, F. W. Notestein, C. V. Kiser, I. B. Taeuber, F. Lorimer, A. J. Lotka, and J. J. Spengler. Of the twenty-two outstanding persons, seventeen are still alive. Nationalities total seventeen for the United States, four for England, and one for France (ten of the books are in English, one in French). Subjects most represented are sociology with ten and economics with six. Major career affiliations are scattered among sixteen organizations, of which the leaders are the London School of Economics, the Metropolitan Life Insurance Company, Princeton University, and the Scripps Foundation. The school granting the most advanced degrees to these men is Columbia University.[13]

Professional demographers normally are trained in scientific method and statistics. They find these techniques of research design and analysis essential in collecting and interpreting data with which to test the hypotheses that are deduced from relevant theoretical stances. Quantification procedures are complicated, and investigators must be painstakingly accurate, but advanced mathematics is rarely required.

COLLECTING DATA

Demographic information is acquired in four ways: by complete enumerations, sample surveys, registration systems, and continuing registers. Complete enumerations or censuses are taken by obtaining information concerning every inhabitant of the area. Also coming into

---

[10] International Union for the Scientific Study of Population, Le Démographie, Paris, No. 9, June 1961, pp. 48-49.

[11] Philip M. Hauser and Otis Dudley Duncan, "Demography as a Profession," in Hauser and Duncan, The Study of Population, op. cit., p. 107.

[12] John D. Durand, "Demography's Three Hundredth Anniversary," Population Index, Vol. XXVIII, No. 4, October 1962, p. 335.

[13] Ralph Thomlinson, "A Note on the Most Frequently Cited Demographers," Population Review, Vol. VII, No. 2, July 1963, pp. 81-83.

increasing use by demographers are sample surveys, conducted by interviewing a part of the population to represent the whole. Registration of births, deaths, marriages, moves, and other demographic phenomena has a long history. Continuous registers maintain information about every individual throughout his lifetime by filing data for each resident on a separate card.

"A census is a sort of social photograph of certain conditions of a population at a given moment which are expressible in numbers, while registration is a continuous, contemporary, movie-camera record of births, marriages, divorces, or deaths."[14] The difference between a census and a registration system may be clarified by analogy. Censuses resemble the annual inventories taken by business concerns; they constitute a complete tabulation of all persons (or stock) in the country (or store). Registrations parallel the sales-slip record that businessmen keep or the records kept by druggists for habit-forming drugs; they represent a running account of additions and subtractions of persons—that is, births and deaths, immigrants and emigrants (or commodities stocked and sold).

Complete registers covering every resident from the time of his birth or immigration to his death or emigration, recording every marriage, divorce, child, move, military enlistment, imprisonment, and so on, are approached only in Finland, Sweden, Norway, Denmark, the Netherlands, and Belgium. Elsewhere, registration systems yield vital information in tabulated frequency distributions but do not keep continuous records for each individual. To extend the preceding analogy, a registry is akin to a store's charge-account bills permanently accumulated for each customer. A properly operated register has the virtue of offering unsurpassed information about the populace and is a superlative source of migration data, but it demands arduous record-keeping, which is not only quite expensive but irritating to citizens who are sensitive concerning infringements on their privacy. Although some Federal and local agencies, notably Social Security, the F.B.I., and state motor vehicle departments, attempt to keep continuing registers for those segments of the population in which they are interested, the United States is far from having a comprehensive register on an individual basis.

Registration Systems

Registration systems, which record and compile the incidence of certain events at or near their times of occurrence, are maintained in

---

[14] Walter F. Willcox, *Studies in American Demography*, Cornell University Press, Ithaca, 1940, p. 195.

many countries. In the United States, vital statistics of births, deaths, marriages, and divorces obtained from local registrars, halls of records, and county courthouses are recorded and tabulated on annual and monthly bases.

HISTORICAL DEVELOPMENT

The origins of registration are ecclesiastical. "Except for fragmentary vital registration during the pre-Christian era, which in Egypt, Greece, and Rome for example appears to have been carried out by civil authorities for revenue or military purposes, the recording of vital events was originally the uncoordinated concern of the individual ecclesiastical authorities. The 'vital events' for which ecclesiastical authorities, then as now, had a responsibility were baptisms, burials, and weddings rather than births, deaths, and marriages."[15] Systematic ecclestiastical registration can be traced back to 720 A.D. in parts of Japan and 1450 in Spain. "The custom of registering deaths and marriages is found in certain parts of Burgundy early in the fourteenth century, and in 1406 the registration of baptisms is mentioned, very probably for the first time, in the records of the Bishop of Nantes."[16]

The first purely civil registration system was established by the Incas in Peru, who used *quipus* (intertwined, knotted strings) to record vital and related statistics. Modern governmental action was foreshadowed by ordinances enacted by terror-stricken sovereigns during plagues requesting the clergy to keep chronicles of baptisms, marriages, and burials in England after 1538, France after 1539, Scotland after 1551, Sweden after 1608, Quebec after 1610, and Japan after 1635.[17] These first annals, usually kept by parish priests, were normally confined to members of the religious bodies concerned, which in some areas was virtually the entire populace. Information so collected was not published but simply kept on file in dusty archives; publication was rare before 1700. Parisian archives of births, deaths, baptisms, and burials were first published in 1670, having been considered state secrets since the inception of the registration system by the Ordinance of 1539.

Europeans who were not members of an established church were omitted from vital statistics until national civil registration was established in Norway in 1685, Sweden in 1756, France in 1792, Belgium in 1796, and England in 1837. Archives were established by several cities before national governments recognized the value of national account-

---

[15] United Nations, *Handbook of Vital Statistics Methods*, New York, 1955, p. 3.
[16] Helen M. Walker, *Studies in the History of Statistical Method*, Williams and Wilkins Co., Baltimore, 1929, p. 33.
[17] United Nations, *Handbook of Vital Statistics Methods*, *op. cit.*, pp. 3-4.

ing of vital events. Augsburg and Brandenburg, Germany, set up vital accounting in 1501 and 1684, respectively. Many other principalities completed compulsory civil registration in the nineteenth and early twentieth centuries. Ordinarily, civil records cover births, deaths, marriages, and divorces; in some cases, information about migration is also included.

Until 1839, vital registration received only fragmentary and desultory treatment. At that time Dr. William Farr was appointed Compiler of Abstracts for England and Wales. Farr had a penetrating impact on international public health statistics, devoting forty years of his life to what was for him the congenial chore of creating and perfecting a thoroughgoing English system of vital statistics, which has been copied around the world. The need for public hygiene and sanitation motivated Edwin Chadwick to persuade the English parliament to establish a national board of health in 1844, but Anglo-Saxon fear of governmental regimentation caused the board to be abolished in 1854. Rudolf Virchow tried unsuccessfully to set up a national health council in Prussia in 1849, but in 1876 the Reichstag, encouraged by Chancellor Bismarck, inaugurated a national health office for the entire German Empire. In the United States, Massachusetts opened the first state board of health in 1869, followed within a decade by nineteen other states. The National Board of Health followed in 1879 after considerable argument.[18] Though these organizations had the primary objective of reforming unsavory health conditions, they incidentally collected useful data. International conferences on sanitation were held beginning in 1851, and in 1920, the League of Nations established a Health Section in its Secretariat. The World Health Organization was founded in 1946 at a United Nations conference.

FEDERAL VITAL REGISTRATION

Although the United States has an admirable census, the country has always been poor in vital statistics registration. Registration in the American colonies began in the Massachusetts Bay and New Plymouth Colonies in 1639. The purpose was not demographic; the legislature wanted only legal documents concerning property and individual rights. As recently as 1833, only six per cent of United States cities registered births and deaths. In 1842 Massachusetts put into effect the first successful state-wide registration statute in this country. But by 1885, registration systems were operating in areas covering only 28 per cent of the population.

---

[18] Richard H. Shryock, *The Development of Modern Medicine*, Alfred A. Knopf, New York, 1947, pp. 233-241.

The Federal Death Registration System was introduced in 1900, the Birth Registration System in 1915. Initially including only ten states and the District of Columbia, these systems became nation-wide with the inclusion of Texas in 1933. Marriage and Divorce Registration Areas were set up in 1957 and 1958. But at the present writing there seems to be little prospect of a Federal migration registration system. At first, registration was performed by the Bureau of the Census, but in 1946 the National Office of Vital Statistics was authorized as a part of the Public Health Service. Further reorganization occurred in 1960, when the National Center for Health Statistics was formed as a part of the Department of Health, Education and Welfare. Its National Vital Statistics Division collects and publishes birth, death, marriage, and divorce data, constructs the official United States life tables and actuarial tables, and performs related functions.

The national system operates through a coordinated flow of statistics from local, state, and Federal agencies. Physicians, funeral directors, clergymen, local government clerks, and court clerks file birth, death, marriage, divorce, and disease certificates with county, city, or district registrars. The city or county health department collates these official reports and forwards them to the state registrar, who in turn transmits transcripts, microfilm copies, or summary reports to the National Center for Health Statistics in Washington, D.C. Finally, the N.C.H.S. tabulates the state records into forms suitable for publication in monthly reports and annual volumes of considerable size. The N.C.H.S. also encourages the district, city, county, and state registrars to adopt uniform certificates so that national statistics may be as complete and accurate as possible.

Census-Taking

The second of the four ways in which population data are obtained is the census, a counting of the entire population at a specified time. In the United States, inhabitants are constitutionally required to be enumerated every ten years. Elsewhere, the interval between countings may be as short as five years, or there may be infrequent and irregular scheduling of censuses according to political and financial considerations.

Modern censuses of population, housing, agriculture, religion, manufacturing, and so forth bear very little resemblance to the embryonic enumerations from which they evolved. Today's uses, techniques, motives, and public images are all different from what they were in the past. In response to a mid-eighteenth-century proposal for a census a member of the English House of Commons commented: "I did not believe that there was any set of men or indeed any individual of the human species, so presumptuous and so abandoned as to make the proposal we have just heard. . . . I hold this project to be totally subversive to the last remains of English liberty."[19]

The word "census" is derived from the Latin *censere*, meaning to value or tax. The original objectives of censuses were not to get data for demographic study, but for military conscription (as among the Romans), for taxation (as in China), and for the determination of political representation (as in the United States). Ordinarily, their limited purposes restricted the census to certain segments of the population: men able to bear arms, heads of families, farmers, merchants, landholders, and others on whom taxes might be levied. Any census was directed toward "the people who count"; today, everyone counts, but in earlier periods of man's development, only a segment of the total number of "live bodies" was worth enumerating—usually the adult males.

Only in the last few centuries have governments been willing to commit themselves to recurring investment in such enterprises. In 1753 the British House of Lords rejected Thomas Potter's bill for an annual census. Many of the early censuses were conducted by private groups; a privately supported census was taken in Scotland by Alexander Webster in 1743-1756.

EARLY ENUMERATIONS

"Five thousand years ago the Sumerians counted their citizens for taxation purposes. At various later times the Egyptians conducted inquiries into the occupations of their people."[20] The Chinese also took limited censuses at early dates. "By the time of the Chou dynasty (circa 1050-247 B.C.) population censuses and registrations had become normal instruments of public administration.[21] These first census-takers played a dual role; if a man were counted in a census, it meant that the census taker would also probably draft him into the army or levy a tax against him. No wonder enumeration was incomplete.

In Biblical times, censuses were undertaken by Moses in 1491 B.C. and David in 1017 B.C.[22] When the Lord directed Moses to "take the sum of the children of Israel" (Numbers 1:1), the count was supposed to include only adult males—"all that are able to go forth to war in Israel."

[19] Registrar-General, *Reports on the Census of Population of England and Wales*, London, 1901, p. 4; quoted in Wladimir S. Woytinsky and Emma S. Woytinsky, *World Population and Production*, Twentieth Century Fund, New York, 1953, p. 32.

[20] Peter R. Cox, *Demography*, Cambridge University Press, London, 1959, p. 14.

[21] John D. Durand, "The Population Statistics of China, A.D. 2-1953," *Population Studies*, Vol. XIII, No. 3, March 1960, p. 209.

[22] Hugh H. Wolfenden, *Population Statistics and Their Compilation*, University of Chicago Press, Chicago, 1954, p. 4.

In honor of this census, the Fourth Book of Moses is named Numbers. David's later census was neither well conceived nor well received: "And Satan stood up against Israel, and provoked David to number Israel. . . . And God was displeased with this thing; therefore he smote Israel" (I Chronicles 21:1,7).

Indian literature dating from the reign of the northern Hindustan King Asoka (c. 270-c. 230 B.C.) also describes methods for taking censuses. The record is subsequently unimpressive, however, until the rule of Akbar, Emperor of Hindustan from 1556 to 1605, when some population data were collected.

The Athenians and other classical Greeks took censuses in times of stress, carefully counting the adult male citizens in wartime and the general populace when the food supply was endangered.[23] The Romans registered adult males and their property for military and administrative purposes. Servius Tullius, who ruled as the sixth king of Rome from 578-534 B.C., is given credit for instituting the census. As part of an annual religious festival, he required each person to contribute money to defray expenses. Each man brought a certain kind of coin, each woman a different coin, and each child a third coin. When the coins were counted, the total population and certain aspects of the age-sex distribution were ascertained.

Charlemagne's Breviary of 762 A.D. listed all the males of military age in the Empire. In 758 Pepin the Short, king of the Franks and the first Carlovingian, collected data concerning Church lands and partially enumerated the serfs. William the Conqueror ordered a land and population inventory of England for 1085-1086. Called the Domesday Book after doomsday or judgment day because it was the final authority, it listed landed proprietors and the nature, size, and value of their holdings. "Domesday was not for curiosity, but for rapacity."[24] Similar inquiries were conducted in succeeding centuries, as for example the Domesday of St. Paul's in 1181. English subsidy rolls of the thirteenth and fourteenth centuries and poll-tax returns of 1379-1381 are early instances of taxation-oriented censuses.

The first known counting of every man, woman, and child occurred in central Europe in 1449, when Nuremberg was enumerated because its leaders feared depletion of a limited food supply under a state of siege; as is often the case in such circumstances, results of the research were considered state secrets. Further attempts to take complete censuses were made in certain Swiss cantons in the fifteenth and sixteenth centuries.

---

[23] A. W. Gomme, *The Population of Athens in the Fifth and Fourth Centuries B.C.*, Basil Blackwood, Oxford, 1933, pp. 1-35.

[24] George Ensor, *The Population of Nations*, London, 1818, p. 28.

In 1662 an numeration of all males over twelve years of age was conducted in Norway for military purposes. Louis XIV ordered a statistical survey of the French provinces; the results were state secrets, but a résumé was published in 1727, a dozen years after his death.

The first complete periodic enumeration began in 1665 in New France (Canada) and continued until 1754 in Quebec. The 154-page report of 1666 included data on total population, sex, age, marital status, and occupation—a remarkable accomplishment at that time.

As noted, results of these early censuses were customarily treated as government secrets. The French statesman Jacques Necker was among the first to advocate free and open interchange of demographic information between countries. As a government official, he planned "the establishment of a special bureau intended solely for the collecting of interesting information, and arranging this information in a clear and easy order."[25]

The difficulty of divorcing censuses from politics has carried over into the twentieth century. The Russian census of 1937 was suppressed and officially disclaimed, supposedly because it contained serious methodological errors. Western observers, however, were inclined to view the "methodological errors" as being essentially a failure to indicate the expected number of inhabitants.[26] When taking the 1939 Soviet census, officials feared sabotage by "enemies of the people," an apprehension which found expression in the press: "One should know that the masked enemy may try to arouse distrust for the census. It is necessary to watch closely for their hostile machinations while this mass political work is conducted."[27]

MODERN CENSUSES

The first modern census system—that is, a continuing complete count taken accurately at regular intervals—began in Sweden in 1749. A national system of parish registers, established in 1686, provided the foundation for this accomplishment. Norway and Denmark conducted general enumerations in 1769.

In this field, the United States made crucial contributions. Local censuses were conducted in Virginia in 1624, in Connecticut in 1756,

---

[25] Jacques Necker, *De l'administration des finances de la France*, Paris, 1784, Vol. III, p. 355; quoted in Abraham Wolf, *A History of Science, Technology, and Philosophy in the Eighteenth Century*, George Allen and Unwin Ltd., London, 1952, p. 703.

[26] Michael K. Roof, "The Russian Population Enigma Reconsidered," *Population Studies*, Vol. XIV, No. 1, July 1960, p. 3.

[27] *Izvestia*, September 6 and October 3, 1938; quoted in Galina V. Selegen and Victor P. Petrov, "Soviet People versus Population Census," *The American Statistician*, Vol. XIII, No. 1, February 1959, p. 15.

and in Massachusetts in 1764. Then in 1787 the new Constitution provided for a national census every ten years to determine the number of representatives each state should have in Congress as well as the tax base of each state. "Representatives and direct taxes shall be apportioned among the several States which may be included within this Union according to their respective numbers. . . . The actual enumeration shall be made within three years after the first meeting of the Congress of the United States, and within every subsequent term of ten years, in such manner as they shall by law direct."[28] This valuable legal underwriting of social research was an outcome of the vituperative and protracted controversy between the large and small states in the power struggle to decide the amount of representation each was to have in the Senate and House of Representatives. It was made necessary by the decision to allot representation in the lower house of Congress according to population. But regardless of the motives for its inception, the first United States census, taken in 1790, constituted a real step forward in census-taking. This census together with the Swedish census of 1749 comprise what may be the two longest strides toward the detailed, accurate censuses of today.

Other noteworthy censuses were taken in England in 1801, Belgium in 1829, France in 1835, Japan in 1873, India in 1881, Egypt in 1897, and Russia in 1897. By mid-nineteenth century, most European countries had adopted the practice of taking a census. Between 1945 and 1954 about 80 per cent of the world's people were enumerated.[29]

Census-takers often encounter their share of resistance and drama. The 1931 Census of India was confronted with a Census Boycott Sunday, and in one province the Bhils "would not have their houses numbered on superstitious grounds. In the Shan States the thirteenth and last survivor of a pre-annexation raid happened to occupy the thirteenth house in a block. As the enumerator inconsiderately refused to rearrange the numbers, the man decided that his (number) was up indeed, went forth into the jungle and committed harakiri. In less law-abiding places the disposition was rather toward disemboweling the enumerator than the enumerated. . . . Here and there wild beasts interfered instead of wild men, and the Administrator of Bastar State, when inspecting census work on the night itself, was attacked by a tiger [which, jumping on the hood of the car but finding the pace and the radiator too hot] failed to make an end either of the inspector or his inspection."[30]

---

[28] *Constitution of the United States*, Article 1, Section 2, Paragraph 4.
[29] Statistical Office of the United Nations, "The 1960 World Population Census Programme," *Population Bulletin of the United Nations*, No. 5, July 1956, p. 2.
[30] *Census of India*, 1931, Vol. I, Part 1, p. x; quoted in Kingsley Davis, *The Population of India and Pakistan*, Princeton University Press, Princeton, 1951, p. 5.

UNITED STATES CENSUSES

In North America another kind of Indian, the Comanches of the Great Plains and Southwest, anticipated the Federal census by many years. Five bundles of reeds represented respectively the number of warriors, the number of young men, the number of women, the number of children, and the number of lodges.

Considerable complexity has been introduced into the United States census since 1790. Whereas the directors of the first census were content just to count the number of residents of each state and territory and record a very limited number of facts about them, the scope has been enlarged with each decade in response to the growing variety of social and economic uses found by commercial and scholarly interests. A capsule story of the growth of the United States Census is presented in Table 3.

TABLE 3. *Growth of the United States Census, 1790-1960**

CENSUS YEAR	NUMBER OF ENUMER- ATORS	LENGTH OF ENUMER- ATION IN MONTHS	TOTAL PAGES IN PUBLISHED REPORTS	COST PER CAPITA	POPULATION ENUMERATED IN CONTINENTAL U.S.
1790	650	18.0	56	$0.01	3,929,000
1810	1,100	10.0	469	0.02	7,239,000
1830	1,519	14.0	214	0.03	12,866,000
1850	3,231	20.5	2,165	0.06	23,191,000
1870	6,530	15.0	3,473	0.09	38,558,000
1890	46,804	1.0	26,408	0.18	62,947,000
1910	70,286	1.0	11,456	0.17	91,972,000
1930	87,756	1.0	32,019	0.32	122,775,000
1950	151,814	1.0	61,394	0.60	150,697,000
1960	160,000	1.0	100,000	0.50	179,323,000

* U. S. Bureau of the Census, *The Story of the Census: 1790–1916*, Government Printing Office, Washington, 1916, p. 22; Leonard Broom and Philip Selznick, *Sociology*, Row, Peterson and Co., Evanston, 1958, p. 313; and recent releases from the Bureau of the Census.

The first census, directed by seventeen marshals beginning in August, 1790, required double the legally stipulated nine months to complete. No clerical force was hired, and the returns were published in a single pamphlet. Industrial statistics were collected for the first time in 1810. Printed schedules were introduced in 1830; before that the marshals' assistants simply used whatever paper they happened to have—a procedure hardly conducive to accuracy and uniformity. Prior to 1850 the family was the basic unit of enumeration, but thereafter, the individual became the unit, making possible a considerable increase in analytical utility. Map presentation was begun in 1870, taking the form of *The Statistical Atlas of the United States*. In 1872 mechanical tallying machines were introduced to analyze census returns. Enumerators and supervisors were specially trained from 1880 on; this date was also the occasion of reduction of the period of enumeration to one month. In 1890 electric machine tabulation was instituted, utilizing the invention of perforated cards by Herman Hollerith, a census bureau employee. In 1902 the Census Office was officially established as a permanent agency; previously, it was set up anew each decade and disbanded upon completion of its immediate task.[31]

Enumerating 180 million people in the 1960 Federal census was a prodigious task requiring 17 permanent regional offices, approximately 300 temporary district offices, about 10,000 crew leaders, and some 160,000 enumerators. Crew leaders and interviewers were recruited locally and given an intensive training program. The over-3,000 counties, 40,000 townships, and 20,000 urban places were divided into a quarter of a million enumeration districts, and millions of maps were made and printed for the occasion.

To help meet such an enormous undertaking, the Bureau of the Census is today becoming automated. Mechanical processing of billions of facts collected in the 1960 Census required almost 1,000 miles of microfilm to feed five FOSDIC's (Film Optical Sensing Device for Input to Computer). FOSDIC "reads" the microfilm and almost instantaneously converts the coded information to a magnetic tape which is then fed into digital computers (four Univac 1105s). The Univac computers are programmed to count, collate, and cross-tabulate this mountain of raw data into usable statistical tables, which are then turned over to a high-speed electronic printer for reproduction at the rate of 600 lines a minute. Given some 100,000 pages of published reports, this automation saves considerable time and money.

de facto or de jure

Census officials have a choice between taking a *de facto* census—a counting of people where they actually are at the moment of enumeration—or a *de jure* census—an allocation according to where the people normally or legally belong. The *de facto* census, favored by Great Britain, records all "warm bodies" wherever they are found, whether their presence in that place be permanent or temporary. It has the advantage of providing a literal accounting of the populace exactly where they are

---

[31] U. S. Bureau of the Census, *The Story of the Census, op. cit.*, pp. 5-16 and 33-34.

at a given moment, without the sometimes arbitrary reallocation of people temporarily away from home. Its disadvantage is that population figures may be inflated or deflated by tourists, traveling salesmen, and other transients.

Some census-takers prefer to have a count of people tabulated by their permanent place of residence. Nations conducting a *de jure* census enumerate people where they are (the personal interview is inherently *de facto*) and then reallocate data for people who are temporarily away from their normal location. United States census officials have traditionally used the *de jure* scheme. Its major strength is that it yields information relatively unaffected by seasonal and other temporary movements of people. Conversely, it has two serious weaknesses: the clerical work of reassigning data from place of interview to place of usual residence is costly, and it is often difficult to be sure just which is a person's usual or legal residence.

> The assumption that each person has one and only one usual place of abode, heretofore implicit in the procedures of the U. S. Census of population, is becoming increasingly invalid with the passage of each decade. Millions of men and women are in the armed forces, large numbers of them stationed abroad; and not only they themselves but the members of their immediate families are shifted from one place to another with considerable frequency. Hundreds of thousands of persons maintain legal residences in states or counties other than the ones in which they actually reside, a phenomenon that is particularly acute on the part of those who live and work in the District of Columbia. Additional hundreds of thousands actually have two residences and spend approximately one half of the year in states such as Florida, Arizona, or California and the other half of the year elsewhere. Finally, the mobility of the population in general is increasing by leaps and bounds, and the elements in the population that have no fixed residence are becoming more numerous year by year. Under these circumstances the definition of population on the *de jure* basis is becoming more and more unsatisfactory.[32]

For these reasons, the United States Census is gradually modifying its traditional legal domicile principle to the more practical one of recording people in the place where they spend more than half of the year; that failing, they classify residence on the basis of plurality. "Each person enumerated in the 1960 Census was counted as an inhabitant of his usual place of abode, which is generally construed to mean the place where he lives and sleeps most of the time. This place is not necessarily

---

[32] T. Lynn Smith, *Fundamentals of Population Study*, J. B. Lippincott Co., Philadelphia, 1960, pp. 43-44.

the same as his legal residence, voting residence, or domicile; however, in the vast majority of cases, the use of these different bases of classification would produce substantially the same statistics, although there may be appreciable differences for a few areas."[33]

Sample Surveys

Since it is expensive to interview everyone in the country, demographers and other social scientists frequently use sample studies to acquire information about residents. In the United States, the ten years between censuses are filled with hundreds of sample surveys on demographic issues, some conducted by the Bureau of the Census and others proceeding from other auspices. Sampling is also used within censuses. In the 1960 census only a few questions were asked of the entire populace; most items were administered to a 25 per cent sample.

Sampling consists of selecting part of a social category to represent the entire category. Making that sample truly representative, however, is surprisingly difficult. Unless the investigator is thoroughly trained in both statistics and research methodology, he almost inevitably fails to achieve representativeness. However, when the sample is properly designed, it offers the virtues of speed, inexpensiveness, and greater attention to each case. If incorrectly designed or carried out, its results may be completely worthless.

Demographic samples can be traced back to the eighteenth century. In France, Messance (pseudonym of de la Michaudière) in 1765, Moheau in 1778, and Lavoisier in 1784 used samples to estimate national population totals, components, livestock supply, and agricultural characteristics. In 1802, Laplace took "a remarkable step forward in attempting to measure the precision of his estimate and announced that the odds were 1161 to 1 that it was not in error by more than 500,000 inhabitants. . . . Even though the method of estimate was crude and the measure of precision not wholly valid, Laplace's effort was much more successful than the complete census of France that was attempted at that time."[34] Similar progress was made in Great Britain, where sampling also preceded the establishment of regular enumerations. Over the last two centuries, sampling has come into increasing use and is now commonplace.

---

[33] U. S. Bureau of the Census, *U. S. Census of Population: 1960*, "Number of Inhabitants: United States Summary," PC(1)-1A, Government Printing Office, Washington, 1961, p. ix.

[34] Frederick F. Stephan, "History of the Uses of Modern Sampling Procedures," *Journal of the American Statistical Association*, Vol. XLIII, 1948, pp. 12-40.

CURRENT POPULATION SURVEY

One of the most efficient, complicated, and generally superior sample designs ever undertaken is the Current Population Survey conducted by the United States Bureau of the Census since 1942. The C.P.S. is a multistage area cluster sample of about 35,000 households spread throughout all fifty states. It is "the source of the monthly statistics on total employment and unemployment and of periodic data on income, migration, education, family status, and many other social and economic characteristics of the population."[35] Results are published in the Monthly Report on the Labor Force and other Census serials. Its quality is extremely high; a comparison of C.P.S. labor force estimates with 1950 decennial Census returns showed that "the C.P.S., in relation to a census, obtains better data," partly as a result of the more highly trained staff of enumerators than may be employed in a continuing sample survey.[36]

Conclusion

Population statistics are highly accurate (although not perfect) in countries with well-developed census and registration systems. These are generally the industrial countries, although a few peasant-agricultural nations also have skilled organizations for collecting and analyzing data. Some countries have excellent coverage of certain items and yet are poor in other respects. The primary sources of the gaps in world demographic knowledge are three lacks: financial resources, trained interviewers and statisticians, and a desire to have detailed data concerning the populace.

Partly as a result of the intensive effort of the United Nations to have enumerations made throughout the world in the mid-century period 1946-1955, we have better knowledge of demographic events and totals for this time than for any other period. Regionally, the most complete and accurate coverage is found in northwest Europe. The least known continent is Africa, although its population is now being studied by the Office of Population Research at Princeton University.

The United States has an excellent census, but its registration system is tardy and incomplete. Federal collection of statistics is a divided responsibility: the Bureau of the Census secures detailed information about

---

[35] U. S. Bureau of the Census, "Expansion of the Current Population Survey Sample: 1956," *Current Population Reports*, Government Printing Office, Washington, Series P-23, No. 3, July 15, 1956, p. 1.

[36] Morris H. Hansen, William N. Hurwitz, and William G. Madow, *Sample Survey Methods and Theory*, John Wiley and Sons, New York, 1953, Vol. I, pp. 581-582.

population characteristics every ten years; the National Center for Health Statistics records vital events such as births, deaths, marriages, divorces, and certain sicknesses; and the Immigration and Naturalization Service organizes data concerning entry and departure. These three agencies, respectively, are parts of the Department of Commerce, the Department of Health, Education and Welfare, and the Department of Justice. In addition, scattered other public and private organizations collect, tabulate, publish, and analyze demographic information.

4 ✕ Population Theories

"The ghost of Parson Malthus is still abroad."[1] The history of population theory can be summarized in three words: pre-Malthusian, Malthusian, and post-Malthusian. Hardly ever in intellectual history does one man so dominate a field as does the Reverend Thomas Robert Malthus in demographic theory. To paraphrase a quotation attributed to Newton, Malthus' shoulders *must* be climbed.

Explanations of population changes have been advanced by writers of many nationalities, religions, occupational specialties, and educational attainments. Independent and dependent variables which have been used for this purpose include total population, density, fertility, mortality, migration, climate, food, topography, energy sources, standard of living, level of aspiration, urbanization, degree of worldliness, transport facilities, technological development, balance of trade, genetic deterioration, age-sex distribution, socioeconomic class, religious belief, type of government, alcohol consumption, state of knowledge, and various combinations thereof. Most of these generalizations are oversimplified or obsolete; some are generally viewed as ludicrous; and a few are brilliant contributions to man's understanding of his own propagation, wandering, and demise.

PRIMARY AND SECONDARY THEORIES

Some theories are formulated for the principal purpose of explaining demographic tendencies; these may be called primary theories. Secondary theories are only incidentally demographic. If a writer's avowed intention

---

[1] David Richard Charles Eversley, *Social Theories of Fertility and the Malthusian Debate*, Oxford University Press, London, 1959, p. 1.

is figuring out the how's, why's, and wherefore's of demographic behavior, his theory is, of course, a primary one. But even if his dominant interest is to analyze economic behavior, social class, or some other nondemographic phenomenon, his resulting theory may have demographic ramifications. Primary theories are easy to identify, but secondary theories are often so indirectly concerned with population matters as to be elusive. While the number of scholars who have devoted their primary attention to population theory is not very large, numerous scholars have included demographic statements of a theoretical nature in writings which were intended for another purpose.

Whereas primary theories are more likely to distinguish and operate through the three demographic variables—fertility, mortality, and migration—than secondary theories, the latter often explore the causes and consequences of population size and growth as if they were unitary phenomena directly creating and responding to physical, biological, geographic, social, economic, and political forces. Greater theoretical sophistication is achieved by examining pluralistically fertility, mortality, and migration as separate but interconnected variables which intertwine with population characteristics and other variables to form a complicated demographic nexus.

Since population as a professional specialty is of fairly recent origin, primary theories are largely post-Malthusian—a situation not directly attributable to the pre-eminence of Reverend Malthus. Prior to the late eighteenth century, population simply did not receive the amount of attention from learned men that we take for granted today.

The Functions of Theory

The object of a theory is to state an order, system, or relation among facts. Theorists want to establish an invariant organization of data, or if that is not possible, at least to demonstrate the nature of the interconnections that affect the subject of their investigations. Demographers share with other scholars the wish to be able to provide a solid theoretical structure that binds together the otherwise disparate facts flowing from empirical research.

The process of theorizing helps demographers to explain existing data and to predict as yet unobserved data (from the future or past). Frequently it is necessary to form unreal or abstract conceptions (such as the life table or standardized birth rates) in order to get at the concept the demographer wishes to study. In analyzing vital rates, it becomes evident that the observed birth and death rates are acceptable for description, but explanation and prediction are better performed not by finding out how many people were born or died, but rather by ascertaining the true or latent propensity to give birth or die—which may vary with many influences, including especially the age-sex composition of the populace.

INDEPENDENT AND DEPENDENT VARIABLES

Population theories deal with total population, the three demographic variables, dozens of population characteristics, and related phenomena. Population components and composition may be used as independent variables, dependent variables, or both. Thus theorists sometimes take population as a "given" with which to explain other phenomena—for example, population pressure as a cause of war. Other theorists treat population as a consequence rather than as a cause, as when they try to figure out what motivates people to hold down their fertility. Or one demographic variable may be assumed to affect another, as in the case of heavy migration altering natural increase among nonmigrants.

NATURAL *versus* SOCIAL THEORIES

Both recent and older population theories may be grouped into two categories: naturalistic and environmental. Naturalistic explanations tend to be mechanistic, stressing the inevitability of certain biological processes and sometimes denying man's ability to adapt himself to these natural forces. Environmental theories try to explain demographic behavior through man-made and therefore man-changeable processes.

The naturalistic theories have of late been losing ground to the environmental theories. Demographers still recognize the part played by heredity, but more and more human events are coming to be understood to be controlled by culture. Nature-made events are fewer than people once believed. The simplicity of naturalistic explanations and their implication that we are not responsible for what happens are tempting, but rigorous research has brought us around to more complicated, but also more realistic, social explanations.

Population phenomena are biological and social, and the processes which affect them are sociocultural, geographic, and biological. Biology and geography set limits, but they are such wide limits that man rarely reaches them (though modern man-made science occasionally enables us to exceed the "natural" prescientific limits—as in the cases of test-tube babies and Ultima Thule). Observed tribal and national variations are fully explained only by using both cultural and physical variables.

Take fertility as an example. Biological capacity to reproduce is a prerequisite to continuation of the species, yet no group of human beings has ever been known to reproduce at its maximum fecundity. Fertility performance, though ultimately limited by the nine-month reproductive cycle and other biological facts, is also partially determined by the social arrangements and the folkways and mores of each culture. Biologists can tell us when puberty begins (though definitions vary), but they cannot predict whether sexual relations will commence before, at, or after pubescence. Sexual behavior, in short, is culturally prescribed in type, amount, and circumstances. Mating occurs according to the dictates of the culture, and observed differences between societies are not correlated with biological capacity to reproduce. In our society, marriage as a precondition for having children is specified; in certain others, a prerequisite for marriage is demonstration of fecundity by bearing a child. Similarly, attitudes toward large families are not given us by nature, but are mutable social values. A couple standing in the classic rank-by-height order with their eleven children are esteemed, rewarded, pitied, or derided according to the prevailing social values of the audience's reference groups.

The situation is similar with respect to death. "Modern longevity is the product of modern enlightenment. Man himself, as a physical and physiological unit, has probably changed but little since remote antiquity. But man's power over his environment has changed immensely, with benefits which find expression in his record of decreasing mortality and increasing longevity."[2] Biological evolution is gradually changing man's physical make-up, but far too slowly to credit with the spectacular drop in the death rate in Western countries in the last few centuries and in non-Western regions in the twentieth century. Furthermore, differentials between continents and disequities within nations are not fully explained by postulating biological differences among men.

In common with other domesticated animals, Homo sapiens deviates from so-called unfettered natural behavior. Since he is self-domesticated, the deviations and fetters are created by his own hand. If he lacks the awareness or courage to accept responsibility for these decisions, he passes the buck to "nature." Ignorant persons still do this; educated men have learned better.

Pre-Malthusian Writings

Early writing on population theory was crammed with moral preconceptions and superficial observations. Generally, scholars failed to differentiate between factual evidence and hearsay or folklore. Other unscientific legacies which beset population theorists included the presumed needs of dealing with basic emotional appetites of lust and greed, of confining one's studies to subjects of prime and immediate importance

---

[2] Louis I. Dublin, Alfred J. Lotka, and Mortimer Spiegelman, *Length of Life*, The Ronald Press Co., New York, 1949, p. 141.

in human affairs, and of being concerned necessarily with matters of policy. Moreover, hypotheses were not tested empirically, and received opinions were slow to die.

Many of the earliest views on the factors affecting fertility show signs of having originated from folk-lore. High living causes sterility: aristocracies die out, towns are graveyards, the countryside teemeth with men. Intellectual pursuits and gallantry diminish power of procreation, whores cannot conceive. Idiots breed like rabbits. Such ideas were learned, we may surmise, by writers in their youth, and they found it hard to rid themselves of such beliefs. Scientific investigations partially confirmed these views, and this helped to keep them alive in their cruder forms. Some of the notions involved must be as old as mankind itself. One has only to read the younger Pliny on the subject of fertility to realize that superstition was a powerful regulator of marriage and the marriage-bed. Juvenal's golden couch[3] and Paley's rice-eaters, Hippocrates' soft airs and the boots that help to beget a male child—all these form part of a powerful web of superstition![4]

EIGHTEENTH CENTURY

Since little of lasting consequence in population theory was written before 1700, this chronological discussion begins with the eighteenth century. Early in the 1700's, Richard Cantillon partially anticipated Malthus' precepts concerning the relation between population growth and standard of living. A businessman writing about commerce, Cantillon had physiocratic leanings. His two primary conclusions were that population increases to as large a size as can be sustained by the prevailing economic system, and that as the standard of living improves the population grows at a decelerating rate. He stressed the importance of the distribution of wealth in distinction to population size.

A few years later, Robert Wallace expressed the then-prevalent view that it was dangerous to raise the standard of living of the poor. He and others opposed the poor laws on the basis of the view that giving financial assistance to the poor would encourage them to have more children and also make it easier for the children to reach adulthood, both of which eventualities would lead to overpopulation, which in turn would wreck schemes for human betterment. In fact, "had it not been for the errors and vices of mankind and the defects of government and education, the Earth must have been much better peopled, perhaps might

---

[3] "But how often does a gilded bed contain a woman that is lying in?"— Juvenal, *Satires*, No. VI, lines 593-594.
[4] Eversley, *Theories of Fertility, op. cit.*, p. 281.

have been overstocked, many ages ago."[5] For similar reasons, Wallace also opposed good government.

> For though happily such governments should be firmly established . . .
> they must at last involve mankind in the deepest perplexity, and in
> universal confusion. For how excellent soever they may be in their own
> nature, they are altogether inconsistent with the present frame of
> nature, and with a limited extent of earth. Under a perfect government
> the inconveniences of having a family would be so entirely removed,
> children would be so well taken care of, and everything become so
> favourable to populousness, that though some sickly seasons or dreadful
> plagues in particular climates might cut off multitudes, yet, in general,
> mankind would increase so prodigiously that the Earth would at last
> be overstocked, and become unable to support its numerous inhabit-
> ants.[6]

This disaster could be averted by sterilization, infanticide, curbing marriages, and killing the aged. "But mankind would never agree about such regulations. Force and arms must at last decide their quarrels, and the deaths of such as fall in battle leave sufficient provisions for the survivors, and make room for others to be born."[7]

Two contemporaries of Thomas Malthus were largely responsible for stimulating him to write about population. The Marquis de Condorcet, a French philosopher, mathematician, and revolutionary, wrote a history of mankind while hiding out in an attic during the French Revolution, under threat of death by ardent terrorists.[8] Condorcet believed that once man was released from the mismanagements of the clergy and royalty, there would be no more inequalities between nations, classes, and individuals. Pure reason would some day prevail, eliminating animosities, limiting diseases, and increasing production. Man's longevity would increase tremendously, but overpopulation would be prevented by recognition of antinatal obligations instead of "the puerile idea of filling the earth with useless and unhappy beings." In England, William Godwin, an unsuccessful minister turned political pamphleteer, also believed in the perfectibility of society and argued that man would one day have no war, no crime, no disease, no govern-ment, and a thirty-minute work day.[9]

---

[5] Robert Wallace, A Dissertation on the Numbers of Mankind in Ancient and Modern Times, Edinburgh, 1753.

[6] Robert Wallace, Various Prospects of Mankind, Nature and Providence, London, 1761, pp. 114-115.

[7] Ibid., p. 119.

[8] Marie Jean Antoine Nicolas de Caritat, Marquis de Condorcet, Esquisse d'un tableau historique des progrès de l'esprit humain, 1793.

[9] William Godwin, Enquiry Concerning Political Justice and Its Influence on Morals and Happiness, London, 1793.

Demographic theorizing along these lines was not confined to the West. Hung Liang-chi, a Chinese poet, philosopher, calligrapher, historian, and patriot, wrote essays contemporaneously with Malthus. He, too, feared overpopulation, but he differed from Malthus in his materialism, anticlericalism, avoidance of statistics, and absence of controversy. Hung favored land reform but did not regard it as a permanent solution to overpopulation.

T. R. Malthus

The Reverend Thomas Robert Malthus was born at The Rookery, Surrey, England, on St. Valentine's Day, 1766. The second son among eight children of a country gentleman who was a friend of Rousseau, Malthus was privately educated until his enrollment at Cambridge University at the age of eighteen. In 1788 he won honors at Cambridge and was ordained in the Church of England. In 1805 he was appointed professor of history and political economy in the East-India College, Haileybury, England, where the cadets of the East India Company were trained. His teaching duties were not onerous, and for most of his life he led the existence of a quiet scholar, though with frequent interruptions for travel and for disputes with other scholars. Malthus married in 1804, was the father of three children, and died in 1834.

At the time of his death, he was internationally famous for his work on population, three books on political economy, and dozens of pamphlets and tracts. He held an M.A. from Jesus College, Cambridge, and was made a Fellow of the Royal Society in 1819 and a Fellow of the Statistical Society posthumously. In 1890, G. T. Bettany wrote in an introduction to a reprinting of the sixth edition of the *Essay*: "A moderate station with comfort, an even mind, able to bear reproaches and to enjoy quiet pleasures, a benevolent heart, ever intent on anything that could really benefit his poorer fellow-creatures, these were the possessions of Malthus."

PURPOSE AND ASSUMPTIONS OF THE *Essay*

In 1798, Malthus published a thin volume on population called "An Essay on the Principle of Population as It Affects The Future Improvement of Society, with Remarks on the Speculations of Mr. Godwin, M. Condorcet, and Other Writers." Immediately successful, the book expanded through five revisions as Malthus added chapters reporting on the demographic situation in various countries with which he became familiar. The sixth edition, dated 1826, was entitled "An Essay on the Principle of Population, or A View of Its Past and Present Effects on

Human Happiness, with An Inquiry into Our Prospects Respecting the Future Removal or Mitigation of the Evils which It Occasions." A seventh edition was published posthumously in 1872.

The choice of words in the title is indicative of the moral tinge of the treatise. Initially conceived as an attack on Condorcet's conjectures regarding the perfectibility of man and Godwin's allegation that the vices of mankind originated in human institutions, Malthus' polemic was founded on an "original sin" attitude.

Malthus' basic assumptions about man as a social animal are directly related to his population theory. "To the laws of property and marriage, and to the apparently narrow principle of self-interest which prompts each individual to exert himself in bettering his condition, we are indebted for all the noblest exertions of human genius, for every thing that distinguishes the civilised from the savage state."[10] Malthus believed man to be indolent by nature and only stimulated into activity by marriage and children, who force him to work to support them. Behind every successful man is a woman—and several voracious children. Since work is good, then marriage must be good because it compels men to work. In this vein, Malthus quoted Benjamin Franklin's remark that "there is no bound to the prolific nature of plants or animals but what is made by their crowding and interfering with each other's means of subsistence."[11]

Malthus' lack of confidence in social progress is indicated by his conviction of "the absolute impossibility from the fixed laws of our nature, that the pressure of want can ever be completely removed from the lower classes." Again, "The structure of society, in its great features, will probably always remain unchanged."[12]

Consistent with his moral views was his assertion concerning birth control: "I should always particularly reprobate any artificial and unnatural modes of checking population, both on account of their immorality and their tendency to remove a necessary stimulus to industry. If it were possible for each married couple to limit by a wish the number of their children, there is certainly reason to fear that the indolence of the human race would be very greatly increased."[13]

Horrified as he was by moral depravity, which he believed to lower the marriage rate, Reverend Malthus could still not accept "immorality" as a preventive, even though he feared overpopulation. "It is impossible

---

[10] Malthus, *Essay*, sixth edition, 1826, p. 543.
[11] Benjamin Franklin, "Observations Concerning the Increase of Mankind and the Peopling of Countries," Boston, 1755; reprinted in *The Interests of Great Britain Considered*, Boston, 1760.
[12] Malthus, *Essay*, sixth edition, *op. cit.*, p. 543.
[13] *Ibid.*, p. 572.

to read the speech of Metellus Numidicus in his censorship without indignation and disgust. 'If it were possible,' he says, 'entirely to go without wives, we would deliver ourselves at once from this evil; but as the laws of nature have so ordered it that we can neither live happy with them nor continue the species without them, we ought to have more regard for our lasting security than for our transient pleasure.' "[14]

CENTRAL THEME OF THE *Essay*

Malthus began the first edition of the *Essay* with two postulates: "First, that food is necessary to the existence of man. Secondly, that the passion between the sexes is necessary and will remain in its present state. These two laws ever since we have had any knowledge of mankind appear to have been fixed laws of our nature; and as we have not hitherto seen any alteration in them, we have no right to conclude that they will ever cease to be what they now are, without an immediate act of power in that Being who first arranged the system of the universe; and for the advantage of His creatures still executes, according to fixed laws, all its various operations."[15] In the second edition, published in 1803, he considerably amplified these remarks, but subsequent editions contained no substantial conceptual alterations. Because of its greater completeness, the sixth and final edition in his lifetime is considered definitive; the heart of the work is expressed in the first three chapters.

Chapter Two of the sixth edition concludes with the following propositions: "1) Population is necessarily limited by the means of subsistence. 2) Population invariably increases where the means of subsistence increase, unless prevented by some very powerful and obvious checks. 3) These checks, and the checks which repress the superior power of population, and keep its effects on a level with the means of subsistence, are all resolvable into moral restraint, vice and misery."[16] By moral restraint, Malthus meant "the restraint from marriage which is not followed by irregular gratifications"; by vice, "promiscuous intercourse, unnatural passions, violations of the marriage bed, and improper arts to conceal the consequences of irregular connexions"; and by misery, "wars, excesses." In addition to these "preventive checks," he postulated the following "positive" population checks: "unwholesome occupations, severe labour and exposure to the seasons, extreme poverty, bad nursing of children, great towns, excesses of all kinds, the whole train of common diseases and epidemics."[17]

---

[14] *Ibid.*, p. 136.
[15] Malthus, *Essay*, first edition, 1798, pp. 5-6.
[16] Malthus, *Essay*, sixth edition, 1826, p. 14.
[17] *Ibid.*, pp. 9-10.

These three propositions form the substance of the theory, of which the fifty-five chapters of the sixth edition are essentially elaboration and documentation. To be sure they are not really original; Malthus' contribution lies not in the newness of his ideas, but in the comprehensiveness and depth of his analysis. Adam Smith, Robert Wallace, and others knew of this relation between population and resources, but none achieved the thoroughness that comes from a lifetime of work devoted to the subject.

One additional element of Malthus' work has received such attention —frequently adverse—as to require comment here. This is his statement that "population, when unchecked, increases in a geometrical ratio. Subsistence increases only in an arithmetical ratio. A slight acquaintance with numbers will show the immensity of the first power in comparison of the second."[18] In this fashion, "the human species would increase as the numbers 1, 2, 4, 8, 16, 32, 64, 128, 256, and subsistence as 1, 2, 3, 4, 5, 6, 7, 8, 9. In two centuries the population would be to the means of subsistence as 256 to 9; in three centuries as 4096 to 13, and in two thousand years the difference would be almost incalculable."[19] This comparison of two progressions was an unfortunate choice for Malthus. It was easy for his opponents to attack by *reductio ad absurdum*, and it has been one of the strongest points of criticism of Malthus over the years. This misleading calculation, however, should not be treated as the basic reasoning of Malthus' theory; in fact, it was added for illustrative purposes after publication of the first edition of the *Essay*.

WEAKNESSES OF THE THEORY

Viewed from the vantage point of the present, Malthus' theory contains four especially important weaknesses. First, he placed undue emphasis on the limitation of the supply of the land. This common mistake is attributable to neglect of the elasticity of substitution of the factors of agricultural production. His predictions did not come about partly because of the nineteenth-century revolution in agricultural methods—crop rotation, chemical fertilizers, plant and animal breeding, and improved livestock feed.

Second, Malthus did not adequately recognize the possibilities for improvement in our standard of living through industrialization, better methods of transportation, and superior distribution techniques. He underestimated our potential for inventions and technological innovations.

Third, he did not take into consideration the faster and more reliable

---

[18] Malthus, *Essay*, second edition, 1803, pp. 13-14.
[19] Malthus, *Essay*, sixth edition, 1826, p. 7.

modes of transport which helped colonial empires to provide additional raw materials, an exploitable labor supply, and new markets for manufactured products. International trade flourished as never before. And huge outpourings of emigrants from crowded European countries afforded temporary relief from population pressure in the home nations.

Finally, his religious beliefs prevented him from grasping the possibility of widespread use of contraceptives. Believing birth control to be immoral, he closed his eyes to its possibilities. He further assumed that only suffering and the fear of more suffering could enjoin the masses to reduce their fertility. But we know now that prudence and hopelessness are incompatible, and restraint and forethought are adjuncts of security.

Sometimes Malthus leaves his readers in doubt as to whether he means that population is in fact increasing faster than the means of subsistence or merely that it might do so if left unchecked. Except for temporary periods, the former situation is clearly impossible for any length of time. "The very fact that numbers are increasing indicates that the means to support them is increasing too. Otherwise mortality would have risen and the population would never have grown to its present size. To think of the world's population as 'outrunning' its normal food supply is like thinking of the hind feet of a horse outrunning the front feet."[20]

IMPACT OF MALTHUS

The rise and fall of interest in Malthus has shown two rather abrupt alterations. Immediately following the publication of his book in 1798, he became a focus of intense controversies. Numerous written responses, sometimes quite heated, both supported and opposed the theory. Clearly, the time was ripe for such a book. Mass destitution was the great problem of the day.

Shortly after Malthus' death in 1834, his theory dropped from favor as new lands and more efficient means of production and distribution temporarily eliminated from men's minds the fears that had made Malthus' book a best-seller during his lifetime. His doctrines held little relevance then because men were finding ways to avoid the pressure of population on the means of subsistence.

The overpopulation (or underfeeding) problems of the twentieth century have encouraged an intense revival of interest in Malthus' ideas throughout the learned world. The force of this revival is attributable to an increased rate of growth, a greater awareness of the consequences of rapid growth, and a widening realization that certain natural resources are being wasted and even exhausted. Whenever there is a real possibility

---

[20] Kingsley Davis, *Human Society*, The Macmillan Co., New York, 1949, p. 612.

of eventual inability to support a growing population, Malthusian principles apply. The force of the birth control movement is augmented by the fact that this "cure for pauperism" can be used by each individual to solve his personal financial problem. It requires no extensive changes in laws, social welfare, or the economic system—although it is helped by legalizing contraception.

Malthus influenced intellectual history in many fields. In economics, his close friend David Ricardo took Malthus' ideas one step further and developed the iron law of wages as a part of a theory of rent and the distribution of wealth: whenever a shortage of labor leads to higher wages, Ricardo reasoned, an increase in population and labor supply follows, succeeded by a consequent reduction of wages to the old level. In other words, fluctuations in the wage level are self-correcting or stabilizing. Thus, in the long run, the poor cannot improve their lot. "The natural price of labor is the price which is necessary to enable the laborers, one with another, to subsist and to perpetuate their race, without either increase or diminution."[21] In our own century, Alfred Marshall called Malthus' work one of the foundation stones of economics and "the first thorough application of the inductive method to social science." The great economist John Maynard Keynes referred to it as the product of a youthful genius.

In biology, both Charles Darwin and Alfred Russel Wallace acknowledged their debt to Malthus for the phrase "struggle for survival" as well as for his suggestion that species may gradually alter through the selection consequent upon their ability to reproduce beyond the supporting capacity of the environment. "In October 1838," Darwin wrote, "I happened to read for amusement 'Malthus on Population' and being very well prepared to appreciate the struggle for existence which everywhere goes on, from long continued observation of the habits of animals and plants, it at once struck me that under these circumstances favorable variations would tend to be preserved, and unfavorable ones to be destroyed. The result would be the formation of a new species. Here then I had a theory by which to work."[22] Modern ecological biologists agree: "Judged by the relative volume of literature . . . the majority of ecologists seem to be neo-Malthusians, and they evince a great concern over the likelihood that food will again play this role of limiting population increase."[23]

---

[21] David Ricardo, *Principles of Political Economy and Taxation*, London, 1817, Chap. V.

[22] Francis Darwin (ed.), *The Life and Letters of Charles Darwin*, London, 1887, Vol. I, p. 83.

[23] Peter W. Frank, "Ecology and Demography," in Philip M. Hauser and Otis Dudley Duncan, *The Study of Population*, University of Chicago Press, Chicago, 1959, p. 673.

Social Darwinists have occasionally used this notion of struggle to buttress their contention that social groups share with biological groups the propensity to evolve and consequently to benefit from an elimination of those individuals least able to meet the unceasing competition and conflict that is inherent in existence. Thus Malthusian pessimism is converted into a force for societal progress.

In sum, "Malthus's work was a great one, written in an opportune time, and though it cannot lay claim to any considerable originality as far as the theories presented are concerned, it was successful in that it showed more fully, perhaps more clearly, and certainly more effectively than had any previous attempt, that population depends on subsistence and that its increase is checked by want, vice, and disease as well as by moral restraint or prudence."[24]

Nineteenth- and Twentieth-Century Theories

Post-Malthusian demographic viewpoints may be grouped into four (somewhat overlapping) categories: economics and politics, social philosophy, biology and ecology, and mathematics. The first two of these involve "secondary" theories, while the others bring together both primary and secondary theoretical formulations. Beliefs about what population actually does are often bound up with what population must do in order to achieve the outcome desired by the writer.

ECONOMICS AND POLITICS

Nineteenth-century political economists of the "right wing" and "center" (to use modern terms) engaged in highly involuted reasoning concerning the relationship between population trends and wage levels, unemployment, production levels, interest, rent, profits, supply of capital, agricultural stability, marginal utility, use of natural resources, and standard of living. None of these theorists claimed to be particularly interested in demographic phenomena, but they did recognize the indispensability of population as a factor in explaining economic conditions, and they used population both as an independent and as a dependent variable. Henry George, for example, attributed overpopulation to inequities in the land ownership system and the tax structure.[25] Certain that Malthus was wrong, he maintained that the problem of the relation of population to resources is simply one of ease of access to land. George's system of land reform was presumed to enable men to support large families comfortably.

---

[24] Charles Emil Stangeland, *Pre-Malthusian Doctrines of Population*, Columbia University Press, New York, 1904, p. 356.
[25] Henry George, *Progress and Poverty*, Appleton Century, New York, 1881.

A more recent economic example takes a quite different line. Gary Becker has put forth a theory analyzing fertility by viewing children as a durable good, primarily a consumer's durable, yielding income, primarily psychic, to parents. Becker postulates that fertility is determined by family income, costs of bearing and rearing children, and preferences and tastes, with increased income and declining prices tending to increase the demand for children. But since children are not bought or sold, each family, rather, producing its own, every uncertainty in the production of children (such as their number and sex) creates a corresponding uncertainty in consumption.[26]

Several nineteenth-century economic and political writers were in reaction against Adam Smith and the classical school of economics, with its emphasis on individualism, unrestricted competition, private property, and self-interest—conceptions dear to the heart of Malthus. Thus Karl Marx took the position that there is no such thing as overpopulation. Rather, an appearance of overpopulation is attributable to the deliberate creation by the capitalist class of a surplus labor force. In this way, the threat of unemployment hangs over the heads of workers, who are thus more readily exploited. Malthus' stress on the biological causation of poverty and population pressure irked Marx extremely. He rejected and found opprobrious Malthus' claim that misery was universal and inevitable Nor could he accept Malthus' opposition to the Poor Laws and other social welfare legislation or the English parson's confidence in individualistic competition and moral prudence. In Marx' eyes, Malthus was an apologist for the exploiting class and a literary oppressor of the underprivileged. Marx' associate Friedrich Engels described Malthus' teaching as "a shameful, degrading doctrine."

Later, Lenin joined Marx in rejecting Malthus. Lenin wanted women to pursue careers! "The main task is to draw the women into socially productive labor, extricate them from domestic slavery."[27] Lubny-Gertsyk and other Communists writing in the 1920's discussed population matters with some objectivity. In 1935 and 1936, Smulevich published two books denouncing bourgeois theories of population, especially Malthusianism, and as late as 1959 he claimed that "the problem of population and public health is fully resolved only in a socialist society." He writes of "distortions of population problems in the bourgeois

---

[26] Gary S. Becker, "An Economic Analysis of Fertility," in National Bureau of Economic Research, *Demographic and Economic Change in Developed Countries*, Princeton University Press, Princeton, 1960, pp. 209-231.

[27] V. I. Lenin, *Women and Society*, International Publishers, New York, 1938, p. 14.

literature" and the "insolubility of population and public health problems within the framework of capitalism."[28]

Although socialists are far removed in most points of political and
economic doctrine from the Communists, they have often agreed with
them in blaming overpopulation on the organization of society. It is
not growth itself but the maldistribution of necessities and luxuries
that must be eliminated. There is, however, this difference: whereas
Communists prefer to deny the existence of population problems,
socialists acknowledge the problems but turn to revision of the social
order for a solution. Recently there has been a swing of socialist thinking
toward the acknowledgement of population *per se* as a source of serious
problems and a consequent espousal of planned parenthood.

SOCIAL PHILOSOPHY

Another social reform group, the utilitarians, sought to make individual
happiness and social utility the sole criteria for evaluating the goodness
of an act. "Actions are right," wrote Mill, "in proportion as they tend to
promote happiness, wrong as they tend to produce the reverse of happiness."[29] Major supporters of this Greatest Happiness Principle were
Jeremy Bentham, James Mill, and his son John Stuart Mill. The school
tried to make happiness the primary aim of morality, and in this way
utilitarianism became a radical social propaganda movement. Indeed, the
utilitarians were quite effective in influencing new legislation promoting
social welfare.

John Stuart Mill may be described as a Malthusian with qualifications.
While agreeing in the main with Malthus, he differed regarding birth
control and the impact of property on fertility. In fact, Mill was one of
the first propagandists of the family planning movement, declaring in
1821 that "the great practical problem is thus to find out how to limit
the number of births." He was perhaps the leading advocate of women's
rights in his time, and his epochal tract *On Liberty* (1859) is still one
of our finest pleas for the rights of the individual. In *The Subjugation of
Women* (1869) he disagreed sharply with the widely-held assumption
that the restriction of women to childbearing, child-rearing, and house-
work was "natural" and inevitable. *Principles of Political Economy*
related population laws to the theory of production: there are three
factors in production, Mill stated—labor, land, and capital—and popula-

---

[28] B. Y. Smulevich, *A Critique of Bourgeois Theories and Population Policy*,
Publishing House of Socio-Economic Literature, Moscow, 1959; quotations are
from G. Akulov, translated by R. A. Feldmesser, in *Sociological Abstracts*, Vol. IX,
No. 2, April 1961, p. 152.
[29] John Stuart Mill, *Utilitarianism*, London, 1861. p. 6.

tion phenomena underlie the supply of labor and less directly influence the availability of land. Mill described the United States as a horrible example of the deification of material possessions, wealth, and population expansion: "the life of the whole of one sex is devoted to dollar-hunting, and of the other to breeding dollar-hunters."[30] The twentieth-century transition theory of Thompson and Notestein has been called "a modern elaboration of Mill's distinction between Malthusian and non-Malthusian populations."[31]

In the traditional view, inimical to Mill, the arch-woman, the peasant woman, was a Mother. Today, however (although it is not perhaps what Mill had in mind) there is the companion-wife, who has mental conflicts instead of children. According to historian Oswald Spengler, the resultant infertility is a major element in the crash of civilizations. Since modern urbanites—unlike primitive men and agricultural peasants who select wives to bear their children—choose a companion who is unfit to be a mother because, as Marchbanks said of G. B. Shaw's Candida, "she belongs to herself," there then begins in all civilizations the stage of "dreadful depopulation. The whole pyramid of human society capable of developing culture disappears."[32]

The less pessimistic philosopher-sociologist Herbert Spencer held that fertility decreases as the complexity of life increases. In societies having complex social organizations, Spencer believed, people tend to increase the proportion of energy devoted to personal development and other nonreproductive activities, at the expense of the birth rate. He saw a natural antagonism between "individuation" and "genesis." Considering his position as a forerunner of sociology, Spencer was remarkably biologistic, postulating that reproductive power declines in people having exceptional cerebral development. "Absolute or relative infertility," he wrote, "is generally produced in women by mental labour carried to excess. . . . The deficiency of reproductive power . . . may be reasonably attributed to the overtaxing of their brains."[33]

Several Frenchmen developed the idea of social capillarity. As a liquid rises in a hair-thin tube through capillary action (the absorption of ink by blotting paper, the rising of sap in trees), so too do persons rise in the social scale. As physical capillarity takes place automatically in the proper circumstances, so the desire to rise is practically universal in an open-class democracy. The crusader Arsène Dumont feared that social

---

[30] J. S. Mill, *Principles of Political Economy*, London, 1857.

[31] Robert Gutman, "In Defense of Population Theory," *American Sociological Review*, Vol. XXV, No. 3, June 1960, p. 328.

[32] Oswald Spengler, *The Decline of the West*, Munich, 1924, Vol. II, p. 125.

[33] Herbert Spencer, *The Principles of Biology*, D. Appleton and Co., New York, 1868, Vol. II, pp. 485-486.

capillarity was causing the break-up of the French family.[34] The more people desire to scale the social ladder, the fewer children they have—to the disadvantage of the nation. Thus French population growth is being strangled by the openness of its class structure; societies with more rigid stratification systems have low capillarity and therefore no tendency for fertility to drop and population to decline. In the same way that a solid impedes capillary action in liquids, a fixed caste system prevents upward movement, thus obviating personal ambition as a motive for smaller families.

Religious affiliation also is said to affect fertility. Max Weber observed that the sexual asceticism of Puritanism differs only in degree from that of Catholic monasticism—and since the former reaches a larger proportion of the populace, its influence on national birth rates is greater than that of the latter.[35]

To sum up, these pioneers, whether adopting population as an independent variable (Mill, Spengler) or as a dependent factor (Spencer, Dumont, Weber), made far less use of population in their social analyses than is customary today. The demographic reasoning of the social philosophers was generally thin, often obvious, and rarely seminal. By contrast, modern social scientists explore interconnections between population and other variables extensively and effectively. Some scholars derive nondemographic ideas from population theories, a recent illustration being Reisman's character typology—tradition-directed, inner-directed, and other-directed people—which was inspired by Thompson's transition theory.[36]

BIOLOGY AND ECOLOGY

The famous heredity *versus* environment dispute in psychology has a counterpart in demography. Prominent among contemporary proponents of heredity as the principal determinant of natality is an Italian, Corrado Gini, who argues that organic degeneration limits biological capacity to reproduce. Without the reinvigoration resulting from cross-breeding of peoples of different stocks, a natural and inevitable "physical exhaustion of the germinal cells" occurs. Furthermore, Gini argues, it is the upper classes especially who tend to experience this deterioration of the reproductive tissues. Nature's cutting off of the reproductive vigor of the upper class is a "providential mechanism for the elimination of

---

[34] Arsène Dumont, *Dépopulation et civilisation*, Paris, 1890; *Natalité et démocratie*, Paris, 1898; *La morale basée sur la démographie*, Paris, 1901.

[35] Max Weber, *The Protestant Ethic and the Spirit of Capitalism* (translated by Talcott Parsons), George Allen and Unwin Ltd., London, 1930, p. 158.

[36] David Reisman, Nathan Glazer, and Reuel Denny, *The Lonely Crowd*, Yale University Press, New Haven, 1950, p. 23.

those family stocks which have fulfilled the cycle of their evolution,"[37] a process which eradicates the weaker strains—scions of inherited wealth and nobility who have reached the stage of exhausted generative power. Paucity of substantiating evidence, however, has led demographers to be highly skeptical of Gini's theory of "demographic metabolism." In fact, in the Growth of American Families study a higher proportion of sub-fecundity (total or partial impairment of ability to reproduce) was disclosed in the lower class than the upper class, though this difference is probably not due to biological sources.[38]

A century earlier, Michael Thomas Sadler wrote that "the fecundity of human beings . . . varies inversely as their numbers on a given space."[39] Population tends to reach a state of equilibrium with density, income, and related variables. But Sadler's contention that nature "abhors" excessive density is as intellectually naïve as Spinoza's "Nature abhors a vacuum."

Eighteen years later Thomas Doubleday propounded as a general law that "whenever a species or genus is endangered, a corresponding effort is invariably made by nature for its preservation and continuance, by an increase of fecundity or fertility; and that this especially takes place whenever such danger arises from a diminution of proper nourishment or food."[40] Thus fecundity varies inversely with the amount and variety of food. The Chinese, Irish, and Scotch, Doubleday claimed, were prolific because of their inadequate diet. He "proved" diet to be responsible by observing that in China, Ireland, and Scotland the diet was poor and fertility high. Quoting Pliny to show that fat people are barren, and finding the birth rate low in France (where people were fat) but high in the slums of England (where people were thin), he concluded that "The plethoric state invariably checks [the population] and the deplethoric state invariably develops it."[41]

Another Englishman, William Paley, attributed the high birth rate of Indians to their dependence on vegetables and rice. Acquisition of a taste for the flesh of animals, he claimed, would induce in a few years a great diminution of population.[42] This assumption that there is an

---

[37] Corrado Gini, "The Cyclical Rise and Fall of Population," in Harris Foundation, *Population,* University of Chicago Press, Chicago, 1930, p. 25.

[38] Ronald Freedman, Pascal Whelpton, and Arthur A. Campbell, *Family Planning, Sterility, and Population Growth,* McGraw-Hill Book Co., New York, 1959, p. 19.

[39] Michael Thomas Sadler, *The Law of Population,* John Murray, London, 1829, p. xxviii.

[40] Thomas Doubleday, *The True Law of Population, Shewn to Be Connected with the Food of the People,* George Pierce, London, 1847, p. 5.

[41] *Ibid.,* p. 20.

[42] William Paley, *The Principles of Moral and Political Philosophy,* London, 1793, Vol. II, p. 355.

inverse relationship between the eating of meat and the bearing of children is found in the folklore of many countries in many centuries.

Currently, the neo-Godwinist physician Josué de Castro echoes this still unverified claim that deficiency of proteins makes undernourished people more fertile than well-fed ones.[43] He cross-tabulated countries according to the protein content of their diets and their birth rates and, finding a negative correlation, assumed a causal relation. But correlation in itself does not demonstrate causation. Furthermore de Castro conveniently omitted many regions which did not support his hypothesis. Nor did he allow adequately for the possibility that other aspects of national life could be responsible for fertility differentials. He might as well have considered the correlation between national fertility and consumption of ice-cream sodas, use of washing machines, or watching of television; as spouses of late-late show addicts have pointed out, the latter is at least connected with sexual behavior.

None of these teleological or dietary views has gained the applause of demographers. Not only do biologistic theories generally assume the existence of a metaphysical will of nature to perpetuate the species— an assumption which demographers cannot accept—but many are marked by choice of causally irrelevant variables to explain correctly reported facts. Because the data are properly cited, lay readers are often deluded into believing the explanatory reasoning to be correct. These speculations share with other naturalistic explanations a tendency to seek immutable laws not subject to human manipulation, whereas in fact the demographic behavior of human beings tends to be strongly under their own control.

Related to these views through the common property of being biological, but differing from them in having a sounder scientific base, are genetics and ecology. Scientific study of genetics began with the Austrian abbot Gregor Mendel, whose epoch-making 1865 paper summarized eight years of painstaking crossbreeding and hybridization of garden peas in a monastery garden and put forth the thesis that, among hybrids, three out of four offspring will display the dominant and one out of four the recessive traits. Further research by such biologists as 1933 Nobel prize winner Thomas Hunt Morgan has elucidated the mechanisms of heredity in terms of mutation, genes, and chromosomes, the carriers of inheritable characteristics.

The word "ecology" was first proposed by a German biologist in 1868 from the Greek *oikos*, meaning "house" or "place to live." Thus ecology is the study of organisms "at home" or "the relations of organisms to the

---

[43] Josué de Castro, *The Geography of Hunger*, Little, Brown and Co., Boston, 1952.

surrounding outer world."[44] It is now a separate branch of biology, dealing with the mutual relations between organisms and their environments. According to ecologists, the symbiotic and commensal associations of plants and animals determine the population size of each species, with one notable exception—civilized man, whose technology enhances his control over his habitat and raises him to the top of the dominance hierarchy. The interacting aggregation of animals, plants, and physical features of the habitat is called an ecosystem. Ecosystems can be of any size—the whole earth and all its animal and plant inhabitants together may be treated as a gigantic ecosystem. Twentieth-century social scientists have borrowed these terms to refer to man's relations with his fellows, his physical surroundings, and his numbers and density. Hutchinson and Deevey even went so far as to coin the term "biodemography" to designate studies of the interaction of environment, density of habitation, fertility, mortality, migratory dispersal, and age distribution among mammals, birds, fish, reptiles, and insects.[45]

Ecological theory has implications both for optimum population and for the carrying capacity—the maximum population attainable in a given area under given conditions—noting that human populations sometimes temporarily exceed the normal carrying capacity, either through release from the subsistence level of living or through assistance from outside areas. For this reason, analogies between animal and human populations are rarely effective, because whereas animal densities are controlled by external forces (weather, predators, unchecked disease, and an uncontrollable food supply), human densities in nonsubsistence societies are largely controlled by man himself. Therefore, if man's population is to level off to a carrying capacity, it must occur at least partially through his own efforts.

MATHEMATICS

As population data improved, mathematicians and mathematically-trained social scientists began to apply sophisticated algebraic and geometric techniques to demography. In 1835, Quételet posited that the obstacles to population growth increase in direct proportion to the square of the rate of increase.[46] As a result, population tends to grow more and more slowly, thus carrying its own built-in self-limiting property.

Three years later Verhulst suggested that the logistic curve might

---

[44] Ernst H. Haeckel, *The History of Creation*, D. Appleton and Co., New York, 1884, Vol. II, p. 354.

[45] G. E. Hutchinson and E. S. Deevey, Jr., "Ecological Studies on Population," *Surveys of Biological Progress*, Vol. I, 1949, pp. 325-359.

[46] Adolphe Quételet, *Sur l'homme et le développement de ses facultés*, Paris, 1835.

be useful in estimating population increase.[47] The logistic is one form of the generic type known as sigmoid curves—that is, curves having the approximate shape of an attenuated letter S. Beginning from a lower limit or horizontal asymptote, the logistic climbs symmetrically toward an upper limit or asymptote. The lower asymptote represents demographic stasis, the sloping portion portrays growth (first at an increasing and then at a decreasing rate), and the upper asymptote shows the carrying capacity.

In the 1920's, Pearl and Reed used the logistic extensively to estimate future populations of various countries,[48] having over the quarter century 1925-1950 a creditable average error of 9 per cent. Unfortunately, projections for some nations were as much as 36 per cent below or 122 per cent above the actual population.

Pearl and Reed developed their curve from observing changes in the number of fruit flies living in a limited and constant environment.[49] The logistic provides an accurate description of the growth of any animal or plant population living in a fixed area under regular climatic conditions and without human intervention. Population growth is slow at first, then becomes very rapid, later slows down as environmental resistance increases, and finally reaches a new equilibrium level. The sigmoid curve applies to fish in a pond, bees in an apiary, pheasants in a field, and sheep in a pasture.[50] The mathematical assumptions of the logistic also make it well suited to studying human population developments in an unchanging or very slowly changing environment (constant area of the country, stable economic and political situation, and uniform level of technology), a condition which has prevailed during most of man's existence. However, in the twentieth century, changes have proceeded too rapidly to fit the assumptions of the logistic.

Demographic histories of several countries have been analyzed by K. W. Taylor through series of three or four sigmoid curves separated by periods of stationary population.[51] Periods of rapid growth reflect the introduction of some productive or other environmental improvement, while static periods reflect continued adjustment to unchanging environmental conditions. Taylor used a curve with three sigmoid growth

---

[47] Pierre F. Verhulst, "Notice sur la loi que la population suit dans son accroissement," in A. Quételet, *Correspondance mathématique et physique*, Brussels, 1838.

[48] Raymond Pearl and Lowell J. Reed, "On the Rate of Growth of the Population of the United States since 1790 and Its Mathematical Representation," *Proceedings of the National Academy of Science*, Vol. VI, No. 6, June 1920, pp. 275-288.

[49] Raymond Pearl, *The Biology of Population Growth*, Alfred A. Knopf, New York, 1925.

[50] Eugene P. Odum, *Fundamentals of Ecology*, W. B. Saunders Co., Philadelphia, 1953, pp. 129-131.

[51] K. W. Taylor, "Some Aspects of Population History," *Canadian Journal of Economics and Political Science*, Vol. XVI, August 1950, pp. 301-313.

stages to describe the population history of France: a first stage ceiling of 5 million under primitive agriculture (200 B.C.), a second ceiling of 20 million under preindustrial civilization (1300-1600 A.D.), and a ceiling of 40 million in the recent past. England has had four growth periods separated by three stable periods: one million under primitive agriculture (100 B.C.), two and a half million as a frontier province of fifteenth-century Europe, and six million as a preindustrial trading power (1700 A.D.). China has had four growth segments, reaching 18 million by 500 B.C., 60 million by 200 A.D., 100 million by 1100 A.D., and 450 million by 1850; at present, China is in a fifth growth stage.

Many other mathematical expressions have been pressed into service to describe or predict population growth, especially straight lines, compound interest curves, and parabolas. They all share with the logistic a record of sometimes succeeding, sometimes failing.

Conclusion

Much has been written in ancient, medieval, and modern times speculating on ways in which populations grow, but very few writers have held intellectual positions that constitute rigorous, systematic population theories. Some *soi-disant* theories are nothing more than empirical generalizations which describe repeatedly observed relationships without offering any understanding of why the conjunction occurs. Others share in a regrettable social science propensity: theory, "instead of meaning the widest body of rigorous reasoning about a set of observed relationships, has come to mean a long stretch of purely verbal analysis. If a publication contains any empirical evidence, particularly of a statistical kind, it is not theory; but if it contains only verbal generalizations, no matter how loosely connected, it is a theory."[52] Many of these speculations are ethical injunctions. Indeed, until quite recently, most men writing of demographic matters produced as a matter of course *obiter dicta* supported by quotations from philosophical and religious sources. And a large proportion of the early doctrines were expounded by parsons and priests. It is only in the last few hundred years that we have gotten away from the sonorous moralistic titles that betoken more ardor than science, more conviction than statistics.

The most prominent theorist continues to be Thomas Robert Malthus, whose main thesis was that population tends to increase faster than the means of subsistence and must therefore be restrained

---

[52] Kingsley Davis, "The Sociology of Demographic Behavior," in Robert K. Merton *et al.* (eds.), *Sociology Today*, Basic Books, New York, 1959, p. 313.

by several powerful checks. The exceptional viability of Malthus' theory may lie in its inclusion of a multiplicity of variables, both natural and social, as well as in its pertinence to problems facing the world today.

Yet the twentieth century has not been without its own prophets. Various kinds of theories have been proposed in the twentieth century. One of these, the Thompson-Notestein transition theory, described in Chapter 2, has gained general acceptance despite scattered critical avowals of oversimplification.[53] This three-stage typology is widely used to describe, interpret, and predict changes in total population and in the demographic components: fertility, mortality, and migration.

---

[53] Paul K. Hatt, Nellie Louise Farr, and Eugene Weinstein, "Types of Population Balance," *American Sociological Review*, Vol. XX, No. 1, February 1955, pp. 14-21.

PART II

MORTALITY, FERTILITY, AND MIGRATION

5 ✕ The Decline of Mortality

Of the three demographic variables, mortality will be discussed first. This order comes about partly because mortality is simplest to analyze and partly because of the chronological primacy of changes in mortality in initiating the demographic revolution.

The over-all picture is one of tremendous improvement in health and length of life in recent centuries—an improvement which is particularly evident in some social groups and in certain countries. "Throughout European history, epidemics had decimated the population at frequent intervals and had disrupted trade and commerce. Infant mortality was very high, and the men and women who survived their first few years lived their lives harassed by 'fevers,' by diseases of malnutrition, and a host of other ill-defined disabling diseases."[1] Man's increased ability to control his environment and thus defeat disease, famine, winter, predatory animals, and other enemies has more than counterbalanced those mortality increases resulting from modern improved death-dealing techniques.

For the first time in history, we are making good the Biblical allotment: "The days of our years are threescore and ten; and if by reason of strength they be fourscore years, yet is their strength labour and sorrow; for it is soon cut off, and we fly away" (Psalms, 90:10). In Moses' day, few people lived beyond seventy, and when they did, their final years ended in "labour and sorrow." Today, things are different. Years lived beyond seventy are accounted an expected bonus beyond what with reasonable luck can be taken for granted; anything less is a

---

[1] Bernhard J. Stern, "The Health of Towns and the Early Public Health Movement," *The Interne*, Vol. XIV, No. 3, March 1948, pp. 83-87; reprinted in Stern, *Historical Sociology*, The Citadel Press, New York, 1959, pp. 386-400.

visitation of misfortune. A few centuries ago, people could expect only one-half as many years of life. "Viewed as a whole the 'problem of aging' is no problem at all. It is only the pessimistic way of looking at a great triumph of civilization."[2]

Preindustrial Conditions

Although there is little solid evidence concerning mortality in ancient times, and virtually no evidence for prehistoric periods, demographers have still been able to make some fairly reliable statements about man's early health and mortality. Paleopathology, the study of disease through fossils and human remains, is a little-known medical specialty which has greatly contributed to our knowledge of the history of epidemiology. The remains of a reptile, Dimetrodon, that lived perhaps 200 million years ago, show evidence of chronic osteomyelitis of the spine. Signs of carious teeth and rheumatic swellings of the joints have been found in numerous Mesozoic fossils; callus and bacterial infections are evidenced in the Paleozoic period.[3] Certainly physical disease antedates man.

ANTHROPOLOGICAL EVIDENCE

Knowledge of early man comes to us in shreds and shards. Population data concerning prehistoric and modern primitive groups are limited in scope and uneven in reliability. And the farther back in time we go, the worse the data become.

All of the vagueness and error stems from one source, that of incomplete collection. Demography of the living deals with a single moment in time, and has the opportunity, seized or not, of knowing the definition of the group (tribe, horde, etc.) with which it is dealing. Archaeological demography, on the other hand, suffers from inability to control these very things, circumscription of the group and contemporaneity. . . . A constant and major problem in archaeology is to know, from all the evidence, how many people were present at one time, not simply how many contributed to all the rubbish, or how many eventually got into a cemetery.[4]

---

[2] Frank W. Notestein, "Some Demographic Aspects of Aging," *Proceedings of the American Philosophical Society*, Vol. XCVIII, No. 1, February 1954, p. 38.

[3] Roy L. Moodie, *The Antiquity of Disease*, University of Chicago Press, Chicago, 1923, pp. 55-56.

[4] William W. Howells, "Estimating Population Numbers through Archaeological and Skeletal Remains," in Robert F. Heizer and Sherburne F. Cook, *The Application of Quantitative Methods in Archaeology*, Viking Fund Publications in Anthropology, No. 28, 1960, pp. 158-159.

Examination of skeletal remains of Paleolithic man shows that he suffered from much the same diseases that affect modern man—tuberculosis, arthritis, and so forth. From the rather small sample of Neanderthal men (who lived about 150,000 to 100,000 years ago) concerning whom we have information, physical anthropologists surmise that only about one-half reached early adulthood and that about 95 per cent died before reaching age forty. For the later Paleolithic (about 35,000 to 8,000 years ago in the Near East—more recently in other parts of the world), skeletal findings indicate around 10 per cent surviving to age forty and a mere 1 per cent reaching the relatively advanced age of fifty. "According to Vallois, none of the known Neanderthal individuals passed the age of fifty; of 102 skeletons of the Upper Paleolithic only one (Oberkassel) did so, possibly passing sixty; and of sixty-five Mesolithic individuals, largely European, only two passed fifty. Of forty-eight Mesolithic skeletons of Northwest Africa none was older than forty-five—no woman older than thirty-five; ninety-four Silesian Neolithic skeletons furnished only four over fifty years of age; 102 west and central Bell Beaker adults furnished only 4.9 per cent of 'senile.' "[5] Excavations from the Middle Bronze age in Lerna, Greece, uncovered 230 bodies, of which 52 per cent were under age ten and only 6 per cent over age forty-five. The 1132 cases found in the Indian Knoll, Kentucky, excavation apparently covered the years 500 B.C. through 500 A.D.; 59 per cent had reached age ten, 49 per cent age twenty, 26 per cent age thirty, and 3 per cent attained age forty.[6]

Archaeological evidence is gathered from skeletons, houses, food remains, and scattered other sources—all highly questionable. For one thing, skeletal remains are not likely to constitute a representative sample of any group, being biased through differential propensities to bury and to care for the remains according to age, sex, family status, ancestry, wealth, migration history, religion, circumstances of death, and other characteristics of the individual who died. Paleodemography, in short, offers almost no solid knowledge; about all we can say with certainty is that people did not live nearly as long in prehistoric times as they do now.

ANCIENT AND MEDIEVAL MORTALITY

Accurate recorded description of symptoms begins with the ancient Greeks, among whom Democritus, Empedocles, and Alcmaeon speculated concerning contagious diseases. The first information useful in diagnosis comes from Hippocrates, the earliest physician for whom we

---

[5] *Ibid.*, pp. 171-172.
[6] *Ibid.*, pp. 169-171. Indian Knoll data are from C. E. Snow; Greek data are from J. L. Angel; approximate life tables were prepared by Howells.

have writings showing a modern approach to medicine—although he was certainly not the first great physician of antiquity. Herodotus states that the Egyptians had dentists, surgeons, internists, and even physicians specializing in one organ of the body. From these accounts, we learn that the ancients were afflicted by a wide variety of infectious diseases.

Data collected from ancient Greek burial stelae place the average length of life in 400 B.C. at approximately thirty years.[7] From epitaphs scattered throughout mainland Greece over the Hellenistic and Roman periods, two students of the subject concluded, precariously, that 62 per cent survived to age ten, 46 per cent to age twenty, 26 per cent to age thirty, 18 per cent to age forty, 13 per cent to age fifty, 9 per cent to age sixty, 4 per cent to age seventy, and 2 per cent to age eighty.[8] Karl Pearson computed the expectation of life at birth for Egyptian mummies as 22.5 years.[9] From Roman tombstone inscriptions, John Durand estimated the expectation of life at birth for the urban population of the western Roman Empire during the first and second centuries to be between fifteen and twenty-five years; for the entire population of the Empire, twenty-five to thirty years.[10] Since data taken from burial inscriptions are likely to contain defects of underrepresentation of deaths of women and children as well as other sources of bias, these figures must be considered crude approximations.

One way to avoid the pitfall of underrepresentation of women and children is to use complete genealogies from selected families. This procedure, however, introduces another kind of nonrepresentativeness: namely, that members of these families may not be subject to the same conditions of life as the general populace. One scholar, using genealogical records for men in the ruling classes of Europe from 1480 to 1579, obtained an average length of life of thirty years.[11]

Estimates for Greece of the average age at death of all persons dying at age fifteen or older (younger ages are omitted because incompleteness is too great) show a rise through Classical times and a fall in the medieval period:[12]

---

[7] V. G. Valaoras, "The Expectation of Life in Ancient Greece," *Pratika de l'académie d'Athènes*, Vol. XIII, 1938, p. 401.

[8] J. L. Angel, "The Length of Life in Ancient Greece," *Journal of Gerontology*, Vol. II, January 1947, pp. 18 ff.; and Howells, "Estimating Population Numbers through Archaeological and Skeletal Remains," *loc. cit.*, pp. 169-171.

[9] Karl Pearson, "On the Change in Expectation of Life in Man During a Period of circa 2000 Years," *Biometrika*, Vol. I, 1901-1902, p. 261.

[10] John D. Durand, "Mortality Estimates from Roman Tombstone Inscriptions," *American Journal of Sociology*, Vol. LXV, No. 4, January 1960, pp. 365-373.

[11] S. Peller, "Studies on Mortality Since the Renaissance," *Bulletin of the History of Medicine*, Vol. XIII, April 1943, pp. 427 ff.; Vol. XVI, November 1944, pp. 362 ff.; and Vol. XXI, January-February 1947, pp. 51 ff..

[12] J. L. Angel, "Human Biology, Health, and History in Greece from First Settlement until Now," *American Philosophical Society Yearbook*, 1954, pp. 168-172.

Pre-Greek	3500 B.C.	31 years
Middle Bronze	2000 B.C.	35
Mycenaean	1450 B.C.	36
Early Iron	1150 B.C.	36
Classical	680 B.C.	41
Hellenistic	300 B.C.	40
Imperial Roman	120 A.D.	38
Medieval	600 A.D.	35
Turkish	1400 A.D.	31
Romantic	1750 A.D.	40

A great pestilence was described by Marcus Aurelius in the second century, and Procopius wrote of a great pandemic—Justinian's plague —that undermined the health of the known world from 540 to 590 A.D. During the seven Crusades of 1096-1270, the Christian army suffered more from epidemics than from Saracen arms. Thus, in 1098, of a Christian army of 300,000 men that laid siege to Antioch, disease and famine killed so many so quickly that the dead could not be buried. Cavalry were rendered immobile in a few months by the death of 5,000 of their 7,000 horses.[13] The leader of the second Crusade, who crawled home with a handful of the half million men who had set off with him from Europe, wrote in his diary: "There came upon us the sickness of the host, which sickness was such that the flesh of our legs dried up, and the skin upon our legs became spotted; black and earth colour like an old book; and with us who had this sickness, the flesh of our gums putrified; nor could anyone escape from this sickness but he had to die. The sign of death was this, that when there was bleeding of the nose, then death was sure."[14] Triumphant over the armies of Europe were scurvy, typhus, and the plague. The Crusaders had indifferent success in killing off infidels and securing Jerusalem. But when it came to infecting and thus destroying their wives, children, and neighbors by diseases contracted during their peregrinations from the Holy Land, the results were phenomenal.

Though immediate mortality was fabulously high, the most serious consequence of these pestilences was the resultant social dislocation. Because of the scarcity of manpower, a manorial lord wanting his fields tilled, his wheat sowed, his vines trimmed, or his animals shepherded, had to pay double wages. Homes were emptied both by death and by affrighted migrants.

---

[13] Charles E. A. Winslow, *The Conquest of Epidemic Disease*, Princeton University Press, Princeton, 1944, p. 210.

[14] Quoted in Hans Zinsser, *Rats, Lice and History*, Little, Brown and Co., Boston, 1935, p. 157.

SEVENTEENTH- AND EIGHTEENTH-CENTURY MORTALITY

Improvements in the collection of death statistics and the development of the life table in the 1600's vastly increased the accuracy of estimates of longevity. Edmund Halley found life expectation to be 35.5 years for the city of Breslau during 1687-1691.[15] While not fully acceptable by modern standards, Halley's work nonetheless contributed much to our knowledge of mortality trends.

For eighteenth-century Western Europe and North America, much more information is available, as suggested by Table 4. Note the greater

TABLE 4. *Expectation of Life at Birth in Eighteenth-Century Europe and America.* *

AUTHOR	PERIOD COVERED	AREA	EXPECTATION OF LIFE AT BIRTH, IN YEARS
Deparcieux	Published 1746	French convents and monasteries	37.5
Price	1735-1780	Northampton	30.0
Barton	1782, 1788-1790	Part of Philadelphia	25.0
Wigglesworth	A period before 1789	Massachusetts and New Hampshire	35.5
Mourgue	1772-1792	Montpellier, Males	23.4
		Females	27.4
Duvillard	A period before 1789	Different parts of France	28.8

* Louis I. Dublin, Alfred J. Lotka, and Mortimer Spiegelman, *Length of Life*, The Ronald Press Co., New York, 1949, pp. 35-36.

longevity of females than males and the higher mortality of urban as compared to rural areas during this period. The dates and areas represented in the table are scattered; knowledge was still scanty, and students of the history of mortality must take their data where they find them.

Reasons for High Rates

Mortality conditions in all countries once resembled those now found in the most underdeveloped countries. The reasons for these high mortality rates are three: acute and chronic food shortage causing famine and malnutrition; epidemic disease; and poor public health conditions, especially in urban areas.

---

[15] Edmund Halley, "An Estimate of the Degrees of Mortality of Mankind," *Philosophical Transactions of the Royal Society of London*, Vol. XVII, 1693, pp. 596-610.

FAMINE

Death-dealing famines and debilitating chronic food shortages were common in Europe as late as the mid-nineteenth century. In Ireland in the 1840's, several hundred thousand people died of starvation. As inadequate transportation systems made each local district dependent upon its own harvest, a crop failure in one area resulted in famine even though the harvest might be normal in adjacent areas.

In Western Europe alone, 450 more or less localized famines were recorded from 1000 to 1855. During the eighteenth century, France, the richest country on the Continent, suffered repeated periods of severe scarcity. At least nine severe harvest failures were recorded in the Scandinavian countries between 1740 and 1800, each resulting in a substantial rise of the death rate. In Norway, the death rate in 1741 was more than three times as high as in 1736–1740; about one person out of fifteen in the whole population perished in that year. The main cause was the acute crop failure which visited all the northern European countries in 1740–1742. In Sweden, during the severe famine of 1773, the death rate rose to 52.5 per thousand population.[16]

In 1315-1317, a severe famine struck all of Europe north of the Pyrenees and the Alps. The price of wheat trebled on the Continent and sextupled in England; other foods rose similarly in price. The poor and lowly "were forced to feed themselves as best they might; they ate dogs, cats, the dung of doves, and even their own children. Cannibalism certainly was common." Thieves in prison, unfed, "ferociously attacked new prisoners and devoured them half alive." Starving people ate freshly buried corpses disinterred from graves. "People tried to relieve the pangs of hunger by eating leaves and roots." As frequently happens, the famine was accompanied by pestilence and "a great increase in crime," including theft of anything that might be bartered for food. "It was common to see the almost lifeless forms of famishing men and women stretched on the ground." Mortality climbed sickeningly in the summer of 1316 and then fell following the autumn harvests, attested by the number of bodies buried during the first week of each month in Ypres, Flanders, a town of about 25,000 population: 54 in May, 107 in June, 167 in July, 191 in August, 124 in September, and 15 in October.[17]

The situation was even worse in Asia, whose great civilizations were said by Mallory to contain "a constant famine factor." From 108 B.C.

---

[16] United Nations, *The Determinants and Consequences of Population Trends*, New York, 1953, p. 51.
[17] H. S. Lucas, "The Great European Famine of 1315, 1316, and 1317," *Speculum*, Vol. V, No. 4, October 1930, pp. 355-369.

to 1911 A.D., China experienced 1,828 famines—nearly one a year.[18] In comparison, the Biblical Egyptian cycle of seven years of plenty followed by seven lean years (Genesis 41) is rather favorable. The Chinese had to expect a famine at any time, triggered by crop failure, droughts, floods, and locusts. In 1877-1878, when four northern provinces were struck, cannibalism occurred frequently, and officials connived at evasion of the laws forbidding sale of children in order "to enable parents to buy a few days' food." The dead were so numerous that they were interred in "ten-thousand-men holes," and dead children were thrown into water wells. An estimated 9 to 13 million persons perished from hunger, disease, or violence.[19]

MALNUTRITION

Because of their spectacular nature, famines causing death from starvation are easily overstressed in comparison to the more deadly malnutrition resulting from continuing insufficiency of food. The latter weakens millions of people to such an extent that they are unable to resist even a mild infection. Men suffering from chronic food shortage of either quantity (calories) or variety (vitamins and minerals) are also often unable to do a full day's work, thus lowering their own incomes (and still further encouraging undernourishment in their families) and failing to make their potential contribution to the production of the community.

Harvest results mold vital rates in agricultural nations; in industrial regions the economic determination is more complicated, but the price index plays its part. The oldest reliable data on this subject are found in Scandinavia. In Denmark, Sweden, and Finland between 1734 and 1800, the crude death rate in years following crop failure or high prices of grain averaged 1.7 above the over-all average, whereas following years of plenty or low prices of grain it averaged 1.9 below the usual level; thus the difference in mortality between years following good and bad harvests was 3.6. Food shortages continuing for several years resulted in reduced population growth and apparently sometimes even in a decline of the total population.[20]

Chronic insufficiency of food beset many European regions until about a century ago, a deficiency especially grievous with regard to meat.

[18] Walter H. Mallory, *China: Land of Famine*, American Geographical Society, New York, 1926, p. 1.

[19] Ping-ti Ho, *Studies on the Population of China: 1368-1953*, Harvard University Press, Cambridge, 1959, pp. 231-232.

[20] Halvor Gille, "The Demographic History of the Northern European Countries in the Eighteenth Century," *Population Studies*, Vol. III, No. 1, June 1949, pp. 45-48.

Describing France in 1855, Le Play said that the peasants of Morvan ate meat once a year; those of Maine, twice a year; and those of Brittany, not at all except at religious festivals. As recently as 1844, "one-third of the population of the United Kingdom and Ireland subsisted on potatoes alone, and another third could add to this only coarse bread and 'refuse of the shambles' twice a week."[21]

EPIDEMIC DISEASE

Epidemiologist Hans Zinsser claims that the course of history has been shaped less by the acts of men than by the chronic and epidemic diseases with which they have had to contend and by superstitions and ignorance concerning medicine and sanitation. Thus concerning war, he writes:

> War is to-day, as much as ever, 75 per cent an engineering and sanitary problem and a little less than 25 per cent a military one. Other things being approximately equal, that army will win which has the best engineering and sanitary services. . . . The only reason why this is not entirely apparent in wars is because the military minds on both sides are too superb to notice that both armies are simultaneously immobilized by the same diseases. Incidentally, medicine has another indirect influence on war which is not negligible. There seems little doubt that some of the reckless courage of the American troops in [World War I] was stimulated by the knowledge that in front of them were only the Germans, but behind them there were the assembled surgeons of America, with sleeves rolled up.[22]

Of the 13,000 amputations performed by French army surgeons in the Franco-Prussian War of 1870-71, 10,000 were fatal.[23] Suppuration, "proud flesh," and "laudable pus" were considered unavoidable. A French army surgeon, de Kerhove, related how Napoleon was helpless to combat the typhus, pneumonia, dysentery, and scurvy that contributed far more than battle losses to reduce a proud force of half a million soldiers to 20,000 half-sick survivors. "The tricks of marching and of shooting and the game called strategy . . . are only the terminal operations engaged in by those remnants of the armies which have survived the camp epidemics. . . . And typhus, with its brothers and sisters—plague, cholera, typhoid, dysentery—has decided more campaigns than Caesar, Hannibal, Napoleon, and all the inspector generals of history."[24]

---

[21] United Nations, *Determinants and Consequences, op. cit.*, p. 51.

[22] Zinsser, *Rats, Lice and History, op. cit.*, p. 132.

[23] Arthur Newsholme, *The Story of Modern Preventive Medicine*, The Williams and Wilkins Co., Baltimore, 1929, p. 30.

[24] Zinsser, *Rats, Lice and History, op. cit.*, pp. 152-153.

Epidemics of plague, smallpox, cholera, typhus, and other contagious diseases were, until recently, commonplace throughout the world. Control was attempted through quarantine and the destruction of animals—usually of dogs and cats—but the sinister rats and dangerous insects were left unmolested. Not only were these precautions ineffective because of lack of knowledge concerning how contagious diseases are spread, but also because of ignorance as to whether or not a disease was even contagious. In addition, there was the orthodox belief that epidemics were caused by night mists and noxious miasmas emanating from swamps and putrescent matter.

Medical diagnoses for most early epidemics are not possible, owing to incomplete and conflicting descriptions of symptoms. The term "plague" was commonly used as a generic label for severe epidemics rather than as identification of a specific disease. Some plagues probably resulted from simultaneous attack of several diseases, encouraged by unsanitary conditions. The first elaborate recorded observation of a major pestilence is Thucydides' description of the Athenian plague of 430-429 B.C., but from his documentation we cannot be sure if the Greeks were suffering from bubonic plague, smallpox, typhus fever, typhoid fever, measles, or ergotism.[25]

THE PLAGUE

Plague itself is of three types: bubonic, a lymphatic swelling resulting from bites of infected rodent fleas; pneumonic, transmitted by human contact and almost invariably fatal; and septicemic, similar to the bubonic type.

In common with other scourges, plague has had far-reaching effects on human history. "Plague, indeed, was probably responsible for the greatest single impetus in the decline of the Roman Empire: the attack of A.D. 166 must have been of serious proportions."[26] Gibbon estimated that the plague which traveled by ship from Egypt to Byzantium in A.D. 543 may have killed 100 million people. Boccaccio mentions the blood-spitting of victims of the pneumonic form of the pestilence and describes the ravaged city of Florence: "Alas, how many great palaces, how many goodly houses, how many noble mansions, once full of families, of lords and ladies abode empty even of the meanest servants! . . . How many valiant men, how many fair ladies, how many sprightly youths . . . breakfasted in the morning with their kinsfolk, comrades,

[25] George Sarton, *A History of Science*, Harvard University Press, Cambridge, 1952-1959, Vol. I, pp. 323-325.
[26] Josiah Cox Russell, "Demographic Pattern in History," *Population Studies*, Vol. I, No. 3, March 1948, p. 394.

and friends, and that same night supped with their ancestors in the other world!"[27]

In 1348 the Black Death was said to have killed 25 million people— one-fourth of the population of Europe. Apparently originating in China, the plague of 1346-1350 moved westward to the Black Sea, to Italian trading ports, and then to every part of Europe. In Bristol, England, "in 1348 the plague raged to such a degree that the living were scarce able to bury the dead."[28] It took its heaviest toll during the summer, and mortality was more severe in urban than in rural areas because the towns had worse sanitary conditions.[29] Also, large populations living in close quarters were conducive to spreading pneumonic plague, and "one cannot doubt that a relation exists between the density of the rat population and that of the human population."[30] Still, rural mortality was high enough for Jarrett to claim the Black Death to be the primary cause of the disintegration of the feudal agricultural system and the evolution of a new pattern of land tenure and land use through decreased supply of labor and consequent increased wages.[31] Guy de Chauliac, the greatest surgeon of fourteenth-century Europe, described the Black Death:

> The great mortality appeared at Avignon in January 1348, when I was in the service of Pope Clement VI. It was of two kinds. The first lasted two months, with continued fever and spitting of blood, and people died of it in three days. The second was all the rest of the time, also with continuous fever, and with tumors in the external parts, chiefly the armpits and groin; and people died in five days. It was so contagious, especially that accompanied by spitting of blood, that not only by staying together, but even by looking at one another, people caught it, with the result that men died without attendants and were buried without priests. The father did not visit his son, nor the son his father. Charity was dead and hope crushed. . . .
>
> For this reason it was useless and shameful for the doctors, the more so as they dared not visit the sick, for fear of being infected. And when they did visit them, they did hardly anything for them and were paid nothing; for all the sick died, except some few at the last who escaped, the buboes being ripened.

---

[27] Giovanni Boccaccio, *The Decameron*, 1348-1353.

[28] Francis A. Gasquet, *The Black Death of 1348 and 1349*, George Bell and Sons, London, 1908, p. 99.

[29] G. T. Salusbury, *Street Life in Medieval England*, Fisher Kight and Co., St. Albans, 1939, pp. 75-125.

[30] R. Pollitzer, *Plague*, World Health Organization, Geneva, 1954, p. 292.

[31] Bede Jarrett, *Social Theories of the Middle Ages: 1200-1500*, Little, Brown and Co., Boston, 1926, pp. 112-149; for an opposing view, see Edward P. Cheyney, *The Dawn of a New Era: 1250-1453*, Harper and Brothers, New York, 1936.

Many were in doubt about the cause of this great mortality. In some places they thought that the Jews had poisoned the world: and so they killed them. In others, that it was the poor deformed; and they drove them out. In others, that it was the nobles: and they feared to go abroad. Finally they reached the point where they kept guards in the cities and villages, and permitted the entry of no one who was not well known. And if powders or unguents were found on anyone the owners, for fear that they were poisons, were forced to swallow them.[32]

The plague killed one-fifth of the persons of London in 1603 and another sixth in 1625. During the four months from mid-June through mid-December, 1665, British Admiralty secretary Pepys entered comments about the plague in his diary on seventy-one days. He continued intermittent references to the plague through April, 1666, and did not abandon the subject until November of that year.

June 15th, 1665. The Towne grows very sickly, and people to be afeard of it; there dying this last week of the plague 112, from 43 the week before.

August 10th, 1665. By and by to the office, where we sat all the morning; in great trouble to see the Bill this week rise so high, to above 4,000 in all, and of them above 3,000 of the plague. . . . The town growing so unhealthy, that a man cannot depend upon living two days to an end.

August 16th, 1665. But, Lord! how sad a sight it is to see the streets empty of people, and very few upon the 'Change. Jealous of every door that one sees shut up, lest it should be the plague; and about us two shops in three, if not more, generally shut up.

August 30th, 1665. But, Lord! how every body's looks, and discourse in the street is of death, and nothing else, and few people going up and down, that the towne is like a place distressed and forsaken.

Sept. 20th, 1665. But, Lord! what a sad time it is to see no boats upon the River; and grass grows all up and down White Hall court, and nobody but poor wretches in the streets! And, which is worst of all, the Duke showed us the number of the plague this week, brought in the last night from the Lord Mayor; that it is encreased from about 600 more than the last, which is quite contrary to all our hopes and expectations, from the coldness of the late season. For the whole general number is 8,297, and of them the plague 7,165.[33]

Defoe was equally revealing on the disruption of life in London:

All trades being stopt, employment ceased, the labour, and, by that, the bread of the poor, were cut off; and at first, indeed, the cries of the

---

[32] Guy de Chauliac, *Great Surgery*, Latin-English translation, 1890.
[33] Samuel Pepys, *Diary*, G. Bell and Sons, London, 1924, Vol. IV, p. 410; Vol. V, pp. 39-40, 44, 57, and 80-81.

poor were most lamentable to hear; though, by the distribution of charity, their misery that way was gently abated. Many, indeed, fled into the country; but thousands of them having stayed in London, till nothing but desperation sent them away, death overtook them on the road, and they served for no better than the messengers of death; indeed, others, carrying the infection along with them, spread it very unhappily into the remotest parts of the kingdom.[34]

Henry Sigerist, the medical historian, points out the close association between famine and the plague: "A drought led to crop failure. The granaries were empty. The rats and other rodents moved closer to man and if there happened to be plague among the rodents there were good chances that the disease would be transmitted to people. And then it spread from man to man like wild fire."[35]

SMALLPOX, CHOLERA, AND TYPHUS

Before 1800, there was little defense against smallpox, "a disease which is every hour devouring its victims; a disease that has ever been considered as the severest scourge of the human race."[36] Outbreaks were frequent and savage, and the chance of escaping infection during an epidemic was remote unless one had previously had the disease. Some people, especially in the Near East, in their attempts to ward off the disease, adopted variolation, which consists of inoculating children with smallpox pus taken from a patient with a mild form of the disease, thereby immunizing them against later attacks, which were apt to be violent or even fatal.[37] Jenner's development of a cowpox vaccine in 1798 eventually resulted in almost complete control, but it required nearly a century to eliminate epidemics. "In London during the ten years from 1681 to 1690 the mortality from this disease averaged over 3 [per year] per thousand population; in the seventeenth and eighteenth centuries it frequently rose to 4.5 per thousand population, accounting for about one-tenth of all deaths."[38] Nearly 20 per cent of Glasgow's deaths between 1780 and 1800 were caused by smallpox. And one-fourth of eighteenth-century Frenchmen were killed, crippled, or permanently disfigured by the disease. Outbreaks occurred in several parts of Europe as recently as 1870-1873. And it is chastening to note that one-fifth of

[34] Daniel Defoe, *History of the Plague in London, 1665* (second edition of *A Journal of the Plague Year*, London, 1722), George Bell and Sons, London, 1905, p. 70.
[35] Henry E. Sigerist, *Civilization and Disease*, Cornell University Press, Ithaca, 1943, p. 9.
[36] Edward Jenner, *An Inquiry into the Causes and Effects of the Variolae Vaccinae*, London, 1798, p. 181.
[37] Mary Wortley Montagu, *Letters from the East*, London, 1716-1718.
[38] United Nations, *Determinants and Consequences, op. cit.*, p. 52.

the reported world cases in 1923-24 were in the United States, where many states lacked compulsory vaccination laws. In Germany, by contrast, the affliction virtually disappeared after vaccination was made compulsory in 1874.

Cholera also killed millions. A London physician described the cholera outbreak of 1824 thus: "Within two hundred and fifty yards of the spot where Cambridge Street joins Broad Street there were upwards of five hundred fatal attacks of cholera in ten days. The mortality in this limited area probably equals any that was ever caused in this country, even by the plague; and it was much more sudden, as the greater number of cases terminated in a few hours. The mortality would undoubtedly have been much greater had it not been for the flight of the population. . . . In less than six days from the commencement of the outbreak the most afflicted streets were deserted by more than three quarters of their inhabitants."[39] An acute infectious disease, cholera apparently originated in the East Indies and is endemic in Asia. Epidemics were recorded in the United States in 1832, 1835-36, 1848-49, 1854, 1866-67, 1873, 1884, and 1892-93. Its cause was discovered by Robert Koch in 1884. Prevention consists primarily of personal cleanliness and public sanitation.

Typhus fever also caused heavy mortality in Europe until the late nineteenth century, before which time it was spread mainly by explorations and wars. Cortez carried it to the Aztecs, and the retreat of the French troops from Moscow in 1812-1813 distributed the disease over Germany. In 1816 and 1819 typhus infected 700,000 of the six million inhabitants of Ireland, striking there again in 1846, and then spreading to England, reaching a total of one million cases. Lice, fleas, and rats are hosts for typhus. "The louse shares with us the misfortune of being prey to the typhus virus. If lice can dread, the nightmare of their lives is the fear of some day inhabiting an infected rat or human being. . . . The ill-starred louse that imbibes the loathsome virus with his nourishment is doomed beyond succor."[40] It was only a historical yesterday that the louse was considered man's inseparable companion— one of life's inevitabilities, like having the flu during final examinations. Lice were even believed to provide protection from certain diseases. In the Middle Ages, the Mayor of Hurdenberg, Sweden, was chosen by having eligible persons assemble with their beards resting on a table, whereupon a louse was put in the center of the table, and the man into whose beard it ventured was the mayor for the ensuing

---

[39] John Snow, *On Cholera*, London, 1824.
[40] Zinsser, *Rats, Lice and History, op. cit.*, p. 168.

year.[41] After the murder of Archbishop Thomas à Becket, the body lay for the night in Canterbury Cathedral; as the corpse grew cold, "the vermin boiled over like water in a simmering cauldron, and the on-lookers burst into alternate weeping and laughter." All of this should not be assigned to a remote past: until very recently, the shaving of heads of United States armed forces draftees was taken as a matter of course.

LACK OF SANITATION

Sanitary conditions have been extremely poor through most of man's history. Absence of knowledge of the medical value of cleanliness, coupled with low standards of living, inadequate personal hygiene, and an absence of communal sanitary facilities resulted in a thoroughly unfavorable standard of sanitation. Rubbish and garbage thrown into the roadway remained there until a scavenger found it worthwhile to cart it away to sell as fertilizer. In some areas, regulations required that sewage be disposed of in large bodies of water; Falstaff complained of being thrown into the Thames "like a barrow of butcher's offal."[42]

In low density areas these health deficiencies were tolerable; only under conditions of very high density or modern industrialization can man pollute his environment enough to endanger the entire populace. But when the same personal hygiene and sanitation habits that had sufficed in the country were carried into the growing cities, health standards were lowered and mortality levels raised.

In the early stages of industrialization, many people lived in over-crowded, grimy tenements grouped around dingy factories. Both the living and working quarters inflicted upon the inhabitants the health hazards of inadequate (and often nonexistent) ventilation, high temperatures, little daylight and poor artificial lighting, insufficient bathing facilities, and filthy toilets. Long and exhausting work days for adults and small children contributed to high accident rates. In 1850, one-thirtieth of the people of New York City lived in cellars, and in Boston "about one-twentieth of the population lived in damp, vermin-ridden, underground rooms."[43] Until the middle of the nineteenth century, the street was the accepted disposal place for the contents of *pots de chambre* and filth of all kinds. On July 5, 1849, the London *Times* published the following letter:

---

[41] Frank Cowan, *Curious Facts in the History of Insects,* J. B. Lippincott & Co., Philadelphia, 1865, p. 316.
[42] William Shakespeare, *The Merry Wives of Windsor,* 1602, Act III, Scene V, line 5.
[43] United Nations, *Determinants and Consequences, op. cit.,* p. 53.

Sur,—May we beg and beseach your proteckshion and power. We are Sur, as it may be, livin in a Wilderness, so far as the rest of London knows anything of us, or as the rich and great people care about. We live in muck and filth. We aint got no priviz, no dust bins, no drains, no water-splies, and no drain or suer in the hole place. The Suer Company, in Greek St., Soho Square, all great, rich powerfool men take no notice whatsomdever of our complaints. The Stenche of a Gulley-hole is disgustin. We all of us suffer, and numbers are ill, and if the Cholera comes Lord help us.

Some gentelmans comed yesterday. . . . They was much surprized to see the sellar in No. 12, Carrier St., in our lane, where a child was dying from fever, and would not believe that Sixty persons sleep in it every night. This here seller you couldent swing a cat in, and the rent is five shillings a week; but theare are greate many sich deare sellers. . . .

Praeye Sir com and see us, for we are livin like piggs, and it aint faire we shoulde be so ill treted. . . .[44]

By modern standards, personal uncleanliness was appalling. In 1831 one observer complained, "We wonder how men can endure the compound of crust of soot, dirt and secretions with which they are enveloped. Throughout the whole of the labouring classes, and indeed among the majority of the middling and upper classes, this subject is strangely neglected. Cleanliness is practised in a very imperfect manner; the whole surface is seldom washed; and in most persons, the body, with the exception of the hands and face, is cleaned only by the removal of those impurities which adhere to the linen."[45] Among the "Rules of Civility" taught to the adolescent George Washington was the admonition: "Kill no vermin, as Fleas, lice, tics, etc. in the sight of others; if you See any filth or thick Spittle, put your foot Dexterously upon it; if it be upon the Cloths of your companions, put it off privately, and if it be upon your own Cloths, return thanks to him who puts it off." Lewis Mumford supplies dramatic documentation of housing and health conditions in "the insensate industrial town" of this period.[46]

Most men approved these unsanitary conditions and even fought the introduction of the cleanliness which we now take so much for granted.

---

[44] Quoted in Richard Harrison Shryock, *The Development of Modern Medicine*, Alfred A. Knopf, New York, 1947, p. 213.

[45] C. T. Thackrah, *The Effects of Arts, Trades and Professions and of Civic States and Habits of Living on Health and Longevity*, London, 1831, pp. 123-124; quoted in United Nations, *Determinants and Consequences, op. cit.*, p. 52.

[46] Lewis Mumford, *The Culture of Cities*, Harcourt, Brace and Co., New York, 1938, Chaps. III and IV.

Dirt, with all its concomitant odors and insects, was once accepted as an unalterable element in the divinely established Order of Things. . . . That there might be a remedy for stink and nastiness—namely soap and water—was a notion almost unthinkable in the thirteenth century. In the first place, there was hardly any soap. . . . Moreover, even if soap had been abundant, its use for mitigating the "stink and nastiness," then inseparable from love, would have seemed, to every right-thinking theologian, an entirely illegitimate, because merely physical, solution to a problem in ontology and morals—an escape, by means of the most vulgarly materialistic trick, from a situation which God Himself had intended, from all eternity, to be as squalid as it was sinful. . . . And finally there was the virtue of modesty. Modesty . . . had its Queensberry Rules—no washing below the belt.[47]

WATER AND SEWAGE SYSTEMS

These conditions of public health were actually worse than sanitation in certain ancient civilizations. On the island of Crete, the Minoans of 2000 B.C. had highly developed systems of water supply, sanitation, and drainage connecting many of the homes of Cnossus. Excavations of palaces at Cnossus, Hagia Triada, Gournia, and Palaikastro contain "remains of drainage systems that excelled anything except the Roman until the nineteenth century A.D. The main drains in the system of the Cnossus palace were large enough for a man to stand upright in them. There was a similar system for the streets and, on a smaller scale, for the better houses. At Cnossus were also latrines with means for flushing."[48] Stone ducts and terra cotta pipes conveyed rainwater through the system.

The Romans, who also faced the problem of sustaining large concentrations of people, provided for the health of the populace through extensive systems for supplying and heating water and for carrying off effluvia. Relics of Roman water circuits have been found in a dozen French and German cities. Huge aqueducts transported water over great distances, and underground sewers like Rome's famous Cloaca Maxima (a woman in Ben Jonson's *Volpone* of 1605 is classified as "the Cloaca Maxima of Venice") attested to the fact that their engineering skills were not restricted to highway construction. A supply of 300 million gallons of purified water was daily piped into private Roman homes through underground conduits. Overhead concrete and stone aqueducts carried on arches in northern Africa, Asia Minor, and Europe stretched across the countryside like a monorail system. The 180-foot-

---

[47] Aldous Huxley, "Sludge and Sanctity," *Esquire*, June 1953.
[48] Albert A. Trever, *History of Ancient Civilization*, Vol. I: "The Ancient Near East and Greece," Harcourt, Brace and Co., New York, 1936, p. 130.

high Pont du Gard in southern France is part of an aqueduct built in 18 B.C. to bring water thirty miles to Nîmes. The Roman aqueduct in Segovia, Spain, is still in use. The city of Rome had fourteen high- and low-pressure aqueducts whose combined length was 265 miles. Pipes were constructed of stone or lead. The better houses had water taps and indoor plumbing, with lead pipes carrying drainage into the central sewage system.

The failure of later Europeans to imitate these sewage systems is attributable to many things, including the Christian otherworldly attitude and acceptance of existing conditions, a different standard of living, and declining concern with engineering and practical arts. "In 1513 the *coutume* (common law) in Paris decreed that every house should have its own privy, but as late as the eighteenth century it was still the prevalent custom to throw refuse into the street. A survey carried out in Madrid in 1773 disclosed that the royal palace did not contain even one privy. . . . In the City of London . . . kites and ravens were protected birds and they and the pigs which roamed about grew fat on the offal in the streets."[49] The water closet or toilet was introduced in England in an elementary form by Sir John Harrington in 1596 and improved in the 1700's, but it was not really effective until connected to municipal sewage systems in the nineteenth century.

As recently as 1850, cities as large as Milwaukee and Providence had no public water system. In the London of 1809, a city of about one million people, water was available only in the basement of most houses; in some quarters, water could be turned on for only three days a week. In new industrial towns, where whole districts were sometimes completely without water, the poor would go begging for it from door to door in the better sections of town.

Under these circumstances, wine drinking became a form of preventive medicine: in the Middle Ages, surmising that their water was contaminated, men drank only wine and other spirits. Lammert, a German physician, adduced failure of the wine supply as a contributing cause in the insurgence of typhus, enteric fever, cholera, and other diseases in the seventeenth century.

Thus the triple threats of food shortage, various epidemic diseases, and unsanitary living conditions combined to produce high levels of mortality through most of man's existence. But in recent centuries men began to achieve partial mastery over these killers, inducing an initially

---

[49] J. Rawlinson, "Sanitary Engineering: Sanitation," in Charles Singer, E. J. Holmyard, A. R. Hall, and Trevor I. Williams (eds.), A *History of Technology*, Oxford University Press, London, 1958, Vol. IV, p. 505.

slow and later rapid reduction of death rates in most regions of the world. The causes of this reduction are approximately opposite to the reasons why death rates were formerly so large.

Causes of the Mortality Decline

Ten factors have been prominent contributors to the decline of mortality that began weakly in the seventeenth century, gathered momentum through the eighteenth and nineteenth centuries, and continues unabated to the present. First, improvements in agricultural techniques made possible considerable increases in the quantity of food produced. Farming methods had remained virtually unchanged for centuries, but beginning in the late 1600's, several innovations were put into practice, notably crop rotation, better fertilizers, and improved machinery and implements.

Second, the change from a home handicraft to a machine factory system increased the amount and variety of products available for use by the public. Although the early influence of this change was to increase mortality because of the grossly unsavory conditions within the factory buildings and environs, the eventual result was a lowering of the death rate because people were supplied with more goods to fend off death (heavy clothing for winter, for example). The advent of the factory system also made feasible the production of large quantities of the commodities required for improvements in agriculture (the iron plowshare), transportation (the steam engine), and most of the other factors in this list of ten causes.

Third, transportation improvements facilitated distribution of these agricultural and industrial products to a wider populace than was formerly possible. Thus the well-being of residents of an area was no longer tied strictly to the productivity of the area itself.

Fourth, the social reforms in the nineteenth and twentieth centuries alleviated many of the hazards of early factory life. Maximum working hours, minimum working ages, and various safety devices all improved working conditions tremendously. One indication of the unsavory way of life once prevailing is the 1802 English act limiting the work of children in cotton mills to twelve hours a day.

In the fifth place, the ability to control temperature and humidity at will in homes and places of work may have contributed to a decline in respiratory infections in winter months and certainly provided more comfort and presumably stimulated more productivity in extreme heat and cold. Today the ability to regulate the climate about us has extended even to our athletic stadiums (with their plastic domes and built-in outlets for electric blankets) and modes of transportation (automobile air conditioning is becoming commonplace and heaters are now standard equipment).

A sixth factor in the mortality decline was the improvement in public sanitation, especially in urban areas. Public utilities were introduced, providing water supply, water purification, and sewage disposal—facilities most cities had gone without until the nineteenth century. The ability to pump water is, of course, essential to an urban water supply. In 1582, the London Bridge Waterworks were erected by a German engineer, "before which time no such thing was known in England as this raising of water," and in the seventeenth century, Edward Somerset built a steam engine that could raise water forty feet.[50] But clean, clear water was not enough; filters were necessary to eliminate cholera bacilli. Simpson's sand filters for Thames River water were introduced into the London water system in 1829.[51] Sand filtration spread quickly across Europe, to be supplemented later by charcoal, pressure, and other methods. The first sand filter to be fully effective against cholera was constructed in Lowell, Massachusetts, in 1893, under the direction of William T. Sedgwick.[52] In modern countries, sanitary engineering applying bacteriological knowledge has practically wiped out cholera, typhoid fever, and other water-borne infections.

Along with preventive health advances made by public agencies, changes in habits of personal hygiene were also very important. Cheap cotton clothing and iron bedsteads facilitated cleanliness. Soap, formerly a luxury, became available to almost everyone. People gradually ceased to think of baths as unnatural, and men came to understand that the body is not kept clean by perspiration. Sedgwick, an apostle of the sanitary awakening of the 1890's, taught that

> one of the most effective vehicles of disease is dirt. The word "dirt" appears to be derived from an old Saxon word *drit*, meaning excrement. . . . Dirt is dangerous, not because it is "of the earth, earthy," but because it is too often *drit* or excrement. . . . Cleanliness, or the absence of dirt, is not merely an aesthetic adornment—though doubtless an acquired taste; it is above all a sanitary safeguard, the importance of which has been learned by hard experience. . . . To be clean is in a measure to be safe from disease. . . . The common drinking cup, wherever found, must be regarded as a sanitary abomination and should not be tolerated any longer.[53]

---

[50] Abraham Wolf, *A History of Science, Technology, and Philosophy in the Sixteenth and Seventeenth Centuries*, George Allen and Unwin Ltd., London, 1935, pp. 534-545. The quotation is Wolf's report of a sixteenth-century observer.

[51] F. E. Bruce, "Water-Supply," in Singer *et al.*, *A History of Technology, op. cit.*, Vol. V, pp. 552-568.

[52] Shryock, *The Development of Modern Medicine, op. cit.*, p. 293.

[53] William Thompson Sedgwick, *The Principles of Sanitary Science and Public Health*, 1901, revised edition, The Macmillan Co., New York, 1935.

Eighth in the list of factors cutting mortality was the late nineteenth-century development of asepsis (the precautionary exclusion of pathogenic microorganisms) and antisepsis (killing or inhibiting the growth of microorganisms already present). Aseptic and antiseptic surgery was founded by Joseph Lister, who introduced the sterilization of instruments, the use of masks, and disinfection of the operating theater by carbolic acid,[54] thereby possibly saving more lives than all the wars of the nineteenth century together had sacrificed. The idea of sepsis could not be accepted, however, until man abandoned the widely-held theory of spontaneous generation, a doctrine which had had long life—from Aristotle to the seventeenth-century belief that frogs were created from mud and eels from river water. But the germ theory finally prevailed. "Life is a germ and a germ is Life. . . . There is no known circumstance in which it has been shown that microscopic beings come into the world without germs, without parents similar to themselves. Those who affirm it have been duped by illusions, by ill-conducted experiments, by errors that they either did not perceive, or did not know how to avoid."[55] Thus bacteriology was born, and from it there developed valuable biochemical applications: the preservation of food through pasteurization and sterilization, and the prevention and cure of infections through asepsis and antisepsis.

A ninth source of mortality decline is immunology. Smallpox was the first malady to yield to artificial immunization, but Jenner's vaccine was a happy accident, and efforts to develop preventive serums for the plague, measles, and syphilis were long unavailing because no one knew how immunity was achieved. (A rejected proposal before the Parisian Academy of Medicine to inoculate the entire youth of France with syphilis was based on the assumption that it was as logical to inoculate with the great pox as with the small.) Finally, through a combination of luck and genius, Robert Koch (1876) and Louis Pasteur (1877) found the key to the basic principle of immunization—namely, that inoculation with an attenuated virus from microbe culture produces a mild case of the disease, which in turn prevents later, serious recurrences. After this breakthrough, Pasteur developed vaccines or drugs for chicken cholera, sheep anthrax, and hydrophobia; Behring and Roux for diphtheria; and Ehrlich, the same, for syphilis. We now have prophylactic antitoxins against tetanus, typhoid, scarlet fever, poliomyelitis, botulism, influenza, some snake venom, and certain plant toxins, developed from filterable viruses, bacteria, and rickettsiae.

[54] Joseph Lister, "On the Antiseptic Principle of the Practice of Surgery," *British Medical Journal*, September 21, 1867.

[55] Louis Pasteur, lecture-demonstration at the Sorbonne in 1864, quoted in René Dubois, *Pasteur and Modern Science*, Doubleday and Co., Garden City, 1960, pp. 60, 62.

Finally, virulent diseases tend to become relatively benign through changes in the disease itself, mutual adaptation between man and the disease, and increased resistance from antibodies (possibly the culmination of selective survival of the medically fit). Bubonic and pneumonic plague, leprosy, and syphilis were once far more acute and lethal than they are today. Measles, diphtheria, and smallpox, when introduced into a society with no natural immunity, strike with much greater violence than in societies where they have long been endemic. These changes began before modern preventive and curative methods exerted any noticeable influence.[56]

THE RISING STANDARD OF LIVING

In general terms, the decline of mortality and the increase in life expectation in the last few centuries is attributable largely to a rising level of living. Better living and working conditions have made survival possible in the face of infections that formerly would have been lethal, and more and more persons now avoid contracting such diseases. But although the twentieth-century decline in mortality is ascribable to the development and widespread application of various scientific methods for the prevention and control of certain diseases, prior accomplishments in controlling mortality are primarily the result of nonmedical improvements. For example, reductions in the death rate from tuberculosis preceded discovery of the tubercle bacillus.

When both a rising living standard and advanced chemical and medical knowledge are operating together toward the reduction of mortality, the effects are phenomenal. During the last half century, when medicine achieved full stature as a science, mortality control increased tremendously. Since World War II the distribution of preventive medicine techniques and supplies to underdeveloped countries has had a startling impact, as can readily be discerned by comparing world and national mortality decreases in the last decade with those of previous decades of man's existence. Chemicals such as the powerful insecticide D.D.T., the antibiotic drugs (beginning with Fleming's 1928 discovery of penicillin), wholesale vaccinations and immunizations, and unique lifesaving drugs and public health innovations may eventually lead to the complete eradication of certain major death-dealing diseases and a world-wide improvement in mortality conditions. To cite an extreme case, antibiotics and D.D.T. cut the death rate in Ceylon from twenty-two to twelve persons per thousand per year over a seven-year period following the second World War.[57]

---

[56] Zinsser, *Rats, Lice and History, op. cit.,* p. 67.
[57] N. K. Sarkar, *The Demography of Ceylon,* Government Press, Colombo, 1957, Epilogue.

Medical Innovations

During the last fifty to one hundred years, medical science has made great advances against the ravages of disease, but the substantial reduction of mortality prior to a century ago can hardly be credited to medicine, since it was only a rudimentary art up to that time. "It is probable that only within this century have medical men and surgeons helped more people than they have injured—one might almost say, cured more persons than they have killed."[58] Pretwentieth century physicians were not much ahead of S. J. Perelman's "I don't know anything about medicine, but I know what I like."

TRADITIONAL MEDICINE

Schools of medicine were founded in Salerno (1077) and Bologna (1156), even before the first students gathered at the nascent universities at Oxford (1167) and Paris (1200), but their teachings were shoddy for many years. For thirteen centuries, Galen (Claudius Galenus, 130-201) remained the undisputed authority, finally yielding to Andreas Vesalius (1514-1564).

Medicine did not share in the scientific advances of the Renaissance; "physic failed to keep up with physics," and an open meeting of the British Association heard medicine referred to as "the withered arm of science."[59] Consider the sort of leadership offered by Dr. Benjamin Rush, Surgeon-General of the Revolutionary Army and a signer of the Declaration of Independence:

> Benjamin Rush, the best-known American physician of his day [evolved a system] based upon a pathology in which all diseases were reduced to one, and all treatments likewise—a performance which greatly impressed his contemporaries. . . . "I have formerly said that there was but one fever in the world. Be not startled, Gentlemen, follow me and I will say there is but one disease in the world. The proximate cause of disease is irregular convulsive or wrong action in the system affected. This, Gentlemen, is a concise view of my theory of diseases." . . . Treatments consisted chiefly of blood-letting and purging, which were supposed to reduce "convulsive action" by a process of "depletion"— a euphonious name for exhaustion. They were, if good for anything, literally "good for what ails you."[60]

---

[58] James B. Conant, *Modern Science and Modern Man*, Doubleday and Co., Garden City, 1952, p. 129.

[59] Shryock, *The Development of Modern Medicine, op. cit.*, p. 19.

[60] *Ibid.*, pp. 3-4; Shryock is quoting from Benjamin Rush, *Lectures on the Practice of Physic*, Philadelphia, 1796. Rush also believed that drinking alcoholic beverages to excess could cause a man to burst into flames by spontaneous combustion, charring his viscera and making smokestacks of his orifices.

MEDICINE BECOMES SCIENTIFIC

Medical practitioners had little valid knowledge to rely on prior to mid-nineteenth-century inventions of instruments and statistical tools. The introduction of the stethoscope (1819), microscope (1830's), clinical thermometer (1830's), hypodermic needle (1840's), ophthalmoscope (1851), sphygmomanometer (1887), and X-ray (1895) enabled physicians for the first time to *examine* their patients rather than simply to observe them, facilitating discovery of causes of illnesses and replacing superficial alleviation of symptoms by treatment of underlying causes. Surgical anesthesia, suggested by Humphrey Davy (1800) and Michael Faraday (1818), was introduced into medical practice by William T. G. Morton and several other physicians and dentists in the 1840's.

Pierre Louis introduced inductive statistics into medicine in 1835, thereby helping to transform medical research into an objective science. Previously, doctors had generalized vaguely from a few cases, but Louis demanded hundreds of cases and methodological controls to allow for individual variations before forming conclusions. This insistence on mathematical exactness won him the encomium "the Bacon of Medicine."

The controlled experiment, which is at the heart of present-day scientific research, dates back in medicine only to 1754, when James Lind described a very crude attempt to evaluate six different treatments for scurvy, a dreadful affliction of navies. The modern "double-blind" experiment, which contains safeguards both against the placebo effect and the undisciplined enthusiasm of physicians administering the medication (both patient and physician are "blind" in that neither knows which tablet contains the drug under test and which is a lactose placebo), was not fully developed until the 1930's.[61] Previous to the adoption of this now standard medical procedure, spurious results were common.

Medical training remained retarded far longer than medical research. The primitive and scandalous quackery then prevalent in medical education in the United States was forcefully exposed by Abraham Flexner in the 1910's and 1920's. His writings resulted in sweeping reforms in medical education; nearly a hundred medical schools closed in the two decades following publication of his report to the Carnegie Foundation.[62]

---

[61] Harry Gold, Nathaniel T. Kwit, and Harold Otto, "Xanthines (Theobromine and Aminophylline) in the Treatment of Cardiac Pain," *The Journal of the American Medical Association*, Vol. CVIII, No. 26, June 26, 1937, pp. 2173-2179.

[62] Abraham Flexner, *Medical Education in the United States and Canada*, Carnegie Fund for the Advancement of Teaching, New York, 1910.

Contemporary medical research and education are redressing these grievous shortcomings, and both preventive and curative medicine are now contributing to reduction of mortality throughout the world. Doubtless these contributions will increase in the years ahead.

6 ❧ Death Rates and Causes

From a preindustrial mortality kept high by chronic malnutrition, frequent famines, pandemic diseases, inadequate sanitation and hygiene, and medical nascency, the more modern countries of the world have reached a remarkable level of control over death and sickness. In only two hundred years, a widespread rise in the standard of living has enabled more than a doubling of expectation of life at birth. This improved ability to meet and conquer his vital enemies must be included among modern man's proudest accomplishments.

Former dread scourges have today been reduced to the status of minor irritations which interrupt childhood play or, when contracted by adults, evoke embarrassing remarks from friends. And it is now possible to conceive of a time when communicable diseases will have vanished. Even the wearing out of parts of the body may cease to kill, as man learns how to replace tissues, bones, and vital organs with spare parts.

Measures of Mortality

Up to this point we have used as measures of mortality the expectation of life at birth and the crude death rate. Actually there are many ways of assessing the magnitude of mortality.

CRUDE DEATH RATE

The simplest measure is the *crude death rate* (C.D.R.)—total number of deaths occurring per year per 1,000 population. To illustrate, if an island had a 1960 population of 50,000 and if 700 islanders died during 1960, then the crude death rate is $\dfrac{700 \times 1000}{50,000} = 14$. That is, for every 1,000 inhabitants, 14 died during 1960. Demographers use the mid-year population when computing death rates, as it is the closest conveniently available approximation to the average number of people exposed to death during the year.

The word "crude" is used advisedly. The C.D.R. tells the rate at which people in a country are dying, without regard for any other characteristics or propensities of the populace; it makes no allowance for the considerable differences in mortality among persons of different types. Age and sex are especially significant omissions. As a result, the crude death rate cannot tell us whether the higher mortality experienced in country A over country B is due to differences in living and health conditions or is merely a product of differences in their age-sex compositions. Specifically, if country A has a large proportion of its residents in the high mortality age-sex classes, and if country B has a large proportion in the low mortality age-sex categories, then country A may have a higher C.D.R. despite identical standards of living and medical care. In short, if we are to understand the propensity to die in a country, or if we want to compare the mortality in two countries, some more sophisticated measure is necessary. Additionally, estimations of future trends can be made more reliably if we know the relationship between mortality conditions and the age-sex structure; the latter is generally rather accurately predictable over a decade or two.

The first improvement is to correct both numerator and denominator for inaccuracies and omissions known to exist in the raw data. When this is done, the result is known as a *corrected death rate*. A particularly troublesome fault in some regions is an underreporting of deaths among babies under one year of age. Another problem is that uncorrected data may have the following inaccuracies concerning age: heaping at ages ending in 0 and 5 and also even digits (not at age, say, 39), overstating age when under 21 (especially of men), understating age when over 21 (especially of women), overstating age when near 65 (to gain pension benefits), overstating age in extreme old age (through pride or ignorance), having unknown ages (through ignorance or refusal to respond), and failing to list all of the people (especially those under two years of age). Elaborate adjustments compensating for misstatements of this kind have been developed by actuaries and statisticians.

SPECIFIC DEATH RATES

A second improvement is to allow for the age and sex structure of the populace. To make international comparisons or study long-term trends, it is necessary to consider variations in age and sex, since they are frequently temporary and therefore may induce artificially high or low crude death rates.

Age-sex specific death rates tell the number of deaths among people of a given age per 1,000 people in that age-sex category. For instance, we may find the age-specific death rate for all men who are 45 years old, or for all women 23 years of age. In practice, five-year age groups are the most useful, as one-year age groups are unnecessarily detailed and require tedious computations, and longer periods are imprecise. Other specific rates may also be calculated—for example, race-specific or urbanization-specific rates—but age and sex are by far the most common.

STANDARDIZED DEATH RATES

Age-sex-specific rates are combined to form standardized rates, which are widely used, especially when we wish to compare different countries or times. These more subtle death rates are obtained by multiplying each age-sex-specific death rate by the number of people in that age-sex category, adding these products, and then dividing that sum by the total population. This yields a kind of weighted average—weighted or adjusted in accordance with a particular age-sex distribution (not necessarily the age-sex distribution actually resident in the area at the given time). These operations result in a final rate which is described as standardized or adjusted for the given age-sex distribution.

For example, if we wished to compare mortality in India with that in the United States, we could start with the crude death rates, observing that India's C.D.R. is higher. But if we stopped there, we could not be sure that India's larger C.D.R. was not merely a function of age-sex differences between the two countries. Therefore we might decide to standardize the rates, using as a standard the population of either country or some outside basis of comparison, such as the population of England in 1951. The term Standard Million designates an age-sex distribution containing exactly a million people arrayed in the proportions of some widely accepted standard. The standardized death rate shows the mortality which would be observed if the actual population (India, 1961, for example) had the same age-sex distribution as the standard population (United States, 1960, for example). Having obtained this standardized rate for India based on the United States age-sex distribution, we might then make our comparison of the mortality tendencies in the two countries, but with the added consideration that we were now "holding age and sex constant" or allowing for differences in the age-sex structures of the two countries. Thus the mortality comparison is made more direct and simple.

These operations may suggest to the nonstatistical reader that demographic measures lack simplicity. But logical simplicity—and what is more to the point, directness—is actually achieved by these quantitative manipulations of the data. Take an instance of a familiar statistical situation: in order to answer a certain question, certain data must be presented in a certain form—but as so often happens, the data were not originally collected and tabulated in that form; to get the figures into proper condition to answer the question at issue we must subtract extraneous material (extraneous for the given question, that is—one question's extraneousness may be another's relevance). The process of deleting this superfluous element may be quite complicated, but the final result is the achievement of a statistic that bears precisely on the point of the question. One of the virtues of careful statistical procedures is that these mathematical techniques often make up for the irrelevancies or imprecisions of the raw data or of the language itself.

The Life Table

The oldest and most successful efforts at demographic measurement originated in the study of mortality—the first aspect of population statistics to be subjected to rigorous analysis. The most penetrating of the resultant methodological techniques is the life table, whose harbinger was John Graunt, a seventeenth-century London haberdasher who used odd moments to study vital statistics. Table 5 summarizes Graunt's

TABLE 5. *Graunt's Table, 1604-1661* *

AGE	NUMBER OF SURVIVORS
0	100
6	64
16	40
26	25
36	16
46	10
56	6
66	3
76	1
80	0

* Adapted from John Graunt, *Natural and Political Observations Made Upon the Bills of Mortality,* London, 1662, reprinted by the Johns Hopkins Press, Baltimore, 1939, pp. 69-70.

work documenting the mortality level prevalent in those times. Graunt's successor, Edmund Halley, a coffee house founder, laid the cornerstone of the life insurance business. In the three succeeding centuries, insurance companies, government experts, and academic scholars have brought the life table to maturation as a valuable tool for demographic analysis.

A major advance in this area was made in 1760 by Leonhard Euler, a Swiss mathematician who set forth the basic principles of the stable population—a population with fixed mortality, fertility, and age-sex distribution. As a result of his work, the life table became intimately bound up with the analysis of stable and stationary (or fixed total size) populations.

The Northampton, England, life table constructed by Richard Price in 1783 was the first to be used to determine life insurance premiums, although the principle of adjusting rates with increasing age was employed by the Equitable company after 1762. The first life table to take thorough account of both deaths and age structure was published in Carlisle, England, in 1815.[1]

The life table was brought to a sophisticated level by A. J. Lotka in articles published in 1907, 1911, and 1925.[2] Lotka probably contributed more to the quantitative analysis of population than any other man. Indeed, his "contribution to demography can be likened in some respects to that of Newton to physics. Both achieved a synthesis in analytical theory which had far-reaching significance, and both set a frame for new empirical investigations.[3]

RATIONALE AND CONSTRUCTION

A life table is the life-and-death history of a category of people, gradually depleted by deaths, telling the probability of surviving from any given age to any other age. It may be generation or current, complete or abridged.

A generation life table follows one cohort (persons born in the same year) throughout their lives. For example, consider the life history of 100,000 persons all born in 1850. The life table would tell us their collective mortality history. But unfortunately, before we could obtain such a table, we would have to wait until nearly all of the original cohort had died, which might make the table obsolete before it was completed. A further defect is that in our rapidly changing society the conditions of life that actuate mortality have varied so much since 1850 that the generation life table would not present an accurate description of any

---

[1] Louis I. Dublin, Alfred J. Lotka, and Mortimer Spiegelman, *Length of Life*, The Ronald Press Co., New York, 1949, pp. 35-36.

[2] Alfred James Lotka, "Studies on the Mode of Growth of Material Aggregates," *American Journal of Science*, Vol. XXIV, No. 141, 1907, pp. 129-216; F. R. Sharpe and A. J. Lotka, "A Problem in Age-Distribution," *Philosophical Magazine*, Vol. XXI, 1911, pp. 435-438; and L. I. Dublin and A. J. Lotka, "On the True Rate of Natural Increase," *Journal of the American Statistical Association*, Vol. XX, 1925, pp. 305-339.

[3] Frank Lorimer, "The Development of Demography," in Philip M. Hauser and Otis Dudley Duncan, *The Study of Population*, University of Chicago Press, Chicago, 1959, p. 156.

one year or decade. It is because of such weaknesses that the generation life table is not often used.

Preferable is the current life table, which is a synthetic product describing a hypothetical population. Based on the present age-sex specific mortality rates for all age groups, rather than the history of any one cohort, it describes what would happen to members of a population who lived their entire lives under current mortality conditions. The mortality conditions implicit in the current life table are those existing in the year (or three or five years) for which it is constructed. This property makes the table and its derivative figures, such as the expectation of life, extremely useful for the portrayal of mortality at a given time. The table shows what mortality would be were the synthetic schedule applied to an actual cohort. Under unchanging mortality conditions, current and generation life tables would be identical. If one is willing to make the assumption that mortality will not change over the next eighty years or so, the current life table can be read as an estimate of the life chances of its component individuals.

Complete life tables are based on one-year intervals—and often one-month intervals during the first year. Since the preparation of a complete life table is tedious, abridged tables based on five-year intervals are sometimes constructed, as in Table 6. To learn some of the properties of the table, look in the first column for your age group and then read across that row until you reach the last column, noting the meaning of each figure by reading the heading over its column. It might be instructive to follow the same procedure for your parents, a child, and others you know who differ considerably in age from yourself.

INTERPRETATION AND APPLICATION

Life tables provide no information concerning future mortality; they describe only the forces of mortality in the given years. A current life table is the death history of a hypothetical group of people who throughout their lives would have the age-sex-specific death rates of the year for which the table was computed. But since the specific death rates used in the current life table are identical with the specific death rates of the existing population, the "life table population" has an immediate though abstract relation to observed data.

Applications of the life table are numerous. It yields the expectation of life at any age; it is useful in computing standardized birth and death rates; it supplies the intrinsic death rate; it measures survival rates (the probability of surviving from any given age to any other given age); and when coupled with other information, it is invaluable in making population projections. Life insurance companies largely base their calculations on life tables.

TABLE 6. Abridged Life Table for the United States, 1960*

Age Interval	Proportion Dying	Of 100,000 Born Alive		Stationary Population		Average Remaining Lifetime
PERIOD OF LIFE BETWEEN TWO EXACT AGES STATED IN YEARS	PROPORTION OF PERSONS ALIVE AT BEGINNING OF AGE INTERVAL DYING DURING INTERVAL	NUMBER LIVING AT BEGINNING OF AGE INTERVAL	NUMBER DYING DURING AGE INTERVAL	IN THE AGE INTERVAL	IN THIS AND ALL SUBSEQUENT AGE INTERVALS	AVERAGE NUMBER OF YEARS OF LIFE REMAINING AT BEGINNING OF AGE INTERVAL
0-1	0.0256	100,000	2,564	97,750	6,966,918	69.7
1-5	.0042	97,436	411	388,751	6,869,168	70.5
5-10	.0024	97,025	237	484,489	6,480,417	66.8
10-15	.0022	96,788	211	483,451	5,995,924	61.9
15-20	.0043	96,577	418	481,915	5,512,477	57.1
20-25	.0058	96,159	558	479,432	5,030,562	52.3
25-30	.0064	95,601	611	476,510	4,551,130	47.6
30-35	.0077	94,990	732	473,205	4,074,620	42.9
35-40	.0119	94,258	1,124	468,657	3,601,415	38.2
40-45	.0185	93,134	1,719	461,666	3,132,758	33.6
45-50	.0284	91,415	2,595	450,993	2,671,092	29.2
50-55	.0449	88,820	3,987	434,716	2,220,099	25.0
55-60	.0662	84,833	5,616	410,855	1,785,383	21.0
60-65	.0999	79,217	7,911	377,114	1,374,528	17.4
65-70	.1561	71,306	11,132	329,752	997,414	14.0
70-75	.2302	60,174	13,851	267,240	667,662	11.1
75-80	.3060	46,323	14,173	196,354	400,422	8.6
80-85	.4474	32,150	14,383	123,718	204,068	6.3
85 and over	1.0000	17,767	17,767	80,350	80,350	4.5

* U. S. National Office of Vital Statistics, Monthly Vital Statistics Report, Vol. IX, No. 13, Part 2, July 28, 1961, p. 6.

And in law cases involving compensation for injuries, they can be used as a basis for adjudication: the gross money value of a man is the present value of his probable future earnings, discounted for interest and chances for survivorship; the net money value of a man is his gross money value minus the present value of what he spends on himself for maintenance and luxuries out of his earnings, discounted for interest and chances of surviving.[4] Personnel statisticians employ life tables to schedule retirement and pension programs and contributions and also to predict probable needs regarding employee replacement. Research physicians use life tables to measure the longevity of persons having specific physical impairments and also to estimate other statistics concerning disease.

Life tables also have been computed for such inanimate objects as furniture, motor vehicles, and factory machines. And they help to solve problems in depreciation and replacement of equipment. There is a story of a young girl who had just begun work at a life insurance company when a maintenance man stopped next to her desk, set up a ladder, pulled a light bulb out of his pocket, and climbed the ladder. Just as he reached toward the overhead light fixture, the old bulb burned out. Seeing the amazement on the girl's face, the janitor explained, "We have everything figured out here."

Any living creature can provide data for a life table—even livestock, although this is hardly standard agricultural practice. Survivorship curves are used by ecologists to describe animal and plant mortality under specified environmental conditions. Figure 2 is plotted semilogarithmically rather than arithmetically to emphasize rates as opposed to absolute increments. Note that whereas fruit flies nearly all live out their inherited life span, oysters have a very high mortality at early ages. Between these extremes are modern man (closer to the flies) and other animals and plants (closer to the oyster). The Hydra (a fresh water polyp) has constant age-specific mortality rates because of its remarkable ability to repair injuries (even if the body is divided into pieces, each piece will grow into a complete animal). The shaded area in the figure represents possible mortality improvement in man. If we could conquer infectious diseases and eliminate accidents, the only significant cause of death (unless new causes entered the historical process) would be the degenerative diseases. Our survivorship curve would then resemble that of flies. Already, man has made a great improvement; human survivorship was once very similar to that of other animals. But even though a larger proportion of men now come close to reaching our

---

[4] Louis I. Dublin and A. J. Lotka, *The Money Value of a Man*, The Ronald Press Co., New York, 1946.

FIGURE 2. *Survivorship Curves for Man and Other Creatures**

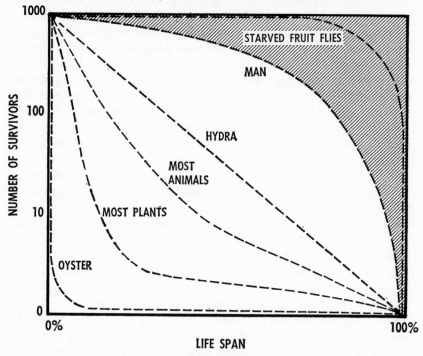

LIFE SPAN

Several types of survivorship curves plotted on the basis of survivors per thousand log scale (vertical coordinate) and age in relative units of mean life span (horizontal coordinate).

* Adapted from Edward S. Deevey, Jr., "The Probability of Death," *Scientific American*, Vol. CLXXXII, No. 4, April 1950, pp. 58-60; and Eugene P. Odum, *Fundamentals of Ecology*, W. B. Saunders Co., Philadelphia, 1959, p. 168.

(present) physiological limit of longevity, we have not increased the ultimate biological limit of human life.

Causes of Death

The leading causes of death have not always been the same. In the preceding chapter it was noted that famine, typhus, smallpox, and the plague—now virtually controllable—once ravaged mankind. Other scourges have also been conquered or are on their way out, for example, typhoid, tuberculosis, cholera, dysentery, influenza, and pneumonia. The ten leading causes of death in the United States in 1900 and 1961 are compared in Table 7. Note that the respiratory diseases (influenza, pneumonia, and tuberculosis) have lost their dominance, dropping from the top of the list to relatively obscure ranks. Circulatory ailments and

TABLE 7. *Ten Leading Causes of Death, United States, 1900 and 1961**

1900

RANK	CAUSE OF DEATH	DEATHS PER 100,000 POPULATION	PER CENT OF ALL DEATHS
	All Causes	1,719	100.0
1	Influenza and pneumonia	202	11.8
2	Tuberculosis (all forms)	195	11.3
3	Gastritis, etc.	143	8.3
4	Diseases of the heart	137	8.0
5	Vascular lesions affecting the central nervous system	107	6.2
6	Chronic nephritis	81	4.7
7	All accidents	72	4.2
8	Malignant neoplasms (cancer)	64	3.7
9	Certain diseases of early infancy	63	3.6
10	Diphtheria	40	2.3
	All other causes	615	35.9

1961

RANK	CAUSE OF DEATH	DEATHS PER 100,000 POPULATION	PER CENT OF ALL DEATHS
	All Causes	930	100.0
1	Diseases of the heart	365	39.3
2	Malignant neoplasms (cancer)	147	15.9
3	Vascular lesions affecting the central nervous system	105	11.3
4	All accidents	51	5.5
5	Certain diseases of early infancy	37	3.9
6	Influenza and pneumonia	30	3.2
7	General arteriosclerosis	19	2.0
8	Diabetes mellitus	16	1.7
9	Congenital malformations	11	1.2
10	Other diseases of the circulatory system	11	1.2
	All other causes	138	14.8

* Monroe Lerner, "Mortality and Morbidity in the United States as Basic Indices of Health Needs," *Annals of the American Academy of Political and Social Science,* Vol. CCCXXXVII, September 1961, p. 4; and National Vital Statistics Division, "Monthly Vital Statistics Report," Vol. X, No. 13, July 31, 1962, p. 14.

cancer now are responsible together for more than half of all deaths in the United States. An interesting comparison is provided by Graunt's tabulation for seventeenth-century England, in which the impoverished state of medical knowledge and death control is evident upon inspection of the leading causes of death: consumption and cough, chrisomes and infants, ague and fever, plague, aged, teeth and worms, flox and small-pox, and dropsy and tympany.[5]

War is an even more variable cause of death than are the epidemic diseases. When a war occurs, it contributes momentously to injury, disablement, and death, but since military deaths are so widely publicized, their numbers and importance may be overestimated by the newspaper reader. However, soldiers and sailors are normally young adults in the prime of their reproductive and occupational careers; hence their deaths are relatively more important for the community than the demise of retired octogenarians. The extreme quality of annual and weekly fluctuations makes it next to impossible to include war deaths in tables of mortality without severe distortion in attempting to measure long-run trends.

A newly recognized factor in mortality is the effect of chance combinations of external events with periodic and random alterations in the physiological state of the individual. To select a simplified illustration, everyone's blood pressure fluctuates about his personal average. If it happens that sudden exertion is made at a time when the blood pressure is at its highest or lowest rating, death might result; if the same exertion occurs when blood pressure is average, no ill effects follow. Other physiological states also oscillate between upper and lower limits; if two or more of these natural processes reach a limit at the same time, health may be adversely affected even though the same value for only one of the conditions would not have dire consequences. Of course, these variations may also operate to one's advantage.

LIFE AND WORKING YEARS LOST

Conventional rankings of causes of death are not fully indicative of the loss to society attributable to each cause of death, largely because they ignore age at death. A disease that kills a person at age 27 obviously creates a greater loss to society than one that kills at age 72. For this reason statisticians have invented two measures: life years lost and working years lost. The number of life years lost is obtained separately for each cause of death by first multiplying the expectation of life at any given age by the number of deaths from that cause at that age and then taking the sum of these age-specific products. The number of working years lost is similarly computed except that the years expected to be lived before age 20 and after age 65 are excluded, thus restricting coverage to "working life expectancy." The units of measurement, respectively,

---

[5] John Graunt, *Natural and Political Observations Made Upon the Bills of Mortality*, London, 1662, reprinted by The John Hopkins Press, Baltimore, 1939. table facing p. 80.

are one "unrealized" year of life and one "unrealized" year of the usual working period of life.[6] Life expectancy values are obtained from life tables. According to the traditional measure compared with the two new ones, ranks of the seven leading causes of death in 1945 were:[7]

BY NUMBER OF DEATHS	BY LIFE YEARS LOST	BY WORKING YEARS LOST
1. heart	1. heart	1. accidents
2. cancer	2. accidents	2. heart
3. cerebrovascular	3. cancer	3. pneumonia
4. accidents	4. pneumonia	4. cancer
5. nephritis	5. cerebrovascular	5. tuberculosis
6. pneumonia	6. tuberculosis	6. nephritis
7. tuberculosis	7. nephritis	7. cerebrovascular

As is evident, when remaining years of total and working life are thus allowed for, the relative importance of the different causes is altered. Heart disease maintains its prominence, cancer declines somewhat, pneumonia appears of greater consequence, and accidents rise to join heart disease at the heads of the columns. As a destroyer of the working years of life—the years constituting the productive and military strength of the nation—fatal accidents outrank every other cause.

SECULAR CHANGES

Changes in causes of death over the last hundred years in the United States may be seen by grouping mortality into the following categories:

    I: Accidents—a) motor vehicle
             b) other
    II: Communicable diseases—a) intestinal
                    b) respiratory
    III: Degenerative diseases—a) heart and circulatory
                  b) other
    IV: Miscellaneous and unknown—a) cancer
                            b) other

I. Accidents are maintained on a fairly steady level. Vehicular accidents have increased considerably, but there have been decreases in some other forms. II. Communicable diseases are gradually being conquered. The intestinal diseases, most dangerous in the summer months, were brought under partial control in the late nineteenth century, followed in the early

---

[6] Frank G. Dickinson and Everett L. Welker, "What Is the Leading Cause of Death," *American Medical Association*, Bulletin No. 64, 1948, p. 3.
[7] *Ibid.*, pp. 7-8.

twentieth century by a successful attack on the respiratory infections, which are most severe during the winter. III. Since people are living longer than they used to, the degenerative diseases are striking a larger percentage of the populace. IV. Cancer has shown a sharp increase, some of which is certainly due to improved diagnostic techniques.

The success of the fight against communicable disease is illustrated in Figure 3. The nineteenth-century Chicago pattern exhibited gross ir-

FIGURE 3. *Death Rates from Typhoid Fever, Chicago, 1860-1942**

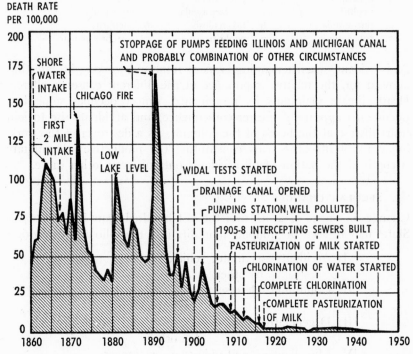

DEATH RATE
PER 100,000

* Louis I. Dublin, Alfred J. Lotka, and Mortimer Spiegelman, *Length of Life*, Revised Edition, p. 159. Copyright 1949 by The Ronald Press Company. Reprinted by permission.

regularities, towering peaks, and troughs that never dipped very low. Twentieth-century maxima are far smaller and the general downward trend is fairly regular.

SEASONAL VARIATIONS

There was a sharp improvement in control over the intestinal infections in the United States between 1850 and 1900 and over respiratory illnesses between 1900 and 1950. By mid-twentieth century, the seasonal variations had almost disappeared.

Pre-1850 mortality causes are not precisely known but may be surmised to have been approximately like those of 1850 as far as seasonal fluctuations are concerned. Mortality statistics from Massachusetts for 1842-1851 indicate a summer peak in August-September which was considerably higher than that of the maximum winter month.[8] Data from other countries in the nineteenth century also presented a marked summer crest.

Three stages can be detected in the seasonal variation of deaths. The first stage, which prevailed about a century ago, was characterized by a very high peak in summer and a secondary high point in mid-winter. Stage two, at about the turn of the century, exhibited a maximum death rate in winter and a moderate high in summer. The United States is now in stage three: a flat curve with a slight maximum in winter and a quite favorable summer. Since it was diarrhea and enteritis which first retreated before the gains of medical science, the summer months were the first to show a substantial decline in mortality. Later, pneumonia, influenza, and respiratory tuberculosis dropped to a death rate of less than 10 per cent of their nineteenth-century level, resulting in the more uniform distribution of deaths which currently prevails. Perhaps the most pronounced change has been in infant mortality. Summer, the most hazardous season before 1900, is now the safest.

Figure 4 illustrates the trend toward seasonal uniformity in the United States death rate during the past six decades. At the turn of the century there was a sharp pinnacle in March, followed by a steep valley reaching a low in June. A secondary peak occurred in July and August, succeeded by lower mortality, having a secondary low point in November. This seasonal distribution of deaths prevailed until World War I. Since 1920 the low point has occurred consistently in August, while January, February, and March bring the greatest number of deaths. Improvements in mortality in recent decades have affected the seasonal pattern by lowering the winter death total slightly more rapidly than the summer total. Thus the monthly distribution curve is approaching a perfect circle. By 1961 the poorest months (December and January) had rates only slightly larger than those of the most favorable month (August).

Among the countries showing a mortality peak in the summer in mid-twentieth century are Egypt, Mexico, Chile, Colombia, the Philippines, and Thailand. Some of the countries having their maximum mortality in the winter are Canada, Japan, France, Germany, Italy, Roumania,

---

[8] Walter Willcox, *Studies in American Demography*, Cornell University Press, Ithaca, 1940, pp. 254-263.

FIGURE 4. *Monthly Death Rates, United States, 1900-1960**

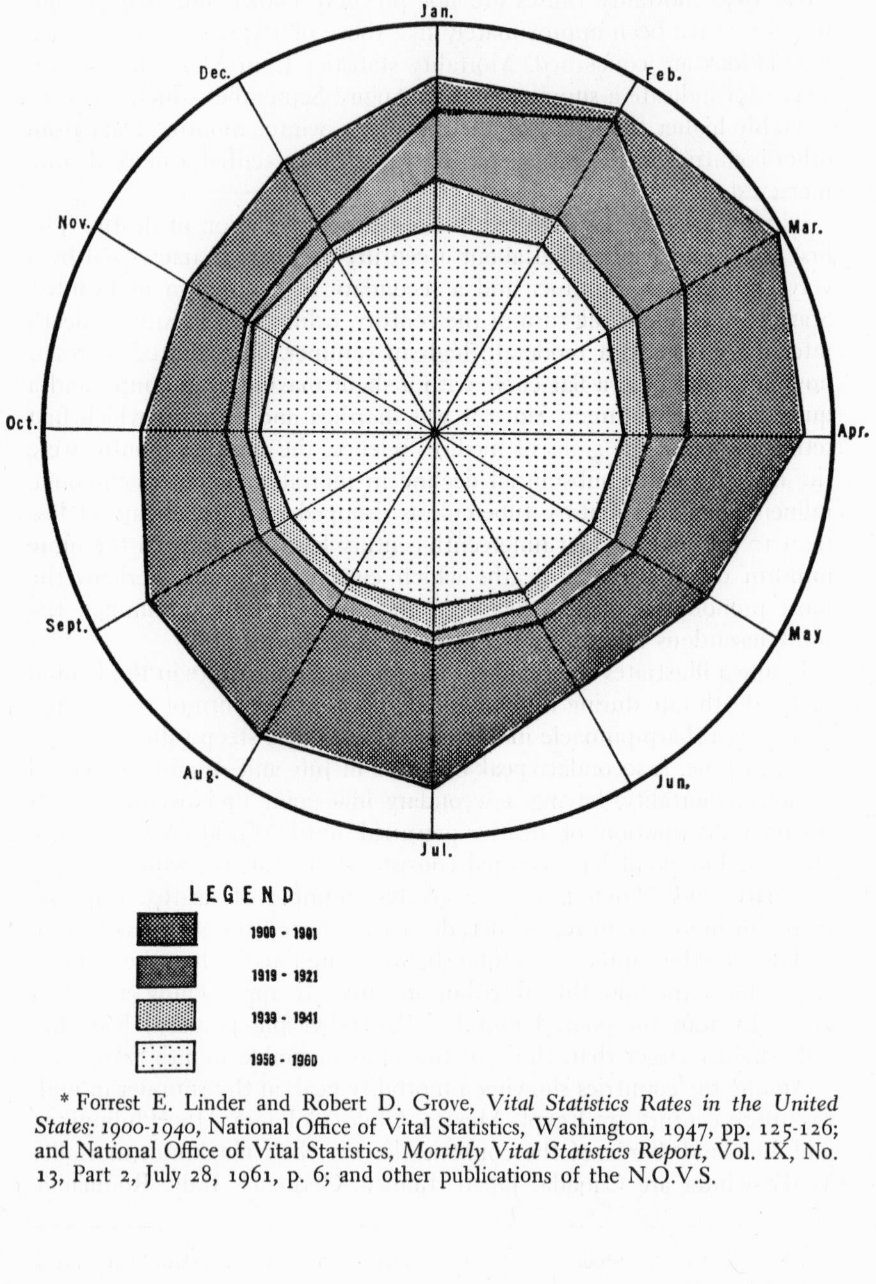
Jan.
Feb.
Mar.
Apr.
May
Jun.
Jul.
Aug.
Sept.
Oct.
Nov.
Dec.
LEGEND
1900 - 1901
1919 - 1921
1939 - 1941
1958 - 1960

* Forrest E. Linder and Robert D. Grove, *Vital Statistics Rates in the United States: 1900-1940*, National Office of Vital Statistics, Washington, 1947, pp. 125-126; and National Office of Vital Statistics, *Monthly Vital Statistics Report*, Vol. IX, No. 13, Part 2, July 28, 1961, p. 6; and other publications of the N.O.V.S.

Spain, and Yugoslavia.[9] Generally the underdeveloped countries tend to have their highest mortality in the summer, while modern industrial countries resemble the twentieth-century United States pattern.

WORLD DISEASE CONTROL

Although all nationalities of men have approximately the same inherent susceptibility to different diseases, the degree of control attained over these diseases varies from region to region. Figure 5 shows four disease regions on a map in which the areas of countries are proportional to their populations in 1950. The prevailing ailments of Region 1 are heart diseases, cancer, mental disorders, tuberculosis, pneumonia, influenza, syphilis, diabetes, the common cold, suicide, and industrial and traffic accidents. These temperate countries, with a total population of about 800 million, are the healthiest part of the world. Region 2, containing about half the world's people, is the zone of tropical diseases. It is ravaged by malaria, amebiasis, dysentery, hookworm, yaws, leprosy, tuberculosis, syphilis, smallpox, cholera, plague, yellow fever, and sleeping sickness. Infant mortality is high, and prevalent diseases tend to be parasitic, largely because the inhabitants have not yet learned how to protect themselves. A tropical climate is not unhealthy *per se* (in fact, it may bear a surprising resemblance to the man-made indoor conditions in Minnesota and Indiana homes, where the thermostat is set high all winter); rather, the diseases persist largely because of human poverty and ignorance. Region 3, containing about 400 million people, is epidemiologically intermediate between and geographically adjacent to Regions 1 and 2 and shares most of their ailments. In addition, inhabitants of Region 3 suffer from dysentery and contagious skin and eye diseases (especially trachoma). The extreme southern area, Region 4, which contains only about 100 million people, is afflicted by typhoid fever, influenza, tuberculosis, syphilis, and flukes. To be sure, this presentation is simplified; individual countries show many deviations from the regional trend. Moreover, importation of preventive medicine from Region 1 is rather rapidly changing the disease patterns of the other regions.

Recent trends in the fight against disease may be summarized as follows:

> 1. Since the turn of the century there has been a decisive decline in mortality from communicable diseases of childhood. Some of them, such as diarrhea and diphtheria, have been practically eradicated; others like whooping cough, measles, and scarlet fever have been made comparatively harmless by new therapies.

---

[9] United Nations Statistical Office, *Demographic Yearbook*, New York, 1951, pp. 206-215.

FIGURE 5. *World Diseases by Four Regions**

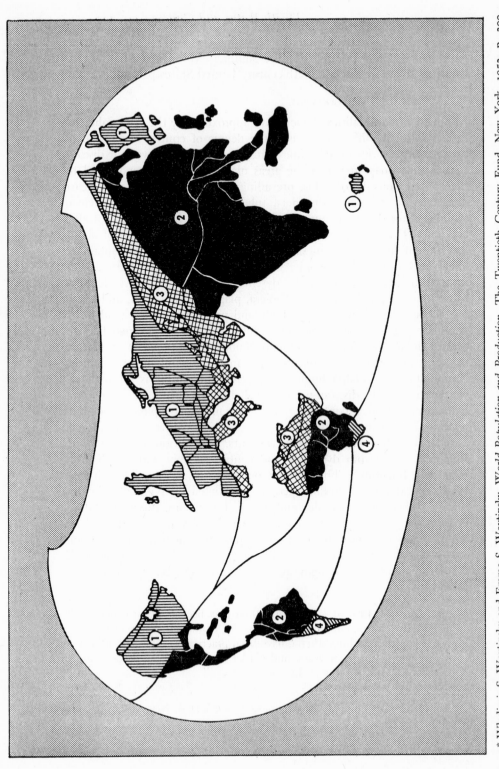

* Wladimir S. Woytinsky and Emma S. Woytinsky, *World Population and Production*, The Twentieth Century Fund, New York, 1953, p. 200,

2. Equally spectacular has been the victory over typhus, typhoid, and paratyphoid fevers and malaria.

3. Substantial, but less decisive, success has been achieved in the campaign against tuberculosis and pneumonia, including influenza, and senile debility.

4. Still unconquered are cancer, diseases of the heart and arteries, including hypertension and arteriosclerosis, nephritis, diseases of the nervous system (including intracranial lesions), and some other ailments, especially diseases peculiar to the first month of life and congenital malformation.

Little improvement, if any, has been recorded in the death rate from violence and from all forms of accidents combined.[10]

The decline in infant mortality has been helped appreciably by improving the quality of milk and water supplies. Impure water and milk once made diarrhea and enteritis responsible for half of all childhood deaths, especially among infants. Also far less dangerous are measles, scarlet fever, diphtheria, and whooping cough, once feared child killers. In the case of diphtheria, prevalence has been reduced, though the case-fatality rate is still high. Scarlet fever, measles, and whooping cough remain widespread, but case-fatality rates have been reduced tremendously.

Regions particularly lacking in modern sanitation and disease prevention are afflicted with ailments almost unknown to Americans. "It is estimated that there are today some 50,000,000 cases of yaws, one of the treponematoses caused by a spirochete similar to that of spyhilis."[11] In some parts of the world syphilis is endemic. Bilharziasis (a disease caused by worms in the blood vessels, in which snails act as intermediate hosts) affects about 150,000,000 people, infestation resulting from poor sanitation. Trachoma, a chronic and contagious form of conjunctivitis resulting in partial or complete blindness, a disease of poverty and promiscuity, affects 400,000,000 persons in parts of the world having low living levels. Filariasis, resulting from infestation by threadlike nematode worms, causing blindness, elephantiasis, and skin lesions, affects some 250,000,000 tropical residents. But there is a promising side to this misery. Yaws, syphilis, trachoma, and the filariases can be cured by antibiotics and sulfa compounds and improved sanitation. Leprosy, now known not to be highly contagious, is gradually coming under control, but, like the filariases and trachoma, remains a problem in Africa and other tropical underdeveloped regions. Trypanosomiasis or sleeping sickness, transmitted by tse-tse flies, was once almost in-

[10] Woytinsky and Woytinsky, *World Population and Production, op. cit.*, p. 201.
[11] United Nations, *Report on the World Social Situation*, New York, 1957, pp. 32-33.

evitably fatal, but modern drugs can prevent or cure it if administered at an early stage.

These infective, parasitic, and virus diseases are prevalent largely in economically underdeveloped regions. In technologically advanced countries, they have been pretty well licked—only to be replaced by chronic degenerative and malignant diseases, which particularly affect older persons. Cancer and cardiovascular diseases are increasingly prevalent in industrial countries, partly because fewer people are dying of other afflictions. As people grow older, there is a greater likelihood of suffering from deterioration of some organ or from malignant growths which enlarge slowly and unobtrusively over several years or decades.

Until the 1950's, paralytic poliomyelitis was practically the only major contagious disease with an increasing rate of incidence. In the United States especially, poliomyelitis rates were very high but the Salk and Sabin vaccines are now placing it under control. Muscular dystrophy and multiple sclerosis remain unsolved problems everywhere.

The mentally ill are most frequently identified and hospitalized in Western nations, but this may be an outcome of different diagnostic practices—or a result of the emotional strains of the accelerated pace of modern urban living. Also, where people are living longer, they are more likely to be affected by arteriosclerotic or senile psychoses. Although statistics on mental health are unreliable and grossly incomplete in most countries, there is evidence to indicate that the number of mentally ill may exceed the number of "physically" ill. In some areas, over one-half of the hospital beds are occupied by persons having mental disorders. Additionally, there are many cases where "nonmental" diseases are apparently wholly or partly psychological in origin.

Farm, industrial, and vehicular accidents continue. The relative apportionment of accidents varies from region to region according to degree of mechanization and motorization and to the vigor and effectiveness of safety measures adopted by governmental and industrial authorities. In underdeveloped regions, the major contributors to fatalities and injuries are falls, drowning, poisoning, suffocation, fire, and explosions. With advancing technology, automobile, railroad, and airplane accidents have been added. Deaths, mutilation, and mutation from artificial irradiation (atomic explosions, radioactive fallout, X-rays, radioactive wastes, and so on) are among the less agreeable by-products of the "march of progress."

Length of Life

Longevity may be conceived as a summary of all the various mortality rates and health conditions prevailing at a given time. It refers to length of life actually lived and must be distinguished from the life span, which is the maximum potential length of life. The usual measure of longevity is the mean duration of life, more commonly called expectation of life at birth. This is the mean number of years lived by a group of persons all born in the same year. Expectation of life is computed through a life table.

EXPECTATION OF LIFE

Life tables for the United States covering the years 1900-1902 yielded the following expectations of life at birth: white males, 48.2 years; white females, 51.1 years; nonwhite males, 32.5 years; nonwhite females, 35.0 years. The improvement in these figures through 1949-1951 was: white males, 18.4 years; white females, 21.5 years; nonwhite males, 26.9 years; nonwhite females, 28.7 years.[12] Clearly, the greatest gains during the first half of the twentieth century were made by females and by nonwhite persons. Table 8 incorporates the right-hand columns of four

TABLE 8. *Expectation of Life by Age, Sex, and Color, United States, 1960**

AGE AT LAST BIRTHDAY	Average years of life remaining after beginning of age interval			
	WHITE MALE	WHITE FEMALE	NONWHITE MALE	NONWHITE FEMALE
0	67.4	74.1	61.1	66.3
1-4	68.2	74.6	63.2	67.9
5-9	64.4	70.8	59.7	64.4
10-14	59.6	66.0	54.9	59.6
15-19	54.8	61.1	50.1	54.7
20-24	50.1	56.2	45.5	49.9
25-29	45.5	51.4	41.1	45.2
30-34	40.8	46.6	36.7	40.7
35-39	36.1	41.8	32.5	36.3
40-44	31.6	37.1	28.4	32.1
45-49	27.2	32.5	24.6	28.0
50-54	23.1	28.0	21.0	24.3
55-59	19.3	23.8	17.8	20.9
60-64	15.9	19.7	14.9	17.7
65-69	12.9	15.9	12.7	15.2
70-74	10.2	12.4	10.7	12.7
75-79	7.9	9.3	8.9	10.4
80-84	5.9	6.8	7.0	8.1
85 and over	4.4	4.9	5.5	6.2

U. S. National Vital Statistics Division, *Vital Statistics of the United States: 1960*, Government Printing Office, Washington, 1963, Vol. II, Section 2, p. 8.

---

[12] National Office of Vital Statistics, "United States Life Tables, 1949-1951," *Vital Statistics—Special Reports*, Vol. XLI, No. 1, November 23, 1954; and "Abridged Life Tables, United States, 1951," *Vital Statistics—Special Reports*, Vol. XXXVII, No. 5, April 30, 1951.

detailed life tables by sex and race. Note that the average remaining lifetime decreases with advancing age with only one exception: mortality in the first year of life is so high that survivors of this hazardous period actually have a higher life expectancy than new-born infants.

Table 9 presents expectation of life in selected countries of newly-

TABLE 9. *Expectation of Life at Various Ages for Selected Countries, 1940-1959*[*]

CONTINENT AND COUNTRY	YEARS	Males			Females		
		BIRTH	AGE 20	AGE 60	BIRTH	AGE 20	AGE 60
NORTH AMERICA							
Canada	1955-57	67.61	51.19	16.54	72.92	55.80	19.34
Mexico	1950	46.67	42.73	15.32	49.85	45.80	15.96
U.S., Continental	1958	66.4	49.4	15.6	72.7	55.2	19.1
SOUTH AMERICA							
Argentina	1947	56.9	45.6	13.8	61.4	49.6	16.5
Brazil	1940-50	39.3	37.9	12.5	45.5	—	—
Chile	1952	49.84	42.67	13.99	53.89	47.08	16.42
Venezuela	1950-51	56.34	46.18	15.70	58.76	48.29	17.48
EUROPE							
Austria	1949-51	61.91	48.68	15.12	66.97	52.62	17.27
Czechoslovakia	1958	67.23	50.59	15.75	72.30	54.90	18.22
Denmark	1951-55	69.87	53.09	17.50	72.60	54.99	18.44
East Germany	1956-57	66.34	51.28	16.23	70.03	54.85	18.46
England and Wales	1959	68.1	50.6	15.1	73.8	55.8	19.0
Finland	1951-55	63.4	47.0	14.1	69.8	52.8	16.9
France	1959	67.0	49.9	15.8	73.6	55.9	19.5
Iceland	1941-50	66.1	50.5	18.2	70.3	54.0	19.6
Ireland	1950-52	64.53	49.31	15.40	67.08	51.15	16.83
Italy	1954-57	65.75	51.04	16.23	70.02	54.68	18.20
Netherlands	1953-55	71.0	53.7	17.8	73.9	56.0	18.9
Norway	1951-55	71.11	54.11	18.52	74.70	56.96	19.93
Poland	1958	62.8	49.9	15.6	68.9	54.9	18.8
Portugal	1957-58	59.8	49.4	15.4	65.0	54.1	18.1
Spain	1950	58.76	47.50	15.18	63.50	52.03	17.69
Sweden	1959	71.69	53.84	17.75	75.24	56.75	19.49
Switzerland	1948-53	66.36	50.16	15.69	70.85	53.86	17.77
Scotland	1959	66.00	48.97	14.24	71.44	53.84	17.56
West Germany	1957-58	66.21	50.12	15.44	71.34	54.44	17.91
Yugoslavia	1952-54	56.92	48.29	14.93	59.33	50.41	16.41
ASIA							
India	1941-50	32.45	33.03	10.13	31.66	32.90	11.33
Israel (Jews)	1959	70.23	53.21	17.09	72.26	54.86	18.43
Japan	1959	65.21	49.31	15.16	69.88	53.45	18.10
Philippines	1946-49	48.81	45.98	17.72	53.36	47.27	18.45
Thailand	1947-48	48.69	39.81	12.69	51.90	42.71	14.20

TABLE 9. (*Continued*)

CONTINENT AND COUNTRY	YEARS	Males			Females		
		BIRTH	AGE 20	AGE 60	BIRTH	AGE 20	AGE 60
AFRICA							
Congo							
African population	1950-52	37.64	34.41	10.63	40.00	36.29	12.27
Kenya							
European population	1946-49	63.8	47.8	15.5	69.3	53.4	17.8
Union of South Africa							
Asiatic	1945-47	50.70	40.22	11.97	49.75	39.30	11.96
Colored	1945-47	41.70	36.83	13.16	44.00	39.42	14.97
European	1945-47	63.78	48.35	15.34	68.31	52.27	18.04
OCEANIA							
Australia	1953-55	67.14	50.10	15.47	72.75	55.06	18.78
New Zealand							
European	1950-52	68.29	51.15	16.19	72.43	54.64	18.53
Maori	1950-52	54.05	42.21	12.81	55.88	43.29	14.41

* *Population Index*, Vol. XXVII, No. 4, October 1961, pp. 377-381.

born infants, young adults, and aging persons. It is noteworthy that female expectations generally exceed those of males, and European nations have the most favorable expectations at all ages. Note also the contrast shown in the Union of South Africa, where life expectancy of European residents exceeds by far that of Asiatics, with Negroes presenting a still less optimistic figure; presumably, *apartheid* and differential life styles are primarily responsible for these differences.

In 1934, Raymond Pearl developed a measure of longevity which applies to an individual and which has the advantage of being extremely easy to compute: the Total Immediate Ancestral Longevity.[13] The T.I.A.L. is the sum of the ages at death of the two parents and the four grandparents of the individual concerned. For example, if one's mother died at age 51, his father at age 82, his mother's mother at age 78, his mother's father at age 68, his father's mother at age 72, and his father's father at age 65, his T.I.A.L. would be 416 (an average of 69 years each) —a figure that augurs well for his own longevity. When one or more of the six forebears is still living, he has two choices for measurement: he can either use that person's present age—yielding a minimum T.I.A.L.; or he can use a life table to estimate the person's probable age at death—yielding an expected T.I.A.L. Ostensibly, this figure gives an indication of the individual's propensity toward longevity, as influenced by the biological stock of his forebears and the social and economic conditions of life of these six ancestors. Unfortunately for users

[13] Raymond Pearl and Ruth DeWitt Pearl, *The Ancestry of the Long-Lived*, Johns Hopkins Press, Baltimore, 1934, pp. 5-7 and 47-49.

of the T.I.A.L., the latter conditions often bear very little relation to the conditions of life for the individual concerned. The highest and lowest values recorded by Pearl were 599 years (an average length of life of 100 years for each ancestor) and 254 years (an average of 42 years). The age of onset of fecundity makes T.I.A.L. totals smaller than 90 almost impossible.

APPROACHING THE LIFE SPAN

Expected future trends regarding longevity include the following: first, accidents will continue, but probably at diminishing rates; communicable diseases will decline in importance and may vanish almost completely; degenerative diseases will receive considerable attention from medical scientists, presumably with partial success; and finally, some of the diseases now imperfectly understood will come under medical control, while others will continue to be troublesome. Assuming that these expectations are realized, the average duration of life should approach closer and closer to the life span—the maximum length of life that can be reasonably expected for a normally endowed human being living under optimal conditions. If deaths from all causes except the degenerative diseases could be eliminated, most people would live to an age approximating our best estimate of the life span: about 120 years. Curiously, Moses is said to have died in his 120th year atop Mount Pisgah. Our approach toward this objective over the past century is documented in Figure 6.

FIGURE 6. *Survivors from Birth to Successive Ages,*
United States, 1850-1959*

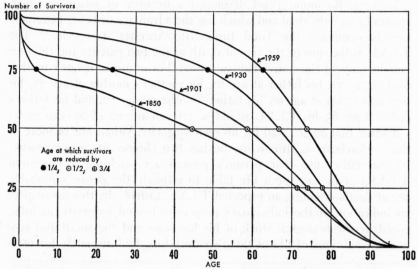

* Metropolitan Life Insurance Company, *Statistical Bulletin,* Vol. XLI, No. 3, March 1960, p. 8.

Increasing longevity to its limit is a generally accepted goal. But it is very difficult to determine just what that limit is. We do not even know the oldest age at death ever attained by a man. Statements regarding the age of very old persons are of highly doubtful accuracy, for after they reach age 60 or so, many people exaggerate their antiquity as a point of pride. Hence, some fantastic "believe-it-or-not" ages are certainly false while others are in disrepute. The greatest age of death having some documentation belongs to Christian Jacobsen Drakenberg, who is supposed to have been born in 1626, worked as a sailor for nearly a century, lived under seven Danish kings, married at age 110, and died in 1772 at the age of 145. He was sturdy, robust, and very impetuous; after 1767—when he reached the age of 141—he is said to have led "quite a respectable" life.[14]

Death from senility or natural causes is not necessarily inevitable. Alexis Carrel kept a bit of chicken embroyo alive for thirty-six years in a nutrient fluid from which metabolic wastes were regularly removed, ending the experiment when it became apparent that the tissue probably could survive indefinitely. In short, there is nothing in the fundamental nature of protoplasm that demands a wearing-out. Why then should people "just wear out"? If biological research supplies appropriate knowledge of the aging process in human beings, it is possible that the life span itself will ultimately be extended—although Shangri-La hardly seems a practical objective at present. Experimentation on cellular growth may provide needed explanations of precisely how human beings become older (biologically, not chronologically or socially). Indeed, one day people may look back on the 120-year life span in the same way that we now regard "Mach 1" or the speed of sound as an obsolete limit to the speed of airplanes.

Inheritance of longevity has been studied by actuaries, physicians, and demographers, yet genealogical and life insurance records concerning the relative roles of heredity and environment in longevity are inconclusive.

> Although evidence favors the common assumption that heredity plays a part in modifying longevity, studies pointing in this direction may have not been freed from the influence of environmental factors. It is impossible, in the present state of knowledge, to estimate the relative share of heredity and of environment. . . . The advantage of better parental longevity . . . has been much less than the gain in expectation of life in the early adult ages which the general population has experienced in less than half a century. Moreover, the possibilities of gain in

---

[14] "Dansk Biografisk Lexikon," quoted in J. F. Steffensen, "Notes on the Life Table and the Limit of Life," *Journal of the Institute of Actuaries*, Vol. LXII, 1931, p. 103.

longevity through control of environment have by no means been exhausted.[15]

It seems that people wishing to maximize their probability of long life should accept Oliver Wendell Holmes' prescription: "One of the best ways to insure a long life is to make a careful and wise selection of grandparents," and then make their environment as favorable as possible by taking honors at college, marrying early, and settling as a professional worker or farmer in a small town in Nebraska.

[15] Dublin, Lotka, and Spiegelman, *Length of Life*, *op. cit.*, pp. 117-118.

7 ⚭ Health and Mortality Differentials

To paraphrase George Orwell, all men are mortal but some are more mortal than others. More accurately, mortality rates are not identical for all segments of the population. Illness too varies from person to person and from group to group within countries as well as among nations.

Before examining these differentials, we should recognize that sickness is more than just a precursor of death: it is demographically consequential in its own right. The vital importance of hospitalization, disability, and preoccupation with sickness is easily underestimated, which has led one expert to point out that "The major world health problem is not death but the chronic infection and infestation which converts man from a productive unit to a liability in society."[1] In short, a chronically sick person requiring continuous care exerts a drag of dependency on the healthy populace. Just as a seriously wounded soldier also removes from the fight those who must care for him, and thus may constitute a greater loss to battle forces than a dead man, so it is in nonmilitary situations: a bedridden man is not a working man supporting his family and producing goods and services useful to his society. Insurance companies often pay more money for a major illness than for a death, and a great fear in lawsuits is that the afflicted person will not die quickly but require years of medical care, which is far more expensive for the liable party. Finally, not even Jeremy Bentham could estimate the total unhappiness and pain produced by sickness affecting loved ones.

---

[1] Henry van Zilde Hyde, "Clean Environment Key to Health," *Public Health Reports*, Vol. LXV, No. 49, December 8, 1950, p. 1613.

Health and Morbidity

The study of illness, called *morbidity*, is important for four reasons: 1) periods of sickness are likely to involve absence from work and a resultant interference with national productivity and family solvency; 2) hospitalization involves economic losses for the individual and for his society; 3) the anguish and preoccupation with illness and pain and the fear of bereavement are matters of serious concern even to those who do not directly experience them; and 4) the social functions and dysfunctions of sickness are integral to the cohesion and disruption of the group.

We cannot generalize from mortality to morbidity; high morbidity is neither necessarily coupled with high mortality, nor *vice versa*. For one thing, some diseases are not fatal. There is, however, some relationship, and for large differences, generalizations assuming a correlation are usually accurate. For example, if country A has a mortality rate four times as high as that of country B, we can safely expect country A to have higher morbidity also. Differentials and causes may fluctuate considerably between morbidity and mortality for diseases differ a great deal as to incidence (new cases), prevalence (existing cases), and fatality (proportion dying).

Because public health officials need quantitative statements of sickness, various morbidity measures have been developed. Incidence rates show the annual number of new cases of a given disease per 100,000 people per year; prevalence rates, the number of persons who have the disease per 100,000 population; and fatality rates, the percentage who die among those contracting the disease. Death rates are computed separately for each cause of death. Rates for one disease or a "family" of similar diseases are calculated on a base of 100,000 rather than the 1,000 that is customary for general death rates; the purpose of this difference in procedure is simply to avoid decimals.

The United States National Health Survey obtains data on chronic conditions from household interviews. Table 10, for example, estimates the prevalence of chronic nondisabling health impairments in the late 1950s. Such data, however, have obvious limitations. For one thing, since they are obtained from interviews in the home, they do not include nonmanifest or undiagnosed cases or conditions which respondents are unwilling to report. They also omit persons in sanitariums, hospitals for the chronically diseased, nursing homes, and homes for the aged. For these reasons, we must regard these figures as minimum frequencies which considerably understate the actual number of people suffering from chronic conditions. Aware of these deficiencies, Federal data collecting agencies are taking steps to improve completeness as well as accuracy of morbidity statistics.

TABLE 10. *Chronic Conditions, United States, 1957-1959**

CONDITIONS	ESTIMATED NATIONAL PREVALENCE (NUMBER OF CASES)
Arthritis and rheumatism	10,800,000
Asthma and hay fever	9,200,000
Bronchitis (chronic)	2,000,000
Deafness (total or partial)	5,800,000
Diabetes	1,500,000
Heart conditions	5,000,000
High blood pressure (without heart condition)	5,200,000
Hernia	2,500,000
Paralysis (major extremities or trunk)	900,000
Peptic ulcer	2,400,000
Sinusitis (chronic)	9,900,000
Visual impairment (total or partial)	3,000,000

* National Office of Vital Statistics, *Health and Vital Statistics for the United States,* Public Health Service, Washington, 1960, p. 31.

One novel effort to make more extensive application of statistics which is lately becoming widespread is a probablity approach to sickness. The likelihood of acquiring or surviving a certain illness under given conditions is sometimes calculated and even conveyed to the patient in percentage terms. Some physicians are seeking ways to use high-speed computing machines to spot individual vulnerability to diseases. By feeding into the machine all relevant information about the person, it is hoped to compute his susceptibility to any given ailment. Should this automatization of the arts of diagnosis and prognosis take place, it will parallel the replacement of bookies by pari-mutuel machines in horse racing—an analogy suggested by the opening sentences of a Damon Runyon short story, "Lonely Heart":

It seems that one spring day, a character by the name of Nicely-Nicely Jones arrives in a ward in a hospital in the City of Newark, N. J., with such a severe case of pneumonia that the attending physician, who is a horse player at heart, and very absentminded, writes 100, 40, and 10 on the chart over Nicely-Nicely's bed. It comes out afterward that what the physician means is that it is a 100-to-1 in his line that Nicely-Nicely does not recover at all, 40-to-1 that he will not last a week, and 10-to-1 that if he does get well he will never be the same again.

DISABILITY

Work disability interferes with income, careers, and morale. From July 1961 through June 1962, the average American civilian resident experienced sixteen days on which his customary activities were substantially reduced because of illness or injury; on six of these days he was confined to bed. The average employed adult lost six days of work, and the average student aged 6 through 16 missed six days of school. Persons aged 65 and over experienced two to four times as many days of restricted activity or confinement to bed as did either children or adults under age 45. Seasonal variations are greater than is the case for mortality, the winter quarter being worst, and spring and summer the best. Sex differentials are consistently one-sided: both restricted activity and bed disability rates are appreciably higher among women. This differential is inconsistent with the differential in mortality rates (women get sick; men die) and with the belief of M. F. Ashley Montagu and others that women are biologically stronger than men—unless one explains these higher rates through social variables. Childbirth is not responsible for the poor showing of the female, as these differences prevail at all ages beyond the fifth year. In this regard, it may be that women and girls stay home or rest more willingly than men and boys; indeed, it is even possible that women live longer than men because they do take better care of themselves when sick—something that male careerism discourages. For both sexes, however, the average number of restricted activity and bed disability days declines with increasing family income; work loss days show the same inverse relation to family income among men, but there is no consistent pattern among women. Occupational groups reporting the highest of these short-term disability rates are famers, private household workers, and retired persons. Rural-farm residents experience higher rates of restricted activity and loss of work than do rural-nonfarm and urban residents. Most of these differentials have prevailed for some years. The rates for such temporary disability are now declining rapidly.[2]

Disability may be total or partial, permanent or temporary. Temporarily disabled people actually represent a greater loss to national productivity than do the permanently disabled because of the larger numbers of workers affected. Table 11 documents injuries on the job in the most dangerous American industries. Criteria for inclusion in the table are a high disability rate or a high ratio of deaths to injuries.

Mental disorders are also influenced by social variables. The anthropologist Malinowski, reporting on the lower incidence and prevalence of neurasthenia and psychoses among the Trobrianders, and observing this and other primitive societies (some having very high rates of mental illness), concluded that culture determines the quantity and types of neu-

---

[2] U. S. National Center for Health Statistics, *Vital and Health Statistics*, Series X, No. 1, "Acute Conditions," 1963; Series X, No. 4, "Disability Days," 1963; and U. S. National Health Survey, *Selected Survey Topics*, "Report B-5," Public Health Service, Washington, 1958.

TABLE 11. *Work Injury and Death in Selected Industries, United States, 1957*[*]

INDUSTRY	DISABLING INJURIES PER 1,000,000 EMPLOYEE HOURS WORKED	DEATHS PER 1,000 DISABLING INJURIES
Logging	62.3	9
Sanitation departments, State and local	53.6	1
Coal mines	44.2	27
Sawmills and planing mills	40.4	4
Roofing and sheet metal work	39.8	0[a]
Highway and street construction	34.8	11
Metal mines	33.0	14[b]
General building contractors	32.4	4
Structural clay products	32.2	2
Warehousing and storage	31.4	2
Structural steel erection and ornamental iron work	31.0	25
Nonmetal mines	26.9	11
Heavy construction, except highway and street	26.6	19
Ship building and repairing	17.3	9
Crude petroleum and natural gas extraction	16.4	11[b]
Electric light and power	5.5	29
Petroleum refining	5.3	13[b]
Blast furnaces and steel mills	4.0	21
Industrial organic chemicals	3.5	17

[a] Less than 1 per 1,000.
[b] Includes permanent total impairments.

[*] Metropolitan Life Insurance Company, *Statistical Bulletin*, Vol. XL, May 1959, p. 10; adapted from U. S. Bureau of Labor Statistics, "Injury Rates by Industry, 1957."

roses and psychoses.[3] In the United States, Robert Faris and H. W. Dunham, studying the ecological etiology of mental disease, found differences in the type and incidence of mental disorders in Chicago by zone of residence.[4] E. Gartly Jaco noted a statistically significant relationship between rates of schizophrenia and the degree of social isolation in the neighborhood, using as data 688 mental patients during 1940-1955 in Austin, Texas.[5] In New Haven, A. B. Hollingshead and F. C. Redlich analyzed

---

[3] Bronislaw Malinowski, *Sex and Repression in Savage Society*, Routledge and Kegan Paul Ltd., London, 1927, pp. 85-90.
[4] Robert E. L. Faris and H. Warren Dunham, *Mental Disorders in Urban Areas*, University of Chicago Press, Chicago, 1939.
[5] E. Gartly Jaco, "The Social Isolation Hypothesis and Schizophrenia," *American Sociological Review*, Vol. XIX, No. 5, October 1954, pp. 567-576.

differential rates of various types of mental illness according to social class, finding significant differentials in the type and amount of treatment given by physicians to patients occupying different positions in the class structure. The New Haven study also uncovered indications of different expectancy and toleration of mental deviance among socioeconomic strata.[6]

SEASONAL INCIDENCE

Communicable diseases exhibit seasonal patterns. In the United States, acute poliomyelitis, typhoid fever, encephalitis, and dysentery show marked peaks in August and September and lows in January through April. Most diseases have less radical seasonal swings. Only one major disease, diphtheria, has an autumn peak. Tularemia, meningococcal infections, and hepatitis have greatest incidences in winter months. Conditions showing spring peaks are primarily childhood afflictions, measles having the greatest seasonal variation of any ailment, reaching a maximum in April and May and declining almost to zero in September.

The largest number of school-loss days occurs in the first few months of the academic year, when children are thrown together after the summer vacation. Loss of work is higher in fall and winter than in spring and summer, and confinement to bed is highest in the autumn. Days of restricted activity exhibit small seasonal variation.

HOSPITALIZATION AND MEDICAL CARE

The use of hospitals by Americans has increased by about 20 per cent during the last quarter century. Yet the almost 80 per cent rise in admission rates is partially counterbalanced by a one-third decrease in average length of stay.[7] Early ambulation is common today, and many of the admissions involve merely overnight stays for examination.

High quality medical service not only requires availability of a large number of trained physicians and nurses but also hospitals with adequate laboratory facilities. International comparisons of the physician-population ratio are difficult because of variations in the minimum standards for qualifications as a doctor, but it is clear that the Western countries have an advantage on this score. The following countries were reported as having at least one physician per thousand inhabitants in 1950-1955: Israel, Austria, the U.S.S.R., the United States, Switzerland, New

---

[6] August B. Hollingshead and Frederick C. Redlich, "Social Stratification and Psychiatric Disorders," *American Sociological Review*, Vol. XVII, No. 2, April 1953, pp. 163-169; and *Social Class and Mental Illness*, John Wiley and Sons, New York, 1958.
[7] Health Information Foundation, "Trends in Use of General Hospitals," *Progress in Health Services*, Vol. VIII, No. 8, October 1959, pp. 1-6.

Zealand, Hungary, Canada, Iceland, Denmark, Spain, Norway, Italy, Greece, Germany, Czechoslovakia, and Belgium. In contrast, many Asian and African nations have fewer than one physician per 20,000 residents.[8] Availability of hospital beds is also higher in Western, industrialized nations. In 1946, for example, China had one hospital bed for each 23,000 inhabitants, compared with one for every 100 persons in the United States. Countries reporting fewer than 100 inhabitants per hospital bed in 1950-1955 were: New Zealand, Australia, Canada, the United Kingdom, Switzerland, Sweden, Ireland, Germany, France, Denmark, and Surinam.[9] The most favorable ratio for physicians is found in Israel (one medical doctor for each 400 persons), and for hospital beds, France (a bed for each 65 persons). Of course, these statistics take no account of the physicians' competence or of the hospitals' equipment, but generally the qualitative and quantitative data correlate well with each other—and with low mortality rates.

National figures, however, often mask considerable internal differentials. Even in as modern a country as the United States, impressive differences exist in the provision of local medical facilities: North-South, urban-rural, rich-poor, and white-Negro contrasts are almost as striking as those between well-supplied Scandinavia and the least favored parts of the world. "In spite of long experience with well-developed local health services in many states," writes one critic, "there are large areas of our country and about 30,000,000 of our fellow citizens lacking even the simplest and most modest local health service."[10]

More than one-half of the hospital beds in the United States are occupied by persons having mental or emotional disorders. Of the half million residents of mental hospitals or psychiatric wards, the overwhelming majority are committed from urban areas, where the demands of everyday living are complicated and institutional facilities relatively more available. The proportions of the total population that are certified are also higher for women, middle-aged and elderly persons, low income persons, and individuals with low IQ scores. Once admitted, their length of confinement is far longer than that of persons undergoing operations.

Differentials in Mortality

Mortality differs according to many background variables: age, sex, race, marital status, urbanization, socioeconomic status, and occupation.

---

[8] United Nations. *Statistical Yearbook.* New York, 1949-50, pp. 478-485; and United Nations, *Report on the World Social Situation,* New York, 1957, pp. 45-48.

[9] United Nations, *Report on the World Social Situation, op. cit.,* pp. 43-45.

[10] Haven Emerson, "Essential Local Public Health Services," *Annals of the American Academy of Political and Social Science,* Vol. CCLXXIII, January 1951, p. 23.

Nor is this list conclusive. Intelligence, for example, may be a relevant independent variable—though we cannot be sure without experimental controls of concomitant and intervening variables. The gifted children (with IQ scores of 135 or more) of Lewis M. Terman's study, who are now in their fifties, have experienced lower mortality and morbidity during the last few decades than has the general population.[11]

This subject is harder to analyze than one might at first suppose. The source of the trouble is the difficulty of sufficiently isolating the intertwined variables to be sure of causal connections. Urban-rural mortality differentials, for example, are influenced by the different proportions of Negroes, foreign born, women, aged, and other groups in urban as opposed to rural areas. Obviously, unless we set up elaborate cross-tabulations involving three or more independent variables acting on the dependent variable, mortality, our conclusions are very apt to be superficial. Fertility and migration differentials present similar problems.

AGE, SEX, AND RACE

The death rate varies of course with age. Mortality declines after conception to a minimum at age 10, after which it rises gradually with each subsequent year. There is only one exception to this rule: immediately after birth, mortality takes an upward jump, as the new-born child is exposed to an exceedingly abrupt transition into a radically new environment and one marked, perhaps not incidentally, by the vicissitudes of child-rearing fads and fashions.

Sex differences in mortality are particularly noteworthy. In the United States women have lower death rates than men at all ages—even in childhood and, as far as we can tell from incomplete evidence, before birth. This differential between the sexes has been attributed to occupational hazards affecting males, military deaths in wars, greater tension among males, and inherent biological superiority of women. The first two explanations are certainly valid, but the latter two are in dispute. Indeed, in some countries female mortality is higher, the mortality differential responding directly to differences in status and hence in health and dietary care. Obviously what is needed to answer this controversial question is a thorough study of large groups in which males and females live under identical health conditions. The closest approach to this kind of investigation is Madigan's research on selected religious orders in the United States from 1900 to 1954, in which it was found that, except for the beginning of the century when the younger women (aged 15-34) had an abnormally high death rate from tuberculosis, the female popula-

---

[11] Lewis M. Terman and Melita H. Oden, *The Gifted Group at Mid-Life*, Stanford University Press, Palo Alto, 1959, p. 29.

tion of these establishments always had a more favorable mortality record and a longer expectation of life than did males of the same age.[12] Yet even if one does accept a consistent biologically induced difference, further questions remain, such as whether female superiority stems from a greater resistance to infection, or from a lower susceptibility to degenerative diseases, or from some other advantage.

In answering this question, male supremacists have a tough row to hoe. From the days of Graunt, the literature of vital statistics in western nations substantiates the higher mortality of men as compared with women. Furthermore, there is incomplete but suggestive evidence of higher male mortality among nonhuman species. Finally, "excess mortality for the male has been found in foetal life, as well as at virtually every age during the whole life span."[13]

Yet while women may be thought to be biologically superior to men, this conclusion is not properly deduced from factually supportable premises. One bit of contrary evidence is the higher mortality rates among females in many underdeveloped areas and in some nonliterate societies. It would appear safer to conclude that mortality differentials by sex are explainable by comparable differentials in status and role resulting in more favorable health treatment of one sex than the other. Possibly both social and biological forces are at work. Analysis of health and occupational records of men and women in the United States indicates that women are more likely than men to acknowledge and treat minor aches, colds, stomach disturbances, headaches, muscular pains, cuts, and bruises—perhaps, as suggested above, because presence on the job is more crucial to men than to women. Thus some physicians have offered the tendency for men to "press on regardless" as a possible explanation of the greater longevity among women. At any rate, the definitive word has certainly not been expressed on this medico-sociological subject.

Comparison of death rates by race is difficult. Not only do conclusions tend to be negative and ambiguous, but very little evidence exists supporting attribution of observed racial mortality differentials to inherent racial differences. And since race is not independent of economic, social, and medical circumstances, observed differences in death rates among races may be due primarily or possibly entirely to socioeconomic differences.[14] Thus while we may safely say that mortality among Negroes

---

[12] Francis C. Madigan, "Are Sex Mortality Differentials Biologically Caused?" *The Milbank Memorial Fund Quarterly*, Vol. XXXV, No. 2, April 1957, pp. 202-223.
[13] Louis I. Dublin, Alfred J. Lotka, and Mortimer Spiegelman, *Length of Life*, The Ronald Press Co., New York, 1949, p. 129.
[14] Forrest E. Linder and Robert D. Grove, *Vital Statistics Rates in the United States: 1900-1940*, Government Printing Office, Washington, 1947, p. 12.

is higher than that among whites in the United States, we should not conclude that the cause of this discrepancy is necessarily biological.

MARITAL STATUS

Married people have lower mortality than those who have never married. This variation arises "partly from the natural selection of healthy lives for marriage, and partly from differences in environment, both biological and social, in which the married and unmarried live."[15] People who are poor insurance risks are less likely to marry than healthy specimens, and married persons usually live more regular lives than single ones. Married, single, widowed, and divorced persons have increasingly higher death rates, in that order.

Rates from all of the leading causes of death are higher among single men than among married men. Married women have lower mortality than have single women for only about half of the major causes of death. Among both men and women, widowed and divorced persons show consistently higher death rates than either single or married ones.[16]

PLACE OF RESIDENCE

Size of community also has implications for mortality rates. Thus in the United States, heart disease, tuberculosis, and cancer exhibit higher rates in urban areas, while pneumonia, influenza, typhoid, and malaria show higher rural rates. Some of this difference is a matter of diagnostic practice and some ascribable to differentials in the age-sex composition of the population, but part of the difference may be the result of contrasts in the life styles of urban and rural people.

Urban-dominant diseases tend to be those that medical science cannot control effectively, whereas the afflictions most common in rural areas are conquerable by modern medicine. The rural prominence of pneumonia, influenza, typhoid, and malaria is largely a function of the lower standard of living plus a lack of preventive medicine and up-to-date diagnostic and curative techniques.

Deaths and illnesses are frequently recorded according to place of occurrence instead of place of residence. (This practice also affects fertility statistics.) Consider the case of the hospital situated in city A with its maternity ward in city B; as one might expect, the *de facto* fertility of city B is artificially high, and the morbidity and mortality of city A correspondingly inflated. To circumvent this difficulty, statisticians reallocate the data for nonresidents, thus securing a *de jure* classification (mortality and fertility data assigned to place of residence of the decedent or mother) rather than a *de facto* classification (data assigned

---

[15] Dublin, Lotka, and Spiegelman, *Length of Life, op. cit.*, p. 140.
[16] *Ibid.*, pp. 137-138.

to geographic unit in which the death or birth occurs). Since hospitals ordinarily are located in urban places, and rural people thus go to the city to get well or to die, comparison of urban and rural morbidity and mortality rates should be made only with a full knowledge of the basis on which the statistics have been collected.

Regional differences suggest the importance of social and cultural factors in influencing mortality differentials. Detailed 1960 figures show that New England had the lowest crude death rates from birth through age 34, whereas the South Central states (from Kentucky through Texas) had the highest. For ages of 35 or more, mortality was lowest in the vicinity of the Dakotas, Iowa, and Kansas, while the highest rates were reported in the Great Lakes area and along the Atlantic Seaboard, with the least favorable results appearing for ages 35-64 along the south Atlantic, for ages 65-84 around New York, and for ages exceeding 85 in Ohio and Wisconsin.

SOCIAL STATUS AND OCCUPATION

Socioeconomic class and its major component, occupation, also constitute relevant variables in explaining mortality phenomena. The renowned physician Sir William Osler described tuberculosis as "a social disease with medical aspects." In England a broad trend toward higher mortality as one moves down the social scale is evident among both men and women. Thus among English men, tuberculosis, influenza, pneumonia, bronchitis, lung cancer, chronic endocarditis, ulcers, and vehicular accidents conform to the general inverse relationship between mortality and social class; whereas coronary artery disease, cerebral hemorrhage, cirrhosis of the liver, and gallbladder disorders show a less usual direct relation.[17]

Mortality differences among social classes are associated primarily with differences in their standards of living. This relation is consistent with the fact that it was a general rise in the living standard that brought about the decreased mortality of the demographic revolution. In Liverpool in 1842, the average age of gentry at death was 35 years, far older than the 15-year average for laborers, which led one contemporary to comment that "The difference in the ages of these several classes presents to my mind a tolerably exact scale of the differences in their abodes."[18] Inadequate housing and slum conditions are still associated with ill health.

---

[17] Great Britain Registrar General, *Decennial Supplement, England and Wales,* 1951, Part II, Vol. I, "Occupational Mortality," London, 1958; and Metropolitan Life Insurance Co., "Mortality and Social Class," *Statistical Bulletin,* Vol. XL, October 1959, p. 10.
[18] Edwin Chadwick, *Report of an Inquiry into the Sanitary Condition of the Labouring Population of Great Britain,* London, 1842, p. 168.

The relative rigidity of the British social structure makes occupation a firmer index of social class than it is in the semi-open class system of the United States. Moreover, the persistence of certain features of the traditional stratification system maintains class-induced mortality differences unchanged over long periods of time; thus mortality ratios of 1920 correlate well by class with those of 1950. In 1954 one demographer noted: "The infant mortality rate . . . is a sensitive index of social conditions. . . . In spite of the tremendous reduction of infant mortality rates during the past thirty years there has been absolutely no narrowing of the difference between the various social classes, that is, no tendency for the gradient to become less steep."[19]

TABLE 12. *Standardized Mortality Ratios by Occupation, United States Adult Working Males, 1930 and 1950**

		1950	
OCCUPATIONAL CLASS	1930	WHITE	TOTAL
All Occupational Classes	100	100	100
Professional occupations	81	82	83
Managerial occupations	85	84	85
Skilled workers	93	96	97
Semiskilled workers	113	97	100
Unskilled workers	151	120	152
Agricultural workers	71	83	96

* Metropolitan Life Insurance Co., *Statistical Bulletin*, Vol. XLI, June 1960, p. 3; basic data taken from articles by Jessamine S. Whitney in 1934 and Lillian Guralnick in 1959.

Income is also a factor in mortality differentials. In both England and the United States, mortality is noticeably lowest for high-income groups, highest for low-income groups, and intermediate for middle-income groups. Disability figures experience even greater jumps between income classes than do death rates. High-income persons of course can afford to spend more money on medical care and they are probably better informed about medical matters.

In broad outline the United States occupational hierarchy resembles the socioeconomic hierarchy (see Table 12). Highest mortality is recorded for both white and nonwhite laborers, while the lowest rates occur among farmers for whites and among managers and proprietors for nonwhites. Occupational differentials are greater among nonwhites: the highest nonwhite ratios are more than double their lowest ratios, while among whites the highest ratios are only about one and one-half times the

[19] W. P. D. Logan, "Social Class Variations in Mortality," *Public Health Reports*, Vol. LXIX, No. 12, December 1954, pp. 1217-1223.

size of their lowest ratios. Racial differences are greatest among unskilled workers. Occupational differences tend to decline with age, a marked convergence of ratios taking place after age 55.[20] Exceptionally favorable standardized mortality ratios (taking the national average as 100) are experienced by college presidents, professors, and instructors, 52; private household workers, 54; social, welfare, and recreation workers, 55; teachers, 61; mechanical engineers, 61; and other professional and kindred workers. Unfavorable ratios apply to transportation laborers, 278; transportation equipment manufacturing laborers, 277; furniture, saw mill, and wood product laborers, 208; chemical manufacturing laborers, 192; food produces manufacturing laborers, 189; and mine operatives and laborers, 185.[21]

Occupational differentials operate in several ways. It is probable that superior physical types, through competition for jobs, attain higher status occupations, leaving the poorer specimens in the less desirable jobs; similarly, emotionally unstable types tend to be culled from high status occupations. And once an occupation is entered, two additional factors come into play. First, certain jobs are hazardous, especially where there is considerable climbing, work with poisons or explosives, exposure to temperature extremes, dangerous machinery, location under the ground or water, or, generally, conditions that stimulate extreme emotional tension. Second, occupation largely determines income, and income determines level of living and health care.

AN ASIDE ON OVERWEIGHT

A currently fashionable concern is that of excess poundage. Data collected and analyzed by the Metropolitan Life Insurance Company covering 4,900,000 policy-holders in the years 1935-1954 show that excess weight definitely is associated with higher mortality. Among men aged 15-69, those who are 10 per cent over the average weight for their age and height show an excess mortality of 13 per cent, for men 20 per cent overweight the excess mortality is 25 per cent, and for men 30 per cent overweight it is 42 per cent.[22] Among women of the same ages, the comparable figures are: 10 per cent overweight, 9 per cent excess mortality; 20 per cent overweight, 21 per cent excess mortality; and 30 per cent overweight, 30 per cent excess mortality.[23] Overweight persons

---

[20] Lillian Guralnick, "Mortality by Occupation and Industry Among Men 20 to 64 Years of Age: United States, 1950," *Vital Statistics—Special Reports*, Vol. LIII, No. 2, September 1962, pp. 59-70.

[21] *Ibid.*, pp. 73-76 and 82-84.

[22] Metropolitan Life Insurance Co., "Mortality Among Overweight Men," *Statistical Bulletin*, Vol. XLI, February 1960, p. 8.

[23] Metropolitan Life Insurance Co., "Mortality Among Overweight Women," *Statistical Bulletin*, Vol. XLI, March 1960, p. 2.

need not despair however; reduction of weight has a favorable effect on mortality and longevity. The 1959 Build and Blood Pressure Study conducted by the Society for Actuaries demonstrated that overweight men who reduce have practically the same mortality as standard risks.[24] Overweight, while not a social factor as are marital status and class, for example, clearly is frequently associated with psychological and thus social conditions.

Reproductive Wastage

It seems fitting to conclude the discussion of mortality with brief consideration of a set of differentials that lead into matters discussed in the following three chapters: the casualties of human reproduction, including infant deaths, maternal deaths, abortions, and stillbirths.

As has been pointed out, the risk of dying is greatest at either end of life. The death rate in the United States during the first year of life is about the same as in the seventieth year; the death rate in the first month is approximately that at age 95; the death rate during the first day is so high that we cannot determine the equivalent period of aged mortality.

PERINATAL MORTALITY

The phrase "reproductive wastage" refers to the loss of life from the time of fertilization of the ovum until the fifth year of age. Reproductive wastage "exceeds by far the wastage in any other period of equal length in the life span" and "causes the loss of at least one-third of each new generation."[25] The more restricted concept, "perinatal mortality," may be defined as the total of fetal deaths of twenty or more weeks of gestation plus deaths within the first week of infancy. Both of these terms group together pregnancy and the period immediately following birth, the rationale being that many of the same factors are associated with the death of young babies as with fetuses.

Perinatal mortality in the United States declined from 51 per 1,000 live births in 1940 to 33 in 1959—a decrease of more than a third. During the same period, the late fetal death rate fell from 28 to 16 and the early neonatal rate from 23 to 17. Race and sex differentials favoring white and female infants have been maintained. The 1940-1941 and 1958-1959 rates are as follows: white males, 50 and 33; white females, 40 and 27;

[24] Metropolitan Life Insurance Co., "Overweights Benefit from Weight Reduction," *Statistical Bulletin*, Vol. XLI, April 1960, pp. 1-3.
[25] United Nations, *Foetal, Infant, and Early Childhood Mortality*, Vol. II: "Biological, Social, and Economic Factors," New York, 1954, p. 40.

nonwhite males, 90 and 56; and nonwhite females, 68 and 46; all four groups experienced an approximately one-third reduction in perinatal rates during this recent period.

Since this is a budding field of statistical investigation, data are not yet accurate enough to warrant definitive statements on the reason why death occurred. Cause of death is often undetermined, and most countries (and states in the United States) have unsatisfactory records. The vocabulary used to state cause of death (prematurity, birth trauma) is itself a confession of ignorance.

Perinatal mortality appears to be particularly prevalent among male babies, premature babies, nonwhite infants, children of low socioeconomic class parents, first-born children, children with high birth orders, children of mothers under 20 and over 40, and offspring of obese mothers, unhealthy mothers, and mothers receiving inadequate prenatal care.

FETAL MORTALITY

At least 5 million pregnancies are required to produce the four million births that occur annually in the United States. Pregnancy wastage (losses between conception and birth) is, however, a little-known area of research. Not only is it extremely difficult to obtain reliable data for the early months of pregnancy, especially because women may never have known, not remember, or be unwilling to disclose information, but hospital records themselves are incomplete.

Our best guess is that fetal mortality is quite high immediately after conception, with subsequent decreases. And it is suspected that pregnancy wastage is a much higher cause of mortality for male infants than for females. Uteral mortality is apparently lower than primitive neonatal mortality, but higher than post-partum mortality when modern medical facilities are available.

Stillbirths are differentiated from abortions (popularly called miscarriages) by the criterion that whereas the former are viable or capable of life, the latter are not. When the fetus squeezed out of the uterus is too unfinished to survive, it is called a spontaneous or induced abortion. There is disagreement concerning the definition of "viable": some countries use 28 weeks as the cutting point while in the United States the figure is 20 weeks; a few authorities prefer to use the weight of the fetus (5½ pounds, for example). However, there is general agreement that if the fetus ever shows life, no matter how briefly, it should be considered a live birth. All of these definitions are somewhat academic, as attending physicians sometimes insist on using their own criteria regardless of the established legal code. ("Stillbirth" contrasts with the archaic term "quickbirth." Those words derive from *quick*, meaning alive, and its antonym *still*, meaning motionless or dead. Thus a stillbirth is the expulsion of a motionless and therefore dead child—in other words, a dead-birth. The New Testament speaks of "the quick and the dead," and Chaucer used the description, "Not fully quyke, ne fully dead they were.")

Stillbirth ratios have declined in the United States in recent decades, but have not yet reached the low level of the Scandinavian countries. Variations in stillbirth ratios between countries are smaller than variations in infant mortality. The probability of a stillbirth (excluding induced abortions to fetuses older than 20 weeks) is lowest for infants of mothers aged 20-24 and fathers aged 20-24, for three-year intervals between births, for single births, and for second children. The chances of having a stillbirth are highest for mothers close to puberty or menopause, for women giving multiple births, for women who have already had a large number of children, and for women who have a previous record of stillbirths or miscarriages. Prenatal mortality appears to be higher for male infants than for females. The primary sex ratio—that is, the sex ratio at conception—is variously estimated at from 130 to 400 males for every 100 females; by the moment of birth, the sex ratio is reduced to about 105.

NEONATAL MORTALITY

Neonatal mortality (deaths of children of less than one month of age) varies remarkably little from country to country, and has shown little susceptibility to reduction under pressure from modern medical science. Apparently, the closer to birth, the less environmental influence applies; mortality in the first day of life has been almost stationary for a long time.

Causes of neonatal mortality are largely intrauterine rather than extrauterine in character. This is to say that, except for deaths caused by accidents during pregnancy and childbirth, almost all deaths of fetuses and neonates are brought about by genetic and developmental factors. However, some evidence is accumulating that environmental factors, such as nutrition and prenatal care, do influence fetal and neonatal mortality; with more knowledge about the precise form of these influences, deaths encouraged by prematurity and congenital malformations should diminish. Major reported causes of mortality during the first week of infancy, in rank order for the United States in 1961, were: immaturity, postnatal asphyxia, congenital malformations, birth injuries, and influenza and pneumonia. The label "immaturity" often represents ignorance or laziness on the part of the person completing the death certificate. Death results from specific, definable ailments, of which immaturity is no more a cause than is senility. Both are predisposing conditions, not proximate causes.

A crucial factor in neonatal and infant mortality is age. More than two-thirds of the deaths during the first year occur in the first month of life; more than one-third, in the first day.[26]

INFANT MORTALITY

Infant mortality (deaths of children of less than one year of age) has lessened considerably in the United States during the twentieth century. With widespread understanding of biological processes and medical causes of ailments among children from the second through the twelfth months of life, the control of illnesses and deaths for post-neonates has greatly improved. Background factors playing an important role in infant mortality include socioeconomic status, age of mother, and sex of child. Specifically, infant mortality is lowest for high status parents, for mothers in their early 20's, and for female children. Negro and white rates are similar when social status is held constant. The highest infant mortality rates are in Alaska and Mississippi, the lowest in Utah and Nebraska. Seasonal variations are negligible.

International differences in infant mortality are shown in Table 13. Note the low rates in Australia, the United Kingdom, Switzerland, Finland, the United States, and Canada; the lowest rates of all are in Sweden and the Netherlands. Infant mortality in many underdeveloped and developing countries is distressingly high. Still more striking is the racial contrast in the Union of South Africa—while rates for Europeans resemble those for Western Europe, Negro infant deaths amount to 12 per cent of the total live births, with the rate for Asiatic residents being intermediate between these two extremes. These variations reflect differences in the standard of living and have no discernible biological cause.

The death rate among children between the ages of one and four is higher in underdeveloped than in industrial countries. In high potential and transitional growth countries, child mortality still shows a summer peak, a seasonal variation which has vanished in most incipient decline countries. Alimentary difficulties appearing several months after birth and continuing into the second year, generally manifested in the summer, contribute to the higher death rates in the less advanced nations. Excess mortality results from inadequate hygienic care, especially in the preparation of food. Under these conditions, the children of the poor and the unlettered pay a heavy tribute through alimentary infections. Other infections add their effects from the second year onward.

---

[26] National Vital Statistics Division, "Infant Mortality," *Vital Statistics—Special Reports*, Vol. LIV, No. 7, December 1, 1961, p. 193.

TABLE 13. *Infant Mortality in Selected Countries, 1959**

CONTINENT AND COUNTRY	INFANT DEATHS PER 1,000 LIVE BIRTHS	CONTINENT AND COUNTRY	INFANT DEATHS PER 1,000 LIVE BIRTHS
NORTH AMERICA		EUROPE (continued)	
Canada	28	Romania	77
Costa Rica	81	Spain	47
Dominican Republic	108	Sweden	17
El Salvador	78	Switzerland	22
Guatemala	90	United Kingdom	23
Honduras	54	England and Wales	22
Jamaica	68	Northern Ireland	28
Mexico	76	Scotland	28
Nicaragua	64	U.S.S.R.	41
Panama	60	Yugoslavia	91
Puerto Rico	48		
Trinidad and Tobago	62	ASIA	
United States	26	Burma, Towns	134
		China, Taiwan	33
SOUTH AMERICA		Cyprus	30
Chile	120	Hong Kong	48
Colombia	97	Indonesia, Registration area	84
Peru	85	Israel	30
Venezuela	59	Japan	34
		Jordan	63
EUROPE		Malaya, Fed. of	66
Albania	76	Ryukyu Islands	11
Austria	40	Sarawak	58
Belgium	30	Singapore	36
Bulgaria	56	Viet-Nam, Rep. of	34
Czechoslovakia	26		
Finland	24	AFRICA	
France	30	Algeria, Europeans	39
Germany		Mauritius	62
Democratic Rep.	50	Union of South Africa	
Federal Rep.	34	Asiatic	65
East Berlin	40	Colored	121
West Berlin	35	European	28
Greece	41		
Hungary	52	OCEANIA	
Ireland	32	Australia	22
Italy	45	New Zealand	24
Netherlands	17		
Poland	72		
Portugal	89		

* *Population Index*, Vol. XXVII, No. 3, July 1961, pp. 282-284 and 290-291.

MATERNAL MORTALITY

In the United States, maternal mortality has experienced dramatic improvement in the last four decades, dropping from 80 maternal deaths per 10,000 live births in 1920 to 67 in 1930, 38 in 1940, 8 in 1950, and 4 in 1961. For 1959, white women experienced a rate of less than 3 in contrast to 10 for nonwhite women. Yet even at that the United States still lags behind the excellent records set in certain other countries, particularly in Scandinavia. In underdeveloped areas, maternal mortality rates are often extremely high.

Puerperal mortality remains the second leading cause of death among American women between 20 and 35 years of age, despite sharp reductions in the late nineteenth century and again in the late 1930's and early 1940's. The most prominent causes of death during childbirth are infection, toxemia, hemorrhage, and trauma—causes that also apply to fetuses and neonates.

Both maternal and neonatal mortality were curbed through the shift from care at home by semiskilled midwives to lying-in hospitals staffed by trained physicians. Prudery once dictated that gynecologists be female —at a time when women doctors were as rare as other educated females. Thus, before 1739, in England, when Richard Manningham established the first lying-in ward, there was no regular provision for obstetrical cases in any London hospital.[27] When physicians finally accepted the contention of Oliver Wendell Holmes in Boston and of Ignaz Semmelweis in Vienna that aseptic precautions are essential to prevent transmission of puerperal fever from patient to patient by attending physicians, maternal mortality dropped sharply.[28]

Conclusion

Improvements in mortality and morbidity have not been shared equally by all groups. One of the prime objectives of social workers, many public health officials, and others is to spread the benefits of decreased mortality to the less privileged residents within each country. Another welfare aim is to bring mortality levels in all countries down to that now experienced in such nations as Denmark, the Netherlands, Sweden, Israel, and New Zealand.

In the more industrialized nations, the discrepancy between the death rates of the upper and lower social classes has diminished and the

---

[27] Richard H. Shryock, *The Development of Modern Medicine*, Alfred A. Knopf, New York, 1947, p. 92.

[28] Oliver Wendell Holmes, "The Contagiousness of Puerperal Fever," *New England Quarterly Journal for Medicine and Surgery*, Boston, 1843.

greatest mortality decline has taken place among infants and young children. Future mortality decreases in such countries will probably depend primarily on two developments: medical advances affecting old persons, and improved living levels and health care among the lower socioeconomic strata (where infant mortality remains relatively high).

Although the magnificent accomplishment of man in keeping himself alive for seven decades, whereas formerly he survived for three, has induced many emotional and practical blessings, it has also unloosed the specter of overpopulation. And with the average person living twice as long as his ancestors, population pressure upon available land and other natural resources sometimes introduces undesirable consequences.

Occasionally motivated by this fear of overpopulation is acquiescence in recurring catastrophes and wars, which was summed up early in this century by a Chinese official who objected to taking measures to avoid the yearly recurrence of bubonic plague "on the ground that there were too many Chinese anyway, and that, by thinning them out and making room for the rest, the plague was a blessing in disguise."[29] A similar feeling was voiced by a South Indian farmer who was quoted as saying, "In the old days wars, pestilence, famine kept the population within manageable limits. You have stopped the working of Nature's laws, and saved myriads of people. What are you going to do with them?"[30]

Thus changes in the death rate have led to social consequences inciting population policies and other national actions discussed in Part Three. But mortality is just one of three major demographic variables affecting human numbers and the conditions of life. The following three chapters analyze the second such variable, fertility.

---

[29] Edward Alsworth Ross, The Changing Chinese, Century Co., New York, 1911, p. 90.
[30] John Chartres Molony, "Population Problems," Contemporary Review, Vol. CLXXIII, No. 889, May 1948, p. 287.

8 ✂ *Fecundity and Social Norms*

Everyone is born and everyone dies, but between these two biological processes there are vast demographic differences. Because only women give birth, analyses of fertility frequently are restricted to the female sex. Because women cannot give birth more often than once in nine months, and then usually to only one child, there are strict upper limits to potential national fertility rates. Because of this physiological limitation, the birth rate is not subject to the large and abrupt increases that sometimes occur for mortality. Because conception originates from a sexual act, social conditioning toward heterosexual behavior becomes relevant. Because conception requires two people and because value systems usually demand a marriage bond, folkways and mores concerning courtship and marriage must be examined. And because the rearing of children normally follows parturition, the nature of the nuclear family is demographically significant.

Biological Limits

Fecundity is to be distinguished from fertility in that the former refers to biological potential, while the latter is a statement of actual performance. We measure fertility by counting the number of children who were born—in relation to some base population. Fecundity is the maximum fertility that could be attained; it is estimated by ascertaining the reproductive limits of human beings.

AGE AND SEX

The limiting conditions imposed on fecundity by age and sex are relatively easy to determine. Human females have a known period of years during which they ordinarily can conceive children; males too have age-determined limitations on their reproductive capacity.

In women, the onset of fecundity is customarily dated from the appearance of menstruation. A study of 142 nationality and ethnic groups around the world yielded an average age at menarche of fifteen, with a range of group means extending from thirteen to seventeen years.[1] Contrary to popular opinion, climate has no discernible effect on these averages; the layman's belief that people living in tropical zones mature earlier than residents of polar regions is not supported by available evidence. Diet is more likely to have an influence; undernourishment and especially mineral and vitamin deficiencies might retard the menarche. As in the case of many other biological phenomena, individual variations *within* racial and nationality groups are greater than variations between groups. This same study found that the cessation of fecundity in females occurred at a mean age of 46 years, with group averages extending as low as 44 and as high as 49.[2] Subtracting 15 from 46 obtains a mean reproductive lifetime of 31 years (presuming the woman lives to age 46).

Among United States females, Kinsey found that the age of first menstruation ranges from 9 to 25 years, with a median of 13.0 years.[3] Nine other studies cited by Kinsey reported mean ages varying from 12.9 through 13.9 years. (Kinsey's data were obtained by recall during interviews of adult women; the other studies were based on direct observation.) Kinsey also found a median age at onset of menopause of 46 years, with a range from 33 to 56.[4] This pair of medians yields an average reproductive lifetime of 33 years. Neither Pearl nor Kinsey can claim to have made a representative sampling of the world's women, but it is probable that the fecundity span is in the vicinity of 31 or 33 years.

To be sure, fecundity is not uniform throughout this span: it is nil immediately following giving birth, and there is some evidence indicating that it is at a low level in the early stages of puberty. The popular assumption that the appearance of menses signals the ability to conceive and reproduce is not supported by biological evidence. The onset of menstruation and the initial release of mature eggs from the ovaries do not necessarily begin at the same time. Sometimes one comes first, sometimes the other: pregnancy has been known to occur before menstruation, and

---

[1] Raymond Pearl, *The Natural History of Population*, Oxford University Press, New York, 1939, p. 49.

[2] *Ibid.*, p. 52.

[3] Alfred C. Kinsey, Wardell B. Pomeroy, Clyde E. Martin, and Paul H. Gebhard, *Sexual Behavior in the Human Female*, W. B. Saunders Co., Philadelphia, 1953, pp. 123 and 131.

[4] *Ibid.*, p. 736.

there is considerable evidence for the existence of a period of so-called adolescent sterility in which the release of fertile eggs is nil or almost nil for a few years following first menstruation. This period of the early teens might be described more accurately as adolescent subfecundity rather than sterility, for in most girls eggs probably are occasionally released during these years. However, from the sixteenth or eighteenth year of age onward, ovulation accompanies each menstrual cycle in the normal woman.[5] This period of adolescent subfecundity may be paralleled by a senescent subfecundity during the ten years preceding menopause. So, too, numerous other variables may alter a woman's capacity to conceive and bear children: certain diseases, nervous stress, general physical condition, hormonal and glandular secretions, and so forth.

Males normally reach puberty between 11 and 14 years of age. Kinsey computed a median age at first ejaculation of 13.8 years.[6] Unlike the female, however, sexual development in the male takes place in a very short period of time (though there are hints of male adolescent sterility). Belief in the earlier maturation of females is the result of confusion of social with biological spheres. Behavioral manifestations of maturity are more a matter of role expectations and performance than of biological readiness to procreate. Indeed, in age- and sex-based status groups, role play sometimes departs drastically from the biological facts of life.

Men also differ from women concerning the upper age limit of fecundity: there is nothing in man corresponding to the female menopause. Instead of the conclusive and sometimes emotional change of the climacteric, men experience a slow, steady decline in sexual prowess after the teens. Capacity for intercourse generally indicates capacity for reproduction. Thus the reproductive lifetime of a man is his age at death minus his age at first ejaculation, which, on the average, is far more than 30-35 years.

THE PRIMACY OF WOMEN

The limiting person in the fecundity of most families is the woman. Indeed it might almost be said that the man's fecundity level is irrelevant—provided, of course, he is not sterile. Man's ability to reproduce is so much greater than woman's as to be almost unlimited by comparison. A Pharaoh of Egypt supposedly begot more than 1,000 children, and the first Khan boasted that his household cavalry troop of 800 men were all his sons—not to mention his some 2,000 other children. Greater plausibility may be attached to the case of Michael Fenelon,

---

[5] *Ibid.*, p. 125.
[6] Alfred C. Kinsey, Wardell B. Pomeroy, and Clyde E. Martin, *Sexual Behavior in the Human Male*, W. B. Saunders Co., Philadelphia, 1948, p. 184.

who died in 1900 having had twenty-five children by his first wife, eighteen by his second, and twenty by his third.

Opinion has shifted regarding the relative importance of the father and the mother in the physiology of reproduction, but Western culture has traditionally assigned responsibility for sterility to the female. Aristotle felt that the man's semen was the source of life, and that the female merely nourished the fetus. Descartes accepted the theory that both sexes emitted semen in coitus and compared the chemistry of reproduction to that of brewing: "The semina of the two sexes mingle and act as yeast, each on the other."[7] The biseminal theory was attacked in 1651 by William Harvey, the discoverer of the circulation of the blood, who founded *ovism*, the doctrine that the female element is decisive in procreation. Carolus Linnaeus summed up Harvey's thesis in an epigram: "Vivum omne ex ovo" (everything living comes from the egg). The Dutch lens-grinder Anton van Leeuwenhoek put semen under his invention, the microscope, and became the first man to see the small swimming creatures which he called spermatozoa—a blow from which the ovists never recovered. Yet it was over two centuries before biologists were able to produce microscopic evidence of the fertilization process in human beings. Today the essentiality of both the male sperm and the female egg are well recognized.

THEORETICAL MAXIMUM FECUNDITY

Were social obstacles not present, birth rates could probably climb extremely high. If a woman had one child every 10 months for 31 years, she would have 37 live births. If she had a child every 15 months (a rate that is maintained for five years or so by many American women), she would produce a total of 25 children.

This does happen. When a daily newspaper in New Jersey sponsored a contest to discover the area resident who had borne the largest number of children (the winner to be awarded prizes by local merchants and a cup inscribed with some such legend as "Mrs. Poly-Prolific of America") the front-runner was a home town woman who had given birth to 27 offspring. But toward the close of the contest another city proclaimed the presence of a woman who had produced the winning total of 28 children, all single births, all still alive, and all by one husband. Yet even this impressive performance is overshadowed by the woman who married at 16 and died at 64, having spawned 39 children with no multiple births.

These heroic performances represent permissive social conditions and

---

[7] René Descartes, *Les traités de l'homme et de la formation du foetus*, Amsterdam, 1680 (published posthumously).

probably exceptional reproductive powers and physical vitality. A more reasonable group limit would be about half that figure, say 13 live births per woman. Given the age structure of the United States, 13 children per woman would mean a crude birth rate of slightly more than 100 per 1,000 population per year.

Yet not only does such a fertility level nowhere exist, but no society produces even half of that potential. The highest crude birth rate ever discovered for an entire country is about 65 per 1,000 per year. However, if the women of India lived through the entire childbearing period, the national crude birth rate would probably reach this theoretical fecundity level.

The age and sex composition of the society is of central importance. A nation composed largely of men would have a relatively low reproductive potential in comparison to a country consisting mostly of women. A country with a very high proportion of its female populace in the prepubertal or postmenopause ages would not be very likely to achieve a high crude birth rate. On the other hand, if an exceptionally large fraction of the females were in the childbearing ages, the production of children conceivably could exceed even the estimated United States potential of 100 births per 1,000 per year.

STERILITY AND SUBFECUNDITY

One limitation on this "unbounded" maximum is the inability of some people to bear children. Infertility apparently has troubled men and women throughout the entire history of the race. Some explanations of barrenness are supernatural: "And Sarah said unto Abraham: Behold now, the Lord hath restrained me from bearing" (Genesis 16:2). Only in the last few decades has the study of sterility been attacked scientifically—with triumphant results for some childless couples. It is only recently that Western culture has approached acceptance of legal equality of the sexes in this regard—a fact that offers little succor to the thousands of wives already divorced for infertility. Divorcing women but not men for failure to bear children is also consistent with our masculine line of descent and inheritance.

Two cures for sterility have aroused wild reactions. Indeed, in several countries artificial insemination, where the donor of semen is not the husband, has been defined by the courts as adultery. A letter to the *New Statesman* declared: "We are in the dawn of a new and secret aristocracy in which even the wisest child may sometimes glance dubiously at its own father." Most of us would agree, however, that this solution is morally preferable to extramarital intercourse, a cure for sterility which has been condoned off and on for many centuries. Pope Clement VII purportedly advised Catherine de Medici, the childless wife of the heir to the throne of François I: "A girl of spirit will never lack children." The aforementioned Sarah bid her husband to "go in unto my maid; it may be that I may obtain children by her." Abraham hearkened to the therapy, and the Egyptian maid Hagar conceived the child Ishmael. Abraham, incidentally, was said to be 86 years old when his son was born.

"Subfecundity," denoting the presence of a physical impairment which substantially reduces the capacity to reproduce, refers to both complete sterility and partial incapacity to bear offspring. About one-third of all the couples in the United States appear to be subfecund, and approximately 10 per cent are definitely sterile, that is, they seem totally incapable of having children. Nine per cent of all American couples have undergone an operation to make conception impossible. Operations to prevent conception are most prevalent in the lower socio-economic strata, particularly among poorly-educated wives and those in their late thirties. Some couples have no difficulty in conceiving, but instead of having a normal birth the wives have a miscarriage or still-birth. Almost all couples who say that they expect to be childless are biologically subfecund; voluntary childlessness is rare in the United States today. Subfecundity and the use or nonuse of some method of birth control are closely related. By the conclusion of the childbearing period, substantially all couples either are subfecund or have tried to regulate their fertility. The incidence of subfecundity increases fairly rapidly according to the age of the wife and the duration of her marriage. It also increases with the number of children she has borne. "There is no evidence of consistent differences in fecundity between most major social and economic strata of our population. Low-status groups . . . are more likely than high-status groups to be classified as subfecund, but it is unlikely that this is due to basic biological differences."[8]

No relationship has been found between fecundity and sexual attractiveness or muscular prowess. A prominent obstetrician and gynecologist has remarked: "Often it seems to me that Nature jokes with us by concealing infertility in a physically perfect body," whereas "an emaciated, used-up-looking woman who appears barely able to sustain herself in the everyday activities of life" produces a child a year. "One of the confusing things about the problem of human infertility is that ordinarily it bestows no physical stigmata upon its victims."[9]

---

[8] Ronald Freedman, Pascal K. Whelpton, and Arthur A. Campbell, *Family Planning, Sterility, and Population Growth*, McGraw-Hill Book Co., New York, 1959, pp. 18-19.
[9] Alan F. Guttmacher, *Babies by Choice or by Chance*, Avon Books, New York, 1961, pp. 181-183.

Sexual Behavior

Since human fertility falls far below fecundity, there must be some explanatory factors. The influences of disease and psychological tension are significant, but they need to be supplemented by other explanations.

One such explanation lies in the frequency and type of sexual intercourse—a highly variable practice. In this regard anthropologists report higher frequencies among most preliterate peoples than the one to three times a week found by Kinsey and others in studying modern urban societies. "In most of the societies in which information is available, every adult normally engages in heterosexual intercourse once daily or nightly during the periods when coitus is permitted."[10] Ford and Beach record societal averages varying from once a week to several times nightly; Chagga men are reported to have intercourse as often as ten times in one night. Accuracy of information on this score, however, is debatable. Age of the husband strongly influences frequency of marital coitus, declining gradually from adolescence to old age. "A belief that very frequent sexual intercourse is weakening or debilitating exists in a a few societies. . . . Despite such suggestions men frequently have intercourse two or three times each night."[11]

LEARNING AND CONDITIONING

Particularly important in both sexual activity and reproductive performance are learning and psychological conditioning. Because of his highly developed forebrain, man seems to be more conditionable than other mammals. Certainly variations in adult human sexual activity probably depend more on cultural training than upon biological variations in anatomy or physiology. The sexual proclivities inherited at birth appear to consist of little more than the essential anatomy and the physiologic capacity to respond to appropriate stimuli. Practically all human males and females are born with such potentialities. "No one has to learn to become tumescent, to build up the neuromuscular tensions which lead to the rhythmic pelvic thrusts of coitus, or to develop any of the other responses which lead to orgasm. But apart from these few inherent capacities, most other aspects of human sexual behavior appear to be the product of learning and conditioning."[12] In sex, as in other things, man is largely a product of his culture.

---

[10] Clellan S. Ford and Frank A. Beach, *Patterns of Sexual Behavior*, Harper and Brothers, New York, 1951, p. 78.

[11] *Ibid.*, p. 79.

[12] Kinsey, Pomeroy, Martin, and Gebhard, *Sexual Behavior in the Human Female*, *op. cit.*, p. 644.

The widely deplored difference in sexual responsiveness between males and females may be principally a cultural or learned phenomenon; certainly it is not accounted for by male-female differences in the anatomy and physiology of sexual orgasm. "We find no reason for believing that the physiologic nature of orgasm in the female or the physical or physiologic or psychologic satisfactions derived from orgasm by the average female are different from those of the average male. But in their capacity to respond to psychosexual stimuli, the average female and the average male do differ."[13] Sex-differentiated conditioning and socialization modify latent sexual and parental drives into varying manifest patterns. When spouses disagree, frequency of intercourse may be lowered, implicitly presaging decreased natality—though not necessarily childlessness. Witness Peter De Vries' acid characterization: "She bore him two children and a good deal of resentment."[14]

FADS AND FOIBLES

Misconceptions about influences on ability to have sexual intercourse and to conceive and produce offspring are vast in number and hard to eradicate. Many substances are assumed to excite sexual desire, to promote conception, or to facilitate carrying the fetus to completion. Indeed, so numerous are these panaceas that it is difficult to find a food, beverage, or herb that has never been suggested as having special sexual or procreative powers. The prevalence in most societies of amulets and charms attests to an almost universal desire for potency. Euripides had Medea tell King Aegeus that "I will make of thee a childless man no more. . . . Such magic herbs I know." Most of these substances fail, however, and some even lower fertility. Narcotics, for example, inhibit erotic responsiveness (addicts are usually sexually inactive) and alcohol is physiologically a depressant, raising the threshold of erectile and ejaculatory reflexes; very large doses often completely halt sexual response, though if the Scottish proverb that "Some men are born two drinks below par" is true, then a brace of cocktails may encourage fertility by promoting bisexual courage or by releasing inhibitions. Rabelais' *Gargantua and Pantagruel* and Shakespeare's *Macbeth* (Act II, Scene 3) both dogmatize on the helpfulness of moderate drinking and the hindrance of intemperance.

Homosexuality, masturbation, and prostitution are often credited with reducing the birth rate on the unverified assumption that channeling sexual desire into aberrant outlets reduces the amount of heterosexual

---

[13] *Ibid.*, p. 688.
[14] Peter De Vries, *Through the Fields of Clover*, Little, Brown and Co., Boston, 1961, p. 162.

coitus. But it seems doubtful that a woman who serves, say, the French or American army actually decreases the frequency of marital intercourse. However, venereal disease, which is at times related to prostitution, may promote sterility.

Throughout the ages, some men have embraced the idea that intellectual activity decreases fertility. To Walter Bagehot, the nineteenth-century English social scientist, the intellectual was an antinatalist martyr: "Men who have to live an intellectual life, or who can be induced to lead one, will be likely not to have so many children as they would otherwise have had. . . . There is only a certain quantum of power in each of our race; if it goes in one way it is spent, and cannot go in another."[15] Herbert Spencer too was inclined toward the assumption that each man is allotted so many ergs of energy; in his opinion, any effort spent on mental or physical activity was permanently lost and not available for reproductive activity. Some boxing managers try to restrict their charges to a monastic life when training for a bout. Even today many Americans and Europeans believe that each male produces a fixed, predetermined quantity of sperm in his lifetime, and that if this generative seed is expended profligately early in life, a man may become prematurely sterile. Alberto Moravia makes incompatibility between creative writing and intense sexual activity a fundamental part of one of his novels—to the extent of inspiring infidelity by the writer-protagonist's dissatisfied wife.[16] By contrast, the physicist-novelist C. P. Snow disputes the public stereotype of the scholarly professor as asexual; actually, says Snow, academic men are exceptionally highly sexed.[17] (Possibly this false belief that intellectual work blasts the germ plasm grew in company with the traditional official association of scholarly activity with a monkish life in medieval days.)

Apropos of both venereal disease and intellectuality is the contention of Harvard Medical School bacteriologist Hans Zinsser that syphilis (which the English called the "French disease," the French called the "Neapolitan disease," the Italians named the "Spanish pox," and so on) must be a potent breeder of genius. "Since so many brilliant men have had syphilis, much of the world's greatest achievement was evidently formulated in brains stimulated by the cerebral irritation of an early general paresis."[18] Other scientists have recorded a similar association between intellectual achievement and cirrhosis of the liver.

---

[15] Walter Bagehot, *Physics and Politics*, London, 1872; Alfred A. Knopf, New York, 1948, pp. 204-205.

[16] Alberto Moravia, *Conjugal Love*, Farrar, Straus and Cudahy Inc., New York, 1951.

[17] Charles P. Snow, *The Affair*, Charles Scribner's Sons, New York, 1960.

[18] Hans Zinsser, *Rats, Lice and History*, Little, Brown and Co., Boston, 1935, p. 62.

Reproductive Norms and Values

Sexual practices and their sometime demographic consequence, fertility, are influenced by various cultural proscriptions on individuals and families. Unfettered reproduction is a chimera. Societies both encourage and discourage having children. Many of these social controls are interiorized to the extent of being practiced unconsciously; furthermore, the biologistic approach is so ingrained that we tend to ignore or disclaim the importance or even the existence of sociological controls. Ignorance motivates some people to think of unrestricted productivity as usual among primitive peoples and to believe that restrictions on fertility are modern inventions. The fact of the matter is that social restrictions on reproduction are imposed in all societies and by all belief systems. Fertility controls that are a part of our own normative system are accepted as God-given or natural, while those social impediments or encouragements foreign to our thinking are recognized as man-made and hence often held to be against nature.

Some of these normative restrictions on natality are known and even deliberate consequences of cultural insistences or proscriptions; others are latent functions of mores designed to satisfy nondemographic social needs. In most cultures, for example, the lineage system, bride price, and rules concerning promiscuity, legitimacy, and inheritance are intended for and supported by religious rather than demographic considerations; nonetheless they do have considerable impact on societal fertility levels. Customs concerning age at marriage and ease of divorce are established and maintained in consistency with other institutions and beliefs and are rarely even acknowledged to influence fertility. But clearly, each year beyond puberty during which marriage is prohibited does decrease the potential childbearing span. Every culture contains many customs having latent consequences for birth as well as for other demographic events. No value system has been discovered which leaves alone fertility, mortality, and migration.

SOCIAL OBSTACLES TO FERTILITY

Kingsley Davis has identified five social impediments to fertility: taboos on the association of males and females (purdah, celibacy, status and financial barriers); taboos on sexual intercourse (after childbirth, against fornication and adultery, marriage age limits); restraints on conception (sterilization, contraception); abortion (sanctioned or condemned); and infanticide (plural births, unwanted females, illegitimate births, deformed children).[19]

---

[19] Kingsley Davis, *Human Society*, The Macmillan Co., New York, 1949, pp. 557-561.

While men often speak as if limiting fertility is inherently bad, they overlook the fact that many such controls are operative in western culture with the full approval of our religious bodies. For example, our insistence both on delaying marriage for several years past the onset of fecundity and on restricting the bearing of children to married people have notable impacts on the fertility level. Further, we share with most cultures the practice of making a social (as opposed to physiological) matter of the rites of passage into adulthood and the privilege of sexual relations and parenthood. "In our own society both men and women remain legally children until long after they are physically adult. . . . Whether a boy is able to breed is less vital to his society than whether he is able to do a man's work and has a man's knowledge."[20] Puberty rites, in short, are more concerned with social than with physical maturity.

Cross-cultural analysis reveals many restrictions on the birth rate. Some cultural norms prohibit bearing a child before or after a certain age, pregnancies occurring outside the permissible ages being often terminated by abortion or infanticide. One Formosan society aborts all pregnancies until the woman is 34 years old, some women having as many as sixteen abortions. And how many children can a woman have after age 34? The Mataco of Argentina are reported to abort all first conceptions. Taboos on intercourse for a stated period following the birth of a child—sometimes as long as three years—are moderately effective; breach of the norm is concealed (and punishment averted) by abortion. This custom limits each woman to at most one child (barring multiple births) every four years. Illegitimate children or those born at an astrologically unpropitious time are often exposed if not previously aborted.

In many times and places, women have found pregnancy and motherhood irksome and even odious. Some men regard pregnant women with disgust. In a de Maupassant story a husband kept his wife pregnant so that she might seem ugly to other men. The act of intercourse is also sometimes denounced as ludicrous and sordid. "What is there . . . more ignoble and more repugnant than that ridiculous act of reproduction of living beings. . . . Since all the organs which have been invented by the economical and malicious Creator serve two purposes, why did he not choose those that were unsullied?"[21]

In medieval Europe inculcation of the principle that a man might not marry until his livelihood was assured exerted a significant check on fertility. Infusion of this institutional safeguard against excessive procreation is implicit in the etymology of two medieval English words: *husband* and *anilepiman*.

---

[20] Ralph Linton, *The Study of Man*, D. Appleton-Century Co., New York, 1936, p. 118.

[21] Guy de Maupassant, "Useless Beauty," *Collected Works*, 1903.

The word husband derives from two words meaning "house" and "dwell," and its original meaning (still preserved in husbandman and husbandry) was a householder, a man who had a home. The Middle English word for a single man was anilepiman ("only man"). These two terms, one referring to property and the other to marital status, gradually became associated as opposites, anilepiman coming to mean a man who had no living and therefore could not marry, and husband a man who was able to care for a family and therefore could get (or, eventually, was) married.[22]

The guilds proscribed marriage during a lengthy apprenticeship (seven years in Elizabethan England) and made it difficult for a period thereafter.

Ireland has one of the oldest average ages at marriage of any country. Although its age-specific birth rate after marriage is rather high, the over-all birth rate is kept low by deferred marriage—a practice more or less forced on the Irish by adherence to old customs coupled with a limited supply of farms to support families and a low level of income.

The proportion of adults ever marrying is also directly relevant to natality rates. Whereas virtually everyone marries in some societies (the United States approaches this condition), in other groups the proportion of unmarried and childless adults is high. For example, in 1936, 55 per cent of Irish women between 25 and 34 years of age and 74 per cent of the Irish men of the same age were unmarried. Since those depression times, the percentage has declined, but it still remains exceptionally high when compared to that of, say, the United States.

SOCIAL ENCOURAGEMENTS TO FERTILITY

Societies encourage fertility in various ways. "Marriage and parenthood become advantageous to the individual not only emotionally but also economically, politically, and spiritually. We often find for example that the permissive enjoyment of sexual intercourse, the ownership of land, the admission to certain offices, the claim to respect, and the attainment of blessedness are made contingent upon marriage."[23] Through idealizing wedlock, giving higher status to parenthood, and extolling virility, a society rewards reproduction.

Social structure has an almost determinative impact on fertility. Thus the prevalence of the old balance in agrarian, familistic societies has been explained by the following cultural inducements to abundant reproduc-

---

[22] William Petersen, "The Demographic Transition in the Netherlands," *American Sociological Review*, Vol. XXV, No. 3, June 1960, p. 341. See also George F. Homans, *English Villagers of the Thirteenth Century*, Harvard University Press, Cambridge, 1941, pp. 136-137.

[23] Davis, *Human Society, op. cit.*, p. 561.

tion. First the financial expense of child-rearing does not fall directly on the parents to the same extent as in societies where the nuclear family has greater independence. Also, as the effort and inconvenience of child care is shared with persons outside the nuclear family, marriage can thus take place at an early age. Because of the heavy emphasis on kin solidarity, the motivation to marry is often quite strong. Wives are encouraged to beget children as soon and as frequently as possible, for the birth of a son or daughter (depending on whether descent, inheritance, and succession are transmitted through the male or female lines) contributes to her husband's lineage (or her own) and therefore to her own rise in rank and esteem. For similar reasons, the husband is powerfully compelled to breed offspring.[24]

Having children is frequently considered a proof of virility. One demographer quotes Puerto Rican men on the subject of masculinity: "A man is anxious to have his son early to prove his *hombría* [manliness]. . . . I mean that he wants to have his first child to prove that he can make sons, that he is not barren." Again, "A large family proves the *hombría* of a man . . . because it takes a real man to maintain and educate a large family." Or, "I wanted a male son . . . so as to know I was a *macho* . . . to show that I am not like the men that have only females."[25] This attitude is not confined to Puerto Ricans or Mexicans; many other Americans describe men with large families as "real men." Psychologists suggest that small or short men who have many children are trying to prove their masculinity. Tourist guides identifying a huge memorial to a prolific man have been known to say that the large stone was necessary "to hold the old boy down."

Most men are fearful of impotence, and those who have been rendered infertile by mumps or who have had themselves sterilized are often regarded as weaker, less virile, misguided, and generally to be pitied. Indeed, both illiterates and intellectuals can be found who assume that fecundity is a cause (necessary but not sufficient) of great vigor, creativity, and artistic sensitivity; and in all educational strata there are men who fear loss of fecundity in the belief that it would strip them of their dynamic vitality, ability to think quickly or profoundly, and, of course, their power to charm women. Ernest Hemingway's castrated war veteran of *The Sun Also Rises* and James M. Cain's singer whose voice lost timbre when he engaged in homosexual activities are fictional cases in point. Nor is this creed restricted to males. Many American women feel that it is essential to have babies in order to prove themselves "com-

---

[24] Kingsley Davis, "Family Patterns Favoring High Fertility in Underdeveloped Areas," *Eugenics Quarterly*, Vol. II, March 1955, pp. 33-39.

[25] J. Mayone Stycos, *Family and Fertility in Puerto Rico*, Columbia University Press, New York, 1955, pp. 173, 177, and 179.

plete women." The ability to conceive and carry a pregnancy to a successful conclusion is a cherished one.

Idealization of marriage and parenthood and the disvaluing of celibacy in many cultures are undoubtedly influential in promoting fertility. In the United States today, childless parents are often chided by their friends as "selfish" or "unfortunate," according to the reasons for the infertility. Many speak of the "blessedness" of parenthood and even of the civic obligation to bear children.

Another encouragement of fertility is the restriction of many privileges to parents or at least to married persons. Reproduction is integrated with other traits, complexes, and patterns in the culture. "Articulation of the parental status with the rest of one's statuses is the supreme encouragement to fertility."[26] Early settlers in New England sometimes required that a person be married before he could own land or vote in elections. Sexual intercourse itself is often legally confined to marriage and the desire to procreate. So too social rank is in some cases affected by the number of one's children. Political pundits sometimes express the opinion that an unmarried man cannot be elected to the White House; Adlai Stevenson's divorce was cited as a vote-losing factor in the 1952 and 1956 Presidential elections. Tax benefits are frequently conferred on persons with large numbers of offspring. In some societies there is an almost confiscatory tax on the incomes and property of bachelors and a huge but less punitive impost on barren couples. Even the salvation of the soul has been related to parentage.

Patriotism too may enjoin the production of children. President Theodore Roosevelt was reported to have said, "To be a worthy citizen, you must have four children, at least." And Julius Caesar promised, "If you have three, you will receive land in the Campania." Governments from Sparta to the Soviet Union have awarded medals and special privileges to citizens having large families.

A more personal and perhaps more potent factor in the promotion of fertility is the desire to carry on one's name. Many people are taught to believe that unless their "seed" and their "name" are continued, they have not fulfilled their major function on earth. Among many ethnic groups the man who dies having produced no surviving male child is considered pitiable, for he leaves no trace of himself. In the classic play of Euripides, the greatest and most loathsome vengeance that Medea could conceive for Jason was to kill his (and her own) sons. Her husband concurred: "Blood-red mother, who didst kill my sons, and make me as the dead."

Another motive for having children is the desire to escape or minimize

---

[26] Davis, *Human Society, op. cit.,* p. 561.

income taxes, military service, or other odious civic obligations. This seems to be a matter of using one issue to avoid another.

CULTURE, BIOLOGY, AND FERTILITY

Let us illustrate the interplay of cultural values and biological impulses by examining a subculture that encourages fertility to the extent of approaching remarkably near the maximum fecundity level. One group in the United States and Canada has rewarded fertility so much that their population is doubling every sixteen years.[27]

The Hutterites (named after Jacob Hutter, a Tyrolean hatmaker who became their first minister) are a religious sect living in Alberta, Montana, and South Dakota. Originating in Switzerland in 1528 as ultrafundamentalist dissenters related to the Mennonites they moved to the Crimea in 1774—after considerable persecution resulting from their refusal to bear arms—under a promise from the Emperor of Russia of one hundred years of freedom from military service. The promise was kept but not renewed, and in 1874, 250 Hutterites emigrated to North America. In both World Wars, they served in camps for conscientious objectors.

The Hutterites are a cooperative agricultural group who live in colonies of about fifteen families each and believe in community ownership of property and goods. Farm and domestic work, leadership, and dealings with outsiders are arranged on a rotation system. They were recently under attack by South Dakota businessmen who unsuccessfully attempted to enact legislation that would make it illegal for them to buy more land—a crippling restriction for such a rapidly growing group.

As a result of their natural increase of over 4 per cent a year, the Hutterites grew from 443 in 1880 to 8,542 in 1950 (there was little migration or conversion). The median number of children ever born to married Hutterite women who have completed the childbearing period varies from nine among the older wives to eleven among the middle-aged ones. The median number of children by age of women varies as follows: age 70-74, 9.2 children; age 65-69, 9.9; 60-64, 10.3; 55-59, 9.9; 50-54, 10.3; and 45-49, 10.9. They have only the usual proportion of multiple births, and extramarital sex relations are strictly prohibited. Only 3 per cent of their marriages are sterile—a far lower proportion than the 10 per cent estimated for the United States or Canada as a whole; probably the major causes of difference stem from the lack of stress and the great security and solidarity of their lives.

[27] Joseph W. Eaton and Albert J. Mayer, "The Social Biology of Very High Fertility among the Hutterites: The Demography of a Unique Population," *Human Biology*, Vol. XXV, No. 3, September 1953, pp. 206-264.

Sterilization is the only conscious interference they tolerate with "natural" fertility. Tietze reports that even with this high a natality rate, one-third of the Hutterite couples have no more children after the wife reaches age 40; since this premature cessation is not attributable to birth control, he assumes that the wife has become sterile.[28]

The fact that fertility rates among Hutterites are more than double those of the general United States population—and still more in excess of natality levels in certain other religious segments—demonstrates that gross differences may exist from group to group within a single country. Even greater differentials are discernible when comparing groups inhabiting different regions of the world or when contrasting different centuries. It would be foolish, certainly, to deny the importance of biological enabling conditions, yet unquestionably culture does play a major role in shaping fertility trends over the world. The results of these natural and social forces are central to the next chapter.

---

[28] Christopher Tietze, "Reproductive Span and Rate of Reproduction among Hutterite Women," *Fertility and Sterility*, Vol. VIII, No. 1, January-February 1957, pp. 89-97.

9 ❧ Fertility Trends and Differentials

Changing folkways and mores of the Western world have recently encouraged a lowering of the birth rate toward the reproductive condition spoken of as "the small family system." Members of various segments of the populace, however, have shown systematic differences in their adaptation of this small family pattern. Especially useful in explaining these past and present differentials is socioeconomic class. And analysis both of over-all tendencies and intergroup variations demands precise measurement of rates.

Measuring Fertility and Replacement

A description of fertility requires rates and ratios similar to those employed in analyzing mortality. Additionally, there are several other measures that apply only to fertility itself. Distinct from fertility *per se* is the concept of replacement of one generation by another—the estimation of the total birth record of a reproductive lifetime. Finally, by comparing birth and death rates we can measure the vital or natural increase of population.

BIRTH RATES AND RATIOS

Crude, corrected, specific, and standardized birth rates correspond to their mortality counterparts. The crude birth rate, which is easy to compute and understand, is widely used as a measure of fertility, but it also has serious drawbacks. First, it requires reasonably complete birth registration, which makes it a deceptive measure in countries and local areas where births are incompletely recorded. Moreover, when used by persons not competent in statistics, it can be highly misleading. Standardized birth rates are superior analytical devices, but they are laborious to compute, and laymen frequently cannot comprehend the standardization idea without lengthy explanation.

The ease of calculation and comprehension of the fertility ratio makes it an extensively used measure wherever the age distribution is accurately known. The *effective fertility ratio* or the *child-woman ratio* equals the number of children under five years of age divided by the number of women in the childbearing ages (ordinarily 15-44 or 15-49, although ages 20-44 and 20-49 are sometimes used). This measure is less affected by minor annual fluctuations than are ordinary birth rates because it describes fertility over a five-year rather than one-year period. The fertility ratio for the Hutterites is .96, meaning that there is almost one child under five for every woman in the fecund ages.

INTERGENERATIONAL REPLACEMENT

Frequently demographers are interested primarily in long-term trends and do not care to use a measure which applies only to the last year or even five years. But unfortunately, indices which best satisfy this kind of demand are deficient in another quality, as they tell us nothing about immediate tendencies and may even obscure important annual variations. Thus we are forced to choose between the above-mentioned measures, which provide the most accurate description of what is happening at any given moment, and the measures described below, which are superior indicators of population replacement on a generational level.

Two popular generational indexes are the *number of children ever born* and *size of completed family* (the number of children there now are in a family whose mother has passed through the fertile ages). But while neither of these measures is seriously affected by temporary conditions, both have the disadvantage that the fertility patterns they describe are those of the last thirty or forty years rather than the current patterns. The first of these two indexes is a superior measure of pure fertility because it is not affected by mortality of the children; the second is a better measure of replacement because it does allow for childhood mortality. Sometimes demographers work with the number of children born or now alive of marriages that have lasted a given number of years.

A related measure, the *total fertility rate*, is constructed in a manner similar to the current life table. It states how many children would be borne by a group of women who lived through their entire childbearing ages under given age-specific birth rates. This synthetic figure is the average number of births that would occur to women experiencing no mortality and remaining throughout the childbearing period subject to the age-specific birth rates of the year for which the rate is calculated. Whereas the number of children ever born (like the generation life table) is simply an observed history of a cohort, the total fertility rate (like the current life table) is a cross-sectional, hypothetical construct.

If we modify the total fertility rate to include only female births (instead of total births), the resultant index is called the *gross reproduction rate*; by adding an additional modification to allow for mortality, we have the *net reproduction rate*. The gross reproduction rate (G.R.R.) is the ratio of 1) the number of daughters who would be born to a cohort of new-born girls if the age-specific fertility rates for female births continued unchanged and if the new-born girls all lived to complete the childbearing period to 2) the number of new-born girls in the original cohort. The net reproduction rate (N.R.R.) is also a ratio of two numbers: 1) the number of daughters that would be born to a cohort of new-born girls if the age-specific fertility rates for female births continued unchanged, including effects of mortality on the original cohort (the effects of mortality are included by using a life table population), and 2) the number of new-born girls in the original cohort. Both the G.R.R. and the N.R.R. show generational fertility trends, but the N.R.R. is more realistic because not all of the girls in the original cohort will live through the entire childbearing period. Thus the N.R.R. is always smaller than the G.R.R. The G.R.R. is a better measure of pure fertility; the N.R.R. is a better measure of replacement of one generation by the next generation. Because of its greater sophistication, the N.R.R. is the more widely used. A net reproduction rate of 1.00 indicates that the population has a static tendency. The Hutterite N.R.R. of 3.66 is one of the highest ever computed. By contrast, France had an N.R.R. of .90 in 1931-1935, and England an N.R.R. of .75 during the same time. As might be imagined, the leaders of both countries were worried about the prospect of a declining population. In 1959 the United States population had a G.R.R. of 1.81 and an N.R.R. of 1.74; the nonwhite population had a G.R.R. of 2.35 and an N.R.R. of 2.20.

COHORT ANALYSIS

Until recently the net reproduction rate was considered the most refined measure of replacement. But as it fails to allow for birth order, a spate of "postponed" births may create a spurious sudden rise. Therefore, demographers are turning increasingly to the cohort approach, a method of analysis in which the experience of cohorts is studied throughout their lives or for specific periods. Cohort analysis begins with a group of women who were all born or married in the same year and then follows them throughout their reproductive lifetimes, recording their production of children. It is particularly useful for exposing trends of a quarter century or more.

By grouping together all women married in, say, 1916-1925, and comparing their attitudes and practices with those married in 1926-1935, 1936-1945, and 1946-1955, we can spot trends more distinctly than if we use other methods of analysis. Also, tables based on such intervals are easy to read and comprehend. This time series method lends itself to either contemporaneous or *ex post facto* experimental designs.

Longitudinal examination of the reproductive histories of several cohorts enables us to compare age-specific fertility patterns through succeeding groups of women. Thus we learn more about child spacing. In America, for example, the increasing tendency of women to shorten the childbearing period, now usually completing their families before they reach age 30, is readily observed by inspecting the reproductive practices of successive cohorts of women as they pass through their twenties and thirties. Cohort analysis exposes changes in timing of reproduction within a few years after they occur, whereas the net reproduction rate does not reflect such trends for two or three decades. This fact makes the cohort approach far more useful for analytical and predictive purposes.

Since cohort analysis is closely linked to the age-sex structure of the population, predictions based on this technique accurately reflect the shape of the population pyramid. Not susceptible to distortion by age-sex variations, it can expose certain misleading inferences drawn from unrefined rates. For example, the present trend toward having children at younger ages inflates the annual birth rates; through cohort analysis, we can see the temporary quality of the deceptive increase and therefore are less likely to overestimate future fertility.

NATURAL INCREASE

Rates of natural increase—comparisons of the birth and death rates—are calculated by subtracting the death rate from the birth rate. They may be either crude, corrected, specific, or standardized. To use the Hutterites as an example, their crude rate of natural increase is the crude birth rate (C.B.R.) of 45.9 minus the crude death rate (C.D.R.) of 4.4, or 41.5 per 1,000 per year. This high a figure is unusual for two reasons: the birth rate is very large, and the crude death rate is low because an exceptionally large part of the population is in the low-mortality ages. The standardized death rate of this group would be higher and would represent a more realistic evaluation of their mortality conditions.

The crude rate of natural increase shares the virtues and defects of its two components. If high-powered analysis is to be performed, the C.R.N.I. is inadequate. Nonetheless, it remains an excellent pure description of natural increase over a given period, since it states simply the number of births minus the number of deaths during the interval, uncontaminated by any other consideration, no matter how pertinent on other grounds.

When a closed population—that is, a population without either in- or out-migration and whose growth therefore depends completely on the difference between births and deaths—experiences constant age-sex-specific fertility and mortality rates over a long time, its total rate of increase will tend to become constant. This constant annual rate is known as the intrinsic or true rate of natural increase. A population which has reached this condition is called a *stable population* because it has an unchanging proportion of persons in each age-sex group. A stable population having a zero rate of natural increase is referred to as a *stationary population*. National populations never reach exact stability because specific birth and death rates continually change, but the use of a life table permits computation of long-term over-all rates as implied by present age-sex-specific vital rates. That is, the intrinsic birth and death rates tell us what ultimately would happen if present age-sex-specific fertility and mortality continue without change. Calculation of the implicit stable population as a model provides a superior index of the national growth potentials as exhibited in the true or intrinsic rate of natural increase.

BIRTHS, AGE STRUCTURE, AND DEATHS

Birth rates obviously affect the pace of population growth or decline by exceeding or falling below death rates. Less directly, fertility also influences total population changes by introducing variations in mortality. Thus the rapid growth of the newly developing countries is attributable to two phenomena—the maintenance of high birth rates and, indirectly, the lowering of death rates by these same high birth rates.

High birth rates generate young populations; nations having high fertility tend to have exceptionally large proportions of their populace in the pre-adult ages. In some cases the population under age 20 exceeds that over 20. Since child and adolescent groups exhibit everywhere the smallest age-specific death rates, then such nations have lower over-all mortality rates than would be the case if their fertility were higher but the state of health remained the same.

In this fashion it is possible to achieve a crude death rate so low as to seem hardly credible. The Hutterites' C.D.R. of 4.4 per 1,000 per year (less than half of the over-all United States rate) is caused by a combination of favorable health conditions and a very young population induced by unusually high fertility. If the entire United States had its present age-specific death rates and the age distribution of the Hutterites—or of any Latin American country—the national C.D.R. would be around 4 instead of 9. Simply altering the age distribution in this manner, without any other change, would lift the national crude rate of natural increase by approximately one-third.

Paradoxically, some underdeveloped countries with unsatisfactory control over sickness and death have crude death rates that rank among the lowest in the world—for example, Chile, Taiwan, and Ceylon. Puerto Rico has one of the lowest living standards of any territory falling within the jurisdiction of the United States, but because of its high fertility, its resulting youth, and its falling mortality, it now has a lower crude death rate than does the mainland. Given these age-induced facts of birth and death, demographers prefer to use more refined measures of both fertility and mortality than the C.B.R. and the C.D.R. provide, especially when engaging in detailed analysis or prediction.

Long-Term and Current Trends

Recent fertility and replacement levels in various countries of the world shown in Table 14 bring to mind the part played by fertility changes in the demographic transition in Western countries. They also encourage speculation concerning the role that natality will play in coming decades. Notice that the N.R.R. for modernized industrial countries is generally between 1.00 and 1.50. Two nations, Hungary and Japan, have N.R.R.'s below the replacement level. Costa Rica and Panama have exceptionally high net reproduction rates resulting from correspondingly high intrinsic birth rates coupled with moderate death rates. Negative intrinsic increase rates have prevailed in Japan since 1956 and Hungary since 1958. In the 1930's many nations exhibited negative natural increase rates: the United States, Austria, Belgium, Czechoslovakia, Denmark, Estonia, Finland, France, Germany, Hungary, Latvia, Norway, Sweden, Switzerland, England and Wales, and Australia. These negative rates generally became positive after 1940, but this portent of decline continued in Sweden and France through 1945, after which the rising fertility following the armistice took effect.

The resurgence of natality following World War II constituted the first and only abiding reversal of the century-long decline in Westernized nations. Fertility levels in most of these countries have not maintained their immediate postwar levels, but they have been persistently higher than those of the 1930's—though not so high as the rates experienced in earlier decades. Causes of this "baby boom" are to be found in higher marriage rates, earlier ages at marriage, and diminishing proportions of childless and only-child marriages. Presumably these demographic changes are the result of several cultural, psychological, and economic independent variables, as for example, folk attitudes toward "only" children and the improved family financial security flowing from the postwar prosperity generally prevalent in Europe and America.

TABLE 14. *Vital Rates in Selected Countries, 1954-1960**

CONTINENT AND COUNTRY	DATE OF VITAL RATES	DATE OF LIFE TABLE	NET REPRO- DUCTION RATE	Intrinsic rate per 1,000 females		
				BIRTH	DEATH	NATURAL INCREASE
NORTH AMERICA						
Canada	1960	1956	1.81	27.6	6.7	20.8
Costa Rica	1960	1950	2.84	43.8	10.8	32.9
Jamaica	1955	1950–52	1.86	33.6	10.9	22.6
Panama	1959	1953	2.18	37.3	9.5	27.8
U.S., Continental	1959	1959	1.74	26.7	6.8	19.9
EUROPE						
England and Wales	1958	1958	1.18	17.0	10.9	6.2
France	1960	1960	1.28	18.7	9.8	9.0
Hungary	1960	1958	0.91	12.6	16.2	−3.6
Netherlands	1960	1951–55	1.46	21.1	8.7	12.5
Norway	1959	1951–55	1.34	19.4	9.2	10.1
Poland	1959	1955–56	1.39	22.3	10.5	11.8
Sweden	1959	1951–55	1.04	14.4	12.9	1.5
Yugoslavia	1959	1952–54	1.08	18.6	15.8	2.8
ASIA						
Japan	1959	1959	0.93	13.0	15.6	−2.5
Thailand	1954	1947–48	1.70	32.1	14.6	17.5
OCEANIA						
Australia	1960	1953–55	1.61	24.6	7.5	17.1
New Zealand	1960	1955–57	1.90	28.6	6.0	22.7

* *Population Index*, Vol. XXVIII, No. 2, April 1962, pp. 197-209.

The United States has grown rapidly since the postwar baby boom combined with the cessation of war deaths to raise the intrinsic rate of natural increase from 4.9 in 1945 to 10.7 in 1946. The rate climbed to 13.3 in 1950, 18.8 in 1955, and 20.5 in 1960. During this period, the intrinsic birth rate rose from 17.4 per 1,000 females in 1945 to 22.1 in 1950, 25.8 in 1955, and 27.2 in 1960.

SECULAR DECLINE IN UNITED STATES

This recent increase in natality should not necessarily be taken as an indication of a long-term increase. "In broad perspective the fertility history of the United States is one of a transition from large families to small families. From 1810 to 1940 there was a virtually uninterrupted decline in the ratio of young children to women."[1] The total fertility rate has dropped consistently; it was 7.04 in 1800, 6.73 in 1820, 6.14 in 1840, 5.21 in 1860, 4.24 in 1880, 3.56 in 1900, 3.17 in 1920, and 2.19 in 1940, after which it rose to 3.52 in 1960.[2]

One reason for this decline is the transition from rural to city living and from agricultural to urban means of livelihood, which has altered the economic value of children. On the farm, children were assets, able to hoe and pitch hay; but in the new urban environment where the family is no longer a productive unit, children increase the family's expenses instead of augmenting its income through productive labor. Indeed, even farm families have become smaller, especially as they have adopted urban norms and technology. "Fundamentally the long decline in fertility during the nineteenth century and the early part of the twentieth century was prompted by desires for higher levels of living for self and for children and by the tangible evidence that levels of living could be further elevated. It was realized that there was a relation between size of family and level of living."[3]

"Between 1910 and 1950, the average number of children ever born to white women 45 to 49 years old at the census date declined from 4.1 to 2.3 and that for nonwhite women declined from 5.9 to 2.7."[4] Table 15 summarizes changes in fertility over the last half century. Note the dip during the depression and the recovery following World War II: 1961 marked the fourth consecutive year that the C.B.R. declined. Between 1960 and 1961, only four states showed an increased C.B.R.

The secular decline of the birth rate has not been uniform throughout the country. The older and more economically advanced New England states, the mid-Atlantic area, and the eastern part of the Midwest had lower fertility from the beginning. Interstate differences have narrowed through time as states with initially high fertility levels (mostly southern) experienced the most rapid declines. These trends are evident among both whites and Negroes. Explanations of this decline

---

[1] Wilson H. Grabill, Clyde V. Kiser, and Pascal K. Whelpton, *The Fertility of American Women*, John Wiley and Sons, New York, 1958, p. 3.

[2] Ansley J. Coale and Melvin Zelnik, *New Estimates of Fertility and Population in the United States*, Princeton University Press, Princeton, 1963, Table 2.

[3] Grabill, Kiser, and Whelpton, *The Fertility of American Women, op. cit.*, p. 3.

[4] *Ibid.*, p. 382.

with narrowing interstate differences turn upon two sets of phenomena: migration from farms to cities and from small towns to large cities, and changes in the age, sex, and nativity composition of the population. Urbanization has contributed much to the decline of Negro fertility, whereas this spatial-density variable has not been particularly important for whites.[5]

Only a few decades ago this seemingly continuous decrease in the national birth rate was inducing demographers and political leaders to expect an eventual decrease in the size of the population. For about a century the United States had been approaching a decreasing rate of natural increase, concealed beneath the bursts of immigrants which contributed so substantially to national growth.

POSTWAR BABY BOOM

This prospect of zero or negative growth rapidly receded as the baby boom of the late 1940's continued through the 1950's and into the 1960's. At first

TABLE 15. *United States Fertility, 1910-1962* *

YEAR	NUMBER OF BIRTHS	BIRTHS PER 1,000 POPULATION
1910	2,777,000	30.1
1915	2,965,000	29.5
1920	2,950,000	27.7
1925	2,909,000	25.1
1930	2,618,000	21.3
1935	2,377,000	18.7
1940	2,559,000	19.4
1945	2,858,000	20.4
1950	3,632,000	24.1
1955	4,098,000	24.9
1960	4,247,000	23.6
1961	4,268,000	23.3
1962	4,167,000	22.4

* National Vital Statistics Division, "Monthly Vital Statistics Report," Vol. X, No. 13, April 30, 1962, p. 3; Vol. XI, No. 12, February 19,1963, p. 1; *Vital Statistics of the United States,* 1961, "Advance Report," November 1962; and earlier publications of the National Office of Vital Statistics.

the fertility surge following World War II appeared to be temporary, as the increased fertility consisted principally of first and second births, many of which had apparently been postponed until the war ended. This kind of fertility does not produce a permanent rapid population growth. But in the 1950's, higher order births increased, a signal to demographers

[5] Bernard Okun, *Trends in Birth Rates in the United States Since 1870,* The Johns Hopkins Press, Baltimore, 1958.

that the baby boom would continue and that the accelerated population growth was here to stay—at least for a while. In the 1960's, a slow but consistent decline in natality has been taking place.

Factors in this postwar rise in natality have been calculated and compared by demographers. Of the four relevant causative variables, the one having the greatest superficial appeal—increased number of children per mother—is the least significant. The proportion of the rise attributable to each of the four variables is as follows: larger number of women, 24 per cent; more women marrying, 30 per cent; more wives bearing a child, 34 per cent; and more total births per mother, 12 per cent.[6] Childlessness is generally involuntary and has declined to a level close to the physiological minimum dictated by sterility.

A mean of 3.2 children was expected by a sample of 2,684 married American couples interviewed in 1960, of which the wives were between ages 18 and 39. The total number of children expected varied as follows: no children, 4 per cent; 1 child, 7 per cent; 2 children, 25 per cent; 3 children, 27 per cent; 4 children, 20 per cent; 5 children, 8 per cent; and 6 or more children, 9 per cent. A smaller sample interviewed in 1962 yielded almost identical expectations.[7]

This expectation is consistent with the increased average size of the United States family in recent decades. The number of children born per 1,000 women aged 15 through 59 ever married rose from about 1,900 in 1940 and 1950 to more than 2,300 in 1960. Cohort analysis indicates that the secular decline in the number of children per woman has halted and perhaps even reversed since World War II. The cohort of 1880 (which reached age 50 in 1930) produced 3.5 children per woman ever married; the cohort of 1910 (which attained age 50 in 1960) bore only 2.3 children per woman; the cohort of 1920 (which has not yet completed the childbearing ages) had already given birth to 2.6 children by age 40; the 1930 cohort bore 2.4 children per woman ever married by age 30. This increase should continue into the 1970's, although without reaching the level of the 1880 cohort.

PARITY AND FAMILY SIZE

The notion of parity—the number of live children a woman has borne—can guide our interpretations still further. A multiparous woman is one who has had more than one child.

Throughout United States history, the birth rate for low orders of

[6] Grabill, Kiser, and Whelpton, *The Fertility of American Women*, op. cit., pp. 368-370.
[7] Morris Axelrod, Ronald Freedman, David Goldberg, and Doris Slesinger, "Fertility Expectations of the United States Population: A Time Series," *Population Index*, Vol. XXIX, No. 1, January 1963, p. 27.

Fertility Trends and Differentials* :: *169

parity (2 or fewer live births) has remained fairly steady. Medium parity births (3 or 4 children ever born) declined somewhat before the depression of the early 1930's and increased thereafter. Fertility of high parity women (5 or more children born) declined tremendously over the past two centuries. It is the higher orders of parity that make for very large families and huge growth by natural increase. Table 16 shows births by parity for six age cohorts of women who have completed the bearing of children. Notice the declining percentages of births of fifth and higher orders and the increasing percentage of first and second order births.

TABLE 16. *Births by Parity and Cohort, United States*
Women Aged 44 Years, 1933-1958*

PER CENT OF TOTAL BIRTHS BY COHORT

Date of birth of women	1889	1894	1899	1904	1909	1914
Year attaining age 44	1933	1938	1943	1948	1953	1958
Birth order						
First and second	46.6	50.1	53.0	57.0	59.5	60.3
Third and fourth	27.1	26.5	25.7	24.4	24.0	24.7
Fifth to seventh	18.1	16.4	15.1	13.2	11.8	11.0
Eighth and higher	8.2	7.0	6.2	5.4	4.7	4.0
Total	100.0	100.0	100.0	100.0	100.0	100.0

* Adapted from National Office of Vital Statistics, *Vital Statistics—Special Reports*, Vol. LI, No. 1, January 29, 1960, Table 4.

Paradoxically, this decline in frequency of large families has not curbed the increasing average family size. The explanation of this situation lies in two facts: first, that "an increasing proportion of couples are having moderate sized families of two to four children instead of the somewhat smaller families of the 1930's and early 1940's"; and secondly, that "the large family of five or more children has been on the decline." Whereas the cohort of 1886-1890 produced 877 fifth or higher order births per 1,000 women by ages 45-49, the 1906-1910 cohort had only 391 such births—a drop of 55 per cent. The proportion of families having five or more children probably will continue to decrease for several years.[8]

We frequently hear of the recent change away from the small families of a generation ago toward the large families of today. The speaker usually intends "large family" to refer to parents with four

---

[8] Anders Lunde, Carl Ortmeyer, and Earl Huyck, "Trends in Marriages, Births, and Population," in National Vital Statistics Division, *Health, Education, and Welfare Indicators*, March 1963, p. xxiv.

or five children. This choice of definition is in itself indicative of the extent of our unconscious acceptance of the fertility decline.

In Colonial days, four or five children were considered a small family, eight or ten children were usual, and twelve to fifteen were frequent. Peter Kalm, a Swedish observer of the Colonial scene, wrote of a New England woman who "has brought sixteen children into the world; and from seven of them only, she had one hundred and seventy-seven grandchildren and great-grandchildren." Another hardy New Englander "could count altogether five hundred children, grandchildren, great-grandchildren, and great-great-grandchildren." "Estimates made by both contemporary and modern authorities, utilizing a variety of techniques and data, place the annual birth rate in the Colonial and early Federal periods at 50 to 57 births per 1,000 inhabitants. The women of completed fertility are variously estimated to have borne an average of eight children."[9] One explanation offered for the high fertility in Colonial times is that the women had little say in such matters, it being largely a man's world.

FAMILY SIZE PREFERENCES

Americans have so thoroughly adopted the small family system common to most urbanized, industrialized, individualized societies that what once was considered a medium sized family is now called large. Today a family with two or three children is regarded as normal and one with nine or twelve as amusing. Indeed, in Revolutionary days, when twelve or thirteen children were not regarded as bizarre, the family comedy *Cheaper by the Dozen* could hardly have been a best seller. Morality and prestige are also involved; in 1882 the moderate political economist Gustav Schmoller inveighed against large families, calling them "a dogma characteristic of a semi-civilized state of culture." In short, large families became *déclassé*.

Even after two decades of the recent United States baby boom, the size of completed families has shown only a slight upward trend— a much smaller change than the decrease previously experienced. Indications that this upward trend may continue are provided by expressions of "ideal" family sizes consisting of two to four children as reported by women interviewed in social surveys over the last twenty years.

The small family ideal is found in many parts of the world. Interviews of West German residents yielded an average expectation of 2.2 children—approximately what is required for replacement under existing mortality conditions. Few West Germans expect to be childless,

---

[9] Grabill, Kiser, and Whelpton, *The Fertility of American Women, op. cit.*, p. 5.

and almost none desire it, yet rather few expect, desire, or idealize large families. Catholics, particularly those with a close attachment to the Church, have, expect, and value larger families than do other religious groups; however, even the Catholics do not want really large families. The greatest occupational difference is that between farmers and urbanites. "Working wives have, expect, and desire fewer offspring than those who do not work. . . . The traditionally negative correlation of fertility and education may be reversing itself with the highest fertility expectations among the best educated in the current generation." Fertility expectations in Western Germany resemble those in the United States, and in both countries in all classes there is widespread agreement about desirable family size.[10] The United States consensus favors three children—slightly more than the German expectation and enough of a difference to distinguish a rapidly growing population from a static one.

THE SMALL FAMILY SYSTEM

The first to adopt the small family system were the French. "From 1770 onwards there was a spread of knowledge of birth control, followed by a fairly general trend towards family limitation, and it is considered that by 1850 some form of control was probably practised by the majority of French families. No other European country can show such a marked development so early in its history."[11] Some scholars have explained this precocious tendency toward limitation of family size as reflecting the efforts of the bourgeoisie to rise into the aristocracy. Others stress the significance of political and religious events, such as the French Revolution and the accompanying decline in the power of the Church. A practical reason for having fewer offspring was the legal change invalidating primogeniture. Under the new laws, inheritances were shared among all the children, thus breaking up family landholdings, a fact which some historians believe to have motivated property owners to restrict the number of their children in order to avoid subdividing traditional family lands into very small portions. Whatever the explanation, for many years fertility barely exceeded mortality in France, and the population increased by only 5 million between 1860 and 1950, of which 2 million was attributable to net immigration.

In the swing toward the small family system, an unresolved argument centers around the relative roles of husbands and wives. The

---

[10] Ronald Freedman, Gerhard Baumert, and Martin Bolte, "Expected Family Size and Family Size Values in West Germany," *Population Studies*, Vol. XIII, No. 2, November 1959, pp. 136-150.

[11] Peter R. Cox, *Demography*, Cambridge University Press, London, 1959, p. 248.

belief that wives are more favorably disposed toward family limitation than are their husbands is supported by public opinion studies in India and elsewhere. If this is true, then the more power of decision the women have, the lower the birth rate will become. The emancipation of women and the trend toward egalitarianism within the family often is credited with the responsibility for a shift to smaller families. Evidence is incomplete regarding this hypothesis, but field research concerning use of and attitudes toward birth control shows that where the husband and wife disagree, the wife's opinion is more likely to determine family policy and action than the husband's. For instance, Catholic wives of Protestant husbands express opinions very similar to those of wives in purely Catholic marriages. However, Protestant wives of Catholic husbands have attitudes somewhat different from those of wives in solely Protestant or Catholic marriages.[12] Similar relations hold for nonreligious independent variables. This situation is consistent with the traditional view that the occupation is the husband's domain, the home the wife's; not only should she stay in it, she rules it.

ECONOMIC CORRELATES OF FERTILITY

The fluctuation of births and marriages with the business cycle has been studied by several sociologists and economists. Research by G. Udny Yule in England, Dorothy Swaine Thomas in the United States, and others has uncovered fairly large product-moment correlation coefficients between marriage rates and various business cycle indexes. These studies also show statistically significant positive associations between business cycles and birth rates.

Data for Sweden from 1736 to 1800 indicate that in years of crop failure the marriage rate averaged 0.4 below average, the crude birth rate 1.4 below average, and the crude death rate 2.5 above average, resulting in a crude rate of natural increase of 2.0. In years of exceptionally good harvests, however, the marriage rate averaged 0.3 above average, the crude birth rate 1.5 above average, and the crude death rate 1.5 below average—the crude rate of natural increase of 8.4 more than quadrupling the rate in years of inadequate harvest.[13]

For the past century in Western Europe and North America there has been a tendency for both nuptial and natality rates to rise in times of prosperity and to decline following the onset of a depression. As

---

[12] Ronald Freedman, Pascal K. Whelpton, and Arthur A. Campbell, *Family Planning, Sterility, and Population Growth*, McGraw-Hill Book Co., New York, 1959, p. 159.

[13] Halvor Gille, "The Demographic History of the Northern European Countries in the Eighteenth Century," *Population Studies*, Vol. III, No. 1, June 1949, p. 46.

long ago as 1885 the English Registrar General of vital statistics wrote: "It is a fair deduction from the facts that the marriage returns in England point out periods of prosperity little less distinctly than the funds measure the hopes and fears of the money market."[14]

Recently the effect of business cycles on marriage rates seems to be weakening: whereas business depressions once precipitated a reluctance to marry (and hence lower fertility), they now lead to abstention from having children after marriage. In the United States, for example, a decrease of both marriages and births obtained in the early depression years of the 1930's; by the middle of the depression people had stopped delaying marriage but continued to delay children; when the depression ended marriages kept on at a fairly high rate and fertility increased. A study of 1920-1958 intercorrelations in the United States concluded that "marriages and births respond sensitively to changes in economic conditions. . . . Economic conditions control about one-half of the annual variance of fertility from its trend."[15] Major secular changes in fertility are not controlled by business cycles—long-range fertility trends are in many respects independent of economic circumstances. "The surface waves are indeed much influenced by economic fluctuations, but the underlying tide appears to be an independent and surprisingly stable force. . . . Economic fluctuations in themselves should not be regarded as primary causes of fertility trends, but as important conditioning influences. . . . Economic costs associated with parenthood presumably bear less heavily in times of prosperity and more heavily in times of depression."[16] But in both cases they merely supplement motivations and behavior of noneconomic origin.

Differential Natality

Group fertility differentials are important for at least three reasons. First, they help demographers identify causes of reproductive behavior. Second, they hint at the proportions of each group that may be present in future generations (if Upper Slobbovians are reproducing more rapidly than denizens of Pogofenokee, they will probably constitute a relatively larger proportion of the world's population thirty years from now). Finally, differentials between subgroups supply clues to future trends for the entire group; that is, if urban residents are reproducing slower than ruralites, and if the area itself is becoming more urban, then we may expect declining fertility levels for the whole region.

---

[14] William Farr, *Vital Statistics*, London, 1885, p. 68.

[15] Dudley Kirk, "The Influence of Business Cycles on Marriage and Birth Rates," in National Bureau of Economic Research, *Demographic and Economic Change in Developed Countries*, Princeton University Press, Princeton, 1960, p. 253.

[16] *Ibid.*, p. 254.

In the United States the over-all trend as regards fertility is toward uniformity. Many long-standing variations are disappearing as groups with high fertility are lowering their notions of ideal family size and adopting birth control practices, and groups with low fertility are beginning to favor a larger family. Both extremes are modifying their ideals and performances toward the average. The Growth of American Families Study indicates that differentials may soon vanish, except for tendencies of working wives to have small families and for Catholics to have large ones.[17]

PHYSICAL AND MENTAL FITNESS

Some differences no doubt are biologically induced. There seem to be what Dr. A. F. Guttmacher has called good breeders and poor breeders. "The longer I am associated with problems of human reproduction, the more I am impressed that women may be readily divided into the same two categories into which we classify domestic animals, good breeders and poor breeders. A good breeder gets pregnant promptly and carries her progeny undisturbed by obstetric and genetic complications. The poor breeder takes a long time to achieve pregnancy and then is quite likely to abort; if not, she is far more prone to pregnancy difficulties."[18]

Psychological fitness, too, modifies fecundity. Thus a study of 1,411 neurotic Philadelphia women showed them to have a higher than normal frequency of nausea, vomiting, unfavorable delivery, Caesarean section, long labor, and prematurity.[19] Another psychological variable that may be affecting American natality rates is intelligence. Terman's gifted children with IQs of 135 or more, who have now reached their fifties, have somewhat fewer children than the population at large—though slightly more than the average of people in similar occupations. Their children appear to have above average intelligence.[20]

Length of marriage is obviously relevant to natality. In the United States, women are now marrying younger than did their mothers and grandmothers. And men too are marrying earlier than those of previous generations. Most childless marriages occur in cases where the women marry late. Fertility is lower among women experiencing broken mar-

[17] Freedman, Whelpton, and Campbell, *Family Planning, op. cit.,* pp. 318-319.

[18] Alan F. Guttmacher, "Discussion" of C. Tietze, "Statistical Contributions to the Study of Human Fertility," *Fertility and Sterility,* Vol. VII, No. 1, January-February 1956, p. 95.

[19] Dorothy G. Wiehl, Katharine Berry, and Winslow T. Tompkins, "Complications of Pregnancy among Prenatal Patients Reporting Previous Nervous Illness," in Benjamin Passamanick (ed.), *Epidemiology of Mental Disorders,* American Association for the Advancement of Science, Washington, 1959, pp. 95-118.

[20] Lewis M. Terman and Melita H. Oden, *The Gifted Group at Mid-Life,* Stanford University Press, Palo Alto, 1959, pp. 132-142.

riages than among those who remain with their husbands. The higher proportion of childless women among nonwhites than among whites is partially explained by the fact that white women are married for an average of two-thirds of their childbearing years, whereas nonwhite women on the average are married for only about half of their potentially fecund age period. In all of these cases, the fertility consequences of length of marriage are modified by the operation of antecedent and intervening variables.

SOCIOECONOMIC CLASS

Socioeconomic class is particularly useful in explaining both contemporary and historical fertility differences. Amos Hawley suggests that there have been three phases in this relationship.[21] At first the classes have either identical fertility or possibly a direct correlation between status and natality. The second phase, beginning in the industrial nineteenth century, is distinguished by a curtailment of the birth rate in high status groups, producing an inverse pattern of fertility differentials. This transitional phase is now yielding in some Western countries to the final phase: direct correlation between birth rates and socioeconomic class. Passage from the second to the third phase takes place in the following manner: high status groups begin their fertility declines early and are the first to stabilize at their new minimums; declines in the lower status groups begin later but eventually stabilize at rates lower than those of the high status groups. Probably the chief explanation in all three periods is the diffusion of family planning from high through middle to low status groups.

Sweden was among the first countries to enter the third stage. In Stockholm during 1918-1930 the fertility of high income persons was well above that of middle and low income persons, who had approximately the same fertility levels. College-educated people had higher birth rates than high school graduates, while the latter were in turn more fertile than those who ceased their formal education with grade school. Occupation was shown to have little influence on fertility: when income was held constant, professional, commercial, and industrial workers had almost identical birth rates.[22]

The United States is now in the latter part of the second phase and is presumedly heading toward the Swedish pattern. Two bits of evidence support the contention that the nation will enter the third

---

[21] Amos H. Hawley, *Human Ecology*, The Ronald Press Co., New York, 1950, pp. 114-120.

[22] Karl A. Edin and Edward P. Hutchinson, *Studies of Differential Fertility in Sweden*, P. S. King and Son, London, 1935, pp. 61 and 78.

phase toward the end of the century. First, Sweden provides a model which the United States has often followed in the past. Second, present United States fertility by social class shows a "buttonhook" pattern: the inverse relation applies in general, but the upper two or three subgroups exhibit a direct correlation between status and natality rates. There appears to be a filtering down from upper to lower classes of birth control knowledge and willingness to deliberately limit fertility. Also, class differentials are influenced by other variables. Two large groups whose birth rates exceed the national average are the Catholics and Negroes, both of which are predominantly lower-class. However, both of these groups, especially the former, are showing a tendency to rise in the socioeconomic scale. If they come to be distributed throughout the class hierarchy in the same proportions as the total population, socioeconomic differentials may change. On the other hand, Negroes and Catholics are likely to alter their reproductive practices somewhat as they rise in status.

UPWARD MOBILITY

Some biologistic theorists have argued that persons occupying high levels of society tend to lose their power to produce children, becoming sterile or at least subfecund. A much more plausible explanation than these "natural laws" is the theory put forth by R. A. Fisher: since persons having few children are more apt to be successful in climbing the social ladder, the upper classes come to contain a disproportionately large share of subfecund persons.[23] With wide acceptance of birth control, this interpretation has now been modified to include the deliberately small families as well as the physiologically limited ones.

In our modern individualized society, recognition of the advantages of traveling with a minimum of economic and emotional baggage is obvious. Investment of income in Pablum, baby shoes, and orthodentistry rarely helps one climb the social ladder—a contention which research on fertility of upward, downward, and nonmobile people has borne out. For example, a study of Philadelphia Main Line families reveals that parents who achieved their socioeconomic status had smaller families on the average than those whose class positions were ascribed.[24] The hypothesis that upward mobile persons tend to limit family size was also supported by a sample survey of 3,000 Frenchmen, which found the proportion of small families to be highest among upward mobile men, lowest among the downward mobile, and intermediate in families

---

[23] Ronald A. Fisher, *The Genetical Theory of Natural Selection*, Dover Publications, New York, 1958, p. 252.

[24] E. Digby Baltzell, *Philadelphia Gentlemen*, The Free Press, Glencoe, 1958, pp. 159-162.

maintaining a consistent status level. Restricted fertility families certainly contain the greatest proportion of persons who have risen socially,[25] and one suspects that fear of loss of status may be the primary motive behind this voluntary curtailment. Paradoxically, the largest families are frequently found in the very highest and the very lowest social classes. To the two extremes of the financial hierarchy— the rich and the very poor—additional children may not be regarded as a threat to status: among the rich, children do not prevent securing other desired items on which status rests, and the lowest classes can hardly drop to a lower position. In intermediate status groups, however, a large family may eventuate in lower standing; "accordingly it is among these classes that we find the birth rate most likely to be curtailed in cultures where effective methods of birth control are known and available."[26] On the other hand, in those communities where social status is tied to large families, the upward mobility motive may encourage a high birth rate.

A random sample of men listed in *Who's Who in America* for 1956-1957 showed that each man averaged about two children. When broken down into five-year groups according to date of birth, the eminent men showed a remarkably stable level of fertility, contrasting sharply with the long-term decline in general fertility over the same period. Thus the selection against prominent people disappeared as the general populace lowered their fertility to approximately the same level as the *Who's Who* members.[27]

RACE AND NATIVITY

In the United States, nonwhite persons consistently evince higher fertility than whites. Take as an indicator the number of children born to women ever married as reported in the 1960 Census. Among white women aged 15 years or older, 16 per cent were childless, 19 per cent had one child, 25 per cent two children, 17 per cent three, 10 per cent four, 8 per cent five or six, and 5 per cent seven or more; the comparable nonwhite distribution was 21, 19, 16, 12, 9, 11, and 12 per cent.[28] From this and other evidence we know that nonwhites have

---

[25] Marcel Bresard, "Mobilité sociale et dimension de la famille," *Population*, Vol. V, No. 3, July-September 1950, p. 563.

[26] George A. Lundberg, Clarence C. Schrag, and Otto N. Larsen, *Sociology*, Harper and Brothers, New York, 1958, pp. 115-116.

[27] Dudley Kirk, "Fertility of a Gifted Group," in Milbank Memorial Fund, *The Nature and Transmission of the Genetic and Cultural Characteristics of Human Populations*, New York, 1957, pp. 78-98.

[28] U. S. Bureau of the Census, *U. S. Census of Population: 1960*, "Detailed Characteristics: United States Summary," PC(1)-1D, Government Printing Office, Washington, 1963, p. 480.

relatively high proportions of childless as well as of high parity women.

The Negro birth rate appears always to have been higher than that of whites. The number of children under five years of age per 1,000 women aged 20-44 in 1850 was 892 among whites and 1,087 among Negroes; by 1950 this child-woman ratio had declined to 587 among whites and 706 among Negroes.[29] Negro fertility after the Civil War substantially exceeded that of the whites, but the differential has narrowed through time because of the more rapid decline of the Negro birth rate. These racial differentials in fertility are largely explained by differences in social and cultural environment.[30]

All other nonwhites also exhibit higher fertility than whites. But fertility rates by color appear likely to continue to converge. Foreign-born women in the nineteenth century were far more fertile than native-born women of comparable age and urbanization. Now, however, there is no observable difference between immigrants and natives.

RELIGION

Religious fertility differentials are world-wide. Mohammedans, Hindus, Confucianists, and Buddhists all have high birth rates. Indeed, Mohammed advised orthodox Moslems to "marry a woman who holds her husband extremely dear, and who is richly fruitful." However, it is difficult to be sure how much of the high fertility can be ascribed to religion *per se*. We do know that religious bodies differ in the values placed on large families and on sons in particular, and that prohibition of family planning is part of the dogma of some religions, one of the most unequivocal stands being the Roman Catholic opposition to certain means of birth control.

But since the United States decennial Census does not include a question on religion, information on this point is confined to what is gathered in Federal and private sample surveys. A study conducted by Princeton University demographers, however, did find religion to be the attribute of greatest single importance among the social and psychological determinants of fertility.[31] In this same study, the number of children desired by American wives varied as follows: Jews, 2.8; Protestants, 3.0; Catholics, 3.6; and mixed Protestant-Catholic marriages, 3.3. Occupational differences observed were negligible, ranging from 3.1

---

[29] Grabill, Kiser, and Whelpton, *The Fertility of American Women, op. cit.*, p. 14.
[30] Okun, *Birth Rates, op. cit.*, p. 16.
[31] Charles F. Westoff, "The 'Family Growth in Metropolitan America' Study: A Progress Report," in Clyde V. Kiser (ed.), *Research in Family Planning*, Princeton University Press, Princeton, 1962, p. 188.

to 3.4, but white-collar Catholics expressed a desire for larger families than did blue-collar Catholics.[32]

In the Current Population Survey of March 1957, which did obtain fertility rates by religion,[33] for Catholics, children ever born per 1,000 married women 45 years old and over amounted to 3,056; for Protestants, 2,753; and for Jews, 2,218. When rates were computed for the younger ages (under 45), however, the Protestant-Catholic differential was negligible: Catholics, 2,210; Protestants, 2,206. Explanation of this discrepancy may lie in a formerly meaningful difference between Catholic and Protestant fertility behavior; yet recent studies show married Catholic women in their twenties and thirties to have substantially the same fertility as married Protestant women of the same age. Mixed Catholic-Protestant marriages are not intermediate in fertility between those purely Catholic or purely Protestant; a sample survey conducted in Indianapolis reported such mixed marriages to have a 10 per cent lower fertility than Protestant couples.[34] The still lower rates of Jews may be explained by their concentration in cities, their higher occupational standing, their higher educational achievement, and their liberal attitudes toward contraception. In the C.P.S. 1957 study, four Protestant denominations were large enough to warrant computation of children ever born per 1,000 married women aged 15-44. The results were: Presbyterians, 1,922; Lutherans, 1,967; Methodists, 2,115; Baptists, 2,381; others, 2,234. Among older women (45 or more) the rates were: Presbyterians, 2,188; Lutherans, 2,382; Methodists, 2,638; Baptists, 3,275; others, 2,702.[35] Remember that many Baptists are Negroes.

Use of birth control varies according to religious affiliation, with the religion of the wife being more determinative than that of the husband. Interviews of a national sample of married white women aged 18 to 39 in 1955 showed the percentage of couples who had ever used birth control to be: both spouses Protestant, 75 per cent; both Catholic, 57 per cent; both Jewish, 86 per cent; wife Protestant, husband Catholic, 68 per cent; wife Catholic, husband Protestant, 55 per cent; all others, 74 per cent. If allegations of intention to use birth control in the future are also included, these percentages rise from 7 to 11 per cent.[36]

---

[32] Charles F. Westoff, Robert G. Potter, Jr., Philip C. Sagi, and Elliot G. Mishler, *Family Growth in Metropolitan America*, Princeton University Press, Princeton, 1961, pp. 185-187.

[33] U. S. Bureau of the Census, *Statistical Abstract of the United States*, Government Printing Office, Washington, 1958, p. 41.

[34] P. K. Whelpton, Clyde V. Kiser, *et al.*, *Social and Psychological Factors Affecting Fertility*, Milbank Memorial Fund, New York, 1943-1958, Vol. I, p. 7.

[35] U. S. Bureau of the Census, *Statistical Abstract of the United States, op. cit.*, p. 41.

[36] Freedman, Whelpton, and Campbell, *Family Planning, op. cit.*, p. 105.

Frequency of church attendance is also relevant. Catholics who seldom or never attend church are more likely to use birth control than are other Catholics. This relation is reversed among Protestants: frequency of church attendance is positively correlated with the proportion of users.[37] The explanation for this appears to be that family planning is discussed less often in Protestant churches, and when it is mentioned, ministers are apt to express favorable attitudes toward birth limitation. Catholics also have a higher proportion of "accidents," that is, pregnancies that occur despite deliberate inhibitory efforts. "Jews begin contraception earlier, use the effective methods, have the longest birth intervals and report the fewest unplanned pregnancies. Catholics are at the opposite end of this pattern and Protestants intermediate."[38]

Catholic-Protestant differences in incidence of use of family limitation methods are not explained away by differences in income, occupation, education, or type of community of present or previous residence. As one study notes:

> Catholics, like Protestants, are more likely to be users as economic status or educational status rises, but the religious differentials persist at each income and educational level. These results contradict the theory that Catholic-Protestant differences in resort to family limitation methods are simply a temporary result of differences in economic status or education, and that they will diminish as the two groups become more alike in these characteristics. Indeed, the differential between the proportion of Catholics and Protestants who try to control conception increases substantially as the amount of schooling goes up.[39]

The traditional Catholic position favoring large families is found more frequently among the better educated.[40] Religious education exerts "a strong influence both on the number of children desired by Catholics as well as on the success of their fertility-planning and the length of time taken to have two children. In general, Catholics educated in secular schools and colleges behave more like Protestants in their fertility behavior than they do like Catholics with religious education."[41] Internalization of dogma appears to be the explanatory variable; parochial education reinforces the position of the Church. "For Catholics, some of the factors affecting fertility appear to be reducible to the

---

[37] Ibid., pp. 107-108.

[38] Westoff, "A Progress Report," in Kiser, Family Planning, op. cit., p. 187.

[39] Freedman, Whelpton, and Campbell, Family Planning, op. cit., p. 109.

[40] Arthur Campbell, "Socio-economic Correlates of Fertility and Fertility Expectations in a Cross-Section of White Married Couples in the United States in 1955," in Milbank Memorial Fund, Thirty Years of Research in Human Fertility: Retrospect and Prospect, New York, 1959, p. 110.

[41] Westoff et al., Family Growth in Metropolitan America, op. cit., p. 211.

degree of adherence to Catholic doctrine."[42] Catholics of Irish background reveal the highest fertility pattern, whereas Catholics of Italian background reveal the lowest, a difference that is maintained when recency of immigration and social status are held constant.[43]

EDUCATION

Although little is known about European fertility differentials attributable to education, the information that is available indicates a higher than average fertility among the well-educated. This pattern has been observable for some years in England and Wales and in Sweden, and has recently become evident in the Netherlands.

Age-specific fertility rates for the United States show particularly sharp differences according to education of the woman. Number of children ever born per married woman aged 45-49 in 1950 varied from 1.4 among college graduates to 3.0 among wives having only an elementary education, with consistent intermediate gradations.[44] This inverse relation, however, is decreasing in magnitude; within the post-high school category, some studies find a direct relation between education and family size. Similar patterns prevail regarding the correlation between family size and the husband's level of education.

These differentials appear to be deliberately induced. The higher the educational level of husband or wife or both, the greater is the probability they are using birth control, the earlier in their marriage they began using it, and the closer the actual family size agrees with their desired family size. Proportions of use are the following: both husband and wife attended college, 86 per cent; one spouse college, one high school, 79 per cent; both high school graduates, 76 per cent; both attended high school, one graduated, 72 per cent; both attended, neither graduated, 63 per cent; one grade school, the other more, 63 per cent; and both grade school, 45 per cent. The wife's education considered alone has a greater influence than does the husband's taken alone.[45]

OCCUPATION AND INCOME

Since occupation and income are components of socioeconomic status, it should not come as a surprise that their relation to fertility in the United States is generally inverse, but with some qualifications. Specifically, fertility differentials by occupation of husband and family income are narrowing. Also, the inverse correlation is not perfect. From

---

[42] *Ibid.*, p. 236.

[43] *Ibid.*, pp. 202-211.

[44] Grabill, Kiser, and Whelpton, *The Fertility of American Women, op. cit.*, p. 205.

[45] Freedman, Whelpton, and Campbell, *Family Planning, op. cit.*, pp. 115-116.

lowest to highest fertility, occupations are ranged as follows: professional, clerical, proprietors, service, craftsmen, operatives, and laborers (the usual rank order in socioeconomic status is: professional, proprietors, clerical, craftsmen, operatives, service, and laborers).

Income of husband relates inversely to fertility: the higher the income, the lower the fertility. This correlation is mild among high income groups and strong for low income groups. Thus married women aged 45 years and over and living with their husbands in 1957 had consistently larger numbers of offspring as the income of husband decreased: incomes under $1,000, 3.8 children ever born; $1,000–1,999, 3.4 children; $2,000–2,999, 3.0 children; $3,000–3,999, 2.8 children; $4,000–4,999, 2.4 children; $5,000–6,999, 2.3 children; and more than $7,000, 2.1 children.[46]

For many years, an inverse relation between income and fertility apparently characterized Western urban-industrial cultures.[47] Demographers are uncertain, however, whether the differential by income is increasing or decreasing, as available evidence is inconsistent.

Broad associations do exist in contemporary United States between the birth rate and occupation and income considered together or separately, but the negative correlation between occupational rank and fertility is much more consistent than that between wealth and fertility. The negative association usually applies in urban communities only below the highest two or three income groups, the highest groups having somewhat more children than those immediately below them but failing to match the fertility levels of groups near the bottom of the income scale. The relation between income and fertility is more fruitfully analyzed when socioeconomic status is held constant. Among persons of similar social class and occupation, the more prosperous families are apt to have greater levels of natality than those with moderate or low incomes.

A substantial majority of United States couples in all income groups use birth control, the size of this majority increasing with the husband's income. Occupationally, the proportion of couples who are users increases with increasing status: lower blue collar (unskilled and semiskilled), upper blue collar (skilled and foremen), lower white collar (clerical and sales), and upper white collar (proprietors and professional). Also, the higher the rank, the earlier the couple begin to plan their family and the more efficient they are (having fewer unwanted

[46] U. S. Bureau of the Census, *Statistical Abstract of the United States: 1961*, Government Printing Office, Washington, 1961, p. 53.

[47] Arthur Newsholme and T. H. C. Stevenson, "The Decline of Human Fertility in the United Kingdom and Other Countries as Shown by Corrected Birth Rates," *Journal of the Royal Statistical Society*, Vol. LXIX, Part I, 1906, pp. 66-68.

pregnancies). Finally, neither occupation nor income has as great a relation to birth control as do education and religion.[48]

COMMUNITY OF RESIDENCE

Along with social class, residence (rural or urban) exerts the most potent influence on fertility variations. After the industrial revolution urbanization of the Western world was a primary force in lowering fertility, but urban-rural birth differentials were observed as long ago as 1760 in Sweden.[49] Rural inhabitants of other European countries have had higher levels of fertility than city residents for at least a century, a difference which has become more pronounced since 1900.

Urban-rural natality differentials probably existed in Anglo-America even in Colonial times. As early as 1703 fertility was appreciably lower in urban Manhattan Island than in the rest of the New York colony (which was almost entirely rural)[50]—a fact noted by Benjamin Franklin. But although today rural fertility still remains higher than urban, the differential has been narrowing since 1940. The higher rural rates are augmented by a greater tendency of rural women to marry and their practice of marrying younger.

Fertility among urban women of childbearing age is inversely correlated with size of city, although an apparent exception is the central city-suburb contrast: in suburban areas fertility is higher than inside the incorporation lines of the dominant city. It must be understood, however, that the entire metropolitan area tends to function as a single socioeconomic entity. Boundary placement is not very important inside this area, and the use of political limits as a basis for sociological or demographic analysis can lead to disastrous oversimplification. Generally, urban sociologists and demographers treat suburbs as a part of the functional metropolitan unit rather than as separate communities. In this light, central city-suburb differentials are seen as internal variations and not as inter-city contrasts.

The relation between size of community of residence and tendency to use birth limitation methods is apparently declining. The highest proportion of users is in suburbs of metropolitan cities (79 per cent), the smallest percentage in farm areas (62 per cent).[51] Dulling of the lines separating urban and rural Americans is producing a more uniform urbanized society in which most people, whether they live in a

[48] Freedman, Whelpton, and Campbell, *Family Planning, op. cit.*, pp. 122, 133-134, and 128.

[49] Abram J. Jaffe, "Urbanization and Fertility," *American Journal of Sociology*, Vol. XLVIII, No. 1, July 1942, p. 50.

[50] Grabill, Kiser, and Whelpton, *The Fertility of American Women, op. cit.*, p. 12.

[51] Freedman, Whelpton, and Campbell, *Family Planning, op. cit.*, p. 148.

metropolis or on a farm, are subjected to the same sorts of environmental pleasures and pressures. When this process is complete—that is, when urbanization of place no longer has a significant influence on the urban-ness of the resident—fertility rates probably will not differ systematically in response to degree of urbanization.

Regionally, birth rates in the United States are highest in the southern and Rocky Mountain areas and lowest in the Northeast. Most of this difference stems from the fact that the proportion of rural residents is high in the South, whereas people in the Northeast are largely urban. Southern fertility is also raised by the large proportion of Negroes. States reporting the highest and lowest crude birth rates in 1962 were, respectively, Alaska (31.6) and Pennsylvania (20.0). Utah has a very low proportion of childless women and a high proportion of high-parity women.

LIFE PLANNING AND HOPE

Family planning and hence the birth rate appear to be related to a propensity to plan other aspects of one's life. Thus the Indianapolis study reported a relationship between the planning of personal affairs and fertility planning, mediated through the socioeconomic status of the couple.[52] The ability of working-class families to plan births seems to be hampered by their relative inability to project their lives into the future. Then too a prevailing attitude of *que sera, sera* may also be accompanied by ignorance of reproductive physiology. The reproductive outcome in the lower class generally is not controlled by the woman—and often the man does not really care.[53]

Ignorance of the biological misunderstandings and ineptitude for planning of lower class persons joined with a belief that the poor are always with us led Malthus to the muddled conclusion that poverty is desirable, for otherwise, he argued, fertility would be untrammeled.

> At the heart of his doctrine is the view that only suffering and the threat of still worse suffering could be relied upon to induce restraint in the masses. Yet there is now clear evidence that abysmal poverty induces more of the same, and not prudence. The poorest must live just for the day to survive. Only when the margins of income are above the minimum can foresight come into play. It was indeed the secure upper and middle classes of Europe's society and not the necessitous masses that started the trend toward reduced fertility. Not poverty and

---

[52] Ronald Freedman and P. K. Whelpton, "The Relationship of General Planning to Fertility Planning and Fertility Rates," in Whelpton and Kiser, *Social and Psychological Factors Affecting Fertility, op. cit.,* Part XII, p. 570.

[53] Lee Rainwater, *And the Poor Get Children,* Quadrangle Books, Chicago, 1960, pp. 33-40 and 93-95.

disease, but improved living conditions and rising aspirations motivated the trend toward birth regulation.[54]

Many writers have expressed the idea that where there is no hope there is no foresight.[55] Both William Godwin[56] and John Stuart Mill maintained that the poor were too hopelessly oppressed under the existing social order ever to practice prudence. Wrote Mill: "The preventive remedy seldom . . . consists in the unaided operation of prudential motives on a class wholly or mainly composed of laborers for hire, and looking forward to no other lot."[57] Samuel Johnson was more succinct: "A man is poor—he thinks, I cannot be worse, so I'll e'en take Peggy."[58]

---

[54] Frank W. Notestein, "Introduction" to Thomas Malthus, Julian Huxley, and Frederick Osborn, *Three Essays on Population*, New American Library, New York, 1960, pp. ix-x.

[55] See, for example, Adolphe Quételet, *Sur l'homme et le développement de ses facultés*, Brussels, 1836.

[56] William Godwin, *Thoughts Occasioned by the Perusal of Dr. Parr's Spital Sermon*, London, 1801.

[57] J. S. Mill, *Principles of Political Economy*, London, 1902, Book II, p. 213.

[58] James Boswell, *Life of Johnson*, London, 1791, Vol. II, p. 101.

10 ✖ Family Planning

Fecundity impairments are much less important determinants of population trends in modern industrial countries than are deliberate measures
for the control of family size. In the United States, "family limitation
is now almost universally approved and is practiced widely and effectively. . . . Although an important proportion of pregnancies come
earlier than desired, a majority of white couples in all social strata do
not have larger families than they want."[1] The proportion of couples
practicing birth control will probably increase in the future, bringing
about further declines in the number of very large families, closer
responsiveness of fertility to social and economic changes (and hence
increased sensitivity of the birth rate), and perhaps less variation in the
marriage rate, as couples will not postpone marriage until they can
afford children but postpone pregnancy instead. "The attraction of the
idea that 'two can live as cheaply as one' is enhanced if the couple is
confident that the numbers will not quickly grow to three or four."[2]

At any rate, Americans are becoming remarkably uniform in their
preferences regarding family size. Lack of historical research hampers
us in knowing for certain whether traditional fertility differentials resulted from differences in wishes of the parents or simply differential
knowledge of how to effectuate their wishes. But nonetheless it appears
safe to infer that all major divisions of the United States population
are heading toward adoption of a common set of values concerning
ideal family size—specifically, the two- to four-child family. This con-

---

[1] Ronald Freedman, Pascal K. Whelpton, and Arthur A. Campbell, *Family Planning, Sterility, and Population Growth*, McGraw-Hill Book Co., New York, 1959, p.
401.
[2] *Ibid.*, p. 402.

sensus plus the almost total rejection of childlessness by American couples and their vigorous disavowal of the one-child family may indicate a resurgence of family values—a reversal of the century-long decline in importance of the family in comparison with other social institutions, which may have been responsible in part for the secular drop in the birth rate.

It should be remembered, of course, that fertility planning may be used to reach this two- to four-child goal as well as to avoid exceeding it. Planned parenthood is not necessarily directed toward curtailing fertility, although that is the most common objective. Birth control may operate either to promote or to retard the birth rate.

Three Aspects of Family Planning

We have just seen in the preceding chapter that different groups of people have different reproductive practices. Changes in socioeconomic fertility differentials were explained through a version of the culture lag hypothesis: high status groups curtail their birth rates first, leading the way in a filtering-down process of successive adoption of the "new balance" fertility habits by the middle class and, finally, by the lower class.

To give thorough answers to the question of why these people have smaller families requires consideration of three dimensions or levels: the concept of individual voluntary limitation of family size, the motive for desiring fewer children, and the techniques of effectuating birth control. Thus family planning has three facets: ideological (concerned with ethics and religion), motivational (concerned with social influences on behavior), and technical (concerned with methods of procedure). Questions asked are: should this end exist? should it be my policy for action? and what means can I use to attain the end?

IDEOLOGICAL DIMENSION

The ideological dimension turns about the recognition and acknowledgment of the legitimacy of planned parenthood. People who respond to the issue in this context address themselves to the question: should anyone deliberately limit the number of his children? The question here is one of belief in certain ends and is closely related to the individual's religious tenets. In short, this is a theological matter concerning moral lawfulness.

The Roman Catholic position was stated by Pope Pius XI in the following words: "Any use whatsoever of matrimony exercised in such a way that the act is deliberately frustrated in its natural power to generate life is an offense against the law of God and of nature, and those who indulge in such are branded with the guilt of a grave sin."[3] And, referring to the Church-sanctioned "rhythm" method of birth control, one Catholic priest has stated:

> The Church upholds and supports the ideal of a large family in every nation, and calls upon her apostolic forces to do the same. One who would advocate the practice of rhythm to a whole nation, however, would tend to destroy the ideal of a large family for members of that nation. . . . The Church speaks of the Christian virtue of raising a numerous progeny for the love of God, the advocate of rhythm proposes an opposite ideal of having few children. To the author it appears that the ideal of the Church, and the ideal of promoters of rhythm on a national scale for the sake of the national economy, are fundamentally irreconcilable.[4]

Indeed, opposition to birth limitation, whether by Catholics or Protestants, is almost entirely on religious grounds. Some Protestants, usually Fundamentalists, believe that interference with the processes of conception and parturition constitutes opposition to the Will of God. Thus one southern rural wife with a permanently disabled husband living in utter destitution rejected contraception (though saying she already had more children than she wanted): "The Good Lord put women here to raise younguns and they oughten to interfere with His business."[5] Some believe that God creates children; the act of coitus is enabling only. "Propagation," wrote Martin Luther, "is not in our will and power. . . . Creation is of God alone." Therefore anyone who fails to have intercourse is not permitting God to exercise His will. However, one can disregard God's will under economic stress: "If people can afford them, they should have as many as God wills them"; or one can hope that God agrees with one's personal desires: "I just hope God doesn't want us to have any more."[6]

We can identify at least five possibilities regarding birth control. First, there are people in the world (though rare in modern countries) who have never heard or thought of birth control. Second, there are those who can conceive of the possibility of family planning but consider its use improper for anyone under any circumstances. Third, some persons believe natality planning suitable for certain individuals but reject it for others (often themselves). Fourth, there are those who consider planning to be desirable both for themselves and for others.

---

[3] Pope Pius XI, Encyclical *Casti Connubii* (On Christian Marriage), The Vatican, Rome, December 30, 1930, p. 17.

[4] Rev. Anthony Zimmerman, *"Overpopulation,"* The Catholic University of America Press, Washington, 1957, p. 102.

[5] Freedman, Whelpton, and Campbell, *Family Planning, op. cit.*, p. 77.

[6] A Catholic wife, quoted *ibid.*, p. 157.

And finally, there are those who believe that failure to plan one's fertility is an irresponsible and immoral act.

Adherents of the fifth stand reason from two premises: that people should be held accountable for the foreseeable consequences of their voluntary actions, and that bringing children into the world is ordinarily a voluntary act of the parents. From these assumptions flows the conclusion that parents are responsible for the offspring they produce. In this view, a couple who have eight children when they can only support three are guilty of committing an irresponsible and socially reprehensible act. Insofar as the additional five children must be cared for by public welfare agencies, the parents are knowingly adding to the taxation burden of the more responsible members of their community. Needless to say, this censorial attitude is far from unanimous.

In the past the first position was common and the fifth attitude highly unusual, but in the last few years the proportion of persons taking each of these five stands has been changing. The passage of time brings fewer representatives of the first two views and more advocates of the last two. Indeed, if espousals of the fifth position become much more numerous, a bitter fight may be precipitated between advocates of the latter and adherents of the second and third views. The existing argument over birth control contrasts a permissive attitude with a restraining one. On the other hand, the possibly virulent conflict now threatening would differ by contrasting the two extreme positions: restraining (for example, against dissemination of birth control advice and supplies) and encouraging (for example, everyone must plan his family size).

MOTIVE DIMENSION

The motive facet in family planning is logically posterior to ideology: unless one's value system justifies voluntary birth limitation, his motivations are irrelevant. However, veneration of logic should not be carried to the point of naïvely ignoring man's ideological flexibility. It has often been observed that when people have a sufficiently strong motive for doing something an ideological rationale is likely to be discovered.

In the early nineteenth century, H. H. Gossen, a German economist of mathematical bent, formulated a principle that has come to be known as Gossen's law: "A person striving for the greatest amount of pleasant sensations stops the gratification of a desire where a continuation in its indulgence would mean less pleasure to him than the gratification of another need, which need he would have to renounce otherwise."[7]

---

[7] Quoted in Roderich von Ungern-Sternberg, *The Causes of the Decline in Birth-Rate within the European Sphere of Civilization*, Eugenics Research Association Monograph Series, No. 4, Cold Spring Harbor, 1931, pp. 33-34.

(This reasoning is cousin to the hedonistic calculus of English utili-
tarianists Jeremy Bentham and John Stuart Mill.) In 1909 Gossen's
proposition was modified by Munich professor Lujo Brentano to bear
directly on the fertility issue: "A person discontinues procreation of
children when an increase in the number of children gives him less
satisfaction than other pleasures of life which otherwise would not be
accessible to him."[8] Brentano's "theory of the competitive enjoyments"
was taken by Ungern-Sternberg as a valid though inconclusive explanation of the decline in fertility in modern Europe. But while this
provocative notion has the usual defects of single-factor theories (supplemented by an "economic man" assumption), it does contain a kernel
of truth. More recently Bernard Okun developed an economic theory
attempting to explain why birth rates declined in the United States
during 1870-1950 despite a rising level of income. Okun contends that
"the rise in income has resulted in a secular rise in the level of living
of children, making children relatively more expensive than commodities, and inducing couples to substitute commodities for children."[9]
In other words, children are being priced out of the market.

Following this line of reasoning, we also need to take into consideration the ideas of the good life and success. In an individualized, urbanized, industrialized society, children, or too many of them, are a liability.
In the spasmodically fierce competitive struggle for advancement, a man
with a large family is definitely at a disadvantage. Ironically, however,
the very openness and mobility inherent in the American class system
promotes overconformity to the rigid, stultifying norms of middle-class
morality.[10] The reasoning behind this quasiparadoxical thesis is that
when there is no chance to rise in the status hierarchy and people are
classified according to their heritage, there is little pressure to conform
in order to gain the esteem of one's fellows. On the other hand, in an
open class system where each person is evaluated according to the
extent to which he complies with the behavioral canons of his peers,
anyone wishing to improve or even to maintain his standing is impelled
to insure the approbation of others by conforming to their criteria of
acceptability. If these norms include having children, the success-
oriented individual will have them. But he should not have too many,

---

[8] Lujo Brentano, "Die Malthusische Lehre und die Bevölkerungsbewegung der
letzten Dezennien," *Abhandlungen der Bayrischen Akademie der Wissenschaften*,
Vol. XXIV, class iii, 1909, pp. 567-606; condensed version published as "The
Doctrines of Malthus and the Increase of Population During the Last Decades,"
Economic Journal, Vol. XX, September 1910, pp. 371-393.

[9] Bernard Okun, *Trends in Birth Rates in the United States Since 1870*, The Johns
Hopkins Press, Baltimore, 1958, p. 17.

[10] Robert S. Lynd, *Knowledge for What?*, Princeton University Press, Princeton,
1939, pp. 60-62 and 100-105.

because he would then have to spend more for housing, food, clothing, medical care, and other necessities. Thus the motivations of Americans toward family planning appear to be determined by a combination of economic considerations and social values.

Noneconomic reasons for wishing to avoid having children include fear of childbirth or of sexual intercourse or both, dislike of children, fear of loss of freedom to do as one wishes when one wishes, prevention of passing on to children an inheritable disease, spacing of wanted children, limiting ultimate size of the family, promoting marital adjustment, and preserving the health of the mother. Among medical ailments for which physicians may recommend avoidance of pregnancy are cardiac disease, pulmonary disease, renal or kidney disease, high blood pressure, diabetes, goiter, recent operation on reproductive organs, anemia, venereal disease, nervous or mental instability, and previous record of being unable to carry a pregnancy through to completion.

Values and habits concerning the planning of one's life and hope for the future are important for both the motivational and ideological dimensions of family planning. As the old saying puts it: "Children should not be brought forth into a world that is going to the dogs." (This folk dictum has been traced back to Roman times, and it is probable that the Romans borrowed it from the Greeks, to whom very likely it had previously diffused from a still earlier civilization.) In stark opposition is the naïvely pronatalist: "Life is so good and enjoyable that everyone should have a chance at it."

One ill-regarded motive is the desire to have licentious intercourse before marriage and outside of marriage without siring illegitimate children. It is widely held that without the restraining effect of dread of having a baby out of wedlock, men and women would run wild and debauch morality by promiscuous libertinism. Against this contention is the anti-Calvinist attitude that people have extramarital relations anyway, and why make their innocent children suffer. The first Swedish Population Commission considered that "birth control outside marriage, although to be discouraged, was more desirable than lack of control."[11]

CATHOLIC-PROTESTANT CONTROVERSY

When reading arguments for and against birth control, it is sometimes difficult to determine whether the writer is discussing the subject on the ideological, motivational, or technical level. The classic dispute is that between Catholic clergy and laymen (not a unitary group) and

---

[11] W. D. Borrie, *Population Trends and Policies*, Australasian Publishing Co., Sydney, 1948, p. 194.

Protestants, Jews, atheists, and agnostics. Sometimes the Catholic source maintains that *any* limitation on fertility by *any* technique whatsoever is morally wrong; ordinarily, however, the disagreement concerns the choice of man-made versus natural methods. For instance, the World Council of Churches (a Protestant organization including 170 church groups in 50 countries) took the position in 1959 that "there appears to be no moral distinction between the means now known and practiced, by the use whether of estimated periods of infertility, or of artificial barriers to the meeting of sperm and ovum—or, indeed, of drugs which would, if made effective and safe, inhibit or control ovulation in a calculable way. It remains that the means employed be acceptable to both husband and wife in Christian conscience, and that, on the best evidence available, they do neither physical nor emotional harm."[12] Father William J. Gibbons, a Fordham sociologist and demographer, is perhaps the outstanding spokesman for the Catholic viewpoint in the United States:

> The Church's objection to artificial birth control is based on the fact that the sexual faculty of man is ordered to reproduction. This does not mean that conception and a pregnancy have to result from intercourse—in the aged or infertile it cannot. But it does mean that one may not place a positive block of any kind—mechanical, chemical, or physical—that would make it impossible for nature to follow its course. The Church's objection to this is that the integrity of the individual sex act is thereby violated. Man has attempted to go contrary to the processes of nature—unlike periodic continence, in which man is following nature and is not introducing any block of his own to conception.
>
> Within marriage itself, it's obvious also that God did not give man sex as a plaything, that it has a purpose and this is related to continuing the race.[13]

The Protestant position, according to one report issued by a conference of leading clergymen, is stated thusly:

> It must be emphasized once again that family planning ought to be the result of thoughtful and prayerful Christian decision. Where it is, Christian husbands and wives need feel no hesitation in offering their decision humbly to God and following it with a clear conscience. The *means* of family planning are in large measure matters of clinical and

---

[12] Special Study Group of the World Council of Churches, "Responsible Parenthood and the Population Problem," *The Ecumenical Review*, Vol. XII, No. 1, October 1959, p. 7.

[13] Rev. William J. Gibbons, S.J., interview reported in "The Birth Control Issue— Why Catholics Reject 'Artificial Birth Control,' " *U. S. News and World Report*, December 29, 1959.

esthetic choice, subject to the requirement that they be admissible to the Christian conscience. Scientific studies can rightly help, and do, in assessing the effects and the usefulness of any particular means; and Christians have every right to use the gifts of science for proper ends.[14]

Catholics sometimes express a willingness to tolerate sexual inter-course not intended for procreation, especially if the aim is the relief of frustration rather than pleasurable lust. Writes Father Gibbons: "The fostering of mutual love, the rendering of the marriage debt, the avoidance of unchastity, are reasonable motives for intercourse."[15] The Church also recognizes man's sexual drive. "In matrimony as well as in the use of the matrimonial rights there are also secondary ends, such as mutual aid, the cultivating of mutual love, and the quieting of con-cupiscence which husband and wife are not forbidden to consider so long as they are subordinated to the primary end and so long as the intrinsic nature of the act is preserved."[16]

The disagreement would probably not be half so heated were it not for resentment by Protestants and others of what they consider the intolerable Catholic claim of being the sole possessor of the universal truth on this subject. Reverend Francis J. Connell, Professor of Moral Theology at the Catholic University of America, writes: "Prohibition to practice contraception is not regarded by the Catholic Church as one of its own laws, binding only Catholics. The Church proclaims this pro-hibition as a law of God, which binds all human beings, whether they be members of the Catholic Church or not." Monsignor George A. Kelly adds: "Many persons think that contraception is a sin only for Catholics. Contraception is a sin for everyone."[17]

EFFECTUATION AND RESULTS

About 60 per cent of United States couples expect to have the number of children they want. About 70 per cent use some means to control their fertility, and another 10 per cent plan to do so in the future. Moreover, about 30 per cent of Catholic couples acknowledge using techniques not approved by the Church. An anomaly arises when one considers that although four-fifths of the couples either have practiced

---

[14] Committee of the Lambeth Conference of the Bishops of the Anglican Com-munion, 1958, quoted in Richard M. Fagley, *The Population Explosion and Christian Responsibility*, Oxford University Press, New York, 1960, Appendix.

[15] Rev. William J. Gibbons, S.J., "The Catholic Value System in Relation to Human Fertility," in George F. Mair (ed.), *Studies in Population*, Princeton Univer-sity Press, Princeton, 1949, pp. 108-134.

[16] Pope Pius XI, Encyclical *Casti Connubii, op. cit.,* p. 18.

[17] George A. Kelly, *Birth Control and Catholics,* Doubleday and Co., New York, 1963, p. 81.

or intend to use some method of fertility restriction, less than two-thirds of the women express unqualified approval and another 12 per cent qualified approval of these procedures.[18] Apparently, some people either use the methods against their better judgment or else are unwilling to state their approval to an interviewer.

Nonetheless, a filtering-down process in this regard is at work in both Britain and the United States. Thus among British women married before 1920, upper-class wives used birth control much more frequently than did lower-class wives; while among women married after 1920, little difference obtained between classes in tendency to use birth control. Also, a larger percentage of upper-class women used the most effective techniques. The percentage of women using any method at any time in their married lives changed as follows: those married before 1910, 15 per cent; married 1910-1919, 40 per cent; 1920-1924, 58 per cent; 1925-1929, 61 per cent; 1930-1934, 63 per cent; and 1935-1939, 66 per cent.[19] Although direct documentation for the United States is not available, indirect evidence indicates a similar trend. Further, among couples who are least successful in applying family planning, fertility is inversely related to socioeconomic status, whereas among the more successful family planners, fertility is directly related to status.[20] Knowledge of this sort raises the possibility that if and when family planning becomes universally practiced, fertility may be positively correlated with socioeconomic status and also with its various components. Or, alternatively, differential fertility may disappear altogether.

Planned families are not inevitably small families. Couples who plan for a small number of children at one time may plan for a large number at another. Thus the possibility of a baby boom is implicit in the increased use of birth control, as family planning introduces the opportunity to alter the timing as well as the quantity of births. Consequently changes in the spacing of children may produce large temporary fluctuations in annual birth rates, even though the average size of completed families remains stable. For a hypothetical illustration of what might happen, let us assume that a prosperous period is followed by a depression and then by a return to prosperity. Suppose also that all couples plan successfully to have an eventual total of three children, but that the couples marrying during the depression postpone

---

[18] Freedman, Whelpton, and Campbell, *Family Planning, op. cit.*, Chaps. 8, 6, and 5 *passim*.

[19] E. Lewis-Fanning, *Report on an Enquiry into Family Limitation and Its Influence on Human Fertility During the Past Fifty Years*, His Majesty's Stationery Office, London, 1949, pp. 7-10.

[20] P. K. Whelpton, Clyde V. Kiser, *et al.*, *Social and Psychological Factors Affecting Fertility*, Milbank Memorial Fund, New York, 1943-1958, Vol. II, Part 9.

having their children until prosperity returns, whereas those marrying in prosperous times have their children as soon as possible. The result would be violent short-run fluctuations in the birth rate: a sharp drop from the "normal" level to very low fertility during the depression, then an upsurge to very high rates while the babies postponed from the depression are born, and finally a return to "normal." The total number of children born and the average size of completed family would be about the same as if there had been even spacing of children throughout all three periods. "Such short-run trends have appeared at some times and places. To a major extent, our high annual birth rate during 1947-57 can be explained in this way as a change in the timing of births. Part of the bumper crop of babies during the war and early postwar years were children postponed by couples in the depression decade."[21]

Techniques of Birth Control

Although the usual connotation of birth control is that of deliberately limiting of the number of births, some techniques are directed toward increasing the birth rate. Among these present and prospective techniques are: artificial insemination (insertion of sperm into the vagina), artificial ovanation (insertion of ova in sterile women), germ-cell preservation (storage of frozen sperm), and artificial parthenogenesis (development of the ovum with chemicals or mechanical stimuli instead of sperm).

Misconceptions abound concerning reproductive processes. In the late nineteenth and early twentieth centuries, Drs. Capellmann, Ogino, and Knaus miscalculated the "safe" period of the menstrual cycle. In 1842 a French physician recommended that the government oblige all women to breast-feed their children for at least three years, on the false assumption that lactating women cannot conceive. In Finland fortune-tellers read melted tin to ascertain what part of the menstrual period was safe, and when they failed, the women sometimes sat on the top (hottest) shelf in the sauna to induce a miscarriage.

INFANTICIDE

Though not strictly a method of controlling births, infanticide does accomplish the same objective: it controls the number of children. In this case, the child is permitted to be born and then killed. Thus it is a death control method employed for birth control purposes. Often it is used by default after other methods have failed or because the parent has not used them.

[21] Freedman, Whelpton, and Campbell, *Family Planning, op. cit.,* pp. 7-8.

Infanticide is widespread throughout the world and is a standard topic in anthropological literature. Ethnological information is summarized by Warren S. Thompson:

> Infanticide was an almost universal custom from very early times and is still quite common in many parts of the world. Almost all the so-called primitive peoples regularly practice infanticide and have done so for ages. Many Australian tribes, many tribes of American Indians, and some of the African peoples belong to this group. Indeed, it is such a common practice that one notices its absence rather than its presence when reading the accounts of explorers and anthropologists. It appears that not infrequently the proportion of infants thus made away with reaches one-half or even more. Among peoples having a more complex social organization infanticide has not been so common, but it was an approved practice among the ancient Greeks of certain communities and certainly was not rare among other Mediterranean peoples in those days. In Europe it was not until well into the Middle Ages that infanticide came to be looked upon as a crime, and there is much evidence that it is by no means absent from the modern world.[22]

Many societies practicing infanticide do not treat it as a device to control population. In common with many other norms having unanticipated demographic consequences, it is often practiced for other culturally defined reasons: inauspicious configurations in the heavens, improper birth order, and various magico-religious mandates and portents. Cultural imperatives regarding fertility are in fact no more rationally demographic in their implications than are social norms dealing with mortality or migration.

ABSTENTION FROM INTERCOURSE

Perhaps the most obvious method of restraining fecundity is reduction in the frequency of intercourse. However, the extent of its use is unknown, and its effectiveness is partial—unless, of course, the frequency is reduced to zero. This is not to say that total abstinence has not been practiced with considerable efficiency by some couples, but for most the degree of self-control required is too great.

Ireland is the best contemporary example of abstinence—achieved in this instance through not marrying. According to the 1951 census, 31 per cent of the men and 26 per cent of the women of age 50 have never married. Average age at first marriage was 31 years for grooms and 27 for brides. Once married, however, the Irish have children at fairly rapid rates. Indeed, except for their habit of marrying late or not at all, their fertility undoubtedly would be quite high.

---

[22] Warren S. Thompson, *Population Problems*, McGraw-Hill Book Co., New York, 1953, pp. 10-11.

For the female, enforced abstinence has been exacted through the chastity belt with which key-carrying medieval husbands planning to be away from home constrained their wives from cohabiting—and, incidentally, from washing. Male abstinence is compelled by infibulation, the fastening of the prepuce over the glans penis with a stick, string, or wire (a practice used by the Greeks and Romans). In Aristophanes' bawdy comedy *Lysistrata* (411 B.C.), abstinence was also induced by the women who forced the end of a war by refusing all sexual relations with their warrior husbands until the men agreed to stop fighting.

Opposition to abstention has been voiced through the ancient and modern belief that regular sexual intercourse is necessary to the physical and moral health of the individual. This idea can be traced back to Hippocrates of Cos, who propounded the doctrine that if the womb is not frequently excited by semen, the blood moves upward in the body, creating shortness of breath and nervousness. Female neuroticism was therefore called hysteria, the disease of the uterus or *hystera*. Its cure is simple: have the patient maintain a satisfying sex life. J. M. Charcot was perhaps thinking of the same thing (though on psychological grounds) when he remarked to a colleague apropos of a female patient, "C'est toujours la chose sexuelle." In those cultures and subcultures that regard appetites for sex and for food as equally fundamental and requiring fulfillment, reduced frequency of intercourse represents a kind of starvation that will not be tolerated and that may even be considered immoral. To some people chastity is a sin against nature; to others it is a cause of serious emotional disturbances and social maladjustment.

THE RHYTHM METHOD

Although the "safe" period was rather extensively used in the years between the two World Wars, its popularity of late is decreasing. Some of this decrease may be due to the conflicting policy statements made by different Catholic authorities plus a gradual recognition that the Pope supported this method only for unusually grave situations. Equivocal approval of periodic continence was affirmed, however, in the Reply of the Sacred Penitentiary in 1853:

> Question: The Bishop of Amiens, France, humbly requests of the Eminent Father of the Sacred Penitentiary the solution of the following difficulty: Certain married people among the faithful, relying on the opinion of learned physicians, are convinced that in each month there are some days on which conception cannot take place in a woman. Are those to be disturbed who do not use marriage except on those days, at least if they have legitimate reasons for refraining from the conjugal act?

Reply: The Sacred Penitentiary, having pondered the proposed case, replies to the Venerable Father in Christ, the Bishop of Amiens, that those mentioned in the petition should not be disturbed, so long as they do nothing to prevent conception.[23]

In 1934 Dr. Leo J. Latz published *The Rhythm* with ecclesiastical approval, but in 1951 Pope Pius XII issued a statement against birth control, including the rhythm method.[24] In fact, contrary to popular opinion, the rhythm method has never had enthusiastic Papal support. One Catholic theologian and professor wrote in 1957 that "papal teachings diametrically oppose the use of rhythm as a deliberate and direct means of lowering a national population growth," although it may in rare instances be used by a few families.[25] Also contrary to popular impression, dissent is possible; Catholic writers who have defended the use of the safe period to alleviate overpopulation include Reverend Stanislaus de Lestapis, S.J., Professor G. H. L. Zeegers, and Reverend William Gibbons, S.J.[26]

The rhythm system is based on body temperature and other guides to identification of the fertile and sterile days during the woman's menstrual cycle. She is supposed to avoid intercourse on the fertile days of each cycle. The technique is also used to promote fertility; in this case, the woman arranges the distribution of acts of coitus so that the maximum frequency falls during the fertile part of the cycle. Irregularities in ovulation, faulty menstrual arithmetic, and lack of sexual discipline weaken reliability.

INDUCED ABORTION

Feticide is a very effective birth control method and far more widely used than is generally realized. One scholar reported that in Berlin in 1929 there were 103 abortions for every 100 births; in Leningrad at the same time, another cited a ratio of 138 abortions to 100 confinements.[27] In France, the number of abortions is said to "greatly exceed the annual number of registered births."[28] Estimates for the United States in the 1960's range from 700,000 to 2,000,000 annually, despite the powerful opposition which has made this country one of the three

---

[23] Quoted in Freedman, Whelpton, and Campbell, *Family Planning, op. cit.*, p. 416.

[24] Pope Pius XII, "Address to the Italian Catholic Union of Midwives," *Acta Apostolicae Sedis*, The Vatican, Rome, Vol. XVIII, October 29, 1951.

[25] Zimmerman, "Overpopulation," *op. cit.*, p. 284 and Chap. IV.

[26] *Ibid.*, pp. 89-90.

[27] Frederick J. Taussig, *Abortion*, The C. V. Mosby Co., St. Louis, 1936, p. 366.

[28] United Nations Population Branch, *Survey of Legislation on Marriage, Divorce, and Related Topics Relevant to Population*, New York, 1956, p. 10.

nations (the other two are England and France) most stringently antipathetic to abortion. Every state in the union has anti-abortion laws. Abortion has been encouraged at times in Japan, the U.S.S.R., and Communist China. Scandinavian nations are permissive.

Abortions occur more often to married than unmarried women. Among wives, 17 per cent of all pregnancies end in induced abortion. And of the women who do have abortions, 74 per cent report no serious physical or psychological consequences.[29] Most abortions are performed on married women aged 20-34 who already have one or more children but who have not previously been aborted. The higher the parity, the higher the percentage of pregnancies terminating in abortions.[30]

In primitive communities abortion is widespread—so much so, in fact, as to have permitted the compilation of a full-sized book on the subject. Abortifacient techniques used are marvelously varied and sometimes uncomfortable even to read about.[31] Although voluntary interruption of pregnancy was sanctioned by law and practiced by the ancient Greeks and Romans, the Christians apparently accepted the old Jewish law forbidding abortion. Thomas Aquinas, striking a fine theological point, believed that the soul did not appear immediately following conception, but rather on the fortieth day of pregnancy for a male fetus and the eightieth day for females. Therefore, he reasoned, abortions induced before that time were not offenses against the moral law of God.

Among both Protestants and Catholics, the question of whether feticide is murder is a very delicate legal point. Pope Pius XI spoke of the "grave sin" of "taking the life of the offspring hidden in the mother's womb. . . . However much we may pity the mother whose health and even life is gravely imperiled in the performance of the duty allotted to her by nature, nevertheless what could ever be a sufficient reason for excusing in any way the direct murder of the innocent?"[32] French law contains the phrase *en ventre sa mère* (in its mother's womb) whereby the fetus is legally deemed alive. Some Catholic theologians consider contraception a worse crime than abortion because whereas feticide is only the murder of a human being, contraception involves prevention of both a human life *and* an eternal soul. After feticide, so runs the argument, the soul continues, but in the case of

[29] Paul H. Gebhard, Wardell B. Pomeroy, Clyde E. Martin, and Cornelia V. Christenson, *Pregnancy, Birth and Abortion*, Harper and Brothers, New York, 1958, pp. 137 and 205.
[30] Christopher Tietze, "Report on a Series of Illegal Abortions Induced by Physicians," in George F. Mair (ed.), *Studies in Population*, Princeton University Press, Princeton, 1949, p. 24.
[31] George Devereux, *A Study of Abortion in Primitive Societies*, Julian Press, New York, 1955.
[32] Pope Pius XI, Encyclical *Casti Connubii, op. cit.*, p. 19.

anticonception techniques, the soul is never created in the first place—a far more heinous sin.

Early Protestant ecclesiastical law held that the soul entered the body at the moment of quickening of the embryo, that is, the first time the woman felt movement in the uterus. (This ordinarily occurs in the fourth month, at which time a normal fetus is not yet viable.) English abortion laws of the nineteenth century reflected this religious norm: prior to 1803, abortion was punishable only after quickening; then in the statutes of 1803 and 1828 (the first laws on feticide) destruction of the embroyo after quickening was declared a capital offense, whereas the penalty for prequickening feticide was imprisonment, transportation, or whipping. In 1837 this distinction was abandoned—though British law did not stay the execution of a pregnant woman until the fourth month of pregnancy.[33] The supposition which ascribes to quickening the acquisition by the fetus of an independent life of its own remains a part of current American folklore.

Greater permissiveness toward abortion is recommended by small but ardent groups of reformers, partially on the basis that abortions take place anyway, and that having them performed by accredited physicians in hospitals would decrease deaths and injuries. The Abortion Law Reform Association, recently formed by a group of eminent Englishmen, proposes a law legalizing abortion by a registered medical practitioner for reason of preservation of life, physical or mental health, economic distress, serious likelihood of a gross congenital deformity or abnormality in the unborn child, pregnancy resulting from rape or incest, pregnancy occurring in a child below the age of consent, and pregnancy in a demented woman.

STERILIZATION

Removal of the ovaries or testes is a highly efficient method of preventing births, but some physicians claim that there may be undesirable aftereffects, particularly when the surgery is performed on a young patient. Before the discovery of the male hormone testosterone and the estrogen stilbestrol, males thus operated upon tended to become impotent, fatten, lose their beards, and have high voices; females suffered from reduced libido, fatness, facial hair, and emotional disturbances.

Severing the tubes through which the sperm or ova pass does not disrupt the glands and permits a normal sex life. Female operations require hospitalization for several days. The tying off or removing sections of the Fallopian tubes between the ovaries and the uterus is called salpingectomy. The discomfort of major surgery, the inconvenience of

---

[33] Gebhard et al., Pregnancy, Birth and Abortion, op. cit., p. 233.

convalescence, and the expense of both result in a general unwillingness to go through the Fallopian ligation unless done in conjunction with an operation or parturition. Cornual cautery is much quicker, but is less frequently successful; in this operation the tissues of the cornua (points at which the Fallopian tubes enter the uterus) are cauterized and healing causes closure.

For males, vasectomy is the severance or removal of a section of the vasa deferentia, the tubes which conduct seminal fluid from the testes to the urethra. Performed in a physician's office under local anesthesia in twenty or thirty minutes, this minor surgery is easy to undertake, not very costly, and about 98 per cent effective. Moreover, it has the further advantage that the vasa deferentia sometimes may be reunited, thus restoring fertility. Urologists report that the reversal operation (reanastomosis) is successful about one-half of the time.

Since one act of sterilization may last a lifetime, sterilization rates have a greater import than their magnitude might indicate at first glance. Thirty-two thousand cases of sterilization were reported in Japan in 1953; the actual number may be five or ten times larger. In the Indian states of Madras and Kerala, men who have at least three children and cannot support more may have a vasectomy performed at government expense. In 1952 Paul Hatt reported 16 per cent of Puerto Rican women to be sterilized.

Sterilization shares with abortion the property of being an ersatz for unsuccessful use of contraception, rhythm, or other methods. When the woman becomes pregnant, the couple may resort to abortion; if this happens repeatedly, they sterilize. Sterilizing operations, according to one demographer, appear to be more frequent among accident-prone couples than others.[34] This is one way of facing the risk period (usually close to twenty years in the United States) between attainment of desired family size and the onset of permanent sterility.

The strict position of the Catholic Church may indirectly encourage sterilization in Puerto Rico. "The embarrassment of recurring confession has been forcing more and more women to find a permanent solution. In increasing numbers, they are rolling many little sins, and a constant aggravation, into one big sin by turning to sterilization as a solution to their problem."[35] So too the Church may have contributed to awareness of *la operación*: "Ironically, it is, in part, the efforts on the part of the strongest moral opponent of birth control, the Roman

---

[34] Robert G. Potter, Jr., "Some Comments on the Evidence Pertaining to Family Limitation in the United States," *Population Studies*, Vol. XIV, No. 1, July 1960, pp. 40-54.

[35] Robert C. Cook, *Human Fertility*, William Sloane Associates, New York, 1951, p. 338.

Catholic Church, that seem to promote the popularity of sterilization. Pastoral letters denouncing its use were instrumental in spreading the knowledge about it."[36]

COITUS INTERRUPTUS

Withdrawal, or onanism, is the major form of male-controlled coitus. "And Onan knew that the seed should not be his; and it came to pass, when he went in unto his brother's wife, that he spilled it on the ground, lest that he should give seed to his brother" (Genesis, 28:9). Its origins dating back to man's early history, interruptus is still the most widely used birth control technique in the world. It requires no mechanical contrivances, no chemicals, no douching, and no money; it is always available, never lost, and easy to use. It has the disadvantage, however, of low reliability: the man's timing must not fail (the sperm count is particularly high in the first few drops of semen), and there is sometimes premature expulsion before the climactic spasm. This method has also been rejected on the grounds of presumed failure to provide complete emotional satisfaction in all cases; the resultant frustration is sometimes held to be a source of neuroticism.

Coitus reservatus, associated with the Oneida colony founded in 1841 in New York, requires even more forbearance. Called *Karezza* in Sanskrit and Hindu literature, this sophisticated technique may involve "as many as a dozen or twenty peaks of response which, while closely approaching the sexual climax, deliberately avoid what we should interpret as actual orgasm."[37] It is not a practical technique for most couples.

CONTRACEPTION

Anticonception methods may be grouped into three categories: those that use an appliance to prevent the sperm from reaching the ovum; those that use chemicals to inactivate the sperm; and those that use both. Traditional female appliances are tampons or vaginal plugs; the male device is the condom or sheath.

The condom, made of rubber or some membranous substance, is widespread and highly effective when properly used. It may have developed from the devices worn by ancient Egyptians to ward off insect bites and tropical diseases. Although condoms were probably in use

---

[36] Kurt W. Back, Reuben Hill, and J. Mayone Stycos, "Population Control in Puerto Rico: The Formal and Informal Framework," *Law and Contemporary Problems*, Vol. XXV, No. 3, Summer 1960, p. 572.

[37] Alfred C. Kinsey, Wardell B. Pomeroy, Clyde E. Martin, and Paul H. Gebhard, *Sexual Behavior in the Human Female*, W. B. Saunders Co., Philadelphia, 1953, p. 625.

some time earlier, the oldest extant description is by the Italian anatomist Gabriello Fallopius, whose 1564 treatise on "the French disease" (syphilis) advised men to "use a small linen cloth" as a safeguard against venereal disease. Madame de Sévigné wrote to her daughter in 1671 of a skin sheath which acts as an "armor against enjoyment, and a spider web against danger." Her contemporary, Casanova, wrote of "the English riding coat," a usage which survives in the current French phrase, *la capote anglaise*. In 1843 the invention of vulcanization of rubber by Hancock in England and Goodyear in the United States made possible mass production of condoms and lowered costs. The United States Food and Drug Administration has supervised quality of condoms since 1938, and the proportion free from defects has increased to about 997 out of 1,000. Domestic sales total about 600 million a year.

Women in numerous primitive societies have been known to place cloth, sponges, or leaves in the vagina to impede passage of semen. The modern occlusive diaphragm was invented in 1838 by Dr. Friedrich Adolph Wilde and perfected by Dr. Wilhelm P. J. Mensinga in 1881 for mass production in rubber form. The cervical cap, a small rubber, metal, or plastic cup, is fitted securely over the cervix (the mouth of the womb). The stem or wishbone pessary, another modern occlusive device, is a Y-shaped metal stem; inserted into the cervix, it holds a small cap over the opening to prevent entrance of the seminal fluid. Intrauterine or Grafenberg rings are small gold, silver, or nylon spirals placed in the uterine cavity; as the body moves, the spirals move about freely, supposedly preventing any fertilized ova from attaching themselves to the wall long enough to grow. All of these mechanical devices must be purchased, and most of them require fitting by a physician. Yet despite their high efficiency, the expense prevents widespread world use—with the notable exception of IUD's.

Spermicidal jellies, creams, and pastes are fairly effective. Less so are foam tablets, powders, and suppositories. Douches of plain water or a mild spermicidal solution have a long record of use and are inexpensive but relatively ineffective.

Greater security against failure is often obtained by using one of the chemical spermicides in conjunction with an occlusive appliance. One of the most common and the most effective preventive methods is the diaphragm and jelly combination. Recent sample surveys in the United States report this combination second in frequency of use after the condom, followed in order by rhythm, douche, and withdrawal.

It goes without saying, of course, that most of these methods demand that at least one of the partners be capable of forethought or deferment of sexual gratification long enough to apply the device or chemical. Even then, however, complexity and cost put many contraceptives out of reach of peasant-agricultural peoples. In highly literate countries, too, individuals of low education and mechanical competence have more than their share of "accidents."

CONTRAGESTION

Recently, medical research has turned toward contragestion or preventing growth after fertilization has occurred, a new approach which offers greater convenience than contraception. Instead of using mechanical or chemical materials every time intercourse takes place, contragestive methods need not be used until after a woman conceives. As soon as she missed a menstrual period, she would take a drug which prevents implantation of the embryo or which causes its absorption if already implanted. Intrauterine rings are contragestive in character.

Since the reproductive systems of both men and women are complex and delicate, many conditions and events must be properly ordered before reproduction is completed. Indeed, it is something of a miracle that children are born at all. Alterations and interruptions of seemingly minor magnitude can break the reproductive chain at numerous points —for example, too much or too little of a normally occurring substance, or a slowing down or speeding up of a physiological process. Malfunctioning of any one of a number of intricate neuro-endocrine mechanisms and hormonal balances may interrupt the processes of fertilization and embryonic development. The importance of the mores is shown in the fact that whereas scientists have developed and the public has accepted many substances designed for the deliberate stimulation or retardation of the digestive, circulatory, and nervous systems, the same thing is only now beginning to be attempted for the reproductive system.

BIRTH CONTROL PILLS

Increasing attention is being brought to bear on the development of a cheap, safe, reliable birth control pill, for obviously oral contraceptives are much more convenient than other techniques. But for an oral pill to be acceptable, it must be inexpensive; it must taste good, have an inoffensive odor, and be of a size that is comfortable to swallow; it must have minimal toxicity, irritation, and cumulative action; it must be demonstrably effective; it should work rapidly; it should permit a return to normal fertility after cessation of administration; and it must act without side-effects that disrupt the complex balanced systems of the body.

Steroid anti-ovulation tablets for women are now on the market, but prescriptions are necessary and prices remain high. Three such pills have been approved by the United States Food and Drug Administration for use as oral contraceptives. The usual dosage of twenty a month costs $3 to $6—cheaper than the price of rearing a child, but still expensive. Increased production and mass sales should lower the price considerably. Certainly the results so far would seem to be promising. Drs. Gregory Pincus and John Rock have conducted experiments reporting 96 to 99 per cent protection against pregnancy. Fertility is restored simply by discontinuance of the pill-taking. Moreover, subjects who took tablets for five years showed no dangerous aftereffects. Nausea and allied discomfort were present in about one-sixth of the women, apparently for the reason that since the pills' effectiveness is based on simulation of certain aspects of pregnancy, taking them did induce some of the same physico-emotional reactions. Pincus and his associates concluded that "the medication used is contraceptively effective; causes no significant abnormalities of the menstrual cycle; has no adverse effect on the reproductive tract and adnexae; has no physiologically adverse effects generally; has no adverse effect on the sex life of the subject; does not impair fertility after cessation of medication; may be used in a low dosage; and is acceptable to users, but to an extent that varies with motivation, economic situation, and other factors."[38]

Research is also proceeding on antipregnancy vaccines which temporarily immunize the wife against her husband's sperm through formation of antibodies. This response may occur spontaneously: certainly an antigen-antibody reaction seems to be responsible for infertility in some couples, even though neither spouse is otherwise sterile.

Oral drugs for men are also in the offing. One compound now being tested induces temporary sterility but not impotence. Two months of pill-taking are required to achieve sterility, after which a booster dose is necessary every few months. Suspension of dosage restores normal fertility. Another oral contraceptive, a diamine compound costing less than a dollar for a month's supply, halts production of sperm as long as the drug is used. Sex drive is unaffected, and normal fecundity restored in five to twelve weeks after ceasing medication. The diamines produce a severe reaction, however, when alcohol is imbibed. Neither drug is yet available commercially.

Underdeveloped countries lacking facilities requisite to other birth control techniques are often highly receptive to a cheap, safe, effective oral contraceptive. India's position was explained by M. C. Chagla, former Ambassador to the United States: "Until we develop an oral contraceptive that works and that we can afford, we must encourage sterilization after the third or fourth child." If birth control pills can be produced and distributed at costs bearable by the Indian populace

---

[38] Gregory Pincus *et al.*, "Effectiveness of an Oral Contraceptive," *Science*, Vol. CXXX, No. 3367, July 10, 1959, pp. 81-83.

or subsidized by the Indian government, sterilization and other procedures may be abandoned in favor of this more efficient and palatable method.

The Development of Planned Parenthood

Birth control is not confined to our time or to Western culture. Contraceptive methods and abortifacient materials are mentioned in a Chinese medical treatise of 2500 B.C., the Petri papyrus of 1800 B.C., Aristotle (384-322 B.C.) and Soranus of Ephesus (second century A.D.), Lucretius (95-55 B.C.) and Pliny (23-79 A.D.), the Holy Bible, Vatsya Yana's *Kama Sutra* (fourth century A.D.), and a Persian medical book of 923 A.D.

CHRISTIAN DOCTRINE

Genesis I:28 reads: "And God blessed them, and God said unto them, Be fruitful and multiply, and replenish the earth, and subdue it; and have dominion over the fish of the sea, and over the fowl of the air, and over every living thing that moveth upon the earth." This contextual emphasis on competition and survival of the fittest has been generally ignored by theologians in favor of an interpretation stressing the desirability of large families for their own sake. In the fifth century, St. Augustine opposed periodic continence as a method of birth limitation: "In marriage, as the marriage law declares, the man and woman come together for the procreation of children."[39] It is this doctrine—that procreation is the sole end of marriage—which became the chief basis of the Scholastic position and subsequent Catholic thought. The Code of Canon Law of 1917 added a second purpose: "The primary end of marriage is the procreation and education of children; its secondary end is mutual aid and the allaying of concupiscence" (Can. 1013, par. 1). In *Casti Connubii* (1930) Pius XI, as noted earlier, added to mutual aid and the quieting of concupiscence another secondary end: "the cultivating of mutual love." Currently the Roman Catholic Church rejects all methods of family planning except abstinence and, under certain circumstances, the rhythm method, as contrary to the law of God. Moreover, the Church "bases its condemnation on the natural law, binding on all men, and not merely on Roman Catholics."[40]

In most countries of nineteenth- and twentieth-century Europe, advocates of family limitation were in active conflict with legal and re-

---

[39] St. Augustine, *On the Morals of Manicheans*, Chap. 65; quoted in Richard M. Fagley, "The Population Problem and Family Planning," *The Ecumenical Review*, Vol. XI, No. 1, October 1958, p. 10.

[40] Norman St. John-Stevas, "A Roman Catholic View of Population Control," *Law and Contemporary Problems*, Vol. XXV, No. 3, Summer 1960, p. 468.

ligious authorities. Even in so advanced a country as Sweden, economist Knut Wicksell was put into prison for "blasphemy"—the blasphemy being advocation of planned parenthood. These so-called neo-Malthusians were often atheists, which added to their aggravating qualities.

ANTI-BIRTH CONTROL LEGISLATION

In 1869 Anthony Comstock and the Society for the Suppression of Vice pushed an anti-obscenity law through the New York state legislature; the law included a section defining birth control writings as obscene. Over the next several years most other states enacted "little Comstock Acts" banning the manufacture and sale of contraceptives or the dissemination of birth control advice. In 1873 Comstock was instrumental in passing Federal legislation which made it a criminal offense to import, send through the United States mails, or transport between states, "any article of medicine for the prevention of conception or for causing abortion." This Protestant crusade was not encouraged by the Catholic Church.

This legislation has not fared particularly well in the twentieth century. The Federal law is still on the books, but its enforcement was invalidated in 1936 by the United States Court of Appeals under Judge Augustus N. Hand in the case of *U.S. vs. One Package* (the package containing diaphragms had been imported by Dr. Hannah Stone and seized by the customs office). In 1944 the Court of Appeals handed down a decision permitting Consumers Union to mail to its members (at their request) a leaflet on products for conception control. The state Comstock laws have been watered down or repealed in every state except Connecticut and Massachusetts, where Catholic pressures keep these Protestant-initiated laws on the books.[41]

The Massachusetts law only makes it difficult to sell contraceptive appliances, but the Connecticut law goes so far as to forbid even their use—a fact which led Dr. A. F. Guttmacher to remark in 1961 that the citizens of Connecticut are "the largest mass criminal population in America."[42] According to the Connecticut law: "Any person who uses any drug, medicinal article or instrument for the purpose of preventing conception shall be fined not less than fifty dollars or imprisoned not less than sixty days nor more than one year, or both fined and imprisoned. Accessories: Any person who assists, abets, counsels, hires or commands another to commit any offense may be prosecuted and

---

[41] Harriet Pilpel and Theodora Zavin, "Birth Control Laws in the United States," in Mary Steichen Calderone (ed.), *Abortion in the United States*, Harper and Brothers, New York, 1958, pp. 196-199.

[42] Alan F. Guttmacher, *Babies by Choice or by Chance*, Avon Books, New York, 1961, p. 88.

punished as if he were the principal offender." In 1960 the Connecticut State Supreme Court upheld the legislation banning the use of birth control even in cases where pregnancy, in the words of one plaintiff, "would result almost inevitably in death."

These two state laws have been attacked repeatedly by several organizations, notably the American Civil Liberties Union, which claims that they run counter to the First, Ninth, Tenth, and Fourteenth Amendments.[43] The Right Reverend James A. Pike, an Episcopal Bishop and lawyer, protests "interference with what the religious and ethical convictions of many of us require. Hence this interference limits the full exercise of religion in violation of the First and Fourteenth Amendments."[44]

CLINICS

The first birth control clinic was established in 1878 in Amsterdam, Holland, by Dr. Aletta Jacobs. The first such clinic in the United States was opened in Brooklyn, New York, in 1916 by Margaret Sanger, a visiting nurse. Mrs. Sanger printed 5,000 handbills in English, Italian, and Yiddish beginning: "MOTHERS! Can you afford to have a large family? Do you want any more children? If not, why do you have them? DO NOT KILL, DO NOT TAKE LIFE, BUT PREVENT." In the first nine days, 464 women visited the clinic. Then on the tenth day several policemen visited it and arrested the three directors on charges of "maintaining a public nuisance." After spending the night in jail, Mrs. Sanger was released on bail, immediately reopened the clinic, was rearrested, tried, and sentenced to thirty days in jail. Following several other arrests, Mrs. Sanger established the first permanent clinic in 1923.

Today there are hundreds of such clinics in operation in the United States. The first state to provide birth control services to mothers through its tax-supported public health program was North Carolina, in 1937. The first five states to provide free contraceptive aid as a part of their public welfare programs were all in the Southeast.

Elsewhere in the world, there are state-supported clinics supplying free advice and occasionally contraceptive devices in Sweden, India, Pakistan, Japan, Singapore, Thailand, Egypt, and several other countries. Spearheading the birth control movement is the International Planned Parenthood Federation, with national and local affiliates and centers for distributing information and promoting legal and social action.

---

[43] American Civil Liberties Union, "A.C.L.U. Attacks Constitutionality of Anti-Birth Control Statutes," *Civil Liberties*, No. 174, November 1959, p. 1.

[44] James A. Pike, address before the National Conference on Social Welfare, San Francisco, Calif., May 26, 1959

MASS COMMUNICATIONS

Not surprisingly, the radio-television industry has been exceedingly slow in acknowledging the existence of birth control. The term was first used on the air in 1935 by Representative Pierce of Oregon, followed by a permissive statement by the National Association of Broadcasters in 1942. To this day, however, there is little mention of this controversial subject on either radio or television.

The press has been more courageous. Newspapers often carry stories reporting various birth control battles. Books advocating contraception were formerly banned but are now widely available.

Advertising of birth control techniques—though widespread in India and certain other nations—is prohibited in the United States by a gentlemen's agreement. But when love comes to Madison Avenue, the resultant jingles will surely not be without precedent. An eighteenth-century English handbill advertising Mrs. Philips' "machines" for "gentlemen going abroad" concluded:

> To guard yourself from shame or fear,
> Votaries to Venus, hasten here;
> None in my wares e'er found a flaw,
> Self preservation's nature's law.[45]

The list of organizations that have made public pronouncements on birth control is large. Associations adopting resolutions favoring birth control include a number of medical and religious groups, such as the national governing bodies of the Unitarians, Presbyterians, Episcopalians, Baptists, Methodists, and the Y.W.C.A. A prominent opposing statement is the encyclical issued by Pope Pius XI in 1931.[46]

In sum, family planning is the most controversial topic in demography today. Although there seem to be few objections to death control, the deliberate control of fertility has raised vociferous and even violent opposition on all three levels: ideology, motive, and method. Whether this conflict will be resolved or intensified—and if resolved, in what direction and how harmoniously—is of considerable import for the future population growth of the world. Indeed, it is upon this demographic outcome, in part, that world peace and the level of living of several billion human beings stand to be decided.

---

[45] Quoted in Guttmacher, *Babies by Choice or by Chance, op. cit.*, p. 72.
[46] Pope Pius XI, Encyclical *Quadragesimo Anno* ("On Reconstructing the Social Order"), The Vatican, Rome, May 15, 1931.

11 ✄ Internal Migration

For the individual, migration may be a step toward a higher rank and better economic or social living conditions. For the society, it can be a means of correcting an imbalance between the supply of workers and jobs and between consumers and production. Migration disturbs the age-sex composition of the population, thus altering marriage prospects and perhaps the birth and death rates. Often, too, it destroys existing social bonds and institutional ties, replacing old allegiances with membership in new churches, schools, factories, and cliques.

The volitional elements implicit in migration are generally far more obvious to the individual than are his actions affecting fertility and mortality. He believes he has the power to move or to stay put, but he accepts death and sickness as beyond his control. Having children is also often regarded as an act of God rather than a human decision. Thus, not surprisingly, this ingredient of conscious personal choice is more evident in migration than in the two vital variables of the demographic triad.

Migration is also a newer subject than either fertility or mortality. Indeed the causes and consequences of shifting fertility and mortality rates are much better understood by demographers, largely because both the collection and the analysis of migration data are comparatively underdeveloped.

Nature and Measurement

Analysis of migration is founded on four subvariables: in, out, gross, and net, referring respectively to movement into an area, movement out of an area, the total in and out movement, and the difference between these movements. We also find it useful to distinguish between internal migration (wholly within one country) and international migration (movement across national boundaries). Internal migration streams are nearly always of larger magnitude than are international migration currents. There being fewer legal restrictions and linguistic and cultural obstacles, the initiative and expense required are smaller; internal migration is therefore more quickly responsive to social and economic changes.

MOVERS AND MIGRANTS

Defining a migrant is not as easy as it may seem at first glance. One might say that he is simply someone who moves. But when, where, why, and for how long? Not all people who change their geographical positions are migrants; for example, commuters, students, shoppers, and tourists are not. In order to be considered a migrant, one must make a move of some consequence. Demographers thus define a person as a migrant if he changes his place of normal habitation for a substantial period of time, crossing a political boundary in the process.

Demographers distinguish between movers and migrants according to a single criterion. A mover is a person who changes his place of residence; a migrant, one whose change of residence takes him into a new political unit. Mover is the inclusive term; thus all migrants are movers, but some movers are not migrants. This distinction is forced upon us by the circumstances under which migration data are collected; it is almost impossible to obtain data for all moves of all persons, but it is feasible to record moves in which people cross political boundaries. (Those few countries that maintain permanent individual migration registers have no need for this distinction.) Thus, in a sense, migration statistics are artificial, depending on whether or not a mobile person happens to cross a boundary line. However, one must not overlook the importance of political boundaries in our lives: a move of ten miles from the United States to Mexico sets in motion changes that may have greater import than a move of 3,000 miles entirely within the United States.

DATA SOURCES

Seven factors, particularly, create difficulties in obtaining accurate migration figures: selection of the political entity of greatest relevance, frequency of placement of boundaries, irregularity of shape of boundaries, boundary changes through time, incomplete knowledge of the purpose of the move, length of the time period involved, and multiple moves during the period by one person.[1] Even so, demographers know

---

[1] Ralph Thomlinson, "Methodological Needs in Migration Research," *Population Review*, Vol. VI, No. 1, January 1962, pp. 59-64.

the primary facts about migration: where people go, how often, and how many.

Statisticians acquire migration information in four ways: by maintaining a continuing individual register; by observing moves when they happen; by asking people about their past moves, previous residences, or place of birth; or by a residual method.

The continuing register is ideal in that it not only collects information about movement, but also permits correlation of migration with other data recorded in the register system. Such registers are maintained, however, in only six small nations; some other countries supply semi-adequate substitutes. In the United States, Social Security records are occasionally used in studying migration, but they yield direct information only about workers participating in O.A.S.I., thereby omitting some employed persons, most housewives, and all children, and missing many residential moves not associated with changes in employment.

The second method, observation, is also excellent when data are complete and accurate. But unfortunately the reliability and validity of officially reported statistics are often unacceptably low. The main sources of observed gross international migration data are official stations at ports, government stations at land frontiers, passports, transport contracts, and coupons detached from certain documents.[2] United States international migration statistics date from 1820, following passage of the Act of 1819 specifying that masters of arriving ships declare the number, age, sex, occupation, and nationality of their passengers. To the regret of demographers, however, these manifests were incomplete and inconsistent. The quality of data did not achieve a satisfactory level until about 1915. Immigration and emigration statistics are now collected and published by the Immigration and Naturalization Service, a part of the Department of Justice. The United States has no such system for collecting internal migration statistics.

The third source, interviewing the population at large or those presumed to have moved, has not proven fully satisfactory. It is expensive, recalled information is inaccurate, and data are not available soon enough following the move.

The residual method uses the formula $P_1 = P_0 + B - D + I - O$. That is, the population of an area is equal to its previous population plus births minus deaths plus in-migrants minus out-migrants. Since we often know or have good estimates for P_1, P_0, B, and D, we can then compute $(I-O)$ from the formula. This method, however, does not permit us to estimate either in- or out-migration, but only net migration.

[2] Brinley Thomas, "International Migration," in Philip M. Hauser and Otis Dudley Duncan (eds.), The Study of Population, University of Chicago Press, Chicago, 1959, p. 511.

COMPUTING MIGRATION RATES

Migration rates are much more troublesome to compute than are birth and death rates. "The numerator (number of migrants) is harder to obtain . . . and the denominator (the base population) is more difficult to ascertain, largely because migration involves two geographic entities rather than one and because a sometimes lengthy time period is involved. Scholars have not reached agreement concerning the most appropriate population base to be used as a denominator in the fraction expressing a crude rate of migration"—though several likely bases have been suggested and evaluated.[3]

To obtain accurate migration rates, we must first know where people move and in what quantities; later comes the more difficult question of why they move. Motives ordinarily must be determined from personal interviews, which are expensive and not terribly accurate; origin-destination data are easier to obtain and more reliable. Therefore the "where" of migration is more completely known than the "why."

Movement within the United States

Internal migration in the United States resembles in motives and general characteristics that of most other countries. People move from farms to cities and from areas of limited opportunities to places offering a greater potential for economic gain. High rates of natural increase promote outward migration; low rates encourage inward migration. Of course, streams dependent upon special geographic or historical circumstances are not reproduced in other lands. There is no frontiering without a frontier, no gold rush without the appearance of gold, no Negro escape to freedom without an ill-treated minority.

Indeed, migrants themselves form a significant minority. "Internal migration is at once one of the most important determinants of population change and the one about which we know least. Every year approximately one American out of every five moves to a different residence, and a considerable fraction of this migration is highly significant in economic and cultural terms. There are no indications that Americans will soon cease to be a nation of nomads."[4]

---

[3] Ralph Thomlinson, "The Determination of a Base Population for Computing Migration Rates," *Milbank Memorial Fund Quarterly*, Vol. XL, No. 3, July 1962, pp. 356-366.
[4] William Petersen, "Internal Migration and Economic Development in Northern America," *Annals of the American Academy of Political and Social Science*, Vol. CCCXVI, March 1958, pp. 52-59.

A NATION OF NOMADS

Of the 159 million persons five years of age or older in the United States in 1960, one-half were living in a different house than they occupied in 1955, one of every six lived in a different county, one of 11 lived in a different state, and one of 78 resided abroad. Residents of the West have been the most mobile; those of the Northeast the least. Regarding degree of urbanization, rural nonfarm residents moved the most, urban people second, and rural farm persons the least. See Figure 7 for differences by state; the proportion moving varies from Pennsylvania at 39 per cent to Alaska and Nevada at 72 and 66 per cent respectively. States having the most 1960 inhabitants who were abroad five years earlier are: Alaska, 4.5 per cent; Hawaii, 3.5 per cent; and California, 2.6 per cent.

More than one-fourth of the United States native population of all ages were born in a different state from the one they resided in at the time of the 1960 Census. In some states more than half of the native-born residents were born in another state of the Union: Nevada, 69 per cent; Alaska, 63 per cent; Arizona, 58 per cent; Florida, 57 per cent; Wyoming, 54 per cent; California, 52 per cent; and Oregon, 50 per cent. States having the fewest such in-migrants were Pennsylvania, 12 per cent; Mississippi, 12 per cent; Alabama, 13 per cent; Kentucky, 13 per cent; and North Carolina, 13 per cent. Seventeen counties had a 1950-1960 population gain attributable to net in-migration of from 100 to 319 per cent—six in Florida, six elsewhere in the South, and five others.

In the United States, six kinds of internal migration are notable: the westward expansion of the frontier, rural-urban moves, Negro migration, nomadic movements, mass movements confined to particular dates, and individual idiosyncratic movements. These types are not mutually exclusive; they are simply a list of types of moves placed in approximate order of their historical importance. Thus a person may participate simultaneously in more than one type of movement; a westward rural-urban move by a Negro construction worker, for instance, exemplifies the first four types.

WESTWARD EXPANSION

The westward movement so cherished by some history teachers and many television and film writers was not of uniform velocity. The seventeenth century, for instance, was characterized by little internal migration. The colonies were being settled and there was ample room along the eastern seaboard. When the Pilgrims landed in Massachusetts in 1620, and later in the century when population clusters developed

FIGURE 7. *Movers as Per Cent of Population, by States, 1955–1960.*

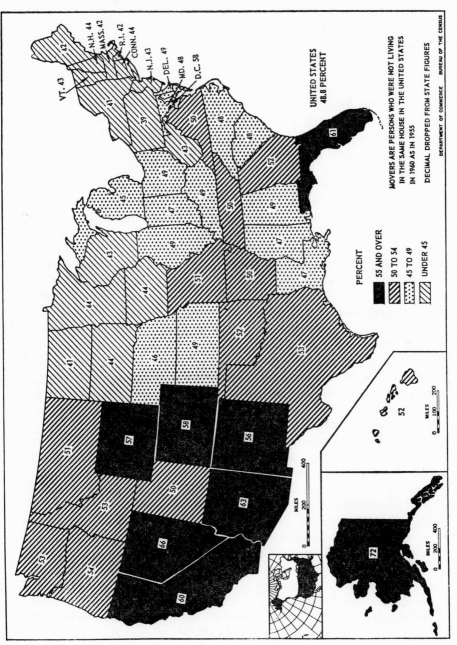

MOVERS ARE PERSONS WHO WERE NOT LIVING
IN THE SAME HOUSE IN THE UNITED STATES
IN 1960 AS IN 1955

DECIMAL DROPPED FROM STATE FIGURES

DEPARTMENT OF COMMERCE   BUREAU OF THE CENSUS

UNITED STATES
48.8 PERCENT

PERCENT

▮ 55 AND OVER

▨ 50 TO 54

⁙ 45 TO 49

▧ UNDER 45

NOTE: Data for both movers and population are confined to persons 5 years of age or older living in the United States in 1960.
* U. S. Bureau of the Census, *U. S. Census of Population: 1960*, "General Social and Economic Characteristics: U. S. Summary," PC (1)-1C. Government Printing Office. Washington, 1962, p. xvii.

in Boston, New York, Philadelphia, and Charleston, the country was primarily agricultural. It is estimated that over a dozen farmers were then needed to produce enough surplus after feeding themselves and their large families to support one city man.

Eighteenth-century migration was largely a filling-in of the territory east of the Appalachians, with a spilling over after midcentury into Kentucky, Tennessee, Ohio, and Indiana. Settlers wanted cheap land for farming, and the Northwest Ordinance of 1787, the Harrison Land Law of 1800, and the Land Act of 1804 were responses to this demand.

It was not until after 1800 that crowding encouraged movement to the west, at which time there was a rapid spreading out to the Great Plains and even to the Pacific, aided by the building of the trans-continental railroad. The Republican 1860 platform—one of the few platforms in American history to be enacted into law—promised dona-tion of land for homesteaders and for colleges. The Homestead Laws beginning in 1862 gave each family head over 21 years of age who was a United States citizen (or declared his intent to become so) a tract of 160 acres in the Great Plains for a fee of about $10.00. If he inhabited, cultivated, and improved the land, the settler acquired title after three years. The government had three principal reasons for passing these laws: it wanted a large income as quickly as possible and pre-ferred the fast return from taxes to the slower income from gradual sale; it wanted to encourage the settlement of the whole country to produce more food and make the United States stronger, and it felt it had to meet the competition of Spain and other powers that were giving free land to agricultural settlers in Latin America.

The twentieth century has been a period of filling-in of the West and of movement to Alaska and Hawaii. Indeed, interregional movement has been generally westward. Recent currents have been primarily from the Northeast and the corn belt to California, from the Southeast and Southwest to California, and from the Southeast to the Northeast. So many persons left the South to populate other sections of the country that this region has become known as the seedbed of national population. The famous directive to "Go West, young man"[5] was well put: they did go, they went West, and they were mostly young and male. Consequently sex ratios in some parts of the West became and have remained highly favorable for young women seeking husbands; even today, practical parents might do well to send their daughters to Wyoming instead of to Bryn Mawr College.

Figure 8 estimates the population gain within each state resulting

---

[5] John B. L. Soule, article in the *Terre Haute Express* (Indiana), 1851; popularized by Horace Greeley in a *New York Tribune* editorial.

from net interstate plus international migration throughout the 1950's. Since net international migration was small compared with net interstate migration, the figure represents largely internal migration. As in previous decades, western states attracted the bulk of the movers, the largest percentage gains being made by Florida, Nevada, Arizona, Alaska, and California. Those states suffering the greatest per cent losses were Arkansas, West Virginia, Mississippi, the Dakotas, Kentucky, Alabama, South Carolina, and Oklahoma. Three states added more than half a million residents by net migration: California (3,145,000), Florida (1,617,000), and New Jersey (577,000). No state lost that many people, but six lost more than a third of a million: Pennsylvania, West Virginia, Mississippi, Arkansas, Kentucky, and Alabama. The migration patterns for 1940-1950 and 1930-1940 were very similar to 1950-1960. For three decades there has been a large exodus from the Great Plains and Deep South toward the Pacific states. This major trend has been supplemented by minor movements away from northern New England and the Appalachians and toward the mid-Atlantic seaboard, the dry Southwest, Florida, Alaska, and the rim of the Great Lakes.

RURAL-URBAN MOVEMENT

The rural to urban current is much greater than the urban to rural trend. Except for 1932 and 1945, the recorded net annual balance has always favored migration toward urban areas. City to city migration involves an increasing number of people as suburbs grow rapidly. Rural to rural movement is greatest in the South, smallest in the Northeast. Of the four possibilities—rural to urban, urban to rural, urban to urban, and rural to rural—the first and third are the most important. Indeed, the first, rural-urban movement, has enhanced maturation of the United States throughout its history. Urban-urban moves have become paramount during the last few decades.

There would also appear to be a tendency to move in stages: farm to small city to large city to metropolis to suburb. "How ya gonna keep 'em down on the farm after they've seen Broadway" is crudely accurate but needs clarification, as it omits steps in the migratory process.

Some metropolises experienced large net in-migration over the 1950-1960 decade. Metropolitan Los Angeles, for example, gained more than a million and a half people. Nineteen other metropolitan areas gained 100,000 to 364,000 people, those gaining a quarter million or more being New York (which, though placing second, added only a fourth as many migrants as did Los Angeles), Miami, San Diego, Chicago, Tampa, San Jose, and San Bernardino. The greatest percentage increases by net migration over the decade were: Fort Lauderdale, 264 per cent;

FIGURE 8. *Net 1950-1960 Migration as a Percentage of 1950 Population, by States**

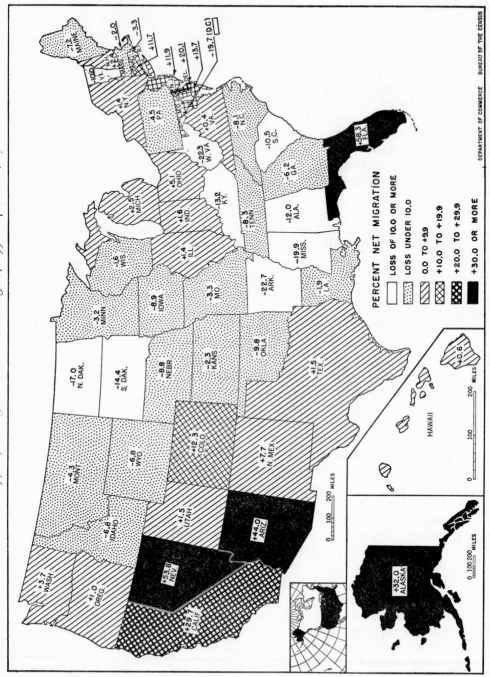

PERCENT NET MIGRATION

LOSS OF 10.0 OR MORE
LOSS UNDER 10.0
0.0 TO +9.9
+10.0 TO +19.9
+20.0 TO +29.9
+30.0 OR MORE

DEPARTMENT OF COMMERCE   BUREAU OF THE CENSUS

Las Vegas, 123 per cent; and fourteen others, 50 to 109 per cent. Pittsburgh and Boston lost over 100,000 population through net out-migration. Of the twenty-nine counties having an excess of in-migrants over out-migrants amounting to 100,000 or more during 1950-1960, all are metropolitan, sixteen are suburban, and ten are located in California or Florida. At the other extreme, all nine counties which lost 100,000 or more net migrants were central counties of giant metropolitan areas.[6]

Cities differ regarding the regions from which they draw their population influx. New England and southern cities are the most provincial in that their in-migrants originating within the United States come heavily from surrounding areas. By contrast, the West Coast cities (especially Los Angeles) are the most cosmopolitan, since they draw huge quantities of migrants from other regions of the country. (These remarks apply only to internal migration. If international migration is included, some of the New England cities must be classed among the most cosmopolitan urban centers, whereas Los Angeles attracts only a moderate number of foreigners.)

The effects of the net migration from farm to city are socially important. For the cities, there is a gain of wealth and of a young energetic labor force, while the rural areas lose population (not necessarily a defect), capital, and perhaps their vigorous future leaders. Moreover, the expense of providing an education is often borne by the rural area, while the benefit goes to the city, since migrants often leave the farm shortly after completing their formal schooling. For the nation, the proportion of the population that is urban increases, and there may be a more equitable distribution of income and economic opportunity. Also noteworthy is the fact that migrants to cities have lower fertility than siblings who stay on the farm (and presumably than they themselves would have had if they too had remained rural), which may contribute to national reduction of fertility and natural increase.

NEGRO EXODUS FROM THE SOUTH

Although the Civil War removed the most pressing legal restrictions on Negro mobility, there was very little voluntary internal Negro migration in the United States before 1890, and for the next twenty-five years the streams of movement, though increasing, were small. Most former slaves were uninformed, poor, and psychologically unprepared to move.

After Emancipation, southern Negroes had four migratory alternatives: leave the country, move West, move North, or move into urban

---

[6] U. S. Bureau of the Census, "Components of Population Change, 1950 to 1960, for Counties, Standard Metropolitan Statistical Areas, State Economic Areas, and Economic Subregions." *Current Population Reports*, Series P-23, No. 7, November 1962, pp. 6-10.

areas within the South itself. A very small number of freedmen emigrated to Liberia and Haiti and a few moved West; usually, however, the North was their choice. Between the two World Wars there was a flood of migrants to the Northeast, mostly to metropolitan centers and mostly on a straight North-South line—from South Carolina to New York, from Georgia to Philadelphia, from Alabama to Detroit, and from Mississippi to Chicago. During the last twenty years, however, the flood has turned westward; there has been a gigantic torrent out of the South to Los Angeles and to other western cities.

The great Negro exodus started in 1915, changing the proportion of Negroes living in the North and West from 10 per cent of all Negroes in 1910 to 24 per cent in 1940 and 40 per cent in 1960. "Recruiting agents travelled South, begging Negroes to come North. They sometimes carried free tickets in their pockets, and always glowing promises on their tongues."[7] Consternation arose quite naturally among southern white leaders; they were in danger of losing a laboring class, and they did not like the prospect. During and shortly after World War I, many communities acted to restrict northern recruiters and Negro would-be-émigrés. In Montgomery, Alabama, fines and jail sentences were imposed upon any "person, firm, or corporation" found guilty of "enticing, persuading or influencing" labor to leave town. The civic leaders of Jacksonville, Florida, in a more subtle maneuver, passed an ordinance requiring labor recruiters from the North to buy a $1,000 license or spend sixty days in jail and pay a $600 fine. This ordinance was too weak for Macon, Georgia; the city council charged $25,000 for a recruiting license, and in case anyone had that much money, they required in addition that the labor agent be recommended by ten local ministers, ten manufacturers, and twenty-five businessmen. In Mississippi, agents were arrested, trains stopped for the removal of North-bound Negroes, and ticket agents intimidated into refusing to sell them tickets. When none of these actions succeeded, the worried citizens tried conciliation and persuasion of the local Negro leaders.[8] But still Negroes migrated from the South.

Gunnar Myrdal estimates that the total net Negro migration from the South to the North and West between 1910 and 1940 was 1,750,000.[9] This was almost wholly a movement toward northern (not western) cities; previously the Negroes had been heavily rural in their distribution.

---

[7] St. Clair Drake and Horace R. Cayton, *Black Metropolis*, Harcourt, Brace and Co., New York, 1945, p. 58.

[8] Emmett J. Scott, *Negro Migration During the War*, Carnegie Endowment for International Peace, "Preliminary Economic Studies of the War," No. 16, Oxford University Press, New York, 1920, pp. 73-79.

[9] Gunnar Myrdal, *An American Dilemma*, Harper and Brothers, New York, 1944, pp. 183 and 1229.

Between 1950 and 1960, about 1,500,000 Negroes left the South, usually going to northern and western metropolises. The states leading the nation in gain and loss due to Negro migration from 1950 to 1960 were California, which acquired almost 350,000 Negroes, and Mississippi, which lost more than 300,000. Five neighboring southern states also lost over 100,000 Negro émigrés, and New York, Illinois, Ohio, and Michigan also received more than 100,000. All in all, the South lost about 14 per cent of its 1950 Negro population through net out-migration by 1960. During this decade, Arkansas, West Virginia, and Mississippi lost an almost unbelievable one-third of their Negroes. By contrast, the white movement out of the South almost exactly equalled white in-migration, and individual southern state losses through departure of whites constituted much smaller percentages, the largest in the nation being those of West Virginia, 21 per cent; Arkansas, 19 per cent; and North Dakota, 17 per cent.[10]

OTHER STREAMS

Most prominent among the nomadic movements are: migratory agricultural workers following crops up and down both seaboards; construction workers going from one dam, bridge, tunnel, or highway to another; military personnel changing assignments; persons moving into and out of winter retirement and resort towns such as St. Augustine, Florida, Provincetown, Massachusetts, and various southwestern communities; and other people with mobile occupations requiring frequent moves.

Three recent currents deserve special mention: southwesterners leaving the Dust Bowl in the 1930's, most often for California; the new employees heading for West Coast war plants during World War II; and the influx of many people to areas of especially warm and dry climates which became pronounced after the Second World War. Most short-term concerted surges of this sort (such as the Gold Rush of the 1840's) are far less important causes of population redistribution than they appear. The moves are frequently temporary, and the publicity is disproportionate to the numbers and lasting effects involved.

EXPECTATIONS FOR THE FUTURE

Our best guesses regarding future internal migration are that the volume will increase and that the following tendencies will obtain in

---

[10] U. S. Bureau of the Census, "Estimates of the Components of Population Change by Color, for States: 1950 to 1960," *Current Population Reports*, Series P-25, No. 247, April 2, 1962, p. 7.

the characteristics and destinations of migrants: 1) the westward trend will continue; 2) interurban migration will become more important; 3) manufacturing cities will gain more slowly than service, political, and commercial cities; 4) suburbanization will continue; 5) Negroes will continue to leave the South; and 6) noneconomic factors such as climate, scenery, and recreation will increase in importance.

This last item represents a striking change. In the past, economic opportunity has been the dominant motive to migration, but with increasing economic security, people think seriously of ideal places to live. What is more, some of them even go there. We want a house with a view; we go to southern California in search of patio living; we insist on residing where the fishing is good or where golf is a year-round sport. But as man gains increasing control over his environment through all-weather heated and air-conditioned automobiles, homes, offices, factories, stores, theaters, and so on, climate and related factors may become irrelevant to migration. So the wheel comes full circle.

Bearing in mind the conditions favorable to out-migration, there is little difficulty in picking the chief areas from which a large part of our net out-migrants are likely to come: (1) the hilly and mountainous areas of the southern Appalachians, of central Kentucky and Tennessee, and of the Ozarks, where the birth rate is high, the land poor, and industrial development lacking; (2) the cutover areas of the northern Great Lakes and of the South, where formerly lumbering furnished a livelihood to a considerable population; (3) the cotton South, especially the Old South, which can no longer compete with the Delta and the new cotton country in Texas and California; (4) the western wheat lands (dust bowl), where drought and the mechanization of agriculture have already combined to oust a considerable number of farmers and where mechanization is not yet complete; (5) the corn belt, where mechanization is also proceeding at a rapid pace and seems likely to continue to do so for some time to come; and finally (6) those areas in which there is a more or less sudden change in industrial employment due to the exhaustion of natural resources (coal or copper mines, and so forth) or to the discovery of new resources elsewhere which are cheaper to exploit, or where temporary conditions have made it expedient to assemble a population which cannot be supported there under normal conditions, or where a long-time shift in industry is taking place, e.g., a shift in the textile industry from New England to the Southeast. The conditions likely to attract immigrants are, of course, just the opposite of the above.[11]

---

[11] Warren S. Thompson, *Population Problems*, McGraw-Hill Book Co., New York, 1953, pp. 309-310.

Forces Generating Moves

Incentives to migration demand more study as migrants increase in quantity and significance. Motives for migration are frequently multiple. People move for combinations of several reasons, and often they are not aware of all the forces urging their move. As with other social causation, there are major and minor causes, predisposing and proximate causes.

Five dichotomies are useful: internal and international, psychosocial versus physicosocial, primary or secondary, habitual or single, and push or pull. 1) Internal and international migration causes are similar, with the qualifications that international moves generally involve greater distances, cultural and linguistic barriers, legislative hindrances, and political barricades. 2) We distinguish psychosocial motives operating through the migrant himself (desire for more money or more pleasant surroundings) from physicosocial ones applying to the area (industrial expansion creating more jobs or a semitropical climate with alluring beaches). However, the two sets of motives are interrelated, because factors inhering in the area may motivate individuals to move, and personal decisions may be based on the character of the intended destination. 3) Some people make conscious decisions or take the primary responsibility for the move, and their families follow. Family members or other migrating groups having no voice in the moving choice are epiphenomenal migrants. In modern times these secondary migrants are usually spouses, children, or other dependents. 4) A few persons have a habit of moving periodically or erratically. Their moves bear little systematic relation to satisfaction with their present surroundings, expectations concerning prospective locations, or other usual variables. They are described colloquially as having wanderlust or itchy feet. A move may return them to a former residence, but usually the destination is new. In itchy-foot human movement, the propelling force is in the long run equal in all directions, though the balance is not perfect at every instant. At times when the balance is grossly uneven, these chronic movers may contribute to nomadic or mass movements.

PUSH *versus* PULL

The traditional approach to the study of migratory motivation makes use of the push-pull dichotomy. Demographers try to determine whether people migrate because they are thrust out of former residences or because they are attracted to new places. Push factors operating at the points of origin are such variables as high rates of natural increase creating a population pressure on the supply of resources (for example, migration away from rural areas); depletion or exhaustion of natural resources (erosion of topsoil in the Southeast causing farmers to migrate westward); droughts, floods, and climatic fluctuations (movement out of the dust bowl of the Great Plains in the 1930's); and acute social, political, and religious maladjustment or conflict (the dramatic shift of the Mormons from Nauvoo, Illinois, to the Great Salt Lake valley in 1847). Pull factors at work in points of destination include the discovery and development of new resources (as gold in California and Alaska), new inventions and industries (as the automobile factories in and around Detroit), and pleasant climatic conditions (as in Arizona and Florida). Some variables may operate as either push or pull factors: technological changes (the factory system pulling people to cities and the tractor creating a surplus agricultural population pushing people out of rural areas); changes in the demand for various products (lower demand for products of a region motivating out-migration just as increased demand for products of another region attracts new residents); governmental policies (the agricultural acreage reduction program of the 1930's displacing many tenant farmers, and land grants bringing settlers to new areas); entertainment and amenities (the profusion of urban facilities and their absence in rural areas); and personal factors (presence or absence of friends or relatives).[12]

RELATIVE DESIRABILITY

A more sophisticated alternative to the push-pull contrast is the concept of differential desirability: a comparison of the attractions of one place with those of another, or several others. The prospective migrant compares the appeal of alternative places of residence, including his present home, and moves to the place with the greatest desirability for him. Or, if the most attractive location is his present residence, he does not move at all. Negro migration from the Deep South to the North is explained in Jelly Roll Morton's song: "Mississippi water tastes like turpentine, but Michigan water tastes like sherry wine."

Comparison of the relative attractiveness of different regions of the United States has been quantified by combining in-, out-, and net migration rates into a composite Force of Attraction. Force of Attraction scores for the nine official Census Divisions for 1935-1940 were: New England (Maine to Connecticut), 44; Middle Atlantic (New York, New Jersey, Pennsylvania), 14; East North Central (Ohio to Wisconsin), 22; West North Central (Minnesota and North Dakota to Missouri and Kansas), 9; South Atlantic (Maryland to Florida), 30; East

---

[12] Lowry Nelson, *Rural Sociology*, American Book Co., New York, 1955, pp. 124-125.

South Central (Kentucky, Tennessee, Alabama, Mississippi), 20; West South Central (Texas, Louisiana, Arkansas, Oklahoma), 0; Mountain (Montana to New Mexico to Nevada), 28; and Pacific (California, Oregon, Washington), 100.[13]

The decision to move or to stay is made essentially on the basis of belief rather than facts. To paraphrase Charles Caleb Colton, immigration is the sincerest flattery. The operative factors are a person's knowledge and opinion of the prospective destinations. Yet even in the United States with its compulsory public education system, knowledge of other parts of the country and of other continents is usually imprecise and often grossly inaccurate. Sociological and economic characteristics are frequently misunderstood, and even landforms and climate may be unknown quantities. One consequence of this misinformation is that many migrants are dissatisfied in their new homes. Some return to their original residences as soon as they are able to finance the passage.

MOTIVATING FACTORS

Factors inciting migration are complex and intertwined. Nonetheless, the possibility of earning more money is generally preeminent among the several operating motives. Sometimes a change in occupation is involved, either through preference or from necessity. Sometimes more education is sought. Related to these incentives is the prospect of a lower cost of living in the new area. Some people move geographically in order to move vertically; by going to where they are not already known, they may be able to improve their status in the social class hierarchy. Another motive is a search for a different way of life—for example, the anonymity, variety, and excitement of urban living. The desire to live within a certain nationality, racial, language, or religious group may act either as a deterrent or as an encouragement, depending on the circumstances. Changes in the family occasionally encourage migration: marriage, divorce, death of a spouse or parent. Resettlement occasioned by retirement is increasingly common. Racial or other oppression may drive some people out of an area. Some move to join friends or relatives who previously moved to the new territory—or to avoid in-laws or unwelcome associates. Internal political boundaries influence migration through the real or supposed quality of schools, fire and police protection, tax rates, and other attributes of local communities. Avoidance of the rigors of winter has driven many people to seek the warmer parts of the country. Others move to get away from

---

[13] Ralph Thomlinson, "A Model for Migration Analysis," *Journal of the American Statistical Association*, Vol. LVI, No. 295, September 1961, p. 684.

high density, or from scarcity of other people. The opening of new territory attracts migrants, as in the land rush of the 1860's to the Great Plains or the 1960's to Alaska and Hawaii. New suburbanites speak proudly of their homes as having light, air, cleanliness, and space, and being "a good place to bring up children." Recreational facilities are central in the lives of many enthusiasts of boating, fishing, and the like. Health, too, is important; Arizona and Switzerland attract tuberculosis and asthma victims. Employees may be transferred to another branch of a large company. The laws of primogeniture may force younger sons to migrate to earn a livelihood. Floods, earthquakes, volcanoes, famines, and epidemics send people away in droves. In sum, people usually move for the objective reason of opportunity or the subjective one of hope.

Obstacles to moving are often the reverse of these factors. In addition, some people are held where they are by pension programs, social welfare benefits, and legal restrictions.

Government control is rarely exercised over internal movement in the United States. Such control is powerful in the Soviet Union and its satellites, but Americans take unrestricted internal migration for granted. Occasionally, however, this policy of free movement has been abandoned. Migrants arriving at the California border from their dust-covered farms in the 1930's found themselves classed as aliens and discouraged from entering the state; validly or not, Californians felt beleaguered by the tattered midwesterners looking for jobs or handouts. Freedom of movement (along with many other freedoms) was denied to Japanese-Americans during World War II. German and Italian minorities were not so treated, but American citizens and aliens of Japanese descent were forcibly transported to detention camps, often suffering crippling financial losses and severe personal unhappiness.[14]

Differential Migration

Just as groups of people exhibit characteristic variations in mortality and fertility, so there are group differences in migration. The study of migration differentials attempts to answer two major questions: In what manner and to what extent do migrants differ from nonmigrants? In what respect and how much do people making certain types of moves differ from those making other kinds of moves?

Despite its importance, the study of attributes of migrants as compared with characteristics of nonmigrants has been seriously neglected.

[14] Dorothy Swaine Thomas and Richard S. Nishimoto, *The Spoilage*, University of California Press, Berkeley, 1946.

The few dozen inconclusive articles contrasting movers with stayers and comparing persons making different types of moves permit only highly qualified conclusions—a hiatus which was repined in the 1960 presidential address before the Population Association of America:

> It is my impression that the study of migration differentials has made very little progress in the past thirty years, despite the fact that this, much more than any other demographic variable, is changing the distribution and characteristics of local population. To take a single example, what have been the effects on the State of Arkansas of the fact that close to half the people born in that State have left her boundaries? Who left or stayed? Is it possible to judge what some of the social implications are?[15]

Differentials appear to exist with regard to age, sex, race, physical fitness, intelligence, education, occupation, marital status, mental illness, deviant behavior, and leadership. Let us consider these characteristics in turn.

BIOLOGICAL CHARACTERISTICS

Demographers have long since concluded that both international and internal voluntary migrants are disproportionately young adults, ranging characteristically from late adolescence through early adulthood, specifically ages 15 to 35. After age 25, the proportion of people who are migrants decreases steadily with advancing age. For many, the first few years after the completion of one's formal education are a time of seeking and searching for essential things: a vocation, a husband or wife, and a place to settle. Moreover, it is easier to move during this period than later in life; ties are not so well fastened, commitments are fewer and weaker, and the world still could be one's oyster if one could only find the right opening. Recently, however, a countertrend has been developing as the aged have become more numerous, more financially independent, and more willing to pull up stakes and move toward the sun.

Sex differentials in migration vary according to the kind of migration under consideration. For long-distance moves, males predominate; for short distances, females. Ordinarily, international migration involves moves of greater distance than internal migration. For both international migration and long-distance internal migration, the available evidence indicates a selectivity favoring males. In the case of moves of relatively few miles, such as rural-urban migration within a single region, females predominate.

---

[15] Dudley Kirk, "Some Reflections on American Demography in the Nineteen Sixties," *Population Index*, Vol. XXVI, No. 4, October 1960, p. 307.

During most of United States history, Negroes were less migratory than whites. But in recent decades Negroes have been making inter-state moves at slightly greater rates than whites. They are also urbanizing more rapidly. Taking all nonwhites together, the 1960 Census found that 2 per cent more nonwhites than whites aged five years or more were living in a different house from the one they occupied in 1955. But whites probably moved greater distances; 11 per cent of nonwhites moved across county boundaries and 6 per cent across state lines in 1955-1960, as compared with 18 and 9 per cent respectively among whites.

The evidence is far from conclusive regarding the physical condition or prowess of migrants. The question has been treated in England, Sweden, and the United States, but data do not permit any conclusion more firm than that farm to city migrants—and perhaps migrants in general—are probably better physical specimens than nonmigrants. It is difficult to obtain suitable information to resolve this uncertainty, because physical examinations are not normally a part of data-collecting procedures for either internal or international moves.

Nor are intelligence tests given with reference to migration. To be sure, migrants to cities score higher on IQ tests than do people who remain on the farm, but urban sedentees also make higher scores than do rural persons. The tests themselves seem to favor urban experiences and skills, and until this defect is removed any inference drawn from test scores must be strongly challenged. Klineberg's study of Negro intelligence and migration loosely supports this contention: "the superi-ority of the northern over the southern Negroes, and the tendency of northern Negroes to approximate the scores of whites, are due to factors in the environment, and not to selective migration."[16]

SOCIAL CHARACTERISTICS

Internal migrants receive more years of schooling than nonmigrants, aggravating disequities in school taxes. But it is possible that the stu-dents who obtain the most schooling may be ill-adjusted to their en-vironment and prefer the ivory tower world of the school; perhaps nonmigrants are more stable emotionally. Looking at the area rather than the individual, outward migration rates tend to vary inversely with the average amount of schooling completed by residents of the region.

Occupational differentials vary according to the character of the move. Rural to urban moves ordinarily betoken a shift from agricultural

---

[16] Otto Klineberg, *Negro Intelligence and Selective Migration*, Columbia University Press, New York, 1935, p. 59.

to nonagricultural pursuits. Internal migrants include an exceptionally high proportion of professional and semiprofessional workers, whereas among international migrants laborers and operatives tend to predominate. Switching our focus from the move to the person, we learn that professional men are of above average mobility, while unskilled and semiskilled workers are among the least mobile segments of the populace. Unemployed persons are more migratory than employed ones.

Data concerning marital status imply that rural-urban migrants in the United States are mostly single. This finding is not substantiated in other countries.

Although there are indications of higher rates of mental disease among migrants than among nonmigrants,[17] research on this subject does not yet permit reliable generalizations. It is doubtful, however, that the migration experience *per se* has psychopathogenic proclivities. Definitive conclusions must await analyses of cross-tabulations involving additional antecedent and intervening independent variables.[18]

Various indexes of social disorganization have been linked to migration by enthusiastic amateurs, but little evidence exists to support the contention that migrants exhibit more deviant behavior than do nonmigrants. In fact, a recent Philadelphia study of 1,062 youths shows that migration does not have the crimogenetic effects attributed to it. The Philadelphia-born population more frequently became delinquent than did the migrant group, though the difference was seldom statistically significant.[19] Legitimate and responsible generalizations must be based on cross-classification into additional categories taking cognizance of the numerous other variables involved in social disorganization. Present knowledge permits no conclusive statements on this subject.

Migrants are sometimes characterized as having more ambition and initiative than sedentees. Thus some forty years ago one sociologist wrote: "In New England there are rural counties which have been losing their best for three or four generations, leaving the coarse, dull, and hidebound. The number of loafers in some slackwater villages of the Middle States indicates that the natural pacemakers of the locality have gone elsewhere to create prosperity. In parts of southern Michigan, Illinois, Wisconsin, and even as far west as Missouri, there are communities which remind one of fished-out ponds populated chiefly by

[17] Benjamin Malzberg and Everett S. Lee, *Migration and Mental Disease*, Social Science Research Council, New York, 1956.

[18] Judith Lazarus, Ben Z. Locke, and Dorothy Swaine Thomas, "Migration Differentials in Mental Disease," *Milbank Memorial Fund Quarterly*, Vol. XLI, No. 1, January 1963, pp. 25-42.

[19] Leonard D. Savitz, "Delinquency and Migration," Commission on Human Relations of the City of Philadelphia, 1960.

bull-heads and suckers."[20] If it is true that some areas do lose the more dynamic elements of their population to the lure of the thriving metropolis and the burgeoning West, then this country is being re-modeled by migration. But there is no really authentic information on this topic.

PERSISTENCE OF DIFFERENCES

Insofar as migrants differ from nonmigrants, how long after the act of migration do the differences persevere? Obviously, the biological differentials of age, sex, and race will not change, and it is doubtful whether physical fitness or intelligence will alter following migration. However, the new settler may change his educational, occupational, or marital status. Other adaptive behavior also might alter, depending on circumstances and the extent to which that particular attribute had motivated the move.

Demographers are especially curious about the effects of migration on the other two basic population variables. Do migrants adopt the reproductive practices of their new locale, or do they maintain their old habits? Does their mortality resemble that of natives of their new area or that of persons remaining in the area of origin? Or do migrants fall in between, that is, do they modify their fertility in the direction of the new region but not so much as to be identical to natives of the new area? Is their longevity half-way between that of stayers and movers?

Answers to these questions are not fully known, but what we have been able to learn is that such change (or refusal to change) varies according to the type of move and various traits of the person moving. Usually, migrants tend to adapt part-way; that is, they no longer re-semble the stayers they left behind, but fail to adopt completely the coloration of their new neighbors. In other words, the truth falls between the two extremes of "chameleon" and "stubborn mule." Some assimila-tion usally occurs in first-generation international migrants, but com-plete assimilation normally awaits passage of several generations—and may not occur even then. Among internal migrants, assimilation may be a matter of a generation, a year, or a week, depending on the gravity of the move. If intensely felt subcultural differences are involved, genera-tions may be required; if a Detroit suburbanite moves to a Chicago suburb, assimilation may be almost immediate. Of course, the adapt-ability of the individual is highly important, as are his new associates and the circumstances of his arrival. In many instances, demographers

---

[20] Edward A. Ross, *The Outlines of Sociology*, Century Company, New York, 1924, pp. 23-24.

can predict the rapidity of adjustment, but our present state of knowledge does not permit a listing of established propositions concerning assimilation of migrants.

Individual and Societal Adjustment

Personal adjustment affects migrants and their new associates whenever they move from one culture or subculture to another, whether or not an international boundary is crossed. Indeed, internal migrants sometimes confront greater changes than persons venturing into foreign lands. The adaptation of the migrant to his new home is related to the existence and perseverance of culturally significant migration differentials. Where cultural differences do exist, and especially when they are powerfully internalized, personal adjustment is slow and painful. Integration trauma are products of social differences between the newcomer and the dominant group into which he moves. Adaptation thus becomes partly a question of how quickly and completely the migrant can transfer his thoughtways from one reference group to another.

The social consequences of migration for sending and receiving areas especially vary with five conditions: the magnitude of gross migration, the significance of variables of differentiation, the amplitude of the differences between migrants and nonmigrants, the roles played by migrants in their new groups, and the receptivity of the receiving region to social changes. Effects may be traced in such divergent subjects as population composition, local politics, national voting patterns, cultural homogeneity, and changes in social values.

CHANGES IN COMPOSITION

Given a large number of migrants entering an area, if they excel in education, occupational skills, or intelligence, the area stands to raise its average performance in these respects, whereas an area from which these migrants originate may experience an inversely related decline. If the migrants are inferior to nonmigrants, then the destination suffers and place of origin gains.

Concentration of attention on the qualities of migrants to the exclusion of attributes of stayers can be misleading. For example, among aged migrants in the United States, the most favored destinations are Florida and southern California. From this fact, one might conclude that these areas would have particularly high proportions of aged— provided he neglected to consider several other facts: the number of nonaged migrating there, the age distribution without this migration, and the effect on the states which the aged left. The population composition of an area is a function of both stayers and movers. In-migration of the aged *per se* increases the median age of an area. Paradoxically, however, unusual age, sex, and other characteristics can arise in a region because people of the *opposite* type move out: for instance, out-migration of the young increases the proportion of aged in an area. Thus an abnormally high percentage of aged persons can be achieved by either disproportionate in-migration of aged or heavy out-migration of nonaged. (Of course, differential mortality is also relevant, as are fluctuations in the birth rate over the past eighty years.) Similarly, if women leave the farms to go to cities, the sex ratio declines in the city and rises in the country. In short, whatever influences migration differentials have, they are exerted both on the area of origin and on the area of destination. To borrow a principle from mechanics, migrants affect sending and receiving regions in equal and opposite fashions—with appropriate allowances for pre-existing population totals and compositions.

CIVIC AFFAIRS AND ELECTIONS

A popular contention is that migrants are less civic-minded than stayers. Having fewer and shallower roots binding them emotionally to their place of residence, they are felt to be less interested in local affairs and generally less responsible. Their allegiance is in doubt—perhaps rightly so. A 1960 letter to the editor of *Harper's Magazine* complained that migrants have no business bragging about the area they have moved to; only natives of the area are entitled to be proud of it. The writer apparently overlooked the fact that migrants choose the area, whereas natives inherit it; on this reasoning, migrants' opinions are perhaps more worthy of respect than the possibly less reflective natives'. If migrants do have less local public spirit and feel less regional sentiment, increasing migration rates should result in lessened feelings of civic responsibility in the nation at large and a lowering of sectional parochialism.

The effects of migration on voting are intriguing. Especially so is the movement out of downtown districts of large cities (usually Democratic) to the traditionally Republican suburbs, a fact which could conceivably alter national voting habits. On this question, two theories have been proposed by political scientists: first, that party preference is stable (once a Democrat, always a Democrat); and second, that voters take on the political coloration of their new community (new suburbanites shift to the Republican party). No one knows which view is correct— or in what situations—but if the chameleon theory prevails, local and national elections may swing toward the Republican side.

Internal as well as international migrants are often disenfranchised; a person who moves during the summer before a fall election is rarely able to vote either in the new area (because he has not resided there long enough) or in his former residence (because he is no longer there). This legal disenfranchisement is often extended by a disinclination to vote until one is accommodated to the new area.

CULTURAL UNIFORMITY AND CHANGING NORMS

By increasing interregional contacts, internal migration encourages the fusion of once disparate regional subcultures. In this manner, migration may be contributing to the social uniformity and cultural monotony so vigorously deplored by Tocqueville, Lord Bryce, Harold Laski, and other foreign visitors to the United States.

> Homogenization of the American population . . . is occurring as the result of migration on the one hand, and of mass media on the other. Will the 1960's see continuing convergence of regional, class, perhaps even of racial, differences in population characteristics? To what extent are there counterforces, such as the increasing school segregation by religion? Many observers see a trend toward greater mobility in our population, particularly insofar as its leadership is concerned. Fewer and fewer remain in their community of birth. The ties of family and local community grow weaker. Are we becoming a single national community, in which regional and class differences and loyalties are being progressively dissolved?[21]

But the knife cuts both ways. On the one hand, migrants introduce into their new groups some of the traits of their old provinces and thus stimulate borrowing and acculturation. On the other, they may constitute a force for modification of folkways and mores away from the traditions of any existing subculture. It has been hypothesized that migrants are innovators. Sociologists have put forward the thesis that migrants are more released from traditional folkways and mores than are nonmigrants. In this respect southern California, the greatest area of gross internal in-migration in the United States, offers some interesting speculations; indeed, it is perhaps more than a coincidence that southern California has such a proliferation of bizarre religious sects, abbreviated apparel for both sexes, emancipated women, and outlandish architecture. So, too, New York City, the major center for immigration from other continents, has long been famed for its exotic gastronomy, the babble of many languages, and a generally cosmopolitan aspect. In the case of southern California, the unorthodoxy is possibly attributable to internal migration; New York's deviations from national norms are more ascribable to the cultural heterodoxy generated by a large proportion

---

[21] Dudley Kirk, "Some Reflections on American Demography in the Nineteen Sixties," *op. cit.*, p. 307.

of international migrants arriving from European subcultures and a variety of other cultures. Confirmed New Yorkers and Californians often find the rest of the United States uniform to the point of monotony. To be sure, this hypothesis that movers have a greater tendency than stayers to be released from received norms has not been verified, but it would seem to be more probable than the converse or null hypotheses.

Thus internal migration may supply a strain toward consistency by intermingling peoples and social values—or it may alter traditional norms by setting a condition favoring unorthodoxy. International migration may foster both of these effects with greater intensity, since it ordinarily involves sharper cultural differences and a more decisive challenge to thoughts and customs of both migrants and those they meet along the way.

12 ✘ International Migration

The effects of migration between countries and cultures are of considerable magnitude and import for the migrant himself, for the nation he leaves, and for his new country. "For many people it has been and still is the only way out of the dead end created in some countries by persistent underemployment."[1] The stimulus of culture contact through intertribal and international migration has been extolled by many scholars. F. J. Teggart wrote of the essential character of "collisions of cultures" in "breaking the cake of custom" and vitalizing the social order.[2] Arnold Toynbee's thinking has some of the same cast. Alfred North Whitehead ascribed the development of culture to "the power of wandering," which along with diversification among communities provides "the incentive and material for the Odyssey of the human spirit. Animals that wander must adapt or die. When man ceases to wander, he will cease to ascend in the scale of being."[3]

Cultural interpenetration and the diffusion of mores and artifacts are accelerated by movement of people across national boundaries. Each migrant carries in his suitcase, habits, and preferences "a bit of old Spain"—or Bali or Latvia or Tannou Touva—thereby diluting the cultural purity of the country of destination. Of course, the mass media of communication also play a vigorous role in, for example, transporting around the world the New York business suit, and mass transportation of goods facilitates widespread consumption of Ford cars, Coca-

---

[1] International Labour Office, *International Migration: 1945-1957*, Geneva, 1959, p. 413.
[2] Frederick J. Teggart, *The Processes of History*, Yale University Press, New Haven, 1918.
[3] Alfred North Whitehead, *Science and the Modern World*, The Macmillan Co., New York, 1925, pp. 297-298.

Cola, and chewing gum. But temporary visits and permanent moves remain potent factors in "peoples talking to peoples."

Historical Types

The history of world migration is divisible into three overlapping periods, each characterized by a different pattern: group migration, free individual migration, and restricted migration. The logical and chronological divisions between the three types are blurred rather than discrete. We cannot assign precise dates to the shift from one pattern to another, and considerable variations obtain within each category. Nonetheless, this tripartite analysis does aid in understanding the changing causes and consequences of international relocation of people.

GROUP MIGRATION

The longest period by far was the first, covering the time before the demographic revolution. Thucydides wrote of preclassical Greece: "The country now called Hellas had in ancient times no settled population. On the contrary, migrations were of frequent occurrence, the several tribes readily abandoning their homes under the pressure of superior numbers."[4]

Group migration refers to the movement of people in clusters larger than a family. When a clan, tribe, or other social group moves as a unit both the motivation and the consequences may be considerably different from the circumstances and effects of individual and family-sized migratory units.

During the period of group movement, migration by a lone individual or nuclear family could be extremely hazardous. Suspicion of strangers even today is a widespread phenomenon among human societies. For most of man's history, a migrating visitor was often regarded with ill-favor, sometimes to the extent of injuring him or even putting him to death. Under these circumstances, expulsion has been considered tantamount to death among many peoples, including the ancient Greeks. Socrates, offered the choice between taking hemlock and ostracism, chose the former.

Several subtypes of group migration can be discerned: invasion, conquest, displacement, forced labor, and colonization. Invasion consists of movement en masse; among the recorded instances of these large-scale movements of entire populations are the wanderings of the Goths, Huns, Vandals, Magyars, Arabs, and Turks. In conquest, the conquerors settle and intermarry with the vanquished, resulting in biological amal-

---

[4] Thucydides, *History of the Peloponnesian War*, c. 400 B.C., Book I, chap. 1.

gamation and often cultural assimilation; examples are provided by the Aryans in India, the Moslems in Spain, and the Spaniards in Mexico. In some cases, the natives are displaced elsewhere, as the Indians of North America were pushed west by the European immigrants. Illustrations of forced labor abound: between 10 and 20 million Negro slaves were taken to the Western Hemisphere between 1550 and 1850; also, some forms of indenture can be considered forced migration. Colonization is familiar to all Americans; that is how the United States came into existence.

VOLUNTARY INDIVIDUAL MIGRATION

In contrast to movement by dozens or thousands, migration in the last few centuries has tended to be in much smaller units: a single person or a married couple accompanied by their children and sometimes by other relatives. The opening up of the world by faster and more reliable transport facilities and the improved knowledge of other countries and continents made possible by new communication media has facilitated migration by small groups desiring to improve their lot. H. P. Fairchild described free migration as the "movement of people, individually or in families, acting on their own individual initiative and responsibility, without official support or compulsion, passing from one well-developed country (usually old and thickly settled), to another well-developed country (usually new and sparsely populated) with the intention of residing there permanently."[5]

Figure 9 shows the major currents of human migration since the beginning of the sixteenth century. These include: from all parts of Europe to Anglo America, 45 million; from Latin countries of Europe to Latin America, 20 million; from Great Britain to South Africa and Australia, 10 million; from Africa to the New World as slaves, 15 million; from China and India to Africa, Indonesia, and neighboring countries, 25 million; from east to west within Anglo America; and from west to east within the Soviet Union. The first five moves are international; the last two are internal under present boundaries, though some of this intracontinental movement was international. Most of the migrants were of the second type (free individual), but a sizeable minority were type one (group).

The huge outpouring from Europe to the Americas and other newly available lands overseas was certainly the most important migratory movement of modern times and possibly the largest in all human history. Beginning in the sixteenth century following the European voyages of discovery and conquest, this exodus attained its climax early in the

---

[5] Henry Pratt Fairchild, *Immigration*, The Macmillan Co., New York, 1925, p. 20.

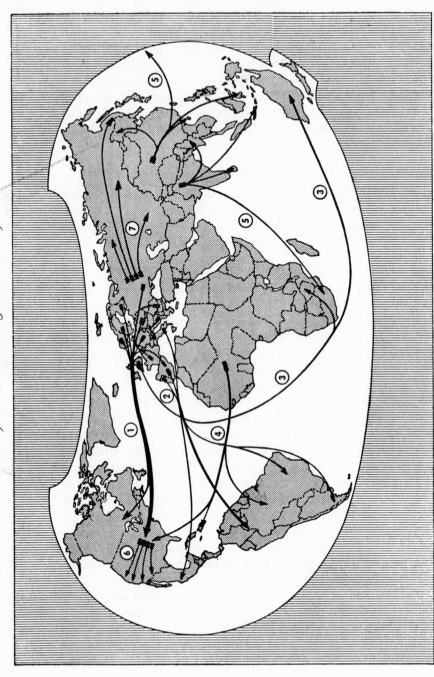

FIGURE 9. *International Migration Since 1500**

The main currents of intercontinental migration since the beginning of the sixteenth century have been: (1) from all parts of Europe to North America; (2) from Latin countries of Europe to Middle and South America; (3) from Great Britain to Africa and Australia; (4) import of slaves from Africa to America. Another current (5), partly intercontinental, partly intracontinental, has flowed from China and India. The most important internal migration has been (6) westward in the United States and (7) eastward in Russia.

* Wladimir S. Woytinsky and Emma S. Woytinsky, *World Population and Production, Twentieth Century Fund, New York, 1953,*

twentieth century and is continuing today, though on a considerably reduced scale. Altogether some 75 million Europeans may have emigrated overseas.

Prior to 1800 this emigration was of relatively small volume. Ocean crossings were difficult and perilous, and land transportation facilities were similarly inadequate, both in Europe and the territories overseas. The almost universal ignorance of conditions in the New World discouraged voyages by persons lacking compelling personal, financial, religious, or political reasons for leaving home. After the Napoleonic Wars, however, millions of people from all sections of the Continent and from all walks of life migrated overseas. Moreover, in contrast to earlier migration, this mass movement was primarily

> a spontaneous movement of individuals; relatively free at its height from legal restrictions, sometimes aided by government subsidies and greatly encouraged by the land policies of some leading countries of immigration. The importance of the expectation of a higher level of living as a cause of this migration is generally recognized. In much of rural Europe land was scarce and was becoming more scarce as population growth accelerated under the impetus of declining mortality. Wages in the European cities were relatively low and periods of unemployment were frequent. According to one view, the development of manufactures and commerce was not rapid enough to match the increase of the labour supply brought about by the excess of births over deaths and by migration from rural areas.[6]

By contrast the New World offered free or inexpensive land to the landless agricultural immigrant and opportunities for employment at higher wages to the urban worker. Also transportation improved: the number, tonnage, and speed of ocean-going vessels increased; new highways and railroads carried migrants from the interior of Europe to the seaports and later transported them from ports of debarkation to inland overseas territories. The timing of the outward migration differed in various regions in Europe. Until about a century ago most emigrants originated from the maritime regions of western Europe; later movement came from the entire continent.

Although none of the other migration currents shown in Figure 9 is quite so impressive, several streams have involved millions of émigrés over the centuries. International migration within Europe has always been fairly extensive. (In the last four decades, the major single stream of migrants has been from Italy into France.) Except for forced exportation of slaves, Africans have never out-migrated in large numbers.

---

[6] Fairchild, *Immigration, op. cit.,* p. 68.

Movement into the African continent has been mostly by Europeans. Asia, too, considering its huge population base, has sent relatively few migrants to other continents in modern times. Intracontinental migration is also small relative to the total Asian population. Anglo and Latin America and Oceania are receiving areas of European and other migration.

RESTRICTED MIGRATION

Controlled migration is now replacing free migration. In the twentieth century, rules governing migration increased in number and restrictiveness. Some nations now prohibit all movement of certain types of people, and others have set up migration quotas which cannot be exceeded, thus curtailing movement severely.

Controls on migration apply to both in- and out-migrants. For example, the United States has a quota system to limit immigration plus a policy of deporting certain undesirables to other countries. Exclusion policies are common; witness the Oriental Exclusion Acts of 1882-1907 in the United States. Limitations on emigration are also spreading, but rules governing emigration are slightly more relaxed than the quotas and prohibitions clamped upon people trying to enter a new land. Even countries that clamor about wanting immigrants sometimes maintain very restrictive immigration laws—Latin American states, for instance. The reasons behind these controls are varied. Immigration restrictions, the first to appear, are usually economically motivated (as are restrictions on the privileges of resident aliens), whereas emigration restrictions are generally enacted for political and military purposes.[7]

A prospective migrant faced with restrictive or prohibitory emigration regulations from his own country and similar immigration ordinances by his intended country of destination appears to have little chance to complete his desired move. In such situations some of the disappointed aspirants resort to illegal departure and entry. Others simply chafe. Still others take advantage of the vague phrasing and even self-contradictory clauses of many migration statutes. Experts on international law often find emigration and immigration regulations impossible to systematize and even to understand; it is no wonder that the rules seem to change at the whim of the official who holds the rubber stamp of permission. Two results of all these confining ordinances are that an enormous potential is being pent up in certain areas, and

---

[7] Edward P. Hutchinson and Wilbert E. Moore, "Pressures and Barriers in Future Migration," in Kingsley Davis (ed.), "World Population in Transition," *Annals of the American Academy of Political and Social Science*, Vol. CCXXXVII, January 1945, pp. 164-171.

inequalities in the distribution of scarce goods and the standard of living are being aggravated.

The displaced persons of World War II and the following decade represent a special case. Approximately 8 million migrants (excluding repatriates) of 1946-1954 were drawn to the following countries: United States, 1,700,000; Canada, 1,100,000; Australia, 900,000; Israel, 800,000; Argentina, 750,000; Venezuela, 500,000; United Kingdom, 450,000; Brazil, 400,000; France, 350,000; and Belgium, 300,000.[8] Many of these migrants were displaced persons. Since the end of the war, millions of people have been ejected from their homelands, and the demographic qualities of entire nations have radically altered. Political upheavals have driven whole populations into exile and created mass migrations far exceeding those normally flowing from regional variations in labor supply and demand throughout the world. Postwar migration may thus be divided into two kinds: economic and political. Economic currents generally have tended to flow at an even pace within fixed channels, whereas the political moves, produced as they were by erratic circumstances, in most cases appeared as precipitously as flash floods and as quickly were spent. Other contrasts between the two types revolve around freedom of choice, degree of permanency, the kinds of persons moving, the effects on the countries of origin and destination as well as on the migrant himself, and finally assimilation. Economic migration is a largely voluntary, individual, temporary movement of young adults, benefitting both emigration and immigration nations by offering an employment outlet for the energies of these men while enabling the migrant worker to better his lot and be absorbed into a new community fairly readily. On the other hand, political migration is ordinarily impelled by threat or coercion imposed upon whole groups of people irrespective of age and sex, who are thus uprooted permanently, exerting a disrupting influence on the economies of the nations of emigration, leading frequently in receiving areas to unemployment, added expenditures, and inflation, and often forcing the refugee to occupy a lower rung of the occupational and social ladder, thereby aggravating existing difficulties of his adjustment to the new environment.[9]

FUTURE PROSPECTS

To anyone who believes that each person should have the freedom to live and move wherever he pleases, future migration prospects are not

---

[8] W. D. Borrie, *The Cultural Integration of Immigrants*, UNESCO, Paris, 1959, p. 17.
[9] International Labour Office, *International Migration, op. cit.*, pp. 1-2.

promising. It is no longer possible to respond to the inciting factors of pressures at home and opportunities abroad by migrating at will because the enabling factor of absence of effective official checks and barriers is not favorable.

Some scholars have recommended that an effectual international migration authority be established, perhaps under the auspices of the United Nations, acting as a clearing house for information and as a labor exchange. In this regard, the International Labour Office and other U.N. organizations have been of some help, but an agency directly and primarily concerned with migration may yet be needed.

Lately, a network of reciprocal migration agreements has arisen, mainly among European nations, covering wages, family allowances, old age pensions, and other benefits to be conferred on each other's citizens. Bilateral and multilateral agreements have been signed by the Scandinavian countries, the Benelux nations, and the United Kingdom. Additional countries have rules protecting people who commute to work across a national boundary.

Countries offering the greatest potential for emigration are China, India, and other dense, land-scarce, rapidly growing nations. Immigration potential results from abundance of scarcely populated land or healthy industrial expansion, coupled with slight natural increase. Today, however, no suitable balance obtains between these two conditions; the immigration potential of the second group is too small to absorb the excess population of the first. Moreover, restrictions on international movement prohibit redress of such economic imbalances.

Immigration into the United States

United States net international migration has been nearly always positive. Much of the country's growth has resulted from the multitudes of immigrants debarking from ships in New York, Boston, and other ports. Since 1820, when the Federal government began to keep immigration statistics, 42 million immigrants have entered the country. Not all settled permanently, but very likely not far from 35 million have remained in the new land. "This is the largest movement of immigrants into any country known to history, and considering the conditions now prevailing in the world, it appears not likely to be surpassed in the near future."[10]

Official immigration figures by decades are reported in Table 17. Annual records show an erratic secular increase from 1820 through

[10] Warren S. Thompson, *Population Problems*, McGraw-Hill Book Co., New York, 1953, p. 277.

TABLE 17. *Immigration to the United States, 1820-1962* *

YEAR	NUMBER OF PERSONS
1820-1962	42,396,068
1820	8,385
1821-1830	143,439
1831-1840	599,125
1841-1850	1,713,251
1851-1860	2,598,214
1861-1870	2,314,824
1871-1880	2,812,191
1881-1890	5,246,613
1891-1900	3,687,564
1901-1910	8,795,386
1911-1920	5,735,811
1921-1930	4,107,209
1931-1940	528,431
1941-1950	1,035,039
1951-1960	2,515,479
1961	271,344
1962	283,763

From 1820 to 1867, figures represent alien passengers arrived; 1868 through 1891 and 1895 through 1897, immigrant aliens arrived; 1892 through 1894 and from 1898 to the present time, immigrant aliens admitted. Since 1868, data are for fiscal years ended June 30.

* U. S. Department of Justice, *Annual Report of the Immigration and Naturalization Service: 1962*, Government Printing Office, Washington, 1963, p. 18.

1907, an irregular decline through 1933, and somewhat larger figures thereafter. For the ten-year period 1905–1914, immigration averaged a million persons a year. The largest annual totals since 1820 were 1,285,349 in 1907 and 1,214,480 in 1914. The smallest figures since 1831 were 23,068 in 1933 and 23,725 in 1943. Recent admissions have hovered between a quarter and a third of a million annually.

Emigration too has been fairly large. Some immigrants came over temporarily, returning to their native lands as soon as they made enough money to set themselves up as farmers or businessmen. Others who came here intending to stay permanently were disillusioned when they found that the glitter in the streets was not gold.

Net foreign-born immigration of whites has been estimated as follows: 1870-1880, 1,876,000; 1880-1890, 3,757,000; 1890-1900, 2,888,000; 1900-1910, 5,188,000; 1910-1920, 2,888,000; 1920-1930, 2,443,000; 1930-1940, minus 122,000; and 1940-1950, 974,000.[11] Net immigration over 1950-

[11] Dorothy Swaine Thomas, "International Migration," in Philip M. Hauser (ed.), *Population and World Politics*, The Free Press, Glencoe, 1958, p. 150.

244 :: MORTALITY, FERTILITY, AND MIGRATION

1960 amounted to almost 2.5 million persons. The depression of the 1930's caused the net outward movement in that decade. Net outward migration has been observed in only four years in this century: 68,000 in 1932; 57,000 in 1933; 10,000 in 1934; and 4,000 in 1935.

FOUR PERIODS OF MIGRATION

There have been four principal stages of migration into the United States. Before the revolution, immigrants were colonists and came mostly from England. At the time of first census, persons of English, Scotch, and Irish descent accounted for 79 per cent of the national population. The British groups together comprised a majority of every state, the English alone attaining 61 per cent of the total and a majority in all states except New Jersey and Pennsylvania (and even there they constituted the largest single group). Aside from the English, the only sizeable concentrations of ethnic groups were the Scotch and Irish in the South, Germans in Pennsylvania and the South, Dutch in New York and New Jersey, Swedish in Delaware, and French and Spanish in territories not yet attaining statehood.[12] The earliest immigrants arrived largely in groups.

After the colonies became the United States, immigration sources widened to other countries—a phenomenon common to many former colonies. During the century following independence, about 95 per cent of the immigrants came from northern and western Europe. England kept its leadership, but large numbers of new settlers began to pour in from Scotland, Ireland, France, and Germany.

This "old immigration" yielded to the "new immigration" around 1880. New-style immigrants came from southern and eastern Europe in addition to the countries already named. Countries of origin included Germany, Sweden, Norway, Italy, Austria, Hungary, Russia, Poland, Turkey, and still, England. Both the old and the new immigrations were preponderantly by individuals and families.

Today, the nation is in a period of restriction dating from the quota regulations enacted in 1921 and 1924. During the last four decades, settlers have been allowed to enter in proportion to the number of existing United States residents whose ancestors came from that country. These quota laws have curtailed immigration severely. Of the 271,344 immigrants admitted in 1960-61, most were from Europe and

---

[12] United States Bureau of the Census, *Historical Statistics of the United States, Colonial Times to 1957*, Government Printing Office, Washington, 1960, p. 756; and American Council of Learned Societies, "Report of Committee on Linguistic and National Stocks of the United States" (based on studies by Howard F. Barker and Marcus L. Hansen), *Annual Report of the American Historical Association, 1931*, Washington, 1932, Vol. I, p. 124.

the Americas; the foremost contributors being Mexico, 41,632; Canada, 32,038; Germany, 29,048; United Kingdom, 22,717; and Italy, 20,652. Mexicans' intended permanent residence is generally California or Texas, Canadians pick California, Germans and British select New York or California, Italians choose New York, and others intend to settle predominantly in New York or California. Almost half of all immigrants intend to reside in either California (64,205) or New York (60,429); other commonly preferred states are Illinois, Texas, New Jersey, Florida, and Massachusetts.[13]

COUNTRIES OF ORIGIN

The largest immigration from a single country since 1820 is Germany's 6.8 million immigrants. Other countries supplying over a million officially recorded immigrants are: Italy, 5.0 million; Ireland, 4.7 million; Great Britain, 4.6 million; Austria-Hungary, 4.3 million; Russia, 3.3 million; Canada, 3.1 million; Sweden, 1.3 million; and Mexico, 1.2 million. Were official records available for years before 1820, the total for Great Britain would be much larger.

In this connection we must not overlook the extent to which the United States is a British country. To be sure, the volume of immigrants from Great Britain has been exceeded by that of other countries on many occasions in United States immigration history, but the influx of British has been moderately large throughout the entire existence of the United States and was dominant in the colonial period. Not only have the English, Scotch, and Irish arrived in quantity— they arrived first. The Italian who came to New York in 1907 now has children and grandchildren. But the Englishman who stepped ashore in 1707 has hundreds of descendants.

Persons of foreign stock—defined by the Bureau of the Census as first-generation (foreign-born) plus second-generation (foreign or mixed parentage) residents—comprised 19 per cent of the total 1960 population—far fewer than the 34 per cent of 1900. As Table 18 shows, the lands contributing 2 million or more to the foreign stock are Italy, Germany, Canada, United Kingdom, Poland, and the U.S.S.R. All the principalities of Asia together (except Asiatic Russia) have supplied the United States with less than one-half as many persons of foreign stock as has the relatively small country of Poland. Italians constitute the largest group of first-generation inhabitants, while Germany leads in the second generation. The state containing the largest number of residents of foreign stock is New York, followed by California and Pennsyl-

---

[13] Department of Justice, *Annual Report of the Immigration and Naturalization Service: 1961*, Government Printing Office, Washington, 1962, pp. 31 and 37.

TABLE 18. *Persons of Foreign Stock, United States, 1960**

COUNTRY OF ORIGIN	POPULATION OF FOREIGN STOCK	PER CENT DISTRIBUTION	STATES IN WHICH MOST NUMEROUS
TOTAL	34,050,406	100.0	N.Y., Calif., Pa.
Italy	4,543,935	13.3	N.Y., N.J., Pa.
Germany	4,320,664	12.7	N.Y., Ill., Wis.
Canada	3,181,051	9.3	Mass., Mich., Calif.
United Kingdom	2,884,651	8.5	N.Y., Calif., Pa.
Poland	2,780,026	8.2	N.Y., Ill., Mich.
U.S.S.R.	2,290,267	6.7	N.Y., Calif., Pa.
Ireland	1,773,312	5.2	N.Y., Mass., Pa.
Mexico	1,735,992	5.1	Calif., Texas, Ariz.
Asia	1,141,839	3.4	Calif., Hawaii, N.Y.
Austria	1,098,630	3.2	N.Y., Pa., N.J.
Sweden	1,046,942	3.1	Minn., Ill., Calif.
Czechoslovakia	917,830	2.7	Pa., Ohio, Ill.
Norway	774,754	2.3	Minn., Calif., Wash.
Hungary	701,637	2.1	N.Y., Ohio, Pa.
All other	4,858,876	14.2	——

* U. S. Bureau of the Census, *U. S. Census of Population: 1960,* "General Social and Economic Characteristics: U. S. Summary," PC(1)-1C, Government Printing Office, Washington, 1962, pp. 203 and 253-254.

vania. Of the 13 places of origin contributing the most foreign stock, New York holds the greatest concentration in eight instances, Massachusetts has the most persons of Canadian stock, California has the most Mexicans and Asiatics, Minnesota the most Swedes and Norwegians, and Pennsylvania the most Czechoslovakians.

Despite the national origins quota system, 2.6 million immigrants were admitted to the United States during 1946-1957, maintaining the nation's position as the largest immigrant-receiving country in the world. These newcomers were, in roughly equal parts: displaced persons and refugees, immigrants from elsewhere in the Western Hemisphere, families of United States citizens, and quota admittances other than displaced persons. The second largest immigrant-receiving country is Canada, which took in 1.5 million persons in 1946-1956, including immigrants from Commonwealth countries, displaced persons, Netherlands farm families, relatives of Canadian residents, and immigrants chosen for occupational placement.[14]

---

[14] Helen F. Eckerson, "United States and Canada: Magnets for Immigration," *Annals of the American Academy of Political and Social Science,* Vol. CCCXVI, March 1958, pp. 34-42.

GOOD SEED OR BAD

From Colonial days until recent decades, the crossing from Europe to the Americas operated as a harsh and brutal filter. Overland in the old world, across the Atlantic, and overland again in the new world, probably few but the hardy survived the dangers and physical difficulties with which they were confronted. Selective factors were both physical and adaptational. Only those who succeeded in adjusting from peasant ways to the challenge of the new urban society could absorb the repeated shocks of migration and its aftermath.

As regards the background of those immigrants there is still some question whether these men and women to whom Walt Whitman said "we opened our gates" were the stalwart survivors of an arduous journey undertaken only by the courageous, ambitious, and far-sighted, or rather the dregs of European society—feeble, stupid, criminal, and incompetent people who could not make a go of their lives and embarked for America in the hope that the competition would be less rugged. Seventh-generation Americans alternately brag of ancestral priority, initiative, and courage and aggressively admit that their foreparents came over when no one but a criminal, a failure, or a fool would step on the new world shores. Thus, according to the disposition of the claimant, the United States was forged out of the best or the worst of metals. Whichever argument is correct, however, does not particularly matter now, for by and large neither the sins nor the virtues of the immigrants are observable in their grandchildren, who eat American hot dogs, attend American schools, and accept the values currently endemic in their generation, regardless of national ancestry.

SETTLEMENT PATTERNS

Settlement patterns of immigrants were guided by several pulls. *Ocean transportation routes:* newcomers tended to settle near the debarkation point of the steamship lines from their countries—for example, Germans clustered in Baltimore. *Reputation of the city or state:* the image that an American area projected in Europe was important in determining the propensity of immigrants to go there. Cities of the northern seaboard had a reputation of providing jobs and residential quarters where an immigrant was welcome; southern cities did not. *Climate:* immigrants tended toward regions having similar weather conditions to the old country. Swedes and Norwegians clustered in Minnesota and Wisconsin. *Fluctuations in regional demands for labor:* the opening of mines in West Virginia and Pennsylvania and fruit growing in California attracted migrants. *River, road, and rail systems:* migrants followed the cheapest and best-known routes of transportation in their trek through interior North America. Cities that were somewhat removed from main routes received few immigrants. *Family and community:* the first member of a family or town to come to this country often wrote letters home to relatives and friends offering advice, information, and help in expediting their settlement in the new land. When the others made the passage, they often moved into the same city or even the same block as the pioneer from their group. Finally, any motive operating in an internal migration situation may apply also to external migration.

As in other countries, immigrants to the United States tend to reside, work, and play together in enclaves comprised of settlers from the same region or even village in the old country. Sometimes this segregation is their own preference; at other times it is forced upon them by the majority. In either case, however, the result is a collection of little communities, each having its own language and customs which are steadily altered by the dominant American culture. Often they have their own grocery store stocked with staples and delicacies with which they were familiar before moving. If the district is populous, it may have its own motion picture theater exhibiting foreign language films with no subtitles.

Waves of immigrants have had a profound effect on the social stratification system of the United States. Their time of arrival, place of settlement, size of group, and other elements all have contributed to ethnic bases of social distinctions. W. Lloyd Warner's Yankee City study clearly illustrates the gradual climb in status of nationality groups as they advance occupationally from mill-worker to foreman to white-collar status and residentially from slums to flats to shabby-genteel houses.[15] The earlier the newcomers began settling in the community, the farther out from the city center is their present median location and the more dispersed their residential pattern. The later they settled, the closer to the city center and the more concentrated and segregated are their residences. Interestingly, a succession of immigrant groups of different nationalities probably accelerates status mobility. That is, each new wave, beginning on the bottom of the social scale, pushes up the ethnic groups of longer residence. As the groups thus make their way up the social ladder, their values change to include such traits as lower fertility and abandonment of patriarchal family structures. Length of residence in the United States is also associated with income, status of occupation, amount of education, participation in community life, and general acceptability to others.

---

[15] W. Lloyd Warner and Paul S. Lunt, *Social Life of a Modern Community*, Yale University Press, New Haven, 1941.

ATTRIBUTES OF IMMIGRANTS

Immigrants' level of living, though appreciably lower on the average than that of most native residents, is usually higher than it was in the old country. They and their children acquire "a small wage but a higher one, a poor house but a better one, a meager sixth-grade education but more than they know enough to want, and it is universal and compulsory."[16]

Demographic attributes of immigrants differ from those of native-born citizens in several respects. The foreign-born population is disproportionately urban; though comprising only 5.4 per cent of the total population in 1960, they constituted 7.2 per cent of the people in metropolitan areas. Their sex ratio, once heavily favoring the males, has declined in every decade since 1910. From 124 in 1850, 115 to 119 during 1860-1900, and 129 in 1910 (after a decade of heavy immigration), it was down to 104 in 1950. Immigration is also selective by age; young adults predominate, attracted by the occupational opportunities offered on the new continent, and they are generally unmarried or newly married without children. Emigration from the United States is similarly selective, favoring young adult males.

Until 1930, the Census year following installation of national quotas, the total number of foreign-born residents had increased with every Census. From 2 million in 1850 the total grew to 14 million in 1930, after which deaths to the foreign-born exceeded immigration, with the result that their numbers declined to 9.7 million in 1960. The resident population born outside the United States had been roughly stable at 13 to 15 per cent through 1920, after which it declined to 5.4 per cent in 1960. Prior to 1920, the national increase through excess of immigrants over emigrants was usually approximately the same as the increase through excess of births over deaths. Unless immigration laws are changed drastically, the foreign-born part of our population may decline to 3 per cent by 1975.[17]

ANTIFOREIGNISM

During the period of maximum immigration rates and high proportions of foreign-born, animus toward interlopers took the form of antiforeignism and religious prejudice. New arrivals were branded as "krautheads," "micks," "polacks," "bohunks," and "wops." Nativist sentiment was directed against the Irish and the Roman Catholic

[16] Donald R. Taft and Richard Robbins, *International Migrations*, Ronald Press Co., New York, 1955, p. 84.

[17] Philip M. Hauser, "The Challenge of Tomorrow's Markets," *Journal of Marketing*, Vol. XXIV, No. 1, July 1959, pp. 1-7.

Church to such a level of animosity that several Catholic churches were burned and numerous riots instigated. Virulent verbal attacks on "them people what cain't talk no English" were supplemented by the workings of the Know-Nothing Party, which flourished in the 1850's for the purpose of repealing laws giving privileges to naturalized citizens. Originating in New York, where the alien population was greatest, the party quickly spread throughout the country, electing seven governors, capturing five state legislatures, and polling almost a million votes for its 1856 Presidential candidate, Millard Fillmore.[18] The Know-Nothing platform contained such planks as "Americans must rule America!" "Hostility to the assumption of the Pope . . . in a republic sanctified by Protestant blood," and "Free and liberal education for all sects and classes, with the Bible, God's holy word, as a universal textbook." Agitation against Jews and the Pope reached another high pitch in the Ku Klux Klan, a nativist organization having 5 million adherents in the South, Ohio, and Indiana in 1925.

Nor did antiforeignism die with the disappearance of the Know-Nothings and the weakening of the Ku Klux Klan. As is seen in the next section, several laws have been passed restricting entry and permitting retraction of privileges granted to immigrants. Present counterparts of the 1798 Alien and Sedition Acts encourage harassment of aliens suspected of being members of subversive organizations.

Federal Laws and Quotas

From the Declaration of Independence to the First World War there was almost no control over immigration or emigration in the United States. A few states along the eastern seaboard had their own immigration laws, and California and other states petitioned Congress to institute regulative measures, but before 1882 there was no Federal restriction of any consequence. Federal action first took the form of invalidating state ordinances: in 1849 the Supreme Court ruled in the Passenger cases that the states could not impose head taxes on entering aliens, and in 1875 the Court declared that state immigration regulations "infringed on Congress's exclusive power over foreign commerce."[19] Until 1921 the Federal government was only concerned with denying admission to Orientals and undesirable individuals, such as prostitutes (barred in 1875), convicts (barred in 1875), the mentally ill (barred

---

[18] Lawrence H. Fuchs, "Some Political Aspects of Immigration," *Law and Contemporary Problems*, Vol. XXI, No. 3, Summer 1956, p. 275.

[19] John Higham, "American Immigration Policy in Historical Perspective," *Law and Contemporary Problems*, Vol. XXI, No. 2, Spring 1956, p. 218.

in 1882), persons likely to become public charges (barred in 1882), contract laborers (barred in 1885), and illiterates (barred in 1917).

A Federal Office of Superintendent of Immigration was established in 1891 as a part of the Treasury Department. Shifted to the Department of Commerce and Labor in 1903, it was reorganized and named the Immigration and Naturalization Service within the Department of Labor in 1933 and was transferred to the Department of Justice in 1940. The I. & N. Service has charge of the entry of immigrants and visitors, determines the status of aliens, enforces exclusion and deportation, and collects statistical and other information about immigrants.

The basic United States immigration law is the Immigration Act of 1917. This and other legislation specify financial, mental, physical, and moral qualifications for entry. All immigrants must secure visas from a United States consul abroad; to obtain a visa, the prospective migrant must be prepared to offer documentary proof of his identity, literacy, solvency, health, and freedom from moral taint. Red tape is an effective screening device. The 1917 Act codified earlier laws excluding pathological or otherwise undesirable individuals:

the physically defective (persons with a "loathsome or contagious disease" or unable to work due to a physical defect); the mentally defective (idiots, imbeciles, the insane, etc., and those with a "constitutional psychopathic inferiority"); the morally defective (a broad phrase for alcoholics, persons convicted of crimes of moral turpitude, polygamists, prostitutes, and previously deported aliens seeking re-admission within a year); the politically defective (another broad phrase covering anarchists and those advocating overthrow of government by force); the educationally defective (all aliens over 16 who could not read English, a foreign language or a dialect); the economically dangerous (those contracted for labor, vagrants, persons likely to become public charges).[20]

Other Federal Acts deserving special mention are: the Oriental Exclusion Acts beginning in 1882, the National Origins Quota Acts of the 1920's, the D. P. and Refugee Acts of 1948-1953, and the McCarran-Walter Act of 1952. The Oriental Exclusion Acts (including the Alien Contract Labor Law of 1885 and the Gentlemen's Agreement with Japan of 1907) deterred Asians from entering the United States—an action instigated on the Pacific Coast. The quota system of the 1920's was enacted primarily to control immigration from southern and eastern European countries. The 1921 Act was originally designed for a one-year emergency; in 1924 the quotas were revised and made permanent.

[20] Taft and Robbins, *International Migrations, op. cit.,* pp. 420-421.

The Immigration and Nationality Act of 1952 codified and strengthened these restrictive principles based on race and nationality.

ORIENTIAL EXCLUSION

The 1882 law—prompted by American fear of cheap "coolie" labor—prohibited entry of Chinese, with the exception of a tiny group of ministers, merchants, and scholars. The Gentlemen's Agreement of 1907 called for Japanese refusal of passports to the United States for laborers (at the suggestion of the United States). In its 1917 Act, Congress set up an Asiatic Barred Zone, declaring natives of India, Burma, Siam, the Malay States, the East Indies, the Polynesian Islands, and parts of China inadmissible to the United States. The 1924 law prohibited immigration of Japanese and other aliens legally declared ineligible for citizenship by the United States Supreme Court in the 1922 case, *Ozawa* v. *United States*. This exclusion policy continued until 1943, when a law was enacted allowing the Chinese an annual quota of 105 persons and ending the ineligibility of resident Chinese aliens to obtain citizenship. The Japanese restriction continued until a 1952 Act brought all Asiatics under the quota system and permitted them to apply for citizenship.

NATIONAL ORIGINS ACTS OF 1921-1929

Senator William P. Dillingham of Vermont, chairman of the United States Immigration Commission, suggested in the 1911 Commission report that the number of each race or nationality arriving each year be limited to a specified percentage of the average of that group's arrivals over a preceding period of years. At the 1919-1921 Congressional Immigration Committee hearings, Sidney Luther Gulick, a former missionary to Japan, proposed allotment of quotas based on the proportion of each nationality now represented in our foreign-born population. To effectuate this "percentage quota" principle, he recommended that immigrants be limited to an annual quota of 3 per cent of the number of their countrymen resident in the United States at the time of the last census. The First Quota Act of 1921, vetoed by President Wilson and later signed by Harding, was a temporary measure embodying Gulick's formula for apportioning a total quota of 357,803 persons.

The Immigration Act of 1924 lowered Gulick's fraction to 2 per cent of the group resident in the United States in 1890. By moving the base date back three censuses, the new law reduced the proportion of admissible immigrants from the "less desirable" countries which had been sending so many new settlers since 1890. This use of outdated population statistics has been called "flagrantly discriminatory," making obvious the motives behind the quota legislation. "The total quota for northern and western European countries was cut by only 29%, whereas that for southern and eastern Europe suffered a cut of 87%. The quota for Italy, for instance, was reduced from 42,057 to 3,845; Poland's from 30,977 to 5,982; Turkey's from 2,654 to 100."[21] Exempt from the quota system were Latin Americans, wives and unmarried minor children of American citizens, a limited number of husbands of American citizens, students over age fifteen, and ministers and professors (and their wives and children under eighteen). Within the quota, 50 per cent of each country's allowance was available to parents of adult American citizens and to skilled farmers and their wives and children under eighteen. Second priority was accorded to wives and unmarried minor children of resident aliens. Beyond that came a complicated system of preferences for aliens in special categories.

The National Origins Provision of the 1924 Act, which took effect in 1929, stipulated that the annual quota for each nationality should bear the same ratio to 154,000 as the number of United States residents of that descent (including both natives and foreign-born) bore to the total population. Thus if Country A had contributed 8.7 per cent of the national populace by 1920, its annual quota would be 8.7 per cent of 154,000. The minimum of 100 per country was maintained. Advocates of this plan contended that it would freeze the ethnic composition of the country, apparently on the ethnocentric assumption that a change would be undesirable. About 84 per cent of the national quotas went to northern and western Europe, 14 per cent to southern and eastern Europe, and 2 per cent to other areas.

Table 19 indicates the favoring of immigrants from northern and western Europe since 1929—the reverse of the pre-1921 trend of immigrants. This legislation assumes innate inferiority and nonassimilability of people from certain countries (apparently the cauldron can only melt down special stocks). Quotas apply to country of birth, not present residence or citizenship. Boundary changes—so frequent in Europe—are practically ignored.

No one knows the precise effect the quota laws have had in curbing immigration. Certainly we cannot separate this cause of the decreased volume from other such powerful influences as the world-wide depression of the 1930's or the Second World War. Be that as it may, the quotas unquestionably reduced immigration from certain countries and had no effect *vis-à-vis* other nations. Admissions reached a nadir of 23,000

---

[21] William S. Bernard, *American Immigration Policy*, Harper and Brothers, New York, 1950, p. 27.

TABLE 19. *Annual Immigartion Quotas by Country, 1929 and 1952**

COUNTRY	QUOTA EFFECTIVE 1929	1952 IMMIGRATION AND NATIONALITY ACT
All countries	153,714	154,657
Europe	150,591	149,667
Austria	1,413	1,405
Belgium	1,304	1,297
Bulgaria	100	100
Czechoslovakia	2,874	2,859
Denmark	1,181	1,175
Finland	569	566
France	3,086	3,069
Germany	25,957	25,814
Great Britain	65,721	65,361
Greece	307	308
Hungary	869	865
Iceland	100	100
Ireland	17,853	17,756
Italy	5,802	5,645
Netherlands	3,153	3,136
Norway	2,377	2,364
Poland	6,524	6,488
Portugal	440	438
Rumania	295	289
Spain	252	250
Sweden	3,314	3,295
Switzerland	1,707	1,698
Turkey	226	225
U.S.S.R.	2,784	2,697
Yugoslavia	845	933
Other Europe	1,538	1,534
Asia	1,323	2,990
Africa	1,200	1,400
Australia	200	600
All others	400	—

* U. S. Bureau of the Census, *Statistical Abstract of the United States*, Government Printing Office, Washington, 1958, Table 103.

in 1933. Between 1931 and 1936, 240,000 more aliens left than were admitted;[22] citizens showed net outward movement in 1932 and 1933.

After World War II, refugees forced a breach in the wall using the Displaced Persons Acts of 1948 and 1950 that allowed people from low-

---

[22] President's Commission on Immigration and Naturalization, *Whom We Shall Welcome*, Government Printing Office, Washington, 1953, p. 29.

quota countries to enter the United States and be charged against future quotas up to a maximum of 50 per cent a year. When immigrants from a given country filled the 1949 quota of, say, 100, then 50 more could be admitted in 1949 under the 1950 quota, another 50 under the 1951 quota, and so forth. In this fashion Latvians mortgaged half of their future quotas through the year 2274. Between 1946 and 1961, some 700,000 immigrants were admitted under the Displaced Persons Acts and the Refugee Relief Act of 1953.

THE 1952 IMMIGRATION ACT

The McCarran-Walter Act of 1952 not only accepted the racist principles implicit in the national origins quota system, but went one step further. Enacted during the early 1950's, when the country was in the grip of a Communist witchhunt, this legislation incorporated various antisubversive provisions borrowed from the Internal Security Act of 1950. This double-barrelled Act has drawn frequent criticism. One sociologist comments:

> Perhaps the most backward aspect of the 1952 Act is its position on civil liberties. Proceeding on the assumption that the Constitution does not protect aliens, it . . . holds that the constitutional safeguards with respect to jury trial, unreasonable searches, and post facto prohibitions, are not applicable. In addition the 1952 Act gives the President power to give governmental functionaries practically unreviewable discretion to exclude aliens and to deport those who have engaged in political activity now proscribed, even if it ceased many years ago, and at the same time was not forbidden by law. By expanding the grounds on which naturalized citizens may lose their citizenship, the 1952 Act has removed the stability of citizenship for naturalized citizens. This, in effect, has created two classes of citizens.[23]

In 1953 the Perlman Commission on Immigration and Naturalization concluded that "the immigration and nationality law embodies policies and principles that are unwise and injurious to the nation. It rests upon an attitude of hostility and distrust against all aliens. It applies discrimination against human beings on account of national origin, race, creed and color."[24] The official report of this Commission recommended the following changes: that the national origins quota system be abolished and replaced by allocation of visas without regard to national origin, race, creed, or color; that the maximum annual quota

---

[23] Simon Marcson, Review of President's Commission, *Whom We Shall Welcome*, in *American Journal of Sociology*, Vol. LXI, No. 1, July 1955, p. 95.
[24] President's Commission, *Whom We Shall Welcome*, *op. cit.*, p. 263.

immigration be one-sixth of 1 per cent of the population of the United States in the most recent census; that the same officials not exercise both enforcement and judicial functions; that aliens be accorded a fair hearing and procedure in exclusion and deportation cases; that conditions for admission and grounds for deportation bear a reasonable relation to national welfare and security, be definite in their meaning and application, and not be retroactive so as to penalize aliens for acts which were not prohibited when committed; and that the law extend to naturalized citizens the same status and rights as enjoyed by the native born.[25]

Because this 1952 Act reflects a spirit of suspicion and hostility toward immigrants, it has had continual opposition from various groups. President Truman vetoed it, but it was repassed over his veto. President Eisenhower called it discriminatory and advised revision "to get the bigotry out of it." And President Kennedy told Congress that national origins immigration quotas are "without basis in either logic or reason" and should be abolished. Civil rights groups were unhappy with the 1952 Act from the beginning. Residents of other countries regard it as insulting and humiliating to their national pride and personal integrity.

CURRENT ADMISSIONS

From 1954 through 1961 only about two-thirds of the total immigration quota was used. Some countries never fill their quotas, while others could fill them many times over if permitted. The United Kingdom used only 38 per cent of its 1954-1961 quota allotment, Ireland 40 per cent, and Sweden 60 per cent. Among nations using over 90 per cent were Portugal, Italy, Germany, Finland, France, Rumania, and Austria.[26]

Establishment of quotas for newly independent countries in Asia and Africa raised the 1952 quota to a total of 156,487 in 1961. During the fiscal year 1960-1961, a total of 96,104 quota immigrants were admitted to the United States, including 25,100 from Great Britain and Northern Ireland, 24,273 from Germany, 6,891 from Poland, 6,273 from Eire, 5,648 from Italy, 24,610 from elsewhere in Europe, 2,014 from Asia, 857 from Africa, and 438 from Oceania. An additional 175,240 persons entered as nonquota immigrants, including 32,551 spouses and children of United States citizens, 112,836 natives of the Western Hemisphere with their spouses and children, 22,840 persons admitted under special legislation (refugees, orphans, and victims of natural calamities), and

---

[25] *Ibid.*, pp. 263-266.

[26] Helen F. Eckerson and Gertrude D. Krichefsky, "Principles of Immigration Law—Part I," *I & N Reporter*, Vol. X, No. 3, January 1962, p. 31.

7,013 others. Nonmigrant aliens admitted on a temporary basis exceed a million persons annually.[27]

DEPORTATION AND NATURALIZATION

As might be expected, deportation reflects immigration policy. In the United States, for example, the rise in the number of deportations has accompanied restrictions on aliens. Yet compulsory return of aliens to their country of birth or entry is more complicated than it might appear to those who see rising deportation figures only as evidence that the Communists are being sent back to where they came from. Essentially, deportation is the basic means for dealing with resident aliens who violate the law and might otherwise be brought to court trial, with the greater guarantees of fair treatment insured by our legal system.[28] It also remains a formal tool for returning illegal entrants, especially Mexican "wetbacks." Of the total 61,801 aliens expelled from the United States, 54,164 conceded deportability and 7,637 were ordered deported by Federal proceedings; most of the deportees were Mexican.[29]

For many immigrants, naturalization is a cherished privilege, and most aliens have availed themselves of the opportunity to become citizens. From 1907 through 1961 some 7,800,000 aliens were naturalized. In the fiscal year 1960-1961, 132,450 aliens were naturalized and 3,175 petitions were denied; 70 per cent of these new citizens formerly owed allegiance to Germany, Italy, the United Kingdom, Canada, Poland, Mexico, Greece, the U.S.S.R., Japan, or Ireland.[30] The opposite of naturalization is revocation of citizenship: the Immigration and Nationality Act of 1952 provided for denaturalization for various reasons, and 3,669 persons were expatriated in 1960-1961. Despite illogicalities and obstacles, naturalization in the United States appears relatively simple and fair when compared to the convoluted and opaque processes of some other nations.

Assimilation of Immigrants

The adjustment of aliens to their new environment—and the adjustment of the environment to them—is rife with difficult problems. Language barriers, job competition, and divergent cultural backgrounds can

[27] Department of Justice, *Annual Report of the Immigration and Naturalization Service: 1961*, pp. 2-3, 22, and 26.

[28] Taft and Robbins, *International Migrations, op. cit.*, p. 431.

[29] Department of Justice, *Annual Report of the Immigration and Naturalization Service: 1962*, pp. 11 and 62-65.

[30] Department of Justice, *Annual Report of the Immigration and Naturalization Service: 1961*, pp. 13 and 78.

create serious disruption both in the migrant's personality and inter-personal relationships. To cite only one illustration, children may suffer from the conflict of loyalties inhering in their attempt to break away from their parents' ways of thinking and acting. In this connection the sociologists W. I. Thomas and Florian Znaniecki proposed as a cause of delinquency the discrepancies between the old world culture of first-generation immigrants and the new folkways and mores that their children learn in school.[31]

THE MARGINAL MAN

The marginal man has been defined as "one who is poised in psychological uncertainty between two (or more) social worlds; reflecting in his soul the discords and harmonies, repulsions and attractions of these worlds"[32]—a pattern of contradictions and ambivalences besetting international migrants entering a culture different from their own. "Only very rarely does such a person succeed in shedding all the old ways and adopting all the new. However far he does go in one direction, he is still tied by a thousand bonds of upbringing, habit, and family to the customs and practices of the culture in which he was raised. These conflicts can sometimes be gracefully reconciled, but usually they are not.[33]

A need to decide consciously about actions that others can perform without thinking is characteristic of the marginal man (or of anyone else who moves from one "reference group" to another). The consequent appearance of seeming stupidity often causes old members of the reference group to assume that the newcomer is of low social rank or dull. Indeed, even if in reality he is more intelligent, informed, and sensitive than the in-groupers he is apt to be treated as an inferior. C. P. Snow expresses the plight of the migrant or social climber in his advice to novelists: "It is a mistake . . . to make your parvenu not know his way about in his new surroundings: it would be truer to make him know his way too well."[34]

CAPACITY TO ABSORB IMMIGRANTS

From the standpoint of the host country, three circumstances pertaining to immigrants are particularly relevant: the capacities to absorb immigrants, to amalgamate them, and to assimilate them. The first is an economic concept; the second, biological; and the last, sociological.

---

[31] William I. Thomas and Florian Znaniecki, *The Polish Peasant in Europe and America*, University of Chicago Press, Chicago, 1918-1920, five volumes.

[32] Everett V. Stonequist, *The Marginal Man*, Scribner's, New York, 1937, p. 8.

[33] Harold R. Isaacs, "A Reporter at Large: Back to Africa," *The New Yorker*, Vol. XXXVII, No. 13, May 13, 1961, p. 116.

[34] Charles P. Snow, *The Search*, The New American Library, New York, 1934, 1958, p. 194.

By capacity to absorb we mean "the annual rate at which a country can receive immigrants without being subject to . . . serious economic derangement."[35] Absorptive capacity is directly related to natural increase as well as to migration. The largest permissible increase through net migration is equal to the maximum tolerable rate of population expansion minus natural increase.

Instead of working with maximums, some economists prefer to speak of optimum immigration rates. Optimum net migration equals optimum total growth minus anticipated natural increase. The optimum rate of population growth is dependent on the availability of jobs, which in turn depends on the optimum expansion of production and distribution of goods.

The relation between immigration and economic development is two-directional. That is, economic prosperity attracts immigrants, and immigrants in turn aid economic growth. Not only do they provide a labor force when it is needed (rather than fifteen or twenty years later, as in the case of fertility) and where it is needed (migrants go where the jobs are), but once in the new country, the immigrants add to the market size, thus contributing to the further expansion of industry and business.

This contribution of immigrants to the economy is sometimes tardy in reaching fruition, as immediate absorption capacity often falls well below the ultimate potential. In the cases of West Germany and Israel, the influx of refugees was so great as to place a great strain on the economy for several years. Later, however, the immigrants supplied an impetus to economic expansion. As explained by the International Labour Office: "The long-term benefits of immigration depend in effect on the strength of the economy and for quite a long time the price which has to be paid for them may appear unduly heavy. This makes it hard for governments, for the sake of distant and possibly uncertain benefits, deliberately to court the risk of short-term and all too certain upheavals. Few countries in fact have been able to derive the full benefit from large-scale immigration during the last twelve years without suffering severe strain in the process."[36]

AMALGAMATION AND ASSIMILATION

Amalgamation is a *biological* fusion of differing racial or ethnic groups. When Hymie Schwartz marries Midori Hayakawa or Virgie Shackleford, their children add to the amalgamation of racial stocks. (Israel Zangwill was thinking of ethnic intermarriage in entitling his 1908 play on American immigration problems "The Melting Pot.")

[35] Julius Isaac, *Economics of Migration*, Oxford University Press, New York, 1947, p. 110.
[36] International Labour Office, *International Migration, op. cit.*, p. 411.

Assimilation is a *social* fusion—a reciprocal merging of norms and values. "In cultural anthropology assimilation means at least relatively intense social interaction and cultural fusion so that a single way of life emerges from a situation of cultural pluralism."[37] Judging from United States immigration laws, a popular assumption seems to be that all foreigners are difficult to assimilate and that some are not assimilable at all. And, indeed, ethnic groups do assimilate at varying rates, exhibiting differences in tendencies to live in separate neighborhoods, to keep old languages and dress, and to intermarry with outsiders. The propensity to intermarry into other groups is probably the best single criterion of assimilation.

Assimilation, like amalgamation, is two-directional: both the immigrant and the receiving culture undergo changes. Thus immigrants to the United States are Americanized, but in the process they also alter the dominant culture, though often too gradually to be detected by the untrained observer. Assimilation also implies conformity, a making alike, but this does not mean total identity. An assimilated person is rather one who has become part of the new community and who resembles its inhabitants, as nearly as possible, in certain essential points. He abides reasonably well by the laws and mores of his new country and severs legal and political ties with the old. He speaks the language, adopts the folkways, and absorbs the major values of his new associates. "An immigrant is assimilated only when he speaks the language of his new country by preference, has adopted its customs, and when his general conduct and way of life become those of his new compatriots and his original outlook gives way to that of his new surroundings."[38] Linguistic and semantic difficulties are associated with incomplete assimilation. (Witness the immigrant who walked into a store in a Midwest town and asked for "a floozie"; after a painful interrogation under the bemused eyes of other customers, the clerk discovered that he wanted to buy a fuse.)

The preponderance of young marriageable males among immigrant groups (especially those from certain countries) may more or less compel intermarriage between persons of different ethnic backgrounds, thus hastening both amalgamation and assimilation. Such cultural cross-fertilization influences fertility, family structure, the status system, and social values. The age-sex structure of immigrants makes it difficult for

---

[37] John J. Honigmann, *The World of Man*, Harper and Brothers, New York, 1959, p. 271.

[38] Henri Bunle, "The Cultural Assimilation of Immigrants," in UNESCO, *Cultural Assimilation of Immigrants*, Supplement to *Population Studies*, Vol. III, March 1950, p. 6.

men to find suitable marriage partners and relatively easy for females to marry above their social status.

Culture shock may be suffered by the marginal men who cannot adjust to their adopted environment, at which point they sometimes return to their homeland. These returnees form the often disregarded countercurrent outward from all countries, including the United States and Israel, nations that migration built.

THE PEOPLING OF ISRAEL

Israel, which has experienced what is possibly the most dramatic immigration history of any nation, has compressed into a few years a remarkable collection of assimilation, amalgamation, and absorption problems. During the first 44 months of its existence (from May 1948 through December 1951) this new country, roughly the area of New Jersey, added 684,000 immigrants to an existing population of about 650,000— the equivalent of an annual immigration to the United States of 50 million. No country ever before had witnessed such a rapid immigration rate. (From 1952 onward immigration restrictions decreased the flow of this *kibbutz galuyoth* or "in-gathering of the exiles.")

In Israel the 1948-1951 wave are called the "old immigrants"; those entering since January 1952 are the "new." The old immigrants were mostly European; the new came largely from the Near East and North Africa. They are very different from each other—in social norms, degree of modernization, and even religious belief.

Immigrants to Israel generally came as a family rather than individually, thus posing a greater than usual dependency burden on the young nation, but offering social-psychological advantages. The old migration also included an unusually large proportion of aged, who are not easily absorbed. Abnormally low standards of health among the immigrants added to the difficulties.

The occupational composition of the incomers was little suited to meet the manpower needs of Israel. In their countries of origin the vast majority had been craftsmen, petty traders, middlemen, and members of professions. In Israel most of them became wage earners in building trades, public works, factories, and farms. The new country especially needed farmers rather than these urban small entrepreneurs who did not want to farm.

Religious and cultural backgrounds varied considerably. Many immigrants had very low standards of education. Yemenite Jews, for example, normally provide only a religious education for their sons—an education which often does not include instruction in writing—and girls receive no formal education at all. Language differences too impeded adjustment. To compound the problems, more than half the new arrivals had come from backward areas, and most were destitute. "Their mentality, scales of value, aspirations and cultural background . . . were those associated with primitive societies. . . . These newcomers had to be absorbed and integrated by a State which had just come into existence, by a society which had not yet established generally accepted norms."[39]

Not surprisingly under the circumstances, a tremendous inflation and a serious housing shortage plagued the Israelis in the early years of the country's existence. In 1951 the nation imported eight times as much as it exported—a grossly unfavorable balance of trade. Capital was needed in large amounts, and Jews in other countries were encouraged to buy Israeli bonds.

"The new State, impoverished by a recent war, poor in natural resources and capital equipment, surrounded by hostile countries, with a total population not larger than that of a medium-sized town, still lacking some important characteristics of a unified and well-balanced nation, and anxious to preserve and consolidate its own identity, yet undertook to double its population within four years through large-scale immigration."[40] Such a sudden growth was bound to impose severe strains on the entire pattern of life.

Israel supplies an extreme but practical example of cultural conflicts arising out of international migration, and of the means—some successful, some not—that may be taken to achieve harmony. Community housing and health, education, employment, and welfare programs were set up to hasten absorption and assimilation of the inflow. The leaders also tried to discourage ethnocentric antagonisms among the Jews. Complete integration of the newcomers will no doubt require many years, but progress has been surprisingly rapid.

Israel joins with the United States, Australia, and other nations in illustrating the fact that international migration sometimes helps to strengthen the links forged between countries. Friendly relations between European powers and certain overseas nations have been prolonged for many years after the territories achieved independence by the presence in the new lands of sizeable clusters of immigrants.

Migration Theories

For migration as for other demographic variables, collection and analysis of data are interrelated; strengths and weaknesses in one reciprocate abundances and deficiencies in the other. But the situation is not

---

[39] Julius Isaac, "Israel—A New Melting Pot?," Chap. XI of W. D. Borrie, *The Cultural Integration of Immigrants*, UNESCO, Paris, 1959, pp. 247-248.
[40] *Ibid.*, p. 239.

circumscribed by the collection-manipulation dyad. The development of both of these aspects of migration research is a function of advances in migration theory.

Theoretical relationships explaining both international and internal migration are often expressed in functional notation. Demographers say, for example, that migration is a function of A and B. This means that there are two variables which are responsible for the frequency of migrants: A and B. It is possible to go one step further and specify the precise form of the relationship: for example, the number of migrants varies directly with A and inversely with the square of B, expressed mathematically as $M = \dfrac{A}{B^2}$. Such a specific functional relation is more valuable (because more precise) than a general association and often rests on a prior general formulation.

GENERAL FUNCTIONAL RELATION

A pioneer effort, in the 1880's, to relate independent variables to the dependent variable, migration, was that of E. G. Ravenstein.[41] His "laws" were the earliest serious attempt to differentiate among the four migration subvariables. From inspection of population movements in Great Britain, Ravenstein related migration to such independent variables as population size, density, and distance. Some of his generalizations follow:

1. Net migration is a small proportion of the gross migration between two areas.
2. For each main stream of migrants, there runs a countercurrent which is usually almost equal in size.
3. The natives of towns are less migratory than those of rural areas.
4. The majority of migrants move only a short distance.
5. Both rural to urban and urban to rural migration tend to proceed by stages.
6. The main currents of migration are from farm to town, town to small city, and small city to large city.
7. The population is shifting toward the great centers of commerce and industry.
8. Females are more migratory than males.
9. Long-distance migrants usually go to large cities.

A few years later, Adna Weber applied Ravenstein's laws to continental cities and modified the theory slightly to include an additional inde-

---

[41] E. G. Ravenstein, "The Laws of Migration," *Journal of the Royal Statistical Society*, Vol. XLVIII, June 1885, pp. 167-235 (esp. pp. 198-199); Vol. LII, June 1889, pp. 241-305 (esp. pp. 286-288).

pendent variable: the demand for labor. "The organization of industry," she wrote, "has steadily demanded an increase in the number of city dwellers. . . . Since the current of migration is toward the cities and yet the bulk of migration is for short distances only, we can see the manner of the movement; it is a migration by stages having for its object the satisfaction of the demand for more labor in the cities."[42]

Frequently offered as a cause of migration is economic disequilibrium, which is brought on by unequal distribution or utilization of natural resources among different nations and regions and gives rise to inequality of economic opportunity. "The lack of correspondence between the distribution of population and the distribution of resources and opportunities to make money often leads to movement of goods, people, or both."[43] Migration is thus seen as a result of economic demand mediated through the prospective migrant's conception of economic conditions in his potential destination.

SPECIFIC FUNCTIONAL RELATION

Princeton astronomer John Q. Stewart has published some dozen articles on "demographic gravitation."[44] Contending with some justification that Newtonian gravitation is susceptible to analogical transfer to demography, Stewart calculated the relative influence or drawing power of two or more concentrations of people. He posits, for example, that the number of migrants to Connecticut from every other state is proportionate to the population of each state of original residence divided by its distance from Connecticut. The same principle is applied to retail sales, truck farming, and commuting. In his formula, N/D (where N is population and D is distance) measures the relative movement. Stewart applied this formula to attendance at the New York World's Fair in 1940 (the number of visitors from each state is proportionate to the state's population divided by its distance from the site of the Fair) and the attendance of students at universities (proportionate attendance from each state equals its population divided by its mileage from the campus). Stewart was partially anticipated by W. J. Reilly's law of retail gravitation, which established the breaking point in trade areas between two cities by dividing the population by the distance squared.[45] Several

---

[42] Adna F. Weber, *The Growth of Cities During the Nineteenth Century*, The Macmillan Co., New York, 1899, pp. 233 and 257.

[43] Ernest F. Penrose, *Population Theories and Their Application*, Food Research Institute, Stanford, 1934, p. 174.

[44] The earliest publications are John Q. Stewart, "The 'Gravitation' or Geographic Drawing Power of a College," *Bulletin of the American Association of University Professors*, Vol. XXVII, February 1941, pp. 70-75; and "A Measure of the Influence of Population at a Distance," *Sociometry*, Vol. V, February 1942, pp. 63-71.

[45] William J. Reilly, *Methods for the Study of Retail Relationships*, University of Texas, Austin, Bulletin No. 2944, November 1929.

sociologists, geographers, and economists have applied Stewart's ideas with partial success. Some scholars have attempted to modify the N/D proportion by finding the best value for the exponent of distance in this gravitational-type formula. This work bears upon the question of whether the relation between migration and distance is inverse-square, as suggested by E. C. Young,[46] inverse-linear, as assumed by Stewart and Zipf, or an inverse improper fraction.[47]

George K. Zipf proposed the P_1P_2/D hypothesis, which states that the number of migrants between any two communities is proportionate to the product of their populations divided by the shortest transportation distance.[48] This gravitational model has been tested and partially verified for passengers on railroads, buses, and airplanes.

In 1940 Samuel A. Stouffer contributed the intervening opportunities hypothesis, which states that "the number of persons going a given distance is directly proportional to the number of opportunities at that distance and inversely proportional to the number of intervening opportunities."[49] Expressed mathematically in increment terminology, this hypothesis has been tentatively supported by several investigators. Stouffer used a formula to estimate the number of persons moving a given distance and then tested his hypothesis by comparing these estimated frequencies with the observed frequencies. Two independent variables (number of opportunities and distance) were causally related to the dependent variable, migration. But although "number of opportunities" is intrinsically interesting to social scientists, it is very difficult to measure. Stouffer himself used housing vacancies as a measure of opportunity; other researchers have used different variables, for example, increase in the size of the labor force. In an attempt to integrate the gravitational and economic demand approaches, Stouffer conceived of distance in terms of the nature of the space rather than the mileage. If the space has a high density of opportunities, then passage of migrants is impeded; if the opportunity density is low, movement is facile. Though

---

[46] E. C. Young, *The Movement of Farm Population*, Cornell Agricultural Experiment Station, Ithaca, Bulletin No. 426, 1928.

[47] Fred Charles Iklé, "Sociological Relationship of Traffic to Population and Distance," *Traffic Quarterly*, Vol. VIII, April 1954, pp. 123-136; and Carl Hammer and Fred Charles Iklé, "Intercity Telephone and Airline Traffic Related to Distance and the 'Propensity to Interact,'" *Sociometry*, Vol. XX, No. 4, December 1957, pp. 306-316.

[48] G. K. Zipf, "The P_1P_2/D Hypothesis: The Case of Railway Express," *Journal of Psychology*, Vol. XXII, July 1946, pp. 3-8; and "The P_1P_2/D Hypothesis: On the Intercity Movement of Persons," *American Sociological Review*, Vol. XI, No. 6, December 1946, pp. 677-685.

[49] Samuel A. Stouffer, "Intervening Opportunities: A Theory Relating Mobility and Distance," *American Sociological Review*, Vol. V, No. 6, December 1940, pp. 845-867.

the number of miles to be traversed is relevant, the determining variable is the total number of opportunities past which the migrant might move. Opportunity is differently defined by different strata of the population, with consequent differences in migration patterns: high-status persons usually must move a greater distance to find better jobs or other opportunities than persons whose skills or aspirations direct them to seek less desirable (and less rare) opportunities; low-status migrants encounter a larger number of intervening opportunities in a given distance than do upper-status persons.

MATHEMATICAL MODELS

Recently scholars have attempted to evolve mathematical models to explain demographic phenomena. These models aid understanding by organizing data into coherent formal systems interrelating possible causative and dependent variables, and ultimately lend themselves to prediction. At present work is proceeding on models for fertility, mortality, morbidity, and marriage in addition to migration. Indeed, increasing attention is being devoted to mathematical models in all facets of demography, and new ones undoubtedly will continue to be invented.

One rather primitive model compares migration streams by controlling for relevant spatial variables in somewhat the same fashion that standardization of mortality and fertility enables us to analyze trends in natural increase. As standardization allows for differences in the age-sex compositions of populations being compared, so this model allows for spatial variables that are important in interpreting migratory behavior. Seven variables are particularly significant: size of area of origin, size of area of destination, shape of area of origin, shape of area of destination, distribution of population within area of origin, distribution of population within area of destination, and distance moved. The model generates theoretical migration frequencies, which are compared with observed frequencies, yielding several indexes of the relative desirability of a given move or area.[50]

In this type of analysis, stochastic processes and Markov chains are especially useful because their underlying assumptions correspond to the interdependence and changing probabilities under which demographic events occur. Demographers in fact are coming to view their subject as a deterministic system in which conditions at any given time are a probabilistic function of the conditions at one or more previous times. The stochastic process is a probability mesasure describing the outcome

[50] Ralph Thomlinson, "A Model for Migration Analysis," *Journal of the American Statistical Association*, Vol. LVI, No. 295, September 1961, p. 684.

of any given stage as dependent upon specified previous stages. A Markov chain is a stochastic process for which "the probability of entering a certain state depends only on the last state occupied."[51] Although the flowering of this new approach is relatively recent—post-World War II—"the first really significant stochastic model of a broad class of phenomena seems to have been provided by Mendel to explain, or to represent, heredity."[52] An origin-destination matrix of migrations consists of a set of numbers, each representing the probability that a resident of a certain area at the beginning of a given time period will reside in a certain other area at the end of the period. Such a first-order process has been used to describe the movement of workers among various industrial groups; modified chains were set up to differentiate between stayers, who have become attached to an industry, and movers, who have not.[53]

Eventually, demographers may be able to analyze migration through higher-order stochastic processes in which the probability of each move is dependent upon several previous residences. Ravenstein's hypothesis of a stage pattern of rural-urban migration (possibly extending over more than one generation) intimates the existence of a multi-order stochastic process. Mathematical models founded on stochastic processes are coming to be applied to more and more fields of knowledge, a trend that is indicative of man's increased comprehension of the complex causal chains underlying human actions.

---

[51] John G. Kemeny and J. Laurie Snell, *Finite Markov Chains*, D. Van Nostrand Co., Princeton, 1960, p. 207.

[52] Jerzy Neyman, "Indeterminism in Science and New Demands on Statisticians," *Journal of the American Statistical Association*, Vol. LV, No. 292, December 1960, p. 630.

[53] Isadore Blumen, Marvin Kogan, and Philip J. McCarthy, *The Industrial Mobility of Labor as a Probability Process*, Cornell Studies in Industrial and Labor Relations, Ithaca, Vol. VI, 1956.

PART III

ISSUES AND
PROBLEMS

13 ⚜ City and Metropolitan Growth

As the world becomes increasingly urban, the attributes and problems of cities are attaining greater and greater importance in human affairs. The city is a widespread physical and social unit of civilization. In advanced countries cities are the principal way of organizing living space. And in all nations they are centers of cultural and social change and foci of wealth and power.

Some historians equate the rise of civilization with the beginnings of urbanization. In *Man Makes Himself*,[1] archaeologist V. Gordon Childe compares "the urban revolution" to the neolithic, industrial, and demographic revolutions. In his *What Happened in History*,[2] Chapters II through IV contain the words "savagery" or "barbarism" in their titles; then after Chapter V, entitled "The Urban Revolution in Mesopotamia," the word "civilization" appears in three consecutive chapter headings.

High densities go surprisingly far back in time. Charles Leonard Woolley claimed that Ur of the Chaldees (in southern Mesopotamia, 140 miles south of Babylon) had a density of about 125,000 persons per square mile (and a total population of half a million) in 2000 B.C. Albert Demangeon, a French geographer writing in the twentieth century, estimated a density as high as 142,000 per square mile in the center of Paris in 1329. According to Lewis Mumford, in the Paris of 1861 the four inner *arrondissements* reached a density of 180,000 per

---

[1] V. Gordon Childe, *Man Makes Himself*, Watts and Co., London, 1936.
[2] V. Gordon Childe, *What Happened in History*, Penguin Books Ltd., Harmondsworth, 1954.

square mile. The highest density achieved by Western man is 350,000 per square mile; this sardine-like concentration was reported by Mark Jefferson for the poorest districts of the Lower East Side of New York City at about 1900. But the busiest beehive of all is Hong Kong, where a restricted town site between mountains and the sea has forced a cramming of the recent population influx up to a density in the worst areas of 800,000 persons per square mile.[3]

URBAN-RURAL CONTRASTS

Urban-rural contrasts in the United States pertain to the three basic demographic variables as well as to other population characteristics. The sex ratio is higher in rural areas, and the proportion of nonwhite is greater. In urban areas there are more foreign-born persons, and the educational attainment is much greater. The ages below 20 are better represented in rural areas, whereas all other age groups are slightly better represented in urban places. There are more working women in cities. Urban incomes are higher.

The urban family tends to have fewer members, smaller quarters, greater mobility, more scattered activities, and less stability than its rural counterpart. City dwellers marry later, produce fewer children, and divorce more frequently. A higher proportion of the rural people are single, and a larger percentage of urban residents are widowed or divorced. There are more housing accommodations and recreational facilities for unmarried people in cities.

The death rate is higher in cities, but not so high as the birth rate. Cities survive through a combination of natural increase and an excess of in- over out-migrants. Rural areas survive through a high natural increase despite a net outward migration. Thus cities are partially "biologically" parasitic on rural areas.

The Rise of Cities

Cities were first made possible by the shift from nomadism to settled agriculture. They were also a response to needs for defense, early manufacturing and processing, commerce, recreation, political centers, and religious centers. To be sure, most of the first cities were very small by twentieth-century standards, but a few did reach the proportions of a modern metropolis. For example, the population of ancient Rome has been estimated at a million persons.

The small size of the cities of antiquity was a result of the inability

---

[3] Colin Clark, "Urban Population Densities," *Bulletin de l'institut international de statistique*, Stockholm, Vol. XXXVI, Part 4, 1957, p. 66.

of the agricultural hinterland to produce and transport daily the huge quantities of food and other necessities required by a large nonagricultural populace. Many of the first cities (if we may so call them) were agricultural bedroom villages, from which people commuted on foot to their farms two or three miles out from the village center.

ANCIENT CITIES

It is very difficult to trace the origins of cities. Most of the early evidence is archaeological, and much of our knowledge fragmentary. The date of the first city is still unknown; it may have been as early as 5000 or 6000 B.C. Our first solid evidence of urban communities stems from about 4000 B.C., the time of settlement of Ubaid, the oldest known city. The precocity of achievement of Ubaid and other Mesopotamian city-states is largely attributable to the surplus food yield of irrigation agriculture and the need for mediators between producers of the various goods that were sold and exchanged.

The Greek city-state or *polis* was an autonomous unit consisting of a city and its immediate environs. The hinterland supplied food for consumption and often products such as olive oil for export. The *polis* (including its surrounding farm land) was self-sufficient and was the basis of the political structure of the ancient Greek world. Demographic knowledge is less fragmentary for Athenian Attica than for any other Greek city-state. In 430 B.C. there were about 40,000 adult male citizens and a total free population of around 150,000, of whom less than one-half lived in the city and its port, Piraeus. There were also some 20,000 aliens resident at Athens or Piraeus and approximately 100,000 slaves.[4] "Hardly more than a score of city-states ever had more than 10,000 citizens"—or a free population of 40,000 or more.[5]

MEDIEVAL CITIES

The city-states of Phoenicia, Greece, and Italy had their counterparts in the medieval communes of Italy and Flanders. However, medieval cities differed from earlier ones in three particularly important respects: they were dependent upon other areas, they were economically specialized, and they contained the first really urban men. The castle fortress (*burgus*) and the market town (*portus*) were not self-sufficient; they imported most of their necessities from other areas. Specialization in industrial and mercantile activities encouraged the rise of the guild

---

[4] A. W. Gomme, *The Population of Athens in the Fifth and Fourth Centuries, B.C.*, Basil Blackwood, Oxford, 1933, pp. 25-29.

[5] Richard E. Wycherly, *How the Greeks Built Cities*, Macmillan Co., London, 1962, p. 14.

system for medieval artisans. One important result of this functional separation of cities from the rest of society was the birth of the middle-class bourgeoisie. The association of a growing middle class with city development is common throughout the world: traditional rural areas often exhibit a two-class system of a few aristocratic landholders and a huge lower class, but city life and urban occupations are not especially consonant with such a feudal class structure.

The cities of the Middle Ages were, in some respects, forerunners of Charles Dickens' and Lewis Mumford's insensate factory-slum. As long ago as the England of 1273 a smoke abatement law was passed, prohibiting the use of sea coal (the old English term for bituminous coal, which produced more smoke than anthracite) as detrimental to health; one violator was prosecuted, condemned, and executed in 1307. But to quote a Scots folk saying, "Where there's smoke, there's money." And the cities soon came to be covered over by a rich layer of soot.

Throughout the Middle Ages a town of 10,000 was considered large. J. C. Russell's estimates for thirteenth- to sixteenth-century Europe show Venice as the largest city at 78,000; following were Paris, Rome, Milan, Florence, and Ghent at between 50,000 and 60,000; London, Bourges, Bordeaux, Genoa, Bologna, Barcelona, Cologne, and Brussels at between 30,000 and 50,000; and several dozen between 10,000 and 30,000.[6] At this time the greatest cities were probably located in China and India. Cortez and his Spanish soldiers were amazed at the size of Mexico City, with its huge public buildings and "60,000 houses, which, by the ordinary rules of reckoning, would give 300,000 souls."[7] In the tenth century the Mayas were said to have had four to six cities larger than 200,000, and about one-third of the people lived in cities of various sizes.[8] Here though, as so often regarding past centuries, scholars are not quite sure of their ground.

MODERN CITIES

Late in the seventeenth century, William Petty gave the following estimates for the largest European cities: London, 696,000; Paris, 488,000; Amsterdam, 187,000; Venice, 132,000; Rome, 125,000; Dublin, 69,000; Rouen, 66,000; and Bristol, 48,000. Petty expected London to double in size every forty years until it leveled off at 5 million around

[6] Josiah Cox Russell, *Late Ancient and Medieval Population*, American Philosophical Society, Philadelphia, 1958, pp. 60-63.
[7] William H. Prescott, *History of the Conquest of Mexico*, 1843, Modern Library edition, pp. 316-317.
[8] Sylvanus Griswold Morley, *The Ancient Maya*, Stanford University Press, Palo Alto, 1946, pp. 312-320.

1800.[9] The rapidity of city growth is illustrated by Paris in Table 20 and the United States in Table 21.

Table 22 shows how the urban population of the world has grown over the last century and a half. In mid-twentieth century 159 million people, about 6.5 per cent of the world population, lived in the 133

TABLE 20. *Population History of Paris, 363-1906**

YEAR	NUMBER OF PEOPLE
363	8,000
510	30,000
1220	120,000
1328	250,000
1596	230,000
1675	540,000
1788	599,000
1801	548,000
1817	714,000
1831	786,000
1851	1,053,000
1856	1,174,000
1861	1,696,000
1866	1,825,000
1872	1,794,000
1876	1,989,000
1886	3,345,000
1906	2,763,000

* Marcel Poète, *L'enfance de Paris*, 1908; cited in Pierre Clerget, *Urbanism: A Historic, Geographic, and Economic Study*, Smithsonian Institution, Washington, 1913.

places of 500,000 or more. The fifty cities including a million or more population contained 101 million residents, 4.2 per cent of the world's people.

World Urban Distribution

Despite its ever increasing urbanization, however, the world today is still primarily rural. As of 1950 about 13 per cent of the people lived in cities of 100,000 or more, occupying about one-seventh of 1 per cent of the world's area. Anyone in doubt concerning these facts can consider what he sees when flying over England or the northeastern part of the United States, two of the most intensely urban areas of the globe. From the air the view gives the impression of a great spread of country-

[9] William Petty, *Politicall Arithmetick*, London, 1676.

TABLE 21. *Urban and Rural Composition, United States, 1790-1960**

YEAR	PER CENT URBAN	PER CENT RURAL
1790	5.1	94.9
1800	6.1	93.9
1810	7.3	92.7
1820	7.2	92.8
1830	8.8	91.2
1840	10.8	89.2
1850	15.3	84.7
1860	19.8	80.2
1870	25.7	74.3
1880	28.2	71.8
1890	35.1	64.9
1900	39.7	60.3
1910	45.7	54.3
1920	51.2	48.8
1930	56.2	43.8
1940	56.5	43.5
1950	64.0	36.0
1960	69.9	30.1

* U. S. Bureau of the Census, U. S. *Census of Population: 1960*, "Number of Inhabitants: United States Summary," PC(1)-1A, Government Printing Office, Washington, 1961, pp. 14-15.

TABLE 22. *Growth of World Urban Population, 1800-1950**

YEAR	WORLD POPU-LATION	Cities 100,000 or More			Cities 20,000 or More			Cities 5,000 or More		
		NUM-BER	POPU-LATION	%	NUM-BER	POPU-LATION	%	NUM-BER	POPU-LATION	%
1800	906	45	15.6	1.7	200	21.7	2.4	750	27.2	3.0
1850	1,171	85	27.5	2.3	660	50.4	4.3	3,400	74.9	6.4
1900	1,608	270	88.6	5.5	1,780	147.9	9.2	9,800	218.7	13.6
1950	2,400	875	313.7	13.1	5,500	502.2	20.9	27,600	716.7	29.8

All population figures are in millions.

* Kingsley Davis and Hilda Hertz, "The World Distribution of Urbanization," *Bulletin of the International Statistical Institute*, Vol. XXXIII, No. 4, 1954, pp. 227-243; and World Urban Resources Index, Bureau of Applied Social Research, New York.

side with an occasional small city consisting of a cluster of a few score buildings. Once in a while there appears a huge city—which is lost in the surrounding rurality until the plane is almost overhead.

Not only are heavily urbanized areas few in number, but they are highly concentrated geographically. Though some degree of urbanization is found over the entire globe, its distribution is very uneven. For a time most city growth was European, but in the last half century Asia has returned to the forefront and once more contains the largest share of the world's urban population. Today Asia has 53 per cent of the world's people and 34 per cent of the world's urban population; Europe, with only 16 per cent of the world's people, contains 28 per cent of the urban population.

Concentration of urbanization is not the same as concentration of population. Oceania, a sparsely inhabitated area consisting mostly of rabbit- and kangaroo-populated wasteland, is the world's most urban continent: 41 per cent of the people live in cities of 100,000 or more. By contrast, even the highly urban United States has only 29 per cent of its people in cities of 100,000 or more and 42 per cent in communities of 20,000 or more. Table 23 provides details of this situation. Spearman's

TABLE 23. *World Urbanization and Population Density, 1950*

CONTINENT	PERSONS PER SQUARE MILE	PER CENT OF POPULATION IN CITIES OF 20,000 OR MORE	PER CENT OF POPULATION IN CITIES OF 100,000 OR MORE	DENSITY RANK	URBANIZA-TION RANK
World	46	21	13	—	—
Oceania	4	47	41	6	1
Anglo America	21	42	29	3	2
Europe	136	34	20	1	3
Latin America	20	25	17	4	4
Asia	79	13	8	2	5
Africa	17	9	5	5	6

rho (a rank-order correlation coefficient) for density versus urbanization turns out to be −.14—very low and slightly negative.

Most of the world's cities lie in the temperate zones. Only 19 per cent of cities containing 100,000 or more people are situated in tropical areas; 81 per cent are in the two temperate zones; and none lie in arctic regions. Of the people living in cities of this size, 89 per cent are in temperate zones and 11 per cent in the tropics. Of the total world population, 66 per cent reside in temperate zones and 34 per cent between the Tropics of Cancer and Capricorn.[10]

THE LARGEST CITIES IN THE WORLD

Currently the largest cities in the world are New York, London, Shanghai, Chicago, Tokyo, Paris, Los Angeles, Berlin, and Moscow. A penchant for superlatives has embroiled us in a nonsensical jumble of arguments concerning just which urban agglomeration is the world's

---

[10] Davis and Hertz, "The World Distribution of Urbanization," *op. cit.*

biggest. Popular publications variously claim this honor for London, New York, and Tokyo. But as long as the different countries use different criteria for bounding cities, international comparability of population size will remain too slender to permit accurate rankings of incorporated places. Not only do national powers define "city" inconsistently with each other, but even in a single country there may be several official and unofficial urban definitions simultaneously in use. For example, when one speaks of New York, does he mean the metropolitan region, Greater New York, the Standard Metropolitan Statistical Area, the urbanized area, the five boroughs, or Manhattan Island? And do the larger units include those parts of the metropolitan community that fall in New Jersey and Connecticut? Other nations also use several definitions, each intended for a particular purpose.

Because the metropolitan region is the operating functional entity (instead of the less sociologically consequential incorporated city), and because international comparability can be maximized by using regional boundaries, metropolitan areas rather than political corporations are reported in Table 24. This table supplies recent census statistics and

TABLE 24. *The Largest Metropolitan Areas in the World, 1953-1957**

AFRICA

Egypt
Alexandria	1,170,000
Cairo	2,770,000

Union of South Africa
Johannesburg	1,825,000

ANGLO AMERICA

Canada
Montreal	1,713,662
Toronto	1,632,149

United States
Baltimore	1,488,300
Boston	2,966,000
Buffalo	1,231,500
Chicago	6,121,600
Cincinnati	1,005,500
Cleveland	1,668,600
Detroit	3,570,000
Houston	1,077,000
Los Angeles	5,640,000
Minneapolis	1,243,500
New York	14,280,500
Philadelphia	4,089,700
Pittsburgh	2,318,500
St. Louis	1,891,000
San Francisco	2,583,500
Washington	1,885,300

LATIN AMERICA

Argentina
Buenos Aires	5,750,000

Brazil
Rio de Janeiro	3,750,000
São Paulo	3,300,000

Chile
Santiago	1,600,000

Cuba
Havana	1,315,000

Mexico
Mexico City	3,900,000

Peru
Lima	1,169,000

Venezuela
Caracas	1,000,000

ASIA

China
Canton	1,598,900†
Chungking	1,772,500†
Harbin	1,163,000†

* International Urban Research, *The World's Metropolitan Areas,* University of California Press, Berkeley, 1959, pp. 34-63.

ASIA

Mukden	2,299,900†
Nanking	1,091,600†
Peking	2,768,149†
Shanghai	6,204,417†
Tientsin	2,693,831†
Wuhan	1,427,300†
Hongkong	
Hongkong	2,535,000
India	
Ahmedabad	1,075,000
Bangalore	1,275,000
Bombay	4,400,000
Calcutta	5,700,000
Delhi	2,435,000
Hyderabad	1,290,000
Madras	2,225,000
Indonesia	
Djakarta	1,871,200†
Iran	
Teheran	1,513,164†
Japan	
Kyoto	1,373,681
Nagoya	1,501,651
Osaka	6,404,749
Tokyo	11,349,339
Yahata	1,658,956
Korea	
Pusan	1,049,363†
Seoul	1,574,868†
Pakistan	
Karachi	1,318,000
Philippines	
Manila	2,348,000
Singapore	
Singapore	1,210,534
Thailand	
Bangkok	1,484,000
Turkey	
Istanbul	1,365,363
Vietnam	
Saigon	2,000,000†

EUROPE

Austria	
Vienna	1,865,000
Belgium	
Brussels	1,371,816
Denmark	
Copenhagen	1,292,915

France	
Paris	6,736,836
Germany	
Berlin (East & West)	4,244,600
Cologne	1,243,900
Essen	5,353,100
Frankfurt am Main	1,520,100
Hamburg	2,107,100
Mannheim	1,278,400
Munich	1,269,000
Stuttgart	1,336,700
Greece	
Athens	1,490,000
Hungary	
Budapest	1,783,000†
Italy	
Milan	2,153,700
Naples	1,565,100
Rome	1,958,600
Turin	1,028,300
Netherlands	
Amsterdam	1,017,042
Poland	
Katowice	1,921,000
Warsaw	1,595,000
Portugal	
Lisbon	1,130,000
Romania	
Bucharest	1,236,905†
Spain	
Barcelona	1,655,000
Madrid	1,840,000
Sweden	
Stockholm	1,021,068
United Kingdom	
Birmingham	2,575,840
Glasgow	1,896,619
Leeds	1,901,420
Liverpool	1,624,510
London	10,490,690
Manchester	2,499,210
Newcastle	1,136,910
U.S.S.R.	
Leningrad	3,500,000
Moscow	7,300,000

OCEANIA

Australia	
Melbourne	1,470,000
Sydney	1,869,000

Where metropolitan area data were not obtainable, the city population is given; daggers identify figures applying to principal cities only.

estimates for all world metropolises known to be larger than a million in residential population.

THE FUTURE OF THE CITY

Lewis Mumford and Kingsley Davis have speculated concerning future prospects of the growth of cities. Mumford, in the 1930's, advanced a "cycle of growth and decay" theory, in which three rising and three descending stages were discerned: 1) Eopolis, the village community; 2) Polis, an association of villages with civic unity; 3) Metropolis, the mother-city of a region; 4) Megalopolis, bigness and power, production and standardization; 5) Tyrannopolis, parasitism and Caesarism; and 6) Nekropolis, empty shells and caricatures. According to Mumford, the United States is now in stage four, the "beginning of the decline," and may continue through to stage six.[11]

Davis is less fanciful:

> It seems unlikely that the growth of existing cities will continue indefinitely. In advanced Western countries the growth of the population in general is coming to a halt. This means that if existing cities are to continue to grow they must do so not simply by draining the rural population of its surplus, as they have done in the past, but also by drastically reducing the rural population. They will draw not only upon the interest but also upon the capital. If, therefore, the growth of existing cities does not stop rather soon, the second aspect of our problem will be raised in an acute form; for we shall all be living in the very largest cities, and eventually in New York City alone. But, as pointed out before, the central cities, as contrasted with the rest of metropolitan districts, are already showing signs of a coming halt in growth. They may actually lose population while the metropolitan districts continue to grow. It may be, therefore, that future metropolitan growth will involve such an expansion of area that the average density of the districts will be either stabilized or decreased.
>
> Even in the advanced industrial nations, already heavily urbanized, the percentage of the population living in cities seems destined to increase for awhile yet. Though in these nations the trend will eventually come to a halt the rest of the world, still overwhelmingly rural, will still have a tremendous urbanization ahead of it. Exactly what the saturation point will be is hard to say, but it is entirely within the bounds of possibility that the entire world will eventually reach the degree of urbanization now attained by only a few advanced industrial nations. Consequently, it is possible that eventually 75 per cent of the world's population will live in places of 10,000 or over.[12]

---

[11] Lewis Mumford, *The Culture of Cities*, Harcourt, Brace and Co., New York, 1938, pp. 283-292.

[12] Kingsley Davis, *Human Society*, The Macmillan Co., New York, 1949, pp. 341-342.

In short, the city of 2000 A.D. may well turn out to be a replica of Los Angeles—a sprawling conglomeration of many small communities having a relatively underdeveloped downtown area and a more uniform density than is traditionally found in large urban clusters. The automobile and other transportation media enabling commuters to journey 50 miles to work in the morning and 50 miles home in the evening at high speeds and reasonable comfort are encouraging people to suburbanize at increasingly long distances into the hinterland. The auto age metropolis with its freeways permitting 60-mile-an-hour speeds throughout the entire urban area negates much of the convenience of living near the central core, especially as employment and recreation centers come to be distributed widely throughout the metropolitan area rather than concentrating centrally as in Chicago's Loop or New York's downtown districts.

Location and Growth of Cities

Many influences are at work in the formation and increase of cities. "Which place could and which place could not develop a city has been a function of the efficiency and peculiarities of the various transport inventions, of the unequal distribution of natural resources, and of the state of the production technology."[13] Certain combinations of these factors make cities possible; other combinations prevent their founding or impede later growth. The less efficient the transport, production, and distribution technologies, the smaller is the economic surplus available to support an urban population.

Reasons for the founding and enlargement of cities show characteristic variations through time. Thus one authoritative article summarizes the situation:

> In early centuries most cities owed both their original location and subsequent growth to considerations of defense. In later centuries London, Paris, Berlin, Vienna, Madrid and Washington have owed much of their growth to political factors, but for the future neither defense nor politics is likely to play much part in the locations and growth of great communities. Among the ten largest cities of the world today there is not a single one that owes its location to a defensible position and only three are political capitals. Trade and industry are the determining factors in the growth of the twentieth century municipality. This is true of city growth in the Orient as well as in Europe and America.[14]

[13] Harlan W. Gilmore, *Transportation and the Growth of Cities*, The Free Press, Glencoe, 1953, p. 3.

[14] William B. Munro, "City," in Edwin R. A. Seligman (ed.), *Encyclopaedia of the Social Sciences*, The Macmillan Co., New York, 1930, Vol. III, pp. 476-477.

Today the hallmarks of a city are industry, commerce, high population density, and closely packed buildings, in contrast to the agricultural pursuits and ordinarily low density of people and structures in rural areas. As Brendan Behan says, "A city is a place where you are least likely to get bitten in the rear by a sheep."

TRANSPORTATION FACILITIES

Four periods are distinguishable in the interplay between transport systems and rural-urban relations. Period I covers man's history through the fourteenth century, when land transport was limited to human and animal sources of power. Wheeled vehicles, very crude mechanically, could carry only very small payloads, and river transport was mostly by downriver barges. "Light boats with little cargo could be gotten upstream by a plentiful expenditure of human effort where the river was navigable and the current was not too swift."[15] Ocean transport was equally primitive. Under these transportation and communication difficulties, large cities tended to be located along the coast. Inland cities grew large only if they were downriver from a productive hinterland. River mouths, combining both of these features, were the most common sites for ancient cities.

During Period II, from the fourteenth through the eighteenth century, land transport was improved by the horseshoe and horse collar, which decreased foot injuries and greatly increased the load a horse could pull. The four-wheeled wagon, however, showed little improvement. A steam carriage was invented by the French engineer Nicholas Cugnot in 1763, but since its speed was limited to two miles an hour—and even at that, it overturned on a busy street corner—it was not copied.[16] Roads were still generally unsurfaced and therefore dusty or muddy. On hilly ground the ruts became water-courses; on flat land they turned into swamps. The highway was hardly distinguishable from an open field. Twenty miles a day was excellent time. River transport remained substantially the same as in Period I, but there were several important inventions in ocean transport. Mariners now had a tacking sailing vessel with a permanent rudder in the stern, navigational aids, drainage pumps, and greater seaworthiness. "For the first time in history, man now had a ship large enough to be seaworthy in which he could sail out of sight of land, keep sailing in a desired direction as long as there was any wind, know in what direction he was going, and know how to get back"[17]—a factor of great importance in this period of exploration, col-

---

[15] Gilmore, *Transportation and the Growth of Cities*, op. cit., p. 7.
[16] Abraham Wolf, *A History of Science, Technology, and Philosophy in the Eighteenth Century*, George Allen and Unwin, London, 1952, p. 554.
[17] Gilmore, *Transportation and the Growth of Cities*, op. cit., p. 28.

onization, and empire. City location remained approximately the same as during the ancient period except that cities now could be somewhat upstream from the mouth of the river.

The one and a half centuries of Period III bred more important transport inventions than all of man's previous existence. The railroad began in England with Watt's steam engine of 1784, Trevithick's steam locomotive of 1801, wrought iron rails, and flanged wheels. River transport was revolutionized by the steamboat, solving the upriver problem for the first time. In many countries canal systems blossomed in the early 1800's, to be superseded by the train and motor truck. On the oceans, the clipper ship reigned supreme for a long time but was eventually supplanted by the steamship. The net effect was that fast, cheap transport became available practically everywhere in industrialized countries. All links were connected by two-way service. The railroad and automobile created suburbanization and urban sprawl. Farmers acquired more of the products of urban industry. Regional agricultural specialization became feasible because farmers were no longer compelled to grow their own subsistence crops; each area could now grow the crop for which it was best fitted. It was in the younger nations which did not already have extensive urban networks that city development was most influenced by the transport improvements of Period III. United States cities, growing up with the new transportation system, tended therefore to have an interdependent reciprocity with rural areas instead of an exploitative relation.

Today the world is entering Period IV: the air age. Already there are cities in Latin America which were built almost entirely on air transport. In fact, some Brazilian cities could hardly be reached by any other means except air for the first few years after their founding. It is not yet known what effect the airplane will have on urban growth. Conceivably, businessmen might commute by helicopter, extending the suburbs of New York City into New Hampshire. Yet whether the airplane is a centralizing or decentralizing force is still moot. It could bring about either a more uniform density distribution or a greater concentration in a few spots, though the first alternative seems more probable. Still, the cheapest form of bulk transport probably will continue for a long time to be the steamship.

GEOGRAPHIC FACTORS

In preindustrial times, under a subsistence economy, when labor was cheap and wars plentiful, defense was an important factor in determining the locations of cities. Athens had its Acropolis—originally a fortress. Etruscan cities were situated on hilltops. Rome had its seven hills. Paris originated from an island in the River Seine selected by the Parisii for economic aggrandizement as well as security. And London started from a protective swamp.

When commerce and trade became predominant in the economy, however, the locations of urban settlements came to depend rather on transportation considerations. Charles H. Cooley's "break in transportation" theory is the standard explanation: "Population and wealth tend to collect wherever there is a break in transportation."[18] Goods are usually transported in stages, and must be unloaded and reloaded at each change—from wagon to raft or train to truck or pack mule or riverboat or ocean steamship. At these interruptions in transit, freight must be stored, machinery repaired, men and animals fed and rested, fuel tanks filled, money exchanged, and office workers fill out forms. These personnel and equipment require warehouses, docks, sidings, hotels, restaurants, laundries, banks, and saloons—in other words, a town. Moreover, factories often take advantage of the presence of these facilities for handling their raw materials and finished products, saving labor, storage, and transit charges by settling nearby.

Thus, according to Cooley, urban settlements usually form where water and land transport routes meet, where two types of water (river and ocean) or land (train and truck) transport meet, at passes in mountain chains, at ferries and other places where bodies of water must be crossed, at places where river rapids require land portage, at intersections of major routes, where a local road meets a highway, where the mountain meets the plain, along the fall line where rivers make sudden descents from a plateau, where goods "break bulk" from a large to a small carrier, at inspection and import stations, where transport equipment needs servicing or replacement, and any other place where goods in transit must be packaged, transferred, or handled. A break in bulk may be either natural or man-made, but ordinarily it is nature rather than man which establishes these breaks.

As industry became increasingly important, a different set of conditions came to affect city location. Manufacturers wanted to be near raw materials, power sources, trained labor, suitable climate (for certain products), and their market. Economic geographers have combined the transport, topographic, and industrial motivations into the following list of favorable locations for modern cities:[19]

1. Head of ocean navigation on streams: Montreal, Bremen, Seville, Bordeaux, London

---

[18] Charles Horton Cooley, "A Theory of Transportation," *Publication of the American Economic Association*, Vol. IX, May 1894, pp. 1-148.

[19] Lester E. Klimm, Otis P. Starkey, and Norman F. Hall, *Introductory Economic Geography*, Harcourt, Brace and Co., New York, 1940, p. 288.

2. Mouth of streams, if there is also important coastwise trade: New York, Shanghai
3. Junction of streams important in inland water commerce or whose valleys are avenues of land travel: Pittsburgh, St. Louis, Albany, Manaos
4. Ends of great lakes important in inland water commerce: Chicago, Duluth, Buffalo
5. Crossings of important land routes, especially railroad: Madrid, Milan, Indianapolis
6. Near power sites if easily accessible to raw materials and markets: Niagara Falls, Minneapolis, Pittsburgh, Birmingham (England)
7. Near bulky raw materials if power and markets are fairly accessible: Birmingham (England), Birmingham (Alabama), Magnitogorsk.

BASIC ECONOMIC FUNCTIONS

Economic efforts in the city may be divided into local and nonlocal types. The local effort is called "nonbasic" by economic geographers because it consists simply of an exchange of money, goods, and services *within* the city, in the fashion of Mark Twain's town those inhabitants all made a living by taking in each other's washing. The nonlocal effort is considered the more important—indeed, as Mark Jefferson observed, the city's life depends on it—because it brings money into the city and justifies the existence of the city to the outside world. Thus whereas laundries, barbershops, grocery stores, movies, and garages essentially serve the city itself and hence involve only a maintenance function, factories and other city-building activities serve the countryside and other cities.

A city which loses its basic functions is in serious trouble. If basic industries close (silk mills in a nylon era) or leave (textiles moving out of New England), they must be replaced or the city will stagnate or decline. If enough primary workers become unemployed, the maintenance activities retrench. Secondary functions only circulate money. Without the purchasing power brought in by basic functions, the financial resources of the city steadily dwindle, and eventually it becomes a ghost town.

THE URBAN NETWORK

Cities are not self-sufficient; they exist rather by virtue of the specialized functions they perform for other areas and for the surrounding hinterlands. There have always been both economic and social relations between cities and surrounding regions—and other cities, but the patterning of cities has not always been the same. Thus colonial and semicolonial areas tend to have a peripheral city pattern; territories whose economy is dominated by outsiders often have their largest cities on the littoral. When local autonomy is achieved, this peripheral colonial system is displaced by a set of regional capitals dispersed through the interior of the country.[20]

Regularities in the development of urban networks have long been noted. Thus Flinders Petrie, writing of ancient Egypt and Mesopotamia, observed "how remarkably similar the distances are between the early nome capitals of the Delta (twenty-one miles on an average) and the early cities of Mesopotamia (averaging twenty miles apart). Some physical cause seems to limit the primitive rule in this way. Is it not the limit of central storage of grain? . . . Supplies could be centralised up to ten miles away; beyond that the cost of transport made it better worth while to have a nearer centre."[21] This notion that there is an optimal size of tributary areas has been seized upon by many scholars, among them Galpin and Isard in the United States and Christaller, Losch, and von Thunen in Germany.

One of the first men to systematically analyze city-hinterland relations was J. H. von Thunen in 1826. In his book *The Isolated State*,[22] he developed the idea that surrounding land uses are conditioned by the distance from the city and other economic factors. He believed that the type of crop grown is determined by the price of the crop in the city market, which in turn is set by the cost of production plus the cost of transport plus the usual margin of profit. Following this line of reasoning, von Thunen visualized an ideal city with six surrounding zones, devoted in order to perishable garden crops, silviculture to supply fuel and building needs, grain, less intensive crops, grazing, and hunting. Since water is the cheapest means of transport, the land use pattern and dense settlement are elongated near rivers and lakes. Von Thunen based his theory on the competition of land uses through economic rent; that use which can pay the highest rent at any given distance from the city is the one which occupies the land.

The most elaborate theory of city patterns is Walter Christaller's hexagonal framework.[23] According to Christaller, cities are disposed in a regular pattern—unless prohibited by topographical features such as mountains or lakes. Urban places are arranged in such manner that tributary areas are hexagonal with a small city located at each corner of each hexagon. The larger the city, the larger the hexagon; large

---

[20] Jacques Tricart, *Cours de géographie humaine*, Vol. II, "L'habitat urbain," Centre de Documentation Universitaire, Paris, 1958, pp. 261-269.

[21] W. M. Flinders Petrie, *Social Life in Ancient Egypt*, Houghton Mifflin, New York, 1923, pp. 3-4.

[22] Johann Heinrich von Thunen, *Der Isolierte Staat in Beziehung auf Landwirtschaft und Nationalökonomie*, Hamburg, 1826.

[23] Walter Christaller, "Rapports fonctionnels entre les agglomérations urbaines et les campagnes," *Comptes Rendus du Congrès International de Géographie*, Amsterdam, 1938, Vol. II: *Géographie humaine*, pp. 123-138.

service areas contain smaller ones, which in turn contain still smaller hexagons, and so forth. The major defect of this theory is its rigidity, ignoring as it does pre-existing roads, industry, density, and type of agriculture. Christaller's rejoinder to this criticism would undoubtedly be that these man-made variables are patterned in consistency with the hexagonal urban network; that is to say, these things all grew together. And he may have a point. Certainly anyone driving through Ohio, Indiana, Illinois, Kansas, Nebraska, and Iowa quickly learns to anticipate his arrival at roads and hamlets; the division of counties into sections and quarters is quite regular, with major and minor roads and towns appearing at periodic intervals.

August Losch extended Christaller's central place concept by deducing a system of city locations as functions of distance, mass production, and competition. He developed what has come to be called a "Losch system," that is a network of market regions of various sizes around each center in a systematic geometric arrangement on an undifferentiated plain with uniform resources. "First we discovered simple market regions surrounding every center of consumption or production in the form of a regular hexagon. Second, for every group of products a net of these market regions was found. And in the third place, a systematic arrangement of these various nets appeared. This self-sufficient system is the ideal type of an economic landscape, or economic region in the narrower sense. Finally, such landscapes are distributed throughout the world like a network and in accordance with definite laws."[24]

THE PRIMATE CITY AND LEAST EFFORT

If the network thesis is carried to its logical extreme, one city is bound to be far larger and more powerful than any other city in the country, in which case it is what Mark Jefferson called the primate city. "All over the world . . . the largest city shall be supereminent, and not merely in size, but in national influence . . . A country's leading city is always disproportionately large and exceptionally expressive of national capacity and feeling."[25] Primate cities such as London, Paris, Berlin, New York, and Moscow dominate the business, political, and intellectual lives of whole countries. Ordinarily, the primate city is at least twice as large and more than twice as significant as the second most important city in the country.

---

[24] August Losch, *Die raumliche Ordnung der Wirtschaft*, Gustav Fisher, Jena, 1939 (translated by W. H. Woglom and W. F. Stolper as *The Economics of Location*, Yale University Press, New Haven, 1954), p. 137.

[25] Mark Jefferson, "The Law of the Primate City," *Geographical Review*, Vol. XXIX, April 1939, pp. 226-232.

This master city whose province is the entire nation can be identified by Zipf's formula: $M = RS$, where M is the population of the largest city in the country, R the rank of each city among those of that country, and S the population of the given city.[26] Identification is simple: the primate city is at or above its theoretical location at the top of Zipf's rank-size curve. In a mature country, all cities fall near the curve; deviations from the curve Zipf takes as indications of improper balance in the pattern of urbanization. Figure 10 compares Zipf's ideal curve with United States cities, urbanized areas, and Standard Metropolitan Statistical Areas. His formula expressing the nonlinear inverse relation between city size and number of cities approximately accords with Christaller's ideas of town size and distribution.

Jefferson's primate city and Zipf's notions of mature urban systems have given rise to international comparison of the primacy rate—the population of the largest city in a country as a percentage of the total population of the four largest cities (see Table 25). Countries with the highest primacy rates are of two types. The first group is characterized by a low per cent urban, low income, and recent political or economic dependency on another country; almost always the primate city is the national capital, and often it is also "the chief port and window to the world" or "the focus of interior transportation routes and a major cultural and economic center." The second (and smaller) group of high primacy countries—such as Austria, Denmark, France, Argentina, and Uruguay—has high incomes and high urbanization. Most of the wealthier countries have moderate or low primacy rates, generally traceable to strong pressures toward regionalism in modern times. Regional identity, multicity development, and low primacy are found also in some middle and low income countries. Regional primacy is conspicuous in countries of large area and population; India and China, having strong urban traditions and large regional centers, have, therefore, low national primacy rates. In sum, though the primate city appears in prosperous and long-established nations, it is more common in poorer and newer states, especially those small enough in territory and people so that one city can easily combine

the functions of national capital, commercial metropole, chief port, and center of the Great Tradition (or nationalism) of the country concerned. On these grounds one could reasonably postulate a high probability for the development of primate cities in countries newly

---

[26] George Kingsley Zipf, *Human Behavior and the Principle of Least Effort*, Addison-Wesley Press, Cambridge, 1949, pp. 374-376; cf. also Felix Auerbach, "Das Gesetz der Bevölkerungskonzentration," *Petermann's Geographische Mitteilungen*, Vol. LIX, 1913, pp. 74-76.

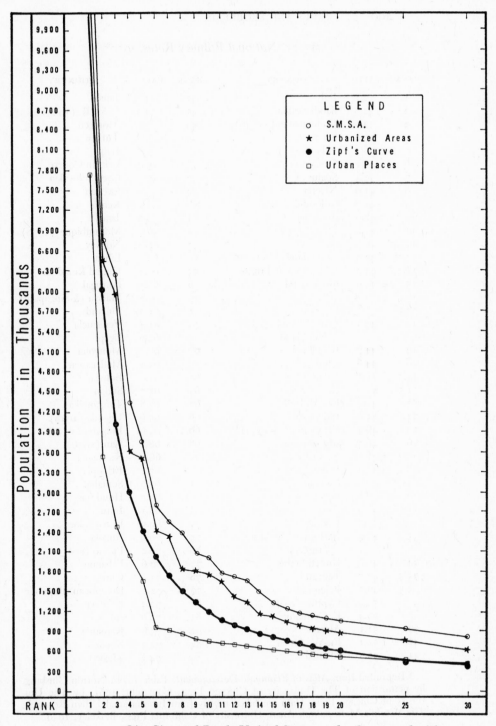

FIGURE 10. *City Size and Rank, United States, 1960, Compared with*
Zipf's Theoretical Curve

TABLE 25. *National Primacy Rates, 1955**

RANK	VALUE	COUNTRY	RANK	VALUE	COUNTRY
1	32.1	Italy	42	54.7	Japan
2	32.8	Saudi Arabia	43	54.8	U.S.S.R. (1959)
3	34.9	Bechuanaland (1946)	44	55.2	Morocco
4	37.8	Syria	46	55.9	Turkey
5	39.7	Poland	46	55.9	Iraq
6	40.1	Canada (1956)	46	55.9	Belgian Congo
7	40.3	Spain	48	56.0	Czechoslovakia
8	41.0	Nigeria	49	57.1	Sweden
9	41.8	Colombia	50	57.5	Kenya
10	42.0	Australia	51	58.3	Israel
11.5	42.2	Yugoslavia	52	59.5	Mozambique (1950)
11.5	42.2	N. Korea	53	60.0	Norway
13.5	43.0	Netherlands	54	60.2	Libya
13.5	43.0	New Zealand (1956)	55	60.3	United Kingdom
15	43.6	Switzerland	56	60.7	Portugal
16.5	44.4	India	57	60.8	Malaya (& Singapore)
16.5	44.4	Luxembourg	58	61.3	Finland
18	44.5	Fed. of Rhodesia & Nyasaland	59	61.4	Venezuela
			60	62.0	Egypt
19	44.7	Brazil	61	62.5	Mongolia
20	44.8	China (1953)	62.5	63.0	Madagascar
21.5	45.2	Pakistan	62.5	63.0	Bolivia
21.5	45.2	Jordan (1952)	64	63.7	Sudan
23	45.5	Br. W. Indies	65	63.8	Tanganyika
24	45.6	Indonesia	66.5	65.6	Uganda (1948)
25	46.4	W. Germany (1956)	66.5	65.6	Bulgaria (1956)
26	46.5	Afghanistan	68	66.1	Iran (1956)
27	46.7	N. Vietnam	69	66.9	Nicaragua
28	47.2	Union of S. Africa	70	67.2	Ethiopia
29	47.6	Cameroons	71	67.6	Somalia
30	47.8	Ghana (1948)	72	67.7	Honduras
31	47.9	S. Korea	73	68.1	Burma
32	48.5	Ecuador	74	69.0	El Salvador
33	49.4	Fr. Equatorial Africa (1950)	75	69.9	Angola
			76	70.2	Puerto Rico
34	49.6	United States	77	70.6	Lebanon
35.5	49.7	Taiwan	78	71.4	Chile
35.5	49.7	Belgium	79	72.0	Dominican Republic
37	50.0	Cyprus	80	72.4	Panama
38	50.4	E. Germany	81	72.6	Aden
39	51.1	Algeria	82	73.8	Rumania
40	52.1	Fr. W. Africa	83	73.9	Nepal
41	52.7	Albania	84	74.3	Mexico

* Reprinted from *Atlas of Economic Development*, Table 12, by Norton Ginsburg, by permission of The University of Chicago Press. Copyright, 1961, by The University of Chicago Press. Data are taken mostly from *International Urban Research, The World's Metropolitan Areas*, University of California Press, Berkeley, 1959.

TABLE 25. *(Continued)*

RANK	VALUE	COUNTRY	RANK	VALUE	COUNTRY
85	74.7	France (1954)	95	79.4	Argentina
86	75.2	Greece	96	81.6	Cambodia
87	75.6	Tunisia	97	81.7	Peru
88	75.8	Ireland (1956)	98	82.0	Philippines
89	76.2	Denmark	99	83.3	Paraguay
90	76.8	Austria	100	83.7	S. Vietnam
91	77.3	Cuba	101	83.9	Guatemala
92	77.8	Haiti	102	84.7	Hungary
93	78.0	Ceylon	103	86.7	Uruguay
94	78.9	Costa Rica	104	94.2	Thailand

independent and with changing economies, as a result of the high localization of increasing political and economic functions in them. This prediction would better fit those states which are comparatively small and compact, with few barriers to a real integration, and with small to medium populations of relative ethnic homogeneity, but without a deep-rooted urban tradition.[27]

Metropolitan Regions

Metropolitan functions have extended into the surrounding area as new means of transportation and communication permit frequent contact throughout a large territory. Subordinate municipalities within the immediate orbit of the metropolis are increasingly oriented about the center. The region thus formed is an integrated functional unit of interdependent constituent cities, towns, villages, and even rural places.

DELINEATION OF REGIONS

A metropolis has at least two boundaries—one which delimits daily contact and another delimiting a larger area dependent upon the center for specialized functions and services.[28] Some scholars include every part of the United States in a metropolitan region; others believe there are intermediate "no man's lands" which are not dependent on any metropolitan centers, or which are equally dependent upon two or more neighboring centers. In other words, two or more regions may interpenetrate.

[27] Norton Ginsburg, *Atlas of Economic Development*, University of Chicago Press, Chicago, 1961, p. 36.
[28] Donald J. Bogue (ed.), *Needed Urban and Metropolitan Research*, Scripps Foundation for Research in Population Problems, Oxford, and Population Research and Training Center, University of Chicago, 1953, pp. 16-17.

The periphery can never be sharply delimited for all purposes, for example, districts for water, electricity, newspaper subscriptions, department store delivery areas, checking accounts in banks, welfare agency service areas, and telephone zones. One may schematically draw a line embracing the central city and those environs which form a unit with it insofar as each criterion is concerned. Thus if a string is placed along each of these boundary lines, the boundary of the region should be found where the strings most frequently coincide, that is, where the wall of string is highest.

Knowing the exact extent of a metropolitan region, however, is not nearly so important as one at first might suppose. The really pressing questions are: Does a metropolitan region exist here? Roughly how many people are in it? And what is its approximate area and shape?

UNITED STATES CENSUS DEFINITIONS

The United States Bureau of the Census has set up special categories for clusters consisting of a major city surrounded by its satellites. At first the term Metropolitan District was used; then in 1960 the Census Bureau began using two units: the Standard Metropolitan Statistical Area, or S.M.S.A. (which replaced the Metropolitan District of 1910-1940 and S.M.A. of 1950), and the urbanized area. Both these areas begin with a central city of 50,000 inhabitants and include surrounding territory and residents if they are metropolitan in character and integrated with the central city. S.M.S.A.'s are delineated using counties as basic units. Urbanized areas are smaller than S.M.S.A.'s and have two components: the central city (or cities) and the built-up urban fringe. The S.M.S.A.'s two components are the central city (or cities) and contiguous related counties.

In the last half-century metropolitan areas and regions have grown rapidly. From 44 Metropolitan Districts in 1910, the United States reached 140 in 1940. There were 212 S.M.S.A.'s in 1960. Relative magnitudes of S.M.S.A.'s including proportions of population within and outside the central cities are shown in Figure 11.

Over the 1950-1960 decade S.M.S.A.'s which doubled their population were Fort Lauderdale-Hollywood, Florida, 298 per cent growth; Las Vegas, Nevada, 163 per cent; Midland, Texas, 163 per cent; Orlando, Florida, 125 per cent; San Jose, California, 121 per cent; Odessa, Texas, 116 per cent; and Phoenix, Arizona, 100 per cent. Note that these areas having the largest percentage growth are mostly scattered along a strip near the southern border. S.M.S.A.'s losing population include Altoona, Pennsylvania, 2 per cent loss; Texarkana, Texas, 3 per cent; Wheeling, West Virginia-Ohio, 3 per cent; Johnstown, Pennsylvania, 4 per cent; St. Joseph, Missouri, 6 per cent; Jersey City, New Jersey, 6

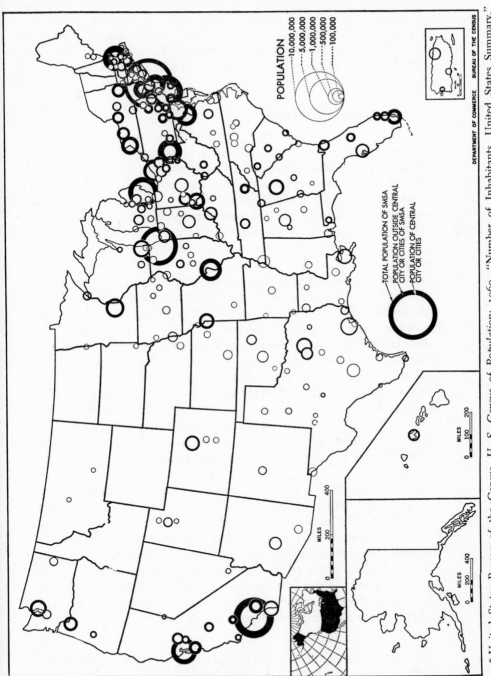

POPULATION

─ 10,000,000
─ 5,000,000
─ 1,000,000
─ 500,000
──── 100,000

TOTAL POPULATION OF SMSA
POPULATION OUTSIDE CENTRAL
CITY OR CITIES OF SMSA
POPULATION OF CENTRAL
CITY OR CITIES

MILES
0   200   400

MILES
0   100   200

MILES
0   200   400

DEPARTMENT OF COMMERCE   BUREAU OF THE CENSUS

* United States Bureau of the Census, *U. S. Census of Population: 1960*, "Number of Inhabitants, United States Summary," PC(1)-1A, Government Printing Office, Washington, 1961, Figure 34, p. S27.

per cent; Scranton, Pennsylvania, 9 per cent; and Wilkes-Barre-Hazleton, Pennsylvania, 12 per cent. Of these eight areas, five are in or bordering on Pennsylvania. The 1950-1960 increase in all S.M.S.A.'s taken together was 26 per cent.

COMMUTING AND TRANSIT

Much of this metropolitan growth has been in suburban areas. "It is hard to realize that not much more than one hundred years ago the only way to travel about in American cities was by private means—on foot, or horseback, or in a horse-drawn vehicle which you either owned or rented. Practically everybody walked to work, and job opportunities from any one residential location were correspondingly limited."[29]

About 1830 mass transportation was introduced with the horse-drawn omnibus, followed by the horse-drawn street railway car, then the suburban railway, the cable car, the elevated railway and electric surface streetcar around 1890, the subway around 1900, and finally the gasoline-powered motorbus after 1920. This tremendous advance in the daily mobility of urban people enabled cities to expand in area and population along the rapid transit routes.

Personal transportation returned with the impetus of the motor car following World War I. As highway systems were built, huge suburban areas were opened up to practically all forms of urban development. The "star" shape of cities changed back to a more circular pattern as the areas between mass transit routes filled up. Moreover, the radius of the circle was far larger than it had been before public transit. For the first time in urban history, the transportation-created emphasis on central location was broken. Suburban land could compete with downtown land.

Today, commuting is taken for granted. But Lewis Mumford (among many others) protests that people have not yet learned to live with the automobile: "The right to have access to every building in the city by private motorcar, in an age when everyone possesses such a vehicle, is actually the right to destroy the city. We still habitually sacrifice all the special values of the city to the function of transportation. . . . But the notion that you can free the motorcar from all restrictions in the city without devastating the city's living spaces is a delusion that will probably cause a lot more damage before it dies."[30] Architect-planner

---

[29] C. McKim Norton, "Metropolitan Transportation," Gerald Breese and Dorothy Whiteman (eds.), *An Approach to Urban Planning*, Princeton University Press, Princeton, 1953, p. 78.
[30] Lewis Mumford, "The Sky Line," *The New Yorker*, Vol. XXXIII, September 28, 1957, pp. 124 ff.

Victor Gruen complains that public improvement of city cores has been brought to a standstill by a new "autocrazity" cult which has chosen as its goddess the private automobile. The autocrats "accept automobile traffic in the same manner that former heathen religions accepted elementary phenomena like the sun and the rain, thunder and earthquakes—as superior elementary forces with which man cannot assume to tangle. . . . How deeply autocrats believe in their dogma may be best illustrated by a statement in a report concerning the rebuilding of Los Angeles downtown, which reads, . . . 'the pedestrian remains as the largest single obstacle to free traffic movement.' "[31]

SUBURBS AND SUBURBANITES

Population increase within central cities contrasts sharply with that of fringe areas. In most instances the peripheral areas are making rapid gains while the inner areas are growing very slowly and in some cases even decreasing. From 1950 to 1960 United States central cities grew 11 per cent in population; outer areas 49 per cent. Nor is the trend subsiding. Suburbanization is becoming increasingly important, particularly in the largest S.M.S.A.'s, where suburbanites constitute a greater proportion of the total population than in the smaller S.M.S.A.'s.

Primarily, the suburbanites are young married couples with children; one-person families are rare. They are generally nuclear families with few relatives. Native-born whites predominate. Suburbanites tend to be well educated, with a heavy proportion of wage earners in the professional and managerial occupations.

The attractions the suburbs hold for these people are multiple—lower mortgage payments, pride of home ownership, the avoidance of crime and expanding racial and ethnic belts, the pull of a presumably more intimate community life, an escape from anonymity, less congestion and more open space, fewer nuisances of noise and dirt, and an impression of space and beauty. Recently, however, there has come to be an awareness that if everyone moves to the suburbs in search of these blessings, the result may be merely a transplanting of urban ailments. Consequently some suburbanites have sold their mortgages, commutation tickets, and power mowers and have returned to apartments in the city.

In fiction and nonfiction, the suburbs have been characterized as matriarchal, filiarchal, and conformity-ridden. Commuting husbands appear to be nighttime residents and weekend guests. Spock replaces

---

[31] Victor Gruen, "Save Urbia for New Urbanites," *Journal of the American Institute of Architects*, Vol. XXXIII, February 1960, pp. 35-38.

the Bible and membership in the Parents-Teachers Association is assumed. "Mow your lawn and keep in line" would appear to be the watchword. And by all means stay exactly even with the Joneses. This congeries of alleged suburban traits has fascinated both psychoanalysts and novelists. In every branch library can be found current critiques of suburbia—or Disturbia[32]—with case histories of overextended income, marital tensions, futility and boredom, and unfulfilled young wives submerged by four walls and a baby. The men become indentured servants to their houses and yards. The women enter a routine of dishes and diapers. C. B. Palmer has described the suburbanite as "a guy with a Little Home, a Little Mortgage, a Little Car, a Little Family, a Little Dog, a Little League, and awfully little time on his hands."[33]

THE METROPOLITAN COMMUNITY

The phrase "metropolitan community" is used to signify the functional unity of the region made up of a central city and its suburban fringe. Four men have been especially prominent in the evolution of this concept: N. S. B. Gras, R. D. McKenzie, Don Bogue, and Christopher Tunnard.

In 1922 Gras used historical and anthropological knowledge to document the contention that each stage of technological development is accompanied by a corresponding form of community organization. According to Gras a causal connection obtains between the independent variable, economic and technological development, and the dependent variable, type of urban pattern. He identified five stages, of which the last is named "the metropolitan economy," and called attention to the bilateral interdependence of the metropolitan center and its tributary adjacent territory. "In studying this organization," he wrote, "we are inclined to emphasize the great metropolitan center; but to forget the large dependent district would be fatal to a correct understanding of the subject. Perhaps, indeed, it is somewhat incorrect to speak of the area as dependent upon the center, for, though that is true, the center is also dependent upon the outlying area with its towns, villages, and scattered homesteads. Interdependence of the parts is really the key to the whole situation."[34]

---

[32] Richard E. Gordon, Katherine K. Gordon, and Max Gunther, *The Split-Level Trap*, B. Geis Associates, New York, 1961.

[33] C. B. Palmer, *Slightly Cooler in the Suburbs*, Doubleday and Co., Garden City, 1950.

[34] N. S. B. Gras, *An Introduction to Economic History*, Harper and Brothers, New York, 1922, p. 187.

A decade later R. D. McKenzie contributed the present label and stressed the role of the motor vehicle in revolutionizing the traditional pattern of urban settlement and local relationships. "The super community . . . absorbs varying numbers of separate local communities into its economic and cultural organizations. In this pattern a dominant city—that is, dominant relative to surrounding settlement—functions as the integrating unit."[35] This functional interdependence, McKenzie noted, began in the motor transport era: "The motor vehicle extended the horizon of the community and introduced a territorial division of labor among local institutions and neighboring centers which is unique in the history of settlement. The large center has been able to extend the radius of its influence; its population and many of its institutions . . . have become widely dispersed throughout surrounding territory. Moreover, formerly independent towns and villages and also rural territory have become part of this enlarged city complex . . . This new type of super community . . . has become the communal unit of local relations throughout the entire nation."[36]

Don Bogue explored the hypothesis that "great cities, or metropolises, dominate the social and economic organization of technologically advanced societies."[37] He divided metropolitan communities into four parts, postulating that a "metropolitan community is an organization of many subdominant, influent, and subinfluent communities, distributed in a definite pattern about a dominant city, and bound together in a territorial division of labor through a dependence upon the activities of the dominant city." The dominant is the central metropolis controlling many of the conditions of life in all the communities surrounding it. Subdominants are satellite hinterland cities which adapt to general dependence upon the center and which function as intermediaries between the metropolis and the outlying areas. Influent populations are rural nonfarm communities of fewer than 2,500 inhabitants, having very small trade areas. Subinfluents are the rural farm population. Proceeding outward along this scale, Bogue notes a diminishing range of dominance and a decreasing number of functions over which dominance is exercised.[38] He credits ecologists for his terminology: "A subdominant has been defined as a species that exhibits a secondary dominance within the area controlled by a dominant. . . . Subdominants

---

[35] Roderick D. McKenzie, *The Metropolitan Community*, McGraw-Hill Book Co., New York, 1933, p. 313.

[36] *Ibid.*, p. 7.

[37] Don J. Bogue, *The Structure of the Metropolitan Community*, University of Michigan, Ann Arbor, 1950, p. 3.

[38] *Ibid.*, pp. 18-20 and 61-63.

298 :: ISSUES AND PROBLEMS

are the successful competitors among the species that accept the conditions imposed by the dominant."[39]

In 1915 Patrick Geddes coined the term "conurbation" to refer to the growing together of two or more large cities, forming an unbroken urban district far larger than a single metropolis.[40] This new urban emergent spread a mass of high density over scores and even hundreds of square miles. These "superregions," resembling those foreseen by H. G. Wells in *Anticipations* (1902) are today threatening to become fact. One city planner has identified the following fifteen such areas in the United States: Atlantic, Steel Belt, Southern Piedmont, Florida Coast, Gulf Coast, Chicago, Minneapolis, St. Louis, Kansas City, Dallas, Denver, Salt Lake, Washington-Oregon, Central California, and Southern California.[41] Another writer has recommended that the emerging megalopolises be given such names as Atlantic-opolis, Lake Michigan-opolis, Pacific-opolis, and the like.[42]

MEGALOPOLIS

In 1960 the Bureau of the Census gave official recognition to this idea by setting up a new megalopolitan unit called the Standard Consolidated Area. The two such areas already delimited are the New York-Northeastern New Jersey S.C.A., which contained 14.8 million people in 1960, and the Chicago-Northwestern Indiana S.C.A., containing 6.8 million people. Each of these S.C.A.'s comprises two or more S.M.S.A.'s.

One 600-mile strip along the Atlantic coast, stretching from Norfolk, Virginia, to Portland, Maine, in a continuous sprawl of urban population, has been called by Christopher Tunnard "a gigantic linear city." Containing one-fifth of the total United States population in a land area constituting only 3 per cent of the national total, it includes the cities of Washington, Baltimore, Philadelphia, Newark, New York, Hartford, Providence, Boston, and Portsmouth. A person driving through this agglomeration can hardly find a rural gap. This northeastern megalopolis encompasses all of Massachusetts, Rhode Island, Connecticut, New Jersey, Delaware, and the District of Columbia, most of Maryland, large chunks of New York and Pennsylvania, and sections of New Hampshire and Virginia. Crowded within its limits is "an extremely distinguished population. It is, on the average, the richest,

[39] Frederick E. Clements and V. E. Shelford, *Bio-Ecology*, John Wiley and Sons, New York, 1939, pp. 239-240; quoted *ibid.*, p. 18.
[40] Patrick Geddes, *Cities in Evolution*, London, 1949, pp. 14-15.
[41] Christopher Tunnard, "America's Super-Cities," *Harper's Magazine*, Vol. CCXIX, August 1958, pp. 59-65.
[42] Philip M. Hauser, *Population Perspectives*, Rutgers University Press, New Brunswick, 1960, pp. 117-119.

best educated, best housed, and best serviced group of similar size in the world. The area is still a focus of attraction for successful or adventurous people from all over America and beyond. . . . The population is on the average healthier, the consumption of goods higher, and the opportunity for advancement greater than in any other region of comparable extent."[43]

---

[43] Jean Gottmann, *Megalopolis: The Urbanized Northeastern Seaboard of the United States*, Twentieth Century Fund, New York, 1961, p. 15.

14 ❧ Resources and Food

Geographic considerations dominate any discussion of settlement patterns, food production, water supply, and resource utilization. Population is important to geographers, but they rarely devote a great deal of attention to demography as such. Rather, they consider it in conjunction with something else—a means to an end. One such end is examination of the potential for human occupancy of the various regions of the world.

There are still large areas on the earth's surface ostensibly available for human settlement where density of human habitation is low. Evaluation of the suitability of such regions for migration and colonizing falls primarily in the purview of geography. In this regard, J. O. M. Broek has identified three climatic zones which offer stubborn resistance to dense settlement but which might support larger populations, though not up to the density common in good lands: "1) areas with low rainfall—the deserts; 2) areas with low temperatures—the polar regions; 3) areas with a combination of year-round high precipitation and high temperatures—the equatorial rain-forest regions."[1] To be sure, these marginal frontier lands cannot be settled without imposing a heavy burden upon the pioneers. To control a new environment, one must discover its properties and devise ways to use them to the greatest advantage. Doubtless modern technology will evolve means of overcoming existing obstacles, but even so, lands having unpropitious climates can be inhabited only through expenditure of considerable effort and money.

---

[1] Jan O. M. Broek, "Climate and Future Settlement," in Department of Agriculture, *Climate and Man*, Government Printing Office, Washington, 1941, pp. 227-236.

Geographic Influences on Population Distribution

Geographic factors affecting the distribution of human density include atmospheric temperature, precipitation, landforms, soils, energy resources, mineral raw materials, and space relationships. Accordingly, a United Nations study notes:

> Some areas appear to have one dominant characteristic restricting their population growth, such as the cold temperatures of the ice-cap area. On the other hand, there are also areas possessing one single physical factor favourable to population growth, such as mineral wealth in a desert or sub-polar area. There are, in addition, other areas where almost all factors appear to be favourable to the support of a high density of population. For example, the alluvial areas of southeast Asia have excellent soils, landforms and climatic conditions; the great plain of western Europe has a striking combination of excellent soils, climate, landforms, mineral resources and spatial position.[2]

The meaning for human settlement and activity of the vast number of such combinations of physical features is constantly changing as cultures change and populations expand.

The functions of these geographic factors may be interpreted either in deterministic or in possibilistic terms. These two schools of thought are not in violent conflict; rather, this is a quiescent controversy. Often the same author inclines toward determinism in one article, only to espouse possibilism in another. Many geographers are in fact difficult to classify consistently: although determinist with regard to one variable (say, topography or temperature), they may be possibilist when the analysis involves different variables (mineral resources, for example).

DETERMINISM

Geographic determinists believe that geographic variables exercise the most fundamental influence on where and how people live. They insist that the physical environment surrounding man is the dominant force in shaping his settlement patterns and even in controlling crucial human events. Geographic determinism "explains the character of culture and social life in terms of climate, rainfall, soil, or other geographic facts. (High civilizations develop only in the temperate zones where the vitality of the people is great.)"[3] According to this view, New York

---

[2] United Nations, *The Determinants and Consequences of Population Trends*, New York, 1953, p. 169.

[3] Francis R. Allen, Hornell Hart, Delbert C. Miller, William F. Ogburn, and Meyer F. Nimkoff, *Technology and Social Change*, Appleton-Century-Crofts, Inc., New York, 1957, p. 77.

was bound to be the largest city in the United States because of the concatenation of its various physical features, notably the harbor. Much deterministic reasoning is in fact accurate and compelling; it is only when a few causative variables get out of hand that this approach becomes faulty. Unfortunately, however, culpability is easy to achieve on this subject. One treads perforce a narrow path when investigating the impact of geographic variables on population distribution. Exponents of geographic determinism include Friedrich Ratzel, a nineteenth-century German who called himself an anthropogeographer; Ellen Semple, a pupil of Ratzel's who tried to explain Mediterranean and American history through geographic variables; and some occasional contemporary geographers who take the view that man is a puny thing in the grasp of powerful geographic influences.

Not all determinism, of course, is geographic. In fact, social science is founded on a deterministic assumption, though most social scientists reject any single type of determinism, believing human behavior to be too complicated to explain through the application of any one set of variables, geographic or other. Indeed the most tenable position seems to be that behavior involves a complex, reciprocally related set of chronological causal chains, in which several varieties of causes may be necessary to an event, but no single set of causes is sufficient.

POSSIBILISM

Possibilists argue that although geographic factors do set limits to man's habitation, these factors are not determinative. An analogy can be made between the determinism-possibilism disagreement and the heredity-environment dispute. Corresponding to hereditary influences are the geographic limiting factors of heat, cold, aridity, dampness, soil condition, topography, and so forth. Proponents of both heredity and determinism argue that the relevant variables are sufficiently influential to set major patterns—in the case of heredity, the personality of the individual; and in the case of geographic determinism, the distribution of individuals. Environmentalists and possibilists both acknowledge the presence and impact of these variables, but they qualify that impact through the use of additional variables taken from other areas. Leading figures among the possibilists are Paul Vidal de la Blanche (who popularized the word possibilism), his student Jean Brunhes, and many modern geographers.

The fundamental identifying trait of possibilist thinking is the possible-impossible duality. Thus a possibilist might argue that human habitation is impossible above and below certain altitudes or temperatures, and that within the band thus identified as possible for human occupance, other variables come into play to affect the density of settlement. To be sure, these bounds of the ecumene are not fixed for all time; they once were closer together than at present, and they are getting farther apart as man improves his technological equipment.

For most of man's history, determinism was a fairly tenable position. However, in the twentieth century, when control over the physical environment has become so great, possibilism is the more realistic approach. Extending this reasoning into the future, man may some day attain such control over his surroundings that the limits of the "possible" will include so many circumstances as to make possibilism a meaningless explanation.

Possibilism and determinism are not strict opposites. Rather, possibilism is a central position between the extremes of determinism (the claim that phenomena can be explained completely by one set of independent variables) and free will (which negates determinism by the assumption that one cannot explain or predict population distribution even in part through the use of the given set of independent variables).

In considering these positions it is important to keep in mind the distinction between a necessary and a sufficient cause. Thus while geographic determinists argue that geographic variables are not only necessary but also sufficient to effect certain results, possibilists contend that these same geographic variables are influential and sometimes even necessary but *not* sufficient. A possibilist would argue, for example, that adequate and regular rainfall is necessary to human existence, but that it alone does not suffice; other factors in the causal nexus must also be favorable. Determinists believe that a single cause or set of causes acting alone will explain events and (given sufficient knowledge) enable us to predict future behavior.

Instead of regarding the causal sequence as proceeding from nature to man, one may reverse the chronology and view the face of the earth as a result rather than a cause of man's culture. Adherents of this viewpoint contend that geographic variables are neither necessary nor sufficient: to their way of thinking, if there is no harbor, one will be created; if temperatures prohibit growing food, food will be imported. In short, the alterations man makes in his natural environment reflect his culture traits. Thus:

> New Zealand today looks far more like England than would have been the case if its dominant European population had been French. . . .
> Man upsets balances of nature both deliberately and unintentionally.
> . . . The natural landscapes of the earth with their topographic, hydrographic, vegetational, and other forms have been converted nearly everywhere into complex cultural landscapes with new forms that vary according to the culture groups who have produced them. Largely un-

altered natural landscapes persist only in relatively uninhabited parts of the earth today.[4]

CLIMATE AND DENSITY

Man's life is influenced by weather, the daily changes in atmospheric conditions, and climate, the average weather condition over a period of years. Weather variations may induce colds, delay pouring cement for new houses, destroy crops, influence horse races, interfere with transport schedules, and make people irritable or relaxed. Climate sets limits upon human settlement, affects which crops may be grown, and motivates us to install patios in the South and storm windows in the North. Failure to prepare for climatic conditions often imposes severe penalties: Napoleon's invasion of Russia in 1812-1813 might not have been a Pyrrhic victory had his troops been adequately prepared for the scorching summer heat and subzero winter. As man's technology improves, however, his subjection to weather and climate fades.

One of the earliest determinist writers was Hippocrates, who gave vogue to the idea that climate shapes human character and temperament.[5] A similar claim was made by Montesquieu (among others) in the eighteenth century. People living in cold climates, he wrote, possess more courage, frankness, curiosity, enterprise, generosity, and vigor. Inhabitants of warm countries are timorous, sensitive, passionate, and slow to change.[6]

The modern geographer Ellsworth Huntington sent questionnaires to leading geographers throughout the Western world asking them to rank the regions of the world regarding the level of civilization attained. By finding the common climatic properties of those regions which achieved the most votes, Huntington felt that he could could identify an optimum climate for human civilization and hence high density. This ideal climate was found to have the following characteristics: 1) an average temperature in the warmest month rarely above 64 degrees— the optimum for physical activity; 2) an average temperature in the coldest month rarely below 38 degrees—the optimum for mental activity; 3) frequent storms and moisture-laden winds maintaining a high relative humidity (except in hot weather) and supplying rainfall in all seasons; and 4) frequent cyclonic storms or winds providing a constant succession of moderate temperature changes. "No region on earth fully satisfies all the requirements," wrote Huntington. "England and the

---

[4] Richard Joel Russell and Fred Bowerman Kniffen, *Culture Worlds*, The Macmillan Co., New York, 1951, p. 5.

[5] Hippocrates of Cos, *Airs, Waters, and Places*, c. 400 B.C., Chap. 24.

[6] Charles Louis de Secondat de Montesquieu, *L'esprit des lois*, Geneva, 1748.

neighboring parts of continental Europe come nearest to the ideal, but [northeastern] United States, a narrow strip close to the Pacific Coast from California to British Columbia, and finally New Zealand fall little if any behind."[7]

Anthropologists do not like Huntington's European-American bias and neglect of the Orient. Also, he has been criticized by geographers for having placed too much emphasis on climate. His approach seems to suffer from the usual weakness of single factor theories: in stressing the importance of climate, he neglects unduly the influence of other relevant variables. However, one must not recoil to the extent of ignoring climate altogether, for it is an extremely important independent variable acting on human moods and actions.

Ironically, the ideal climate for promoting progress and supporting a high density appears to be one of moderate adversity rather than the abundantly productive situation which obtains in the tropics. The reasoning behind this paradox is that the presence of an unfruitful agricultural season (too cold or dry) leads to forethought in working and saving habits. Once man is able to store food or save money he keeps on working even when he does not need to. Without storage facilities, there is no point in producing more than enough for present demands; when a man has enough, he stops.

Up to now we have considered the influence of climate on man; the following 1953 letter to the editor of *The New Yorker* magazine reverses this order and treats climate as the dependent variable.

> In a recent issue, you mention the theory of Mr. William Baxter that the hot weather of the tropics is gradually moving north and that New York City and its environs will soon be even more uncomfortable to live in than they are right now. Mr. Baxter proposes that young people move to the Pacific Northwest, where it's still cool. I would like to say that this is no solution at all, for people of any age. It shows that Mr. Baxter not only has failed to think the problem through but is unaware of what has caused the problem in the first place. I agree with Mr. Baxter that the climate is changing, *and I know why.* The answer can be given in two little words: body heat. The temperature of the human body—at least, of most human bodies—is 98.6°. Now, the population of the world is going up by leaps and bounds and more and more body heat is being poured out into the atmosphere. It stands to reason, therefore, that the weather can't help but get warmer and warmer. According to calculations I have made, if the present rate of population increase continues unchanged, the entire earth will reach a uniform temperature of

---

[7] Ellsworth Huntington, *Principles of Human Geography*, John Wiley and Sons, New York, 1940, pp. 348-349. See also his *Civilization and Climate*, Yale University Press, New Haven, 1935.

98.6 by the year 2033. I hope some of your younger readers will be here then to check my figures.

Meanwhile, the more people who follow Mr. Baxter's advice, the sooner the Northwest will become a perfect oven.[8]

EUROPEAN DENSITY PATTERNS

Dudley Kirk has applied possibilist principles toward achieving a better understanding of the population distribution of Europe. According to Kirk, the continental pattern is a response to five limiting geographic factors. 1) People tend to flow downhill. In Europe, as in other continents, they avoid mountains—the Alps, the Carpathians, the Balkans, the Scandinavian backbone, and even the relatively low Scottish hills. (See Table 26 for world data supporting this thesis.) 2) Cold tempera-

TABLE 26. *The Distribution of World Population by Elevation Above Sea Level**

WORLD DATA	UP TO 200 METERS	200- 500 METERS	500- 1000 METERS	1000- 1500 METERS	1500- 2000 METERS	ABOVE 2000 METERS	TOTAL
Population (per cent)	56.2	24.0	11.6	4.4	2.3	1.5	100.0
Area (per cent)	27.8	29.5	21.2	9.7	5.6	6.2	100.0
Density (per square kilometer)	34.8	14.0	9.4	8.3	6.8	4.1	17.1

* Josef Staszewski, *Vertical Distribution of World Population*, Polish Academy of Sciences, Geographical Studies No. 14, Warsaw, 1957, pp. 17-18.

tures inhibit population from spreading into northern Scandinavia and Russia. 3) Aridity led to thin settlement in central Spain, the Balkans, the steppes of southern Russia, and other excessively dry regions. 4) Excessive dampness checked growth in northern Scotland, parts of Norway, and the Pripet Marshes of White Russia. 5) Poor soil north and east of the Elbe River discouraged agricultural settlement. The density was much higher south of the Elbe, where the soil is good. Thus climate, topography, and other physiographic features set limits to the kinds of uses that men can make of their territory. And within these limits, Kirk reasoned, density patterns are affected by other variables. "Within the European regions suitable for primitive agriculture the pattern of population distribution is much more complex than might be suggested by

---

[8] Eglise Barnard, "Department of Amplification," *The New Yorker*, Vol. XXIX, No. 37, October 31, 1953, p. 87.

the more elementary geographical features. The development of natural resources, the degree of industrialization, the location of markets, the lines of transportation have all created a continental pattern of distribution that is shaped only in its broad outlines by the sharper limits of topography and climate."[9]

In Europe as elsewhere the greatest clusters of people are found in lowlands along rivers or near seaports, where agriculture, commerce, and industry can flourish. Europe, west of Russia, is about five times as densely populated as is the generality of the world's surface. Kirk notes two great axes of high density: a major axis stretching east-west through central and southern England, Flanders, the Netherlands, the lower Rhine Valley, central Germany, Poland, and the black earth regions of Russia; and a minor north-south axis running through the Rhine valley, Switzerland, and Italy (though broken by the Alps). These axes seem to be unaffected by political boundaries. In fact Kirk goes so far as to suggest that North America, where political boundaries are fewer and less important, is a mirror image of Europe.[10] The largest population density in North America, as in Europe, is located on the Atlantic Seaboard. The European east-west axis with its industrial production in the England-West Germany area gradually yields to farming as we move east; corresponding to this distribution is North America's east-west manufacturing belt extending from New York to Chicago yielding to agriculture as we go west. The Anglo American secondary axis is north-south (as in Europe) from Boston through New York, Philadelphia, Baltimore, Washington, and Norfolk. Canada, though less dense, resembles Scandinavia in its settlement pattern. The Great Lakes are similar in location and function to the Baltic Sea. In the American Middle West, as in European Russia, the density falls gradually to that of the Great Plains, which correspond in topography and settlement to the Russian steppes. The American South, with its rurality and slowness to industrialize, reminds one of Spain, southern Italy, and the Balkans. After we reach the great north-south mountain chains of the Rockies and the Urals, the resemblance ends.

It is even conceivable to posit social counterparts to these geomorphological resemblances, for example, the proud graciousness of Georgia and Spain. Lest this analogy be taken too seriously, it must be pointed out that some observers have used geographic characteristics to explain differences between the United States and Europe. For example, André Siegfried speaks of America's "great scale," space, and "freedom from

---

[9] Dudley Kirk, *Europe's Population in the Interwar Years*, League of Nations, Geneva, 1946, p. 6.
[10] *Ibid.*, p. 8.

and imposition on nature" as providing an incentive for wastage of resources and territory, urban sprawl, ecological irregularities, a spirit of adventure, initiative, and energy.[11]

Migration and natural increase trends have altered Europe's population distribution many times over the centuries of recorded history. In the ancient period the Mediterranean Sea was the center, with the highest densities clustered first in Greece and, then, as colonization proceeded westward, along the entire Mediterranean littoral; elsewhere, population was sparse. With the coming of the Middle Ages, mature settled agriculture moved north to France and the Low Countries, but despite the shifting toward the northwest, the highest density was still in Italy. This frontier was pushed to the northern limits of the continent by the seventeenth century, at which time the greatest concentration was in France. The demographic, agricultural, and industrial revolutions brought additional changes, moving the population center still further toward the northwest. As Kirk has noted: "The great urban concentrations of Northwestern Europe are clearly a function of the fact that the processes of industrialization first took foothold in this region. Their predominant weight in the distribution of the European population is therefore a creation of the modern era. Throughout most of its early history the population of Europe had a Mediterranean orientation, in which the chief population clusters and areas of dense settlement were to be found in the countries bordering that sea."[12] Now, in the twentieth century, the enormous growth in southern and eastern Europe is shifting the density pattern once more, this time in the reverse of the earlier direction.

These changes are often used as evidence against the deterministic school of geography. If geographic variables are truly determinative, so runs the argument, then why should the density pattern show such marked alterations? The answer appears to lie in the changing conditions of life. Differences in economic organization, transportation, manufacturing methods, power sources, marketing, and natural resources create different patterns of population settlement. In short, just as a man is the product of his times, so is his density of habitation.

Utilization of Natural Resources

The interrelationships between population and resources have fascinated geographers, economists, and conservationists for many years. This in-

---

[11] André Siegfried, *America at Mid-Century*, Harcourt, Brace and Co., New York, 1955.
[12] Kirk, *Europe's Population, op. cit.*, p. 241.

terest appears destined to increase, for as human numbers enlarge, the wasteful practices that have prevailed in man's dealings with natural resources have come to have more and more harmful consequences. As the population is felt to press upon the earth's productivity, social scientists and laymen alike have grasped their pen-shaped cudgels and sailed into combat against the senseless things we have been doing to our topsoil and the water table.

WASTE AND CONSERVATION

John Ruskin called land "the most precious 'property' that human beings can possess" and decried its unesthetic use at the hand of man. Objections by lovers of beauty have been supplemented by mundane, materialistic fears that in time there won't be enough of everything to go around. Witness Malthus: "Man is necessarily confined in room. When acre has been added to acre till all the fertile land is occupied, the yearly increase of food must depend upon the melioration of the land already in possession. This is a fund, which, from the nature of all soils, instead of increasing, must be gradually diminishing."[13] Or, in our own time: "Above all, we must learn to know—to feel to the core of our beings—our dependence upon the earth and the riches with which it sustains us. We can no longer believe valid our assumptions that we live in independence. No longer can we rest secure in the certainty that somehow, from somewhere, our wants will be supplied. We, even we fortunate Americans, are pressing hard on our means of subsistence. Our neighbors on five continents know what it means to find their cupboards bare."[14] Thus there are two bases of complaint: first, that we scar beautiful hills by strip mining and deform quiet meadows with auto muffler shops; second, that we breed more mouths and stomachs which require more food and water.

Small wonder that resource use and depletion is becoming an urgent policy issue. The waste that characterized nineteenth-century United States resource recovery and application is finally yielding place before conservationist arguments. Three factors are primarily responsible for this trend: population increments add to the number of potential resource consumers; underdeveloped areas are now industrializing; and intensity of use is increasing in industrialized nations. Thus more people are making more intense use of minerals and energy. If per capita use

---

[13] Thomas R. Malthus, *An Essay on the Principle of Population*, London, sixth edition, 1826, p. 4.
[14] William Vogt, *Road to Survival*, William Sloane Associates, Inc., New York, 1948, p. 286.

of materials and energy triples and population size doubles, the total demand upon the earth's natural resources will be multiplied by six.

POPULATION-RESOURCES RATIO

The contemporary social scientist Samuel Ordway has proposed a theory governing the limit of population growth based on two premises: 1) that "levels of human living are constantly rising with mounting use of natural resources"; and 2) that "despite technological progress we are spending each year more resource capital than is created." Ordway contends that "if this cycle continues long enough, basic resources will come into such short supply that rising costs will make their use in additional production unprofitable, industrial expansion will cease, and we shall have reached the limit of growth."[15]

One geographer has classified the regions of the world into five types according to their technological level and population-resources ratio (see Figure 12). Present characteristics and future prospects of these types are as follows: 1) United States type: "Little resource limitation on numbers, some on standard of living; economically strong competition for product of foreign countries"; 2) European type: "Strong pressure for attachment to foreign resources; where frustrated, crisis possible"; 3) Brazil type: "Little resource limitation on numbers; domestic orientation"; 4) China type: "Continual consciousness of impending crisis; increasing pressure for attachment to foreign resources"; 5) Arctic-desert type: "Development by type 1, 2, 4 countries inevitable; strong competition for resources; however, few people."[16]

OPTIMISTS *versus* PESSIMISTS

In recent decades there has been a running conflict concerning population growth *versus* resource growth. The opponents may be classified with reasonable accuracy into the two camps of optimism and pessimism, two viewpoints concerning the Malthusian dilemma that were parodied by Kenneth Boulding in a 1955 Princeton University symposium:[17]

---

[15] Samuel H. Ordway, Jr., "Possible Limits of Raw-Material Consumption," in William L. Thomas, Jr. (ed.), *Man's Role in Changing the Face of the Earth*, University of Chicago Press, Chicago, 1956, p. 992. See also Ordway, *Resources and the American Dream*, Ronald Press, New York, 1953, pp. 31-35.

[16] Edward A. Ackerman, "Population and Natural Resources," in Philip M. Hauser and Otis Dudley Duncan (eds.), *The Study of Population*, University of Chicago Press, Chicago, 1959, p. 645.

[17] Kenneth E. Boulding, Discussion of "Limits of the Earth: Materials and Ideas," in Thomas, *Man's Role in Changing the Face of the Earth, op. cit.*, p. 1087.

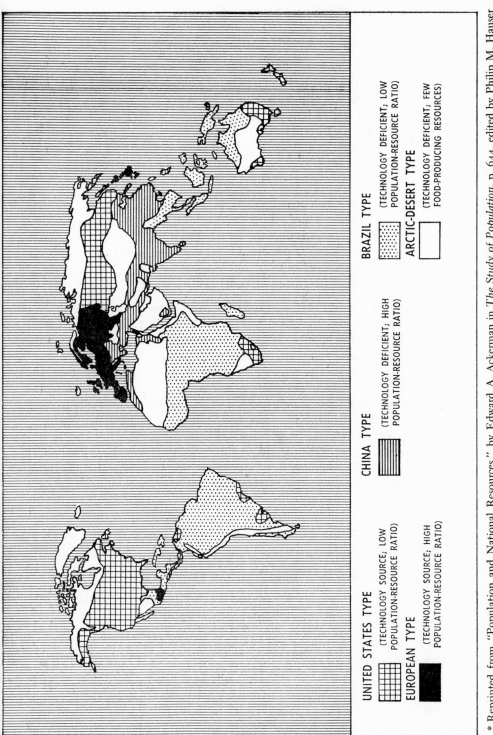

UNITED STATES TYPE
(TECHNOLOGY SOURCE; LOW
POPULATION-RESOURCE RATIO)

EUROPEAN TYPE
(TECHNOLOGY SOURCE; HIGH
POPULATION-RESOURCE RATIO)

CHINA TYPE
(TECHNOLOGY DEFICIENT; HIGH
POPULATION-RESOURCE RATIO)

BRAZIL TYPE
(TECHNOLOGY DEFICIENT; LOW
POPULATION-RESOURCE RATIO)

ARCTIC-DESERT TYPE
(TECHNOLOGY DEFICIENT; FEW
FOOD-PRODUCING RESOURCES)

A CONSERVATIONIST'S LAMENT

The World is finite, resources are scarce,
Things are bad and will be worse . . .
Fire will rage with man to fan it,
Soon we'll have a plundered planet.
People breed like fertile rabbits,
People have disgusting habits.

THE TECHNOLOGIST'S REPLY

Man's potential is quite terrific
You can't go back to the Neolithic.
The cream is there for us to skim it,
Knowledge is power and the sky's the limit . . .
Men can grow to pastures greener
Till all the earth is Pasadena.

Optimist Kirtley Mather expressed the minority viewpoint in his book *Enough and to Spare*, written just before the end of World War II, when the population sprint of the 1950's was not yet conceived. Yet then as today, opposing best-selling books by several authors visualized humanity on the verge of disaster.[18] Sometimes a writer seems to have made a sudden personal discovery of the population problem which has fired him with enough fervor to write a book about the disasters implicit in the situation. In chemistry, biology, and economics departments—to name only a few—experts are leaping on the bandwagon—except most demographers and sociologists, who have lived with this problem long enough to be used to it. We have here the spectacle of reputable scholars in vociferous disagreement for three reasons: because the controversy relates to the future (it is always difficult to obtain agreement about the future), because we are unable to set up controlled experiments on the subject, and because the scientific issue is intermixed with ethical and political issues.

RENEWABLE AND NONRENEWABLE RESOURCES

In any discussion of resource depletion it is helpful to distinguish between resources that are renewable and those that are not. Renewable resources—the sun, wind, tides, precipitation, and gravitational attraction—maintain a roughly stable potential regardless of use. Nonrenewable resources—coal, oil, and gas—can be used only once. Some

---

[18] See Recommended Readings: Resource Utilization (p. 552), references to Harrison Brown, Fairfield Osborn, Karl Sax, and William Vogt.

resources (such as soil fertility) are renewable if properly managed but may be so depleted by inadequate care as to become nonrenewable.

Although the renewable resources do not present difficult problems, the nonrenewable ones must be closely watched; otherwise they may be thrown away like the excellent timber reserve formerly held by the United States. Following exhaustion of the supply of a nonrenewable resource (or the anticipation thereof), it is sometimes physically possible and financially feasible to shift to another nonrenewable resource as a substitute; in certain cases this procedure is quicker and cheaper than the staggering cost of attempting to restore renewable resources.

Similarly, one must not overlook the future development of presently unknown (nor even yet conceived) resources as a solution to the problem of resource depletion. The history of technology provides copious documentation of the fact that certain hitherto unknown or poorly valued substances can be extremely useful for industrial processes. One hundred years ago, how many people suspected that oil or uranium would be so valuable to man? There is no reason why similar discoveries should not take place in the future.

WATER SUPPLY AND USE

Among the many articles written advocating maximum or at least increased efforts toward conserving both renewable and nonrenewable resources, water, an absolute necessity, is prominently featured. Some writers warn that there is or soon will be an insufficient total quantity of water available to meet man's increasing demands. Others place the onus on misuse of existing water supplies, which, "especially in the arid regions of the West, are grossly misallocated as a result of unwise water policies and laws of the past and present. There is, furthermore, some reason to believe that these policies will be continued and even expanded in the future."[19]

A gallon of water or an inch of precipitation does not always have the same significance. Precipitation may or may not add to usable water resources. Seasonal variations in both supply and demand force us to build huge reservoirs. Of special importance is the quality of water: water contains bacteria, organic matter, and dissolved or suspended salts and acids which require purification. In turn, purity requirements differ according to use—for drinking, industrial processes, and so forth. We need also be concerned with palatability, softness or hardness, corrosiveness, and temperature.

Gross distribution of water withdrawals in the United States is shown

---

[19] Jack Hirshleifer, James C. De Haven, and Jerome W. Milliman, *Water Supply*, University of Chicago Press, Chicago, 1960, p. 6.

TABLE 27. *Estimated United States Water Withdrawals, 1955**

USE CATEGORY	WITHDRAWALS IN BILLION GALLONS PER DAY	PERCENTAGE OF TOTAL
Domestic residential	8.7	3.6
Industrial and commercial	47.2	19.6
Steam-electric power	72.2	30.0
Public municipal (fire, parks, etc.)	0.9	0.4
Agriculture	111.5	46.4
Total	240.5	100.0
Water power	1,500	...

* Reprinted from *Water Supply*, p. 25, by Jack Hirshleifer, J. C. De Haven, and Jerome W. Milliman, by permission of The University of Chicago Press. Copyright, 1960, by The University of Chicago Press.

in Table 27. Nonwithdrawal uses as involved in navigation, waste disposal, recreation, and fish and wildlife conservation are not included. The withdrawals used in generating electric power are noted because (although not strictly depleting the water supply) such withdrawals often make the water unavailable for other purposes.

East-West differences regarding water withdrawals contrast sharply. Most water withdrawn in the East is used by industry, whereas a majority of that in the West goes into irrigation. "Beyond the Missouri River water has been almost a sacred commodity—accorded the same passionate respect that it received in Bible lands. There is an old frontier saying: 'Steal my horse, carry off my wife, but damn you, don't touch my water.' And from the time that the first farmer fenced off a water-hole on the open range, water has been the West's chief source of conflict."[20] Western history abounds with stories of cattle dying of thirst across from a fenced-off water hole, dynamiting of aqueducts, and interstate water rights feuds. Lately, fear of water shortage has been spreading throughout the country; indeed, in some areas it is illegal to water lawns on certain days of the week.

In the United States per capita use of water is soaring annually. Four-gallon-a-minute showers and five-gallon toilet flushes are supplemented by growing industrial demands. Increased rates per capita, coupled with a larger population, mean that the United States is using eight times as much water as it did in 1900.

Nor is this trend likely to let up. To make a ton of steel takes 50,000 to 100,000 gallons of water. One gallon of gasoline represents

[20] Remi Nadeau, *Los Angeles: From Mission to Modern City*, Longmans, Green and Co., New York, 1960, p. 161.

an investment of about 15 gallons of water. Eight gallons of water are expended in brewing one gallon of beer. Five gallons of water go into each gallon of milk, 40 to a gallon of whiskey or a pound of finished cloth, 80 to a kilowatt-hour of electricity, and 300 to a pound of synthetic rubber. A steer and its pastureland consume something like 4,000 gallons of water for each pound of beef; thus regarded, steak is more expensive in water than in money. Even a slice of bread, one of the cheapest of commodities, requires (including the growing of the wheat) some 30 gallons of precious water.

In many parts of the country the water table (the top level of underground water) is falling steadily. This dangerous drop is due not to drought, but to demand. Americans appear to have formed the habit of wasting whatever is abundant. Regarding water, United States inhabitants have been using, misusing, polluting, and abusing it as though there would never be a tomorrow.

A present hope is the conversion of sea water to fresh water, now reduced to a cost of about one dollar per 1,000 gallons—some three times the average price of municipal water. Further reductions in conversion costs should follow application of scientific knowledge under pressure from population growth and increasing per capita use. Eventually the necessity for desalinated water should make salt water conversion a standard practice. Yet even if all the water in the oceans were fresh enough to drink, there would still remain the considerable expense of pumping it from sea level up to the height at which it is to be used—and most farms, factories, and people are located hundreds or thousands of feet above ocean level.

In 1961 the United States Office of Saline Water estimated that, by 1980, national consumption of water will exceed "readily available" supplies, forcing partial dependence upon converted salt water. Milking rain clouds is a very distant prospect. For the near future, pipelines, conservation, and pollution control are more likely hopes. Los Angeles has brought water hundreds of miles to supply its arid steppes. Governmental agencies are turning to stream regulation, watershed and anti-erosion control, improved sewage systems, and small dams. Manufacturers could do much to recirculate water used for cooling, reclaim lost water, and treat waste water to avoid pollution.

AGRICULTURAL LAND

From the classic conservation doctrine that land is a constant parameter in the resource equation, the modern view has evolved the theory that land is a variable, though with ascertainable limits. Writes Karl Polanyi: "Land is an element of nature inextricably interwoven with man's institutions. To isolate it and form a market of it was perhaps the weirdest of all undertakings of our ancestors. . . . Land is thus tied up with organizations of kinship, neighborhood, craft, and creed—with tribe and temple, village, guild, and church."[21]

The amount of support that land yields to man is a function of at least four independent variables: the accumulating knowledge of techniques of cultivation, the substitution of industrial transformations for processes occurring in plants and animals (for example, the development of sucrose and glucose refining and the preparation of edible fats and oils from vegetable sources), the magnitude of population, and the available quantity of land.[22] The first two variables are being brought under control with the advances of physical and biological science. Control of the third is largely a matter of family planning. And the land supply is affected by both geographic and cultural circumstances.

International differences with regard to the acreage of land per capita under cultivation are considerable. Thus the United States has approximately twice the per capita acreage under cultivation of Germany, which in turn has much more than double the equivalent proportion to be found in China or Japan. Figure 13 illustrates the sometimes sharp disjunctions between land area and population around the world.

The man-land ratio is a crude statement of the relationship between population and the cultivated land area. A rough symbolic expression of this relationship is: $\dfrac{P}{L} = \dfrac{E}{S}$ where P = population, L = productive land, E = economic organization, and S = standard of living. These concepts are placed in mathematical form not because they are quantitatively manipulable, but because that is the clearest way to state the relationships among them. According to Malthus, population tends to increase up to the supporting power of the land for any given economic organization and standard of living. To illustrate:

United States: $\quad \dfrac{1}{1} = \dfrac{1}{1}$

Japan: $\quad \dfrac{.50}{.05} = \dfrac{.50}{.05}$

Java: $\quad \dfrac{.333}{.018} = \dfrac{.100}{.005}$

---

[21] Karl Polanyi, *The Great Transformation*, The Beacon Press, Boston, 1957, p. 178.

[22] J. B. Canning, quoted in E. F. Penrose, *Population Theories and Their Application*, Food Research Institute, Stanford University, 1934, p. 15.

FIGURE 13. *Comparison of Land Area and Population**

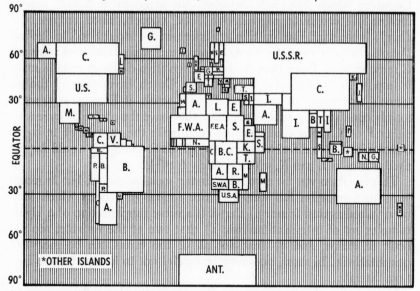

A. DISTRIBUTION OF LAND

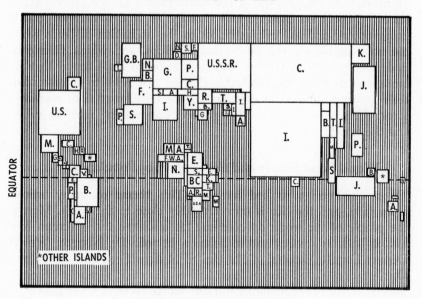

B. DISTRIBUTION OF POPULATION

* Prepared by the Institut National de la Statistique et des Études Économiques, Paris, 1949.

Countries which insist on raising S (the standard of living) cannot inprove E (economic organization) fast enough, since ordinarily L (land) is constant, thus putting a pressure on P (population) to decline. Put otherwise, if a country wants to increase P while L remains constant, E must increase faster than S—but conservative elements usually make it impossible to change E rapidly. The Dutch have adopted the extremely rare policy of increasing L; as a result, if E remains approximately constant (the usual situation), they have the choice of increasing either P or S. Many countries, however, make the mistake of trying to increase both P and S simultaneously, although to do this would require similar rises in L and E, which is rarely feasible.

This equation was once popular among social scientists, but in recent years its reputation has waned. Three serious objections which have been voiced against it are: 1) that it is a naïve simplification of a highly complex set of interrelationships; 2) that two of the variables are difficult to define; and 3) that not all of the terms can be measured quantitatively. In short, one must be careful not to interpret these fractions literally.

Not surprisingly, an excessively dense agricultural population may be an obstacle to effective use of the land. Thus a United Nation report states: "Population pressure and shortage of land sometimes lead to over-cropping and soil exhaustion or to the utilization of lands which are not suitable for the production of crops, and which deteriorate under the plough. A United Nations mission to Haiti found that the farmers in that country, constantly clearing new fields to accommodate their growing numbers, had stripped steep hillsides of their protective forest cover with the result that the soil was washing into the valleys and the sea."[23]

World Food Supply and the Support of Population

"Most children go to bed hungry." This theme of many articles, radio talks, and the like is uncomfortably close to the truth. Most of the people of the world do consume far less than the optimum food intake, both in amount and in balance. In 1960 Dr. Norman Wright, Deputy Director-General of the United Nations Food and Agricultural Organization, stated that at least half of the world's people are either undernourished or malnourished. Daily intake averages fewer than 2,000 calories in countries containing 60 per cent of the world's population.

The very idea that most people should reach an optimum food

---

[23] United Nations, *Population Growth and the Standard of Living in Underdeveloped Countries*, New York, 1954, p. 4.

consumption has only recently attained popularity. Arnold Toynbee has predicted that the achievement for which our generation will best be known in future eras is the initiation, for the first time in human history, of a universal aspiration toward high standards of living.

In the United States the chronic food problem is overeating, and many persons buy nostrums which purportedly enable them to eat as much as they wish without getting too fat. Living among such a plentiful overabundance of things to eat, Americans often have difficulty understanding that the usual problem for man is not how to restrain him from eating too much, but rather how to obtain enough food to maintain health and vigor.

The Eltonian pyramid (100 pounds of plants are required to support 10 pounds of herbivores, which in turn can support one pound of carnivores)[24] implicitly poses limits to human density and numbers. Edward Deevey modifies Elton's reasoning:

> Plants capture the solar energy impinging on a given area with an efficiency of about .1 per cent. (Higher values often quoted are based on some fraction of the total radiation, such as visible light.) Herbivores capture about a 10th of the plants' energy, and carnivores convert about 10 per cent of the energy captured by herbivores (or other carnivores). This means, of course, that carnivores, feeding on plants at second hand, can scarcely do so with better than 1 per cent efficiency (1/10 × 1/10 equals 1/100). Eugene I. Rabinowitch of the University of Illinois has calculated that the current crop of men represents an ultimate conversion of about 1 per cent of the energy trapped by land vegetation. Recently, however, I have re-examined the base figure—the efficiency of the land-plant production—and believe it should be raised by a factor of three or four. The old value came from estimates made in 1919 and in 1937. A good deal has been learned since those days. The biggest surprise is the high productivity of forests, especially the forests of the Temperate Zone.
>
> If my new figures are correct, the population could theoretically increase by 30 or 40 times. But man would have to displace all other herbivores and utilize all the vegetation with the 10 per cent efficiency established by the ecological rule of tithes. No land that now supports greenery could be spared for nonagricultural purposes; the populace would have to reside in the polar regions, or on artificial "green isles in the sea, love"—scummed over, of course, by 10 inches of Chlorella culture.[25]

---

[24] Charles S. Elton, *Animal Ecology*, Sedgwick and Jackson Ltd., London, 1927, pp. 68-70.

[25] Edward S. Deevey, Jr., "The Human Population," *Scientific American*, Vol. CCIII, No. 3, September 1960. The "green isles" quotation is from Edgar Allan Poe, "To One in Paradise."

AMOUNT AND VARIETY OF FOOD NEEDED

On the quantity side, nutritionists speak of the adult minimum number of calories per day needed to function efficiently, that is, to do one's job properly. On the quality side, people need certain vitamins, proteins, carbohydrates, minerals, and so forth. But in many regions animal protein (the richest protein) is simply not to be had. The inexpensive, energy-giving carbohydrates make up four-fifths of the diet of some peoples—a diet which is not only nutritionally inadequate, but boring as well. Spices are often used to offset the monotony. Yet how many ways can one cook rice without meat, fish, or fowl? The notion that "bread is the staff of life"[26] is not correct for the world; it shows that the writer comes from a wheat-growing rather than a rice-growing society. (Rice is not moist enough to hold together as wheat does in forming bread.) Unfortunately, rice is the poorest of the staple cereals because it loses more nutritional value in cooking than do other grains. This lack of edible variety is responsible for the endemic nutrition deficiency diseases in Asia such as beri-beri, symptomized by neuritis, rigidity, and debility. "They that die by famine die by inches."[27]

Nor is the problem simply one of inadequate distribution, as some would like to believe. To satisfy the adult daily caloric and other dietary requirements of everyone in the world would require doubling the production of milk, fruits, and vegetables and making substantial increases in man's production of sugar, meat, fats and oils, roots and tubers, and cereals. Some scholars have even suggested that sending food to relieve alimentary distress in undersupplied regions of the world would merely result in a larger number of half-starved people than before. Ironically, the greatest potential population growth is found in those areas having the greatest deficiency in the food supply.

In an effort to cope with this problem through international cooperation, the Food and Agriculture Organization was formally established as an affiliate agency of the United Nations in 1945. The F.A.O., with 79 member countries, has as its principal aim the coordination of national efforts to improve food production, distribution, and consumption. It does not produce, buy, or distribute food, but merely advises and consults. F.A.O. has three functions: information—statistical surveys, publications, technical information service; international consultation—staff and machinery for conferences, especially on pest and disease control; and technical assistance—advice to member governments, recruiting of specialists.

---

[26] Jonathan Swift, *Tale of a Tub*, 1704, Preface.
[27] Mathew Henry, *A Commentary on the Holy Bible*, 6 vols., London, 1708-1710, Genesis III, Psalm LIX.

The world food situation could be enhanced by bringing new land under cultivation, making better use of land already cultivated, increasing the supply of food taken from water sources, producing non-agricultural or manufactured food, improving the processing and distribution of food, or persuading people to eat food now considered inedible and therefore wasted.

INCREASING LAND UNDER CULTIVATION

At present only about 8 per cent of the world's land (excluding Antarctica) is used for growing crops and 12 per cent for pasture and meadows. The remaining 80 per cent is, for various reasons, unable to be put into immediate agricultural use: insufficient rainfall, poorly distributed rainfall, not enough sunlight, heavy tropical vegetation needing clearing, irregular topography, poor soil composition, swampy marsh, poor temperature conditions, or too high density of people and man-made structures. Some of these debilities are permanent, others temporary. Improving any one of them, however, would increase slightly the proportion of land available for agricultural use, and removal of several difficulties could ensure a significant augmentation of the total agricultural land.

New land may be brought into cultivation in several ways, though on a world-wide basis the expense of such accomplishment would be tremendous and, at present, too great to finance. Scientific control of rainfall, improved fertilizers, and the development of new hybrid and mutant crops and farm animals hold varying degrees of promise for the future. Drainage of marshes and swamps and irrigation of arid land could add considerably to the acreage under cultivation, but, again, the cost is a deterrent. Also, as noted above, the adequacy of the water supply is already challenged in some places. As population increases and the per capita industrial and personal use of water climbs, the people of the world are faced with the prospect of decreasing the amount of water available for crop irrigation. Added to these troubles are inadequate treatment of watersheds and silting up of reservoirs.

Moreover, should the world population double by the end of this century (as will happen if the present rate of growth continues), far more land will probably be needed for housing. Some of the land now used for farming and grazing will certainly be taken over by builders to construct dwellings. Even today, consider how much once agriculturally productive land has been turned into suburban housing tracts. This expansion of housing will be paralleled by the construction of new factories, warehouses, stores, and offices, all of which occupy land. Superhighways also pre-empt farm land. Jonathan Swift and Voltaire both extolled the service to mankind of anyone who could make two blades of grass grow where only one grew before; today, however, man replaces a hundred thousand blades of grass by one cloverleaf.

An unusual resolution of the land shortage problem was devised by the Dutch. They simply created new farm land by uncovering it; drainage of the polders has partially solved their overpopulation problem. Reclamation of land from the Zuiderzee involves five stages, each consisting of the construction of an independent polder; the final polder now planned should be finished in the 1970's. Completion of the five will add 10 per cent to the farm land of the Netherlands.[28]

More land is not a solution in and of itself. The mere existence of unoccupied land does not guarantee room for an increasing agricultural population. Much of the world's land remains uncultivated because it is not suitable for farming, and much technically usable land is of poor quality or inaccessible. To bring such land under cultivation ordinarily requires substantial capital investment plus a technical knowledge which the people of the region may not possess. Immigrants may be deterred by legal restrictions discouraging entry supplementing the high cost of moving and resettling their families in new homes. Frequently, too, the location is unattractive to newcomers because of its remoteness, an unpleasant climate, unsavory prospective neighbors, or an unappetizing political setting. Finally, if the land is held by private owners, they may prefer to wait for speculative gains or put it to nonagricultural uses.

INCREASING PRODUCTIVITY OF CULTIVATED LAND

Productivity of land already being cultivated may be raised by some of the same techniques that would bring new land into cultivation, for example, irrigation, fertilizers, and new crops. "In the more densely populated regions at least, intensive development of agriculture on the lands already in use offers greater possibilities than extension of the cultivated area. Crop yields per unit of land could be greatly increased in all the under-developed countries if full advantage were taken of present technical knowledge."[29]

There are three basic methods for maintaining the nutrients in cultivated land: the medieval practice of letting it lie fallow every third year, planting restorative crops (also an old practice), and fertilizing. Yet all three methods have serious deficiencies. The fallow method is wasteful because one-third of the land is always out of production. Restorative crops are wasteful because generally they do not produce as

[28] A. K. Constandse, "L'aménagement d'un polder aux Pays-bas," *Population*, Vol. XII, No. 3, July-September 1957, pp. 401-412.
[29] United Nations, *Population Growth and the Standard of Living, op. cit.*, pp. 4-5.

much return in bushels of beans or in money at the market as does the regular crop. High capitalization is needed for the industrial production of phosphorus-, nitrogen-, and potassium-based fertilizers, and its price to the consumer is too high for most of the world's farmers, especially to those in regions of the world where there is the greatest pressure of population on the food supply.

Chemical sprays and disease-resistant plants have greatly reduced pests and diseases. But disease-resisting plants are designed to resist only presently known diseases. As mutations of disease germs and pests adjust to the new varieties of plants, the gain is wiped out. Thus agricultural experiment stations are kept busy developing new strains to resist new forms of disease that did not exist a decade earlier. The financially desirable procedure of planting huge areas in a single crop also has its drawback: once a disease gains entrance to the area, it rapidly sweeps through the entire area because all of the plants are susceptible to the same ailment. In contrast, when farms are composed of small patches with each patch planted with a different crop, the disease may be quickly contained; that is, there may only be one acre of crops in the vicinity susceptible to a given disease. Thus we observe a boomerang effect in agricultural improvements.

Breeding animals and plants for higher production is fruitful. Hybrid corn, swine with more bacon, and similar genetic attainments have increased agricultural productivity in the United States and elsewhere. Unfortunately, however, the expense both of initial research and of acquisition by the farmer is too great to be borne in most countries. Also, in some cultures the scientific manipulations involved in the development of these new animals and plants are objectionable on religious grounds. Moreover, since improved varieties of plants usually take more nutrients out of the soil than the traditional varieties removed, production may soon return to the original level or even lower—unless the correct expensive fertilizer is available.

The legal and social framework within which agriculture is usually pursued can hardly be considered efficient. Not only is production handicapped by many systems of land tenure and inheritance, but land speculators and absentee landlords are often agriculturally dysfunctional. In some countries a deceased farmer's land is divided into as many plots as he has sons; carried on for several generations, this promotes a crazy-quilt pattern of land ownership. Religious beliefs and local customs also interfere with agricultural productivity. In China until quite recently, thousands and possibly millions are said to have starved while land was kept out of cultivation by such non-agricultural uses as ancestral grave mounds which no one could disturb.

One highly effective way to increase the quantity of food available to people would be to decrease the amount fed to farm animals. Animals are inefficient converters of plant nutrients to food for the human beings. We eat beef and ham because we like them, but cattle and pigs are profligate users of land and for this reason are expensive to buy. Indeed, it is quite possible that population increase will emphasize this inefficiency to the extent of pricing meat out of the market, so that an ordinary American family will consider itself lucky to eat steak once a month and hamburger once a week.

Not all plants are equally efficient producers of calories and other vital nutrients. For instance, potatoes and sugar beets yield about twice as many edible calories per acre per year as do cereal crops, partly because cereals involve a higher proportion of stalks, hulls, and other inedible residues. However, some soil and climatic conditions do not permit very efficient raising of crops. Table 28 compares protein production of various methods of farming.

TABLE 28. *Production of Protein Per Acre by Different Methods of Land Management**

METHOD OF LAND MANAGEMENT	METHOD OF RECOVERING PROTEIN	POUNDS OF EDIBLE PROTEIN PER ACRE PER YEAR
Planted to forage, grain, fed to steers	as beef	43
Planted to forage, silage, fed to cows	as milk	77
Planted to soybeans	as soybeans	450
Planted to alfalfa, U.S. average crop	as extracted protein	600
Planted to alfalfa, Western U.S. irrigated	as extracted protein	1500

* Harrison Brown, James Bonner, and John Weir, *The Next Hundred Years*, The Viking Press, New York, 1957, p. 71. Reprinted by permission.

Mechanization has been frequently suggested as a way to increase output. But mechanized farms are not more efficient, either on an acreage basis or on a monetary basis, except in areas where human labor is expensive. Also, machinery can rarely be used effectively unless farm land is divided into rather large parcels. The mechanized American farmer produces approximately 25 calories of food for each calory of input; the Japanese farmer's output-input ratio is about the same. Farmers in this country are highly efficient as measured by edible output per calory input of human energy, but they are prodigal in using inanimate energy (which is too expensive for the Japanese farmer— and for farmers in underdeveloped countries). The Japanese make more efficient use of supplementary energy sources, but output per man-hour is relatively low. Contrasting the hoe with the plow, it is the more primitive instrument that yields more calories per acre. Tractors and combines do not necessarily produce more food—though they do produce almost as much with far greater comfort. And what is accomplished by saving man-hours from farm work only to have men sitting about looking for something to do because there are no other job outlets? Notes one sociologist: "If the objective is the secure support of the largest possible population, hand methods of intensive cultivation provide the answer."[30]

WATER SOURCES OF FOOD

Farming the ocean for edible flora and fauna is a relatively undeveloped possibility. Much additional food could be obtained from oceans, rivers, lakes, and other water sources. The annual world fish catch could be doubled without depleting supplies. Certainly, better exploitation of the seas is possible through scientific control of catches, businesslike organization of individual entrepreneurs, development and stocking of new species, and other elements of farming the depths. Lakes and ponds are now stocked for fishing sport by United States state and county game agencies; this pond cultivation and restocking could be carried out more extensively and with an eye toward food production rather than recreation. Moreover, fish excel over animals as efficient converters of plants to human food. Stocking flooded rice paddies could induce a spectacular rise in the protein supply in some underdeveloped areas. The yield of fish is greater in the northern than the southern hemisphere, despite the far larger area and volume of water south of the equator. The reason for this differential is probably the greater economy of fishing close to the home port; most home ports, like most people, are in the northern half of the world. Finally, much food is lost in the wasteful processing of fresh water fish and salt water seafood; cutting down on losses through inefficient transporting and canning operations would help.

One day man may have an aquaculture system in which ocean farmers and ranchers cultivate and stock edible plant life and fish. Floating factories may move through the ocean farms, harvesting and processing at the point of production, thus cutting both transport cost and spoilage. Floating housing for workers might even be developed in mid-ocean beds of seaweed and schools of fish.

The ocean has great depth; the deepest ocean trench is farther

[30] Fred Cottrell, *Energy and Society*, McGraw-Hill Book Co., New York, 1955, p. 143.

below the surface than the highest mountain rises above sea level. This depth can be used in aquaculture. Sea food of many varieties can be farmed at depths extending thousands of feet below the surface. Land cultivation, on the other hand, is confined to the surface and a few feet into the soil. Thus there is not only more water surface than land surface on earth, but the water has a productive depth far exceeding that of land. Moreover, the oceans are less likely than land to be appropriated for nonagricultural uses such as housing, industry, retail stores, and parking lots. And even if the water surface is occupied by houseboats, water plants can still grow and fish still swim.

One weakness of both the seas and hydroponics is that water-grown plants are largely microscopic algae which, since they are smaller than land plants, respire away a larger percentage of the carbon they fix. Thus although the culture of the fresh-water alga chlorella, an undeniably promising source of food, offers exceptionally efficient photosynthesis as compared with land plants, it demands large flat areas exposed to sunlight.

With world population increasing at its present rate, it is not likely that improvements in the production of food from bodies of water (or from new land or better use of cultivated land) could easily approach the increased food supply that will be needed to feed the additional people. If the world's population doubles by the end of the twentieth century, the food supply to keep pace must also be doubled. And if we are to avoid having billions of people alive but inadequately fed, we will need to at least triple the present food supply.

MANUFACTURED FOOD

The possibility of deriving edible products from wood, plant stems, corn cobs, and various chemical substances has opened the door to a room of auditorium-like magnitude. But although chemical synthesis of food has been attempted, it is still a rather remote cure for man's alimentary insufficiencies. During World War II the German government synthesized fats through hydrogenation of coal and other industrial processes, but such ersatz food so far has been a product of dire emergency.

Chemical synthesis of bulk dietary calories is impractical at present, but dietary supplements (vitamins and minerals) are now produced in quantity. Bear in mind, however, that the daily requirements of all dietary supplements combined are minute in comparison to the rest of the diet. Persons in underdeveloped countries with an inadequate supply of proteins and a diet consisting primarily of cereals frequently suffer from amino acid deficiencies. Synthetically produced amino acids would cost at present about $40 a year per person—a small sum to Americans, but prohibitive for a family of six in China or India.

Manufacturing food differs from ordinary farming in that it demands a large initial capital investment for equipment. Yet the countries most in need of supplementary food supplies are precisely the ones least prepared to invest money and materials in setting up hydroponic and other food-producing factories. In addition, purchase of the product requires a larger family income than the levels prevalent in under-developed areas. At present, the people who do not need manufactured food are the only ones who can afford it.

DISTRIBUTION AND PROCESSING OF FOOD

People who oppose family planning frequently support their contention with the statement that the problem is not one of population but rather of the production and distribution of goods. Unfortunately, however, the total production of food in the world would be inadequate even if it were perfectly distributed. To be sure more uniform distribution would improve the situation in that many families would be able to eat better by getting a larger proportion of the food available locally. Yet it is doubtful that equitable distribution would constitute a solution on a world level.

At present, food distribution is severely hindered by poor marketing methods. The information farmers have on the subject is frequently poor, interest rates are often prohibitively high, inadequate storage facilities and careless handling cause spoilage, prices are unstable, and land is idle because carriers are not available to transport crops. In some areas, surpluses accumulate and rot at the same time that severe shortages and even famines are occurring elsewhere. A heartening example of what can be done in this situation is the distribution of surplus dried milk by UNICEF (the United Nations Children's Fund) to children around the world—some of whom had never tasted cow's milk.

More careful processing of food could decrease wastage. Food processing plants, wholesale and retail groceries, and restaurants are primarily oriented (as they are supposed to be in most Western countries) toward profit rather than conservation. As a result much food is thrown away in preference to taking a chance on interfering with the marketing process or the price structure. However, even improvement in this area would not make a significant dent in the food shortage.

Cooking is another problem. Many people lack electricity, gas, or adequate supplies of coal or wood for fuel. Increasing timber production could make more wood available for fuel in the kitchen. It might also have helpful side effects: erosion prevention (because people would not remove grass and shrubs for fuel), improved livestock food supply (for the same reason), and increased food production (estimated at

15 per cent in India) through use of dried manure for fertilization rather than burning.

Dispensing food by machines is becoming commonplace. The purported invention of a coin-operated holy-water dispenser in the second century B.C. by Ctesibius of Alexandria perhaps was the first step of a triumphant march of the dispensing machine to its current apogee: a restaurant staffed entirely by machines. Whether this promising development will be cut off by the universal adoption of food pills as a replacement for eating is problematical. In the latter case, problems of world food supply should be practically solved.

SOCIOLOGY OF FOOD PREFERENCES

Getting people to eat edible products that they now consider to be unsuitable for human consumption is a difficult sociological problem. People of all countries have emotional reactions to food which make it impossible for them to enjoy certain edible products—or even to eat them at all. Canned grasshoppers, ants, oysters, rattlesnake, and tripe wait on shelves for the delectation of the customer who does not agree with the clerk's remark, "I don't see how people can eat that stuff!"

Often the taste is attached to the label; consider the teen-agers who pounced ravenously on a bowl of hamburger and then, on discovering it was really dog food, vomited up the meat they had so recently consumed with gusto. People's digestive functions seem to be tied to their emotional preconceptions about the food; in a group of hardened pizza-eaters, it is the dubious newcomer who is most likely to become sick in the middle of the night.

Societies exhibit wide differences in the use of spices and other dietary practices, as for instance the number of meals in a day. Americans' "three squares a day" (now often a coffee breakfast, a stand-up lunch, a coffee break, a full dinner, and a three-hour evening snack) are not universal. Cultural variations include such societal daily norms as one huge meal plus irregular snacking, two regular meals, five or six regular meals, and one continuous almost day-long meal. Changes occur even within the same society. Witness variations in English eating habits over a few centuries: "Whereas in the Middle Ages two meals a day were generally considered sufficient, four were not uncommon in the sixteenth century. The main meal was usually at noon, followed by a supper at about seven or eight o'clock in the evening, but by the eighteenth century gentlefolk had their main meal in the late afternoon, a light lunch preceding it and tea following."[31]

[31] R. J. Forbes, "Food and Drink," in Charles Singer et al., A History of Technology, Oxford University Press, London, 1957, Vol. III, pp. 19-20.

Human beings seem able to exist indefinitely on some very strange diets. Indeed so long as the person believes that the diet is suitable, the human stomach is apparently adaptable to a wide range of gastronomical adventures. On the other hand, an experiment involving feeding a group of people ordinary food that was dyed unusual colors (purple mashed potatoes, green steak, and so forth) was marked by pronounced gastronomic distress. Man eats with his eyes and nose as much as with his mouth.

How many of us shudder when reading Jonathan Swift's outcry: "A young healthy child well nursed is at a year old a most delicious, nourishing, and wholesome food, whether stewed, roasted, baked, or boiled, and I make no doubt it will equally serve in a Fricassee, or a ragout."[32] Without our inbred horror of cannibalism, the Irish clergyman's savagely satirical attack on the English would be just mildly amusing or merely commonplace.

The food supply itself and the rate of population increase are not the only keys to the problem. Malnutrition and starvation cannot be conquered simply by having fewer people or making food plentiful. Hunger can and does exist next door to surpluses. The people who are hungry just do not have enough money to buy the necessary food. Sometimes the poor are compelled to purchase only the cheapest foods (cereals and starchy roots), which are rarely the most nutritious. Meat, eggs, milk, and fruit are too expensive. The solution to this problem is a higher real income rather than more food. Effective policies for the promotion of greater purchasing power among the impoverished majority are sorely needed. Thus the food problem is in part a problem of general economic well-being.

---

[32] Jonathan Swift, *A Modest Proposal for Preventing the Children of Poor People from Being a Burthen to Their Parents or Country, and for Making Them Beneficial to the Public*, Dublin, 1729.

15 ✖ Industrialization and Level of Living

Remarkably few groups resist efforts to raise their standard of living. A desire for more and better material possessions and comfort-enhancing conveniences is nearly universal. The wide currency of this attitude adds poignancy and a threat of violence to the fact that some countries are rich in these material desiderata while others are not.

Income data and energy consumption may be used as indicators of level of living. Table 29 summarizes total and per capita income by continents. Note that the 55 per cent of the world's people who live in

TABLE 29. *Population, Income, and Energy Consumed, by Continents, 1950*[*]

AREA	Total Population		Aggregate Income		PER CAPITA INCOME ($)	ENERGY CONSUMED PER CAPITA (KW-HR)
	NUMBER (MILLIONS)	PER CENT	DOLLARS (BILLIONS)	PER CENT		
World	2,497	100.0	556	100.0	223	1,676
Africa	199	8.0	15	2.7	75	686
North America	219	8.8	241	43.3	1100	10,074
South America	112	4.5	19	3.4	170	741
Asia (except U.S.S.R.)	1,380	55.3	69	12.4	50	286
Europe (excl. U.S.S.R.)	393	15.7	149	26.8	380	3,117
U.S.S.R.	181	7.2	56	10.1	310	1,873
Oceania	13	0.5	7	1.3	560	3,543

[*] Philip M. Hauser, *Population Perspectives*, Rutgers University Press, New Brunswick, 1960, p. 12; data are mostly from the United Nations.

Asia have only 12 per cent of the world's income, whereas in North America, 9 per cent of the world's inhabitants are able to divide among themselves a whopping 43 per cent of the world's income. Per capita income in North America is twice that of the second most favored continent (Oceania) and 22 times that of impoverished Asia. Thus more than one-half of all the world's people inhabit a continent with an average annual income equivalent to $50—or $250 for a family of five. Kilowatt-hours of energy consumed by the average person shows an even greater range, the ratio between North America and Asia standing at 35 to 1. Regarding both income and energy utilization, Asia and Africa are truly have-not continents.

INCOME AND DENSITY

The have *versus* have-not situation may be attacked by combining income and density differences into four categories: high income-high density, high income-low density, low income-low density, and low income-high density.[1]

The high income-high density countries of western Europe have long been dependent upon food imports to support their heavily clustered populations. As long—but only as long—as they can continue to trade industrial products for overseas food surpluses, they will not have serious population pressure. Japan is in a somewhat similar position.

Principal high income-low density countries are the United States, Canada, Argentina, Australia, and the U.S.S.R. Their vast grasslands are the world's most vital food surplus producers, and they are decidedly capable of absorbing more people (though not too rapidly, or internal disruption may result).

The major low income-low density areas include most of Africa south of the Sahara Desert, much of Latin America, and the large islands of New Guinea, Borneo, and Madagascar. At first glance these regions would seem to be the most promising of the world's underdeveloped areas. Optimists envision tropical agriculture developed to the point where Africa and South America may become new granaries for the world. But the argument may be made, as by L. Dudley Stamp, that the agricultural techniques best suited to tropical climate, topography, and soils have yet to be discovered, and that extensive agricultural research will be necessary before one can be sanguine about such prospects.[2] Indeed there is little hope that in the near future either Africa or Latin

---

[1] Dennis Wrong, *Population*, Random House, New York, 1959, pp. 108-117.

[2] L. Dudley Stamp, *Land for Tomorrow*, Indiana University Press, Bloomington, 1952, pp. 57-59.

America will contribute to solving the world food supply problems. At present both continents are growing rapidly and both need capital.

Low income and high density conditions prevail in North Africa, the Caribbean Islands, and the Asian countries of China, India, Pakistan, Ceylon, and Indonesia. These "Malthusian" nations are suffering from a deteriorated food supply attributable to population growth, political instability, and wars. Economic progress is extremely difficult because their dense and rapidly increasing populations require a huge proportion of the national effort simply to prevent starvation. Moreover, the density of habitation leaves little room for enlargement of crop acreage, and poverty retards conversion to industrial processes. On both farm and factory development, population increase exerts a powerful drag, and as mortality falls the augmented growth will still further impede attempts to improve living conditions by demanding the diversion to food production of resources that might otherwise promote economic development. Pakistani President Ayub Khan warns, "If we continue to increase at the present rate it will ultimately lead to a standard of living which will be little better than that of animals."

Industrial and Demographic Needs and Supplies

In order to raise the standard of living in all countries to the level already reached in the leading countries it will be necessary to industrialize every continent. To accomplish this, capital, technological knowledge, sources of power, and a desire to industrialize are needed.

As with food, the level of living problem is not simply one of maldistribution. A completely equitable redistribution of world money and products would be hopeless to effectuate an appreciable improvement in the average income or level of living throughout the world. As Table 29 shows, equal distribution of world income in 1950 would have resulted in a per capita world annual income of $223, only one-fifth of that of North America. But although this average was three to four times that of Africa and Asia, it would still be inadequate, demonstrating the spuriousness of the argument that overpopulation problems can be overcome by equitable dispersal of goods and services. "The miserably low level of living of most of the world's population is attributed not so much to maldistribution as to low aggregate product, the result of the low productivity of most of the world's peoples."[3] The author of this assertion states further:

The total world product of goods and services in 1950 could have supported approximately 500 million persons at the North American level

[3] Hauser, *Population Perspectives, op. cit.*, p. 11.

of living, and some 1.5 billion at the European level. The actual world population in 1950 was 2.5 billion. Although this is admittedly an over-simplification of the problem, the difference between these figures may be taken as indicating either world overpopulation in 1950, or a world shortage in the production of goods and services. For average world income to have matched income in North America, aggregate income would have had to be increased about five-fold. To bring world per capita income by 1975 to the level enjoyed in North America in 1950 would require about a 7.5 fold increase of the 1950 level in twenty-five years. To do the same by 2000 would require a twelve-fold increase in the 1950 world income within fifty years.[4]

ADDING CAPITAL AND EQUIPMENT

A growing population assists industrialization by supplying a ready labor force to staff new factories and exploit natural resources. Additionally, it supplies an enlarging market in which to sell the mass-produced products. A crucial problem in underdeveloped areas appears to be how to acquire the huge capital and large store of technical equipment necessary to launch a large-scale program of industrialization. Without capital, the potential assets of a growing labor force and market remain the liabilities of overdense agricultural and consumption millstones. And even if financial backing is forthcoming, scarcity of skilled machinists and engineers may cripple efforts at maintaining machinery and operating factories efficiently. Peasant farmers do not provide a plentiful source for industrial trainees; in a traditionally stable and ostensibly (but never actually) changeless culture many peasants find an insurmountable obstacle in the geographic and status mobility that is required. Sheer inability to read and write hinders training and adaptation to an urban-industrial milieu. In the face of all these difficulties, underdeveloped countries not surprisingly are slow to industrialize and to compete successfully with established nations for a portion of the world market. Their low per capita purchasing power not only limits local markets but also fails to support a vigorous program of industrialization. "The hoe cannot be asked to produce enough both to feed its owner today and purchase a tractor tomorrow."[5]

The chronic shortage of capital in peasant-agricultural societies is intensified by rapid population growth. Thus a United Nations report notes:

> The faster the population grows, the more investments are necessary to keep up a given level of per capita production. In a country with a

---

[4] *Ibid.*, pp. 9-10.
[5] United Nations, *Population Growth and the Standard of Living in Under-Developed Countries*, New York, 1954, p. 6.

constant population, it is necessary only to replace the equipment which is worn out or becomes obsolete, in order to see that each generation is as well provided with the tools of production as the preceding one. Where the population is growing, an additional investment is required to maintain the same average amount of equipment per worker. An improvement of equipment which would permit a larger average product per worker and a higher standard of living can only be obtained by a further investment, over and above what is required by the growth of population. The further investment, which an under-developed country can actually afford to spare from its annual income, is smaller if the population is growing rapidly than if it is growing slowly.[6]

For such states trying to elevate themselves by their own bootstraps, the required investment of human capital is also staggering. Rearing and educating the next generation is an investment which may pay handsomely in the future gross national product and local prosperity, but the expense of education falls on the adult workers, and the ponderosity of the burden depends on the child-youth dependency ratio. Inexpediently, it is the countries most in need of improving educational standards and training industrial workers that have the highest proportion of dependent children in their populations. A commonly adopted solution to excessive child dependency is to put children to work at an early age, a practice which interferes with education of the children and hence retards national advancement toward a higher level of living. High infant and child mortality is another source of loss; whatever is invested in rearing and training a youth is lost if he dies before attaining an age at which he can add to productivity. And again in this regard it is the underdeveloped countries which suffer the greatest drain.

PER CAPITA OUTPUT AND DEMAND

In industrial nations the situation is similar in some respects, different in others. Fertility, the age distribution, international and internal migration, and other demographic attributes produce alterations in demand and productivity. Changes in mortality appear less influential than fertility changes, except that lowering infant mortality is tantamount to increasing fertility, and reductions in mortality among the aged tend to increase the post-retirement population, thus increasing dependency unless the retirement age is advanced—as is quite likely in view of the improved health and vigor that accompany lowered mortality.

Ansley Coale, contrasting the effects on industrial economies of low fertility (as in France, England, or Scandinavia) with those of high

---

[6] *Ibid.*

fertility (as in the United States or Canada), found that population changes flowing from high fertility stimulate aggregate demand.[7] Rapid growth carries the prospect of larger returns from producers' investments through increased numbers of people who purchase durable and consumable products. High fertility also produces an age distribution with a relatively small fraction in the ages of labor force participation. Thus the labor force has more dependents per worker to support when recent and current fertility is high. This higher dependent-to-earner ratio raises consumption at the expense of savings and investment and also exerts an upward pressure on education and other government expenditures. Thus an industrialized country with high fertility and low mortality has many children in relation to its adult population and therefore many persistent pressures toward inflation.

Variations in fertility also affect productivity per capita. Labor input is affected by demographic factors. Other things being equal, low fertility yields a larger labor force in proportion to total population, for two reasons: low fertility implies an age distribution with relatively many persons of labor force age, and release from childbearing and rearing increases the possibility of women's entering the labor force. Then there is the relation of labor input to resources under given conditions of population size and growth. As Coale notes: "High fertility ultimately produces more workers, and the problem is whether economies of scale in using resources tend to offset tendencies toward diminishing returns. There is no clear-cut answer except in the long run. . . . Ultimately, high fertility produces a population that overwhelms *any* finite resources, and diminishing returns must sometimes become more important than economies of scale."[8] But high rates of natural increase do not necessarily place insupportable strains on resources in the short run; indeed, they might not decrease the per capita output for many years—that is, in industrial countries having ample capital.

In both industrial and underdeveloped countries, the availability of capital per worker is altered by population changes. "High fertility, by increasing the ultimate rate of growth of the labor force, increases the need for current investment in order merely to keep output per worker constant. If the labor force grows by 3 per cent a year, an investment of perhaps 9 per cent of annual output is needed merely to equip new

---

[7] Ansley Coale, "Introduction," in National Bureau of Economic Research, *Demographic and Economic Change in Developed Countries*, Princeton University Press, Princeton, 1960, pp. 10-14. For details, see Simon Kuznets, "Population Change and Aggregate Output," pp. 324-340; and Ansley J. Coale, "Population Change and Demand, Prices, and the Level of Employment," pp. 352-371; both in the N.B.E.R. volume.

[8] *Ibid.*, p. 12.

workers."[9] Thus a large natural increase adds considerably to the proportion of the national income that must be channeled into producers' goods to keep from sliding backward; to increase per capita output perceptibly, additional investment is necessary—amounting in the illustration above to a total of perhaps 12 to 15 per cent of the national income. Since a burgeoning population with more dependents per earner has more mouths to feed, backs to clothe, heads to roof over, and generally requires more consumers' goods, it tends to depress the portion of national capital available for investment.

In sum, then, high fertility presents an economic paradox. The resultant growth increases aggregate demand, but at the same time it tends to reduce the capability of the economy to achieve an increased output per head.

ENERGY SOURCES

Man is the only creature able to store and later release large amounts of energy without first converting it by bodily metabolism. Human use of energy extends from "readily available but low-yield sources, such as plant life and draft animals, to more complicated but high-yield forms, such as steam power and electricity. . . . The amounts and types of energy employed condition man's way of life materially and set somewhat predictable limits on what he can do and on how society will be organized. The influence of energy is seen to be ubiquitous, with economic, political, social, psychological, and ethical consequences intermeshed."[10]

Power sources are fundamental to industrial progress. "During the last 250 years five great new prime movers have produced what is often called the Machine Age. The eighteenth century brought the steam-engine; the nineteenth the water-turbine, the internal combustion engine, and the steam-turbine; and the twentieth the gas-turbine. . . . Such is 'The Industrial Revolution,' the title for a development often described as starting in the early eighteenth century and extending through much of the nineteenth. It was a slow movement, but wrought changes so profound in their combination of material progress and social dislocation that collectively they may well be described as revolutionary."[11] These technological changes opened "an essentially new stage in mechanical technique."[12] The basic technical achievements of

---

[9] *Ibid.*, p. 13.

[10] Joseph Mayer, "Foreword," in Fred Cottrell, *Energy and Society*, McGraw-Hill Book Co., New York, 1955, p. vii.

[11] R. J. Forbes, "Power to 1850," in Charles Singer *et al.*, *A History of Technology*, Oxford University Press, London, 1958, Vol. IV, p. 148.

[12] Abbott Payson Usher, *A History of Mechanical Inventions*, Harvard University Press, Cambridge, 1954, p. 160.

the industrial revolution were replacement of hand tools by machines, introduction of new prime movers, making prime movers mobile, and emergence of the factory as a new form of organization and production.[13]

ANIMATE AND INANIMATE POWER

Sources of energy have changed considerably in the last century. Energy sources may be divided into two types: animate and inanimate. The quantity of animate energy available for use varies with the number of people and work animals alive at any given time. Potential animate energy has increased over the last hundred years, but not tremendously. On the other hand, inanimate energy has shown a many-fold increase as the technological level has advanced. In 1800, animals and human beings contributed about 17 billion horsepower hours of energy in the United States; by 1950 the figure had almost doubled to 33 billion. Most of this increase was derived from human population growth. In contrast, the same 150-year period witnessed a growth of inanimate energy from 1 billion to more than 400 billion horsepower hours. Between 1850 and 1950 the distribution of energy used in the United States changed as follows: human, 13 to 1 per cent; animal, 52 to 1 per cent; machine, 35 to 98 per cent.[14]

One reason for the greater increase of inanimate sources is that man has more discretion in the amount he can develop: that is, machinery is under closer control than animals. Secondly, inanimate energy is much easier to use; instead of harnessing a mule to a heavy piece of lumber, an electric cord is plugged into a socket. Third, inanimate energy is faster and more efficient. Fourth, some industrial operations could not be performed with animate energy sources; how many revolutions per minute of a turret lathe can be generated by a horse-driven set of gears? Finally, animal energy is not capable of propelling land, sea, and air vehicles at rapid speeds.

The development of electric power is one of man's most significant accomplishments. "No doubt the most conspicuous change in production methods during the nineteenth century was the greater substitution of energy derived from coal and falling water in place of energy derived from muscles in the operation of tools and machines."[15] The invention of electric generators, transmission lines, and induction motors during

---

[13] Forbes, "Power to 1850," *op. cit.,* pp. 150-151.

[14] J. Frederick Dewhurst, *America's Needs and Resources,* The Twentieth Century Fund, New York, 1955, p. 908.

[15] W. Paul Strassmann, *Risk and Technological Innovation,* Cornell University Press, Ithaca, 1959, p. 158.

the last third of the nineteenth century made it possible to produce and distribute electric power economically over long distances, and a new era in industrialization was born. In three decades electrical manufacturing grew to be a huge industry.

Man is making increasing use of natural resources through the discovery of new power sources—things that already were there but not previously known to be useful sources of power. As one resource is depleted, another is found. If this process can be maintained indefinitely, men need have no fears concerning the exhaustion of world energy resources. However, the transition to new sources can be and often is unpleasant and expensive, as some entrepreneurs are driven out of business and workers are unemployed before they can learn new skills. Consider the succession of major inanimate power sources. First, trees were used as firewood. Then coal was discovered and unearthed as a fuel. Later other fossil fuels, natural gas and oil, came into demand; then hydroelectric power from dams in areas having mountains, rivers, or high-tension electric transmission lines. Today atomic energy resources are being tapped. Use of the sun's rays is promising. The energy sources of the twenty-first century are difficult to imagine, but some possibilities will probably involve energy derived from the center of the earth, from cosmic and other radiation, and from the ocean.

MEN *versus* MACHINES OR ANIMALS

Population enters the scene with consideration of the relative costs of men *versus* machines. In most Western countries it is cheaper to buy machines than to hire men, but in underdeveloped areas with manpower surpluses men are the cheaper element of production. Americans keep a spare typewriter in the office to be sure of making full use of clerk-typists if a typewriter breaks down. In contrasting countries men spend many hours hunting and cherishing worn machinery (hence the possibly apocryphal anecdote of the Asian factory that kept spare men available to tend machines when the regular workers were absent ten minutes for coffee or calls of nature). The economic man hypothesis stands up well here, for employers do tend to purchase whichever is cheaper—men or equipment.

Men may even be put to work in preference to draft animals. "In a 10-hour working day a man can deliver from 1/10 to 1/20 as much mechanical power as a horse, but his caloric intake and thus his dependence on plants is also only about 1/10 to 1/20 as much. Where land is plentiful, population sparse, and draft animals available, there may be an economy in substituting draft animals for manpower; but with increased population and competition of land for the production of food and feed, the situation may be reversed, the survival of man being more important than the feeding of work animals."[16]

Ready availability of sufficient manpower at slight expense may discourage inventions. The ancient Greeks, for instance, developed many new scientific ideas but failed to make the relatively simple translation of these ideas into practical applications. The usual explanation of this engineering sluggishness is that their ample supply of slaves made labor-saving machines pointless.[17]

Demographic Impediments to Industrialization

Underdeveloped areas contain about two-thirds of the world's population. Such areas are not likely to be developed by industrial countries; therefore they must develop themselves. And the considerable capital and the technical manpower and equipment required for industrialization make the process a slow one in most nonindustrial countries.

HIGH AGRARIAN DENSITY

Density of population interferes for a variety of reasons with the accumulation of capital necessary for industrialization. The tremendous inertia resulting from the large dense population in peasant-agricultural countries like India is so great as almost to prevent industrialization. In writing of India and Pakistan, Kingsley Davis has posited seven ways in which a high agrarian density combined with rapid population growth tends to impede industrial development:

1) In general the consequence is to focus economic effort on consumption goods rather than heavy industry, and thus to discount future advantage against present advantage. . . . Everything is expended on sheer maintenance of life. . . . Its labor is like the labor of Sisyphus, except that the stone grows constantly larger.

2) The amount of land per cultivator has steadily declined. . . . This has tended to increase poverty, to limit investment in the soil, and thus to hold down productivity. . . . Caught in this vicious circle, the over-numerous farm population is in no condition to furnish the economic surplus with which an industrial system can be built.

3) A high ratio of farm population to agricultural resources means that most of the land is devoted to food crops for sustenance rather than to export crops for an investment surplus. . . . This situation reaches its ultimate futility when the food requirements of the swollen population

---

[16] Mayer, "Foreword" to Cottrell, *Energy and Society, op. cit.,* p. viii.

[17] See, for example, Benjamin Farrington, *Greek Science,* Penguin Books, Harmondsworth, England, 1953, pp. 150 and 304.

become so great that an agricultural country becomes an importer of agricultural produce.

4) In a dense agrarian economy, labor is immediately cheaper than machinery. . . . The measure of industrialization is precisely the degree to which machinery is substituted for human labor; to the extent that a dense agrarian economy impedes this substitution, it impedes industrialism.

5) A rapid population growth attributable to an extremely high fertility and a high but somewhat lower death rate produces an unusual burden of young-age dependency. . . . Much of the dependency is wasted. . . . Women are pregnant, give birth to and nurse millions of babies each year who die before they reach a productive age. Energy, food, and supplies are wasted on them. Thus the young-age dependency is a greater drain on the economy than the sheer proportion of dependents would indicate.

6) The high mortality . . . is associated with a high morbidity. Disease, undernourishment, malnutrition, and injury lead to lethargy, absenteeism, and inefficiency. As a consequence the productivity per worker is low, independently of capital equipment.

7) The state of public enlightenment is so low and the poverty is so great that the political stability is hard to maintain. The citizenry is prey to any humor of illusion that will promise relief from the round of disaster and despair. . . . Under disturbed political conditions, industrial enterprise cannot thrive.[18]

RAPID GROWTH

Another demographic obstacle to industrialization is rapid growth. Increasing at rates of 2 per cent a year or even higher, some underdeveloped nations are in the position of a losing football team in the last quarter of the game when the announcer intones impassionately that "time is becoming increasingly a factor." In the words of the President of the International Bank for Reconstruction and Development: "Unless foreign aid can be increased, a country in this position is faced with a stark alternative. It must reduce its savings or lower its living standards —although both are already inadequate. . . . I find myself increasingly doubtful whether domestic savings and foreign aid together will be sufficient to allow real progress, if present rates of population growth continue for long."[19]

Two contemporary examples of attempts at industrialization of rapidly growing, overpopulated agricultural areas are India and Puerto Rico.

---

[18] Kingsley Davis, *The Population of India and Pakistan*, Princeton University Press, Princeton, 1951, pp. 218-219.

[19] Eugene R. Black, address presented before the Economic and Social Council of the United Nations, New York, April 24, 1961.

Both societies have been moving toward industrialization, but with varying results. Let us explore some of the reasons for these differences in progress.

INDIA—A DIFFICULT PROGNOSIS

Under the impelling force of independence and a realization of the need to improve the living standard, Indian leaders have been fostering industrial development. The country has many resources essential for industrialization (iron, coal, water power, manpower, aluminum, manganese, textiles, mica, agriculture), and long-term prospects are favorable. In the 1947 partition, India got the manufacturing, Pakistan the agrarian parts of the economy.

However, India's problem is not alone that of becoming industrialized, but of doing it in the face of a tremendous population increase which swallows up much of the technological advance. The immediate purpose of keeping the production of food and consumer durables and expendables abreast of population growth interferes with future expansion. In a sense the object is not to advance, but rather to keep from sliding backwards. Under these conditions the need to increase production of producers goods and export items is very difficult to satisfy. Progress is being made, however, from T.V.A.-like river valley developments to the building of factories.

India's broad program of economic development recognizes the imperative need for new housing, roads, water supplies, sewage systems, hospitals, schools, and jobs. Yet all of this requires enormous investments of capital, and unfortunately population increase does not produce investment capital. In fact the situation is quite the reverse. Population growth spreads investment funds increasingly thinly over the labor forces. Thus unless capital increases rapidly, each pair of hands will continue to be backed by fewer dollars, productivity will suffer, and living standards will improve very slowly.

PUERTO RICO—A PROPITIOUS CONTRAST

A quarter century ago the situation in Puerto Rico seemed as hopeless as that in India. The densely settled island was poverty ridden and economically stagnant. A Senate committee used the word "unsolvable" to describe the scandal of slums, poverty, and disease. "Of all the important indices," said H. S. Perloff, "only the index of population growth showed a sustained and uninterrupted rise."

The improvement in Puerto Rico's standard of living since then has been striking. Real income per capita has more than doubled, and the living standard is one of the highest in Latin America. "Operation Bootstrap," launched by Governor Luis Muñoz Marin in 1948, has built hundreds of new factories and created thousands of new jobs. This induced boom has played an important part in the increased life expectancy, higher school enrollment, better roads, and superior health care of this American possession. The crude death rate fell precipitately from 19 per 1,000 in 1940 to 8 in 1960. Since the crude birth rate stayed around 40 per 1,000, natural increase advanced half again as rapidly in 1960 as the already rapid rate of 1940.

Reasons for Puerto Rico's rapid improvement as compared to the much slower progress made in India are not hard to come by. First, the number of people is small enough to profit by emigration; whereas the excess population can be absorbed by the continental United States, the surplus people of India would swamp any country but China. Second, since Puerto Rico is part of the United States, the escape valve for population growth is easy to open. The absence of international boundaries and the attendant quotas, coupled with the short transport distance and frequent commercial airline trips, make the hop to Anglo American cities relatively painless. Third, the subsidization of industries by the government has helped. (A full-page advertisement entitled "Now Puerto Rico Offers 100% Tax Exemption to New Industry," with a text signed by Beardsley Ruml, appeared in *The New Yorker* for April 30, 1955.) Fourth, capital available through the export of rum and other commodities is relatively greater than in India. Fifth, World War II occurred at the right time for Puerto Rico. Expansion of Federal activities in connection with defense and war fortuitously and thus somewhat artificially aided economic advances. Sixth, being a part of the United States facilitated accumulation of capital assets during World War II by individual islanders. Seventh, birth control is spreading rapidly throughout the population. Finally, some people have suggested that leadership has been superior (or at least more concentrated on achieving industrialization), although other authorities dispute this statement with considerable elan. Demographically, the smallness of the population and the ease of migration have facilitated the island's almost unprecedented rapidity of the economic maturation.

This same expenditure of effort would probably have raised the Puerto Rican level of living even more had the population growth been smaller. "There is every reason to believe that the economic development of Puerto Rico, impressive as it has been, has been retarded and hindered by the growth of numbers, and that the level of living is much lower than it would have been had the population not grown at all."[20] Although the insular net income doubled in the 1940's, "almost a third of

---

[20] Kingsley Davis, "Puerto Rico: A Crowded Island," *Annals of the American Academy of Political and Social Science*, Vol. CCLXXXV, January 1953, p. 120.

the gain was absorbed by the increase in the number of consumers."[21]
Even this rapid economic advance is not sufficient to employ all island
residents; unemployment and underemployment are heavy burdens.
Furthermore, population growth has impeded substitution of inanimate
power and equipment for human hands and energy. Food is imported.
In the face of their continued population growth, "one cannot help
wondering whether the fortunate developments from 1940 to 1952 will
prove temporary. The birth rate seems likely to fall in the next thirty
years, but not fast enough to prevent rapid population growth. Only if
the decline can be hastened deliberately, with continued stimulation of
economic development and continued massive emigration, can the level
of living keep on rising in the next few decades."[22]

Solutions to Problems of Rapid Growth

The present explosive surge of world population has both desirable and
undesirable aspects. On the debit side, it limits the benefits of economic
growth by "retarding capital formation, accelerating the rate of depletion
of the world's limited store of nonreplaceable resources, augmenting
the rise of costs in increasing cost industries, and decelerating the rate
of increase of per capita income."[23] Frank W. Notestein has estimated
the economy of India to be advancing at 3 per cent per year—identical
to the United States figure. But the Indian population is growing at 2 per
cent per year, thus absorbing two-thirds of her economic growth. India,
in common with all other countries, must first care for the immediate needs of her population; then, with whatever surplus remains, she
can concentrate on the economic development her leaders want so
badly.

In some countries the rate of population growth even exceeds that of
economic progress. In this situation the level of living may even retro-
gress despite an expanding productivity, presenting an Alice-in-Wonder-
land picture of running as fast as you can to remain in the same place:
"If you want to get somewhere else, you must run at least twice as
fast."[24]

Nor are these problems simply ones of economics and technology.

[21] Puerto Rican Planning Board, *Economic Development*, 1940-50, 1951-60, Office
of the Governor, San Juan, 1951, p. 16; quoted *ibid.*, p. 121.

[22] *Ibid.*, p. 122.

[23] Joseph J. Spengler, "The Population Obstacle to Economic Betterment," *American Economic Review*, Vol. XLI, May 1951, pp. 343-354.

[24] Lewis Carroll (C. L. Dodgson), *Alice's Adventures in Wonderland and Through
the Looking-Glass*, Random House, New York, 1946, Vol. II, p. 32 (originally published in 1865 and 1871).

J. S. Mill pointed out a century ago how they may restrict man's freedom of space for contemplation and pleasant living:

> There is room in the world, no doubt, and even in old countries, for a great increase of population, supposing the arts of life to go on improving, and capital to increase. But even if innocuous, I confess I see very little reason for desiring it. . . . A population may be too crowded, though all be amply supplied with food and raiment. It is not good for man to be kept perforce at all times in the presence of his species. A world from which solitude is extirpated is a very poor ideal. Solitude, in the sense of being often alone, is . . . essential to any depth of meditation or of character. . . . Nor is there much satisfaction in contemplating the world with nothing left to the spontaneous activity of nature; with every rood of land brought into cultivation, which is capable of growing food for human beings; every flowery waste or natural pasture ploughed up, all quadrupeds or birds which are not domesticated for man's use exterminated as his rivals for food, every hedgerow or superfluous tree rooted out, and scarcely a place left where a wild shrub or flower could grow without being eradicated as a weed in the name of improved agriculture.[25]

Charles Dickens' *Pickwick Papers* of 1836-1837 provides fictional expression of this feeling for openness. Pickwick and his friends conspicuously enjoy the pleasures of living in a relatively low density England, with its open pastures and accessible river banks. Of course, many people prefer the social norms and intellectual benefits of high density metropolitan living—"They'd get D.T.'s if they heard a cricket chirp."[26]

LIMITS OF THE EARTH

Population is exploding rapidly enough to cause us to wonder what might be the upper limit of the earth's ability to support it. Estimates of the carrying capacity of the earth vary according to the assumptions underlying each prognostication; reputable authorities have suggested figures varying from 5 to 16 billion.[27] Some writers have advanced potential limits as generous as 50 billion,[28] based on such presently unrealistic assumptions as unlimited ability to produce, distribute, and purchase food and the infinite elasticity of land through creation of artificial satellites and migration to other planets, solar systems, and galaxies.

---

[25] John Stuart Mill, *Principles of Political Economy*, D. Appleton and Co., New York, 1868, Vol. II, p. 339.

[26] Eugene O'Neill, *The Iceman Cometh*, 1946, Act I, Scene 3.

[27] United Nations, *The Determinants and Consequences of Population Trends*, New York, 1953, p. 185.

[28] Richard L. Meier, *Science and Economic Development*, Massachusetts Institute of Technology, New York, 1956, pp. 73, 141, and 236.

One of the more optimistic sets of limits has been suggested by J. F. Bonner, professor of biology at the California Institute of Technology:

> The most generous estimate of people supportable by our earth is roughly 50 billion people. This estimate has been made both by Meier and by myself. . . . It would require the cultivation of all potentially cultivable land; it would require the irrigation with reclaimed sea water of the earth's deserts, and so on. It would be a highly vulnerable culture in which any major catastrophe, such as breakdown of the industrial power network, would result in starvation of 9 out of 10 of the population. It would be a crowded world—20 times as crowded as today. It would be a world in which all animal protoplasm would be replaced by human protoplasm. One could not afford the luxury of maintaining pigs or cows or horses or dogs or cats, or even, probably, strange creatures in zoos. All edible material would have to go down the throats of hungry people.
>
> A less intensive food economy—one approximating that of Japan today—would suffice to support about 16 billion people. In such a world, the present Japanese level of agricultural productivity would have to spread over not only all of the world's presently cultivated acres but all over an additional area which would increase the total by 50%. The world's peoples would have to all agree to a vegetarian diet and to deny themselves the luxury of animal products with their inherent caloric inefficiency. This is clearly an intensive economy even though it is much less intensive than my first model.
>
> Finally, a population of some 8 to 10 billion people should be supportable on the earth's surface under a food production program characterized by the efficiency of present day Japan, spread over all of Asia, and by the efficiency of present day western Europe, spread over all of rest of the earth's agricultural acres which have in the meantime been expanded by 50%. This level of agricultural productivity should in principle be attainable within another 75 to 100 years at the rate of 2% increase per year.[29]

A more philosophical answer to the question "What is the maximum number of people that the earth can hold?" is *cui bono*—to whose benefit? In other words, what purpose would be served by having five times as many people as today living on a barely tolerable diet and a depressed standard of living? This reflection has been expressed by Kingsley Davis and A. B. Wolfe in the twentieth century and by John Stuart Mill and Matthew Arnold in the nineteenth. Arnold, regarding the worship of wealth and population size as "unintelligent and vulgarising," wrote derisively of "people, fresh from reading certain articles

---

[29] James F. Bonner, "Exploding Population," *Pasadena Star-News and Independent,* January 2, 1961, pp. C-6 and C-7.

346 :: ISSUES AND PROBLEMS

of the *Times* on the Registrar-General's returns of marriages and births in this country, who would talk of our large English families in quite a solemn strain, as if they had something in itself beautiful, elevating, and meritorious in them; as if the British Philistine would have only to present himself before the Great Judge with his twelve children, in order to be received among the sheep as a matter of right."[30]

Harrison Brown, one of Bonner's colleagues, believes the nub of the issue to be not what the limit is, but rather that there is a limit. "We know that by proper application of technology the earth could support a considerably larger population than now exists. But no matter where we place the limit of the number of persons that can be comfortably supported, at some point in history population growth must stop."[31] The paucity of thoughtful arguments favoring limitless expandability of human population supports Brown's position.

CAUSE FOR OPTIMISM

Colin Clark prefers to think that there is no limit. If the earth becomes crowded, he reasons, extra people can be blasted off in huge satellites[32] or artificial planets orbiting about the sun. Yet providing billions of satellite-dwellers with food, air, water, housing, and other necessities would offer a logistics problem of a magnitude unapproached in military history. Popular discussions suggest extraterrestrial migration, but other planets of our solar system are probably not suitable abodes, and the nearest star, Alpha Centauri, is so distant that "Americans, by cutting our standard of living down to 18 per cent of its present level, could in one year's time set aside enough capital to finance the exportation of one day's increase in the population of the entire world."[33] On the other hand, Evgeny K. Fedorov, secretary-general of the Soviet Academy of Sciences, entertains the prospect of settling on new planets within a generation.

Prospective technological discoveries and plasticity of the earth's power to produce food and other necessities of life hold forth the possibility of supporting a population that is far larger than is presently supported or supportable. Solar and nuclear energy have barely been tapped. And modern agricultural skills and machinery are applied

---

[30] Matthew Arnold, *Culture and Anarchy*, Cambridge University Press, Cambridge, 1935, pp. 52-53 (originally published in 1869, revised to present edition in 1875).
[31] Harrison Brown, *The Challenge of Man's Future*, The Viking Press, New York, 1954, p. 236.
[32] Colin Clark, Newmarch Lectures, University College, London, published as "World Population," *Nature*, Vol. CLXXXI, No. 4618, May 3, 1958, p. 1236.
[33] Gilbert Hardin, "Interstellar Migration and the Population Problem," *The Journal of Heredity*, Vol. L, No. 2, March-April 1959, p. 69.

in only a small minority of the world's farmland. Economists Arnold C. Harberger and Simon Kuznets fancifully remind us too that since the larger populations of the future presumably should contain more geniuses, their intellects may solve the problem of feeding still more people. In a similar vein, Colin Clark claims that higher densities will intensify competition and sharpen everyone's wits.

In any case, social and economic organization are not today geared to an optimal use of existing scientific knowledge, a fact repined in a United Nations report:

> Scientists have pointed out that, in any case, there is not much practical value in trying to calculate how many people the earth could eventually support if all its resources were fully utilized. It is the consequence of human frailty that what is technically possible is not always practically feasible. Ignorance, greed, strife, superstition, and blind adherence to tradition prevent men from accomplishing what is in their power, even though the alternative may be misery or starvation. A realistic view of the population problem must take these obstacles into account. The question is, whether or not, in the world as it is, increasing population hinders progress toward the twin goals of prosperity and peace.[34]

The answer to this question is complicated, and it varies according to the time and the area. For China and India, the two largest countries of the world, the reply is incontestably, "Yes." For countries of about 100 million or more—the U.S.S.R., the United States, Japan, Indonesia, and Pakistan—the response varies. For the world as a whole, responsible demographic opinion inclines sharply toward the affirmative.

POSSIBLE POLICIES

Problems introduced by the revolutionary surge of world population might be alleviated by any one or combination of the following steps:

1. Stack people up in layers. (We are already doing this with our 20-story apartment buildings in metropolitan centers.) But this is only a palliative, not a solution.
2. Extend human habitation into the tropics, the arctic, deserts, mountains, swamps, and other heretofore uninhabitable areas. But this too offers only temporary relief.
3. Redistribute people more evenly over the habitable areas of the earth. But there are no longer any empty hemispheres awaiting settlement.

---

[34] United Nations, *Population Growth and the Standard of Living, op. cit.*, p. 1.

4. Develop new foods and more efficient methods of food production. To date, however, such methods appear very costly—and the food is often tasteless.
5. Distribute food and other needed supplies in a more equitable fashion. But unless we can also increase the quantity of food available, improved distribution procedures will not suffice.
6. Lower the birth rate. This is the choice made by Western peoples, but it is difficult to agree on methods of family limitation.
7. Raise the death rate. Such an unpleasant outcome could occur in some countries if they do not lower their fertility.
8. Kill people off as they reach a certain age. Polar Eskimos and Fiji Islanders used to expose their aged, but this is not really an effective solution—or a popular one.
9. Establish a permanent, controlled war using as soldiers only those too old to be productive to society. This would help the economy, lessen the dependency of the aged, provide something for the old folks to do, and make them feel wanted. But our attitudes oppose it.
10. Place people on man-made satellites. But this would account only for a few extra people, barring tremendous technological improvements.
11. Disperse excess people through the heavens by interplanetary or intergalactic travel in a modern adaptation of the solution for overpopulation chosen by the ancient Greeks. But we are not yet ready for this new colonization.
12. Live inside the earth in the same way that H. G. Wells' moondwellers lived in the moon. But room is limited here.

EVALUATION OF THESE POLICIES

Most of these possible solutions do not seem to be realistic today. Indeed, only proposals 3 (migration), 4 and 5 (food supply), and 6 (fertility) have any serious supporters.

International migration is often advanced as a remedy for population growing pains. But planned resettlement is neither a prophylactic, a cure, nor an analgesic. Not only are the necessary capital investments prohibitive, but empty lands are virtually nonexisitent, and sparsely inhabited territory is rare and often unsuitable for occupancy. To be sure, international movement once provided an escape valve for Europe, but it cannot solve Asia's present problem. "The base populations in Asia are so huge and the rates of population growth are so high that European size movements would have little demographic effect, even if they were possible. The United States received 34 million migrants from Europe in the years from 1820 to 1955. This number of migrants would represent less than a single year's population growth in Asia."[35] If emigration were to succor the overpopulated countries of Asia, it would have to surpass by a large margin the most numerous exodus ever experienced from European countries during the era of the great transatlantic movement to the United States and Latin America. A feat of this magnitude seems to be highly unlikely.

Some people place their faith in agricultural production to solve the population problem: "In a chronic condition where we have more people than food, the logical answer would be, not to decrease the number of people but to increase the food supply."[36] Others advocate fertility control: "If mortality gains are to be retained, then, the only way to reduce explosive population growth is to decrease the birth rate. That is, the death control mankind has achieved can be retained only if it is accompanied by birth control. In view of prevalent value systems, this proposition provides heated debate, even though it flows directly from the demographic facts of life."[37]

Perhaps the most effective (though not necessarily the most desirable) policy would be to adopt both the above lines of attack—augmenting world food supplies, and controlling population through family planning. In any event, to speedily improve the standard of living throughout the world, men need to go to work on both demographic and economic variables.

Basically the problem is one of timing. World economic growth is not apt to accelerate as fast as population growth. When the demographic transition occurred in Europe, the inhabitants had time to adapt. But Asia today has no time to spare: its population is increasing so rapidly that industrial development has little prospect of keeping pace.

Even so, however, we do have a reasonable chance of winning through. But it will require the cooperation of all nations. All countries may one day be compelled to recognize their responsibility to keep their natural increase slower than their economic expansion. As scientist Julian Huxley stresses: "The remedy is to stop thinking in terms of a race, and to begin thinking in terms of a balance. . . . We must give up the false belief that an increase in the number of human

---

[35] Irene B. Taeuber, testimony presented to the Subcommittee on Immigration and Nationality of the Committee of the Judiciary of the U.S. House of Representatives on September 13, 1962; extracts reprinted in *Population Bulletin*, Vol. XVIII, No. 8, December 1962, p. 168.

[36] National Catholic Welfare Conference, "Explosion or Backfire?," November 26, 1959.

[37] Hauser, *Population Perspectives, op. cit.*, p. 163.

beings is necessarily desirable; and the despairing belief that increase
is inevitable; and the fatuous over-optimism that shuts its eyes to the
grievous effects of over-population; and the airy assertion that 'science'
will surely find a way out."[38]

---

[38] Julian Huxley, *New Bottles for New Wine*, Harper and Brothers, New York,
1958.

16 ✂ Politics and Power

One of the oldest anecdotes about population tells of an elderly Chinese mandarin who receives messages reporting progress of a war with Japan. "Two hundred thousand Chinese killed," says the messenger. The old man frowns. Then the messenger adds, "Five thousand Japanese killed." "Ah, good," smiles the old Chinaman, "pretty soon, no more Japanese."

Population size, density, and characteristics depend on and in turn drastically influence the utilization of natural resources, the food supply, and the industrialization process. But population is itself a resource.

Population is, indeed, a nation's greatest resource, though like other resources it may be squandered or misused. What greater asset can a nation have than a multitude of able-bodied citizens, ready to stoke its furnaces, work its mines, run its machinery, harvest its crops, build its cities, raise its children, produce its art, and provide the vast array of goods and services that make a nation prosperous and content? On the other hand, what greater liability can a nation have than a mass of surplus people, living in hunger and poverty, scratching at tiny plots of land whose produce will not feed them all, swarming into cities where there are no more jobs, living in huts or dying in the street, sitting in apathy or smouldering with discontent, and ever begetting more children to share their misery? The relationship between numbers and wealth and power is not simple, but surely it is significant.

And what of population pressure as a cause of war? May not an overcrowded nation turn in anger and frustration upon its neighbors, seizing their land and wealth in an effort to find space for its multiplying millions? Germany, Italy, and Japan all argued in the years before World War II that their increasing numbers required more space, and there are those who fear that China and India may make such claims in the future.

It would be oversimple, of course, always to see population as the cause of other happenings, political and economic, for often cause and effect run the other way. Wars, depressions, and national policies have profound effects upon fertility, mortality, and migration, the three factors responsible for population trends. To do this topic justice, one must trace not only the ways in which population affects world power and world politics, but also the ways in which the major trends of our time affect the world's population.[1]

POPULATION AS DETERMINANT OR CONSEQUENT

Is population an independent or a dependent variable, that is, is it a determinant or a result of other variables? The view of population as a determinant of such phenomena as standard of living and hot and cold wars is resisted by many people, both for rational and for nonrational reasons. Social scientists tend to be habituated by their disciplines to think of something else as the primary determinant, although in most fields population is considered very important. Political and religious thought is often directed by dogma or ambition away from accepting demographic variables as independent. Many leaders desire some national expansion. Religious and racial groups sometimes want to outnumber competing groups. Others simply resist an intellectual position which is contrary to the ideology of their reference group.

Population as a determinant is favored by other leaders and intellectuals, also for both rational and emotional reasons. It is easy to grasp (and therefore leads to ready oversimplification), it provides an excuse for placing blame for poverty and other distress on the people themselves, and frequently it even appears for sound scholarly or scientific reasons to be the most satisfactory explanation of the phenomena being studied.

On the other hand, the view of population as a dependent variable is often rejected or adopted for similar, though contrasting, reasons, both dogmatic and intellectual.

In fact, demographic variables and sub-variables are sometimes independent, sometimes dependent, and rarely operating alone in the causal chains of human behavior. For instance, popular opinion tends to go too far in emphasizing the importance of population pressure as a determinant of war; a more realistic position would be to accept the pressure of population as one among many powerful independent variables. And as we have seen, population phenomena in turn depend on many influences: folkways and mores concerning sexual relations,

---

[1] Katherine Organski and A. F. K. Organski, *Population and World Power*, Alfred A. Knopf, New York, 1961, pp. 3-4.

the structure of the family, medical knowledge and health practices, and so forth.

The determinant-*versus*-consequent issue has ramifications in peacetime competition between nations for power, the internecine conflict known as war, and power struggles within nations. In all three cases, population size and composition play both cause and effect roles. This chapter is principally concerned with population factors—particularly total size—as independent variables affecting internal harmony and discord, international diplomacy, and war. Attempts by governments to manipulate population trends—that is, to treat population as a dependent variable—are discussed in Chapter 18.

Internal Affairs

The role of demographic trends in promoting or making impossible internal peace has been the subject of much discussion by both academic and governmental authorities. Agreement is slight and opinions are strong. Even at the onset of World War II Gunnar Myrdal wrote: "To my mind no other factor—not even that of peace or war—is so tremendously fatal for the long-time destinies of democracies as the factor of population. . . . Democracy, not only as a political form but with all its content of civic ideals and human life, must either solve this problem or perish."[2]

But the answer to this problem is not likely to be speedily or easily found; the relationship between demographic variables and social, economic, and political disruption within a nation needs considerably more study before definitive conclusions can be reached. Scholars are in doubt, for instance, as to the validity of the causal relationship imputed to exist between the independent variable, percentage of the population belonging to a minority group, and the dependent variable, frequency and virulence of attacks on that minority group.

Consider internal migration as an example of an independent variable. Migration redistributes population and balances population-resources ratios. When migrants differ from nonmigrants in their biological, social, and economic attributes, the national and regional distribution of characteristics may be altered. The changes—as well as fertility and mortality variations—influence internal affairs in numerous ways.

DENSITY AND RISING GOVERNMENT POWER

Population growth and pressure may eventuate in fascism and totalitarianism. Thus one professor of law: "Population growth will create

---

[2] Gunnar Myrdal, *Population*, Harvard University Press, Cambridge, 1940, p. 33.

the need for more organization, which, in turn, will result in the further enhancement of group rather than individual values. If continued, the tendency could result in such a diminution of personal freedoms as to approximate the conditions of totalitarianism."[3] A conservationist adds: "The more people we have, the more government we must have. . . . With roads jammed with cars, skies filled with jets and schools overstuffed with children, personal freedom of action must shrink."[4] And a biologist: "As populations increase and as they press more heavily upon the available resources there arises the need for increased efficiency, and more elaborate organizations are required to produce sufficient food, to extract the necessary raw materials, and to fabricate and distribute the finished products. In the future we can expect that the greater the population density of an industrial society becomes, the more elaborate will be its organizational structure and the more regimented will be its people."[5]

This line of reasoning is a direct extrapolation of present tendencies. As density increases, formal means of social control tend to increase. In low density areas in the United States, dogs run free, cars are driven at speeds determined by the driver, and waste can be thrown on the ground. In high density areas, dogs must be leashed or confined to the yard, drivers obey stop lights and drive at speeds dictated by surrounding cars, and waste is collected and disposed of in specified sanitary fashions. The more people a man encounters in a day, the more his behavior is circumscribed by formal and informal norms. He cannot take off his shirt in public when he is hot nor go for a walk unfettered by WAIT signs and pedestrian traffic jams, and laws even prohibit his burning down his own house. To be sure, there is method in this madness. Dense populations must be regulated to prevent spread of contagious diseases, and human behavior has to be made more predictable if large clusters of people are to survive without conflict. The freedom of the frontier or simple rural life must under conditions of high density be exchanged for the regulations of complex urban society. Thus regimentation, however necessary and justified, does accompany population growth.

GROWTH AND PROSPERITY

In the minds of many business leaders national economic vigor is frequently associated with a growing population. Vance Packard collected

---

[3] Arthur S. Miller, "Some Observations on the Political Economy of Population Growth," *Law and Contemporary Problems*, Vol. XXV, No. 3, Summer 1960, p. 614.

[4] William Vogt, *People!*, William Morrow and Co., New York, 1960, p. 59.

[5] Harrison Brown, *The Challenge of Man's Future*, The Viking Press, New York, 1954, p. 256.

quotations from advertisers and popular magazines extolling the idea of "progress through proliferation of people":

"A Bonanza for Industry—Babies. Sixty Million More U. S. Consumers in Next Nineteen Years. . . . America's greatest boom is in people. Business, workers, government will be kept busy providing for an exploding population."—*U.S. News and World Report.*

"This Bird Means Business"—caption accompanying picture of a nesting stork circulated by the Advertising Council.

"New Population Score Card Can Help You Strike It Rich—The country's booming population growth spells money in the bank for the alert construction man. . . . It means more homebuilding, more community facilities, more roads, more commercial buildings, more factories, more transportation facilities."—*Engineering News Record.*

"Look at those happy little dollar signs."—a businessman driving past a schoolyard filled with children.[6]

Boosterism and profit-seeking, however, are not reliable clues to the future. Sir Charles Darwin calls the United States "one of the most dangerously increasing countries in the world." Economist J. J. Spengler explains that population growth fails to guarantee endless prosperity. "It solves only temporarily certain problems whilst creating bigger ones. It resembles the dope a sick man takes, only in the end to become a dope addict, and hence sicker than ever." Population growth is actually income-depressing and "continuation of population growth is likely to intensify various social and economic problems, solutions to which will be sought largely through state intervention. Should this come to pass, the economy would become less flexible and the freedom of individuals to do as they please would tend to become highly circumscribed. In this event the stork would have managed to do what the followers of Marx had found themselves unable to do for all they tried—fasten fetters on mankind."[7]

International Relations and War

World unity can be disrupted by many things, including inequities in population density and characteristics such as age, sex, race, language, religion, education, literacy, occupation, and income. Some scholars are concerned about the international imbalance between population distribution and the distribution of sought-after goods. Others talk

---

[6] Vance Packard, *The Waste Makers*, David McKay Co., New York, 1960, pp. 171-174.

[7] Joseph J. Spengler, "Population Threatens Prosperity," *Harvard Business Review*, Vol. XXXIV, No. 1, January-February 1956, pp. 85-94.

avidly about the pressure of population size and growth against the supporting power of the land and resources of the country, giving the impression that some countries are likely to burst from this pressure, overrunning other countries in the process. Equal ardor is devoted to disparities in income, education, race, ethnic stock, and occupation.

But the foremost topic of all is fertility. Early in the century, the sociologist E. A. Ross wrote: "There are good reasons for believing that, whatever motives for aggression may lie on the surface, the real enemy of the dove of peace is not the eagle of pride, nor the vulture of greed, but the stork."[8] And recently the demographer Warren S. Thompson stated more cautiously:

> It seems to the author that the growth of population and especially the differential growth of peoples has been an underlying factor of great importance in bringing about both a change in the need of a people for resources and a change in the military power essential to conquest. Hence, a world in which large differentials in population growth exist is likely to be an unstable world and one in which the acquisition of larger resources by the growing peoples would be governed chiefly by their ability to take them forcibly from weaker peoples. This belief rests, in part, on the further assumption that even if unused resources needed by the more rapidly expanding peoples were available they would not be made accessible to them by the peoples that already hold title to them. It has long appeared to the author, therefore, that the changing needs of peoples for resources, arising, in part, from differential rates of population growth was a very significant factor in creating international tensions which could readily lead to war.[9]

So much for population as a determinant. Now consider population variables as dependent. War has long been known to have both positive and negative demographic consequences. Social Darwinists argue on the positive side that war accelerates the endless struggle for the survival of the fittest; in their view war favors the noblest emotions and the finest human specimens, eliminating the weak and incompetent individuals and nations. Opposing arguments claim that war kills off the most vigorous young men because they are the ones at the front; the physical and emotional rejects left at home marry the girls and run the factories. Nor are the consequences of war confined to mortality differentials: fertility declines when enough men are away from home for long periods of time—although there may be a partially compensat-

[8] E. A. Ross, *Standing Room Only?*, D. Appleton-Century Co., New York, 1927, p. 166.

[9] Warren S. Thompson, *Population Problems*, McGraw-Hill Book Co., New York, 1953, p. 347.

ing upsurge of births after the armistice. But there is no truth to the folk belief that nature compensates for military deaths by arranging for a higher proportion of male births during and following a war. Migration is also affected; witness the millions of displaced persons following World War II. Often resources are depleted; always they are wasted. To be sure, war is a spur to the economy and an inspiration for new inventions, but at what costs.

POPULATION PRESSURE AND *Lebensraum*

Population pressure has been defined by E. W. Hofstee as a "social tension originating from an absolute or relative disproportion between population and available resources." An absolute disproportion exists when "it endangers the provision for the minimum needs of the population and thereby endangers the lives of a considerable part of the population, as is the case in different parts of Southeastern Asia. We can take it for granted that such a proportion will always cause dissatisfaction, even though it may not lead to collective action." A relative disproportion exists when, without truly endangering provision of minimum needs, the ratio is reacted upon with a feeling of dissatisfaction.[10] The converse of population pressure is the approximate adjustment between population and resources that may be regarded as the optimum population.

Population pressure is more a feeling in people's minds than an objective economic distress. A complex subjective phenomenon made up of income, density, standard of living, ambition, and social values, it is not always consciously recognized as such; tensions and dissatisfactions arising from population pressure are often indistinguishable from complaints arising from other social ailments. Yet ignorance of the sources of one's disquiet does not make that disquiet any less serious; more often perhaps the reverse reaction applies—that is, ignorance converts worry into terror.

Military aggression is sometimes attributed to demographic aggression. Ancient and modern conquistadors have often claimed population problems as the justification for an expansionist war as well as for other means of acquiring new territory. But the validity of this argument is questionable. In fact, no single cause is adequate to explain why a war begins. But although population pressure alone will not inevitably lead to war, it may be a contributory factor supplementing other predisposing conditions. Some countries under severe population pressure do not go to war. Some wars begin without assistance from

---

[10] E. W. Hofstee, "Population Pressure and the Future of Western Civilization in Europe," *American Journal of Sociology*, Vol. LV, No. 6, May 1950, p. 523.

population pressure. So although demographic pressure has been used as an argument by Germans, Italians, Japanese, French, and many other national groups, it appears to be more an excuse than an explanation. To adapt the image of Scotsman Andrew Lang, militaristic rulers use population statistics "as a drunken man uses lampposts— for support rather than for illumination."

Conquest is not of course the only alternative for overcrowded countries. Indeed expansion of territory is a temporary solution at best —and sometimes it is not even that. Two other options are increasing a country's efficiency of production of food and other marketable commodities, or decreasing its population growth. However, improvements in economic organization are difficult to effectuate. That leaves as choices only population checks, the foremost of which are birth control and emigration.

Observers of the actions and speeches of political leaders claiming a need for *Lebensraum* have descried a tendency to distort the facts. Thus at the same time that Mussolini and Hitler were excusing their forceful seizure of, respectively, Ethiopia and Czechoslovakia by claiming a pressing need for more population space, they were doing their utmost to increase fertility in their own two countries. Clearly, demographic factors were used here as *ex post facto* explanations in lieu of the actual motives.

Once war begins, population factors may have something to do with the conduct of the fighting. High growth nations may take maximum advantage of their manpower supply in an attempt to overwhelm the enemy by sheer weight of numbers; killing off a few million warriors from an overpopulated country may be viewed as little loss and even as a gain. Countries with stationary populations adopt a different strategy; they are more likely to husband their manpower, expending other resources instead.

Arnold Toynbee used population pressure as an explanation of historical actions in three city-states of ancient Greece. Athens engaged in manufacturing and the production of agricultural specialties like olive oil for sale in outer markets. Sparta turned to military aggression against neighboring city-states. Corinth established agricultural colonies abroad. Each city chose a different policy in response to the pressure of expanding population: development of commerce and shipping, military conquest, and expansion by colonization.

WORLD GOVERNMENT

A few people have expressed the belief that a powerful international organization could serve as a mechanism through which demographic and other inequalities between nations might be minimized. This result

would be achieved through encouraging the industrialization of backward areas, eliminating national migration restrictions, and promulgat-
ing one or more methods of family limitation.

The most prominent world organization we know, however—the
United Nations—seems to be an ineffective instrument for these ends.
Many if not most member nations oppose one or all three of the above
proposals. Moreover, the United Nations, like the League of Nations
before it, lacks adequate power to perform this function. Nor does it
focus sufficient attention on demographic matters.

The World Association of World Federalists and its affiliate, the
United World Federalists, are enthusiastically attempting to strengthen
the United Nations and establish a U. N. International Police Force.
Their fear-inspired optimism is evident in the following quotation from
Adlai E. Stevenson: "The greatest seers of our generation have proclaimed again and again that mankind's only hope of survival lies in
rising above nationalist parochialism and building the minimum
institutions of world order." Similar emotions underlie this remark by
British political leader Clement Attlee: "Today, all the nations of the
world are jay-walking in a dangerous, busy thoroughfare. It is time
to call the policeman to help establish rules of the road."

But most citizens seem unwilling to tolerate any organization that
stands above their own country. We are conditioned to nationalism by
parents, peers, teachers, and the mass media. Small wonder that the
League of Nations failed, that the United Nations is regarded with
suspicion, and that the World Federalists are often eyed narrowly as
impractical do-gooders and subversives. Under these circumstances,
concerted and effective international action to modify demographic
events and policies seems highly improbable and perhaps even visionary.

This coin has two sides, however. Not only does world-wide governmental cooperation affect demographic patterns, but population influences international political relations. Bertrand Russell contends that
"World Government cannot be stable until every important country
has a nearly stationary population."[11]

Struggle for World Dominance

The continents and culture areas of the world have had very dis-
similar histories of population growth. Figure 14 depicts regional differences in population size over the past millennium and projects them
for the next few decades. The area of each circle is proportionate to the

---

[11] Bertrand Russell, *New Hopes for a Changing World*, Allen and Unwin, London,
1951, p. 99.

FIGURE 14. *Distribution of World Population, 1000-2000* A.D.*

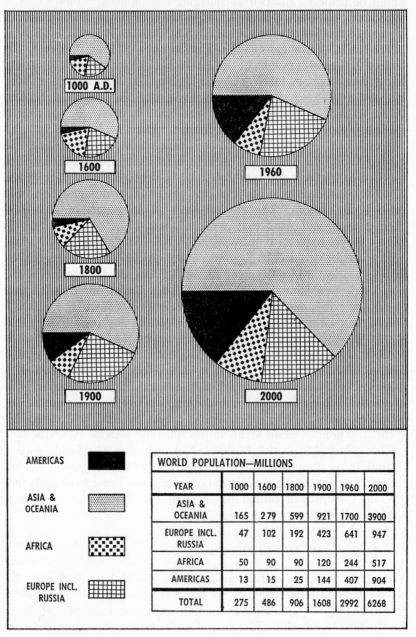

WORLD POPULATION—MILLIONS						
YEAR	1000	1600	1800	1900	1960	2000
ASIA & OCEANIA	165	279	599	921	1700	3900
EUROPE INCL. RUSSIA	47	102	192	423	641	947
AFRICA	50	90	90	120	244	517
AMERICAS	13	15	25	144	407	904
TOTAL	275	486	906	1608	2992	6268

AMERICAS

ASIA & OCEANIA

AFRICA

EUROPE INCL. RUSSIA

* Population Reference Bureau, "How Many People Have Ever Lived on Earth?," *Population Bulletin*, Vol. XVIII, No. 1, February 1962, p. 11.

total world population at that time. Note that Asia (with its demo-graphically minuscule neighbor Oceania) contains over half of the world's people at all six of the dates depicted by the pie charts. The wedge representing Europe grew through 1900 and thereafter declined in proportion to the pie as a whole. The slice portraying population in the Americas exhibits a widening angle from 1800 through 2000.

This unevenness of growth has contributed to the changing fortunes of factions in the competition for world power. Four conflicts now being waged are Orient against Occident, political independence *versus* colonialism, high standard of living *contra* subsistence level, and the free world-Communist cold war. Obviously, many nondemographic in-fluences are at work on these four issues—some intensifying conflict, others smoothing things over.

> There are three major determinants of national power: the size of a nation's population, the level of its economic development, and the skill and efficiency of its government. High standing in one respect may compensate to some degree for lack in another, but no nation can attain first rank without all three. Canada possesses a modern economy and an efficient government and has in addition rich resources, exten-sive territory, and high morale; but her population of less than 20 million relegates her forever to second rank. India has a giant population and a government of considerable efficiency; but until she succeeds in modernizing her economy she will have trouble even in defending her own frontiers. . . .
>
> No matter how efficient or how troublesome, no nation of small or even moderate size can push its way into the ranks of the great powers today. Admission to this ever shrinking circle requires a population of at least 45 million; tomorrow the minimum may well be 200 million, for size becomes more important as the years go by. To be a great power, a nation needs many millions of citizens to serve as cannon fodder, labor force, world market and—most important of all—as taxpayers.[12]

EAST AGAINST WEST

Caucasoid racists are deeply perturbed by the dread thought that "Mongol hordes" (the "yellow peril") will one day "reduce" the world to the Oriental level. These Occidentals are ensnared by the illusion that race determines culture, ignoring the fact that the recent dominance of European culture and people is neither natural, God-given, nor neces-sarily desirable.

The priority of Western Europe over the rest of the world in achiev-ing both the industrial and demographic revolutions resulted in an abrupt change in the relative magnitude of Eastern and Western

---

[12] Organski and Organski, *Population and World Power, op. cit.*, pp. 27 and 13.

populations. Europeans multiplied themselves sixfold in three centuries, while the total of all other peoples was augmented only threefold. From about 20 per cent of the world's population in 1650, Europeans increased to almost 40 per cent in 1950. The slowing of their rate of increase since 1900 bodes a declining share of world population in future generations. The estimates of population by continents shown in Table 30 portray a steady and decisive increase in the population of European

TABLE 30. *World Population by Continents, 1650-1950**

DATE	WORLD	AFRICA	ANGLO AMER-ICA	LATIN AMER-ICA	ASIA	EUROPE	OCEANIA	AREA OF EURO-PEAN SETTLE-MENT
1650	545	100	1	12	330	100	2	118
1750	728	95	1	11	479	140	2	158
1800	906	90	6	19	602	187	2	219
1850	1,171	95	26	33	749	266	2	335
1900	1,608	120	81	63	937	401	6	573
1930	2,008	155	134	110	1,069	530	10	784
1950	2,406	199	166	162	1,272	594	13	935

All population figures are in millions.

* A. M. Carr-Saunders, *World Population*, The Clarendon Press, Oxford, 1936, p. 42; and United Nations, *The Determinants and Consequences of Population Trends*, New York, 1953, p. 11.

descent: the 1950 total of 935 million persons is almost exactly eight times their magnitude three centuries earlier.

This enormous demographic expansion played a large part in the international spread of European culture and in the military and economic dominance of Europe over other continents. More than 50 million Europeans emigrated to other areas during the last century— including the United States, Australia, South Africa, and various South American countries. White supremacy, thus placed in its historical and demographic context, is seen to depend not on superior mental or physical endowments, but on rapid population increase and technological improvements. "Whatever happens we have got,/ the Maxim gun and they have not."[13]

With so much of Asia's population just entering the stage of transitional growth, an ethnocentric fear has arisen among some Westerns that, by the end of the century, Europe and Anglo America will be

---

[13] Hilaire Belloc, "The Modern Traveler," a comic narrative poem of about 1900.

overwhelmed by Asia, who will change our way of life to fit its Oriental customs. To be sure, Asia is now by far the most populous continent; before long Asian people may constitute two-thirds of the world's population. If they act together, they will undoubtedly have tremendous strength.

But as Asians make the economic and scientific changes necessary to reduce mortality, they almost inevitably participate in a process of Westernization. Scientific techniques cannot be borrowed without also borrowing parts of the Western educational system, its this-world orientation, and other segments of the social structure and value system. In some measure, to beat us, they must join us. Either way, large parts of Western culture prevail.

AUTONOMY *versus* COLONIALISM

Recent declarations of independence in Africa and Southeast Asia have marked a swelling surge of colonial peoples toward political inde-pendence. Along with their avaricious hunger for industrial products has come a highly successful drive toward freedom from colonial status and external domination. These newly formed nations—amounting to more than three dozen since January 1, 1960—are on the average considerably smaller in population than are the older countries.

Enthusiastic claims to the contrary, demographic trends have probably played but a small causal role in these movements toward independence —though population is a powerful predisposing cause. On the other hand, attainment of political autonomy significantly alters population growth, income per capita, mortality, pattern of urbanization, labor force, education, agricultural density, literacy, international and internal migration, and other demographic variables and characteristics.

HAVES *versus* HAVE-NOTS

World conflict in the twentieth century seems to be turning into a battle between the "haves" and "have-nots." The "have" countries try to maintain or preferably to increase their present favorable position *vis-à-vis* their less fortunate brethren. The "have-not" countries do their best to join the haves so that they too may partake more copiously of the world's choice goods. But their prospects on this score are not bright. Not only is the gap between the have and have-not powers increasing rather than decreasing, but it probably will continue to widen unless economic development programs are able to outrun population growth.

According to Jessie Bernard, the nations of the world have now reached a point where accurate description requires a third category: the "have-mores." The fabulous material gains of the United States—

TABLE 31. *Countries of Twenty Million or More Residents, 1960**

RANK	COUNTRY	APPROXIMATE MID-YEAR POPULATION	ANNUAL PERCENTAGE GROWTH SINCE PREVIOUS CENSUS OR ESTIMATE
1	Mainland China	669,000,000[a]	2.46
2	India	432,417,000	2.04
3	U.S.S.R.	214,400,000	1.78
4	United States	179,977,000	1.73
5	Japan	93,200,000	0.99
6	Pakistan	92,727,000	2.14
7	Indonesia	92,600,000	1.44
8	Brazil	65,743,000	2.35
9	West Germany	55,577,000	1.27
10	United Kingdom	52,539,000	0.47
11	Italy	49,361,000	0.51
12	France	45,540,000	0.98
13	Mexico	34,626,000	2.95
14	Nigeria	34,296,000	2.02
15	Spain	30,128,000	0.78
16	Poland	29,703,000	1.73
17	Turkey	27,561,000	2.90
18	Philippines	27,500,000	3.14
19	Egypt	25,929,000	3.51
20	Thailand	25,520,000	5.74
21	Republic of Korea	24,665,000	2.84
22	Argentina	20,956,000	1.72
23	Burma	20,662,000	1.01
24	Iran	20,182,000	1.87

[a] 1959.

While data for most countries on this list are fairly accurate, some of these figures are crude approximations.

* *Population Index*, Vol. XXVIII, No. 1, January 1962, pp. 86-91; Vol. XXVII, No. 1, January 1961, pp. 92-97; and United Nations, *Demographic Yearbook: 1959*, New York, 1960, pp. 109-126.

alternately (and often simultaneously) reviled, adulated, and imitated by other nations—illustrate this new economic type.

Inspection of Table 31 presses home the fact that the have-not nations comprise the bulk of mankind. China and India alone encompass over a billion people. Of all living human beings, one out of every three is a resident of either China or India. Of the seven largest countries, five are in Asia and four are have-nots. Since they contain a decisive majority of the world's inhabitants, on a democratic basis they hold the voting power; and on the emotionally surcharged basis of wants and needs, they may have much to gain and little to lose by listening to the clamorous voices of demagogues. The haves will do well to heed the have-nots' pleas—if only in their own self-interest.

If the underdeveloped areas continue to increase their population so precipitously, and if they are frustrated in their efforts to achieve better living conditions, there may be political friction and even military conflict. Certainly the larger among these countries are not likely to remain hungry without at least observing the territory available in other nations for their emigrants—be those emigrants colonists or conquerors. Writing of the possibility that the denser countries of Asia may want to expand into more sparsely settled territory, Warren Thompson warns that people in the Americas and even parts of Africa might feel the aggressive force resulting from population pressure in the Far East. The demographic situation in Communist China, India, Pakistan, and Japan may encourage them to resort to force to secure access to additional land and natural resources. Smaller countries unable to use force may require intervention of outside aid to prevent internal chaos or bitter boundary disputes.[14]

Nor are the have-not countries confined to the Far East. To be sure, the internal political instability and revolutionary ardor of the nations of Latin America, the Middle East, and Africa are generally caused by economic, religious, and ethnic diversities rather than by population pressures. But as rapid population expansion persists, it augments existing chronic tensions in these areas.

Envy of the have-nots over land and other resources held (and frequently not used) by the haves may eventuate in another war. Thus Warren Thompson beholds the effect of differential rates of population growth in different nations as stimulating alterations in the pressure of population on available resources and possibly as provoking armed conflict.[15] As the people of have-not countries become more and more aware of and responsive to these increased pressures, initially lawful and, that failing, ultimately violent attempts to effect new adjustments are highly likely to occur. What is more, the tensions thus inspired will probably increase with augmentation of the industrial might of these growing nations as well as with more unified political organization enabling them to enforce what they are coming to believe are fair demands for a greater share in the world's goods.

FREE AND COMMUNIST BLOCS

Each of the three major political blocs into which the world is now divided—the free nations, the Communist nations, and the uncom-

---

[14] Warren S. Thompson, *Population and Progress in the Far East*, University of Chicago Press, Chicago, 1959.

[15] Thompson, *Population Problems, op. cit.*, p. 349.

mitted nations—has approximately the same population. Thus the free and Communist blocs have much to gain in the global struggle for the remaining, uncommitted third. "This titanic competition is focused primarily on South and Southeast Asia at the present time, because the bulk of the world's politically uncommitted population is located there."[16]

For some nations, however, it is difficult to determine into which of these three categories they should be placed; confusion exists especially between the free and uncommitted blocs. Kingsley Davis ignores the uncommitted category by defining "free" as "non-communist," thus placing most doubtful cases in the free category. He divides the people of the world into two groups, having the following demographic features as of 1950: number of countries—70 free, 11 communist; total population —1,450,000,000 free, 800,000,000 Communist; land area in square kilometers—68,000,000 free, 103,000,000 Communist; persons per square kilometer—21 free, 23 Communist.[17]

The weapons which are getting the most exercise in this conflict are propagandistic. The Communists, calling attention to the wide gap between the levels of living of the have and have-not nations, place responsibility for the misery of the have-nots on the exploitative, imperialistic, and colonial practices of the capitalistic haves. "Needless to say, the fire of this propaganda is effectively fed by the frustrations of the underdeveloped areas in their efforts to advance their levels of living, and in their efforts to win independence from imperial powers where this is not yet accomplished."[18]

The major armament of the free nations in this cold war is the provision of material assistance to the undecided have-nots to assist them in achieving their economic goals. With the greater economic surplus of the anti-Communist powers, this weapon has a high propagandistic potential.

Two great struggles are under way between the leaders of the free and Communist factions—the United States and Soviet Russia—and between the mammoths, India and China. Thus the four giant nations in the world are locked in a two-by-two struggle: two behemoths, Communist China and the quasi-free subcontinent of India, and the two less populous but more powerful combatants, the U.S.S.R. and the United States. The outcome of this struggle may well decide the political future of the globe for many years to come.

---

[16] Philip M. Hauser, *Population Perspectives*, Rutgers University Press, New Brunswick, 1960, p. 26.

[17] Kingsley Davis, "Population and Power in the Free World," in Philip M. Hauser (ed.), *Population and World Politics*, The Free Press, Glencoe, 1958, p. 200.

[18] Hauser, *Population Perspectives, op. cit.*, p. 27.

17 ❧ *Ideals and Preferences*

Population policy may be divided into two segments: the practical and the idealistic. The practical side consists of the formulation and expedition of action programs, usually on a national scale. The idealistic aspect involves writing and speculating in terms of specific values— implicitly held or explicitly stated.

Modern policies actually practiced are discussed in the next chapter; ancient edicts and modern recommendations and exhortations form the substance of the present chapter. Here we will discuss what certain individuals and private organizations believe should be put into practice— plus a few obsolete imperial fiats. The following chapter delineates what has been done by twentieth-century sovereigns and legislatures.

Early Writings

Pre-Malthusian meditation about population often led to exhortation toward action. Sometimes a public leader adopted a program which was at least partially dictated by his acceptance of sycophantic or independent visions. And then as now idealistic canons were transformed into action by governmental bodies who feared that their territories would be outdistanced in the breeding race or, in contrasting circumstances, worried about the economic and political turmoil that might accompany excessive population growth. Religious doctrines or authorities frequently dominated either or both the hortatory musing or the action program.

THE ORIENT

Ancient non-Western ideas on population must be sought almost exclusively in religious writings, for here as in the Occident, population was not viewed as a purely secular matter. The early Hebrews considered marriage a religious duty; according to the Talmud, authorities could compel a man to marry and anyone who lived alone at the age of twenty was cursed by God in the same manner as a murderer.[1]

Zoroaster lauded three meritorious actions: to plant a tree, to cultivate a field, and to give life to children. The Zend-Avesta is packed with religious counsels concerning marriage and paternity: "Marry young so that your son can succeed you and that the family chain is not broken." Herodotus indicated that the Persians' religious motives were reinforced by military considerations: "After military virtues, they regarded with great merit the having of many children. . . . Force consists of great numbers."

Nirvana, the Buddhist and Hindu ideal of extinguishing self and the desire for life, appears a-natalist, but the Vedantic Upanishads advise marrying early, having children, and, in the case of sterility, adopting a son. Though Buddha admired the contemplative and ascetic life, the masses of India and China did not accept renunciation and monasticism.

The Laws of Manu, the most renowned legal treatise of the ancient Hindus, speak of the sacred obligations of marriage and paternity. Law 96: "Women were created to bring children into the world, men to perpetuate the species." Law 106: "As soon as a man becomes a father of a son, he is freed of his debt toward the spirits of his ancestors." Law 107: "This son through which he pays his debt and obtains immortality is the child of duty; the others are children of love." Law 137: "Through a son, one conquers worlds; through a grandson, one obtains immortality; but through a great-grandson, one secures the universe." However, even if one is prevented from reaching Heaven because his children are all girls, if one of his daughters bears him a grandson, he can enter Heaven through the back door.

Confucius mentioned the undesirability of excessive population growth for an empire, but advised individuals that "To die without offspring is one of the three gravest unfilial acts." Other ancient Chinese writers sought ideal proportions between land and population.

ANCIENT GREECE

The demographic thought of the ancient Greeks must be recognized as falling within the context of their focus on the ideal harmony in all things, the mystical and religious significance of geometric forms and numbers, a basically static conception of life tolerating little expectation of change, and their attitudes toward the family and the role of women as procreative rather than companionate.

---

[1] René Gonnard, *Histoire des doctrines de la population*, Nouvelle Librairie Nationale, Paris, 1923, p. 13.

To the Greeks the ideal population was one that was good rather than large. The aim of Greek institutions was to permit the fit to survive as citizens. In population as in other matters, the Greeks strove for *arete* or excellence. *Arete* required exuberant, all-inclusive intellectual, physical, practical, and ethical perfection. Odysseus had *arete* because he was skilled at boxing, public speaking, sailing, farming, track and field, cooking, singing, and outwitting an opponent by wily schemes and because he exhibited strength, courage, intelligence, sentimentality, wisdom, fatherly love, and when ill-used by the gods, resignation.

The Greeks were also preoccupied with optimum size. Athenians felt that the Assembly, their legislative body comprising a meeting of all native male adults, should never become too large to permit a citizen to speak and be heard before the entire assemblage. By this criterion, no city-state should exceed the number of assembled citizens that could be reached by the unaided human voice.

Plato and Aristotle both stressed proportion and quality in population.[2] Plato was in fact a eugenicist. Although he did not know enough about the biological mechanisms of human reproduction to speak of genes and chromosomes, he recommended ideal matings arranged by matching desirable traits in the man and the woman. He further advised restriction by law of the childbearing period to ages 30 to 35 among men and ages 20 to 40 among women.

Plato also voiced the hardly original opinion that women's health depends on their being kept almost continually pregnant. "Whenever the matrix or womb, as it is called—which is an indwelling creature desirous of childbearing—remains without fruit long beyond the due season, it is vexed and takes it ill; and by straying all ways through the body and blocking up the passages of the breath and preventing respiration it casts the body into the uttermost distress, and causes, moreover, all kinds of maladies; until the desire and love of the two sexes unite them."[3]

Plato proposed 5,040 as the ideal number of citizens for a city-state, which would make the total population including women, children, slaves, and aliens number about 50,000 people. (Athens was some four times larger than this figure in Plato's lifetime.) Both Plato and Aristotle wanted a polis large enough to ensure economic self-sufficiency and military defense, but not too large to permit a constitutional government with considerable contact between citizens.

Aristotle recommended abortion as a means toward birth control and accepted abandonment of deformed infants as a eugenic measure. He also proposed that the city-state set a limit on the number of children

---

[2] Plato, *Laws* and *Republic*; Aristotle, *Politics* and *Ethics*.
[3] Plato, *Timaeus*, Loeb edition, Vol. VII, p. 249.

each person might have. He complained that giving large dowries aggravated the inequality of property distribution (women owned two-fifths of the land) and was detrimental to an adequate supply of warrior-citizens.

Ancient Greek literature, history, and philosophy make it clear that the citizenry neither practiced the ideals nor held to the goals set forth by their pundits. The Faustian, orgiastic cult of Dionysus, the god of wine, existed side by side with the temperate, ordered cult of Apollo, the peaceful guardian of flocks and villages. Acrimony and war forced the Greeks to abandon (sometimes enthusiastically, it seems) their harmonious image of civil life.

Bellicose Philip of Macedon, the father of Alexander the Great, enacted pronatalist legislation and encouraged immigration by the Thracians, who were believed to be more fertile than the Macedonians.[4] Several city-states were in the habit of passing laws encouraging marriage and natality following wars. In Hellenistic times, marriage and family cares were often regarded as evils necessary for propagation of the group. Polybius opined that the taste for conspicuous consumption and luxurious living thwarted population growth.[5]

THE ROMAN EMPIRE

The perspective of a great empire is different from that of a small city-state. The Romans wanted a large population increase in order to expand their empire. Identifying numbers with power, they enacted pronatalist legislation. There is evidence, however, that the Roman population failed to increase as fast as their leaders wished. Concern was especially expressed over the low fertility and consequent lack of replacement of the upper classes. Fertility deterrents were celibacy, late marriage resulting from long military service, and unpopular inheritance laws.

In an attempt to reinvigorate Roman family life, Augustus, the first Emperor, enacted sumptuary laws regulating eating, drinking, wearing apparel, and the general style of living. He also enacted eugenic measures designed to promote fertility among the upper classes. He exempted married couples with children from certain inheritance taxes, forbade the unmarried to inherit at all under certain circumstances and made their taxation burdensome, and established heavy penalties for adultery. To encourage prolificity, he permitted concubinage and offered legal advantages to children of such unions.

After the third-century taxation reform of the Emperor Diocletian, "the theory of population was well expressed by the term, *stabilitas cen-*

[4] Livy, *Histories*, Book XXXIX, par. 24.
[5] Polybius, *Histories*, Vol. IV, Book cxxiii.

sus, that is, stability of the population with respect to tillage."[6] The land was divided into sections of varying size, each large enough to support one farmer and his family. Controlled migration from overpopulated to underpopulated areas was attempted to maintain the desired stability.

The Christian ecclesiastic Tertullian, a Carthaginian who lived in Rome around 200 A.D., adumbrated Malthus in writing of the difficulties awaiting the Roman Empire:

> We find in the records of the Antiquities of Man that the human race has progressed with a gradual growth of population. . . . Surely it is obvious enough, if one looks at the whole world, that it is becoming better cultivated and more fully peopled than anciently. . . . What most frequently meets our view is our teeming population; our numbers are burdensome to the world, which can hardly supply us from its natural elements; our wants grow more and more keen, and our complaints more bitter in all mouths, whilst nature fails in affording us her usual sustenance. In very deed, pestilence, and famine, and wars, and earthquakes have to be regarded as a remedy for nations, as a means of pruning the luxuriance of the human race.[7]

THE MIDDLE AGES

To medieval Christian writers population was a moral issue; their discussions on the subject centered around the ethical superiority of celibacy, chastity, and virginity. The religious dogma of the time, stressing as it did the unimportance of the present life, did not generate treatises on population problems. Practically all Christian sects agreed that population was not a fundamental matter.

Nevertheless a few ecclesiastics did write on the subject. As early as the fifth century St. Augustine opposed birth control, declaring that "intercourse even with one's legitimate wife is unlawful and wicked where the conception of the offspring is prevented. Onan, the son of Juda, did this and the Lord killed him for it."[8] Eight centuries later Thomas Aquinas stated that the power and prestige of a political unit are functions of its population. In the sixteenth century Martin Luther counseled his followers not to worry about overpopulation: "God makes children, and He will also nourish them." Neither Luther nor John Calvin regarded marriage as a sacrament, preferring to conceive it as a remedy for allaying concupiscence in man's state of sin—the first epistle

---

[6] Josiah Cox Russell, *Late Ancient and Medieval Population*, American Philosophical Society, Philadelphia, 1958, p. 132.

[7] Quoted in Harrison Brown, *The Challenge of Man's Future*, The Viking Press, New York, 1954, p. 30.

[8] St. Augustine, *De Adulterinas Conjugiis*, Vol. II, Chap. 12.

of Apostle Paul proclaims: "It is better to marry than to burn" (*I Corinthians:* VII, 9).

The fourteenth-century Moslem Ibn Khaldoun posited a cyclical theory of history. According to this view, societies develop from small and hardy nomadic groups through various stages of economic and demographic growth to periods of luxury and decline of fertility and hence to death of the state. This pattern repeats itself indefinitely. Later thinkers added subtlety to the notion of periodic recurrence, transmuting the cycles into spirals. Khaldoun's analogy between the maturation of an individual organism and the growth of a society (birth, happy childhood, growing youth, vigorous manhood, solid maturity, withering senescence, and death) is very tempting. In the last hundred years, this misleading scenario entranced among others philosopher Herbert Spencer, geographer Griffith Taylor, architect Le Corbusier, and demographer Corrado Gini.

THE RENAISSANCE

The Humanists returned emphasis to this life, but visionary utopias were also popular. In Thomas More's *Utopia* (1516), a perfect island society of 54 cities of 5,000 to 6,000 people each, everyone except slaves worked six-hour days and spent two years in the country for every one in the city. Marriages were fertile, families contained ten to sixteen adults, and excess population was to be drained off by colonizing other islands. Tommaso Campanella's *City of the Sun* (1623) promised a four-hour work day, Francis Bacon's *New Atlantis* (1627) provided special honors for large families, and James Harrington's *Oceania* (1658) offered freedom from taxation for families with children. Le Maître's *La Métropolitée* (1682), a regional plan for an urban network anticipating Mark Jefferson's primate city, assumed that population growth promotes production, commerce, and national strength; therefore high birth rates, agricultural productivity, and immigration are desirable.

The Florentine statesman and political commentator Niccolo Machiavelli, writing in *The Prince* and *The History of Florence*, acknowledged that population did play a part in the power struggle of states. But he stressed that a great state is not created by a large population alone; also necessary are high agricultural and nonagricultural production and shrewd leadership.

SEVENTEENTH AND EIGHTEENTH CENTURIES

In the seventeenth century, the opening of the New World and the development of trade and commerce fostered mercantilism—an economic doctrine which flourished from the mid-sixteenth to the mid-eighteenth century and betokened a concern with money and foreign commerce, particularly the importation of gold and silver from America. Accompanying this transition to a money economy instead of payment in kind and services was the breakup of the old feudal régime. The supplanting of feudalism by nationalism encouraged statesmen to think that national power, wealth, and glory were ensured by out-populating other countries. Mercantilists favored governmental adoption of strong "bigger and better" policies and stressed the military and commercial advantages of a constantly increasing populace. To their way of thinking a larger population meant greater production and commerce as well as more men to colonize and exploit other areas. Cromwell, Colbert, Frederick the Great, and other prominent exponents of mercantilism all wanted a large natural increase. Spain and Russia encouraged immigration, and nascent states hurried to build merchant marines.

Revolting against the mercantilist emphasis on industry, trade, and wealth, the eighteenth-century physiocrats, followers of François Quesnay, believed that since nature is the source of all prosperity, we must arrange our laws and customs so as not to encroach upon the natural, immutable laws affecting production. The best possible governmental regulation, they argued, is abstention from meddling. The physiocrats embodied this tenet of noninterference in the maxims: *laissez faire et laissez passer*—leave (people) alone and let (things) take their own course, attributed to Jean Claude de Gournay, and *le monde va de lui-même*—the world goes of itself. The physiocrats also introduced the systematic distinction between productive and unproductive labor: productive labor adds something material to the world's goods; unproductive labor does not. They claimed that only extractive industries (agriculture, mining, and fishing) are productive, whereas commerce and manufacturing are not because they merely give new forms and locations to materials. For these reasons they wanted a substantial supply of farmers but did not care what happened to the urban population. Ironically, the physiocrats helped lay the groundwork of both conservative capitalism and radical socialism: their slogan, *laissez faire*, became the motto of the right wing; their insistence on the difference between productive and unproductive labor prefigured the labor theory of value.

Adam Smith, the "father of political economy," built upon (and overthrew) the labors of both the mercantilists and physiocrats. His epochal and catholic *Wealth of Nations*[9] begins with the idea that the source of national income is labor. Like Cantillon, he distinguished three economic classes: landowners, entrepreneurs, and wage-earners. Demographically, the working ages are most important—although dependent

---

[9] Adam Smith, *An Inquiry into the Nature and Causes of the Wealth of Nations*, London, 1776.

children, women, and aged are valuable as consumers. Smith and Malthus gave impetus to the classical school of economics.

Various essayists and philosophers also displayed some concern with population. Francis Bacon warned that "Generally it is to be foreseen that the population of a Kingdom (especially if it be not mown down by wars) do not exceed the stock of the Kingdom which should maintain them."[10] Thomas Hobbes believed war to be the principal impediment to human security and happiness, and overpopulation to be the chief cause of war; therefore, he argued, governments should hold down the population in order to secure peace. Hobbes anticipated Malthus by writing of the dependence of population on subsistence, especially food. Montesquieu pointed out that human society limits the birth rate; but that people who have nothing will have many children, as it costs them nothing. Voltaire wrote that demographic matters should be so arranged as to improve man's lot. Finally, in what is possibly the bitterest satire ever written, the Irish clergyman Jonathan Swift proposed that five-sixths of the children of Ireland "may at a year old be offered in sale to the persons of quality, and fortune, throughout the kingdom, always advising the mother to let them suck plentifully in the last month, so as to render them plump, and fat for a good table. . . . Ask the parents of these mortals whether they would not at this day think it a great happiness to have been sold for food at a year old . . . and thereby have avoided such a perpetual scene of misfortunes as they have since gone through."[11]

Optimum Population

The population pressure felt by the Irish may be contrasted to an optimal condition; when people need—or believe they need—*Lebensraum*, they are exceeding or convincing themselves that they have exceeded the optimum. The concept of an optimum differs from absence of population pressure in that the former can be objectively defined, whereas the latter is essentially subjective and not necessarily an accurate reflection of prevailing conditions. When the citizens are fully informed, the two concepts are in accord: where population and resources are in balance, no pressure is felt; where disequilibrium exists, pressure is felt and policy recommendations may follow.

The idea of an optimum has been enthusiastically supported by many

---

[10] Francis Bacon, "Of Seditions and Troubles," *Essays or Counsels: Civil and Moral*, London, 1625.

[11] Jonathan Swift, *A Modest Proposal for Preventing the Children of Poor People from Being a Burthen to Their Parents or Country, and for Making Them Beneficial to the Public*, Dublin, 1729.

economists of both the right and left wings. The Marxian socialist Karl Kautsky believed that in the perfect socialist society, population would always tend toward the ideal size: whenever population starts to deviate from the optimum, public opinion and individual conscience will make women's duty clear. The conservative economist-demographer A. M. Carr-Saunders approved of the theory that societies inherently tend to move toward an optimum—that is, he postulated a feedback mechanism whereby considerable deviation above or below the optimum size introduces self-corrective tendencies. John Maynard Keynes, an ardent admirer of Malthus who wrote panegyrically of the *Essay on Population*, stated that the determination of an optimum population is an important national matter: "The time has already come when each country needs a considered national policy about what size of population, whether larger or smaller than at present, or the same, is more expedient. And having settled this policy, we must take steps to carry it into operation."[12]

An upper limit of population is set by available resources, the existing state of technology, and the efficiency of social organization. If population begins to exceed this number, the Malthusian checks come into operation. A lower limit is determined by the necessities of replacement; below a certain reproductive minimum, the species heads toward extinction. Between the maximum supportable by the earth and the minimum required for survival of the species, there is a very wide range within which the value system of the society is largely determinative. It is in this area that such questions as "How highly are children valued in comparison to material satisfactions?" or "How sacred are the taboos against premarital and extramarital intercourse, early marriage, or birth control?" come to be answered.

Even if an optimum size and growth rate could be established for a region, it would be foolish to insist on immediate conformance to that size or rate of increase. Indeed, where a country is too large and growing too fast, the most constructive course of action might be to continue to let it grow, but at a slower pace. The contrasting policy of attempting to decrease population (even assuming that practical control methods were available for use) until it reaches the optimal magnitude might easily create internal disruption of catastrophic dimensions. This is a case of choosing the lesser of two evils: maintaining (but reducing) non-optimum conditions *versus* suddenly (but disruptively) achieving the optimum. Changes toward optimum size or growth should be gradual.

Nor is optimum population simply a matter of total number or growth.

---

[12] John Maynard Keynes, *The Economic Consequences of the Peace*, London, 1920, p. 8.

Also of concern is the optimum composition of the populace—the preferred proportion of college graduates, churchgoers, married couples, literate persons, skilled machinists, beautiful women, aged men, and so forth.

CRITERIA FOR OPTIMA

There are at least two major weaknesses inherent in the concept of population optima. First, one must ask: optimum for what? There are many criteria, and not all are mutually compatible: total production, per capita output, wages, unemployment, military strength, longevity, quantity and quality of food, population density, social services, internal peace or disruption, and so forth. The ideal population size for military strength is rarely the same as the optimum for standard of living or the food supply or social welfare. Sometimes the criteria are otherworldly: "The concept of a God who glories in a large number of worshippers, much as a monarch might preen himself on the adulation of great numbers of people, has at times led to the belief that the increase in the number of worshippers was of more importance than the earthly welfare of these worshippers."[13]

Second, even if we could determine the optimum size of the population of a country in a given year, we could hardly expect it to apply unchanged to the different conditions of social, industrial, agricultural, and military life of 1975 or 1984. An optimum population must be related to the circumstances under which life is lived. In periods of rapid change, such as the present century, an optimum may become obsolete in a few years. It is perhaps precisely because of this prospect of obsolescence that the concept of optimum population has not attracted as much expert attention as it did in former—and more static—eras. For social, military, and economic planning, what we need to know is not the present optimum, but rather a future optimum toward which we can aim. In other words, if the optimum idea is to be applied to policy instead of remaining merely a theoretical notion, demographers should learn how to approximate optima for ten, twenty, or perhaps fifty years in the future—an impossible task at the present time.

Demographers today are moving away from the idea of a precise, fixed optimum to an optimum band resembling a statistical confidence interval. Within this band are found several ideal population sizes suggested by the criteria noted above. Thus Sauvy placed the optimum population of France between 50 and 75 million people, while Whelpton recommended an optimum range for the United States extending from

---

[13] Warren S. Thompson, *Population Problems*, McGraw-Hill Book Co., New York, 1953, p. 456.

100 to 140 million.[14] Sauvy's optimum interval is larger than the present national population; Whelpton's is smaller. However, intervals this wide have rather little practical value; nor are demographers able to specify narrower bands with any confidence. Here are two definitions of optimum population, the first by an economist, the second by a sociologist-anthropologist team. According to the economist the optimum size of population is "that which furnishes the labor supply which, fully utilized, is necessary to operate the total resources of land, materials, and instrumental capital at the point of least (labor) cost per unit of product or income."[15] To the sociologists the "optimum population of a given society is one of such size and composition that it interposes no hindrances to the fullest possible utilization of the natural resources and the greatest possible development of personal and social relations in terms of the techniques, ideals, values, and general cultural system of its particular society."[16] Note that where the economist talks of "per capita income," the sociologists substitute "personal and social relations."

The latter definition resembles the ethical system of Jeremy Bentham and John Stuart Mill, who held that the best action is that which provides the greatest balance of pleasure over pain, or the greatest happiness for the greatest number of people. By this reasoning, that population is best which brings about the greatest total human happiness. One should estimate as closely as possible the usefulness of the consequences (both intentional and unanticipated) of each policy, of whatever type, thus exposing which is the superior.

E. F. Penrose has contrasted the income optimum population with the welfare optimum population but acknowledges the possibility of relating the two.

> The per capita income concept of the optimum can be made to coincide with the per capita welfare concept on the assumption that this income is spent in the consumption of the kinds and amounts of goods and services that make the maximum contribution to welfare. The more nearly rational the choices of consumers in a community, or, in other words, the more these choices are influenced by scientific knowledge, the more closely will the per capita income optimum approach the per capita welfare optimum. There are reasons for supposing that in many

---

[14] P. K. Whelpton, *Forecasts of the Population of the United States: 1945-1975*, Bureau of the Census, Washington, 1947, p. 64.

[15] A. B. Wolfe, "The Theory of Optimum Population," in Louis I. Dublin (ed.), "The American People: Studies in Population," *Annals of the American Academy of Political and Social Science*, Vol. CLXXXVII, November 1936, pp. 243-249.

[16] John L. Gillin and John P. Gillin, *Cultural Sociology*, The Macmillan Co., New York, 1948, p. 98.

countries choices of consumers have become more rational in recent years.[17]

The three demographic variables come into play in any full consideration of population optima. For example, the Indian sociologist Mukerjee defines optimum population in terms of maximum survival or longevity.[18] Conceivably one could measure an optimum through highest fertility, exact balance of birth and death rates, maximum surplus of births over deaths, maximum surplus of deaths over births, or any number of other arrangements of vital phenomena. Migration, too, can be introduced: maximum immigration, zero net immigration, maximum internal migration, and so forth. Or one can consider total population growth, including both migration and natural increase, as do the authorities cited above.

OVERPOPULATION

Although it is difficult these days to find a demographer who is willing to speak of optimum population, demographic experts frequently refer to countries as over- or underpopulated. Between these two conditions there lies a wide optimum band, but no one feels he has both the necessity and the ability to locate a precise optimum point.

Overpopulation in particular has been given considerable attention. Frank Lorimer suggests three definitions: an area is overpopulated if fewer people would lead to a higher level of living, if population increase is more rapid than possible production increase, or if continuance of present growth trends would check economic advances.[19] Using the first definition, about 95 per cent of the world is overpopulated; using the second, there is little overpopulation; and using the third, about one-half of the world is overpopulated.

OPTIMUM GROWTH

Concern over ideal population size has lately been yielding place to the notion of optimum rate of growth. In highly industrialized countries the population can vary within wide limits without having a serious effect on the level of real income or other criteria of optima. Underdeveloped countries, however, lack this flexibility; for them questions of over- and underpopulation are extremely important. A United Nations report comments:

---

[17] Ernest F. Penrose, *Population Theories and Their Application*, Food Research Institute, Stanford, 1934, p. 83.

[18] Radhakamal Mukerjee, *The Philosophy of Social Science*, Macmillan and Co., London, 1960, pp. 117-120.

[19] Frank Lorimer, "Issues of Population Policy," in Kingsley Davis (ed.), "World Population in Transition," *The Annals of the American Academy of Political and Social Science*, Vol. CCXXXVII, January 1945, pp. 193-203.

In the more highly developed industrial countries there is at present probably a wide range of population sizes, within which income could be maintained at satisfactory levels. Consequently, in such countries the size of the optimum population and the presence or absence of over-population or under-population appear much less important than they do in densely populated under-developed countries. At least, so far as the highly industrialized countries are concerned, the question of the optimum rate of population growth may be more important than the size of the optimum population.[20]

As more and more segments of the world become industrialized, the idea of optimum population may recede farther into the background until it is completely replaced by the concept of optimum rate of increase.

The desirability of a steadily increasing population long has been extolled by religious, political, and military leaders. Said Benjamin Franklin: "We can never have too many people (nor too much money)." But an increasing population is neither necessarily healthy nor desirable. Thus a present-day essayist asks: "Even supposing we could support a vastly increased world population, do we really want to? . . . Do we really want the earth turned into a human ant-heap?"[21]

Some religious and other spokesmen acknowledge the possibility of overpopulation while denying the legitimacy of conceding to it. In other words, avoidance of overpopulation or overly rapid growth takes second place in importance behind the religious obligation to have large families. In the opinion of The Reverend Anthony Francis Zimmerman of the Catholic Universities of America and Nagoya: "The family has not only a right but, in principle, a most sacred duty to expand at a normal rate. It has no duty to restrict the number of children because of consideration for the community, that is, in order to avoid overpopulation. It must keep itself uncontaminated by the view of those who scoff at the virtue of having a rich crown of children. The family which courageously and even heroically rears a large number of children in an overpopulated area merits special praise for its virtue."[22]

If a nation is to be healthy, population growth should not exceed increases in food supply, industrial goods, and other production. Primary, secondary, and tertiary economic activities must be balanced against the demands set by population size and intensity of use of these extracted and manufactured products. Also vital is the ratio between population

[20] United Nations, *The Determinants and Consequences of Population Trends,* New York, 1953, p. 237.
[21] Frank L. Lucas, "The Greatest Problem of To-Day," in *The Greatest Problem and Other Essays,* Cassell and Co., London, 1960, p. 320.
[22] Anthony Zimmerman, "*Overpopulation,*" The Catholic University of America Press, Washington, 1957, p. 103.

and the output and distribution of food, water, and other necessities. This is not simply a matter of the supply divided by the population; the interrelationships are convoluted and often reciprocal. This issue embraces national and local laws with regard to land use and ownership, water utilization and allocation, industrial regulations and planning, transportation facilities and subsidies, national power and military strength, housing and other construction, wholesaling and retailing systems, consumer buying practices and installment credit policies, and many other important public activities.

Quality and Eugenics

By population quality we mean the level attained regarding various personal and social characteristics. We speak of level of education, amount of intelligence, degree of physical strength, and manual dexterity. These and other characteristics may be ordered hierarchically; hence the term "population quality." Quality relates to social variables (income, literacy) as well as to biological ones (height, club feet). Indeed, these two categories actually overlap—for example, musculature is a product of genetic, nutritional, and exercise variables. Quality refers also to both genetic and acquired characteristics, though this distinction can be easily overstressed, since most phenotypes or observed characteristics of adults are influenced both by genotypes or inherited factors and by environmental factors.

The subject of eugenics is related to quality in that both are concerned with human abilities and accomplishments. They differ, however, in that quality is descriptive and essentially objective, whereas eugenics is aimed at improvement of the species. Eugenics may be either positive—intending to increase the proportion of persons having desirable traits, or negative—intending to decrease the proportion having undesirable attributes.

Based on the science of genetics, the eugenics movement was founded by Francis Galton, a cousin of Charles Darwin. Galton advocated both increased breeding of the fit and decreased breeding of the unfit. On his death he bequeathed his fortune to the University of London to support a chair in eugenics and the Eugenics Laboratory, which he had established in 1904. His biometric research at the Laboratory was continued by Karl Pearson and Ronald A. Fisher.

IMPROVEMENT *versus* DECLINE OF QUALITY

Geneticists disagree whether various desirable attributes are waning in human beings as a result of the inverse relation between fertility and several socioeconomic variables. Given the fact that in the United States the lowest classes produce the largest portions of the next generation, and assuming that there is a causal association between success and genetic endowment, Robert Cook (among others) takes the stand that "today's differential birth rate makes a decline in intelligence inevitable."[23] But many scholars disagree with this view, holding with O. D. Duncan that the hypothesis of declining intelligence is untenable—and that the "modern dilemma" in that respect is "most unfortunately misstated."[24] Similar arguments arise with regard to mental disease, feeble-mindedness, and other types of defectives.

The dispute centers on whether current practices are dysgenic—declining or retrogressing in quality, genetically neutral—holding steady with no change, or eugenic—improving the species. Darwin postulated the natural selection of the fittest specimens through competition, and there have been many men who have opposed giving alms to the poor on the basis that such eleemosynary activity would harm *Homo sapiens* because it prevents natural selection from occurring. In modern industrialized countries, however, where the high standards of living are far removed from the subsistence level, survival of the fittest tends to be negated in favor of no selection at all. Corrado Gini, among others, has argued that negative selection is actually occurring through deterioration of genetic endowments. In any case, random genetic drift (sometimes called the Sewall Wright effect) toward the mean in succeeding generations does exercise a normalizing influence.

Carrying Cook's thesis from heredity toward environment, Harold Dorn observes that

> Even though we do not have sufficient scientific evidence to determine the effects of differential fertility upon the genetic qualities of our population, we do have sufficient evidence to be sure that a large proportion of the recruits of the next generation come from the classes of our population which are the least able to provide maximum cultural and health advantages. So long as differential fertility operates in a way that denies opportunity for maximum development of innate ability it acts counter to the professed ideals of our society and as such is a matter of serious concern.[25]

EUGENICS POLICIES

In 1906, Francis Galton closed his autobiography by stating the aims of eugenics: "Its first object is to check the birth rate of the Unfit, instead

---

[23] Robert C. Cook, *Human Fertility: The Modern Dilemma*, William Sloane Associates, New York, 1951, p. 261.
[24] Otis Dudley Duncan, "Is the Intelligence of the General Population Declining?," *American Sociological Review*, Vol. XVII, August 1952, pp. 401-407.
[25] Harold F. Dorn, "Present Knowledge Concerning the Effects of Differential Fertility," *Milbank Memorial Fund Quarterly*, Vol. XXV, October 1947, p. 366.

of allowing them to come into being, though doomed in large numbers to perish prematurely. The second object is the improvement of the race by furthering the productivity of the Fit by early marriages and healthful rearing of their children. Natural Selection rests upon excessive production and wholesale destruction; Eugenics on bringing no more individuals into the world than can be properly cared for, and those only of the best stock."[26]

Eugenics is thus a program for improving the human species through application of genetic principles. Eugenicists generally try to encourage fertility among responsible parents and to diminish fertility among the nonresponsible. This, of course, is what Sweden is doing with its national program to make fertility—and nonfertility—voluntary. A reform movement aiming at the betterment of mankind, eugenics is based on genetic knowledge and on generally accepted notions of what constitutes quality in human beings.

So far eugenic efforts have had both positive and negative emphases. Some eugenicists have advocated a program of more children by the "better" persons; others have concentrated on sterilizing the unfit or making it difficult for them to have children. A complete program calls for a graduated scale in which the number of children a person should have varies directly with his genetic and social endowment, thus embracing both the quality of his chromosomes and the kind of upbringing he can offer his children.

Early eugenics writing stressed hereditary defects and superiorities and the consequences of these characteristics for offspring. Thus Phi Beta Kappa football players were urged to have many children whereas congenitally deficient adults were urged to have none, lest they pass along their inferior genetic endowment to the next generation, who in turn might continue this deterioration of *Homo sapiens*.

Today, however, this "six foot two, brilliant too" idea has been superseded by emphasis on the environmental advantages that responsible people can offer their children. This situation, reflecting a decline in acceptability of determinism through heredity and a swing toward environmental influences, has had a decided effect on eugenicists. If behaviorist psychologist John Watson's dozen new-born infants could be made into whatever kinds of adults were requested (within broadly defined limits), then surely the more of the world's infants who are placed in the hands of well-meaning and capable parents, the better off the world will be.

Parenthood, according to eugenicists, is important enough to deserve training and competence. The first director of the World Health Organi-

[26] Francis Galton, *Memories of My Life*, Methuen & Co., London, 1906, p. 323.

zation, Dr. Brock Chisholm, pleaded in 1946 for the application of modern scientific knowledge to child rearing: "If your son is going to raise pigs for a living he goes to a college for three or four years to study under experienced teachers. But if he is merely raising children he commonly learns nothing; nor appreciates, even dimly, that there is anything that he has to learn. Surely the rearing of children is greatly more important, and more complicated, than the raising of pigs."[27] (Some young parents now take this admonition so seriously that they hardly dare breathe in the presence of their delicate and awesome offspring.)

Eugenics has of late been watered down by some supporters to a rather innocuous "we want children reared better" policy. Related to this approach to eugenics is euthenics—a striving for the improvement of physical surroundings and the betterment of living conditions to make people's lives more efficient and comfortable.

CRITICISMS OF EUGENICS

Not surprisingly, eugenics programs have been criticized on half a dozen grounds. First, ask its opponents, who is to decide which people are most fit to bear or rear children? And how is one to restrict unfit— that is, prevent undesirables from bearing and bringing up their offspring? Finally, if we are all equal—an assumption thoroughly drilled into most Americans—why all the fuss? The pervasive emotional democratism that infects the United States makes it virtually impossible to promulgate any program based on an assumption that some people are inherently superior to other people.

Another complaint is that eugenics improvement takes a long time before showing any benefit. But then so does forest conservation.

A third objection is that eugenics is unnatural and immoral. But the enthusiastically adopted modern miracle drugs are also unnatural; that is, they too were invented by man and do not occur in pristine nature. Nor is tampering with fate or heredity necessarily immoral; most of us accept human decisions, for example, to electrocute certain criminals. Some people resist taking penicillin, oral contraceptives, or even aspirin on the basis that meddling with the body chemistry is dangerous and hence undesirable. Of course, the opposing view is powerfully entrenched; Thomas Gray's twentieth-century descendant might write of "mute inglorious Miltowns."

A fourth issue, and one that is particularly difficult for eugenicists to handle, centers on the question: How do we agree on what to breed or rear for? An action program must work toward some end; what are the

---

[27] G. Brock Chisholm, "The Reestablishment of Peacetime Society: The Responsibility of Psychiatrists," *Psychiatry*, Vol. IX, No. 1, February 1946, pp. 19-20.

384 :: ISSUES AND PROBLEMS

appropriate ends for this program? Should it strive to make people taller or stronger or more intelligent or more honest or more spiritual or more aggressive or more patient or more industrious or more courteous or what? Goals are often contradictory: Which person should have more children—the bright but puny intellectual or the stupid but powerful giant? The couple combining two average persons or the combination of one superlative spouse and a frail reed? (An actress was said to have written George Bernard Shaw that his brilliance coupled with her beauty would make a superb child. Declining the offer, Shaw replied that the offspring of such a union might well turn out to have his beauty and her intelligence.) To be sure, the problem would seem to be insoluble, yet it is no more so than most of the goal selections we are compelled to make. However, the final equation might be a complicated system of weighted variables requiring a thorough psychological profile of every individual—an extremely costly and perhaps demeaning procedure. For while we are unable to achieve unanimity on goals for improvement, there is a rough concordance regarding what a good man should be like. And on the negative side, even though we are not sure precisely what traits are wholly objectionable, we have arrived at a strong enough consensus to have enacted sterilization laws affecting persons having certain hereditary defects. Eighteen American states, for example, have sterilization laws applicable to epileptics, and in ten states epileptics are forbidden to marry (although medical authorities have stated that the genetic element in epilepsy is not significant). As of 1952, compulsory sterilization of defective persons was legal in 23 states; voluntary sterilization with the consent of the defective, his spouse, or his guardian was legalized in two; and provisions for either compulsory or voluntary sterilization existed in three.[28]

A fifth criticism frequently espoused is that eugenic selection might result in personal uniformity. Eventually, every man would be, say, six feet three, regular featured, highly intelligent, and morally reliable. In countering this argument eugenicists have two mutually inconsistent ripostes: First, that we strive for uniformity in other respects (courtesy, dress, driving behavior, ethics)—so why is such an objective so undesirable here? Secondly, that the result would not be uniformity; that is, in the language of the statistician, the mean would increase, but the standard deviation would not be reduced. In Aldous Huxley's *Brave New World*, application of controlled eugenic policies results in a deliberately increased standard deviation for the populace (although the value of sigma is decreased within each subgroup).

---

[28] Hope T. Eldridge, *Population Policies*, International Union for the Scientific Study of Population, Washington, 1954, pp. 105-106.

A sixth argument is that the state should not force couples to have a specified number of children. Such procedure would be contrary to many received ideas concerning both mate selection and the freedom to decide the number of children one wants. In some circles, however, this freedom is now coming to be considered irresponsible license. We must separate two kinds of eugenic suggestions: on the one hand, the usual ideas of sterilizing the unfit, mildly encouraging fertility of the fit, and improving rearing knowledge and habits; and, on the other hand, rigidly determined breeding in which the individual's fertility is computed through a formula and enforced by law. Advocates of eugenic principles are bound by the democratic framework. Aside from a small lunatic fringe, they do not propose that governmental or other organizations compel people to have specified numbers of children. Actual performance would this be left to the wishes of the marital partners, a circumstance that would severely weaken the impact of the program, even if it were adopted.

In view of the narrowing of traditional fertility differentials in the United States as in many other countries, the eugenics argument is becoming less and less timely. One might say that the eugenicists are being killed off by success: lower class fertility is declining, and upper class fertility shows signs of permanent increase. Furthermore, interclass differences in levels of living are being reduced by rising minimum wage levels and the extinction of the very rich, supplemented by converging per capita incomes as poor couples divide the family income among only as many people as the high income families. Family subsidies and free public education are also reducing the force of existing differentials.

SCIENTIFIC BREEDING

Plants and animals are improved by scientific breeding. Genetic, nutritional, and other knowledge is used to modify farm animals to obtain a closer approximation to the ideal type for that animal. Thus if we can make larger or stronger swine or chickens, why not do the same for human beings? Present knowledge of hereditary and environmental influences on animal development are adequate to the task of "improving the breed" of people.

The crucial point, however, is that we do not want to do this, although we are not always willing to admit that this is the case. Human beings are regarded as sacred and not to be tampered with; they are *us*. Eugenic breeding is interpreted as *lèse-majesté*—a crime against dignity and human sovereignty. Thus whereas we are perfectly willing to breed Chihuahuas, we would attack the same operations applied to people with emotional frenzy—and perhaps with some justification. After all, people's imperfections are often taken as proof of their humanness: "To err is human" (Alexander Pope); "We are all mortals, and as mortals err" (Royall Tyler). Works of art are often considered superior because they are marked by the mistakes of the human artisan, thus demonstrating that they were not made by a too-perfect machine.

INBREEDING

Inbreeding, the mating of close relatives, is implicit in genetic improvement of animals. It is purposely used by breeders of animals as a means of increasing the probability that offspring will have certain desirable traits. Certainly it could be used to better the human breed. But here too there is resistance. Almost all societies, including our own, forbid intermarriage between members of the nuclear family. And 28 American states have laws prohibiting marriage between first cousins.

Inbreeding increases the probability of crossing two rare traits; that is, recessive traits are emphasized. Since biologists have identified far more undesirable traits than desirable ones, the process is often considered essentially harmful. But a more accurate evaluation is that inbreeding *per se* is neither good nor bad.

Through experiments with white mice and other animals, we know that inbreeding can result in localizing and identifying disease; by preventing diseased animals from reproducing (by killing them, usually), we can eliminate the strain. Presumably, if we were to use the same techniques on human beings, we could eradicate certain inherited diseases. But we are not willing to inbreed, we disapprove of this non-romantic principle of mate-selection, and we oppose killing unfit offspring.

There are claims that inbreeding decreases fertility. And it does seem to decrease litter size in animals, but the mechanism is uncertain. Probably the lower birth rate is caused by fetal deaths rather than a smaller number of conceptions. This lower rate of procreation, however, is not necessarily undesirable.

INCEST TABOOS

Anthropological evidence is sometimes cited by biologists who oppose inbreeding of human beings. Pointing to widespread incest taboos in human groups, they conclude that there is probably some biological reason for these prohibitions. But how could these primitive groups (a few of whom show little comprehension of the details of procreation) have the observational ability to recognize the biological consequences of different levels of inbreeding? Ethnography supplies "little evidence of a precise knowledge of the reproductive process or of the principles of heredity among simple peoples. It is particularly hard to understand, for example, how a tribe ignorant of the very fact of physical paternity, like the Arunta or the Trobrianders, could have arrived at prohibitions on such a basis."[29]

A second objection to the biologists' hypothesis is that incest means different things to different groups. Thus whereas inbreeding is a biological term susceptible to a uniform definition applicable to all mankind, incest is an anthropological concept and is defined differently by different cultures and constituent subcultures. Incest rules in short are culturally prescribed rather than biologically defined. For this reason "legalized incest" is a contradiction in terms. Incest does not necessarily mean inbreeding; it refers to sexual intercourse between persons for whom such relations are prohibited—sometimes these persons are closely related, sometimes not. Further, not all closely related persons are prohibited by incest regulations from having sexual intercourse. "Incest taboos do not apply universally to any relative of opposite sex outside the nuclear family. . . . Incest taboos, in their applications to persons outside the nuclear family, fail strikingly to coincide with nearness of actual biological relationship."[30] This discrepancy betweeen incest taboos and degree of biological relation is also found in the United States: 22 states, for example, prohibit marriage between a man and his stepdaughter.[31] Voltaire satirized French mores in his account of the difficulties experienced by a Huron Indian in attempting to marry his godmother, Mademoiselle de St. Yves.[32] To sum up, universal but differing incest taboos do not vindicate *our own* incest taboos, which are far from universal.

Some societies and family trees contain evidence of successful inbreeding of brothers, sisters, and parents. Brother-sister marriages were preferred in the Inca royal family and in the old Hawaiian aristocracy. Father-daughter intercourse has been practiced by Azande kings and the Thonga. A long-term institutionalized pattern of brother-sister, brother-half-sister, and father-daughter marriage persisted among Egyptian royalty and commoners from the fifteenth century B.C. through the second century A.D. Balinese permit twins to marry on the presumption that they have already been intimate in their mother's womb. Dobuans tolerate intercourse between sons and mothers, provided the father is dead. Many European aristocrats marry first cousins; commoners too—the Mozart family was very closely inbred. In some preliterate societies first cousin marriage is the formal rule; in others

[29] George Peter Murdock, *Social Structure*, The Macmillan Co., New York, 1949, p. 289.
[30] *Ibid.*, pp. 285 and 286.
[31] Alfred Louis Kroeber, *Anthropology*, Harcourt, Brace and Co., New York, 1948, pp. 399-400.
[32] François Marie Arouet de Voltaire, *L'ingénu*, Cramer, Geneva, 1767.

388 :: ISSUES AND PROBLEMS

even closer marriages are legitimate. "We cannot too strongly emphasize the fact that the varied forms incest regulations take are wholly cultural in nature, and have nothing to do with biological considerations."[33] Just how harmful, then, is inbreeding? The truth of the matter would seem to be that we know much less on this subject than we think.

A powerful and to many persons fully sufficient reason for incest taboos is the social one that the institution of the family is more easily preserved in its present form if incest is prohibited. Allowing sexual relations within the nuclear family and therefore sexual competition and jealousy might be seriously disruptive. The authority of the parent could break down, and interfamily conflicts might easily rise to such a level as to interfere with the performance of the family's societal functions. Taboos on inbreeding force people to marry outside the family, thus diffusing knowledge between families as well as binding them closer together, as among the Five Nations of the Iroquois. Since the family is our most important institution, anything that weakens it is dysfunctional both for the society and for its members. Structural-functional analysis identifies good sociological reasons for incest regulations; it should not be necessary to invent biological ones.

SOCIAL STRATIFICATION AND MARRIAGE NORMS

The interrelations between genetic selection and social organization are socially and demographically important. For illustration, let us first inspect marital structure and then turn to the effects of stratification systems on eugenics.

Although monogamy is a legitimate form of marriage in all societies, polygyny (a plurality of wives) is not only practiced in most but is more popular than monogamy in those societies where both forms exist.[34] Polyandry (a plurality of husbands) is too infrequent to be of much demographic consequence. Under polygyny, it is generally the more successful males who can afford the greater number of wives and hence have the most offspring. This situation may give rise to a favorable eugenic selection of the next generation. Under monogamy, successful men are limited in the number of children that they produce through having only one wife. The contrast between the two systems is not crucial for women. Thus (again assuming that success implies better parental prospects), the polygynous system offers better eugenic selection than monogamy.

A caste system is one which is closed to upward and downward

---

[33] Ralph L. Beals and Harry Hoijer, *An Introduction to Anthropology*, The Macmillan Co., New York, 1959, p. 476.
[34] Murdock, *Social Structure, op. cit.*, pp. 23-33.

mobility; everyone (or nearly everyone—no caste system is completely immobile) remains fixed in the position into which he is placed, usually at birth. A class system on the other hand does permit vertical mobility up and down the social ladder. In a caste system there is almost no recruitment of the most capable individuals into the elite group. There-fore the upper castes probably are not biologically superior, and inter-caste fertility differentials are irrelevant to eugenics. However, the lower standard of living and higher mortality commonly found in lower castes may make the society "eugenic in the brutal manner"—that is, the less desirable people die sooner than the desirable ones. (Nonetheless, there may be birth rate differentials between genetically different people within caste groups.) In sum, caste systems are probably neither eugenic nor dysgenic.

Open class systems normally presuppose considerable selection of the more intelligent and vigorous people into the higher classes. When the upper classes have higher fertility than the lower ones, eugenic selection takes place. However, in the United States (and elsewhere) it is the unsuccessful people who have the most children. Therefore scholars who do not want the next generation to be produced largely by failures write treatises advocating eugenic programs. Some people in this competitive society are successful largely because they are intelligent or ambitious enough to avoid saddling themselves with children; they realize that a large family is often an obstacle to success. And as long as national reproductive habits persist in supplying the lower classes with the most children, the result will be dysgenic. Ironically, the very openness of the stratification system, of which Americans are so proud, may be the cause. It should be stressed that these remarks assume that biological differences do play a part in the shifting of people into social classes; if this assumption is not met, these conclusions are unwarranted.

The preceding discussion considers population quality as the de-pendent variable and social stratification as the independent variable. Reversal of this causal chain also affords an instructive view. That is, if the upper class or caste has a very low fertility, it fails to reproduce it-self; and if the lower class or caste has a very high fertility, it comes to represent an increasingly large proportion of the population. This situation is not necessarily catastrophic. In fact, it may promote social mobility into the upper stratum, and if the successful strivers are Darwin's fittest specimens, the result is a continual refreshing and strengthening of the quality of the uppermost level by this vertical movement. But moving the "best genes" to the upper class thereupon may lower their fertility, to the disadvantage of the next generation. Conceivably, if a caste system had an extremely high negative correla-tion between caste level and natality, a change toward greater openness might be induced. To members of that caste society, this might indeed be a catastrophe; to Americans, of course, it would be a humanitarian refinement. This reasoning is purely conjectural, as verifying evidence is not available.

Birth and Death Control

Among the demographic variables, fertility is the main conscious and contentious concern of policy-makers, with migration, especially immigration, second in importance. Since almost everyone agrees to the desirability of lowering mortality and there is general agreement on the methods to do so, there is little discussion of death control policies.

Whatever the techniques, birth control is physically easier to manage than is death control. If there is any doubt about this, one need only consider how long mankind has been fighting mortality, with what unanimity and consistency, and using what scientific and religious weapons as compared to the relatively paltry scientific ingenuity and financial support which have gone into fertility control. Yet we are far closer to complete biological (though certainly not social) control over fertility than over mortality.

The demographic inflation consequent upon achievement of death control without birth control has been deplored by many, including Marriner S. Eccles, former chairman of the Board of Governors of the United States Federal Reserve System: "This situation has largely been brought about by our well-meant interference with the controlling laws of nature. From the most humanitarian motives we have drastically lowered the death rates, but have neglected to exert a compensating influence on the birth rates. Our policy has been to work for death control without taking the necessary steps to reduce the number of births, and so offset the consequent runaway inflation of people."

BIRTH CONTROL CONTROVERSY

Substantial disagreement exists regarding the legitimacy and necessity for separating sexual intercourse from impregnation and hence fertility. Traditional gentility abhors even acknowledging this issue, and world political, economic, and nutritional problems indite it.

The controversy rages among religious, scientific, and political personages. Views vary from those of Robert C. Cook, Director of the Population Reference Bureau: "Unless population growth is controlled in some underdeveloped countries, world chaos is inevitable"; and Sir Julian Huxley, former head of UNESCO: "Birth control is necessary, on a world scale and as soon as possible"; to those of the Roman Catholic Bishops of the National Catholic Welfare Conference:

"Artificial birth prevention is a morally, humanly, psychologically, and politically disastrous approach to the population problem"; and the Soviet delegate to a United Nations meeting: "The key to progress does not lie in a limitation of population through artificial reduction of the birth rate, but in the speedy defeat of the economic backwardness."[35] All four of these authorities agree on the presence of "the very real problem of population pressures."[36] The difference of opinion concerns the causes, seriousness, and solutions. Communists claim that overpopulation is really a capitalist plot to exploit the working classes. Roman Catholics decry the "hysterical terrorism of alarmists." Most biological and social scientists support a two-pronged thrust to raise the level of living through birth control and an increase in food and other resources. As Huxley says, if two weapons are available, why not use both?

Currently, birth control is the most controversial issue affecting demography. Ironically however, the controversy exists mainly outside of demography. Within the field itself, there is very little disagreement: the great majority of demographers favor planned parenthood through use of the most effective techniques available.

---

[35] Quoted in National Catholic Welfare Conference, "Explosion or Backfire?", November 26, 1959.
[36] *Ibid.*

18 ✕ National Policies

Population policy should not be confused with population theory and practice. A population practice is simply what people do. A population theory is what someone thinks causes people to act as they do. A population policy is what someone in authority thinks people ought to do and tries to implement. The three are sometimes independent of each other, sometimes interrelated. Government policy may be at variance with practice, perhaps because it does not rest on sound theoretical grounds. Or it may deliberately deviate from the practices of the citizenry.

Many practices are, inadvertently, policies. Cultural norms designed to achieve religious, economic, status, or other objectives often also have consequences for population size or composition—for example, preferential infanticide of female babies. Members of the society may be completely unaware that a given practice has demographic implications, in which case it is hardly appropriate to speak of population policy. But if the leaders are aware of these implications (even though laymen are not), we may consider the practice to be an indirect or partial population policy. In other cases leaders deliberately introduce a practice for demographic purposes without informing the people of their intent. Even today, but especially in the past, few individuals are fully aware of the demographic implications of their customs and institutions. To the ordinary citizen, folkways and mores (including those that are instruments for population control) represent merely the traditional, expected reactions of his group; the norms are conformed to without raising questions about their ramifications for social policy. Conversely, some practices controvert the normative policies—surreptitiously or openly, deliberately or unintentionally.

Population Control

"Ever since the dawn of history," writes demographer Warren S. Thompson, "there have been peoples who made more or less successful efforts to control population for the welfare of the community."[1] Their aims were usually quantitative, but a few societies did have qualitative goals, for example, Spartans exposed deformed infants. In many societies and normally in Western society, reproduction was not considered an individual concern. The nineteenth- and early twentieth-century American treatment of fertility as a purely personal matter which was "nobody else's business" was exceptional; ordinarily community feeling is a prime consideration. Now, in mid-twentieth century, rumblings about "social duty" and "civic responsibility" not to have too many children are beginning to be heard in the land.

Since the population of any area is determined by fertility, mortality, and migration, control of population must therefore take place through a manipulation of one or all of these three variables. When one studies population control, he should consider five facets:

1) control of what—total, components, characteristics?
2) to what ends—military, production, welfare?
3) by what means—fertility, mortality, migration?
4) in what direction—growth, decline, neither?
5) with what result—success, stalemate, failure?

LAWS AFFECTING POPULATION

In studying the laws which affect population, it is not sufficient to analyze only those that admit to being population policies. Demographic implications are present in a considerable variety of legislative enactments. Three kinds of laws have demographic significance: those determined entirely or in part by population, those indirectly affecting population, and those having a direct effect on population.[2] In the first category is legislation specifically enacted to cope with demographic phenomena, such as the aging of the population, ethnic compositon, population size, labor force composition, and geographic distribution. The second class consists principally of laws concerning marriage and the family, sexual relations, and economic matters—for example, minimum age at marriage, rights and privileges of illegitimate children, economic assistance for the family, legal obligations of the father to

---

[1] Warren S. Thompson, *Plenty of People*, The Ronald Press Co., New York, 1948, p. 232.
[2] Jacques Doublet, "Les lois dans leurs rapports avec la population," *Population*, Vol. IV, No. 1, January-March 1949, pp. 39-56.

support his family, divorce regulations, provision of housing for families, hereditary succession to family agricultural holdings, full employment laws, trade or commerce statutes affecting the labor force, certain agricultural legislation, laws establishing new cities or territories, and laws concerning the rights of women and children to work and to receive education. In the third category are laws directed toward mortality (sanitation, preventive medicine, and communicable diseases), natality (contraception, abortion, compulsory marriage, exemption of fathers from military service, and special employment privileges for fathers of large families), and migration (encouragement of immigrants of certain types, discouragement of others).

Enactment of a law is not necessarily evidence of pursuance of a given policy, even when the effect of that law on population is direct and obvious. Existence of legal provisions does not guarantee their enforcement. Generally there is here as elsewhere a gap between legal codes and actual practice. The discretionary powers of the courts also make caution necessary in drawing inferences from the letter of the law; legal interpretation is the prerogative of the court.[3] As regards the legislators themselves, they may or may not be aware of the demographic implications of the laws they enact. Many bills are so complicated that no one can foresee all of their repercussions. In other cases the consequences are there to see, but lawmakers have neither the knowledge nor time to trace them. In such situations laws designed for other purposes may have unintended but nonetheless real demographic results.

FREE ENTERPRISE AND SOCIALISM

The traditional and continuing lack of deliberate Federal population policy in the United States is a part of the conservative conviction that the less the government has to do with the actions of private persons, the better off will be the nation and its citizens. But decade by decade, this position becomes increasingly inconsistent with the facts as governmental authority extends into more areas of activity and modes of thought. The result is inconsistency. People fight socialized medicine, but take pride in the socialized water supply and sewage disposal systems. The Federal government operates the postal system, but the nationwide postal telegraph and telephone networks are handled privately. Americans subsidize shipbuilders, nationalize highways, and permit municipally owned and operated streetcars and subways, but oppose nationalization of railroads. Large corporations share in this

---

[3] United Nations Population Branch, *Survey of Legislation on Marriage, Divorce and Related Topics Relevant to Population*, New York, 1956, mimeographed, pp. 9-10.

confusion. "Every so often I hear my seniors at the corporation inveigh against socialism, and it seems strange. I think that our company resembles nothing so much as a private socialist system."[4] Social welfare policies are conceived and adopted by business concerns for the purpose of assuring security to both employees and the company—at the expense of individual responsibility and initiative.

United States laws having demographic import include the homestead laws which began in 1862 (having a strong effect on internal migration and urbanization); the exclusion and quota laws of 1882 and the 1920's (strong effect on immigration); child labor laws (moderate effect on mortality); anti-birth control laws (uncertain effect on fertility); marriage and divorce laws (strong influence on fertility); a spate of laws regarding sewage disposal, water supplies, quarantines, and other public health problems (strong effect on mortality); and the Social Security Act of 1935 and other social welfare legislation (strong but variable effect on fertility and mortality). Population composition or characteristics may be altered by racial segregation laws, unemployment insurance, public assistance for the needy, fair employment practices acts, free compulsory public education, and many other Federal and local statutes. Related but doubtfully potent for population trends are the income tax laws which began in 1913, food and drug laws, prohibition and repeal, the Mann Act, the death penalty, military conscription, and a host of other regulations. Any subject as fundamental as population is bound to be affected directly or indirectly by a wide range of ordinances, despite the fact that most of them were enacted with no intent or even realization of demographic repercussions. In sum, the United States has laws affecting population but no concerted population policy.

RELIGIOUS CONVICTIONS

Religious as well as political beliefs are intertwined with demographic policies. Theological dogmas contend that certain forms of birth control are immoral, or that particular techniques for death control are highly desirable, or that everyone has a God-given right to unimpeded migration. Few people are willing—or even desire—to fly in the face of such inbred doctrines. Just as there are no songs like the old songs, so there are no demographic practices like the ones of our formative years.

Religious feelings about marriage and sex run especially strong. Pope Pius XI said: "Since . . . the conjugal act is destined primarily by nature for the begetting of children, those who in exercising it deliberately

---

[4] Alan Harrington, *Life in the Crystal Palace*, Alfred A. Knopf, New York, 1959, p. 12.

frustrate its natural power and purpose sin against nature and commit a deed which is shameful and intrinsically vicious. Small wonder, therefore, if Holy Writ bear witness, that the Divine Majesty regards with greatest detestation this horrible crime and at times has punished it with death."[5]

Companionate marriage—deliberate childless marriages dissoluble at the wish of both parties without alimony or trial—was advocated by Judge Ben B. Lindsey in the 1920's. About the same time temporary or trial marriage was proposed by Bertrand Russell: "In a rational ethic, marriage would not count as such in the absence of children. . . . No marriage should be legally binding until the wife's first pregnancy."[6] Not surprisingly, proposals of this kind, running counter to existing mores, aroused much indignation, with the result that Lindsey was dismissed from his magistracy of the juvenile court in Denver and Russell's appointment at the College of the City of New York was revoked. Comments Alfred Kinsey: "Sex is so clearly a moral issue that many persons in the group consider it a religious obligation to impose their code upon all other segments of the population."[7]

Varieties of Policies

National population policies may be classified as expansive, restrictive, both, neither, or distributive. 1) Expansive policies operate through aids to child-bearing and rearing and subsidization of immigrants. 2) Restrictive policies embrace family planning and out-migration. 3) Both approaches are combined by some countries in a bipolar policy. 4) It is possible expressly to ignore the expansion-restriction dichotomy. 5) Policies may aim at altering the regional or rural-urban proportionment. Illustrations of the five viewpoints are to be seen, respectively, in France, the Netherlands, Great Britain, the United States, and the Soviet Union. These, as all, demographic policies operate through the three primary variables: fertility (as in the cases of pronatalist and antinatalist policies along with the sometimes demographically neutral family subsidies), mortality (and its ancillary variable, morbidity), and migration (both international and internal).

PRONATALIST

Most national policies have been directed toward increasing population growth. These pronatalist and pro-immigration policies are desired for

---

[5] Pope Pius XI, Encyclical *Casti Connubii* ("On Christian Marriage"), The Vatican, Rome, December 30, 1930, p. 17.

[6] Bertrand Russell, *Marriage and Morals*, Horace Liveright, New York, 1929, pp. 156 and 166; cf. also Benjamin B. Lindsey and Wainwright Evans, *The Companionate Marriage*, Boni and Liveright, New York, 1927.

[7] Alfred C. Kinsey, Wardell B. Pomeroy, and Clyde E. Martin, *Sexual Behavior in the Human Male*, W. B. Saunders Co., Philadelphia, 1948, p. 385.

such various purposes and feelings as military strength, economic production, national pride, and the like.

Once adopted, a pronatalist policy may be effectuated by at least three methods. The first is to accept existing values and attitudes and eliminate or diminish the economic liability of having children. Most pronatalist policies try to ease the economic disadvantages of parentage through the provision of cash, goods, schooling, or services. Major methods of distribution consist of cash grants to parents, graduation of wages according to family needs, graduated taxes according to family size, and free services such as public schools, medical and dental examinations, and milk for babies. (Even staunch conservatives often accept socialistic measures so long as they are confined to children.) Cash grants appear to be effective in influencing the lower and middle classes, but such economic rewards do not motivate the upper income groups, thus introducing the possibility of a dysgenic fertility pattern. Given enough subsidy, lower-class people might be able to make a reasonably good living by merely having children. (Conceivably a professional child-rearing class could arise, which might be an improvement over the present amateur, untrained parents.) In short, such economic policies do influence the value system: the more economic support governments give, the more they may break down existing values and social institutions.

A second approach which has been used to effectuate pronatalist policy is to try to modify the norms by glorifying values concerning reproduction. Leaders institute advertising campaigns championing pregnancy, medals for mothers, and other noneconomic rewards. Hitler tried this, with inconclusive success. Rulers might also take advantage of the fashion element of fertility: have children because the neighbors are having them, or go them one better. Legal moves include lowering the minimum age for marriage and reinstating the old custom of divorce on grounds of infertility.

Relaxing the taboos on illegitimacy is a third possibility. The Nazis also used this method, extolling the German Aryan mother even if she were not married. However, many cultures contain such well-entrenched opposing mores that the program would be virtually defeated before it began. Even today fear of the consequences of removal of stigma from "love babies" leads many people to refuse to accord illegitimate children equality of treatment.

All three of these methods have been adopted at one time or another, and often together. Hitler tried them all simultaneously. The first approach commits the government to considerable expenditure of money, but legislators are able to convince themselves and their constituents that they are not tampering with citizens' beliefs. In the second case, existing pronatalist attitudes need to be strengthened and new ones formed, which requires such techniques as advertising, indoctrination, and brainwashing; money is spent, but not directly for children. The third possibility involves both money and deliberate value formation; if such a campaign is effective, the government must be prepared to bear the cost of rearing resultant illegitimate offspring.

ANTINATALIST

Birth limitation policies can be attempted via changes in the normative structure in somewhat the same fashion as for the pronatalist policies, or by relying on various birth control methods. Scientists are now within striking distance of the ideal contraceptive: one that is inexpensive, simple to use, long-lasting, nonirritating, applied at a time remote from the sexual act, and easy for governments to administer in mass campaigns.

John Stuart Mill wanted the English Parliament to change the normative structure through legislation: "No advance in public morality can be looked for until numerous families come to be regarded with the same contempt as drunkenness and other corporeal excesses. The moral obligation not to have too many children could, if the case called for it, be changed into a legal obligation."[8] Mill's youthful attempts to distribute birth control literature to working-class readers brought him before a magistrate. But although he ceased disseminating leaflets, he remained throughout his life an unrepentant advocate of neo-Malthusianism. Dr. B. L. Raina, Secretary of the Central Family Planning Board of the Indian Ministry of Health, favors gradualism: "My motto is, let the whole country hum with family planning, but it takes time and patience to change the mores of a people as numerous as ours. . . . We must create a demand for family planning—and then provide the services."

The policy of deliberately limiting fertility has two especially well-intentioned, well-organized, and powerful opponents—the Communist Party and the Roman Catholic Church. Interpretation of birth control as "an instrument by which imperialist capitalist powers attempt to achieve their objective of subduing and exploiting the 'have not' peoples of the world, is one that the U.S.S.R., rich in land and resources, can probably afford for the time being. But the quite different situation of China led her recently to break with the U.S.S.R. on this position, and although China's stand on birth control is ambiguous at

---

[8] John Stuart Mill, *Principles of Political Economy*, London, 1857, Vol. I, pp. 362-363.

present, this may well be one of the policies over which China will part
company with the U.S.S.R."[9] Catholic values influence policy—sometimes effectively, sometimes not—in the United States, France, India,
and many other countries.

FAMILY SUBSIDIES

Advocacy of governmental assistance to families may be motivated
by one or more of four principles: the belief that the "natural" unit of
society is not the individual but the family, the egalitarian conviction
that all children are entitled to equal portions of the world's goods, the
welfare assumption that children of large families often need help, and
fear concerning declining national fertility levels.[10] Only the last of
these motives is explicitly demographic, but demographic results may
flow from any of the four stances.

Conviction of governmental responsibility in matters concerning the
family has spread to the point where "more than half of the world's
sovereign nations now have constitutions that carry some recognition of
'social rights' as distinct from personal or individuals rights and make
some commitment with respect to family security or social security or
both. These 47 countries are distributed as follows: 20 in Europe (including the U.S.S.R.); 18 in North and South America; 9 in Asia."[11]
Family or children's allowances have had a rapid development following their introduction as national laws by New Zealand in 1926 and
Belgium in 1930 (many countries had such schemes for limited segments of the populace at earlier dates). A quarter century later, forty
other countries had joined the first pair. Today every European country
except the Federal Republic of Germany has adopted family subsidies.[12]
The universal purpose of the subsidies is the betterment of living
conditions of children by setting a minimum standard that will be
ensured regardless of family income or unemployment. They nearly
always take the form of cash payments scaled according to the number
of children in the family. Often services (concerning health, housing,
education, and the like) are provided. Sometimes (but not usually) the
grants are withheld from families with only one or two children. In a
few countries the amount supplied increases progressively with parity,
but usually a flat rate applies. Generally the amount is too small to bring

[9] Philip M. Hauser, *Population Perspectives*, Rutgers University Press, New
Brunswick, 1960, pp. 163-164.
[10] William Petersen, "Family Subsidies in the Netherlands," *Marriage and Family
Living*, Vol. XVII, August 1955, pp. 260-266.
[11] Hope T. Eldridge, *Population Policies*, International Union for the Scientific
Study of Population, Washington, 1954, pp. 21-23.
[12] *Ibid.*, p. 26.

out the profit motive—and consequent rises in the birth rate. Occasionally the size of the allowance is scaled according to family income. Some countries grant bonuses or long-term loans to enable young people to marry early.

Functional analysis of reproductive outcomes of welfare measures has exposed a possible unanticipated consequence, one which Kingsley Davis noted as far back as 1937:

> Undoubtedly, as many people fear, some families at the bottom of the social scale (and perhaps others) would find this a delightfully easy method of earning a livelihood. Now see what would happen. The Government would meet this situation by commanding that persons who live by producing children must prove their fitness. It would thereby produce, gradually and probably unwittingly, a new profession —the profession of child-bearing. It would take only one step more to introduce required training for the professional child-rearers, thus elevating both the standards and the social status of this occupational group. With training there would come specialization. The different subsidiary functions in the creation of new citizens would be taken over by specialized groups within the profession. Some women would merely *bear* children, others would care for them physically, others would educate them. Thus, by a gradual evolution unforeseen at the start, the use of monetary rewards for having children would lead to a system in which the father's role is assumed by the state, the mother's role by professional women paid by the state for their services. A new kind of reproductive organization compatible with modern society would have been substituted for the family.[13]

The family has in fact lost many functions it formerly held. We entrust the plastic minds of our children to outsiders (for example, schoolteachers), and we have willingly and occasionally even enthusiastically abandoned other once familial functions to such nonfamilial groups as the church and the employer. What would happen if a nation set up a group of professional childbearers (of exceptional physique, intelligence, and personality) and professional child-rearers who would be trained for the job and who could be fired for neglecting the children or deliberately mistreating them? Although this interesting speculation is not a likely policy in the United States, many local communities do have all-day nurseries for children of working mothers, and Americans show signs of heading toward widespread adoption of the Swedish and Israeli practices of sending children to week-long nurseries and schools.

---

[13] Kingsley Davis, "Reproductive Institutions and the Pressure for Population," *Sociological Review*, Vol. XXIX, July 1937, pp. 289-306.

MORTALITY

Mortality and morbidity control favoring long life are now taken for granted, but world history is replete with instances of dysfunctional attitudes toward death and sickness. "There are situations in which, by definite social prescription, death or physical injury is required. More numerous are the situations in which, though not planned that way, the individual is forced by rivalry and mental conflict to injure his own health or take his life. Still more frequent are the situations in which the aim is to promote health but the result, through superstition and error, is to accomplish exactly the opposite. And innumerable are the situations in which actions regarded as irrelevant to health nevertheless injure it."[14] Illustrations are easy to find: suttee in India, harakiri in Japan, war everywhere, blood-letting in Europe, faith healing, quack doctors, many patent medicines in the United States, ceremonial sacrifices in many societies, tight corsets on Victorian women, and polished rice in the Orient.

Mortality policies occasionally are consciously negative. The most sweeping such policy ever conceived is genocide, the killing of whole groups of people. The word was coined to describe the liquidation of the Jews by Hitler, though similar attempts to eliminate unwanted groups had been made before. On a smaller scale is the killing of individuals judged to have undesirable attributes. Societies eliminate certain criminal offenders by capital punishment, a retribution for breach of the law. In such cases as infanticide of deformed neonates, killing of infirm aged, destruction of feeble-minded and crippled adults, and liquidation of ideological deviants, the society is supposedly strengthened by the action. The United States condones the public taking of life as punishment for misdeeds but abhors any such action taken in the interests of the betterment of the group.

HEALTH AND SICKNESS

Accompanying a concern with mortality are programs designed to curb illness and its social and economic after-effects. Many countries have national boards of health which attempt to eliminate or reduce un-healthful conditions. In addition, local health offices work toward improving sanitation, applying preventive medicine, teaching better habits of personal hygiene, and immunizing the populace. This type of public health movement began in mid-nineteenth-century Europe.

Compulsory health insurance has been adopted in Germany (1883), Austria (1888), all other European countries except Spain, all Latin

---

[14] Kingsley Davis, *Human Society*, The Macmillan Co., New York, 1949, p. 564.

American nations, and several other states. Subsidization of health societies began in Italy in 1886, Sweden in 1891, Denmark in 1892, and Belgium in 1894. Complete health care has been tried in the U.S.S.R., Great Britain, and other countries.

In America, however, resistance to such programs has won the day. Though proud of their socialized highway and education systems, Americans so far have rejected socialized medicine—except for children and members of the Armed Services. A health insurance bill resembling the British system and promoted by the Association for Labor Legislation was passed in the New York State Senate in 1919, but it failed in the Assembly on the grounds that it was too expensive and that our late enemies, the Germans, were doing the same thing. The United States remains "the only great industrial country without a compulsory nation-wide program of health insurance or sickness benefits. Costs of sickness and medical service in the nation are met largely by consumers. . . . There is ample evidence, however, of a shift of public opinion toward handling medical care as a predictable and insurable risk and collective responsibility."[15]

Americans elect rather to join individual and group health insurance programs offered largely by Blue Cross-Blue Shield and other insurance companies. During the last two decades prepayment plans covering hospital, surgical, and other medical expenses have gained widespread public favor. The percentage of United States civilians covered by these programs has increased as follows: hospital—10 per cent in 1940, 50 per cent in 1950, and 73 per cent in 1960; surgical—4 per cent in 1940, 36 per cent in 1950, and 67 per cent in 1960; regular medical— 2 per cent in 1940, 14 per cent in 1950, and 49 per cent in 1960; major medical—less than 1 per cent in 1940 and 1950, 15 per cent in 1960.[16] The readiness of the public to enroll in these programs is often offered as evidence that they might shortly have accepted government health insurance had private systems not been developed. Many employers today pay one-half or even all of the monthly premiums. And although these programs are ostensibly voluntary, some of the insuring companies offer lower premiums to groups in which 100 or 75 per cent of the employees enroll, thus creating a powerful group pressure on recalcitrant workers who prefer the pay-as-you-go system. Under these conditions, personnel officers and bosses are tempted to coerce refractory individualists who take their old-line capitalism seriously.

---

[15] Wladimir S. Woytinsky and Emma S. Woytinsky, *World Population and Production*, Twentieth Century Fund, New York, 1953, p. 238.

[16] Health Information Foundation, "The Growth of Voluntary Health Insurance," *Progress in Health Services*, Vol. X, No. 9, November 1961, pp. 1-2.

INTERNATIONAL MIGRATION

Restrictions on migration are increasing as governments institute additional rules limiting both entry into and exit from their domains. Moreover, we can expect migration policies to be even more restrictive through the rest of this century, although some form of international organization may eventually become powerful enough to tear down the thick legislative walls now facing anyone who wants to cross an international boundary.

The International Labour Office and the United Nations-sponsored organizations founded to help displaced persons after World War II are steps in this direction. The I.L.O. is permanent and antedates the United Nations. Founded in 1919 with headquarters in Geneva, Switzerland, it has some 80 member countries and became allied with the United Nations in 1946. Its purposes are to collect and disseminate information about labor and social conditions throughout the world and to formulate international labor standards and supervise their application in various countries. Specifically, it has prompted the adopting of workmen's compensation laws in 38 countries, health insurance in 30 countries, unemployment compensation in 14 countries, old-age insurance in 36 countries, and family allowance plans in 17 countries. Although its main interest is in labor conditions, this organization does have some involvement in international migration.

INTERNAL MIGRATION

Migration policies may be internal as well as external. The Russians, for example, have moved millions of people within their domain—a policy of governmental control over population distribution in sharp contrast with United States policy, which regards internal migration as a constitutional privilege not easily withdrawn. Nonetheless, occasional states in this country have imposed restrictions on movement across their boundaries, usually in an effort to keep out "undesirables."

The most glaring exception to this Federal laissez-faire policy has been the government's treatment of the American Indian. During most of its existence, the United States has moved the Indian population into those sections of the country that the whites do not want. Indians have had particular trouble in maintaining their rights to land "given" to them and then taken away (the white man's version of Indian giving) when the land was found to be more desirable than had been thought at the time of ceding. Witness the struggle between the Paiutes and Italian-American settlers in Nevada over water rights; Senator McCarran supported the squatting of the whites on Indian land and aided these modern "Sooners" in their attempts to drive out the

Indians by causing their cattle to die of thirst. The Bureau of Indian Affairs, a Federal agency, established relocation centers in major cities to promote the movement of Indians from reservations into metropolitan areas; this policy, however, has been disastrously ineffectual, which is not surprising in view of the grossly inadequate resources of thought, personnel, and money made available. The Federal program for Indians, in spite of some improvements beginning in the 1930's, has been one of the sorriest accomplishments of the nation. Indeed, foreign newspapers which complain of mistreatment of the Negro could make a much better case for the "poor red man."

Governmental Action in Industrial Countries

Although industrial countries have policies concerning mortality and migration, it is fertility which receives the greatest attention. Recent policies are exemplified by Hitler's pronatalism, French family subsidies, Swedish welfare and egalitarian measures, the generally "hands-off" United States attitude, the heavy-handed Soviet stand, Japan's antinatalism, and Australia's immigration program.

GERMANY

German demographic policy under Hitler was definitely pronatalist. Negative birth stimulants—prohibiting abortion and making it difficult to obtain contraceptive advice and devices—restricted the practice of birth control. Positive economic measures—marriage loans, family allowances, and remission of taxes—relieved the financial burden of rearing a family. And psychological conditioning—talk of the spiritual rebirth of the "master race," stress upon the function of women as mothers—encouraged favorable attitudes toward large families.

The success of these methods was uncertain. The crude birth rate did rise enormously after 1933, but the rise might have been a consequence of economic recovery rather than Hitler's population policy. Since fertility at any given time is partially a result of past fertility (in other words, the 1935 birth rate is not independent of the 1930 birth rate), it might be that the German rate increased because it had recently been low—that is, in 1935 people might have had children that had been postponed in 1930. In addition, the size of completed families did not show much change, indicating that family-building habits may have remained substantially the same. Also, the increased fertility came from first, second, and third births.[17]

---

[17] John Hajnal, "The Analysis of Birth Statistics in the Light of the Recent International Recovery of the Birth Rate," *Population Studies*, Vol. I, No. 2, September 1947, pp. 144-150.

In sum, then, we cannot state definitely that these policies either increased or decreased fertility. Nor without experimental control, which would require comparison of German experience with that of another country similar to Germany that did not adopt these pronatalist policies, can we say conclusively that they had no effect at all on natality.

FRANCE

French policy, though also pronatalist, differs in rationale and expression from the policies of Hitler and Mussolini. Though predominantly Catholic, France was the first nation to show the substantial decline in fertility characteristic of the transition to the new balance and small family system. In the period between the two World Wars, fertility fell so low as to inspire Joseph J. Spengler to call a book *France Faces Depopulation*—a title which hardly anyone then found unreasonable. The net reproduction rate hovered just above 1.00 in the 1800's, plunged below replacement in 1890, fell to .59 in the war years 1916-1920, and stood at .95 in 1921-1925, .92 in 1926-1930, .90 in 1931-1935, and .80 in 1936-1939.[18] More recently Spengler wrote: "For at least three quarters of a century the Devil of Declining Growth has been present at French council tables, at policy-making conferences, and in the minds of strategically situated decision makers. The Devil has not always been present in the flesh, since that is not the way of devils. But he has always been at the shoulders of the holders of power, and they have usually taken him into account implicitly when not explicitly."[19]

As far back as the reign of Louis XIV, comptroller-general Jean Baptiste Colbert included population measures in his sweeping reform of French finances. Edicts of 1666 and 1667 granted partial tax exemption for early marriage, life-time exemption to fathers of ten children, and pensions for men with twelve children or ten legitimate children. Immigration was encouraged, and emigration prohibited on penalty of death. After Colbert's death in 1683, these edicts were revoked, and for a long time thereafter population policy efforts were sporadic.[20] The Franco-Prussian War, which stimulated nationalistic discussion, may have been a factor in bringing about adoption of the child and maternal welfare laws of the 1870's, including child labor statutes, extension of public education, public aid to pregnant women, and "suckling bonuses for those who nursed their children."

---

[18] Alfred Sauvy, *Richesse et population*, Payot, Paris, 1943, p. 225.
[19] Joseph J. Spengler, "Notes on France's Response to Her Declining Rate of Demographic Growth," *Journal of Economic History*, Vol. XI, Fall 1951, p. 403.
[20] Frederick Osborn, *Preface to Eugenics*, Harper and Brothers, New York, 1951, p. 205.

Family allowances began privately with a Family Fund established in a factory in 1854. In the period of rising prices between 1917 and 1932, payment of salary supplements to employees with families spread throughout French industry, partly to reduce labor turnover and partly to permit families to maintain a standard of living roughly comparable to that of childless employees. Although the intended effect of these supplements on the birth rate may at first have been somewhat incidental, by the time the family allowance movement was taken under the government's wing in 1932, stimulation of births had become a central motive and was a major force in gaining official approval of the system.

The French Government Act of 1932 provided for gradual extension of the industrial system to all occupations, including farm labor. The French Family Code of 1939 completed extension of the system to all families and provided for payment of a lump sum for first children equal to two months' salary for the average industrial worker, graduated continuing allowances for second and subsequent children, and additional allowances to mothers with young children. The head of a family of four children received, on the average, a monthly allowance equalling 60 per cent of his basic earnings. This money was paid out of a family allowance fund to which the wage-earners contributed, with provision for government subsidy in regions where the drain was excessive. A 1947 study reported that among couples in which wives had not been working before the advent of children, the level of living changed very little with the arrival of offspring. Since family allowances contribute an income increment almost proportionate to the increased family needs introduced by the addition of children, the level of living of a family with four children, for instance, is reduced only to 89 per cent of that of a childless couple.[21] There are other aids to large families, including a law protecting employed women against discharge from jobs upon confinement, but the distinctive attribute of French policy is the family allowance system.

Availability of birth control knowledge and devices is deliberately restricted by laws such as the one subjecting birth control propagandists to fines. However, these laws are ineffective, and contraception materials are widely sold under the guise of preventing venereal disease.

Private organizations lobby for pronatalist assistance. The National Alliance for the Increase of the French Population was established in 1896, and in 1921 some one hundred small pronatalist groups formed the Federation of Associations of Large Families of France. The chronically rampant French chauvinism (after all, Chauvin was a soldier

[21] *Ibid.*, p. 209.

of Napoleon) is manifested in the exuberant sensationalism of the Association's monthly newspaper.

So far the effect of these measures on the birth rate is not known, having been obscured by the drastic changes of the depression, World War II, and recent economic and political disturbances.

SWEDEN

Whereas German policies are representative of measures adopted by authoritarian governments without regard for the civil rights of their citizens, in Sweden policies were developed by social scientists under governmental sponsorship motivated by fear of population loss but never forgetting demographic principles. Moreover, Hitler's motives were expansionistic, whereas Sweden's leaders desired a stationary population. That Sweden had avoided war for more than a century contributed to a popular psychology of peaceful normality. "Particularly important in explaining the psychology of the 1930's, during which social policy made its most rapid advances, is the fact that an extreme trust in national security was to be discerned in Scandinavia while all the rest of Europe lived in a state of war scare."[22]

Modern Swedish population policy began in 1935 with the appointment of a nine-member Royal Commission.[23] The government, fearful of an impending population decline, charged the commission with the task of examining the facts and issues scientifically preparatory to passing legislation. A second Population Commission, appointed in 1941, was assigned the task of formulating practical proposals for transferring substantial parts of the costs of rearing children away from the family and onto the nation. Among the measures proposed were marriage loans and loans to individuals with university training; free delivery care and comprehensive maternity benefits; grants in aid for family expenses such as rent, food, medicine, and clothing; and spread of knowledge about birth control techniques (about 60 per cent of married couples had been using only coitus interruptus). In this way the cost of bearing children and much of that of rearing them was borne by the central government. Today these proposals have been modified and the intent is overtly neither pronatalist nor antinalist, but the welfare program is so solidly established that no political party would dare criticize the principle (although there are occasional outbursts against its administration).

---

[22] Alva Myrdal, *Nation and Family*, Kegan Paul, Trench, Trubner, and Co., London, 1945, p. 11.

[23] Halvor Gille, "Recent Developments in Swedish Population Policy," *Population Studies*, Vol. II, No. 1, June 1948, pp. 3-70; and Vol. II, No. 2, September 1948, pp. 129-184.

These provisions, which absorb over 10 per cent of the national income (but less than one-half of the expenditures for military defense), include free lunches for school children, free dental care for all children, hospitalization at a total cost averaging fifty cents a day, free medical examinations and confinement for expectant mothers, subsidized maternity and infant homes, free travel and inexpensive annual vacations at resorts for mothers and children, a cash maternity allowance, and a yearly cash allowance. In this context, a child is defined as anyone below age 16.

Birth control information is openly supplied to both adults and adolescents. Sex education is scheduled in all high schools. Contraception advice is offered when requested at Maternity Welfare Centers and by district medical officers, midwives, and nurses. Advertising of contraceptives is prohibited by law, but there is little religious resistance against their use, and pharmacies routinely supply them.[24]

The salient characteristic of this program is its objective of allowing people as much choice as possible regarding having children. People who want children but who cannot afford them are given money and services; people who do not want children but who do not know how to prevent them are given information and equipment for contraception; people who want and who can afford children, along with those who have both the knowledge and desire to avoid offspring, may keep their existing preferences and practices. The chief goal is to minimize the differences in living standards so that all children (and mothers) will have the same opportunity for comforts and health, regardless of the size of the family. Swedish policy assumes that parenthood should be voluntary—in both directions.

The effect of all these provisions on the marriage and birth rates cannot be definitively ascertained. Gunnar Myrdal, one of the architects of the program, comments: "It must be remembered that this question is not a crucial one for the type of family reforms here envisaged as constituting the economic ingredients in democratic population policy. The reforms are primarily motivated as investments in the happiness, health, and productive quality of the rising generation and should from this point of view be undertaken even if their quantitative effects upon the population trend were slight."[25]

UNITED STATES

The United States has no deliberate fertility policy of any consequence. Nor has it had concerted policies in the past—although through most

---

[24] Gunnar af Geijerstam, "Abortion in Sweden," in Mary Steichen Calderone (ed.), *Abortion in the United States*, Harper and Brothers, New York, 1958, p. 29.
[25] Gunnar Myrdal, *Population: A Problem for Democracy.* Harvard University Press, Cambridge, 1940, p. 216.

of its history there has been a wandering theme of expansionism. Supporters of General John C. Frémont in the 1856 Presidential campaign ridiculed James Buchanan's bachelor status with the song lyric: "Old bachelors are low in rate; they'd never populate a state!" (We cannot be sure, however, whether Buchanan's victory should be attributed to lack of popular pronatalist sentiment or to the public's good taste in music.) President Eisenhower said: "I cannot imagine anything more emphatically a subject that is not a proper political or governmental activity or function or responsibility. . . . This government has no, and will not . . . as long as I am here, have a positive political doctrine in its program that has to do with this problem of birth control. That's not our business."[26] This laissez-faire approach represents the prevailing opinion that if people are left alone, the country will continue to grow as it should.

Be that as it may, an over-all increase is generally preferred. Federal and local governmental agencies have (usually inadvertently and never systematically) provided slight demographic propulsion through such welfare programs as socialized education, community-sponsored child care, subsidized housing, income tax exemptions for dependents, and free land for Western settlers. But few of these actions have been demographic in intent or in effects.

An exception is the "keep America for Americans" *soi-disant* policy of discouraging the arrival of "dirty" immigrants and pushing the Indians into the less-favored hinterland. "The nation was barely founded before a Congressman rose to say on the floor of the House of Representatives in 1797 that while a liberal immigration policy was satisfactory when the country was new and unsettled, now that the United States had reached maturity and was fully populated, further immigration should be stopped. . . . In 1921, the Immigration Committee of the House of Representatives again recommended complete termination of all immigration."[27] Perhaps the words of Emma Lazarus graven in the pedestal of the Statue of Liberty meant nothing more to most people than a schoolteacher's shibboleth.

Yet the time for demographic inaction may have passed. As Philip Hauser cautions: "The facts for the United States indicate explosive growth with crisis implications. . . . It would not be sound national policy to maintain our present national rate of increase indefinitely, as it would double our population about every 40 years."[28] Given present

---

[26] President Dwight D. Eisenhower, news conference, Washington, December 2, 1959, reported in *The New York Times*, Vol. CIX, No. 37,203, December 3, 1959, p. 18.
[27] President's Commission on Immigration and Naturalization, *Whom We Shall Welcome*, Government Printing Office, Washington, 1953, p. 27.
[28] Hauser, *Population Perspectives, op. cit.*, p. 168.

mortality, a drastically lowered fertility would be needed to produce a stationary population. Hauser goes on to ask:

> How is our birth rate to be further reduced? The answer is, of course, by a continuation on a larger scale of the policies and behavior which already characterize the reproductive practices of the American people. Our present birth rate, well below its historical levels, is the result of voluntary planned parenthood, of individual couples deliberately restricting the number of their offspring. To dampen the present explosive rate of United States population growth, birth control methods must be somewhat more widely employed than is already the case.[29]

The Federal and local governments are faced with three kinds of options regarding birth control: they can be restrictive, permissive, or encouraging. Thus far most legislation has been restrictive, prohibiting or limiting dissemination of advice, sale of contraceptive supplies, and so forth. As regards the permissive and encouraging positions, many people fail to see the difference between the two. A government encourages birth control when it uses public funds actively to promote that end; it is permissive when it allows private organizations to manufacture, advertise, and sell contraceptive equipment but does not itself engage in these activities. Both proponents and opponents of birth control tend to equate this permissive moderate attitude with the stand opposite their own, following the time-honored conviction that "If you're not with me, you're agin' me." United States governmental agencies are often restrictive, sometimes laissez-faire, and occasionally encouraging. If one accepts the doctrine that decisions concerning birth control belong to the individual, then the middle or hands-off policy seems most appropriate.

Table 32 summarizes traditional and contemporary governmental positions regarding population. Virtually no one favors deliberately

TABLE 32. *United States Governmental Attitudes Regarding Population*

ISSUE	RESTRICTIVE	Type of Attitude PERMISSIVE	PROMOTIONAL	EXTENT OF AGREEMENT
Low mortality	Rare	Former	Present	Almost unanimous
Birth control	Former and present	Present and near future	Distant future?	Strong controversy
International migration	Present	Former	Former	Mild controversy
Internal migration	Rare	Former and present	Rare	General agreement

[29] *Ibid.*, p. 170.

raising mortality or even leaving it undisturbed (though a few sects occasionally resist efforts of physicians); authorities are nearly unanimous in attempting to lower death and sickness rates—though a noninterference policy was once prevalent. Actions concerning fertility vary from state to state. No state actively encourages a high birth rate, but some have passed and continue to enforce legislation making it difficult for individuals to practice birth control; other states permit use or nonuse of birth control techniques, leaving the decision to the discretion of the individual. Immigration is restricted by quotas unknown a century ago, and emigration too is under governmental control; formerly, both entering and leaving the country were simply matters of raising passage money and boarding a ship. Except for such unusual instances as Californians refusing admittance of "Okies" in the 1930's and southern "state sovereignty commissions" impeding departure of Negroes during and before the 1960's, internal migration has been accepted as a birthright not to be disturbed. The general trend, however, is toward increasing government intervention with respect to all three demographic variables, especially mortality and migration. Contemporary portents permit the envisaging of governmental compulsions toward long life and limited migration—for example, compulsory inoculations, reporting of diseases, and quarantines (as at present); and controls over immigration (as at present), emigration (increasing present restrictions), and internal redistribution (a political bombshell).

U.S.S.R.

Government policy in the Soviet sphere contrasts sharply with that of the United States. It too is not always consistent, but it is always there. "Demographic movements, more directly mortality and migration, and less directly, fertility, are dominated by direct government intervention on a scale far exceeding that in the West. Such intervention introduces an essential predictability and regularity to demographic movements with a proviso, however, that discontinuous changes may take place suddenly."[30]

Russian population policies have varied with shifts in political power. For three years after the 1917 revolution the U.S.S.R. followed the Tsarist tradition. Then in 1920 abortions were legalized, primarily (according to statements made at the time) to protect the lives and health of women who were determined to end their pregnancies by abortion. A Soviet woman could have a cost-free abortion virtually on demand—

---

[30] Demitri B. Shimkin, "Demographic Changes and Socio-Economic Forces within the Soviet Union, 1939-1959," in Milbank Memorial Fund, *Population Trends in Eastern Europe, The USSR and Mainland China,* New York, 1960, p. 245.

and many did, particularly residents of cities. In 1935 about 150,000 abortions were recorded in Moscow—more than twice the 70,000 live births. Both Moscow and Leningrad had hospitals called Abortariums.

Worries over the low birth rate and consequent slow rate of population increase were among the reasons that led Russian leaders to revoke legalization of abortions in 1936 (except where pregnancy constituted a serious threat to the health or life of the woman). Thereafter the birth rate rose rapidly, though the influence of the prohibition of abortion remains uncertain. An American physician visiting Russia in 1934 reported "a very intensive movement all over Russia to try to fight the abortion evil by disseminating information on contraception, and in most of the hospitals I visited, especially in the gynecological departments, there were large posters on the walls which read, 'Go to the prophylactic center (the birth control clinic) and avoid abortions.' "[31]

In 1955 abortion was once more legalized by the Presidium of the Supreme Soviet with the proclamation that the efforts of the government to increase maternity had been so successful that the ban on abortion could be abolished completely. However, operations can be performed only in public clinics. Results of this new dispensation are as yet indeterminable.

Soviet interest in contraception appears to be limited to its value in controlling abortions. Their over-all attitude is pronatalist.

In 1936 the U.S.S.R. adopted a family allowance program of payments to mothers of seven or more children, a policy which was extended in 1944 to cover three or more children. This elaborate and expensive system includes maternity bonuses, monthly allowances, and a graduated schedule of honors. Mothers of five living children (or of children who died in military service) receive a motherhood medal, second class. For ten living or war-dead children, women are awarded the Order of Mother Heroine (Gold Star), plus a scroll from the Presidium of the Supreme Soviet. Unmarried mothers receive larger payments than do married ones to compensate for the absence of the husband's income. Men between the ages of 20 and 50 and women between 20 and 45 who have fewer than three children must pay special taxes. The 1944 Edict also provided for nursery schools and made divorce more difficult to obtain.[32] Payments under the program in 1947 amounted to slightly more than one per cent of the total national budget. One American demographer complains: "The whole scheme is

[31] Abraham Stone, "Abortion in the U.S.S.R.," in Calderone, *Abortion in the United States, op. cit.,* pp. 207-208.
[32] W. Parker Mauldin, "Fertility Control in Communist Countries: Policy and Practice," in Milbank Memorial Fund, *Population Trends in Eastern Europe, the USSR and Mainland China, op. cit.,* pp. 209-215.

a blatant pro-natalist program, rather than a plan designed to meet the economic needs of families. Though alleged welfare goals are emphasized in the preface of the Edict, one of its stated goals is 'to encourage large families.' . . . Even the celebrated pro-natalist measures of Mussolini and Hitler were hardly so blatant."[33]

The exceedingly restrictive Soviet policy concerning international migration—both inward and outward—is well known. Flight abroad, considered high treason, is punishable by death, confiscation of property, or ten years imprisonment. Internal migration is also under close governmental surveillance. Forced internal redistribution is common.

In view of the firm though changeful policies taken by Soviet authorities in dealing with fertility and migration (they have been even firmer regarding mortality, but since their attitude has consistently resembled that of any other nation—holding the death rate to a minimum—it need not be discussed), it may be somewhat difficult to accept Stalin's denial of the importance of population as a determinant of the character of the social system or the level of economic development. Moreover, he avowedly favored an increasing population. Present-day Russian leaders argue that seeming overpopulation is a capitalist plot: there is and could be no overpopulation problem in the U.S.S.R. In 1958 Premier Khrushchev stated the official attitude toward population growth: "Bourgeois ideology invented many cannibalistic theories, among them the theory of overpopulation. Their concern is to cut down the birth rate, reduce the rate of population increase. It is quite different with us, comrades. If about 100 million people were added to our 200 million, even that would not be enough."[34]

JAPAN

Japan suffers from an acute population problem. From 35 million in 1872 and 70 million in 1935, the population climbed to 92 million in 1958, making Japan the fifth largest nation in the world. On a group of small islands are concentrated several of the world's largest cities. Furthermore, Japan's agricultural density is extremely high. The overall national density is exceeded only by the Netherlands, Belgium, and Taiwan. "Japan is undoubtedly the most overpopulated great and powerful country there has ever been."[35]

The Japanese government, recognizing this problem, is taking steps to control it. A bulletin circulated on October 27, 1954, by the Japanese

---

[33] Frank Lorimer, "Population Policy and Politics in the Communist World," in Philip M. Hauser (ed.), *Population and World Politics*, The Free Press, Glencoe, 1958, pp. 224-225.

[34] Nikita S. Khrushchev, Radio Moscow Broadcast to Southeast Asia, July 4, 1958.

[35] Political and Economic Planning, *World Population and Resources*, George Allen and Unwin, London, 1955, p. 150.

Embassy in Washington admitted that the population problem under-
lies all vital issues confronting modern Japan. In 1949 a Population
Problems Council was formed within the Japanese Cabinet, and currently two agencies in the Ministry of Health are engaged in population research.

In Japan abortion is legal and bears no stigma. Abortionists (physicians) are licensed by the government, and their fees are small; if
the family is too destitute to afford the several dollars charge, the state
sometimes pays it; many factories and other employers pay for an
abortion in the interest of improving the worker's morale. Remembering
Hiroshima, one Japanese observed: "A people which has had the opportunity of experiencing at first hand the full expression of modern
warfare will not be too compunctious over the removal of a few grams
of protoplasm from the uterus." Since 1953 reported abortions have
exceeded a million a year; the national total may surpass 2 million
annually (about the number of live births).

The government is also endeavoring to popularize contraception,
working particularly through midwives, who deliver some 90 per cent
of the babies. Sale of appliances is legal, and educational films on contraception are shown. Contraceptives are distributed freely to the poor.

Sterilization is also a part of Japan's tripartite effort to check population increase. Indeed, Japan was the first country which officially
favored sterilization to achieve this objective. Sterilization of women is
increasing, but male sterilization is not commonly practiced. Between
1949 and 1957, 258,000 sterilizations were reported.

This antinatalist policy set by the Eugenic Protection Law of 1948
represents an about-face from the attitude of the Japanese government
during and shortly before World War II, when their desire for a
powerful army and abundant manpower fostered opposition to fertility
control measures. Nor did the American occupation forces of 1945-
1952 favor birth control. Earlier, however, under the Shoguns, abortion
and infanticide had been for many generations a part of the Japanese
cultural pattern. And since very early times, Japanese culture has accepted conscious control of fertility. Neither Shinto nor Buddhism
categorically opposes birth control, including abortion.

The results of Japan's antinatalist program seem more evident than
those of most national policies. Abortions are now giving way to the
more efficient and less complicated contraception techniques. Intensive
studies made in selected districts indicate a sudden drop in the birth
rate.[36] From 34 per 1,000 in 1947, the birth rate fell to 18 in 1956 and
17 in 1961. The popularity of family planning is indicated by the recent

---

[36] Yoshio Koya, "Population Problems and Family Planning in Japan," *Eugenics
Quarterly*, Vol. IV, No. 3, September 1957, pp. 157-161.

election of "the Margaret Sanger of Japan," Mrs. Kanju Kato, to the Upper House of the Japanese Diet.

AUSTRALIA

Countries with large tracts of unoccupied land sometimes encourage immigrants—though often they neither seek nor receive the kind of immigrant they most need. Australia's population policy is qualifiedly pro-immigrant. Since World War II this rising young country has been "receiving immigrants at a ratio to population far exceeding that for the United States even at our greatest period of immigration."[37] In the decade 1947-1956, Australia accepted over a million immigrants, constituting a mean annual population increment of 1.1 per cent. Encouragement of immigration sprang originally from humanitarian motives, later from military objectives, and more recently from a belief in the economic advantage of fuller utilization of natural resources and relief of the labor shortage. Even so, government policy has discriminated against nonwhites, with the result that almost one-half of all immigrants are British. Immigrants, as compared with the rest of the population, are disproportionately young, male, and in the working force, though their occupational distribution is much like that of the general populace. About 55 per cent of all new settlers are financially assisted in immigrating through treaties with various European nations and international organizations.[38]

The Australian demographer W. D. Borrie credits this heavy immigration as having been of great assistance in helping to attain national policy objectives: "The post-war immigrants have been absorbed at a time when the natural increase of the population of working age has been at a very low ebb. For the ten years ending June 1957 there would have been a decrease of more than a hundred thousand persons in the age-group 20-29 years had there been no immigration. Immigration filled this gap and converted a decrease into an increase of eighty-six thousand."[39]

The government's previously mentioned "white Australia" policy keeps out the Chinese, Indians, and Japanese, who have been casting longing glances at Australia's open spaces. Had they won the Second World War, the Japanese might well have resettled millions of their people in Australia.

---

[37] Dudley Kirk and Earl Huyck, "Overseas Migration from Europe since World War II," *American Sociological Review*, Vol. XIX, No. 4, August 1954, p. 448.

[38] Frank Meissner, "Australia's Postwar Immigrants," *American Journal of Economics and Sociology*, Vol. XIX, No. 2, January 1960, pp. 169-177.

[39] W. D. Borrie, "Foreword" to Jerzy Zubrzycki, *Immigrants in Australia*, Melbourne University Press, Victoria, 1960, p. vii.

Yet ironically Australia's open spaces are largely a mirage. Only about 8 per cent of the land can be brought under cultivation even with irrigation. The present proportion cultivated is 3 per cent. Nonetheless, Australia could still benefit from more people and remains one of the few countries accurately describable as underpopulated. The present rate of immigration is probably about as great as the country can tolerate without disruption.

Government Programs in Underdeveloped Countries

If the peasant-agricultural countries that contain two-thirds of the world's population undergo the same demographic transition that Europe experienced, they are likely to end with a standard of living too low to permit the industrial development and modernization they so earnestly seek. The problem appears to be one of introducing fertility control *before* industrialization rather than afterwards, as was the case in Europe. Some social scientists believe that this cannot be done. But the demographic experiences of Asia, Africa, and Latin America need not necessarily follow exactly those of Europe and Anglo America. As George Barclay has stressed:

> Today it is doubtful whether any non-industrial nation, desirous of securing for itself the advantages of an industrial system of production, can afford to rely on this "automatic" decline in fertility, even if it is prepared to let the social changes run their course. The time is too short, the starting position too precarious, and the large empty areas of the world are no longer open to migration if fertility fails to fall. The increase of people would probably have to be suppressed, either by accident or by design, through a restoration of high mortality. Agrarian countries that wish to play safe in their plans for development are now left with little choice but to promote the idea of deliberative fertility control among their people.[40]

One Indian economist subscribes to the view that "in many parts of the world, food and natural resources are not only not increasing with the growth of population but that instead a steady depletion of these resources is taking place. . . . Eventual starvation of large numbers is in store unless population growth is severely restricted. . . . Our only road to survival is through a drastic reduction of human fertility. . . . What is needed in Asia is to make every woman deliver one baby where she delivered two or more before and make two blades of grass grow where

---

[40] George W. Barclay, *Colonial Development and Population in Taiwan*, Princeton University Press, Princeton, 1954, p. 262.

one grew before."[41] The author of this statement, Sripati Chandrasekhar, envisions a world population policy simultaneously attacking on political, economic, and social fronts through political freedom for all colonial peoples, universal adoption of birth control, planned international migration, large-scale and rapid industrialization, and intensive agricultural development.[42] Clearly, however, this five-point program is too ambitious to be completed in the near future.

INDIA

Of the many nonindustrial nations which face high density or rapid population growth, one of those with the most distressing pressure is India. The 1961 population was officially put at 438 million, representing an increase of 22 per cent in the preceding decade—considerably more than the 1941-1951 increase of 13 per cent. Before 1941, population growth was substantial but not phenomenal: between 1872 and 1941 the population increased about 8 per cent a decade. Today, however, more than 300 Indians are resident on an average square mile of land, and their per capita daily diet is estimated at a meagre 1,700 calories. India embodies on a massive scale the major problems of all the heavily populated agricultural countries of the Orient. Her cities are so crowded and impoverished that each night an overflow of people with nowhere else to sleep must share the streets with roaming cattle.

Ironically, the fact that India does have demographic problems was at first denied by national leaders. In 1948 Jawaharlal Nehru answered British charges of overpopulation by contending that India's poverty was caused by British exploitation and that "if this population is put to work for production, then we are not overpopulated."[43] Reversing his position, the Prime Minister later recognized "the utmost importance" of curbing the birth rate of his country: "Our Five Year Plans have no meaning if the population grows at a rate one can never catch up with." Indian government officials have informed the United States that the effect of the $3 billion of American aid which India has received since independence is being negated by the population increase.

To popularize family planning, the government of India spent $1,500,000 in the first Five-Year Plan (1951-1956) and $10,000,000 during its second Five-Year Plan (1956-1961) and has allocated $52,000,000 in the third such Plan (1961-1966), which places birth control at the

---

[41] Sripati Chandrasekhar, *Hungry People and Empty Lands*, Indian Institute for Population Studies, Baroda, 1952, pp. 12 and 271.
[42] *Ibid.*, pp. 16 and 246-271.
[43] Quoted in N. V. Sovani, "The Problems of Fertility Control in India: Cultural Factors and Development of Policy," in Milbank Memorial Fund, *Approaches to Problems of High Fertility in Agrarian Societies*, New York, 1952, pp. 62-73.

center of planned development. Nehru, once skeptical, boasted shortly before his death that there was more talk and action by official agencies about birth control in India than in any other nation.

Of the three demographic variables, fertility is the only one which offers a realistic solution to the problem of countries like India. Few other lands could absorb or would accept the Indian natural increase, and raising the death rate would be inconsistent with existing values. Lowering the birth rate could be accomplished indirectly by industrializing, modernizing, and urbanizing the country and then hopefully waiting for the people to adopt reproductive patterns normally associated with an industrial, modern, urban society. But the slowness of this method permits a huge interim growth; were this indirect pattern to unfold in the same manner as Europe experienced it in the nineteenth century, India could reach a population of a billion by about the turn of the century. The direct method involves bringing birth control deliberately and vigorously into the country. To be sure, technological, economic, and sociological obstacles are large, but they are not insurmountable.

Kingsley Davis concluded his large study on the population of India and Pakistan with these forthright remarks about demographic policy and the probable future of these countries: "We must admit that the demographic situation in Pakistan and India will get worse before it gets better. Also, it will get better later than it would if the two governments successfully carried through a comprehensive population policy. The main stumbling block to attempting such a comprehensive policy is birth control; yet if the benefits of civilization are to come increasingly to the people of this region, the birth rate must be brought down."[44]

Mahatma Gandhi's ascetic espousal of self-control and self-restraint and abhorrence of self-indulgence led him to oppose "artificial" methods of birth control, contending that if they become the order of the day "moral degradation" will result. But by 1951 the tide had turned so far that Health Minister Rajkumari Amrit Kaur, a loyal Gandhian, helped to launch the first Five-Year Plan. The Registrar General of the 1951 Census said that reduction of the incidence of "improvident maternity" would bring about a "visible reduction of human suffering and promotion of human happiness." Improvident maternity was defined as births above the third order of parity. Even the official 1951 Census contained this entreaty:

> The task before the nation is first of all to bring about such a change
> in the climate of public opinion that every married couple will accept
> it as their duty (to themselves, to their family, and to that larger family

---

[44] Kingsley Davis, *The Population of India and Pakistan*, Princeton University Press, Princeton, 1951, p. 231.

—the nation) that they should avoid improvident maternity. The occurrence of improvident maternity should evoke social disapproval, as any other form of anti-social self-indulgence. This is necessary; but not enough. There should be standing arrangements for ensuring that advice is given to every married couple on the various ways open to them for discharging this duty and to make available the necessary facilities.[45]

Clearly the Registrar General recognized the need to forward birth control on all three levels: ideological, motivational, and technical.

Interviews of urban civil servants and illiterate peasants indicate a remarkable willingness and even desire to learn how to limit family size, especially among women.[46] Traditionally, well-wishers greeted new brides with "May you bear this man ten children and treat him as the eleventh." But this simple arithmetic of an increasing population and a fixed land supply evoke the lament, "There used to be enough land in our village to divide among our sons, and we ate two meals a day. Now there is no more land, and we are eating one meal a day. We cannot afford to have large families."[47]

Governmental programs are conducted in the face of ignorance in rural areas, vigorous opposition from the leaders of India's 5 million Roman Catholics, and sporadic though relatively ineffective opposition from orthodox Hindus and Gandhiites. Government advocacy of birth control embraces several kinds of activity—from posters in buses proclaiming "Many a Progeny—Many an Agony" to the officially declared "All-India Family Planning Day." The Madras State Family Planning Officer proffers "Advice to Every Married Couple: Please buy and read a copy of the *Family Planning Manual*."

Four thousand fertility planning centers have been established to distribute contraceptive information and devices under the slogan: "Don't delay the first child, don't hurry with the second, don't have the third." In one effort to educate the peasants, inexpensive strings of colored beads were given to impoverished villagers to facilitate use of the rhythm method (green for "safe" days, red for "dangerous" days); the woman were instructed to move one bead each day. But difficulties arose: the beads' color could not be determined at night (an important consideration in homes without electricity), some women moved the beads in the wrong direction (corrected later by a ratchet which permitted movement in only one direction), and superstitious peasant

---

[45] R. A. Gopalaswami, *Census of India, 1951*, Vol. I, Part I-A, "Report," 1953, pp. 218-219.

[46] S. N. Agarwala, "Population Control in India: Progress and Prospects," *Law and Contemporary Problems*, Vol. XXV, No. 3, Summer 1960, pp. 577-593.

[47] Quoted in Jean Lyon, " 'Safe Days' and 'Baby Days,' " *The Reporter*, September 14, 1954.

women thought the beads had magical properties and slid them along the string until they reached a green bead before engaging in sexual intercourse.

The Government of India and some of the fifteen State Governments have tried to inform the populace of the safe period, coitus interruptus, the condom, foam tablets, and diaphragms. But experience has led them to believe that reliance on these methods can only insignificantly reduce fertility in the present century. Therefore they have turned to sterilization, which has the additional virtue of being performed only once in a lifetime instead of continuing throughout the childbearing period, thus being about one-fifteenth as costly as mechanical and chemical methods —an important consideration to a "have-not" country like India.[48]

Vasectomy, although repugnant to many Indians, is gaining widespread acceptance. In the state of Madras, men who already have three or more children are operated upon without charge and are awarded a bonus of about $8.00. Some 40,000 such sterilizations were performed in 1960.

Sterilization of women is much more difficult and is not encouraged by authorities because the operation requires hospitilization. Mrs. Sushili Singli, general secretary of the Bengal office of the Family Planning Association, remarked in 1961: "It is difficult to get hospital beds, particularly for women. The maternity cases crowd us out."

Whether or not these officially endorsed measures will achieve the hoped-for 50 per cent reduction in births is debatable.

Thus Donald Bogue writes:

As yet, the program of family planning in India has not produced the results its sponsors and friends hoped it would when it was launched. ... The number and percentage of couples who are availing themselves of family planning services and information is discouragingly low. Several surveys have reported that a preponderant majority of Indian couples, even in the remote villages, want smaller families. They also want to learn more about how to control fertility. In the Hindu religion there seem to be few overpoweringly strong religious or moral taboos against the practice of family planning. [Nevertheless,] unless something is done to accelerate the program, and if India must rely upon the official family planning programs to reduce her birth rates, it will require a century or more to attain the desired effect.[49]

---

[48] R. A. Gopalaswami, "Family Planning: Outlook for Government Action in India," in Clyde V. Kiser (ed.), Research in Family Planning, Princeton University Press, Princeton, 1962, pp. 67-81.

[49] Donald J. Bogue, "Some Tentative Recommendations for a 'Sociologically Correct' Family Planning Communication and Motivation Program in India," in Kiser, op. cit., pp. 503-504.

CHINA

The largest country in the world is among the nations for which we have the least information, as regards both factual population data and national policies. Nor is this situation a phenomenon of the Communist regime alone; China has never had an adequate census or a monolithic policy. The Communists do seem to be improving the quality of census and registration data, plus instituting a concerted population program; but the problem now is mainly one of communication through the Bamboo Curtain.

In the face of a fabulous increase in what for centuries has been the world's most populous country, the leaders of Communist China encouraged high fertility until 1953 and then adopted a policy of toleration toward birth limitation. Communist China, Russia, and Japan are the only countries that have fully legalized abortion in recent times. The first official pro-birth control statement in China was released in 1954, activated apparently by fears of overpopulation. From 1954 through 1958 birth control was advertised in newspapers, magazines, government pamphlets, posters, and billboards. Illustrated lectures publicized birth control techniques. Then in 1958 the official policy relaxed from its strenuous effort to promote family planning to an attitude of permissiveness. Contraceptives are still sold and abortion remains legal, but a visitor from India was told that 650 million people were not enough: "China is really underpopulated and there is an acute labor shortage."[50] Malthus is labeled "reactionary," and birth control is attacked in the press. Dissenting voices do remain, however, and there is no assurance that this pronatalist policy will continue. At present Peking leaders seem to be "waiting hopefully for good news from the agricultural front before undertaking another major policy revision"; disappointment of this hope will mean that Communist China is failing to control population growth in the interests of economic development, a circumstance that will exert "an incalculable impact on the world political scene."[51]

From its infancy, the Peoples Republic has had to combat an extremely high mortality, particularly of neonates and pregnant women. To counter the death rate, laws were adopted in 1951, 1953, and 1956 which contributed social security services, including, among other provisions, retirement and disability pensions. The precise impact of these welfare programs is not known, but they are almost certain to lower mortality.

[50] Sripati Chandrasekhar, "China's Population Problems: A Report," *Population Review*, Vol. III, No. 2, July 1959, pp. 17-38.
[51] John S. Aird, "Population Policy in Mainland China," *Population Studies*, Vol. XVI, No. 1, July 1962, pp. 38-57.

Restrictions on immigration and emigration are severe, following the policy of the U.S.S.R. Pre-Communist heavy "blind infiltration" of peasants into cities helped motivate the Party to introduce a registration system providing strict controls over unplanned internal migration. The new system was adopted in January 1958. "As a result of these new regulations, it is virtually impossible to move from one residence to another without the knowledge and consent of the local authorities. . . . The regulations . . . seem to have effectively terminated most of the unauthorized population movements."[52]

The desire to increase productivity has resulted in policies of redeploying both industries and people away from the dense coastal provinces and toward the relatively untapped resources of the western provinces. Consequently inland cities are growing rapidly, though more from rural-urban peasant migration within the province than from interregional migration. Nonetheless there is a general westward movement accompanying capital investment for industrial development. Westward migration has also been induced by revision of the agricultural system as the Communist government moves individuals and families to work new farm lands in the west and north. But these industrial and agricultural transfers are not very significant for the regional population distribution.

In sum, the effect of seemingly shifting population policies upon demographic trends in China are largely questions for future study when, hopefully, more adequate information will become available. And stereotypes of party leaders notwithstanding, it must be recognized that Chinese Communist officials differ from their Russian counterparts in exhibiting a remarkably great toleration of diverging views, even to the extent of sometimes permitting disagreements to be published in the newspapers.

INTERVENTION BY OTHER POWERS

During the last few years demographers and governmental organizations in industrial nations have become increasingly worried about the extreme rapidity of growth of the have-not countries. The underdeveloped, heavily populated nations are today highly contested pawns in the struggle between the free world and the Communists. To the extent that the allegiance of uncommitted factions can be secured through provision of economic and other assistance, the free and Communist blocs stand to gain or lose considerably by proffering desired equipment or information. If birth control devices or knowledge are useful to such countries,

---

[52] Leo A. Orleans, "Population Redistribution in Communist China," in Milbank Memorial Fund, *Population Trends in Eastern Europe, the USSR and Mainland China, op. cit.,* pp. 144-145.

the cold war combatant that supplies the need may add to its own strength. On the other hand, uncommitted countries that want to avoid birth control will be best pleased by a policy of nonintervention. In any case the wishes of the contested nations are significant.

This situation has become so serious that the Draper Committee, appointed by President Eisenhower to reassess United States foreign aid, recommended in 1959 that "the United States assist those countries with which it is cooperating in economic aid programs, on request, in the formulation of their plans designed to deal with the problem of rapid population growth" and that the Federal government give financial support to research on this problem.[53] Despite these unusually forward recommendations, the government did nothing until December 1962, when it offered to provide other nations, upon their request, with information and technical assistance on birth control.

In the absence of Federal action, private organizations have taken the lead. During the last few years several groups have been established to ask the public for financial contributions to promote planned parenthood in overpopulated countries. In 1960 a conference at Princeton, New Jersey, witnessed the founding of the World Population Emergency Campaign, which group immediately instituted a mail canvass seeking contributions. The organization's Statement of Purpose is provocative:

> The poor are getting poorer in the second half of the Twentieth Century. Nearly two thirds of the world's people, more than one billion six hundred million, live in countries which have an annual per capita income of less than $200. More than one billion people, 40 per cent of the world's population, live in countries whose 1957 income averaged $120 per person. . . . These statistics, whose meaning is human misery, are worsening year by year in most countries having the lowest income levels. Unchecked population growth robs their peoples of any gains from capital investment, foreign aid or technological advance. If this fantastic growth continues during the next decades, the pauperization of humanity will stagger the imagination and be beyond remedy.[54]

Comparable programs are under way in other countries. On August 18, 1961, the governments of Sweden and Denmark requested the United Nations General Assembly to study the effects of population growth upon the standard of living in underdeveloped countries and to provide technical assistance to those countries desiring to limit their growth.

---

[53] President's Committee to Study the United States Military Assistance Program, *Third Interim Report: Economic Assistance Programs and Administration*, Section V: "The Population Question," Government Printing Office, Washington, July 13, 1959.
[54] World Population Emergency Campaign, "Statement of Purpose," Founding Conference, Princeton, March 20, 1960.

Such efforts are not always received with open arms. National sensitivity in have-not countries encourages resistance toward foreign attempts—especially by the haves—to limit their fertility. This reaction is heightened by the personal nature of the actions involved in birth control. Probably no family planning program will ever be adopted primarily as a result of outside pressures. In fertility planning as in other welfare concerns, "do-gooders" must be careful to avoid inadvertently antagonizing the presumed benefactors of their good will. Results are far more likely to be positive if a needy nation requests assistance (or if propagandizers are sufficiently subtle). This *caveat* is weakened by a marked receptivity of many individuals in overpopulated countries to conveyance of birth control knowledge and materials.

PART IV

COMPOSITION AND DESCRIPTION

19 ❧ Ascribed Characteristics

All populations have both structure and movement. Mortality, fertility, and migration form the movement of a population, while its structure consists of various characteristics. The composition or characteristics of the population are such attributes as age, sex, race, nationality, marital status, education, literacy, occupation, income, language, and religion.

In general, these characteristics are less valuable in demographic analysis than are the three fundamental demographic variables. However, this is not to say that population composition is unimportant. On the contrary, these attributes are very useful for many purposes—for instance, the age and sex distribution of a population seriously affect birth rates, martial rates, death rates, military manpower, the gross national product, size and type of housing, needed educational facilities, and attitudes toward youth and age. Some characteristics are peripheral to demography. Many are assigned separate courses or departments in the academic curriculum: religion, economics, marriage, language, education, and race.

Characteristics, like statuses, are of two types. Ascribed characteristics are those which are assigned to the individual; achieved characteristics are those which are (or are assumed to be) open to individual choice. Most statuses and the most important characteristics in any society are nonvolitional or ascribed, especially those having to do with the conduct of day-to-day existence. This chapter considers biological attributes along with those characteristics that are assigned by the culture. Sex, race, and nativity are immutable. Age advances intransigently. Language and religion ordinarily remain fixed for life. The following chapter focuses on mutable social traits subject to frequent individual alteration in many societies, including Western culture.

Age and Sex Composition

The basic characteristics of any demographic group are age and sex; their pervasive quality causes them to be discussed first in this chapter. As fundamental "givens" of human existence, they are the variables most frequently held constant in computing specific birth and death rates. For the same reason, age and sex differentials are prominent factors affecting marriage, fertility, mortality, morbidity, and internal and international migration. A wise manufacturer knows the sex ratio and distribution of population by age in the locality in which he intends to sell his products. Indeed there is hardly a phase of social, economic, and political life that escapes the influence of the age-sex structure. Its significance for population policy is extremely high.

STATUS AND ROLE

The biological attributes of sex and age are prime sources of ascribed status. They are very important to sociologists because they are visible, indisputable, and convenient indicators of status in all societies, and because the corresponding roles are essential ingredients in the family, occupational division of labor, education, and the other social institutions. Yet although most societies attempt to rationalize their cultural prescriptions in terms of physiological differences between age and sex groups, the actual ascriptions are largely culturally rather than biologically determined. "Our own idea of women as ministering angels contrasts sharply with the ingenuity of women as torturers among the Iroquois and the sadistic delight they took in the process."[1] In our own social system, the modest, shy, and delicate damsel of the late nineteenth century (if she ever truly existed) has yielded to the outspoken, emancipated partner, with the result that the fainting, nonperspiring lady reared years ago may be conducted about town by an aggressive girl taxi driver.

Three age categories are recognized as important in all social orders: child, adult, and aged. One might think that the transition from childhood to adulthood would have a physiological basis, but actually the rites of passage take place at the time when the boy is considered ready to do a man's job. In the United States, both sexes remain legally under age until long after they are physically adults. "The child becomes a man not when he is physically mature but when he is formally recognized as a man by his society."[2]

---

[1] Ralph Linton, *The Study of Man*, D. Appleton-Century Co., New York, 1936, p. 116.
[2] *Ibid.*, p. 118.

The passage from adulthood to old age also varies considerably from one society to another and is generally given less emphasis than the passage from adolescence. In some social systems the status ascribed to the aged is quite high: the old are respected as the repositories of wisdom, and their role is that of honored consultant. In other societies, especially those which stress physical achievement as a source of status, the aged are looked down upon and given the more unpleasant and monotonous tasks. In the United States, which has been described as having a "youth cult," the aged tend to be regarded as encumbrances. Social workers are hired to make them feel useful and wanted, and the euphemism "senior citizen" is substituted in a vain effort to pretend that they are not really old.

Several criteria of aging are available for societal choice: biological—physical condition; chronological—aged at 60, 65, or older; economic—too old to work; psychological—how old the individual feels; and social—change of roles. Regardless of these local variations in cultural definition, demographers emphasize chronological aging, largely because of its greater susceptibility to precise measurement and international comparisons.

THE SEX RATIO

The universal demographic measure of sex distribution is the sex ratio, which is the number of males per 100 females. The use of females as the base or denominator is consistent with other demographic reasoning, particularly regarding fertility.

The sex ratio in the United States in 1960 was 97.1. The secular trend is toward a lower ratio: in 1900 it was 104.4. At the mid-century United States Census—the first in which the sex ratio of the total population dropped below 100—some component sex ratios were: total population, 98.1; native whites, 97.8; foreign-born whites, 102.2; and Negroes, 97.6. A century earlier the corresponding figures were 104.3, 103.1, 123.8, and 99.1. The greatest change occurred among the foreign-born. Certain groups of immigrants were almost entirely male: the sex ratio of Filipinos in 1930 was 1,438; of Japanese in 1900, 2,370; and of Chinese in 1910, 3,307.

Throughout the world the sex ratio at birth is consistently about 105. National deviations from this figure are slight. Anyone wishing to earn a little money may possibly do so by always betting that babies will be male (although this is not a good way to make a living because the pay-off of 21 to 20 will not yield a large percentage profit).

If the sex ratio at birth is 105, one might well ask why the total United States sex ratio is so much lower. The answer lies in the simple fact that men have higher death rates than women. The preponderance of males in the younger ages is eaten away by differential mortality until a balance is reached at about age 48. After that, the proportion of women gradually increases with increasing age, until beyond age 95 there are about twice as many women as men. This fact helps to explain why widowers have so much easier a time remarrying than do widows; the old man may pick and choose (assuming he confines his attention to his own age group), but the old woman must seek out her quarry. However, in nations where females receive inferior treatment, the death rate may be higher among females than among males, and the sex ratio may climb above 105 in adult ages.

Frontier communities and colonies ordinarily have high sex ratios since differential immigration of males to newly-settled, hazardous areas creates a deficit of females. Thus for many years Alaska's sex ratio exceeded 150, though it is now expected to decline as a consequence of the greater stability associated with statehood. Conversely, areas of emigration tend to have low sex ratios, as for example the nations of southern and eastern Europe which have sent many men to America and elsewhere, but few women. In the United States, western states tend to have higher sex ratios than do eastern ones. The very highest are the Pacific Northwest and Rocky Mountain states; the lowest are in New England.

Another factor affecting the sex ratio is that of occupation. Areas dominated by mining, lumbering, herding, or heavy industry attract unmarried males, whereas commercial, service, administrative, and political towns attract females. Washington, D.C., has so many female government white-collar workers that transient infantrymen claim that a soldier who cannot pick up a girl in the national capital cannot pick one up anywhere. In the United States and other industrial countries, cities have lower sex ratios than farm areas, but the ratios are reversed in India and some other underdeveloped lands.

Sex ratios below 90 or above 115 are regarded as out of balance—a tribute in part to the internalization of monogamy. Irregular sexual morality and other aberrant behavior are sometimes attributed to a disproportionate sex ratio, but this explanation is incomplete. For instance, the instability and violence of towns in the "Wild West" were also connected with high mobility, relative absence of strong group norms, self-selection of deviants, placement of pride above life in the scale of values, and other social and cultural conditions.

Deviations in the sex ratio away from 100 may influence the marriage norms toward polygyny (a plurality of females) or toward polyandry (a plurality of males). However, it is probably just as likely that the form of marriage may itself affect the sex ratio. Possibly the most realistic interpretation is that both the marital system and the sex ratio are integral and reciprocally interacting parts of the social system, influencing and being influenced in turn by other social and cultural elements. The causal chain appears convoluted, plural, and multidirectional.

AGE-SEX PYRAMIDS

Obviously the number of people at each year of age must be smaller than in the previous year—that is, unless no one dies, young people emigrate, or old people immigrate. This tendency is clearly reproduced in the population pyramids of Figures 15 and 16. These age-sex "trees" provide graphic statements of the current age and sex distributions of various areas; they also tell us something about the social attributes of the inhabitants concerned.

An age-sex tree reflects the history of the country over the past two or three generations. For example, the population pyramid of France is affected by the severe military losses suffered by young adult males in World War I, creating a marked indentation in the upper part of the male side of the pyramid. Younger age groups are also affected, since the men who died in the war did not father the children they might otherwise have bred. The concavities at ages 40-44 in both male and female sides are caused by the absence of these potential parents killed in the war. A quarter century later, the influence of military losses of World War I combined with the depression of the 1930's to form dents for both sexes at ages 10 to 24 and especially 15 to 19.

As also can be seen in Figure 15, Ceylon and Mexico have young populations. The age-sex profile of the United States once resembled these two pyramids. Today the United States profile has been tending more and more to resemble that of Sweden and France, which are representative of old populations. Irregularities of these profiles are products of historical events peculiar to each country. But two general shapes may be detected: the triangular shape of the young population and the almost rectangular pattern of the old.

Demographers use the terms "stable" and "stationary" to refer to age distributions of populations. A stable population is one having unchanging age-specific fertility and mortality rates (and hence eventually a constant natural increase rate); under these conditions the proportions of persons in different age groups remain constant and the population pyramid always maintains the same shape (though the area may change). A stable population having equal birth and death rates, no migration, and thus a fixed total size is called stationary.

AN AGING POPULATION

The long-term trend in the United States age distribution is one of growing older. The median age has increased from 16.0 years in 1800

FIGURE 15. *Age-Sex Pyramids, Various Countries, 1950-1959**

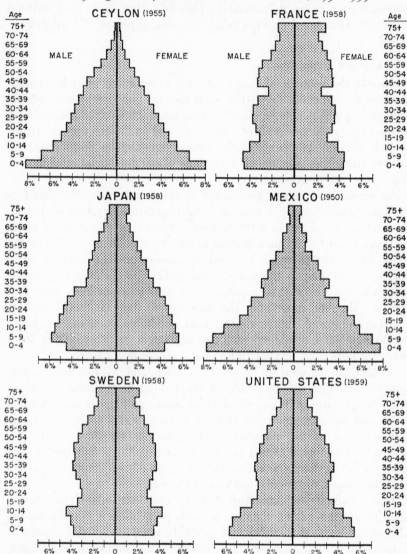

* Population Reference Bureau, *Population Bulletin*, Vol. XVI, No. 8, December 1960, p. 159.

and 19.1 years in 1850[3] to 29.5 years in 1960. The proportion of the population over 65 increased from 4 per cent at the turn of the century to 9 per cent in the last census. The prospect is that by the end of this

[3] Henry D. Sheldon, *The Older Population of the United States*, John Wiley and Sons, New York, 1958, p. 138.

FIGURE 16. *Age-Sex Pyramids, Various Urban Areas, Seattle, 1940**

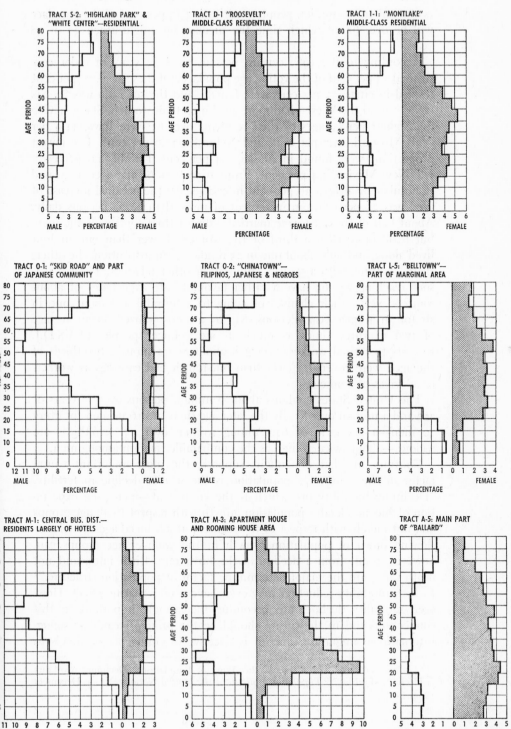

* Calvin F. Schmid, *Social Trends in Seattle*, University of Washington Press, Seattle, 1944, p. 92. Reprinted by permission.

century about 30 million people constituting 13 per cent of the populace will be over 65, at which time the median age might reach 37 or 38 years.

According to the 1960 census, persons aged 65 years or older constituted 15 per cent of the voting age populace. Of these aged, 70 per cent resided in cities, 55 per cent were female, and the sex ratio was 83. Six states—all in the West—had more aged men than women. States having the highest percentages of their residents over 65 were Iowa, 11.9 per cent; Missouri, 11.7 per cent; and Nebraska, 11.6 per cent. The lowest proportions were found in Alaska, 2.4 per cent; Hawaii, 4.6 per cent; and New Mexico, 5.4 per cent. From 1950 to 1960 the aged increased in number by at least 10 per cent in every state; the national increase of aged was 35 per cent, an increment of more than 1,000 persons daily. About half of the aged were married—almost three-fourths of the men, but little more than a third of the women. Fewer than one in four lived alone, and only about one in 25 resided in an institution; the others shared housing with a spouse, children, or other relatives. Though persons reaching age 65 have a rather favorable life expectancy of about fourteen years, their chances of going to a hospital are about one in six for an average year. Persons over 65 are hospitalized on an average of two or three times as much as are younger people. O.A.S.D.I. benefits to retired workers averaged about $76 a month; two-thirds of the aged were covered. Fewer than one-fourth had earnings as workers or as wives of workers.

The United States contains about 6 million persons over 75 years of age and a million over 85. By the later age there are 16 women for every 10 men—a sex ratio of 64. Among women over 75, two-thirds are widows—about twice as high as the comparable fraction among men.

Contrary to what one might suppose, the most important causal factor in the aging of a population is the secular decline in fertility. "Declining mortality or—which is the equivalent—increasing expectation of life, accelerates population growth with respect to all age groups and not merely with respect to the segment at advanced ages. A relative slowing down of population growth in the younger age groups can, however, result from a decline in the birth rate. Birth rates, and not death rates, are the major determining factor of population structure."[4] In fact, mortality reduction may even have a rejuvenating effect. However, mortality declines are becoming increasingly important in this connection, and in the future should be the principal cause of aging International migration, since it is selective of young people, tends to

---

[4] United Nations, "The Cause of the Aging of Populations: Declining Mortality or Declining Fertility?," *Population Bulletin of the United Nations*, No. 4, December 1954, p. 30.

accelerate the aging process in countries of emigration and to retard aging in countries of immigration, such as the United States. When lowered birth rates induce an increase in the proportion of aged, an increased incidence of the disabilities of old age is not necessarily entailed. If death rates are low, persons of advanced ages are usually in better health than where mortality is high. Where fertility has ceased to decline, the aging process will eventually halt, except for whatever additional gains in survival at extreme ages may be achieved by advances in medicine. In populations where natality has recently risen, aging will at some future time give way to temporary or partial rejuvenation. In areas where birth rates have remained at a high level, no appreciable aging is to be expected, irrespective of the extent and rapidity of the decline in death rates. "Marked aging can occur only after the onset of a decline in fertility. For most parts of the world, the emergence of such a trend cannot yet be foreseen."[5]

Table 33 shows the United States age distribution divided into four rough categories: preworking, young workers, old workers, and retired.

TABLE 33. *Age Distribution in the United States, 1820-1960*[*]

AGE AND OCCUPATIONAL CHARACTER	1820[a]	1860	1900	1940	1950	1960
Under 20—preworking force	58%	51%	44%	34%	34%	39%
20-44—young working force	30	36	38	39	38	32
45-64—old working force	10	10	14	20	20	20
Over 65—retired	2	3	4	7	8	9
Total	100	100	100	100	100	100
Median age	17.0	19.6	22.9	29.0	30.2	29.5

[a] Whites only. This restriction overstates the median age.
[*] U. S. Bureau of the Census, various publications.

The proportion of persons in the under-20 age class has been declining steadily. The people in the too-young-to-work and retired categories represent dependency drains on the national productivity. People in the two middle classes contribute the bulk of the gross national product.

Several consequences of aging require attention. First, pension schemes are arranged so that the amount contributed before retirement will be balanced against the payments that must be made after retirement; as people live longer, they draw more money from the pension fund and force increases in premiums. (The French railroad system actually has more men on pension rolls than active permanent employees.) Second, as the aged come to represent a larger proportion of

[5] *Ibid.,* p. 38.

the population, recreation facilities, housing, and other conveniences are needed to provide the types of facilities demanded by older citizens. Third, politicians can be expected to direct more and more speeches and slogans to the aged, and bills introduced in legislative bodies may reflect the changing age structure. Fourth, the normal retirement age will perhaps be increased by several years. Not only do people live longer, but they are healthier. A few employers now use medical criteria instead of sheer age in determining when a person should retire; perhaps this practice will spread. Fifth, medical and welfare services for the aged must be expanded. In sociology and medicine, specialties dealing with the aged are thriving. Sixth, the combination of longer survival and the tendency to complete childbearing at an earlier age have lengthened the "empty nest" stage—the period after the last child has left home. Increasing geographic mobility aggravates the loneliness in the lives of aged parents. Seventh, it is possible that attitudes toward age and youth may change also, but this prospect is difficult to evaluate. Eighth, the prevalent belief that aged persons are inherently conservative is over-emphasized. "It does seem true that the average person tends to grow more conservative with age. Yet part of this tendency may be due, not to a change of one's views in a conservative direction, but to a change in the social milieu. In a dynamic society the radicalisms of yesterday become the conservatisms of today. The old person, who acquired his basic ideas long ago, may become conservative simply by hanging on to his original views.[6] Finally, responsibility for care of the aged is undergoing a change in the United States from the family (especially children) to the individual himself (through pensions and annuities) and the government (social security).

GROWING YOUNGER

Although the long-term trend in the United States has been toward an aging population, the country has recently begun to grow younger. The demographic cause of this new trend is the reverse of the cause of the aging trend—that is, a spectacular rise in fertility since the Second World War. Repercussions of this change are already being felt in the pressures for more schools. A drift toward a younger population is common in underdeveloped countries, but the United States is one of the very few highly industrialized nations experiencing a shift toward the younger ages.

This is not to say that the nation has ceased adding to the proportion

---

[6] Kingsley Davis and J. W. Combs, Jr., "The Sociology of an Aging Population," in Proceedings of the Eastern States Health Education Conference, *The Social and Biological Challenge of Our Aging Population,* Columbia University Press, New York, 1950, p. 163.

of aged. Both the youngest and the oldest age groups are enlarging in size and proportion, while the intermediate ages are relatively stagnant. Figure 17 compares the 1950 and 1960 age-sex compositions. During this decade the only age categories that lost population were those from 20 to 24 and 25 to 29. The largest absolute increase occurred among children. Percentage increases were great at both ends of the age scale. The number of persons younger than 18 and 65 or older increased by 37 and

FIGURE 17. *Age-Sex Pyramid, United States, 1950-1960**

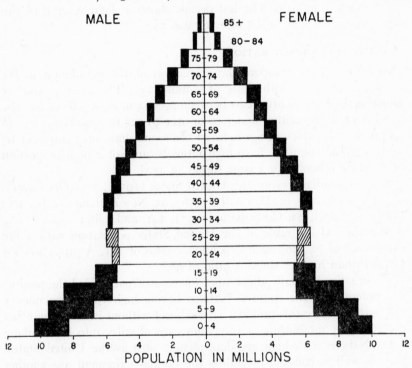

POPULATION IN MILLIONS

███ 1960 MORE THAN 1950   ▨▨ 1960 LESS THAN 1950

NOTE: ALASKA AND HAWAII INCLUDED IN BOTH YEARS.
SOURCE: DEPARTMENT OF COMMERCE, BUREAU OF THE CENSUS.

* U. S. Bureau of the Census, *U.S. Census of Population: 1960,* "General Population Characteristics: United States Summary," PC(1)-1B, Government Printing Office, Washington, 1961, Figure 2, p. xiii.

35 per cent respectively, whereas persons of ages 18 to 64 increased by only 7 per cent and the age group 20 to 29 (born during the 1930's, a period of low fertility), even decreased by 9 per cent. Because of these unequal rates of growth, the proportion of the population aged 18 to 64 declined from 61 per cent in 1950 to 55 per cent in 1960, whereas the

percentage under 18 rose from 31 to 36 per cent and that 65 and older rose from 8 to 9 per cent. As a result, the median age declined slightly, marking the first time in the recorded history of the nation that the median age fell during an intercensal period.[7]

V. G. Valaoras suggests an index of aging consisting of the number of aged persons divided by the number of dependent young persons, expressed as a percentage.[8] American occupational norms favor cutting points at ages 15 and 65. The index of aging for the United States increased consistently and rapidly from about 6 before 1850 to 11.8 in 1900 and 30.2 in 1950. The last decade shows a slight reversal of this aging trend: the 1960 index of aging was 29.7.

THE DEPENDENCY RATIO

Dependency ratios compare the proportion of the population in the nonproductive ages with those of working age. The most productive period is the forty to fifty years between ages 15 or 20 and 60 or 65. The number of persons either under 20 or over 59 per 100 adults aged 20 to 59 provides an index of age-induced economic drain on manpower resources. Some countries have high ratios because of a high proportion of children; others have a large supply of aged.

Some dependency ratios are: United States (1950), 73; India (1951), 113; France (1957), 92; Denmark (1956), 93; New Zealand (1956), 106; Belgium (1956), 83; Costa Rica (1957), 141; and Libya (1954), 129. A hypothetical life table of the United States population with a life expectancy of 83 projects a dependency ratio of 111. A projection for Great Britain in 2017 shows a ratio of 98.[9]

These ratios naturally affect labor force participation and the productive potential of the country. Nations having high youth dependency can partially solve this problem (though not without introducing other problems) by establishing a very young age of entry into the working force. Nations with high age dependency, such as the United States, may do well to consider extending the normal retirement age another several years.

Dependency ratios also influence investment, savings, pensions, and governmental expenditures.

---

[7] U. S. Bureau of the Census, *U.S. Census of Population: 1960*, "General Population Characteristices: United States Summary," PC(1)-1B, Government Printing Office, Washington, 1961, pp. xii-xiii.

[8] Vasilios G. Valaoras, "Patterns of Aging of Human Populations," in Proceedings of the Eastern States Health Education Conference, *The Social and Biological Challenge of Our Aging Population, op. cit.*, pp. 67-85.

[9] Kingsley Davis, "Population and Welfare in Industrial Societies," *Health Education Monographs*, No. 9, 1960, p. 5.

Thus Hauser comments:

An increase in younger dependents requires a larger allocation of savings for purposes of "social investment," that is, investment in the rearing and education of the young. This is achieved only at the expense, in some measure, of decreased savings allocated to "productive investment," or investment designed specifically to increase product per head. A rise in the number of older dependents increases the claims on current production of that part of the population which tends no longer to contribute to increased product. Thus, apart from raising the ratio of dependents to workers, increased dependency, all other things being equal, operates in these other ways to reduce product per head and therefore to affect level of living adversely.[10]

Past and prospective changes in United States dependency ratios are shown in Table 34. The present rising trend is attributable primarily to the fertility resurgence since World War II, which, as Hauser puts it, "introduced changes in the age structure which, all other things being equal, would bring about the first decrease in product per head in our history. That is, prior to World War II the combination of forces affecting the age structure of the population of the United States produced 'hands' faster than 'mouths.' As the result of the sharp upturn in birth rate in the postwar period, mouths began to be generated more rapidly than hands."[11]

Whether a person is dependent is not solely a matter of age, but also of health, financial standing, and normal working ages in his culture. In Western society, people now begin work at a much later age than they did before enactment of the child-labor laws. Early twentieth century American folkways concerning work-age and social class were castigated by Sarah Cleghorn:[12]

> The golf links lie so near the mill
> That almost every day
> The laboring children can look out
> And see the men at play.

Race and Nativity

Since a person's race is virtually unchangeable, it is therefore viewed as an ascribed status like age and sex. However, where "passing" is

---

[10] Philip M. Hauser, *Population Perspectives*, Rutgers University Press, New Brunswick, 1960, pp. 72-73.

[11] *Ibid.*, pp. 70-71.

[12] Sarah N. Cleghorn, quatrain published in Franklin P. Adams, "The Conning Tower," *New York Tribune*, 1919.

frequent, race in effect can become an achieved status. Many societies contain several racial groups, each with its own status and role. Nativity or place of birth is also unchangeable. Citizenship can be altered by conforming to (or breaking) certain regulations.

TABLE 34. *Dependency Ratios for the United States, 1820-1980**

	Dependents Per 100 Persons of Working Age (20-64 Years)		
YEAR AND SOURCE	YOUNG (UNDER 20)	OLD (65 OR MORE)	YOUNG AND OLD
1820 (census)	146	7	153
1850 (census)	117	6	123
1900 (census)	86	8	94
1950 (census)	59	14	73
1960 (census)	74	17	91
1970 (projection)	80	18	98
1980 (projection)	85	19	104

* Philip M. Hauser, *Population Perspectives*, Rutgers University Press, New Brunswick, 1960, p. 71; and U. S. Bureau of the Census, U. S. *Census of Population: 1960*, PC(1)-1B, p. 146.

Race and nationality are both difficult to define. Nationality is an ambiguous term taking on such meanings as: place of birth of the individual, citizenship of the individual, place of birth of his ancestors, or citizenship of his ancestors. The situation is particularly confusing regarding naturalized citizens. For demographic study the greatest value inheres in the first and third interpretations as identifications of the foreign-born and the foreign stock.

The subjectivity of laymen's definitions of race is an obstacle to scientific classification and analysis. Skin color is overemphasized to the extent that all other criteria are subordinated to it. Physical anthropologists, on the other hand, supplement physical measurements with blood type and other sophisticated measures to identify racial groupings. Given present knowledge, race is best viewed as a constellation of characteristics. Furthermore, migration and intermarriage have eliminated pure strains.

The racial classification system adopted by the United States Bureau of the Census is not based on a detailed analysis of physical characteristics—and for very good reason. It would be impossible to have all residents of the country examined by physical anthropologists to ensure their proper racial classification. Instead, local definition is used: for example, if a person is considered to be Negro by other members of

TABLE 35. *Race by Sex and Region, Urban and Rural, United States, 1960**

| | Number of Persons (In Thousands) | | | | | | | Percentage Distribution | | |
	WHITE	NEGRO	INDIAN	JAPANESE	CHINESE	FILIPINO	OTHER	WHITE	NEGRO	ALL OTHER
Total	158,832	18,872	524	464	237	176	218	88.6	10.5	0.9
Urban	110,428	13,808	146	381	227	130	150	88.2	11.0	0.8
Rural	48,403	5,064	378	83	11	47	68	89.5	9.4	1.1
Male	78,367	9,113	263	225	136	112	115	88.7	10.3	1.0
Female	80,465	9,758	260	240	102	64	103	88.4	10.7	0.8
Northeast	41,522	3,028	26	18	54	11	18	92.9	6.8	0.3
North Central	48,003	3,446	99	29	18	9	16	93.0	6.7	0.3
South	43,477	11,312	128	16	17	11	13	79.1	20.6	0.3
West	25,830	1,086	271	401	148	146	171	92.1	3.9	4.1

* U. S. Bureau of the Census, U. S. *Census of Population: 1960*, PC(1)-1B, pp. 144 and 164.

his community, he is listed as Negro, even if he is 15/16 white—or even if he is entirely of white ancestry. Occasionally, users of census statistics are disturbed by the "unscientific" quality of this approach to racial classification. However, strict adherence to principles established by physical anthropology would yield data that would in most cases be less useful than the pragmatic attitude which now characterizes the Census Bureau. For most purposes, if a person is treated as white, he is in effect white. The social facts of life do not always correspond to the physical facts. In the words of W. I. Thomas, "If men define situations as real, they are real in their consequences." Furthermore, anthropologists are coming increasingly to consider racial types as cultural rather than physical.

NONWHITE DISTRIBUTION

The largest racial group in the United States is the Caucasoid, popularly called white and renamed by E. M. Forster "pinko-grey." Other racial and quasi-racial groups large enough and identifiable enough to warrant recording by the Bureau of the Census are Negro, American Indian, Japanese, Chinese, and Filipino. As is shown in Table 35, the Chinese are almost exclusively urban, the Indians are predominantly rural, and the others are heavily urban. Sex ratios are fairly well balanced except among the Filipinos and Chinese. All nonwhite groups are overwhelmingly Western except the Negroes and Indians. State distributions are presented in Table 36. Note the clustering of Orientals in Hawaii and California, American Indians in Arizona, and Negroes by total number in New York and by percentage in Mississippi. In no state are Negroes a majority. Hawaii has by far the lowest proportion of whites in its populace, being 32 per cent white, 1 per cent Negro, and 67 per cent other nonwhite. The New England states and the northernmost Great Plains and Rocky Mountains states are the most heavily white; no nonwhite group is well represented in any of these districts.

As regards the American Indian, the demography is terra incognita. About all we can be sure of is that they constitute the second largest nonwhite group in the United States and are growing rapidly. The reservation style of life is not conductive to accurate enumeration and vital registration by normal census procedures. Since 1958, however, the University of Arizona Bureau of Ethnic Research has been collecting data on the Prima and Papago tribes for I.B.M. analysis as a part of establishing an anthropo-demography center.[13] According to the data gath-

---

[13] Robert A. Hackenberg, *Papago Population Study*, University of Arizona, Tucson, 1961, pp. 166-177.

TABLE 36. Nonwhite Population, Selected States, 1960*

Negro				Indian		Japanese		Chinese		Filipino		Population Neither Negro nor White	
STATE	NUMBER	STATE	PER CENT	STATE	NUMBER	STATE	NUMBER	STATE	NUMBER	STATE	NUMBER	STATE	PER CENT
N.Y.	1,417,511	Miss.	42.0	Ariz.	83,387	Hawaii	203,455	Calif.	95,600	Hawaii	69,070	Hawaii	67.3
Tex.	1,187,125	S. Car.	34.8	Okla.	64,689	Calif.	157,317	Hawaii	38,197	Calif.	65,459	Alaska	19.8
Ga.	1,122,596	La.	31.9	N. Mex.	56,255	Wash.	16,652	N.Y.	37,573	N.Y.	5,403	Ariz.	6.9
N. Car.	1,116,021	Ala.	30.0	Calif.	39,014	Ill.	14,074	Ill.	7,047	Ill.	3,587	N. Mex.	6.1
La.	1,039,207	Ga.	28.5	N. Car.	38,129	N.Y.	8,702	Mass.	6,745			S. Dak.	3.9
Ill.	1,037,470	N. Car.	24.5	S. Dak.	25,794	Oreg.	5,016	Wash.	5,491				
		Ark.	21.8	Mont.	21,181								
		Va.	20.6	Wash.	21,076								
...	...	...	...	...	...	...	...	...	...	...	...	N. Hamp.	0.1
												Vt.	0.1
		Hawaii	0.8									Pa.	0.1
		Wyo.	0.7			Ark.	237					Ohio	0.1
		Minn.	0.7			N. Hamp.	207					Ind.	0.1
		Utah	0.5			R.I.	192					Iowa	0.1
		N. Hamp.	0.3			S. Dak.	188					Mo.	0.1
N. Hamp.	1,903	Maine	0.3	Hawaii	472	Miss.	178	W. Va.	138	Del.	67	S. Car.	0.1
Idaho	1,502	S. Dak.	0.2	Ky.	391	W. Va.	176	Alaska	137	Miss.	59	Ga.	0.1
Mont.	1,467	Idaho	0.2	W. Va.	181	Del.	152	Maine	123	S. Dak.	59	Ky.	0.1
S. Dak.	1,114	Mont.	0.2	N. Hamp.	135	N. Dak.	127	N. Dak.	100	N. Dak.	47	Tenn.	0.1
N. Dak.	777	N. Dak.	0.1	Vt.	57	Vt.	79	S. Dak.	89	N. Hamp.	41	Ala.	0.1
Vt.	519	Vt.	0.1					Vt.	68	Vt.	25	Ark.	0.1
												W. Va.	0.0

* U. S. Bureau of the Census, U. S. Census of Population: 1960, PC(1)-1B, p. 164.

ered so far, the Papago age distribution shows heavy concentrations in the age groups below 20; people older than 35 are rare relative to the total United States population; persons over 65 constitute only 4 per cent of the tribal totals. Racial mixture is proceeding rather slowly. Twenty per cent of Papago children have a parent who is not a full-blooded Papago; thirty years ago the proportion was 10 per cent, and sixty years ago 3 per cent. Out-marrying Papagos tend to marry other Indians rather than non-Indians. An increasing proportion of Papagos attend school, though there seems to be a preference for reservation over integrated schools. Three-fourths of employment is off the reservation. Initially commuters, many Indians later move away from the reservation to be nearer their jobs. Women especially have far greater work opportunity off the reservation. This case is probably fairly characteristic of several Indian groups in the Southwest.

NEGROES

Negroes make up by far the largest of the nonwhite groups in the United States, constituting almost 19 million people or 10.5 per cent of the 1960 population; all other nonwhites combined comprised 0.9 per cent. In 1950 the 15 million Negroes accounted for 10.0 per cent of the total population; thus they are increasing somewhat faster than the total population. New York has the largest number of both whites and Negroes. The six states having more than a million Negroes in 1960 were New York, Texas, Georgia, North Carolina, Louisiana, and Illinois.

The Negro population has been steadily diffusing through all regions of the country. In 1860, 95 per cent of all Negroes lived in the South, 5 per cent in the North, and fewer than 1 per cent west of the Mississippi River—a distribution that remained almost constant until World War I.[14] By 1940, however, the proportions reached 76 per cent in the South and 24 per cent in the West and North combined. In 1960 the percentage distribution was: Northeast, 16 per cent; North Central, 18 per cent; South, 60 per cent; and West, 6 per cent. From 1920 through 1950 the southern Negro population increased by 18 per cent, a slower rate of growth than that of the nation as a whole. Outside the South, during the same time, the Negro populace grew by a whopping 210 per cent. The Northeast added the greatest numbers of Negroes, though the Pacific states experienced the largest percentage gain—

[14] Gunnar Myrdal, *An American Dilemma*, Harper and Brothers, New York, 1944, p. 182.

970 per cent.[15] Nearly all of this differential growth is attributable to migration rather than natural increase. The heaviest losers of Negroes by migration are the "black belt" areas; thus Arkansas, Georgia, and South Carolina even had fewer Negro residents in 1950 than in 1920 despite a sizeable excess of births over deaths; Mississippi, Alabama, and North Carolina also lost large numbers of Negroes through migration. The most frequent states of destination are New York, Illinois, Michigan, and California.

Once predominantly rural, Negroes today are urbanizing rapidly. The per cent urban within the nonwhite population (which is nine-tenths Negro) increased from 62 per cent in 1950 to 72 per cent in 1960; 1950 and 1960 nonwhite proportions living in urbanized areas were 45 and 59 per cent. The increase in nonwhite population through the 1950's was 49 per cent for urban dwellers and 65 per cent in urbanized areas; rural nonwhites lost 9 per cent in population. Over-all nonwhite increase over the decade was 27 per cent.[16]

Should the present rate of natural increase among nonwhites continue, they will number over 50 million by 2000 A.D.; that is, one of every seven inhabitants will be non-Caucasoid. And a century from now, 21 per cent of the United States population would be nonwhite[17] —a proportion roughly equivalent to that in 1776.

The magnitude of this minority growth may presage intensification of existing intergroup frictions. Adjustment of the stream of Negro emigrants from the rural South to the urban North and West may be aggravated by the amplitude of their numbers. If there is any truth in the hypothesis that tensions increase directly with the size of the minority group, then the Negroes are in for continued difficulty concerning housing, employment, and other outlets for prejudice. The hoped-for transition to attainment of equality might be easier were the tempo of Negro growth retarded.

Another problem stemming from the large excess of Negro births over deaths is that the larger the family to be supported by a given income, the lower the income per child. High Negro fertility may be helping to depress their standard of living; certainly it augments difficulties in sending children to college.

---

[15] Lawson Purdy, "Negro Migration in the United States," *American Journal of Economics and Sociology*, Vol. XIII, July 1954, p. 358.

[16] U. S. Bureau of the Census, *U. S. Census of Population: 1960*, PC(1)-1B, p. 143.

[17] Donald J. Bogue, *The Population of the United States*, The Free Press, Glencoe, 1959, p. 761.

FOREIGN-BORN

In 1960 there were 9.7 million foreign-born persons residing in the United States—a marked decrease from the 14.3 million in 1930. One-seventh of the 1960 foreign-born came from Italy, with substantial proportions also originating in Canada, Germany, Russia, and Poland. Figure 18 shows long-term trends in place of origin of foreign-born residents.

Most of these immigrants settle in the urban Northeast, whereas very few reside in southern states. Less than one-half of 1 per cent of the inhabitants of Mississippi, Tennessee, and Arkansas in 1960 were born outside the United States; contiguous states too are almost entirely populated by native-born citizens. The highest percentages of foreign-born are in New York (14 per cent) and Connecticut (11 per cent). What few foreign-born persons there are in the South tend to be of German birth. States along the Mexican and Canadian borders have, as might be expected, heavy proportions of Mexican and Canadian settlers.

Over the next few decades the foreign-born populace will remain approximately constant in absolute size but will decrease as a percentage of the total population. This stability may assist assimilation.

The foreign-born population is more urban than is the general population. Four cities of over 50,000 population are made up of 20 per cent or more foreign-born persons: Miami Beach, Florida, 33 per cent; Passaic, New Jersey, 23 per cent; East Los Angeles, California, 20 per cent; and New York, New York, 20 per cent. At the opposite extreme are Gadsden, Alabama, 0.3 per cent; and 0.4 per cent for High Point, North Carolina, Macon, Georgia, and Tuscaloosa, Alabama. Gadsden has an additional 0.7 per cent of natives who have at least one foreign parent, making a total of exactly 1 per cent first- and second-generation residents—a far cry from Miami Beach's 66 per cent or New York City's 49 per cent.

FOREIGN STOCK

People who were born elsewhere and moved to the United States form only a part of the "melting pot" story. Table 37 provides data concerning the foreign stock, which is defined by the Bureau of the Census as all foreign-born persons plus natives having one or both parents foreign-born. These first- and second-generation residents now constitute nearly one-fifth of the national population and reach almost two-fifths throughout New England. Ranking the states by the percentage of population that is of foreign stock emphasizes the extreme regional differences: the four leading states are in the Northeast, while the twelve states at the

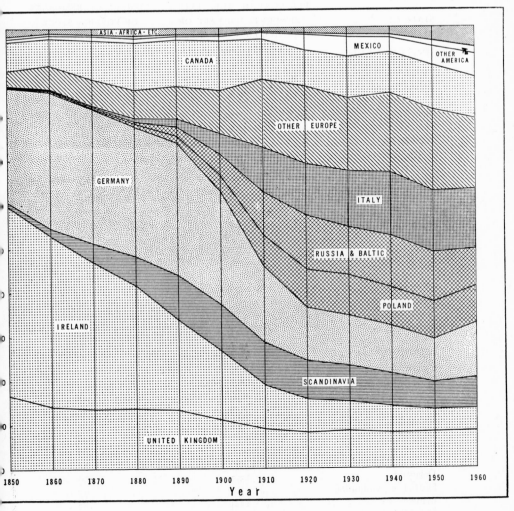

* U. S. Bureau of the Census, *Historical Statistics of the United States: 1789-1945,*
Government Printing Office, Washington, 1949, p. 32; *U. S. Census of Population:*
1950, Vol. II, "Characteristics of the Population," Part 1, United States Summary,
Government Printing Office, Washington, 1953, p. 98; and *U. S. Census of Pop-*
ulation: 1960, "General Social and Economic Characteristics: U. S. Summary,"
PC(1)-1C, 1962, p. 203. Data for 1910-1950 are for whites only; other data represent
total foreign-born.

TABLE 37. *State of Residence of Foreign Stock, United States, 1960**

STATE OF RESIDENCE	PER CENT OF THE STATE'S RESIDENTS WHO ARE OF FOREIGN STOCK	NUMBER OF RESIDENTS OF FOREIGN STOCK (IN THOUSANDS)
UNITED STATES	19.0	34,050
Massachusetts	40.0	2,058
Rhode Island	39.5	340
Connecticut	38.9	982
New York	38.6	6,487
Hawaii	38.3	243
New Jersey	34.7	2,109
North Dakota	30.0	190
New Hampshire	29.2	177
Minnesota	25.6	875
California	25.4	3,994
Michigan	24.3	1,899
Illinois	24.3	2,449
Maine	23.3	226
Wisconsin	23.1	914
Washington	22.9	654
Pennsylvania	22.1	2,502
Montana	22.1	150
Vermont	22.0	86
South Dakota	20.8	142
Nebraska	18.3	258
Arizona	18.1	236
Nevada	17.5	50
Oregon	17.0	301
Utah	15.6	139
Ohio	15.4	1,491
Florida	14.8	733
Colorado	14.8	261
Wyoming	14.6	48
Iowa	14.0	388
Alaska	13.7	31
Delaware	13.2	59
District of Columbia	12.6	97
Idaho	12.4	83
Maryland	11.9	372
Texas	11.3	1,082
Kansas	9.4	206
Missouri	8.5	367
New Mexico	8.4	79
Indiana	8.1	377
West Virginia	4.9	91
Virginia	4.5	178
Oklahoma	3.9	89
Louisiana	3.8	124

TABLE 37—*continued*

STATE OF RESIDENCE	PER CENT OF THE STATE'S RESIDENTS WHO ARE OF FOREIGN STOCK	NUMBER OF RESIDENTS OF FOREIGN STOCK (IN THOUSANDS)
Kentucky	2.5	75
Georgia	1.9	78
Arkansas	1.9	34
Alabama	1.7	55
South Carolina	1.6	38
Tennessee	1.6	59
North Carolina	1.5	68
Mississippi	1.3	29

* U. S. Bureau of the Census, *U. S. Census of Population:* 1960, PC(1)-1C, pp. 248 and 253-254.

bottom of the list are all southern. In most states, persons of Italian stock are fairly numerous. Noteworthy clusters include Canadians in the northern border states, Mexicans in the Southwest, Scandinavians in Minnesota and the Dakotas, and Germans in the South.

The "melting pot" idea discussed in Chapter 12 is being replaced in intellectual thinking by the more realistic concept of cultural pluralism. This concept refers to ethnic diversity, though its broader meaning includes any type of cultural diversity: race, ethnicity, religion, degree of urbanization, occupation, income, or standard of living.[18] For example, the ethnic diversity of the United States is based on initial Indian occupancy, British colonization and attempted extermination of Indians (and failing that, segregation on reservations), importation of Negro slaves, and influxes of free immigrants (mostly European). Many scholars believe that cultural pluralism makes a positive contribution to the maturation of the United States; as one of them avers, "through recognizing the fact of cultural pluralism we achieve cultural democracy."[19] And, of course, many other Americans disagree—one result of the altercation being the fight over immigration policies.

Language and Religion

Closely related to nationality and a part of ethnicity is the language (or languages) that one speaks fluently. In the United States, fluency in a foreign language generally indicates foreign birth. Once learned well, a language is not easily forgotten; it is one of the more persistent attributes of immigrants.

---

[18] Clyde V. Kiser, "Cultural Pluralism," *Annals of the American Academy of Political and Social Science*, Vol. CCLXII, March 1949, pp. 117-130.

[19] E. George Payne, "Education and Minority Peoples," in Francis J. Brown and Joseph S. Roucek (eds.), *One America*, Prentice-Hall, New York, 1945, p. 501.

Religion is also relevant to ethnic status and national origin. Most people accept the religion of their parents or another creed prevalent in the region where they spent their formative years. Once adopted, religious affiliation usually persists unchanged throughout the individual's life.

LANGUAGES OF THE WORLD

Of the two to four thousand languages of the world, most are spoken by rather few people. Indo-European language speakers are by far the most numerous, although the language with the greatest number of speakers —Mandarin Chinese—is of another linguistic family. The list of major languages in Table 38 showing the number of speakers in 1960 reflects customary terminology and grouping into families. Only languages having at least 10 million users are included, and all figures are rounded to one or two significant digits. One word of caution: as there is considerable disagreement among linguists regarding family relationship, labeling, and even the total number of world languages, the list is not definitive. Similarly, the population data should not be regarded as exact but rather as crude approximations.[20]

TABLE 38. *Number of Speakers of Major World Languages, 1960*

Indo-European family: 1,600,000,000
  Teutonic subfamily (derived from speech of Angles, Jutes, Saxons, Norsemen, others): 500,000,000
    German: 100,000,000
    Dutch: 20,000,000
    English (most widely distributed language): 300,000,000
  Italic subfamily: 400,000,000
    Spanish: 150,000,000
    Portuguese: 70,000,000
    French (second most widely distributed language): 80,000,000
    Italian: 60,000,000
    Roumanian: 15,000,000
  Greek (second oldest known Indo-European language, after Sanscrit): 10,000,000
  Balto-Slavic subfamily: 300,000,000
    Serbo-Croatian (Yugoslavia): 10,000,000
    Czech: 10,000,000
    Polish: 30,000,000
    Russian: 150,000,000
    Ukranian (Little Russia): 40,000,000
  Indo-Iranian subfamily: 450,000,000
    Persian: 20,000,000
    Pushtu (Afghan): 10,000,000

[20] Cf. for example C. F. and F. M. Voegelin, "Languages Now Spoken by Over a Million Speakers," *Anthropological Linguistics*, Vol. III, No. 8, November 1961, pp. 13-22.

Hindustani (like Sanscrit; northern India): 30,000,000
Hindi (northern India): 70,000,000
Urdu (Hindustani with Persian and Arabic influences; Moslem; northern
    India): 70,000,000
Bengali (eastern India, Bengal, Calcutta): 70,000,000
Punjabi (northern India, Punjab, Pakistan): 30,000,000
Marathi (western India, Bombay): 30,000,000
Rajasithani (northwestern India): 20,000,000
Oriya (eastern India): 15,000,000
Gujarati (western India, north of Bombay): 20,000,000
Bihari (northeast India): 30,000,000

Semitic-Hamitic family: 120,000,000
Arabic (Semitic; named for Shem, son of Noah): 80,000,000
Hausa (Hamitic, after Ham, son of Noah; Nigeria): 10,000,000

Ural-Altaic family: 100,000,000
Magyar (Hungarian, Ugric; Uralic subfamily): 15,000,000
Turkish (Siberia, northwest China, Turkey, Iraq; Altaic subfamily): 20,000,-
    000

Sino-Tibetan family: 800,000,000
Mandarin Chinese (Kuo-Yu; northern China; national literary language):
    450,000,000
Wu (Shanghai): 50,000,000
Foochow (Fukien, Min; south coastal China): 50,000,000
Cantonese (Yueh; most common Chinese dialect in United States): 50,000,-
    000
Hakka (southeastern China): 15,000,000
Burmese: 20,000,000
Thai (Siamese): 15,000,000
Vietnamese (Annamese, Tonkinese): 20,000,000

Japanese family: 130,000,000
Japanese: 100,000,000
Korean (questionable relation to Japanese): 30,000,000

Dravidian family: 100,000,000
Tamil (southeastern India, Ceylon): 30,000,000
Telugu (southeastern India, Madras): 40,000,000
Canarese (southwestern India, south of Bombay): 15,000,000
Malayalam (southwestern India): 15,000,000

Malayo-Polynesian family: 100,000,000
Malay (Indonesia): 20,000,000
Javanese: 40,000,000
Sundanese (Indonesia): 10,000,000
Visayan (Philippines): 10,000,000

African family (quasi-related family of over 300 languages): 150,000,000
Swahili (Bantu subfamily; modified by Arabic; commercial lingua franca of
    eastern Africa): 20,000,000

MOTHER TONGUE

The most common mother tongue among United States foreign-born
in 1960 was English, followed closely by German and Italian and less

closely by Spanish, Polish, and Yiddish. German speakers are most prevalent in New York, California, and Illinois; Italian speakers in New York, New Jersey, and Pennsylvania; Spanish as a mother tongue is heavily concentrated in California and Texas; Polish and Yiddish in New York.[21]

Sociologists and others are interested in the extent to which immigrants have become adapted to American culture. Clinging to the old language probably is correlated with a lack of assimilation; those immigrants who teach their American-born children their ancestral speech are likely also to have refused to abandoned the "old country" ways of thinking, believing, and acting. As we are unable to ask questions in censuses regarding social organization and values, the mother tongue variable has been used as a substitute for these complicated aspects of culture. Of 22 million people reporting non-English mother tongues in the 1940 census, 8 million were foreign-born and 14 million were native-born; they represented almost one-fifth of the total white population of the United States and three-fourths of the foreign-born residents. The largest group was the Germans, two-thirds of whom were born in the United States. Of the foreign languages reported by natives of native parentage, those most frequently mentioned (and therefore perhaps indicative of little assimilation) were: Spanish, 39 per cent; French, 37 per cent; German, 19 per cent; Czech, 16 per cent; and Norwegian, 12 per cent. High linguistic assimilation possibly is indicated by low percentages of such third- and higher-generation speakers: Russian, 2 per cent; Yiddish, 3 per cent; and Swedish, 4 per cent.[22]

RELIGIOUS AFFILIATION

Adequate data concerning the extent of religious devoutness or "real" church membership are not available; neither are reliable statistics concerning church membership as such. Once a person joins a church, he may be kept on the rolls for years after he has ceased to attend or even care; duplication is also commonplace. In a country where people switch their denominational affiliations as frequently as they do in the United States, this error involves millions of people.

Indeed, the only religious item for which data are accurate enough to warrant reproduction is the affiliation reported by persons being interviewed. And even these data are imperfect, as some people resent

---

[21] U. S. Bureau of the Census, *U. S. Census of Population: 1960*, PC(1)-1C, pp. 255-256.

[22] U. S. Bureau of the Census, *Sixteenth Census of the United States: 1940*, "Nativity and Parentage of the White Population: Mother Tongue," Government Printing Office, Washington, 1943, pp. 2 and 7.

TABLE 39. *Religion by Color and Sex, United States, 1957**

| | Number of Persons (In Thousands) | | | | | Per Cent Distribution | | | | |
| | | WHITE | | NONWHITE | | | WHITE | | NONWHITE | |
RELIGION	TOTAL	MALE	FEMALE	MALE	FEMALE	TOTAL	MALE	FEMALE	MALE	FEMALE
Total, 14 years old and over	119,333	51,791	55,570	5,679	6,293	100	100	100	100	100
Protestant	78,952	32,320	36,155	4,851	5,626	66	62	65	85	89
Baptist	23,525	7,822	8,450	3,354	3,899	20	15	15	59	62
Lutheran	8,417	4,084	4,301	17	15	7	8	8	0	0
Methodist	16,676	6,788	7,821	968	1,099	14	13	14	17	18
Presbyterian	6,656	3,000	3,549	57	50	6	6	6	1	1
Other Protestant	23,678	10,626	12,034	455	563	20	20	22	8	9
Roman Catholic	30,669	14,396	15,499	361	413	26	28	28	6	7
Jewish	3,868	1,860	1,999	1	8	3	4	4	0	0
Other religion	1,545	688	676	88	93	1	1	1	2	2
No religion	3,195	2,051	730	306	108	3	4	1	5	2
Religion not reported	1,104	476	511	72	45	1	1	1	1	1

* United States Bureau of the Census, "Religion Reported by the Civilian Population of the United States: March 1957," *Current Population Reports*, Series P-20, No. 79, February 2, 1958, p. 6.

the question or for other reasons refuse to answer or give a false reply. However, tests conducted by the Bureau of the Census to evaluate incorporation of a question on religion in the 1960 Census led their experts to conclude that resistance to the question was rather low. Nonetheless the item was dropped from the 1960 Census plans at the insistence of groups who considered it an invasion of privacy. The decennial census has never included a direct question on religious preference or affiliation, although data have been secured from organized religious bodies intermittently since 1850, and religious questions are occasionally included in the Current Population Survey.

Table 39 documents the prevalence of Protestantism in the United States. Note, however, that no single Protestant denomination has as many adherents as the Roman Catholic Church. Protestants, Catholics, and Jews taken together constitute 95 per cent of the population aged 14 years or more. Regional strongholds are the South among Baptists, the North Central area among Lutherans, and the Northeast among Roman Catholics and Jews.

Religious organizations such as the National Council of Churches do refer to the proportion of United States residents that are church-connected, but the latter term is so vague in definition that imprecision of measurement is to be expected. The current fraction is reported as three-fifths—the highest percentage in the nation's history; 100 years ago it was one-fifth. Sunday schools are expanding, and the construction of new churches absorbed 13 per cent of the national public building budget in 1960.

Demographic characteristics of major national religious groups have been studied by the University of Michigan Survey Research Center, one report of which states:

> The analysis indicates only slight differences in sex composition, marital status, and age structure among Protestants, Roman Catholics, and Jews except for a middle-aged concentration among Episcopalians and Presbyterians. People who report they are without a religion are heavily male and have a larger percentage single than does the nation as a whole. The number of children in Jewish, Episcopalian, and Presbyterian families is similar, but smaller than the number in other religious groups. On education, occupation, and income, the religious groups can be separated into three descending ranks: 1) a top rank, having large percentages of college graduates and white collar workers, and enjoying high incomes, composed of Episcopalians, Jews, and Presbyterians; 2) a middle rank, containing smaller percentages of college graduates and white collar workers, and earning less income, consisting of Methodists, Lutherans, Roman Catholics, and the "no

religion" group; 3) the bottom ranked Baptists with few college graduates or white collar workers and low family incomes.[23]

Research conducted by the National Opinion Research Center
substantiates and supplements these conclusions (see Table 40). According to this study the highest proportions of proprietary and profes-

TABLE 40. *Occupation, Education, and Income by Religious
Affiliation, United States, 1955**

Occupational Distribution by Percentage

RELIGIOUS AFFILIATION	PROPRI-ETARY, PROFES-SIONAL, TECH-NICAL	FARM OPER-ATORS OR MAN-AGERS	OPER-ATIVES	LABOR-ERS, NON-FARM	MEDIAN YEARS OF SCHOOL COM-PLETED	MEDIAN INCOME
Total	10.0	10.8	20.3	6.1	9.5	$4,094
Protestant	9.5	12.9	19.7	7.0	9.5	3,933
Baptist	6.0	13.3	25.3	10.0	7.8	3,174
Methodist	10.2	15.7	16.6	5.5	10.7	4,235
Presbyterian	15.3	8.0	15.8	3.6	11.0	4,586
Episcopal	19.6	1.5	9.6	5.3	11.8	5,000
Lutheran	8.0	15.6	15.1	5.2	9.6	4,278
Other Protestant	10.4	11.6	21.6	6.8	9.3	4,008
Roman Catholic	9.6	5.4	23.8	4.6	9.4	4,340
Jewish	17.6	1.3	12.0	1.3	11.4	5,954
Other	17.7	4.6	16.9	6.8	8.8	3,875
No religion	11.7	13.0	19.6	3.0	9.2	4,320

* Special tabulations of survey data from National Opinion Research Center,
Jacob J. Feldman, Senior Study Director; quoted in Donald Bogue, *The Population
of the United States*, The Free Press, Glencoe, 1959, pp. 703, 704, and 706.

sional people is found among Episcopalians, Jews, and "Other"; laborers
and operatives are most often Baptists and Roman Catholics. Educational achievement varies from above average performances by Episcopalians, Jews, Presbyterians, and Methodists to low schooling among
Baptists. Income is highest among Jews and lowest among Baptists.

Estimates of worldwide membership in religious organizations are
informed guesses. World totals for 1962, rounded to the nearest 50
million, were: Roman Catholic, 550; Moslem, 450; Hindu, 350; Con-

[23] Bernard Lazerwitz, "A Comparison of Major United States Religious Groups,"
Journal of the American Statistical Association, Vol. LVI, No. 295, September
1961, p. 568.

fucian, 350; Protestant, 200; Buddhist, 150; Eastern Orthodox, 150; Shinto, 50; Taoist, 50; and other or no religion, 700.[24] The three Christian groups, totaling 900 million, will probably grow more slowly than others because most Christians live in countries with small rates of increase. Islam should grow moderately, and the others more rapidly.

---

[24] Encyclopædia Britannica, *Britannica Book of the Year*, Chicago, 1963, p. 270.

20 ❧ Achieved Characteristics

In the preceding chapter some statistics were presented regarding the more abiding characteristics of human populations. This chapter focuses on the changeable social and economic traits of marital status, education, literacy, occupation, and income. Here as previously, emphasis is placed on the United States.

Marital Status

In modern censuses, marital conditions are often subsumed into six categories: 1) never married, 2) married—spouse present, 3) married—spouse absent, 4) widowed, 5) divorced, and 6) miscellaneous. This last classification may be split into several subcategories in order to differentiate among common-law mating, civil versus religious marriage, concubinage, morganatic marriage, and the variegated other types of marital sexual union that are practiced. The legal and religious obligations involved vary from none (as in certain consensual arrangements) through diverse shadings of rights and responsibilities toward spouse, offspring, and relatives.

MARRIAGE RATES

The marital composition of the United States is shown in Figure 19. Notice the Gibraltar-like pre-eminence of the married condition in both sexes. Note also the striking difference in proportion widowed at all ages.

The marital status of United States males 14 years of age and older was reported in the 1960 Census as follows: single, 25.0 per cent; married, spouse present, 66.0 per cent; married, separated, 1.4 per cent; married, spouse absent but not separated, 2.1 per cent; widowed, 3.4

FIGURE 19. *Marital Status by Age and Sex, United States, 1960**

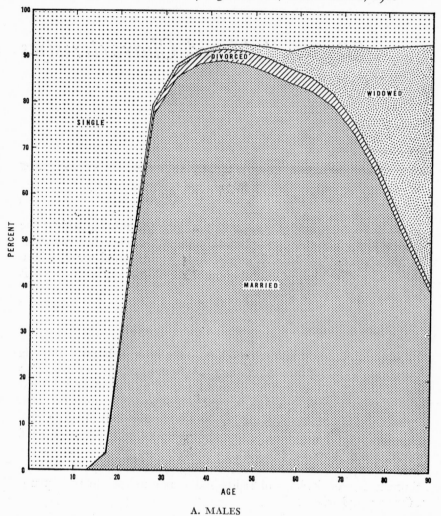

A. MALES

* U. S. Bureau of the Census, *U. S. Census of Population:* 1960, "Detailed Characteristics: United States Summary," PC(1)-1D, Government Printing Office, Washington, 1963, pp. 424-435.

per cent; divorced, 2.1 per cent. Comparable figures for females aged 14 or more were: single, 19.0 per cent; married, spouse present, 62.1 per cent; married, separated, 2.0 per cent; married, spouse absent but not separated, 1.9 per cent; widowed, 12.1 per cent; and divorced, 2.9 per cent. Among men who ever married, 14.0 per cent married more

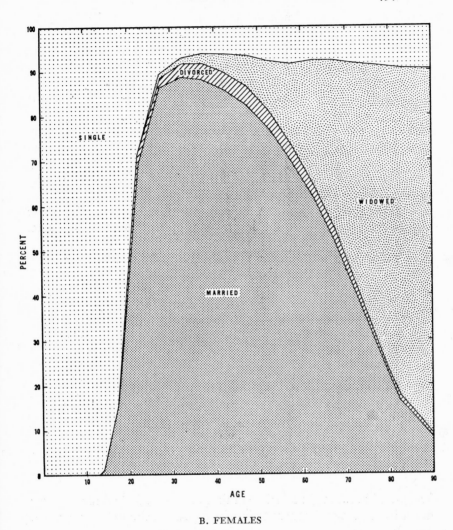

PERCENT

AGE

B. FEMALES

than once; among women who ever married, 14.1 per cent married two or more times.

Over the last century the marriage rate has fluctuated substantially from year to year but has shown a slight secular propensity to rise. The highest recorded rate since 1860 is 16.2 per 1,000 population in 1946; lowest rates are 7.7 in 1863 and 7.9 in 1862 and 1932.[1]

Recent alterations in marriage and divorce rates reflect changes in the

[1] Paul H. Jacobson, *American Marriage and Divorce*, Rinehart and Co., New York, 1959, p. 21.

normative system. The median age at first marriage continues its long-term decline, being 22.8 for men and 20.2 for women in 1961. About two-fifths of all brides and one-eighth of all grooms are in their teens. Americans are also completing reproduction earlier in life, which means that women can enter the labor force in increasing numbers. Marriage is becoming a smaller financial commitment for the man. Breaking the marriage ties—and vows—is taken more lightly than formerly. And for many persons marriage has become a more personal thing; companionate marriage, though still not accepted in all its aspects, is more common. Divorce is increasing, but because of lower mortality and a greater tendency toward remarriage, the total of marriages broken by divorce or death has remained remarkably steady.

The life cycle of American women has altered in reflecting these changes. Table 41 shows the lengthening of the "empty nest" state.

TABLE 41. *The Changing Life Cycle of Men and Women, United States, 1890 and 1950**

STAGE OF THE LIFE CYCLE OF THE FAMILY	MEDIAN AGE OF HUSBAND		MEDIAN AGE OF WIFE	
	1950	1890	1950	1890
First marriage	22.8	26.1	20.1	22.0
Birth of last child	28.8	36.0	26.1	31.9
Marriage of last child	50.3	59.4	47.6	55.3
Death of one spouse[a]	64.1	57.4	61.4	53.3
Death of other spouse[b]	71.6	66.4	77.2	67.7

[a] Husband and wife survive jointly from marriage to specified age.
[b] Husband or wife survives separately from marriage to specified age.

* Paul C. Glick, "The Life Cycle of the Family," *Marriage and Family Living*, Vol. XVII, February 1955, pp. 3-9.

The period between the marriage of the youngest child and the mother's death has increased by more than fifteen years in the last half century. This demographic change, supplemented by modified folkways regulating the behavior of matrons, has created new social and occupational patterns in the United States.

Marriage rates are also influenced by political events. War affects the marriage rate in proportion to the proximity of the actual fighting and to the nature and intensity of its impact on the citizenry. A brief conflict (like the Spanish-American War of 1898) which hardly disturbs the customary activities occasions only a small dent in the marriage rate. On the other hand, in a country overrun by battles (such as France in World Wars I and II) reaction is immediate and pronounced.

Marriage regulation in the United States is the exclusive province of each state; local variations exist regarding age at first marriage, the waiting period, premarital examinations, nonresident marriages, parental permission for minors, and total marriage rates. The preference for June marriages among new brides is a national phenomenon (though less pronounced in the South and West), as is the practically uniform monthly rate for second and later marriages. Approximately three-fourths of American marriages are celebrated with religious ceremonies.

HOUSEHOLD FORMATION

When people marry, they generally establish a household—a socio-economic unit consisting of a group of individuals living together. In the United States this unit normally comprises an adult man, an adult woman, and their children. Demographers also speak of one-person households—that is, individuals living alone forming separate social and economic units. The household sometimes includes relatives, servants, boarders, and guests. The distinctive element is that of residing together in one dwelling place, whether it be a house, apartment, trailer, tent, or igloo. The members need not be biologically or maritally related as long as they share living quarters and housekeeping arrangements.

In the twentieth century the number of households in the United States has trebled. For that matter, throughout the nation's existence, household formation has exceeded population increase. This means that the average number of persons per household has become smaller —a consequence both of declining fertility and of restriction of the family to two generations instead of three. Grandparents are coming to be classified as "close relatives" rather than "immediate family." In 1950, there were in the United States 43 million households, a total that will probably increase by about 10 million every decade for the rest of the twentieth century. In 1960 the 53 million households contained an average of 3.3 persons each. Three-fourths of the households included both husband and wife.

DIVORCE RATES

Marriage is the only civil contract in the United States that cannot be dissolved officially at the will of the persons involved. In divorce proceedings the state is always a third and interested party. For seventy years before it allowed divorce in 1949, South Carolina was the only state in the Union which did not grant divorce for any cause, and legal separations there amounted to "little more than a score annually during the 1940's."[2]

---

[2] *Ibid.*, p. 109.

Marital dissolution takes five forms: desertion, legal separation, annulment, divorce, and death. Desertion (sometimes described as the poor man's divorce) does not alter legal status: persons cannot remarry and financial responsibility remains. Legal separation seems to be a device to satisfy religious strictures prohibiting divorce; by keeping to the letter of the church law, it provides the disadvantages of divorce without its benefits. Annulment is a legal proclamation that there never was a marriage in the first place; where divorce is difficult (as in New York State), annulment rates may exceed divorce rates.

The long-term United States divorce trend is definitely upward. The rate has multiplied several times in the past one hundred years, and it offers every prospect of continuing to rise in the foreseeable future. In 1959 divorces and annulments in the United States numbered 395,000— one for every 3.8 weddings. Divorces per 1,000 married females 15 years of age or older declined from a maximum of 17.9 in 1946 to 8.9 in 1958 and thereupon increased to 9.3 in 1959.[3] In the sixteen states officially reporting such data, 67 per cent of the decrees were granted to the wife and 39 per cent were granted to families with no children under 18 years of age. Legal grounds for the decree were: adultery, 1.2 per cent; bigamy, 0.5 per cent; conviction of crime, 0.6 per cent; cruelty, 51.6 per cent; desertion, 23.2 per cent; drunkenness, 1.2 per cent; fraud, 0.3 per cent; insanity, 0.1 per cent; nonsupport, 4.1 per cent; under age, 0.1 per cent; other and not stated, 17.2 per cent. The highest rate of divorces per 1,000 midyear population was in Nevada (34); other leaders were Oklahoma (6) and Arizona and Alabama (5). The lowest rates (including annulments) were reported for New York (0.5), New Jersey (0.7), and North Dakota (0.9). The number of divorces granted was highest in California, Texas, Illinois, and Ohio; these four states together accounted for almost one-third of the national total.[4] Monthly variations were negligible.

Amateur sociologists are sometimes prone to attribute social disorganization to climbing divorce rates. Juvenile delinquency, for example, is said to be caused by marital break-ups, on the basis of the view that two parents are necessary to the proper rearing of a child. On this reasoning, homes broken by death must also be considered. Marriages may end either "naturally" through death of a spouse or "civilly" through divorce or annulment. The total marital dissolution rate from death and divorce combined is fairly constant. The rising divorce rate is ap-

---

[3] National Office of Vital Statistics, *Vital Statistics of the United States: 1959*, Section 2: "Marriage and Divorce Statistics," Government Printing Office, Washington, 1961, p. 17.

[4] *Ibid.*, pp. 28, 29, and 31.

proximately balanced by a declining proportion of marriages broken by death of a spouse. It has been reported that the United States divorce rate rose from 1.2 per 1,000 existing marriages in 1860 to 9.3 in 1956, whereas the dissolution rate by death declined over the same period from 28.4 to 17.5. Total marital dissolutions have hovered around 30 per 1,000 since 1860, with a maximum rate of 39.6 in 1918 (caused by the influenza epidemic) and a low of 26.7 in 1954 and 1955.[5] Through the years the relative importance of death and divorce has altered considerably: a century ago, divorce accounted for less than one-twentieth of dissolved marriages; this figure is now about one-third. Since remarriage of divorced and widowed persons is rising, the proportion of permanently broken homes may even be decreasing.

WIDOWS AND WIDOWERS

At the time of the 1960 Census the 1,313,000 divorced men (not including 908,000 separated males) and 1,839,000 divorced women (excluding 1,306,000 separated females) were outnumbered by the 2,219,000 widowers and 7,945,000 widows. Widows, by far the most numerous type of once-married persons, have been increasing by more than 100,000 annually for two decades. This increment results from the surplus of accretions to the group as wives become widows (550,000 in 1961) over remarriage or death of women previously widowed.

Widows outnumber widowers by a steadily widening margin, for two reasons: mortality is higher among males than among females; and the remarriage rate is higher among widowers than among widows, probably because of the very low sex ratio at the relevant ages. The median age of widowers in 1961 was 72 years, of widows 67 years. Today there are almost four widows for every widower, as compared to the two to one ratio at the turn of the century. Of United States women aged 65 years or older, 55 per cent are widowed, as compared with 24 per cent of men of the same age.[6]

Widowhood is less frequent among whites than among nonwhites for both sexes. Widows comprise a smaller proportion of farm women than of urban women; farm-city differences among males are negligible. The proportion of men in each state who are widowed also does not vary greatly; Maine, New Hampshire, and Pennsylvania reach 4.3 per cent, and aside from Alaska at 1.9 per cent and Utah at 2.3 per cent, no state falls below 2.8 per cent. Interstate variations in their proportion of widowed women are much greater, ranging from 14.0 per cent in Mis-

---

[5] Jacobson, *American Marriage and Divorce*, *op. cit.*, p. 142.
[6] U. S. Bureau of the Census, "Marital Status and Family Status: March 1961," *Current Population Reports*, Series P-20, No. 114, January 31, 1962, pp. 1 and 7-8.

sissippi and Arkansas to 4.7 per cent in Alaska, 7.8 per cent in Hawaii, and an average of 10.0 per cent in the Rocky Mountain states.[7]

According to life tables, the average widowed woman can expect to live another fifteen years after her husband's death. This fact often results in acute economic stress, as many widows must nurture young children, and those over 45 face great difficulty securing employment because of their age and frequently protracted absence from the working force.

Education and Literacy

There is a great deal of talk about the importance of maintaining a high level of literacy and education in countries where citizens are expected to make informed, intelligent choices in elections. In nondemocratic countries it is also desirable to have an educated populace—a major obstacle to industrial and other advances is frequently the lack of necessary training in the physical and social sciences. The national supply of scientific, technological, and scholarly manpower is of vital concern for a country's resource development, invention and discovery, and military strength.

SCHOOL ENROLLMENT

Students attending classes in elementary, secondary, collegiate, professional, graduate, and vocational schools form an increasingly large segment of the United States population (see Table 42). Undoubtedly the most visible result of the changing age structure since World War II is the demand for enlarged elementary school facilities. Early in the 1950's primary schools were inundated by a tidal wave of babies reaching school entrance age; high schools faced this same flood eight years later. Today, large-scale building programs and a leveling of accretions to this age group are relieving pressure on elementary schools. But school boards must devote additional attention to expansion of secondary school facilities. The relentless surge carries inevitably through successive age levels, and an increasing proclivity to attend institutions of higher learning helps presage a severe test for collegiate instructional and housing facilities. Next to weather the onslaught will be graduate and professional schools.

Given the expected increases in the school age population and the greater propensity to prolong schooling through high school and col-

---

[7] U. S. Bureau of the Census, U. S. *Census of Population: 1960*, "General Population Characteristics: United States Summary," PC(1)-1B, Government Printing Office, Washington, 1961, pp. 156 and 174.

TABLE 42. *School Enrollment by Level and Age, United States, 1950-1960**

LEVEL OF SCHOOL AND AGE	OCTOBER 1950	OCTOBER 1960	Increase, 1950 to 1960	
			NUMBER	PER CENT
Total, 5 to 34 years	30,276,000	46,259,000	15,983,000	52.8
Level of School				
Kindergarten	902,000	2,092,000	1,190,000	131.9
Elementary school (grades 1 to 8)	20,504,000	30,349,000	9,845,000	48.0
High school (grades 9 to 12)	6,656,000	10,249,000	3,593,000	54.0
College or professional school	2,214,000	3,570,000	1,356,000	61.2
Age				
5 and 6 years	4,061,000	6,438,000	2,377,000	58.5
7 to 13 years	16,655,000	25,621,000	8,966,000	53.8
14 to 17 years	6,953,000	10,242,000	3,289,000	47.3
18 to 24 years	2,149,000	3,167,000	1,018,000	47.4
25 to 34 years	458,000	792,000	334,000	72.9

* U. S. Bureau of the Census, "Fall School Enrollment at 46 Million," *Current Population Reports*, P-20, No. 107, January 16, 1961, p. 1.

lege, the United States should require large additions to the supply of school teachers and college professors. Some persons fear that instructional staffs will not be able to keep up with increasing enrollments and that the quality of education will suffer. On the other hand, departments of education and graduate schools are turning out larger numbers of teachers and Ph.D.'s, causing some observers to be optimistic. Bernard Berelson, for one, sees little chance of our running out of college professors:

> The sense of Crisis that makes discussions of graduate education sound shrill these days is unwarranted and misleading. . . . Forecasts have traditionally been pessimistic in this field. What is the problem? It is that within a fifteen-year period we shall be doubling our baccalaureate ranks. But baccalaureate degrees have doubled, or more, every fifteen years or so in this century—whereas doctorates have kept ahead of that pace by doubling every decade or so. . . . The numbers game is by no means lost.[8]

[8] Bernard Berelson, *Graduate Education in the United States*, McGraw-Hill Book Co., New York, 1960, pp. 79-80.

Of course, much depends on the proportion of potential professors who are drawn into industry by high salaries, research opportunities, and other inducements.

EDUCATIONAL ATTAINMENT

The United States educational level is steadily rising, as measured by the median number of school years completed by persons 25 years of age and older. During the last two decades every state showed an increase. The national median improved from 8.6 years in 1940 to 10.6 in 1960. Census Bureau projections published in 1959 anticipate increases to 12.0 in 1970 and 12.3 in 1980. The percentage completing four years of college rose from 4.6 per cent in 1940 to 7.7 per cent in 1960, and high school graduates increased from 24.1 per cent in 1940 to 41.1 per cent in 1960, while those who failed to finish a single year of school decreased from 3.7 to 2.3 per cent. Projections by the Bureau of the Census are: four years of college—9.0 to 9.2 per cent in 1970 and 10.4 to 11.0 per cent in 1980; four years of high school or more—50.0 to 50.7 per cent in 1970 and 57.5 to 59.7 per cent in 1980; and no years of schooling completed—1.2 per cent in 1970 and 0.8 to 0.9 per cent in 1980.[9]

A sample survey conducted by the Bureau of the Census in October 1960 showed the following distribution of educational attainment among men aged 20-24 years: 32 per cent did not graduate from high school, 32 per cent graduated from high school but did not attend college, 10 per cent attended college but did not graduate, 20 per cent are currently enrolled in college, and 6 per cent graduated from college. Of those whose fathers were college graduates, about 78 per cent were currently attending or had graduated from college; of those whose fathers did not graduate from high school, only 16 per cent were attending or had completed college. About half of the men interviewed had already reached a higher level of education than had their fathers, about two-fifths had reached the same level, and only one-tenth had not attained their fathers' educational peak.[10]

Table 43 shows the magnitude of urban-rural, racial, sex, regional, and state differences prevailing in 1960. Note that educational attainment was greater in urban than in rural areas, though this difference was not so great as is the white-nonwhite differential, which was ob-

---

[9] Charles B. Nam, "Projections of Educational Attainment in the United States: 1960 to 1980," *Current Population Reports*, Series P-20, No. 91, January 12, 1959, pp. 6-9.

[10] U. S. Bureau of the Census, "School Enrollment and Education of Young Adults and Their Fathers: October 1960," *Current Population Reports*, Series P-20, No. 110, July 24, 1961, p. 1.

TABLE 43. *Years of Schooling Completed by Persons 25 Years Old and Over, by Urbanization, Race, Sex, and Region, United States, 1950-1960* *

MEDIAN YEARS OF SCHOOL COMPLETED

	1950	1960
TOTAL	9.3	10.6
Urban	10.2	11.1
Rural nonfarm	8.8	9.5
Rural farm	8.4	8.8
White	9.7	10.9
Nonwhite	6.9	8.2
Male	9.0	10.3
Female	9.6	10.9
Northeast	9.6	10.7
North Central	9.4	10.7
South	8.6	9.6
West	11.3	12.0
Highest state	12.0 (Utah)	12.2 (Utah)
Lowest state	7.6 (La., S.C.)	8.7 (Ky., S.C.)

PER CENT BY YEARS OF SCHOOL COMPLETED

	1950	1960
4 years of college	6.2%	7.7%
Highest state	8.1 (Calif., Colo.)	10.7 (Colo.)
Lowest state	3.1 (Ark.)	4.8 (Ark.)
4 years of high school or more	34.2	41.1
No years	2.6	2.3
Lowest state	0.6 (Iowa)	0.5 (Iowa)
Highest state	9.1 (La.)	6.6 (La., Hawaii)

* U. S. Bureau of the Census, *U. S. Census of Population: 1950*, Vol. II, "Characteristics of the Population," Part 1, U. S. Summary, Government Printing Office, Washington, 1953, pp. 96 and 118; *U. S. Census of Population: 1960*, "General Social and Economic Characteristics: United States Summary," PC(1)-1C, pp. 207-209, 248, and 260.

servable in all states except New Hampshire and is pronounced in the South. Women's years of schooling exceeded that of men in every state except Rhode Island and Utah. Of the seven states in which the majority of residents aged 25 and over have finished high school, all were in the West. The nine states in which the majority have not completed the ninth grade were all in the South. Nonwhites in South Carolina averaged only 5.9 years of schooling. Utah's outstanding record was attributable to the high value placed on schooling by Mormons. Colorado had more than twice as high a percentage of college graduates as did Arkansas. For two decades Louisiana has had the highest proportion of residents who have not finished a single year of school; in 1940, 12.8 per cent of all Louisianans older than 25 were in this category.

The superiority of the West and the poor showing of the South are also reflected in performances on the Federal selective service mental test. The lowest percentages of failures, 4.7 per cent, were recorded in Utah and Washington; the five foremost states are all in the West. The highest percentages of mental test failures are credited to South Carolina at 54.6 per cent and Mississippi at 54.5 per cent; the eleven weakest states on this mental test are all southern.

It is frequently stated that the nation is becoming more homogeneous in educational attainment, that is, that existing differences are vanishing. But this is not true in all instances; some existing inequalities are being maintained and even enlarged. Between 1940 and 1950 the highest percentage increase in median years of schooling completed among all states in the South was smaller than the lowest percentage increase of any state in the West; absolute increases showed an even greater tendency for the South to slip further behind the West. These statistics measure educational practices over the last half century. Since migration is selective of better educated persons, and since the South has lost and the West gained by migration, these increased differentials may be attributable to differential migration. Between 1950 and 1960 the gap between the South and the West declined as regards median years of schooling, though only from 2.7 to 2.4. White-nonwhite and male-female differentials remained about the same during the 1950's. The urban-rural farm difference closed from 1.8 years to 1.3.

Cities exhibit striking variations in educational attainment of their inhabitants. The best records are achieved by college towns and the better residential suburbs surrounding such cities as New York, Chicago, and Cleveland; the worst, by communities bordering the Rio Grande and lower Mississippi Rivers and by old New England mill towns and cities receiving substantial proportions of immigrants. In 1960 among cities of 50,000 or more, the highest median years of school completed among persons 25 years of age or older were found in Bethesda, Maryland, 15.0; Ann Arbor, Michigan, 13.7; and Palo Alto, California, 13.3. Lowest medians appeared in Fall River and New Bedford, Massachusetts, 8.4; and Laredo, Texas, whose famous streets are traversed by people averaging an unimpressive 6.4 years of schooling. Until 1960 no decennial census had ever reported a single incorporated community in the United States as having 50 per cent college graduates among its population over 25 years of age; in the last census, however, this barrier was crashed by Swarthmore, Pennsylvania, which contains 52 per cent college graduates (and no one reporting less than a year of schooling). There still remain cities whose median years of schooling fall below five years—for example, San Pedro, Texas, at 2.0.[11]

HIGHER EDUCATION

Some states are grossly deficient in higher education facilities. Regional disequities are illuminated in Table 44, compiled from prominent academic indicators. Schools are identified as superior through either absolute or relative bases; for example, a college may be outstanding for its total production of distinguished scholars or for the number of such scholars per student. The leadership of the Northeast is partly attributable to the sheer number of institutions of higher education in the region. The South is last on every criterion. Schools making the best showings regarding the eight criteria and composite index are, in order: universities—Harvard, Chicago, Yale, Columbia, Princeton, California, Michigan, Wisconsin, Cornell; technical schools—Massachusetts Institute of Technology, California Institute of Technology; colleges—Oberlin, Swarthmore, Haverford, Bryn Mawr.

Paul Glick and Herman Miller have tried to determine the monetary value of formal schooling.[12] Using 1950 Census data for men, they found the income increment that was associated with additional schooling. This annual increment was about $150, $250, and $500 respectively for each year of elementary school, high school, and college, with an extra increment for graduation. A life table showed estimated lifetime earnings to be $58,000 for persons having no formal schooling, $116,000 for elementary school graduates, $135,000 for those with one to three years of high school, $165,000 for high school graduates, $190,000 for those with one to three years of college, and $268,000 for college graduates. This study lacked experimental controls for intelligence, ambition, and other relevant background variables, but we may nonetheless conclude that investment in education does pay off in the long run.

The correlation between income and educational attainment is mediated largely through the intervening variable, occupation. "Education qualifies the individual for participation in occupational life, and pursuit of an occupation yields him a return in the form of income. . . . Well-educated persons engage disproportionately in high-income occupations and poorly-educated persons in low-income occupations."[13]

[11] U. S. Bureau of the Census, *U. S. Census of Population: 1960*, PC(1)-1C, Table 153, and PC(1)-2C through PC(1)-53C, Tables 73 and 81.
[12] Paul C. Glick and Herman P. Miller, "Educational Level and Potential Income," *American Sociological Review*, Vol. XXI, No. 3, June 1956, pp. 307-312.
[13] Otis Dudley Duncan, "Occupational Components of Educational Differences in Income," *Journal of the American Statistical Association*, Vol. LVI, No. 296, December 1961, pp. 783-784.

TABLE 44. *Regional Distribution of Academically Superior Colleges, United States*

Number of Outstanding Colleges

CRITERION	NORTHEAST	NORTH CENTRAL	SOUTH	WEST
Graduate Schools[a]	7	10	1	4
Production of Professors[b]	14	14	1	5
Faculty Salaries[c]	18	5	2	3
Libraries[d]	13	2	2	3
Doctorates Granted[e]	7	5	0	1
Scholarships Awarded[f]	18	6	2	4
Production of Scholars[g]	8	9	0	3
Educational Expenditures[h]	13	2	0	1
Composite Index	26	10	2	7

[a] Berelson, *Graduate Education in the United States*; Hayward Keniston, *Graduate Study and Research in the Arts and Sciences at the University of Pennsylvania*, The Educational Survey of the University of Pennsylvania, Philadelphia, 1958.

[b] Allan O. Pfnister, *A Report on the Baccalaureate Origins of College Faculties*, Association of American Colleges, Washington, 1961; National Research Council, *Doctorate Production in United States Universities, 1936-56*, National Academy of Sciences Publication 582, Washington, 1958.

[c] Committee Z, "The Economic Status of the Profession," *Bulletin of the American Association of University Professors*, Vol. XLVII, No. 2, June 1961, pp. 101-134; Vol. XLVI, No. 2, June 1960, pp. 156-193; Vol. XLV, No. 2, June 1959, pp. 157-194.

[d] John C. Rather and Doris C. Holladay, *Library Statistics of Colleges and Universities, 1960-61*, U. S. Office of Education, Washington, 1962, pp. 1-51; Dale M. Bentz, "College and University Library Statistics, 1954-55," *College and Research Libraries*, Vol. XVII, No. 1, January 1956, pp. 56-83.

[e] Mary Irwin (ed.), *American Universities and Colleges*, American Council on Education, Washington, 1956; publications of various professional societies; Walter Crosby Eells, several publications.

[f] Annual reports, Educational Testing Service, National Merit Scholarships, Fulbright Scholarships, International Educational Exchange Service, and Institute of International Education, 1951-1960; Frank Aydelotte, *The American Rhodes Scholarships*, Princeton University Press, Princeton, 1946.

[g] Robert H. Knapp and Joseph J. Greenbaum, *The Younger American Scholar*, University of Chicago Press, Chicago, 1953; Robert H. Knapp and H. B. Goodrich, *Origins of American Scientists*, University of Chicago Press, Chicago, 1952.

[h] American Council on Education, *American Universities and Colleges*, 1960, 1956, 1952, and 1948.

LITERACY

On a world basis, schooling data are not very useful because the duration and intensity of school years provide poor international comparability. For that matter, it can be said that no two persons anywhere obtain exactly the same educational benefit from a year of formal schooling. The basic meaningful minimum is literacy.

Literacy rates are often difficult to determine. Fortunately the choice of measure is not a crucial one; for most purposes almost any line dividing literacy from illiteracy suffices, since what is needed is mainly a rough national indicator of ability to use written materials. A usual definition of percentage literate is persons with the ability to read and write one's name in a language commonly used in the country of residence, as a proportion of all persons 10 years of age and older. If a person can read and write only a language not customarily encountered where he lives and works, he is functionally illiterate—no matter how well versed he may be in Latin and Sanscrit.

From 1930 to 1955 world literacy has increased from an estimated 40 per cent to about 56 per cent. Regional variations are extensive: 95 per cent in most of Europe, Anglo America, Oceania, and the Soviet Union; 80 per cent in southern Europe; 60 per cent in Latin America; 55 per cent in east Asia; 35 per cent in southeast Asia; 25 per cent in southwest Asia; and 20 per cent in south central Asia and Africa.[14] National variations are even greater; continental averages mask a wide range by country, just as national averages obscure local variations. In underdeveloped areas men are likely to have literacy percentages several times higher than those for women.

In nations having many impoverished subjects a serious problem is school and literacy wastage: that is, the loss of literacy or the forgetting of knowledge through atrophy. Where books and newspapers are not available, or when citizens cannot afford to purchase or otherwise gain access to them, people may actually forget how to read.

Illiteracy in the United States is surprisingly high. Less than a century ago, in 1870, 18 per cent of the men and 22 per cent of the women were illiterate. By 1900 these figures had dropped to 10 and 12 per cent respectively. Yet even in 1960 the nation was still 2.4 per cent illiterate, at which time there were 3 million illiterates of age 14 or older; as in earlier years, rates were generally highest in the South.[15] The highest illiteracy rate in the country is held by the American Indian: data are only casually accurate, but Indian illiteracy was estimated at 56 per cent in 1900; it is less than half that great at present. Negroes have also made appreciable gains, from some 16 per cent illiterate in 1939 to about 5 per cent today. Table 45 shows illiteracy by Census divisions. The lowest percentages by states in 1950 were Iowa at 0.9 per cent followed by Nebraska and Oregon at 1.2 per cent; highest illiteracy rates obtained in Louisiana, 9.8 per cent; South Carolina, 7.9 per cent; and Mississippi, 7.1 per cent. In 1900 the extreme

---

[14] United Nations, *Report on the World Social Situation*, New York, 1957, p. 65.
[15] U. S. Bureau of the Census, "Estimates of Illiteracy, by States: 1960," *Current Population Reports*, P-23, No. 8, February 12, 1963, pp. 1-2.

TABLE 45. *Illiteracy by Divisions, United States, 1900 and 1950**

DIVISION	NUMBER ILLITERATE, 1950	PER CENT ILLITERATE, 1950	PER CENT ILLITERATE, 1900
United States	3,623,000	3.2	11.2
New England (Me., N.H., Vt., Mass., R.I., Conn.)	195,000	2.7	6.6
Middle Atlantic (N.Y., N.J., Pa.)	731,000	3.1	6.4
East North Central (Ohio, Ind., Ill., Mich., Wis.)	445,000	2.0	4.9
West North Central (Minn., Iowa, Mo., N.D., S.D., Nebr., Kans.)	161,000	1.5	4.6
South Atlantic (Del., Md., D.C., Va., W.Va., N.C., S.C., Ga., Fla.)	744,000	4.9	25.1
East South Central (Ky., Tenn., Ala., Miss.)	438,000	5.5	26.3
West South Central (Ark., La., Okla., Texas)	591,000	5.7	21.4
Mountain (Mont., Idaho, Wyo., Colo., N.M., Ariz., Utah, Nev.)	107,000	3.1	10.3
Pacific (Wash., Oreg., Calif.)	210,000	1.9	4.6

* U. S. Bureau of the Census, "Estimates of Illiteracy, by States: 1950," *Current Population Report*, Series P-23, No. 6, November 1950, p. 2. 1950 data refer to people 14 years old and over; 1900 data refer to the population aged 15 years or more.

positions were held by Nebraska with 2.6 per cent and Louisiana with 39.7. These state and division rankings vary in much the same manner as do state and regional education ratings. (Illiteracy may never vanish completely, as some people are physically or mentally incapable of learning to read and write.)

Economic Composition

More time and money probably go into the collecting and publishing of decennial, annual, and monthly data on employment, occupation, and income than is expended on any other category of statistics collected through the Bureau of the Census, the Bureau of Labor Statistics of the Department of Labor, and allied Federal agencies. The reason lies in the obvious importance for the individual, his family, the community, and the nation of occupational skills, earnings, unemployment, and productivity.

JOB SUPPLY AND DEMAND

The age-sex structure of the population is highly significant for employment. The dependency ratio is particularly revelatory. Since sex-based occupational differentiation is universal, the sex ratio of adults is also relevant.

Youngsters born during a depression are likely to enter the labor force in a seller's market caused by the dearth of young adults; those young men who were born during a baby boom are faced with stiffer competition in seeking jobs—throughout their careers, *ceteris paribus*, they may have to face slower promotions and faster layoffs. From the employer's standpoint the 1960's will provide a relatively large reservoir of new employees in the United States, counterbalanced by the need to use older workers as larger proportions of the labor supply exceed 45 years of age. Other factors, especially expansion or contraction of the economy, may countervail or surpass this demographic influence on the unemployment level.

The number of jobs is increasing rapidly, partly in response to the larger working-age population. In the 1940's Henry Wallace was ridiculed by some people as a visionary for insisting that the national economy must expand to provide 60 million jobs.[16] Having accomplished this "unrealistic" objective, the nation is now faced with the goal of 90 million jobs by 1975. This formidable task (especially so under conditions of increasing automation) is born upon the nation's leaders by population increase resulting from a high birth rate coupled with a low death rate. Failure to provide this many jobs will presumably create increases in the number of unemployed adults.

Population size, growth, and age-sex make-up are not the only influences on the labor supply. Paradoxically, a major obstacle to economic development is the manpower shortages existing even in what are generally considered to be overpopulated nations. One reason for this situation is the young age structure, providing an insufficient number of adults in proportion to the total population. Additionally, social customs sometimes remove many adults from employment and therefore prevent their contributing to national economic development. Of greater importance are qualitative deficiencies: for example, in some regions where public health is poor, many if not most workers would be unacceptable to employers insisting on rigid medical standards. The most critical qualitative deficiency lies in training—the lack of skilled workers for industry, literate clerks for business, and educated managerial and professional personnel.[17]

---

[16] Henry A. Wallace, *Sixty Million Jobs*, Simon and Schuster, New York, 1945.
[17] United Nations, *The Determinants and Consequences of Population Trends*, New York, 1953, p. 265.

THE LABOR FORCE

Figure 20 contrasts the terms working force, labor force, and manpower. The working force is synonymous with the employed persons. The labor force includes all people in the labor market—that is, either working or seeking work. Manpower is the potential labor force—that is, the labor force plus everyone able to work but preferring to avoid remunerative employment (housewives, for example). The term "raw manpower" is sometimes used to refer to all those of certain ages (for example, 14 to 65), without regard for sex, health, or occupational skills.

FIGURE 20. *Terms Used to Describe the Economic Composition of the Population*

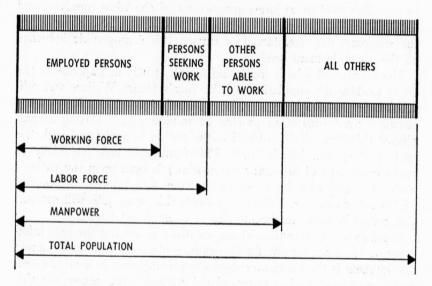

These terms are fuzzy and hard to define, partly because they are based not on the amount of effort a person expends, but rather on the criterion of whether pay or profit is involved. For instance, a housewife is not included in the working force by virtue of her unpaid work in and around the home, regardless of the amount of cleaning, dishwashing, and baby-tending she may do. However, her hired cleaning woman is a member of the working force. This information is normally obtained by asking how many hours of the preceding week were spent in gainful employment, plus some supplementary related questions. Both the labor force and the gross national product are measured in terms of price; if a service or good does not command a formal price, its contribution to national well-being is omitted from such data.

The United States labor force includes persons 14 years of age and over who are either working at a job or looking for work. It is comprised of members of the armed forces, unemployed persons seeking work or temporarily laid off, persons at work full or part time for pay or profit as employees or in their own business or profession, persons working without pay for fifteen hours a week or more in a family business or farm, and those temporarily absent from work because of vacation, sickness, labor-management disputes, bad weather, or similar reasons. Not included in the labor force are children under age 14, inmates of institutions, housewives and other unpaid household workers, full-time students, permanently disabled persons, retired persons, seasonal workers in the "off" season, and the voluntarily idle.[18]

Some economists believe that labor force definitions and statistics should be oriented toward the gross national product: the total value of all goods and services to which the society gives a money value and which are socially acceptable. The gross national product (GNP) equals all manufactured goods plus all agricultural products plus all mining products, and so forth. However, several ambiguous situations make this concept a difficult one to define exactly: 1) subsistence consumption of products not marketed (for example, the farmer who eats his own tomatoes, the shoemaker who wears his own shoes); 2) free services (for example, volunteer workers for "good causes," housewives); 3) military service (servicemen, who usually do not produce anything, but who work for a salary); and 4) illegal services and products (gamblers, bootleggers). Functional analysis contributes to the understanding of the last point. Thus Robert Merton writes:

> It would be peculiar to argue that prior to 1920 (when the 18th Amendment became effective), the provision of liquor constituted an economic service, that from 1920 to 1933, its production and sale no longer constituted an economic service dispensed in a market, and that from 1934 to the present, it once again took on a serviceable aspect. . . . Can it be held that in European countries, with registered and legalized prostitution, the prostitute contributed an economic service, whereas in this country, lacking legal sanction, the prostitute provides no such service? . . . The failure to recognize that these businesses are only morally and not economically distinguishable from "legitimate" businesses has led to badly scrambled analysis.[19]

And several years earlier, criminologists had observed: "The prostitute, the pimp, the peddler of dope, the operator of the gambling hall, the

---

[18] U. S. Bureau of the Census, "The Monthly Report on the Labor Force: June 1959," *Current Population Reports*, Series P-57, No. 204, June 30, 1959, pp. 7-8.
[19] Robert K. Merton, *Social Theory and Social Structure*, The Free Press, Glencoe, 1949, pp. 78-79.

vendor of obscene pictures, the bootlegger, the abortionist, all are productive, all produce services or goods which people desire and for which they are willing to pay. It happens that society has put these goods and services under the ban, but people go on producing them and people go on comsuming them, and an act of the legislature does not make them any less a part of the economic system."[20]

EMPLOYMENT STATUS

In 1961 the United States labor force included 74 million persons, of whom two-thirds were male (see Table 46). Once in the labor force,

TABLE 46. *Employment Status of the Noninstitutional Population 14 Years of Age and Over, by Sex, United States, 1961*[*]

	BOTH SEXES	MALE	FEMALE
Total noninstitutional population aged 14 years and over	127,852,000	62,147,000	65,705,000
Labor force including Armed Forces	74,175,000	49,918,000	24,257,000
Per cent of population	58.0	80.3	36.9
Civilian labor force	71,603,000	47,378,000	24,225,000
Employed	66,796,000	44,318,000	22,478,000
Agricultural	5,463,000	4,508,000	955,010
Nonagricultural	61,333,000	39,811,000	21,523,000
Unemployed	4,806,000	3,060,000	1,747,000
Per cent of civilian labor force	6.7	6.5	7.2
Not in labor force	53,677,000	12,229,000	41,448,000
Keeping house	34,897,000	106,000	34,791,000
In school	9,001,000	4,560,000	4,440,000
Unable to work	1,759,000	1,077,000	682,000
Other	8,020,000	6,486,000	1,534,000

* Carol Kalish, Frazier Kellogg, and Matthew Kessler, "Labor Force and Employment in 1961," *Monthly Labor Review*, June 1962 (reprinted as U. S. Bureau of Labor Statistics, Special Labor Force Report No. 23), p. A-7.

women do not have a strikingly higher unemployment rate than do men, but they do have a far greater tendency to stay out of the labor force, generally in order to keep house. Of the noninstitutionalized population aged 14 years or more who remain outside the labor force, almost two-thirds are females engaged in housekeeping; another one-sixth (evenly divided between both sexes) attend school. Eighty per

---

[20] E. R. Hawkins and Willard Waller, "Critical Notes on the Cost of Crime," *Journal of Criminal Law and Criminology*, Vol. XXVI, January-February 1936, p. 684; quoted *ibid.*, p. 373.

cent of male manpower is in the labor force, as compared with 37 per cent among females.

The 4.8 million unemployed persons, who constitute the difference between the working force and the labor force, comprised 6.7 per cent of the civilian labor force in 1961. Both the number of persons and the rate were "about the same as for the recession year 1958 and substantially higher than in any other year in the postwar period."[21] Unemployment rates are particularly unfavorable among certain segments of the labor force: nonwhites, older workers, unskilled workers, and poorly educated or functionally illiterate workers—described by the folk complaint, "Last to be hired, first to be fired."

OCCUPATION

Occupation is even more difficult to measure than labor force. To begin with, differentiation must be made between "regular" and "actual" occupations (when is an actress really a waitress or a hat check girl?). There is also the problem of allocation of retired persons who work occasionally (at carpentry, painting, or odd jobs), or those who refuse to admit they have finished their occupational careers (Willy Loman in Arthur Miller's *Death of a Salesman*). Fully effective analysis requires identification and differentiation of: usual occupation, present occupation, previous occupation, prospective occupation, occupation for which one has been trained, and highest rank occupation ever held. Sometimes these are all the same, but often they are not—as in the case of workers receiving promotions or demotions. Persons holding two or more jobs of different types (for example, the school teacher who works in a shoe store on Saturdays) complicate the picture still further.

A common occupational classification is: 1) managerial and professional, 2) clerical and kindred, 3) skilled craftsmen, and 4) laborers. The first two categories are "white collar," the last two "blue collar." It is often difficult to be sure where a particular occupational group is to be placed; for example, novices must be careful not to accept the hairdressers' claim to being "professional"—an occupational label normally restricted to positions requiring at least a master's degree.

In census reports of economic characteristics, "occupation" refers to the activity of the person: professional, manager, foreman, clerk, laborer, and so forth. "Industry" refers to the activity of the organization employing the person: agriculture, manufacturing, transport, trade, and so on. "Class" refers to the relation of the person to other persons: self-

---

[21] Carol Kalish, Frazier Kellogg, and Matthew Kessler, "Labor Force and Employment in 1961," *Monthly Labor Review*, June 1962 (reprinted as U. S. Bureau of Labor Statistics, Special Labor Force Report No. 23), p. 628.

employed, government-employed, privately employed. Industry and class are not particularly difficult to handle, but no one has ever been able to figure out a fully satisfactory classification system for occupations.

Particularly salient industrial trends are a rise in the proportion of workers employed in service and transportation and a decline in those gainfully occupied in agriculture. In the early 1800's around 85 per cent of United States workers were engaged in agriculture; by 1870 this proportion had dwindled to about 50 per cent; at present less than 10 per cent of the labor force is occupied in farming.[22] Regarding occupation, laborers have declined while professional and clerical workers have increased. Table 47 shows half-century changes in occupational structure in the United States.

Between 1950 and 1960, changes in the occupational distribution of

TABLE 47. *Occupation of Economically Active Civilians, United States, 1900-1950**

MAJOR OCCUPATION GROUP	PER CENT DISTRIBUTION		PER CENT CHANGE,
	1900	1950	1900-1950
Total	100.0	100.0	+103
White-collar workers	17.6	36.6	+322
Professional, technical, and kindred workers	4.3	8.6	+312
Managers, officials, and proprietors, except farm	5.8	8.7	+204
Clerical and kindred workers	3.0	12.3	+725
Sales workers	4.5	7.0	+216
Manual and service workers	44.9	51.6	+134
Manual workers	35.8	41.1	+133
Craftsmen, foremen, and kindred workers	10.5	14.1	+173
Operatives and kindred workers	12.8	20.4	+223
Laborers, except farm and mine	12.5	6.6	+ 7
Service workers	9.0	10.5	+135
Private household workers	5.4	2.6	− 3
Service workers, except private household	3.6	7.9	+343
Farm workers	37.5	11.8	− 36
Farmers and farm managers	19.9	7.4	− 24
Farm laborers and foremen	17.7	4.4	− 50

* David L. Kaplan and M. Claire Casey, "Occupational Trends in the United States, 1900 to 1950," U. S. Bureau of the Census, Working Paper No. 5, Washington, 1958, pp. 7-8.

[22] Conrad Taeuber, "Some Recent Population Changes in the United States," *Journal of Intergroup Relations*, Vol. I, No. 2, Spring 1960, p. 115.

men, ranked in order of percentage increase, were: professional, technical, and kindred, 51 per cent; sales, 16 per cent; clerical and kindred, 14 per cent; craftsmen, foremen, and kindred, 12 per cent; service, 9 per cent; managers, officials, and proprietors (except farm), 6 per cent; operatives and kindred, 6 per cent; laborers (except farm and mine), −9 per cent; farm laborers and foremen, −39 per cent, and farmers and farm managers, −43 per cent. Comparable rates of change among women were: service (except private household), 48 per cent; clerical and kindred, 46 per cent; professional, technical, and kindred, 41 per cent; sales, 25 per cent; private household, 24 per cent; managers, officials, and proprietors, 13 per cent; and operatives and kindred, 8 per cent.[23]

In 1960 four groups comprised more than 60 per cent of all those employed: operatives and kindred workers, 19 per cent; clerical and kindred workers, 15 per cent; craftsmen, foremen, and kindred workers, 14 per cent; and professional, technical, and kindred workers, 12 per cent.[24]

WORK AND LEISURE TIME

The 168 hours in a week are apportioned among three kinds of activity: work, maintenance, and leisure. In the first category are the hours spent in remunerative employment and commuting. Maintenance activities include the various personal and household chores necessary to keep going—eating, sleeping, washing, mowing the lawn, sewing, sweeping the floor, getting a haircut, and so forth. Whatever remains is leisure time, to be spent in loafing, watching television, playing with the dog, reading, traveling, and other recreational pleasures. Clearly, enjoyment is not the criterion for these distinctions (although work may be pleasurable, and many people enjoy edging the lawn or mending socks); rather they are based on the primary manifest function of the activity itself.

The work week in the United States has shortened on the average from 72 hours in 1850 to 56 hours in 1900 to 40 hours in 1950. (Although as recently as 1923 certain types of steelworkers had a 12-hour, seven-day work week.) Today the 35-hour week is common, and there is talk of a universal 30-hour week in the near future. Days off have been added: first Sunday, then Saturday, then an afternoon in the middle of the week. In a few instances the four-day week is already an actuality.

---

[23] U. S. Bureau of the Census, *U. S. Census of Population:* 1960, PC(1)-1C, p. 219.
[24] U. S. Bureau of the Census, *U. S. Census of Population:* 1960, PC(1)-1D, p. xxxv.

Holidays have been added, and three-week annual vacations are becoming usual. In the last half century, the working year of the typical industrial employee has dropped from 3,000 to 2,000 hours.

Complementing the decrease in time consumed in earning a living is the increase in free time at the disposal of the individual: from an estimated 11 hours a week in 1850 to 27 hours in 1900 to 43 hours in 1950. By the end of this century Americans may have a work week of only 24 hours, with leisure time amounting to about 75 hours. Ironically, however, a good many wage-earners are taking advantage of the shorter working hours to obtain additional employment ("moonlighting") in order to increase their income.

WORKING WOMEN

Folkways concerning working women have undergone a striking change since the nineteenth century. Just as men who do not work deviate from the traditional norms of American culture, so do women who work outside the home. Formerly, if a married woman worked, her husband was apt to be ashamed because he presumably could not provide for the family properly, and a "good provider" was—and is—a highly valued role. Clinging to the old folkway is most common in the lower class, where, not incidentally, competition between men and women is at a maximum. Opposition to working women stems also from widespread though diminishing resentment of higher family incomes derived from two salaries (although differentials in family earnings by double income are not as great as differentials in income among men alone) as well as from the fallacious idea that there is only a fixed number of jobs and that women who work are therefore taking jobs away from men. In a few communities these social values have resulted in stringent antinepotism rules.

Nonworking women today have been at times characterized as a major social loss and the largest group of time-wasters in the country. Modern housewives who do not have young children to superintend or paying jobs often must develop skills in finding "make-work" activities to justify their daily existence (social welfare work) and to keep from being bored (afternoon bridge clubs and discussion groups). Economically, the female population and more particularly the married women constitute a reserve manpower supply capable of exerting a steadying influence on the employment situation in times of distress. Sociologically, the whole set of statuses held by women in Western culture is undergoing a mild transition.[25]

---

[25] Alva Myrdal, *Women's Two Roles*, Routledge and Kegan Paul Ltd., London, 1956.

The proportion of wives working outside the home approximately doubled between 1940 and 1960 in the United States, changing from one-seventh to one-third; in 1890 less than one wife in 20 was in the labor force. There are now two-thirds more working mothers than there were a decade ago; these women have about 15 million children under age 18, including 4 million under age 6. For the family the consequences of this trend toward working mothers remains moot; some observers decry the absence of mothers from the home, while others claim that both mothers and children benefit from the temporary separation and change of companions.

In 1960 the total number of employed females reached 21 million, an increase over 1950 of 34 per cent; comparable male figures were 43.5 million workers in 1960 and an increase of 7 per cent. No major female occupational group decreased in size over the decade. Between 1940 and 1960 the male working force gained 28 per cent additional members, whereas the number of employed female workers increased by 89 per cent—almost doubling in twenty years.[26]

Participation in the labor force strongly reflects marital conditions, though not so sharply as in previous generations. The 1960 distribution among women 14 years old and over was: single, 43 per cent in labor force; married, husband present, 31 per cent; married, husband present, and children under age 6, 19 per cent; married, husband absent, 48 per cent; widowed, 28 per cent; and divorced, 71 per cent.[27]

INCOME

The average income in the United States is higher than it has ever been. Table 48 documents the impressive recent rise. Nonetheless, poverty is still with us: 22 per cent of all American families make ends meet with an income of less than $3,000—well below the minimum needed to secure adequate food, medical care, and other necessities for two adults and one or two children. If $7,000 is assumed as a minimum necessary for "comfortable" living, only one-third of the families are so provided. As Table 49 shows, current income differentials with regard to race, region, size of community, and type of occupation resemble those for educational attainment.

The 1960 Census reported that male college graduates averaged $7,646 annually and high school graduates $5,437, as contrasted with $3,885 among men with eight years of school and a mere $1,439 for men who completed less than a single academic year. Presence of dependent

---

[26] U. S. Bureau of the Census, *U.S. Census of Population: 1960,* PC(1)-1C, p. 219.
[27] U. S. Bureau of the Census, *U.S. Census of Population: 1960,* PC(1)-1D, p. 501.

TABLE 48. *Annual Income of Families, United States, 1947-1960**

TOTAL MONEY INCOME	1947	1950	1955	1960
Number	37,237,000	39,929,000	42,843,000	45,435,000
Median income	$3,031	$3,319	$4,421	$5,620
Per cent	100	100	100	100
Under $3,000	49	43	29	22
$3,000 to 4,999	31	34	30	20
$5,000 to 6,999	12	14	22	24
$7,000 to 7,999	5	6	13	20
$10,000 to 14,999			5	10
$15,000 and over	3	3	1	4

* U. S. Bureau of the Census, "Income of Families and Persons in the United States: 1960," *Current Population Reports*, P-60, No. 37, January 17, 1962, p. 3.

children is also a relevant variable: median income reached a peak in families having two children under 18 and was smallest in families with four or more children (childless families were intermediate); the difference, however, was only about $800. Three occupational categories had median earnings above $10,000; in order, they were physicians and surgeons, dentists, and lawyers and judges.[28]

By states, the highest median family earnings in 1960 were $7,305 in Alaska and $6,887 in Connecticut; the lowest were less than half as great; $2,884 in Mississippi and $3,184 in Arkansas. Differences in the cost of living may reduce the effect of these differentials on the living standard, but powerful discrepancies do remain.

Among urban places of 50,000 population or more, ten cities had median family incomes exceeding $9,000. Two cities surpassed $10,000: Bethesda, Maryland, $12,357; and Lower Merion, Pennsylvania, $12,204. Cities with family incomes between $9,000 and $10,000 were, in rank order, West Hartford, Connecticut, Skokie, Illinois, Greenwich, Connecticut, Silver Spring, Maryland, Evanston, Illinois, Palo Alto, California, Oak Park, Illinois, and Newton, Massachusetts. The six communities of the 50,000-class averaging below $4,000 were all in the South. Laredo, Texas, occupied the extreme position by virtue of its median income of $2,935; the other five, from the lowest, were, Augusta, Georgia, Charleston, South Carolina, Nashville, Tennessee, Monroe, Louisiana, and Lexington, Kentucky. Smaller communities were more extreme in both directions—witness Scarsdale, New York, at $22,177, and Eudora, Arkansas, San Pedro, Texas, and Tallulah, Louisiana, at $1,706, $1,800,

---

[28] *Ibid.*, pp. 590, 601, and 553-556.

TABLE 49. *Income by Selected Characteristics, United States, 1960**

	Median Income of Year-Round Full-Time Workers	
SELECTED CHARACTERISTICS	MALE	FEMALE
Total	$5,435	$3,296
REGION		
Northeast	5,538	3,369
North Central	5,525	3,325
South	4,501	2,772
West	6,259	4,044
FARM-NONFARM RESIDENCE		
Urban and rural nonfarm	5,631	3,338
Rural farm	2,423	2,178
COLOR		
White	5,572	3,377
Nonwhite	3,683	2,289
OCCUPATION		
Professional, technical, and kindred workers	7,115	4,358
Self-employed	10,858	—
Salaried	6,954	4,365
Teachers, elementary and secondary schools	6,063	4,581
Other salaried workers	7,143	4,285
Farmers and farm managers	2,004	—
Managers, officials, proprietors, except farm	6,648	3,514
Self-employed	5,258	1,800
In retail trade	4,757	—
Other self-employed	5,950	—
Salaried	7,472	4,220
Clerical and kindred workers	5,291	3,575
Sales workers	5,842	2,389
Craftsmen, foremen, and kindred workers	5,826	—
Operatives and kindred workers	4,997	2,969
Private household workers	—	1,156
Service workers, except private household	4,088	2,340
Farm laborers and foremen	1,686	—
Laborers, except farm and mine	4,017	—

* U. S. Bureau of the Census, "Average Income of Families Up Slightly in 1960," *Current Population Reports*, P-60, No. 36, June 9, 1961, p. 4.

and $1,880 respectively.[29] The most superior performance in income as well as in education is found in an elliptical area having foci at Chicago and Cleveland, with other leaders located in the vicinity of New York City. As with educational attainment, the worst income records are achieved by rural areas and by cities in southern Texas, especially those along the Rio Grande River. One wonders if these people ever heard the words of Sholem Aleichem: "Poverty is no disgrace—but it's no honor either."

---

[29] U. S. Bureau of the Census, *U. S. Census of Population: 1960*, PC(1)-1C, Tables 106 and 154; PC(1)-2C through PC(1)-53C, Tables 76 and 81.

21 ✕ World Population by Regions

World population growth is very uneven geographically as well as temporally. Some continents and countries are growing far more rapidly than others. Table 50, showing population growth by continents over the last millennium, should be read with caution. These figures are not to be accepted literally; most of them are crude approximations, and many are rash guesses. Relative credibility varies widely: data for the Americas, Europe, India, and Japan are fairly reliable; those for China, Southwest Asia, Southeast Asia, and Oceania are questionable though somewhat credible; and statistics concerning Africa and Asiatic Russia are highly conjectural. Population statistics for some parts of the world may best be evaluated by Gibbon's epigram on the condition of Corsica as "easier to deplore than to describe."

HISTORICAL CHANGES

Within the last thousand years the world's population has multiplied itself by about eight or nine times. The population of the world in 1000 A.D. was probably less than half that of the population of Europe in 1950. In one century—the fourteenth—world population did not increase at all, but declined. More people (800 million) were added to the world's population from 1900 to 1950 than in the 800 years between 1000 and 1800 A.D.

Portions of Table 50 require special explanation.[1] The cessation of growth in Japan from 1750 to 1850 is explained by Japanese historians mainly in terms of the prevalence of infanticide during the Tokugawa era. The decline in the Americas from 1000 to 1050 reflects a famine.

---

[1] Merrill Kelley Bennett, *The World's Food*, Harper & Brothers, New York, 1954, pp. 17-19.

TABLE 50. *Population of the World and Its Subdivisions, 1000-1949**

YEAR	EUROPE	ASIATIC RUSSIA	SOUTHWEST ASIA	INDIA	CHINA MAJOR	JAPAN	SOUTHEAST ASIA AND OCEANIA	AFRICA	THE AMERICAS	TOTAL
1000	42	5	32	48	70	4	11	50	13	275
1050	46	5	32	49	74	5	12	52	12	287
1100	48	6	33	50	79	6	12	55	17	306
1150	50	6	33	50	84	7	13	58	20	321
1200	61	7	34	51	89	8	14	61	23	348
1250	69	7	35	49	94	10	14	64	27	369
1300	73	8	33	50	99	11	15	67	28	384
1350	51	9	30	47	106	12	16	70	29	370
1400	45	9	27	46	112	14	16	74	30	373
1450	60	10	28	51	118	15	18	78	35	413
1500	69	11	29	54	125	16	19	82	41	446
1550	78	12	30	60	132	18	20	86	23	459
1600	89	13	30	68	140	20	21	90	15	486
1650	100	14	30	80	150	23	22	90	9	518
1700	115	15	31	100	205	27	24	90	10	617
1750	140	16	32	130	270	32	28	90	11	749
1800	188	17	33	157	345	28	32	90	29	919
1850	266	19	34	190	430	33	37	95	59	1,163
1900	401	20	35	290	430	44	71	120	144	1,555
1949	548	45	74	439	503	82	158	198	321	2,368

* Merrill Kelley Bennett, *The World's Food,* Harper & Brothers, New York, 1954, p. 9. Reprinted by permission.

The sharp drop in the Americas from 1500 to 1650 shows the impact of European diseases, notably smallpox and measles, upon a population which had never before experienced these illnesses and was therefore weak to resist them. (The Americas' "thank-you" package in return is thought by some medical historians to be syphilis.) Native Americans also suffered from general disruption of their cultures, governments, and systems of food production under the enslavement, war, and mass murder accompanying European conquest. The decline in Europe from 1300 to 1400 reflects the impact of famine and plague. Statistics for India also reflect the ravages of the fourteenth-century plague. Southwest Asia too suffered the plague at that time. This devastation was further augmented by successive wars and invasions by the Seljuk Turks, the Crusaders, and the Mongols; internal warfare between Persians and Arabs, Turks and Byzantines; the terrible campaigns of Tamerlane toward the close of the fourteenth century; and conquests of the Ottoman Turks. Historical data for China show no population decline from Mongol conquest and domination in the thirteenth and fourteenth centuries or in the first half of the seventeenth century during the successive Manchu wars, for the reason that the probable gyrations of population growth baffle quantitative expression.

Nomadic and hunting tribal groups provided chronic warfare in Africa, southwest Asia, southeast Asia, Oceania, and the Americas. The persistent killing diseases (infections, dysentery, respiratory ailments, malaria, and leprosy) suppressed population growth steadily, year by year; by contrast, the great pandemic diseases struck with fury in some years and were barely felt in others. The rapid growth of Japan before 1750 and the Americas before 1500 reflected not only freedom from pandemics but also a narrower range of diseases than prevailed elsewhere. The most important reasons for the slow growth of world population before 1650 were "great pandemics exemplified by the bubonic plague, persistent rather than episodic diseases, the diffusion of Old World diseases to the New World, wars of conquest, intertribal warfare, slave raiding, famines, and infanticide and abortion."[2]

Present Population Distribution

The world's population has grown by more than a billion persons since 1920. International differences in birth and death rates are portrayed in Figure 21. The estimated world total in 1962 was 3,115 million persons, distributed by continents as follows: Africa, 267 millions; Asia, 1,747; North America, 278; South America, 152; Europe, 433; Oceania, 17; and

---

[2] *Ibid.*, p. 20.

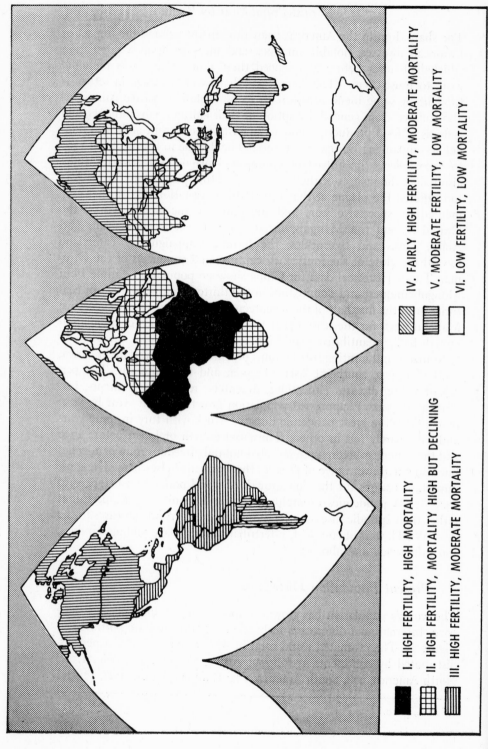

FIGURE 21. *World Regions by Types of Demographic Situation, 1950-1955**

I. HIGH FERTILITY, HIGH MORTALITY

II. HIGH FERTILITY, MORTALITY HIGH BUT DECLINING

III. HIGH FERTILITY, MODERATE MORTALITY

IV. FAIRLY HIGH FERTILITY, MODERATE MORTALITY

V. MODERATE FERTILITY, LOW MORTALITY

VI. LOW FERTILITY, LOW MORTALITY

the Soviet Union, 221. National population statistics for 1962 form the subject of Table 51. Countries and territories growing fast enough to double their population in twenty years or less include Israel, Syria, North Borneo, the Philippines, Singapore, South Viet-Nam, Taiwan, Hong Kong, Costa Rica, the Dominican Republic, and El Salvador. Three areas lost population between 1953 and 1962: East Germany, Ireland, and North Viet-Nam. The highest observed natural increase rate was Costa Rica's 47.5 per 1,000 per year. No principality reported a negative natural increase, but in a few cases net out-migration exceeds natural increase.

Certain of these regions and nations—Latin America, Africa, Australia, the U.S.S.R., and Communist China—warrant discussion by virtue of their extreme rapidity of growth, present size, density, or prominence in the world power struggle.

LATIN AMERICA

Latin America is the fastest growing major region in the world, having a percentage increase almost double that of the world as a whole. One Dominican Republic official has complained, "The period of gestation here is three months." The most rapid growth in this fastest growing continent is in the Central American countries—Mexico, Costa Rica, El Salvador, Guatemala, Honduras, Nicaragua, and Panama, all of which are doubling their population in a quarter century or less.

Mexico's population has been rising by an average of 3 per cent annually since 1950. In recent decades the death rate has been cut in half, while the birth rate has slightly increased. The result is a burgeoning population with ever-growing food supply problems. Corn, the staple food, dominates the Mexican agricultural spectrum, occupying as much land as all other farm products combined; Mexico devotes a larger proportion of its arable land to corn than any other country of comparable size. However, methods of cultivation are primitive and production per acre is only about one-third that of Anglo America. As yet Mexicans are not suffering from extreme population pressure, but they will soon be compelled to rapidly increase both industrial and agricultural productivity.

The Caribbean Islands, extending in an arc from the Gulf of Mexico over 2,000 miles to the coast of Venezuela, is the most densely peopled section of all Latin America. It is also the only part of the Western Hemisphere that is already suffering from overpopulation. Densities vary from less than 150 persons per square mile in Cuba and the Dominican Republic to 1,400 per square mile in Barbados, one of the most crowded agricultural areas of the world. With a total land area of only 86,000 square miles, the Antilles have a population of 18 million, which,

TABLE 51. *Population, Density, and Vital Rates for 127 Countries, 1959-1962**

CONTINENT & COUNTRY	POPULATION ESTIMATES MID-1962 (MILLIONS)	POPULATION PER SQUARE KILOMETER, 1960	ANNUAL PER CENT INCREASE SINCE 1953	BIRTH RATE (LATEST SINCE 1959)	DEATH RATE (LATEST SINCE 1959)
AFRICA					
Northern Africa		(9)		(45)	(23)
Algeria	11.7	5	2.3		
Ethiopia	20.0	17	—		
Libya	1.2	1	1.6		
Morocco	12.3	26	3.0		
Somalia	2.0	3	—		
Sudan	12.4	5	2.9ᵃ		
Tunisia	4.3	33	1.5	45	26
United Arab Republic	27.2	26	2.4		
Tropical & Southern Africa		(8)		(48)	(27)
Angola†	4.9	4	1.1		
Cameroun	4.2	9	0.8		
Central African Republic	1.3	2	1.7	48	26
Chad	2.7	2	1.7		
Congo (Brazzaville)	0.9	3	2.6	47	27
Congo (Leopoldville)	14.8	6	2.2		
Dahomey	2.1	17	2.8	55	27
Gabon	0.5	2	0.8	38	28
Ghana	7.2	28	3.0ᵃ	55.8	25.6
Guinea	3.2	12	3.1		
Ivory Coast	3.4	10	2.2ᵃ	56.1	33.3
Kenya†	7.5	12	2.3		
Liberia	1.3ᵇ	12	—		
Mali	4.3	3	2.1	56	30
Malagasy Republic	5.7	—	2.6		
Mauritania	0.7	1	—		
Mauritius†	0.7	342	3.1	39.7	9.9
Mozambique†	6.7	8	1.1		
Niger	3.1	2	—	59	32
Nigeria	36.4	38	1.9		
Rhodesia & Nyasaland†	8.8	7	2.6		
Senegal	3.0	15	—	40	18

* Information Service, Population Reference Bureau, Washington, September 1962; United Nations, *Demographic Yearbook: 1961*, New York, 1962, pp. 101-125; and other United Nations publications.

TABLE 51—continued

CONTINENT & COUNTRY	POPULATION ESTIMATES MID-1962 (MILLIONS)	POPULATION PER SQUARE KILOMETER, 1960	ANNUAL PER CENT INCREASE SINCE 1953	BIRTH RATE (LATEST SINCE 1959)	DEATH RATE (LATEST SINCE 1959)
Sierra Leone	2.6	34	2.6		
Tanganyika	9.6	10	1.8		
Togo	1.5	25	2.8[a]	53	32
Uganda†	7.0	27	2.5	42	20
Union of South Africa	16.5	13	2.4		
Upper Volta	4.4	16	1.6	49.1	30.6
ASIA					
Southwest Asia		(14)		(48)	(21)
Cyprus	0.6	61	1.5		
Iran	21.2	12	2.1		
Iraq	7.5	16	2.9		
Israel	2.3	102	3.6	24.9	5.9
Jordan	1.8	17	3.2		
Kuwait	0.3	14	2.3		
Lebanon	1.7	158	2.8		
Saudi Arabia	6.0	4	—		
Syria	5.1	25	3.5		
Turkey	29.2	35	2.9		
Yemen	5.0	26	—		
South Central Asia		(109)		(41)	(24)
Afghanistan	13.8[a]	21	—		
Bhutan	0.7	13	1.6		
Ceylon	10.5	151	2.7	37.0	9.1
India	448.3	136	1.9		
Nepal	9.5	67	1.5		
Pakistan	96.6	98	1.9		
Southeast Asia		(48)		(41)	(21)
Burma	21.7	30	—		
Cambodia	5.2	29	2.2[c]	41.4	19.7
Indonesia	96.6	62	2.2		
Laos	2.0	8	3.2		
Malaya	7.4	53	3.0	40.9	9.5
New Guinea†	0.8	2	0.7		
North Borneo†	0.5	6	3.6		
Philippines	29.6	93	3.8		
Sarawak†	0.8	6	3.3		
Singapore†	1.7	2813	4.6	35.5	6.0
Thailand	28.0	51	3.1[a]		
Viet-Nam, North	16.6	103	−0.2		
Viet-Nam, South	15.3	83	5.4		

TABLE 51—*continued*

CONTINENT & COUNTRY	POPULATION ESTIMATES MID-1962 (MILLIONS)	POPULATION PER SQUARE KILOMETER, 1960	ANNUAL PER CENT INCREASE SINCE 1953	BIRTH RATE (LATEST SINCE 1959)	DEATH RATE (LATEST SINCE 1959)
East Asia		(71)		(40)	(20)
China (Mainland)	716.5	68	2.3		
China (Taiwan)	11.4	295	3.6	38.3	6.7
Hong Kong†	3.3	2891	4.1	34.2	5.9
Japan	94.9	252	1.0	16.9	7.4
Korea, North	8.3	67	—		
Korea, South	26.1	250	2.0		
Mongolia	1.0	1	2.2		
AMERICA					
North America		(9)		(24)	(9)
Canada	18.6	2	2.6	26.0	7.7
United States	186.7	19	1.7	23.4	9.3
Middle America		(24)		(45)	(18)
Costa Rica	1.3	23	4.1	55.4	7.9
Cuba	6.8	59	2.1		
Dominican Republic	3.2	61	3.5		
El Salvador	2.8	117	3.5	49.6	11.4
Guatemala	4.0	35	3.0	49.5	17.5
Haiti	4.3	126	1.2		
Honduras	2.0	17	2.5		
Jamaica	1.7	142	1.2	42.7	8.9
Mexico	37.2	18	3.2	44.9	10.6
Nicaragua	1.6	10	3.4		
Panama	1.1	14	2.7		
Puerto Rico†	2.5	265	1.1	31.0	6.7
Trinidad & Tobago	0.9	165	3.2	32.4	6.9
South America		(8)		(42)	(19)
Argentina	21.3	7	1.2	22.3	8.1
Bolivia	3.6	3	1.5^e		
Brazil	75.3	8	3.4		
British Guiana	0.6	3	3.1	41.8	8.3
Chile	7.9	10	1.8	35.4	11.9
Colombia	14.8	12	2.2	42.5	12.0
Ecuador	4.6	16	3.2	45.9	14.3
Paraguay	1.9	4	2.4		
Peru	10.6	8	1.9		
Uruguay	3.0	15	1.6	21.3	8.1
Venezuela	7.8	8	2.6^d		

TABLE 51—*continued*

CONTINENT & COUNTRY	POPU-LATION ESTIMATES MID-1962 (MIL-LIONS)	POPU-LATION PER SQUARE KILO-METER, 1960	ANNUAL PER CENT INCREASE SINCE 1953	BIRTH RATE (LAT-EST SINCE 1959)	DEATH RATE (LAT-EST SINCE 1959)
EUROPE		(86)		(19)	(11)
Albania	1.7	56	3.1	41.9	9.8
Austria	7.1	84	0.2	18.5	12.0
Belgium	9.3	300	0.6	17.0	11.7
Bulgaria	8.0	71	1.0	17.8	8.1
Czechoslovakia	13.9	107	0.9	15.8	9.2
Denmark	4.6	106	0.7	16.6	9.5
Finland	4.5	13	1.0	18.4	9.0
France	46.4	83	0.9	18.3	10.9
Germany, East[e]	17.2	150	−0.7	17.4	12.8
Germany, West[f]	54.7	215	1.2	18.3	11.0
Greece	8.5	64	0.9		
Hungary	10.1	107	0.6	14.0	9.6
Iceland	0.2	2	2.2	27.4	6.6
Ireland	2.8	40	−0.6	21.3	12.3
Italy	49.8	164	0.5	18.8	9.4
Luxembourg	0.3	121	0.7	16.0	11.8
Netherlands	11.8	342	1.3	21.2	7.6
Norway	3.6	11	0.9	17.5	9.1
Poland	30.4	95	1.8	20.7	7.6
Portugal	9.3	97	0.5	23.6	10.7
Romania	18.8	77	1.3	17.5	8.7
Spain	30.6	60	0.8	21.3	8.6
Sweden	7.6	17	0.6	13.9	9.8
Switzerland	5.6	130	1.3	18.1	9.3
United Kingdom	53.2	215	0.5	17.8	12.0
Yugoslavia	18.8	72	1.1	22.6	9.0
OCEANIA		(2)		(24)	(9)
Australia	10.7	1	2.2	22.8	8.5
New Zealand	2.5	9	2.1	27.1	9.0
U.S.S.R.	221.0	10	1.7	24.9	7.1

Daggers identify nonself-governing countries.

[a] 1960-1961.

[b] 1960.

[c] 1959-1960.

[d] 1961-1962.

[e] Excludes East Berlin, pop. 1.2 million.

[f] Excludes West Berlin, pop. 2.2 million.

given continuance of present rates, could reach 48 million by the end of the century. Since these countries are "now experiencing difficulties in raising the low levels of living of the present population," one scholar observes, "such an increase in numbers would prove disastrous."[3] In the Caribbean the more than fifty inhabited islands, long accustomed to a colonial economy, have attained varying degrees of independence. The major political units are Cuba, the Dominican Republic, Haiti, Jamaica, Puerto Rico, and Trinidad and Tobago.

> With high population densities, large proportions dependent on agriculture, and rates of natural increase generally in excess of 2% per year, the Caribbean exemplifies all the modern demographic problems of the underdeveloped areas of the world. Fertility remains high, though there is some suggestion of a decline in Puerto Rico, and mortality has declined steeply in nearly all the islands. Recent emigration has reduced rates of growth in Puerto Rico and the British Islands, but the indications are that massive increments are to be expected unless definite policies of fertility control materialize.[4]

Efforts have been made to curb illiteracy and promote industrialization, but a sharp drop in population growth does not appear imminent. "With Barbados the only island in which the government has publicly committed itself to a policy of fertility control, there is little likelihood of any sharp decline in the rate of natural increase for the area as a whole."[5]

Tropical South America includes Bolivia, Brazil, Colombia, Ecuador, Peru, and Venezuela. Rapidity of growth varies from Ecuador and Venezuela, which are doubling in population every quarter century, to Bolivia, which is taking half a century to double. Population densities are generally low: Brazil, Peru, and Venezuela have 15 to 20 persons per square mile; Ecuador, the most dense, only 35. The economies are basically agricultural or extractive. Birth rates are high—often around 45 per 1,000 per year.

Temperate South America, in contrast, is growing much more slowly. In this area of topographic and climatic contrasts are grouped Argentina, Chile, Paraguay, and Uruguay, comprising about one-fourth of the area of the continent and roughly the same proportion of the population. Densities are low and population increase is gradual.

The largest country in the New World in land area is Brazil, which occupies half of South America and is the fourth largest country in the

---

[3] Harold L. Geisert, *The Caribbean: Population and Resources*, The George Washington University, Washington, 1960, p. 3.

[4] G. W. Roberts, "The Caribbean Islands," *Annals of the American Academy of Political and Social Science*, Vol. CCCXVI, March 1958, pp. 127-136 (abstract).

[5] Geisert, *The Caribbean, op. cit.*, p. 44.

world in area. Its population numbers about 2 per cent of the world total. In the Western Hemisphere, Brazil is second in population only to the United States. Throughout the nineteenth century Brazil grew much more slowly than did the United States, but in the last few decades this situation has been reversed. Brazil's foremost demographer, Giorgio Mortara, has said that the birth rate is "exceptionally high" and declining slowly, while the still high death rate has a marked downward trend. According to Mortara: "Improvidence is the main factor in high natality; poverty and ignorance are the principal factors of high mortality. The standard of life is very low for the majority of the population, owing to obsolete techniques, imperfect organization, low labor productivity and to scarcity of capital, lack of enterprise, deficiency of communications and ineptitude of governmental action."[6] The sex ratio is balanced. There are very few old people, but the very high proportion in the infant and adolescent ages creates a high dependency ratio. Immigration, scanty in the 1930's and 1940's, is resuming importance. The population is less than one-third urban.

Territorially, the most significant feature of Brazil's population is its concentration along the Atlantic seacoast. The coast between the mouth of the Amazon River and the Uruguay border is relatively heavily populated, and most of the large cities are concentrated in this narrow coastal band. The major areas of population concentration are in the southeastern coast from Rio de Janeiro to São Paulo and in the easternmost corner from Salvador to Natal. Racially, Brazil surpasses the United States as a melting pot, though three strains predominate: the native Indians, the original Portuguese colonists, and the millions of Negro slaves imported from Africa beginning in the sixteenth century. Brazil's population history and national policies have been influenced by the need for a cheap supply of agricultural labor, open territory in the interior, and huge landed estates. The country is predominantly agricultural, and coffee is king, having supplanted rubber, cotton, gold, sugar, and brazilwood. Even so Brazil is the most industrialized country in Latin America, with industry and population being greatest in the southeastern states—particularly in the environs of Rio de Janeiro, São Paulo, and Belo Horizonte. Yet while its territorial extent is tremendous (2,300 miles from north to south, 2,300 miles from east to west, and a coastline of 4,500 miles), about half of the country consists of the forbidding and hardly habitable Amazonas basin—a fact which policy makers should not overlook. Unreflective inspection of density figures could produce excessively optimistic forecasts of Brazilian demographic prospects.

[6] Giorgio Mortara, "The Development and Structure of Brazil's Population," *Population Studies*, Vol. VIII, No. 2, November 1954, pp. 121-139.

One of the salient demographic traits of Latin America in general is the prominence of primate cities. The most extreme case is Uruguay, where one-third of the inhabitants live in Montevideo; similarly, more than one-fifth of the people of Argentina, Chile, Panama, Cuba, and Costa Rica live in the largest city. If the same proportions of the United States population lived in New York City, it would contain either 60 or 35 million people.

AFRICA

Though its growth started much later, Africa is today moving toward the Latin American pattern. Virtually stationary for many centuries, Africa's population grew slowly in the nineteenth century and is now entering a period of rapid increase.

North Africa—the area between the Mediterranean Sea and the Sahara Desert—is heavily Moslem. The population is concentrated along the coast and the Nile River in deference to the aridity of the interior. The countries are largely rural; a narrow but agriculturally fertile strip stretches along the Mediterranean coast and the Nile valley. Death rates are high but declining, and birth rates are higher and steady. The level of living is low, and the area is underdeveloped economically. Literacy and education are sadly deficient. A French scholar declares: "The relation between population and resources is the fundamental problem of North Africa and the Moslem world."[7]

The only North African country for which we have reasonably accurate and extensive statistics is Egypt. The population in Pharaonic, Roman, and early Arab times was approximately 6 or 7 million. Five and a half centuries of Mameluke misrule combined with diversion of trade routes away from Egypt played a major role in decreasing the population to about 2.5 million at the end of the eighteenth century. By the time of the British occupation in 1882, it had climbed back to 7 million, from which it began a rise to 25 million in 1958, when Egypt and Syria formed the United Arab Republic. Virtually all of these people are compressed at very high density into the Nile Valley and the Delta, the remaining 95 per cent of Egypt's land being practically uninhabitable desert. All but 2 million Coptic Christians are Moslem, of which about 80 per cent are fellaheen or peasant farmers. Their depressed level of living is attributable to "the maldistribution of wealth, the population pressure, and the persistent fall in the prices of agricultural products, especially cotton."[8] Population pressure on the

[7] Louis Chevalier, "France et Tunisie," *Population*, Vol. XII, No. 4, October-December 1947, pp. 607-614.

[8] Charles Issawi, "Population and Wealth in Egypt," *Milbank Memorial Fund Quarterly*, Vol. XXVII, January 1949, p. 99.

exiguous land has forced up land values and contributed to political uneasiness. Great strides will be necessary to relieve the massive poverty of the fellaheen.

Middle African boundaries and political statuses are changing rapidly. Here poverty is severe and malnutrition omniprevalent. Fertility is generally high, but high mortality curbs natural increase. Huge expanses of land are practically uninhabitable. However, the bulk of the region is not overpopulated. Resources are plentiful and could support far more agricultural and industrial enterprises.

South Africa is partitioned into several political subdivisions, the Union of South Africa occupying the southernmost tip of the continent. Here the dominant whites have neglected to compile thorough and accurate statistics for the Negro inhabitants, so we have little solid knowledge of demographic trends in the indigenous population. The Union of South Africa is the most highly developed country south of the Sahara Desert. However while the whites living in its growing cities have relatively high incomes and high standards of living, the Bantu and other Negroes do not (although the dark-skinned residents of the Union, increasing nearly twice as fast as the already far outnumbered whites, are bringing pressure to bear on the apartheid policy of segregation and discrimination). To a racial problem which dwarfs that of the American South, differential rates of increase are adding new meaning and importance. During the 1950's whites increased by 16 per cent to a total slightly over 3 million, Negroes increased 26 per cent to almost 11 million, Eurafrican mulattoes gained 35 per cent to one and one-half million, and Asiatics increased 30 per cent to a total of half a million. By 1980 the Negro population will probably reach 15 million, by 2000 some 21 million. The National Party government policy of developing tribal homelands into seven economically self-sufficient and eventually self-governing bantustans seems unlikely to solve the severe racial problems besetting the white stronghold.

AUSTRALIA

Another white supremacy area, Australia, is demographically unusual because of its extreme contrasts in density. In 1788, at the time of the first British settlement, the aboriginal population numbered about 150,000. In 1800 the English total was approximately 5,000. For a time, convicts sent to this dismal outpost by English authorities outnumbered free settlers, and for many years the relation between convicts, natives, and independent colonists was insecure, to say the least. One of the early inducements to settle in Australia was the offer of convict labor at very low wages. Then because this policy tended to deter freemen from doing hard manual labor, the government substituted land grants.

A bounty arrangement was begun in 1835 whereby older settlers were paid to bring in immigrants. The discovery of gold in 1851 stimulated a rush of adventurers. A literacy test was established in 1866 to exclude the Chinese.

"White Australia," like New Zealand, is heavily British. Yet although its area is roughly that of the United States, the nation's population is smaller than that of metropolitan New York. The vast interior is not conducive to human habitation, and most Australians live in a few coastal cities. Australia is in fact a highly urban country of considerable industrialization with only 15 per cent of the labor force working at rural occupations. "The most thinly populated nation-state on earth, with only three persons per square mile, Australia has at the same time one of the world's most highly urbanized societies, with . . . 79 per cent living in all urban areas."[9] In 1958 Australia's birth rate was 22.6, the death rate 8.5, and the natural increase rate of 14.1 was supplemented by a net immigration rate of 6.6.[10]

THE SOVIET UNION

The Russian population grew from 18 million in 1724 to 59 million in 1859 to 94 million in 1897 and 209 million in 1959.[11] Boundary changes interfere with strict comparisons—not to mention the inaccuracies of the earlier estimates. Between the 1939 and 1959 Soviet censuses, population increased 22 per cent or 38 million. Slightly over half of this growth was by annexation; the population within present boundaries grew by 10 per cent or 18 million people.

The regions with the largest percentage increases between 1939 and 1959 were: Far East, 70; Central Asia and Kazakhstan, 38; East Siberia, 34; Urals, 32; and West Siberia, 24. All of these regions are in Asia; the seven economic regions in European Russia grew more slowly. In 1939 one-fourth of the Soviet population lived in or east of the Urals; today one-third live there. Almost one-half of the Asiatic Russian growth resulted from redistribution by internal migration. Migration is also responsible for the change from 18 per cent urban in 1926 to 32 per cent in 1939 and 48 per cent in 1959.

Perhaps the most striking revelation of the Soviet 1959 census was

---

[9] W. D. Borrie, "Demographic Cycles and Economic Development: Some Observations based upon Australian Experience," *Population Index*, Vol. XXVI, No. 1, January 1960, p. 3.

[10] *Ibid.*, p. 4.

[11] Frank Lorimer, *The Population of the Soviet Union*, League of Nations, Geneva, 1946, p. 10; and Galina V. Selegen, "The First Report on the Recent Population Census in the Soviet Union," *Population Studies*, Vol. XIV, No. 1, July 1960, p. 18.

how severely the male population was decimated during the Second World War. Instead of the generally accepted estimate of losses as 7 million men, the census implies losses of from 15 to 20 million. Today males comprise only 45 per cent of the populace. The entire disparity in the sex ratio is concentrated in the ages older than 32; below that age the sex ratio is normal. Clearly the Soviet Union was far weaker in manpower resources at the end of World War II than Western powers realized. As one demographer has noted: "There no longer seems any reasonable doubt . . . that specialists in the West were misled concerning the size of the post-war Soviet population, and that the Soviet government possessed information—at least by 1950—to this effect, but the government did not choose to publicize this information until the middle 1950's.[12] The impact of the war will remain for many years: "Projecting prewar population growth rates, it appears that the U.S.S.R. would now have 30 to 40 million more people, were it not for the grievously heavy war losses and the lower birth rate during the war years. . . . The widespread use of women in all labor, from cleaning streets to the professional level, came as much from necessity as it did from the desire to 'emancipate' women."[13] Furthermore the entrance of large numbers of women into the labor force has partially frustrated efforts to increase Soviet fertility. As regards mass purges it is impossible to gauge their effects on population depletions, but they appear to be selective regarding age and sex, thus exerting an effect on birth and death rates for a generation or longer.

This serious manpower weakness, which might have impaired Russia's bargaining power, undoubtedly contributed to an "almost pathologically secretive" guarding of population data.

This might also partly explain Soviet bellicose behavior in postwar years as well as her forceful enslavement of satellite countries such as East Germany and Hungary, which are dubious economic assets. The satellites . . . represent a supplement to the manpower of the U.S.S.R. . . . A rigid demographic blackout combined with poker-playing bluff concealed her inherent weakness. . . . What course would history have taken in the postwar years had the U.S.S.R.'s true population profile been available? When searching for a clue to that riddle, the reader must recognize that demographic ignorance can be disastrous, not only to the diplomat, but to all persons who are charged with the formation of national policy.[14]

---

[12] Michael K. Roof, "The Russian Population Enigma Reconsidered," *Population Studies*, Vol. XIV, No. 1, July 1960, p. 15.
[13] Robert C. Cook, "USSR Census: A Power Myth Exposed," *Population Bulletin*, Vol. XV, No. 4, July 1959, pp. 61-62.
[14] *Ibid.*, pp. 64-65.

The Russian people are experienced in dealing with demographic catastrophes. The repercussions of war, revolution, forced labor, and famine have left many scars on the Russian population. From 1913 to 1959 population losses from such forces plus birth deficits and modest emigration amounted to the staggering total of from 70 to 80 million people. "Losses from World War I, revolution, and turmoils of the initial post-revolution period have been assessed at more than 25 million; losses during 1931-33 collectivization of agriculture with its attendant famine have been estimated at over five million; and losses associated directly or indirectly with World War II have been placed at 45 million."[15]

About one-half of the Soviet population consists of Great Russians, one-fourth of Little Russians (Ukrainians) and White Russians (Belorussians), and the other fourth a large number of other ethnic groups.

According to the 1959 census, the crude birth rate was 25, the crude death rate 8; thus the crude rate of natural increase was about 17. Though this reported death rate of 8 is extremely low and may be in error, the young age distribution (and perhaps also the high proportion of women) makes the rate appear somewhat credible.

Twentieth-century population growth of the Soviet Union has been slightly slower than that of the United States, but present growth rates of the two nations appear about even. Russia has a larger population, but this demographic leverage may be offset by the vast military losses of World War II.

COMMUNIST CHINA

Mainland China, long "one of the great uncertainties of demography,"[16] is by far the largest country in the world. One out of every five people now alive resides in China. Before the 1953 census, one American demographer was fond of remarking that the population of China was so large and so imprecisely known that if the entire population of the United States were suddenly transported to China, the increment would not be noticeable. This statement is a trifle exaggerated, but it hews closely enough to the truth to convince us of the tremendous significance of the Chinese in world population trends and the relative inconsequence of the United States population.

After a careful inspection of extant records, John Durand prepared the emended series of estimates reproduced in Table 52. Defective and inconsistent statistics are copiously available; the first remotely reliable

[15] Robert C. Cook, Georgine Ogden, and Addabelle Desmond, "Population Trends in the USSR," *Population Bulletin*, Vol. XVII, No. 6, October 1961, p. 112.

[16] Alfred Sauvy, "La population de la Chine," *Population*, Vol. XII, No. 4, October-December 1957, pp. 695-706.

TABLE 52. *Population Growth in China, A.D. 2-1953**

DYNASTY AND YEAR (A.D.)	POPULATION (MILLIONS)
Western Han:	
2	71
Eastern Han:	
88	43
105	53
125	56
140	56
156	62
Sui:	
606	54
T'ang:	
705	37
726	41
732	45
742	51
755	52
Sung:	
1014	60
1029	61
1048	64
1065	77
1075	94
1086	108
1094	115
1103	123
Sung-Ch'in:	
1193-1195	123
Ming:	
1381	60
1393	61
Ching:	
1751	207
1781	270
1791	294
1811	347
1821	344
1831	383
1841	400
1851	417
People's Republic:	
1953	518

* John D. Durand, "The Population Statistics of China, A.D. 2-1953," *Population Studies*, Vol. XIII, No. 3, March 1960, p. 249.

account of China's population was the "well done and accurate" census of 1953.[17] Although "there is no evidence that demographic data are fabricated for propaganda purposes,"[18] analysts complain of under-enumeration of females and infants and distortion of the age-sex structure. Indeed underreporting is a chronic census problem everywhere, especially besetting inexperienced census-takers. Underenumeration of women and infants is an error that results more frequently from poor methodology than from deliberate misrepresentation. John Aird contends "that the demographic data of Mainland China are substantially in error, that the population was undercounted in 1953-1954 and has been underregistered since, and that the State Statistical Bureau knows this and is trying as inconspicuously as possible to revise its figures upward."[19]

Official releases of the Chinese State Statistical Bureau claimed in 1957 a total population of 647 million and in 1958 some 663 million, a growth in one year of 16 million persons at a rate of 2.5 per cent. The Foreign Manpower Research Office of the United States Bureau of the Census estimated the Mainland Chinese population at 687 million in 1958 and 723 million in 1960. The F.M.R.O. estimates that the Chinese are increasing at an accelerating rate, with annual increments of 2 per cent through 1948-1954 and 2.5 per cent through 1955-1960.[20]

The Peiping government uses population data for policy and planning. Birth control policy was altered in 1954, almost immediately following completion of the official enumeration. "Registration data and certain economic statistics disclosed that the urban labor force was increasing more rapidly than the capacity of urban industry to absorb it. Registration statistics also showed an increasing urban nonproductive population. Consequently, current policy discourages migration of rural residents to the cities, and large numbers of urban residents are being drafted for work in the countryside. These major policy decisions testify to the acceptance of official population data."[21]

The Ministry of Public Security set up a registration system for major cities in 1951 and extended it to rural areas in 1955. From data thus

---

[17] Ta Chen, "New China's Population Census of 1953 and Its Relations to National Reconstruction and Demographic Research," *Bulletin de l'Institut International de Statistique*, Stockholm, 1957, Vol. XXXVI, Part 2, pp. 255-271.

[18] Lawrence Krader and John Aird, "Sources of Demographic Data on Mainland China," *American Sociological Review*, Vol. XXIV, No. 5, October 1959, p. 623.

[19] John S. Aird, "The Present and Prospective Population of Mainland China," in Milbank Memorial Fund, *Population Trends in Eastern Europe, The USSR, and Mainland China*, New York, 1960, p. 94.

[20] *Ibid.*, p. 129.

[21] Krader and Aird, "Sources of Demographic Data on Mainland China," *op. cit.*, p. 630.

collected, supplemented by sample surveys, the present birth rate is approximately 40 to 45 per 1,000 per year and the death rate somewhere in the vicinity of 20. Subtraction yields a probable crude rate of natural increase of 20 to 25. The death rate appears to be falling rapidly.

In the 1953 census the age structure was reported to contain 36 per cent under age 15 and 3 per cent over age 65; corrected figures are 40 and 3 per cent, respectively.[22] The sex ratio was officially given as 105 at birth, rising to 117 at ages 10 to 14, falling thereafter to below 100 after age 55 and dropping to 45 at age 85 and older. In 1957, 37 per cent of all adults were represented as being literate, though literacy data are extremely shaky and definition susceptible to complaint.[23]

The Chinese density pattern is highly uneven. Ninety-six per cent of the people are concentrated on 40 per cent of the land area in the eastern and southern parts of the nation. Sections of Sinkiang, Tsinghai, and Tibet are virtually uninhabited, whereas the density in the Chengtu plain in Szechuan Province approaches 2,500 per square mile. Density pressure is intensified by heavy internal migration of peasants to the cities. Between 1949 and 1956 approximately 20 million people moved from rural to urban areas—one of the largest recorded internal shifts in such a short time anywhere in the world. Overflowing cities reported "serious shortages of food, drastic lack of housing, and growing unemployment."[24]

The extremely low level of living prevailing in China is not likely to be improved in the near future. Ma Yin-chu, President of Peking University until 1960 and a proponent of birth control, argues that increasing population makes it difficult to improve the standard of living, despite large production increases. This attitude contrasts sharply with the party-line doctrine that human labor organized and directed in Communist fashion can accomplish anything, and that population control is an admission that poverty and economic ills could be caused by forces other than non-Communist sociopolitical systems.

Although Malthusian reasoning is regarded by China's officialdom as bourgeois and reactionary, high fertility and overpopulation are feared by some authorities as instigators of economic distress. Marx maintained that "the poverty of the peasant and worker grows from feudalism and class exploitation, underproduction and maldistribution, and quickly

[22] Aird, "The Present and Prospective Population of Mainland China," *op. cit.,* pp. 105 and 124.
[23] Sripati Chandrasekhar, *China's Population,* Hong Kong University Press, Hong Kong, 1960, p. 51.
[24] Leo A. Orleans, "Population Redistribution in Communist China," in Milbank Memorial Fund, *Population Trends in Eastern Europe, the USSR, and Mainland China,* p. 144.

vanishes under Communism where a nation's resources are fully exploited." In its early years, the Communist government of China contended that neo-Malthusian birth control was a device to delude the workers into believing they were personally responsible for their own poverty. Some officials still maintain that China is underpopulated and confronted with an acute labor shortage. Others accept the panegyric: "There is nothing the Chinese people under Communism cannot achieve."

Estimation Techniques

Of the four objectives of demography identified in the first chapter, the final one is the estimation of future population size, distribution, and characteristics. Professional and amateur demographers have been trying to forecast population growth for many years; population prediction is in fact as old as demography itself. Yet despite this long history, attempts to ascertain future population are still of doubtful accuracy—and they will undoubtedly remain so for a long time to come.

In this connection, five facts should be kept in mind. First, subjectivity cannot be eliminated from any estimate; at best, it can only be minimized. Second, the longer the time period over which the estimate is made, the greater the chance for error. Third, the smaller the area, the more difficult is projecting its growth into the future, because the inertia or tendency to continue existing trends is much less for small areas than for large ones. Migration is especially troublesome in this regard; the opening or closing of one factory can double or halve the population of a town in a single year. Fourth, population forecasting implicitly and inescapably involves forecasting social, economic, political, and physical environmental conditions—an almost impossible task. Lastly, despite these weaknesses, a well-made estimate is generally better than no estimate at all or a random or biased guess. Kingsley Davis perceptively writes:

> A forecast . . . is a population projection based on assumptions regarded as most likely to hold true. The assumptions of the demographer relate to births, deaths, and migration. Given them, he can grind out the figures for the future population by well-known operations. Since, however, these demographic processes are affected by economic and political occurrences, a really accurate population forecast would have, at the same time, to be an accurate politico-economic forecast. Unhappily, the economists and political scientists cannot foresee the future in their fields five, ten, or fifteen years in advance; and even if they could, there is as yet no known technique by which these events can be operationally—i.e., quantitatively—connected with the demographic

processes. The American birth rate, for example, continued a steady decline through the prosperous 1920's, but it rose amazingly during the prosperous 1940's. The demographer is therefore forced to resort to what may be called featherbed assumptions. He says that *if* economic conditions remain good, or *if* there is no war, or *if* no catastrophe occurs, his assumptions with reference to fertility, mortality, and migration will likely hold true. But he has no way of ascertaining whether or not these politico-economic conditions will or will not prove real; his statements about them are spongy and amorphous, because these conditions are not quantitatively defined and cannot be mathematically connected with demographic events. Seen in this light, population forecasts are obviously hazardous undertakings. They resemble the prediction that a drunken driver will reach his destination by a certain time *if* he has enough gasoline, *if* he stays on the road, and *if* he does not decide to go elsewhere; his gasoline supply can be ascertained, but it is impossible to assess in advance the other two factors.[25]

Population estimates involve five dimensions or decisions: 1) total population or components; 2) pre-, inter-, or post-censal dates; 3) world, country, province, county, ward, tract, or other area; 4) one, two, three, or many estimates presented together; and 5) projection, prediction, or prophecy. The first of these distinctions compares use of the entire population in contrast with making separate estimates of birth, deaths, and migration. The second refers to the timing of the estimates; intercensal estimates are more secure than either pre- or post-censal ones, for the reason that interpolation is easier and safer than extrapolation. Third, population forecasts may apply to geographic and political areas of various sizes and kinds. The fourth facet differentiates those statisticians who prefer to make several estimates—high, medium, and low, for example, each dependent upon certain conditions—from those who prepare only a single statement. The fifth aspect contrasts mathematical projection based on certain specified assumptions, careful predictions based on informed judgment and experience with the material (a shrewd guess), and intuitive conjecture or speculation founded on faith or wishful thinking. In practice, population estimates usually take either of two forms: mathematical extrapolation of total population or component projections based on birth, death, and migration trends.

MATHEMATICAL EXTRAPOLATION

Mathematical extrapolation generally assumes that the population will continue to grow exactly as it has in the recent past—founded on the prior assumption that the economic and political situation will not

---

[25] Kingsley Davis, "Future Population Trends and Their Significance," *Transactions of the Eighteenth North American Wildlife Conference*, Wildlife Management Institute, 1953, pp. 9-10.

change drastically. A pure extrapolation avoids the implication of prediction, since it is literally a direct extension of present tendencies.

Curves may be fitted by inspection (freehand "eye-balling it in" or using such drafting aids as the French curve, ship's curve, spline, or snake); smoothing (weighted or unweighted moving averages); or mathematical formulas (straight line, logistic, Gompertz curve, compound interest curve, quadratic parabola, cubic parabola, hyperbola, or catenary). Time series analysis provides a method of breaking up a growth curve into the secular trend (long-term changes), cyclical movements (recurring infrequent fluctuations), periodic movements (systematic and frequent repetitions), and irregular variations (random, unexplained, or accidental).

Projections must be made very carefully. Great discretion is necessary in the choice of a mathematical curve to be fitted. In his first message to Congress, Abraham Lincoln predicted (by incorrect selection of a straight line extrapolation of 1790-1860 growth) that the population of the United States would reach 250 million persons early in the twentieth century; his second message revised the forecast to 217 million by 1925.[26] In 1852 retired merchant Francis Bonynge predicted a total United States population of 290 million in 1960 and 703 million by 2000 A.D.[27] In fairness it should be pointed out that Bonynge's short-term estimates (under fifty years) were within 3 per cent of the census enumerations. H. S. Pritchett, a professor of mathematics and astronomy at Washington University, had such faith in the third degree parabola that he published forecasts for ten centuries in advance; his projections for the United States of 222 million in 1960, 386 million in 2000, and 41 billion in 2900 A.D. bespeak an overly rigid clinging to one growth formula.[28]

COMPONENT PROJECTION

Component projection, the most widely used technique for estimating future population, begins with a certain assumption or set of assumptions regarding future trends concerning each of the three basic demographic variables. From these assumptions one traces the number of births, deaths, and net migrants expected. The estimate of total popula-

---

[26] J. J. Spengler, "Population Prediction in Nineteenth-century America," *American Sociological Review*, Vol. I, 1936, pp. 905-921.

[27] Francis Bonynge, *The Future Wealth of America*, New York, 1852; cited in Harold F. Dorn, "Pitfalls in Population Forecasts and Projections," *Journal of the American Statistical Association*, Vol. XLIV, September 1950, pp. 311-334.

[28] H. S. Pritchett, "A Formula for Predicting the Population of the United States," *Transactions of the Academy of Science of St. Louis*, December 1890, p. 12; and "The Population of the United States during the Next Ten Decades," *Popular Science Monthly*, Vol. LVIII, 1900-1901, pp. 49-53.

tion is obtained only after these future births, deaths, and migrants have been estimated.

After the demographic variables are projected separately, they are combined using the equation $P_e = P_i + B - D + I - E$, which reads: the estimated population equals the initial population plus births minus deaths plus immigrants minus emigrants. P_i is known at the start, D is fairly stable, and with luck B is not terribly hard to estimate. However, I and E are refractory, depending as they do on volitional and frequently transient factors. Demographers sometimes project natural increase only, on the assumption that since they cannot estimate migration properly they should not attempt it at all. Relevant variables that may be used supplementarily are marriage rate, age at marriage, age-sex structure, race, occupation, employment, socioeconomic status, and level of living.

Demographers may make several projections for each variable (high, medium, and low, for example). This procedure results in a dozen or so total projections, which may strike the uninitiated as hedging. But actually this is a much more realistic approach than simply providing one estimate, as it supplies the reader with a better understanding of the ways in which the estimator has proceeded. Also, it permits the user to apply his own judgment by selecting whichever assumptions regarding social, political, and economic conditions he most expects. In 1947 P. K. Whelpton made six series of thirty-year projections for the United States by combining assumptions regarding fertility (high, medium, low), mortality (high, medium, or low), and migration (high or low).[29] And in 1949 the English Royal Commission on Population prepared sixteen different projections through the year 2047 by making two to five assumptions each for mortality, fertility, migration, and nuptiality.[30]

Component methods take several forms. We may find demographically advanced areas to use as a guide.[31] We project births, deaths, and marriages by using the life table. We project symptomatic data such as school enrollment or industrial activity (Crosetti and Schmitt claim considerable success using a multiple regression equation made up of live births, public school enrollment, and registered motor vehicles).[32] We carefully assess recent trends and prospective developments and

[29] Pascal K. Whelpton, *Forecasts of the Population of the United States: 1945-1975*, U. S. Bureau of the Census, Washington, 1947.

[30] Royal Commission on Population, *Report*, His Majesty's Stationery Office, London, 1949, pp. 80-99.

[31] Frank W. Notestein *et al., The Future Population of Europe and the Soviet Union*, League of Nations, Geneva, 1944, pp. 199-211.

[32] Albert H. Crosetti and Robert C. Schmitt, "A Method of Estimating the Intercensal Population of Counties," *Journal of the American Statistical Association*, Vol. LI, No. 276, December 1956, pp. 587-590.

form judgments of their probable demographic repercussions; thus we may ask—and calculate tentative answers to—such questions as: What do we expect to be the impact of D.D.T. or a new vaccine on death rates? Is governmental action regarding birth control being altered? Will the government repeal immigration laws, and with what demographic consequences?

Component methods have three advantages over extrapolation of totals: they do not require as long a series of data, they can yield many forecasts, and they are generally considered more valid. Advantages on the side of fitting curves to totals are that usually they are simpler and more condensed, they are always faster once the curve has been obtained, they lend themselves better to making estimates for dates other than those originally intended, and they are sometimes conceptually valuable.

Future Growth Expectations

At present the world's population is increasing at a breakneck pace. It will probably reach 6 billion—roughly twice the present number—by the year 2000. The United States alone has only to continue growing at its present speed to reach a billion by 2050—and it is unlikely the rate will remain constant. Realization of these facts is the essential first step toward facing social, economic, and political demands which world and national leaders will have to meet.

Timing is exceedingly important. A United Nations report written in 1957 complains: "More disturbing than the projected figure of a population amounting to 6,000 or 7,000 million is the fact that it will probably be attained so soon. . . . Not only technical achievement but progress in international co-operation and organization will have to be more effective than during the past 43 years if the expected numbers of mankind are to be organizationally and technologically accommodated to the minimum conditions required for human dignity."[33]

Comparing technologically developed and underdeveloped parts of the world, the latter segment is destined to grow far more rapidly in our lifetimes. "The technologically advanced areas contain now slightly more than one-third of the world population. This share, according to the seemingly most plausible expectations, will drop to less than one-quarter by the end of the century."[34] In effect a majority of the next generation will be born and reared in parts of the world that are not well equipped by contemporary Western standards to nurture and educate future citizens. And unless technological and economic develop-

---

[33] United Nations, *The Future Growth of World Population, op. cit.*, p. 22.
[34] *Ibid.*, p. 23.

ment can be forced to exceed population growth, these child-rearing functions will not be performed as well as they might.

Regional groupings provide useful bases for highlighting long-range demographic anticipations. The rapid population growth of Latin America, Asia, and Africa is indicated in Table 53. Population growth in the 37 leading nations is reviewed in Table 54. The estimates in these two tables were prepared by the United Nations Population Branch using component projection techniques of a rather complicated nature based on several assumptions regarding future fertility and mortality. According to these estimates, the seven largest countries will maintain their present rank order for another decade or so, with the United States holding to its fourth position. China should reach a hardly believable total of a billion people by about 1980. Well before then, India will pass the half-billion mark, and the Soviet Union will exceed a quarter of a billion.

LATIN AMERICA

By the end of the century, the Latin part of the New World will probably have to feed, clothe, and house about 600 million people—four times its 1950 population. Yet although nearly every country will double its 1950 population by 1980, the density should not become insupportable. Rapid growth in Central and South America should continue for many years before falling birth rates offset the newly lowered mortality accompanying the transition to industrialization and modernization. Fortunately, Latin America possesses plentiful natural resources, which will go far toward meeting the alimentary and other needs of the larger population. Growth pains, though serious, should not prove insurmountable or excessively disruptive so long as civic leaders apply intelligence and forethought to the exploitation of the natural riches of the land. But the class structure and omnipresent poverty are impediments. Dennis Wrong comments:

> Without extensive social reform and increased capital expenditures, it is unlikely that Latin America's empty spaces will be fully developed and settled. Meanwhile population is growing more rapidly than anywhere else in the world and the danger exists that here, as in more densely populated areas, agricultural expansion will merely augment the area's capacity to support more people at low living standards. Nevertheless, South America has plenty of time left to undergo economic development and to make the transition to low birth rates before its population becomes too large to permit the necessary changes to occur without great social dislocation and loss of life.[35]

---

[35] Dennis H. Wrong, *Population*, Random House, New York, 1959, p. 111.

TABLE 53. *Estimated Population Increases by Continents, 1900-2000**

ESTIMATE AND YEAR	WORLD	AFRICA	ANGLO AMERICA	LATIN AMERICA	ASIA (EXCLUDING U.S.S.R.)	EUROPE (INCLUDING U.S.S.R.)	OCEANIA
Population (millions)							
1900	1,550	120	81	63	857	423	6
1925	1,907	147	126	99	1,020	505	10
1950	2,497	199	168	163	1,380	574	13
1975	3,828	303	240	303	2,210	751	21
2000	6,267	517	312	592	3,870	947	29
Percentage of world population contained in each continent							
1900	100.0	7.7	5.2	4.1	55.3	27.3	0.4
1950	100.0	8.0	6.7	6.5	55.2	23.0	0.5
2000	100.0	8.2	5.0	9.4	61.8	15.1	0.5
Increase							
1900-1950	947	79	87	100	523	151	7
1950-2000	3,770	318	144	429	2,490	373	16
Per cent increase							
1900-1950	61	66	107	159	61	36	117
1950-2000	151	160	86	263	180	65	113
Percent of increase in each continent							
1900-1950	100	8	9	11	55	16	1
1950-2000	100	8	4	11	66	10	1

* United Nations, *The Future Growth of World Population*, New York, 1958, pp. 23-24; and Donald J. Bogue, *The Population of the United States*, The Free Press, Glencoe, 1959, p. 789.

TABLE 54. *Expected Population Growth in the Largest Nations,*
*1960-1975**

RANK IN 1960	NATION	PROJECTED POPULATION (MILLIONS) 1960	1975	INCREASE 1960-1975 (MILLIONS)	PERCENTAGE CHANGE 1960-1975	DIFFERENCE IN RATE FROM U.S. RATE
1	China	654.0	894.0	240.0	37	+16
2	India	417.0	563.0	146.0	35	+14
3	U.S.S.R.	215.0	275.0	60.0	28	+7
4	United States	179.0	217.0	38.0	21	—
5	Japan	95.1	116.0	20.9	22	+1
6	Pakistan	92.2	128.0	35.8	39	+18
7	Indonesia	89.3	122.0	32.7	37	+16
8	Germany	73.0	80.5	7.5	10	−11
9	Brazil	67.1	102.0	34.9	52	+31
10	United Kingdom	51.6	55.5	3.9	8	−13
11	Italy	49.5	56.1	6.6	13	−8
12	France	44.5	49.1	4.6	10	−11
13	Mexico	34.2	53.3	19.1	56	+35
14	Nigeria	34.0	42.3	8.3	24	+3
15	Korea	31.5	43.0	11.5	37	+16
16	Spain	30.0	34.4	4.4	15	−6
17	Poland	29.4	34.4	5.0	17	−4
18	Viet Nam	29.1	40.4	11.3	39	+18
19	Turkey	27.5	40.0	12.5	45	+24
20	Egypt	26.0	38.3	12.3	47	+26
21	Philippines	24.4	34.1	9.7	40	+19
22	Iran	24.3	34.3	10.0	41	+20
23	Thailand	22.9	32.1	9.2	40	+19
24	Argentina	21.3	27.2	5.9	28	+7
25	Burma	20.7	27.4	6.7	32	+11
26	Federated West Africa	20.2	24.7	4.5	22	+1
27	Yugoslavia	19.0	22.6	3.6	19	−2
28	Romania	18.5	21.7	3.2	17	−4
29	Canada	17.6	22.3	4.7	27	+6
30	Union of South Africa	15.2	21.9	6.7	44	+23
31	Colombia	14.3	21.6	7.3	51	+30
32	Belgian Congo	13.9	17.6	3.7	27	+6
33	Czechoslovakia	13.7	15.5	1.8	13	−8
34	Afghanistan	12.8	16.9	4.1	32	+11
35	Ethiopia	12.2	14.4	2.2	18	−3
36	Netherlands	11.3	12.8	1.5	13	−8
37	Sudan	10.5	12.2	1.7	16	−5

* United Nations, *The Future Growth of World Population,* New York, 1958, pp. 72-75; and Donald J. Bogue, *The Population of the United States,* The Free Press, Glencoe, 1959, p. 790.

EURASIA

Throughout what remains of the twentieth century the nations of north-west and central Europe will probably experience small gains in population. Southern and eastern Europe are expected to grow moderately. With the exception of little Albania, no country of Europe is on the way to doubling its population in less than a third of a century. The populations of all the southeastern nations are doubling in less than one hundred years, but the continent as a whole does not promise a rapid rate of increase. Northwest Europe, having initiated the "swarming of Europe," is now growing sedately. Unique in northern and western Europe is the Netherlands, which has retained its relatively high fertility and rate of natural increase; its density of 865 persons per square mile makes it the densest nation in the world—followed in order by Belgium, Taiwan, Japan, and South Korea.

In contrast, the huge Asian population is due for a gigantic increase to approximately 4 billion by the year 2000. Asia's phase of accelerated growth began and continues under unpropitious skies. Deterrents to harmonious population expansion are otherworldly religions, traditions of servile political status and a resultant lack of experience in self-government, strong feelings of nationalism, dense agricultural population, few outlets for emigration, modernization borrowed incompletely from the outside, disharmony resulting from culture lags, low levels of capital, education, and literacy, and a huge base population.

That one Asian country, Japan, has adopted European ways has led to a belief that other Asiatic nations will shortly follow. But this would seem to be an extremely dubious presumption. Relevance of the demographic transition in Japan to that of other Asian countries is uncertain. Irene Taeuber, a distinguished specialist on Japan, points out Japan's uniqueness:

> Neither the timing, the magnitude, nor the interrelations of the changes is likely to be identical with or predictable from those in Japan. . . . The first complete transition outside the Western world has occurred in Japan. The completion came swiftly, but the course involved more than a century of industrial and urban development and educational advance. The means whereby the transition proceeded, perhaps even its course and speed, were associated intimately with the indigenous and the developing culture of the Japanese.[36]

---

[36] Irene B. Taeuber, "Japan's Demographic Transition Re-examined," *Population Studies*, Vol. XIV, No. 1, July 1960, p. 39; cf. also Irene B. Taeuber, *The Population of Japan*, Princeton University Press, Princeton, 1958.

AFRICA

The continent of Africa should approximately double its population by the year 2000. Her population potential, like her resources, is huge and almost untapped. As regards her resources, however, they are very unevenly distributed, and the capital necessary for their development will be difficult to accumulate. If Africans can effectively exploit their impressive supplies of minerals, many of which have scarcely been touched, they may look forward to a bright future. But in order to extract and export their abundant metallic ores, they must first purchase machinery, train skilled technicians, and build highways, railroads, and harbor facilities—all of which demand investment capital that is sadly lacking. Subsistence farmers produce only a slow trickle of capital, and neither augmentation of agricultural output nor large-scale industrialization offers the quick solution that is sought. But although the difficulties of surmounting their present poverty are considerable, they are not overwhelming. "In view of the magnitude of the task of developing African agricultural resources, the race between population and food supply will probably be a close one until the area is over the hump of economic development."[37]

The major problem of Africa, as of most underdeveloped and rapidly growing areas, is one of time. Eventually any region should be able to industrialize and to modernize its agriculture. But these are long jumps requiring money, a trained labor force, leadership, and a great deal of sheer determination. And while each of these requisites can be acquired, even the more fortunate nations cannot acquire them all in the space of a few decades.

In some cases, too, the modernization process presupposes a fundamental change in people's values and philosophies—a difficult and often heartrending operation. The people of Africa are only now winning their political freedom from Western colonial dominance. Resentment of things European may make them unwilling to plunge suddenly into the clock-watching, machine-oriented, disciplined mass society which makes possible telephones that work and gasoline stations in every community.

Africa's development problems are pervious to solution. Unlike Asia, Africa is beginning its demographic explosion with a fairly small and relatively sparse population. If tragedy and disaster do come, they will result from poor timing. Indeed, time is the one resource they can least afford to squander.

---

[37] Wrong, *Population, op. cit.*, p. 111.

22 ✺ Population of the United States

The lobby of the United States Department of Commerce building is decorated with a "population clock" on which the Bureau of the Census ticks off population changes. In the center is a register resembling the odometer on an automobile dashboard. Its nine dials show the population at any moment. Every eleven seconds, the right-hand wheel rolls to a new number, thus demonstrating the rapidity of over-all increase. A blue bulb denoting births flashes every eight seconds. A purple light is illuminated every twenty seconds, indicating that someone has died. A green bulb lights up each ninety seconds, symbolizing the arrival of an immigrant. A red bulb, which reports on emigration, winks every twenty minutes.

Periods of Growth

In this final chapter, we first review the demographic history of the United States. Before 1790, data are incomplete and based on crude estimates. Before 1600, statistical information is at best fragmentary and often nonexistent.

As can be seen in Table 55, population rose in every decade of the three and one-half centuries following the initial European settlement. During Colonial times, percentage increases were irregular, varying from estimates of 19 to 49 per cent per decade between 1660 and 1790. Nineteenth-century growth was rapid and steady, never deviating more than 2 per cent from intercensal increases of 34 per cent in the ante-bellum period, and then slowing to gains of 20 to 30 per cent from 1860 through

TABLE 55. *Population Growth of the American Colonies and the United States, 1610-1960**

YEAR	POPULATION	Increase Over Preceding Period		POPU-LATION PER SQUARE MILE
		NUMBER	PER CENT	
1610	350	—	—	—
1620	2,302	1,952	557.7	—
1630	4,646	2,344	101.4	—
1640	26,634	21,988	473.3	—
1650	50,368	23,734	89.1	—
1660	75,058	24,690	49.0	—
1670	111,935	36,877	49.1	—
1680	151,597	39,662	35.4	—
1690	210,372	58,775	38.8	—
1700	250,888	40,516	19.3	—
1710	331,711	80,823	32.2	—
1720	466,185	134,474	40.3	—
1730	629,445	163,260	35.0	—
1740	905,563	276,118	43.9	—
1750	1,170,760	265,197	29.3	—
1760	1,593,625	422,865	36.1	—
1770	2,148,076	554,451	34.8	—
1780	2,780,369	632,293	29.4	—
1790	3,929,214	1,148,845	41.3	4.5
1800	5,308,483	1,379,269	35.1	6.1
1810	7,239,881	1,931,398	36.4	4.3
1820	9,638,453	2,398,572	33.1	5.5
1830	12,866,020	3,227,567	33.5	7.4
1840	17,069,453	4,203,433	32.7	9.8
1850	23,191,876	6,122,423	35.9	7.9
1860	31,443,321	8,251,445	35.6	10.6
1870	38,558,371	7,115,050	22.6	13.0
1880	50,189,209	11,630,838	30.2	16.9
1890	62,979,766	12,790,557	25.5	21.2
1900	76,212,168	13,232,402	21.0	25.6
1910	92,228,496	16,016,328	21.0	31.0
1920	106,021,537	13,793,041	15.0	35.6
1930	123,202,624	17,181,087	16.2	41.2
1940	132,164,569	8,961,945	7.3	44.2
1950	151,325,798	19,161,229	14.5	50.7
1960	179,323,175	27,997,377	18.5	60.1

* Pre-1790 data were computed from U. S. Bureau of the Census, *Historical Statistics of the United States, Colonial Times to 1957,* Government Printing Office, Washington, 1960, p. 756; post-1790 data were taken from Bureau of the Census, U. S. *Census of Population: 1960,* "Number of Inhabitants: United States Summary," PC(1)-1A, Government Printing Office, Washington, 1961, p. 4. Pre-1790 figures are estimates. Intercensal intervals were not always exactly 10 years; the range is from 9 years and 9 months to 10 years and 3 months. Indians living in Indian territory or on reservations were not included in the population count until 1890. Negroes were included after 1620.

1910. Except for the depression decade of the 1930's, growth in the last fifty years has remained between 14 and 18 per cent per decade. Density shows a strong secular increase, with occasional declines attributable to inclusion of large areas of new territory under the jurisdiction of the United States, some of which were sparsely settled in the years preceding statehood.

INDIAN AND COLONIAL POPULATIONS

The American Indians kept extremely poor demographic records; hence we are obliged to use whatever estimates we can lay our hands on. Possibly the best estimates are those of anthropologists A. L. Kroeber and J. H. Steward, who based their findings on previous work by James Mooney. All three men took as their date the period of first contact of each group with settling whites, a time which varied among different regions of North America. Mooney assessed the total Indian population at 1,150,000; Kroeber preferred the figure 900,000; and Steward estimated 1,000,000.[1]

In the sixteenth and seventeenth centuries the largest and densest aboriginal groups were the Pueblo in the Southwest, the Pomo in central California, the Ojibwa near the Great Lakes, the Chinook in the Pacific Northwest, and the Cherokee and Creek in the Southeast. Densities exceeding one person per square mile were found only in parts of New Mexico and Arizona and along the Pacific coast from Mexico to Canada.[2] The fact that there were such gross differences between the twentieth-century national settlement pattern and the earlier Indian density distribution is evidence against the operation of strict geographic determinism.

For several centuries before 1800 the native Indian population apparently held steady at approximately a million. Then in the early nineteenth century, warfare, hardships associated with tribal transfers, smallpox, tuberculosis, and malnutrition reduced their numbers to about a quarter of a million. Holding to this total from the Civil War to World War I, the Indians have in recent decades begun the rapid increase that follows a sharply declining mortality.

Beginning with the first effective settlement of Europeans in 1607, the white population has shown a phenomenal growth. From an estimated 48,000 in 1650, the colonies reached 223,000 by 1700—fivefold in

---

[1] Alfred Louis Kroeber, *Cultural and Natural Areas of Native North America,* University of California Press, Berkeley, 1939, pp. 131-181; and Julian H. Steward, "The Native Population of South America," in Steward (ed.), *Handbook of South American Indians,* Smithsonian Institution, Bureau of American Ethnology Bulletin 143, Washington, 1946-1950, Vol. V, Part 3, p. 656.
[2] Kroeber, *Cultural and Natural Areas of Native North America, op. cit.,* p. 134.

fifty years—through a combination of immigration and high natural increment. By 1750 the number of whites reached 934,000—fourfold in fifty years. The first Census, in 1790, recorded a white population of 3,172,000, tripling the size in forty years. During the preceding century and a half, the annual increase was more than 3 per cent, or approximately double the present rate of growth. In those days, of course, there was far more room in which to put the increment. Most of the growth resulted from an excess of births over deaths; fertility was very high. After the initial few decades of settlement, immigration did not contribute nearly as much to population growth as did natural increase.

1790 TO 1950

After the founding of the United States the demographic situation changed. Immigration became a greater contributor to population growth, while natural increase fell off somewhat. As noted earlier, the nineteenth-century immigration into the United States was the largest movement of people into a single country in man's history. Immigrants came from every nation of Europe and also from Asia and Africa. But even the very heavy surge of immigrants immediately preceding World War I did not equal the excess of births over deaths. Natural increase during 1910 to 1913 amounted to an annual average one and one-half to five times larger than the net immigration.[3]

In 1800 the birth rate was more than double the death rate. Then for a time, the greater rapidity of fertility decline brought the rates closer together, but by 1950 the birth rate was again twice the death rate. Since both rates decreased by more than 50 per cent between 1800 and 1950, the rate of natural increase was much smaller in 1950 than in the early years of the century.

Other changes during the period from 1800 to 1950 are shown in Table 56. Population, density, and urban areas grew very rapidly. The proportion of farmers declined considerably. The median age almost doubled. And the gross national product and expenditure of energy increased vastly. All these changes reflect transformation from an agrarian to an urban-industrial society.

1950 TO PRESENT

Since World War II the United States has been increasing in population at its greatest rate in half a century. The nation experienced annual increases ranging from 1.59 to 1.94 per cent during 1946 to 1960, a rate of growth approximately twice that of the 1930's and early 1940's. The

---

[3] Warren S. Thompson and P. K. Whelpton, *Population Trends in the United States*, McGraw-Hill Book Co., New York, 1933, p. 301.

overwhelming portion of this increase resulted from an excess of births over deaths; net gains from migration have been small since 1925.

From 1950 to 1960 the nation added 40 million babies and lost 15 million persons through deaths, resulting in a natural increase of 25 million people in ten years. During this period net immigration was slightly below 3 million, a paltry figure by comparison. Total increase amounted to 19 per cent, or just below 3 million a year.

Since the 1960 Census the population has continued to grow at a rate of about 1.6 per cent a year. The April 1, 1963 population reached an estimated 187,888,000 (excluding Armed Forces abroad), an increase of 8,557,000 or 4.8 per cent since April 1, 1960. Currently the national population is growing by approximately 200,000 a month. When Armed Forces abroad are included, the estimated total as of April 1, 1963, is 188,643,000.[4]

The 1959-1960 vital statistics picture is exhibited in Figure 22. Note that the birth rate fluctuated between 22 and 26 per 1,000, while the death rate was less than half that. The June peak in the marriage rate was attributable to school graduation and the symbolic value of a June

TABLE 56. *Selected Statistics for the United States, 1800-1950**

	1800[a]	1850[a]	1900	1950
Population in millions	5	23	76	152
Density of persons per square mile	6	8	26	51
Crude birth rate	55	43	32	24
Crude death rate	26	21	17	10
Crude rate of natural increase	29	22	15	14
Child-woman ratio	1342	892	666	587
Median age in years	16	19	23	30
Proportion urban	6%	15%	40%	59%
Number of urban places	33	236	1737	4023
Proportion of occupied persons in agriculture	85%	64%	37%	12%
Proportion foreign-born	b	10%	14%	7%
Proportion Negro	19%	16%	12%	10%

[a] 1800 and 1850 figures are often imprecise estimates.
[b] Not available or meaningful.

* William Petersen, *Population*, The Macmillan Co., New York, 1961; U. S. Bureau of the Census, *Historical Statistics of the United States: Colonial Times to 1957*; Ansley J. Coale and Melvin Zelnik, *New Estimates of Fertility and Population in the United States*, Princeton University Press, Princeton, 1963; and Conrad and Irene B. Taeuber, *The Changing Population of the United States*, John Wiley and Sons, New York, 1958.

---

[4] U. S. Bureau of the Census, "Estimates of the Population of the United States: January 1, 1950, to April 1, 1963," *Current Population Reports*, Series P-25, No. 266, May 22, 1963, pp. 1-2.

FIGURE 22. *Monthly Vital Rates, United States, 1959-1960*

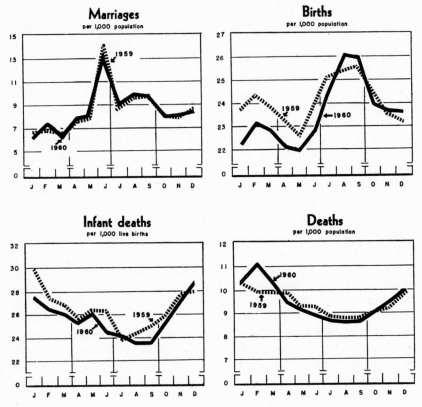

* U. S. National Office of Vital Statistics, *Monthly Vital Statistics Report,* Vol. IX, No. 13, Part 1, May 31, 1961, p. 1.

wedding for first marriages. Contrary to popular opinion, the fertility maximum was not in March or April—that is, nine or ten months after the June wedding date. The birth rate was remarkably even throughout the year, except for a small peak in August and September. The death rate still showed a winter maximum, though monthly variations were smaller than they used to be. Seasonal fluctuations of infant mortality resembled those of the total mortality pattern.

Regional and State Distribution

The official justification for a decennial census is the provision of an equitable basis for apportionment of members of the House of Representatives. Except for 1920, reapportionment has followed every census since 1790. Because total membership in the House is now stabilized at 435, some states gain and others lose following each census. Changes in 1950-1960 were as follows: California gained eight representatives; Florida four; Hawaii two; Alaska, Arizona, Maryland, Michigan, New Jersey, Ohio, and Texas gained one each; Alabama, Illinois, Iowa, Kansas, Kentucky, Maine, Minnesota, Mississippi, Missouri, Nebraska, North Carolina, and West Virginia lost one each; Arkansas, Massachusetts, and New York lost two each; and Pennsylvania lost three. Regionally, the West gained and the Midwest, South, and East lost.

The population changes inducing these legislative shifts are documented in Table 57. The highest rates of population growth between 1950 and 1960 occurred in Florida, 79 per cent; Nevada, 78; Alaska, 76; Arizona, 74; California, 48; Delaware, 40; New Mexico, 40; Colorado, 32; and Maryland, 32 per cent. States losing population during the decade were West Virginia, 7 per cent; Arkansas, 6 per cent; Mississippi, less than 1 per cent; and also the District of Columbia, 5 per cent.

Between 1950 and 1960 all states had an excess of births over deaths. Natural increase was highest in the Deep South and Mountain states and lowest in the Northeast. Net international migration made a relatively minor contribution to national growth during the decade, amounting to less than one-tenth of the total population change. Consequently, the net migration gain and loss for most states was largely a result of internal redistribution among the states themselves rather than an influx of immigrants from abroad. Although 27 states and the District of Columbia experienced a net loss of population through migration, natural increase was large enough to make up the migration deficit in all but the four instances noted above. Because of the relatively small interstate variation in rates of natural increase, most differentials in rates of over-all change were caused by variation in migration rates. The rank order of states by percentage growth during the last two decades is quite similar to the rank according to per cent of net migration.

Natality and mortality statistics for 1961 reported a live birth rate of 23.3 and a death rate of 9.3. States having the highest crude birth rates were Alaska (32.3), New Mexico (30.5), and Utah (28.9); those having the lowest birth rates were Rhode Island (21.2), West Virginia (21.1), and Pennsylvania (21.0). Maximum crude death rates were found in Vermont (10.9), Maine (10.8), New Hampshire (10.8), and Missouri (10.8); minimum death rates were in New Mexico (6.5), Alaska (5.4), and Hawaii (5.2). The crude rate of natural increase was highest in Alaska (26.9), New Mexico (24.0) and Utah (22.2); slowest growing states were Rhode Island (11.0), New York (10.8), and Pennsylvania (10.5). Regionally, the Pacific and Rocky Mountain states had the highest fertility and lowest mortality, whereas the northeastern

TABLE 57. *Population Growth and Density by Divisions and States, United States, 1960**

	1960 POPULATION	Increase, 1950-1960 NUMBER	PER CENT	1960 RANK	1960 DENSITY
AREA					
Total	183,285,009	29,051,775	18.8	—	—
50 states and D.C.	179,323,175	27,997,377	18.5	—	50.5
Puerto Rico	2,349,544	138,841	6.3	—	686.4
Outlying areas	237,869	22,681	10.5	—	—
Population abroad	1,374,421	892,876	185.4	—	—
Regions					
Northeast	44,677,819	5,199,833	13.2	—	273.1
North Central	51,619,139	7,158,377	16.1	—	68.4
South	54,973,113	7,776,025	16.5	—	62.7
West	28,053,104	7,863,142	38.9	—	16.0
Northeast					
New England	10,509,367	1,194,914	12.8	—	166.5
Middle Atlantic	34,168,452	4,004,919	13.3	—	340.1
North Central					
East North Central	36,225,024	5,825,656	19.2	—	148.0
West North Central	15,394,115	1,332,721	9.5	—	30.2
South					
South Atlantic	25,971,732	4,789,397	22.6	—	97.0
East South Central	12,050,126	572,945	5.0	—	67.0
West South Central	16,951,255	2,413,683	16.6	—	39.5
West					
Mountain	6,855,060	1,780,062	35.1	—	8.0
Pacific	21,198,044	6,083,080	40.2	—	23.6
New England					
Maine	969,265	55,491	6.1	36	31.3
New Hampshire	606,921	73,679	13.8	46	67.3
Vermont	389,881	12,134	3.2	48	42.0
Massachusetts	5,148,578	458,064	9.8	9	654.5
Rhode Island	859,488	67,592	8.5	39	812.4
Connecticut	2,535,234	527,954	26.3	25	517.5
Middle Atlantic					
New York	16,782,304	1,952,112	13.2	1	350.1
New Jersey	6,066,782	1,231,453	25.5	8	806.7
Pennsylvania	11,319,366	821,354	7.8	3	251.5
East North Central					
Ohio	9,706,397	1,759,770	22.1	5	236.9
Indiana	4,662,498	728,274	18.5	11	128.9
Illinois	10,081,158	1,368,982	15.7	4	180.3
Michigan	7,823,194	1,451,428	22.8	7	137.2
Wisconsin	3,951,777	517,202	15.1	15	72.2

* U. S. Bureau of the Census, *U. S. Census of Population: 1960*, PC(1)-1A, pp. xii, 16, 18, 20, and 25.

TABLE 57—(continued)

Increase, 1950-1960

AREA	1960 POPULATION	NUMBER	PER CENT	1960 RANK	1960 DENSITY
West North Central					
Minnesota	3,413,864	431,381	14.5	18	42.7
Iowa	2,757,537	136,464	5.2	24	49.2
Missouri	4,319,813	365,160	9.2	13	62.5
North Dakota	632,446	12,810	2.1	45	9.1
South Dakota	680,514	27,774	4.3	41	8.9
Nebraska	1,411,330	85,820	6.5	34	18.4
Kansas	2,178,611	273,312	14.3	28	26.6
South Atlantic					
Delaware	446,292	128,207	40.3	47	225.6
Maryland	3,100,689	757,688	32.3	21	314.0
District of Columbia	763,956	−38,222	−4.8	40	12,523.9
Virginia	3,966,949	648,269	19.5	14	99.6
West Virginia	1,860,421	−145,131	−7.2	30	77.3
North Carolina	4,556,155	494,226	12.2	12	92.9
South Carolina	2,382,594	265,567	12.5	26	78.7
Georgia	3,943,116	498,538	14.5	16	67.7
Florida	4,951,560	2,180,255	78.7	10	91.3
East South Central					
Kentucky	3,038,156	93,350	3.2	22	76.2
Tennessee	3,567,089	275,371	8.4	17	85.4
Alabama	3,266,740	204,997	6.7	19	64.0
Mississippi	2,178,141	−773	—	29	46.1
West South Central					
Arkansas	1,786,272	−123,239	−6.5	31	34.0
Louisiana	3,257,022	573,560	21.4	20	72.2
Oklahoma	2,328,284	94,933	4.3	27	33.8
Texas	9,579,677	1,868,483	24.2	6	36.5
Mountain					
Montana	674,767	83,743	14.2	42	4.6
Idaho	667,191	78,554	13.3	43	8.1
Wyoming	330,066	39,537	13.6	49	3.4
Colorado	1,753,947	428,858	32.4	33	16.9
New Mexico	951,023	269,836	39.6	37	7.8
Arizona	1,302,161	552,574	73.7	35	11.5
Utah	890,627	201,765	29.3	38	10.8
Nevada	285,278	125,195	78.2	50	2.6
Pacific					
Washington	2,853,214	474,251	19.9	23	42.8
Oregon	1,768,687	247,346	16.3	32	18.4
California	15,717,204	5,130,981	48.5	2	100.4
Alaska	226,167	97,524	75.8	51	0.4
Hawaii	632,772	132,978	26.6	44	98.6

states had the lowest natality and the highest mortality. The fact that median ages were highest in the Northeast and lowest in the Far West contributed powerfully to these regional and state variations.

DENSITY VARIATIONS

With regard to area and density of the four Census regions in 1960, the Northeast contained only 5 per cent of the land area but 25 per cent of the population, the North Central accounted for 21 per cent of the land and 29 per cent of the people, the South for 25 per cent of the land and 31 per cent of the people, and the West an overwhelming 49 per cent of the land but only 16 per cent of the population.[5] Thus, as Table 57 shows, the Northeast has by far the greatest density, 273 persons per square mile of land area, and the West is easily the least dense region, at 16. Among the nine divisions, the Middle Atlantic is the most dense, with 340 persons per square mile, followed by New England at 166 and the East North Central with 148. The Mountain division has only 8 persons per square mile; next lowest are the Pacific at 24, the West North Central at 30, and the West South Central at 40.

Figure 23 is a dot map of the 1960 population. The heaviest clusterings of dots obviously denote the presence of cities. Of the seven urbanized areas exceeding two million in population, five are in the East and North Central regions and two in California. In rank order, these largest communities are New York, Los Angeles, Chicago, Philadelphia, Detroit, San Francisco, and Boston. Exactly half of the sixteen urbanized areas exceeding one million population are located on an approximately straight line from Boston to Chicago and all but three fall in the industrial cluster bounded by the four lines connecting Boston, Baltimore, St. Louis, and Minneapolis. Small city, village, and rural densities are also greatest in the northeastern quadrant of the nation and least in the Great Plains, Rocky Mountain, and southwestern territories.

Figure 24 shows which counties have experienced gains and losses over the past censal period. That the bulk of the counties attaining increases of 50 per cent or more are located in the West indicates a diminution of density differentials as Pacific and Mountain districts gradually catch up with other parts of the country. From 1950 to 1960 about one-tenth of the nation's 3,134 counties doubled in population, and seven (all but one in the West or South) tripled. Yet despite the substantial growth of the nation generally, many counties lost population over the 1950-1960 decade.

---

[5] U. S. Bureau of the Census, *U. S. Census of Population: 1960*, "Number of Inhabitants: United States Summary," PC(1)-1A, Government Printing Office, Washington, 1961, p. xvi.

FIGURE 23. *United States Population Distribution, 1960**

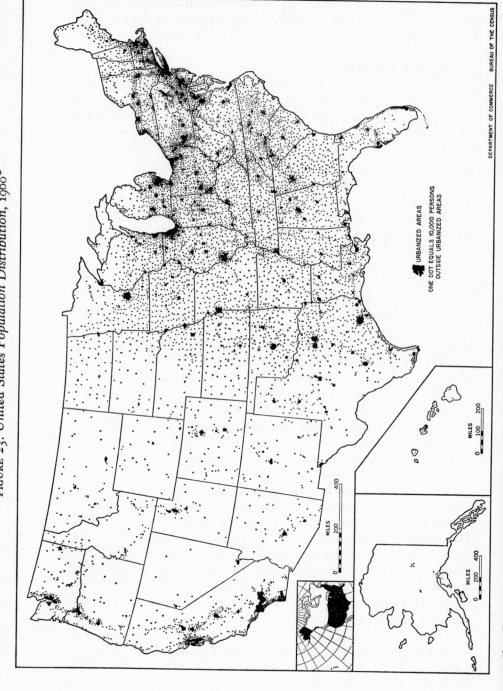

URBANIZED AREAS

ONE DOT EQUALS 10,000 PERSONS
OUTSIDE URBANIZED AREAS

DEPARTMENT OF COMMERCE   BUREAU OF THE CENSUS

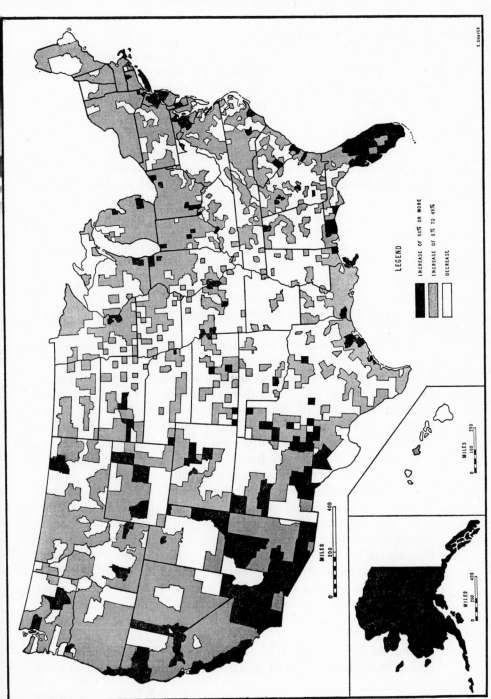

LEGEND

INCREASE OF 50% OR MORE

INCREASE OF 0% TO 49%

DECREASE

E. SHAFER

MILES
0   200   400

MILES
0   200   400

MILES
0 100 200

* Adapted from U. S. Bureau of the Census, *U. S. Census of Population: 1960,* PC(1)-1A, Government Printing Office, 1961, Figure 24, p. S20, and pp. 51-63.

CENTERS OF POPULATION

Changes in the internal distribution of population are reflected in the movement of the center of population. The mean point or pivotal point or center of gravity is located by a trial and error process involving calculation of first moments (population times distance) on two perpendicular (North-South and East-West) lines. If we prepare a contour population map in which density is represented by thickness, the map would balance on this center point. If everyone in the country flew directly to a national convention, the population center would come close to requiring the least total mileage traveled (the absolute minimum aggregate travel point is based on different calculations but falls near the mean point). This property makes the center of population useful in locating administrative headquarters for governmental and business organizations so as to minimize communication and transportation costs. Centers of population calculated from the Censuses of 1790 through 1960 are shown in Figure 25. Plotting the successive centers of gravity summarizes regional trends in national population shifts. Note the consistency of westward movement since 1790 and the slight southward tendency since 1910.

Another spatial measure of central tendency is the population potential, which has its closest analogue in the magnetic or electric field familiar to physics students and high fidelity buffs. The potential at any point is the sum of the reciprocals of the distances of every person from the given point. It is the population density weighted by the reciprocal of distance. The rationale underlying population potential is the assumption that the influence of persons on any given place is inversely proportional to their distance from that place—a postulate amplified by Dudley Kirk as follows: "In so far as geographical distance is a factor in social relations it is obviously a negative rather than a positive influence. Proximity facilitates social intercourse, distance impedes it. . . . A man is far more influenced by his neighbors than by unknown persons at the other end of the continent. The intensity of human relationships is inversely rather than directly associated with distance."[6] Maximum potentials are found at nodal or central points of the urban network. In Figure 26, the primacy of New York is evident. In the future, a secondary focal point should develop around Los Angeles.

NORTHEAST

During the 1950-1960 decade, the Northeast, the oldest part of the United States, had the slowest growth of any of the four national Census

---

[6] Dudley Kirk, *Europe's Population in the Interwar Years*, League of Nations, Geneva, 1946, p. 8.

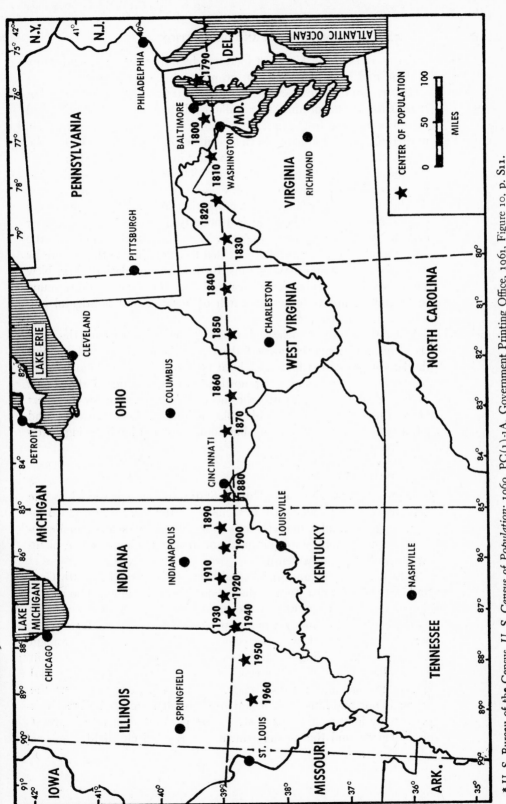

* U. S. Bureau of the Census, U. S. Census of Population: 1960, PC(1)-1A, Government Printing Office, 1961, Figure 10, p. S11.

regions—13 per cent. Vermont increased by only 3 per cent, while Connecticut and New Jersey grew by 26 per cent.

This region includes New York, which in 1960 was the most populous state, with a total of almost 17 million inhabitants. New York ranked first in population from 1810, when it took the lead from Pennsylvania, until 1963, when it apparently yielded its leading position to California.

The Northeast is the most urban region in the United States; 80 per cent of its residents live in urban areas. (The West is not far behind at 78 per cent, followed by the North Central region, 69 per cent, and the South, 58 per cent.) The highest proportions urban by state are 89 per cent in New Jersey; 86 per cent in Rhode Island and California; 85 per cent in New York; and 84 per cent in Massachusetts. In these areas the once prevalent rural values have yielded to coloration of the culture by industrial activity and urban norms. Birth rates are relatively low. New York City in particular is an area of ingress of the ambitious young southerner or midwesterner in search of lucrative and prestigeful outlets for his talents.

Not only has the Northeast been the debarkation area for the great waves of immigrants that created the United States, but it still contains the largest proportion of foreign-born residents. Immigrants arriving in New York, Boston, and other northeastern ports tend to stay there. New Yorkers take for granted the incomprehensible tongues they hear in the subway and on the sidewalks. Ethnic theaters, groceries, and restaurants reflect this exciting but sometimes tension-inducing heterogeneity.

NORTH CENTRAL

The great heartland of the United States—often represented as the most orthodox and least bizarre segment of the country, the setter of mores, and exemplar of behavior—is fittingly intermediate in demographic qualities. Its states are medium in size, medium in rate of increase, and medium in density.

Both demographic and sociological characteristics of the North Central area show fewer extremes than those of other regions. The area is closer (or tied for closest) to the national average than is any other region in the following attributes: per cent of persons under age 18, per cent aged 65 and over, per cent foreign-born, per cent of foreign stock, per cent residing in their state of birth, per cent of workers in white-collar occupations, per cent in manufacturing, per capita and family income, and median school years completed. However, the region is not middling with regard to every characteristic: illiteracy is particularly low in midwestern states, the per cent nonwhite is lowest of all regions, and the unemployment rate is relatively slight.

FIGURE 26. *Isolines of Population Potential, United States, 1950**

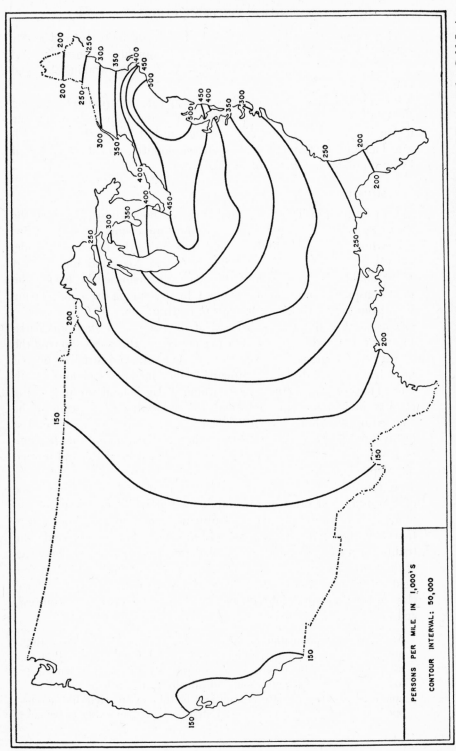

PERSONS PER MILE IN 1,000'S

CONTOUR INTERVAL: 50,000

* Otis Dudley Duncan, "Population Distribution and Community Structure," in *Population Studies: Animal Ecology and Demography*, Cold Spring Harbor Symposia on Quantitative Biology, Vol. XXII, 1957, p. 368; and Otis Dudley Duncan, "The Measurement of Population Distribution," *Population Studies*, Vol. XI, No. 1, July 1957, p. 36.

These demographic traits probably both contribute to and partly reflect the region's striking homogeneity of morality, gastronomy, and social norms. The area is characterized by a prevailing working-class and middle-class Protestantism.

Possibly the blandness and regularity of life contribute to making the West North Central the healthiest of the nine Census divisions (the region has the lowest mortality and the greatest longevity). Its health care facilities are among the best in the country, and its standard of living promotes low levels of morbidity.

SOUTH

As can be seen in Table 57 and Figure 24, population growth in the South varies considerably from state to state and county to county. Thus while three southern states lost population during the 1950-1960 decade, Florida grew very rapidly, and Delaware and Maryland increased at about double the national rate. Florida is distinguished by having the most conspicuous improvement in rank by size among the states, having risen from twentieth largest in 1950 to tenth in 1960.

The South is the least urban part of the country. Aside from Alaska (10 per cent) and North Dakota (11 per cent), the states showing the lowest per cent urban are preponderantly southern. Industrialization and urbanization are advancing, bringing higher incomes and lower birth rates. However, southern states continue to lag behind the rest of the country in income and education. (Modernization does seem to be eradicating the "hillbillies," described with some legitimacy as the last of the nation's rugged individualists. Their vestigial independence is impossible in a high density, urban society governed by clocks and mutual interdependence.)

Unlike the Northeast, the South has escaped the leavening influence of European and other immigrants who bring different customs and unfamiliar dress and languages. Southerners are almost without exception native-born, sharing a common history and ethnic background. The traditional pre-Civil War pattern is changing, but there are still heritages of the plantation system ruled by white Protestant families clinging to a rigid social code. Thus the word "Southern" connotes sharply defined class distinctions, prideful resistance to modern ways, gracious courtesy, and relaxed living. Two sociologists support this view:

At the root of population problems peculiar to the Southeast lie the unique cultural and long-standing traditions of the Old South. Protestantism. Sabbath observance, strong family integration with a tendency toward patriarchal organization, individualism, and a high regard for honor are among the cultural traditions of this region. Here has developed a more rigid system of social stratification than exists anywhere else in rural America. . . . All of these factors in the culture pattern have a definite relationship to family tradition, to the exercise of reproductive functions, to health and mortality rates, and to the exodus of large numbers to other regions.[7]

The most distinctive demographic characteristic of the South is its high proportion of Negroes. Until the twentieth century, approximately 90 per cent of all Negro Americans lived in southern states. The recent migration to the North and West is gradually lowering this proportion, although some of the rural Negro out-migration is being absorbed into southern cities.

Nor have Negroes been the only ones to leave. Residents of the West South Central Division suffered the financial and sometimes spiritual ruin of having their topsoil swept away in the Dust Bowl panic of the 1930's. So great was the westward movement from this district that the term "Okies" was coined to identify the impoverished nomad families who picked oranges in California and sold handmade wicker baskets to sympathetic housewives.

Consistent with its predominant agrarianism, the South (especially the Southeast) is commonly described as the seedbed of the nation. It has a high birth rate, heavy out-migration, and a young population. Indeed, as the South contributes so many people to other parts of the country, the southern heritage influences in many subtle ways the entire nation.

The southern standard of living and level of education, as noted earlier, are easily the lowest in the nation. When H. L. Mencken ranked the states according to wealth, education, health, and public order, Mississippi was last on three of the four indices. On the composite score, southern states occupied the lowest nine positions, and no southern state ranked in the upper half.[8] Objective indices show no radical changes since Mencken's study.

WEST

The West has achieved the most rapid growth in the nation for several decades. Its 1950-1960 increase of 39 per cent was more than double that of the second fastest growing region. Most of this 6 million-person increase in the West occurred in the Pacific Division. California, though ranking only fifth in percentage growth, was far and away the national leader in number of inhabitants added during 1950-1960, gaining more

---

[7] Paul H. Landis and Paul K. Hatt, *Population Problems*, American Book Co., New York, 1954, pp. 367-368.

[8] Charles Angoff and H. L. Mencken, "The Worst American State," *The American Mercury*, Vol. XXIV, Nos. 93-95, September-November 1931, pp. 1-16, 175-188, and 355-371.

than 5 million residents during the decade, while only one other state (Florida) added 2 million, and six states gained one million persons apiece.

The eight states comprising the Mountain Division are among the least dense in the country. After Alaska, those most sparsely settled are Nevada and Wyoming, with three persons per square mile. At the other extreme is Rhode Island's density of 812.

As to urbanization, the West is an area of great contrasts. Thus whereas California leads all fifty states in having the highest percentage of its population in Standard Metropolitan Statistical Areas, Idaho, Alaska, and Wyoming are three of the only four states that completely lack metropolitan areas (the other is Vermont). Two of the three states which doubled their urban population between 1950 and 1960 were in the West: Arizona, 133 per cent gain, and Nevada, 119 per cent; the third was Florida, 101 per cent. (No state showed a loss in urban population over the decade; the least growth was exhibited by New Hampshire at 2 per cent.)

Westward migration has made the Pacific Division the most mixed internally. However, the West is not particularly well supplied with foreign-born persons. California abounds in Chinese and Japanese, having almost half of the national totals of each group. American Indians are concentrated in Arizona, Oklahoma, and New Mexico.

The Far West has the highest per capita income in the country. It also has the highest educational expenditures per pupil, and its states and cities are among the leaders in median years of school completed by adults and in percentage of college graduates.

ALASKA

After years of effort, Alaska and Hawaii were admitted to statehood in 1958 and 1959 respectively. They are included in the Pacific Division of the West region, but their recency of achieving statehood, their geographic isolation, and their demographic irregularities warrant special treatment.

Of all the fifty states Alaska is the least populous, least dense, least urban, and largest in area. Birth and death rates are both higher than the national averages. The sex ratio is by far the highest of all states. Alaska's median age is 23.3 years, making it the third youngest of the states (after New Mexico and Utah). Alaska's northern location, its frigid climate, its rugged topography, and its geographic isolation have deterred settlement, but its per cent increase between 1950 and 1960 was third greatest among all states.

Alaska's even more rapid growth since attaining statehood contrasts sharply with its demographic history. In prehistoric times most of the area was sparsely settled, though there was moderate density along the Pacific shores—a settlement pattern that persisted, along with Mesolithic and Neolithic cultures, into the nineteenth and even the twentieth centuries. Although some influences of advanced East Asian cultures penetrated into the area, isolation from the outer world was not really broken until the arrival of eastward moving Russians and westward moving Americans. And even when these groups did make contact with indigenous Alaskans beginning in the eighteenth century, their representatives were not colonists, but rather explorers, traders, soldiers, and missionaries.[9] For decades after the Russian scientific expedition of 1741 the fur trade was dominant. Financial and political difficulties motivated Russia to sell Alaska to the United States in 1867 for $7 million.

Since then, the Indian, Eskimo, and Aleut populations have remained fairly constant at a total of about 30,000, but the white colonists have increased in number to about 200,000 in 1960. The three indigenous groups are overwhelmingly rural. Total population was 33,000 in 1880, 64,000 in 1900, 74,000 in 1940, 129,000 in 1950, and 226,000 in 1960. The military population was very large in the 1940's and is still rather large at present. In 1961 Alaska had the highest crude birth rate (32.3) and the second lowest crude death rate (5.4) of any state. The largest employer by far is the Federal government, which employs a greater percentage of the residents in Alaska than in any other state. In the summer the population is swollen by vacationers and seasonal workers in fishing, mining, construction, and other occupations that are difficult to pursue in the extremely cold winter months. Anchorage, at 44,000 in 1960, is the largest city.

HAWAII

The 1778 visit of Captain James Cook to the Sandwich Islands (known today as the Hawaiian Islands) was a nomenclatural coincidence: the Islands were named in honor of the English Earl of Sandwich, the eighteenth-century First Lord of the Admiralty. Initial white settlement was accompanied by a declining native population, followed by a period of rapid increase of both indigenous and immigrant populations. The first migrants to enter Hawaii in any numbers were the Chinese, mostly from the Canton delta. Small numbers were imported as early as 1867, and 1878 there were 15,000 "coolies" under contract for plantation work. But as soon as they accumulated enough money from work in the cane fields, many of the Chinese opened small shops which were so

---

[9] Irene B. Taeuber, "The Population of the Forty-Ninth State," *Population Index*, Vol. XXV, No. 2, April 1959, p. 93.

successful that *haole* (white) merchants successfully supported legislation restricting Chinese immigration in 1883 and stopping it altogether in 1886 (although the demand for cheap labor on plantations did reopen immigration in 1893 for a few years). Since then Portuguese, Filipino, and Japanese immigration, particularly, has contributed to the singularly polyglot Hawaiian population. The seven inhabited and many small uninhabited islands became a territory of the United States in 1898.

Hawaii's ethnic composition was comprised in 1950 of 37 per cent Japanese, 23 per cent Caucasian, 17 per cent Hawaiian, 12 per cent Filipino, 6 per cent Chinese, 2 per cent Puerto Rican, 1 per cent Korean, and 1 per cent Negro. It has the most heterogeneous population of any American state—as well as the greatest marital intermingling and ethnic amalgamation. The total population was 84,000 in 1850, 154,000 in 1900, 499,000 in 1950, and 632,000 in 1960. Only three states—Rhode Island, Delaware, and Connecticut—have smaller land areas. Hawaii's young age distribution was partly responsible for its crude death rate of 5.2 in 1961—the lowest of any state. Hawaii is predominantly urban. Metropolitan Honolulu contains 79 per cent of the islands' people—a primate city indeed.

TERRITORIES AND POSSESSIONS

Outlying areas under American jurisdiction include Puerto Rico, 2,350,000 people; Guam, 67,000; the Virgin Islands, 32,000; Samoa, 20,000; Midway Islands, 2,000; Wake Island, 1,000; Canton and Enderbury Islands, 320; Johnston and Sand Islands, 156; Swan Islands, 28; the Canal Zone, 42,000; Corn Islands, 2,000; and the Trust Territory of the Pacific Islands, 71,000.

The Commonwealth of Puerto Rico is the only demographically significant area not established as a state. It is more than twice as large in population as Hawaii and Alaska combined. The island is the easternmost and smallest of the Greater Antilles. The birth rate of 36 and death rate of 8 yield a natural increase of 28 per 1,000 per year. Puerto Ricans have a median age of 18.5 years, more than four years younger than any state. Only 5 per cent are 65 or older. Both men and women have a higher per cent of single persons than their counterparts in any state. The sex ratio is almost identical with the national average. The Commonwealth is 44 per cent urban and more dense (686 persons per square mile) than any state except Rhode Island and New Jersey. Its three Standard Metropolitan Statistical Areas are San Juan with 588,000 persons, Ponce with 145,000, and Mayaguez with 83,000.

The 138,000 residents added to Puerto Rico's population between 1950 and 1960 represent an increase of only 6 per cent, far below the national increase of 19 per cent, thanks to migration to the mainland.

Moves into New York City accounted for most of the 493,000 residents lost by migration between 1950 and 1960. This relatively slow growth made the 1950's the first decade since 1900 to 1910 that the Commonwealth grew slower than the country as a whole.

Although Puerto Rico was ceded to the United States by Spain in 1898, its inhabitants were not declared United States citizens until 1917. Most persons are of Spanish descent; minority ethnic groups are Negro, French, Corsican, other Europeans, and a smattering of Indians. The predominant language is Spanish (although educated Puerto Ricans are bilingual). Customs are a mixture of Spanish, Anglo American, and Latin American.

Projections

Projections of vital rates in the United States by the Bureau of the Census indicate a lowering mortality, steady fertility, and high increase. Estimates for 1975-1980 show crude birth and death rates of 24.0 to 26.7 and 8.2 to 8.5 respectively, which would bring about an annual natural increase of about 16 persons per 1,000. The gross reproduction rate for 1975-1980 is placed at 154 to 179.[10]

Donald Bogue has published projections of the total United States population based on the assumptions that fertility will continue at the 1955-1957 level, mortality decline moderately, and net immigration average 300,000 annually. On this basis, by 1980 the population would reach 260 million, by 2000 about 375 million, by 2050 about 939 million, and by 2100, some 2 billion 350 million.[11] By 1980 Bogue estimates that the proportion nonwhite will increase to 13 per cent, the sex ratio decline to 97.2 (with the supply of surplus females reaching 3.5 million), the foreign born keep approximately the same numbers but decrease in proportion to the total population (to 4.7 per cent), the proportion urban climb to 73 per cent, and the number of persons attending colleges and professional schools reach between 11 and 12 million.[12]

ANTICIPATIONS

In contrast with the depressing situation prevalent in much of the world, the population picture in the United States future may appear rosy. Yet naive optimism can be dangerous. In the 1940's the nation shifted from a surplus to a deficit regarding raw materials. At the turn of the century

---

[10] U. S. Bureau of the Census, "Interim Revised Projections of the Population of the United States, by Age and Sex: 1975 and 1980," *Current Population Reports*, Series P-25, No. 251, July 6, 1962, pp. 2-3.

[11] Donald J. Bogue, *The Population of the United States*, The Free Press, Glencoe, 1959, p. 761.

[12] *Ibid.*, pp. 761, 768, 771, 778, and 784.

the United States produced 15 per cent more raw materials than it consumed (excluding food); by mid-century the country was consuming about 10 per cent more raw materials than it produced.[13] Population increases and advancing industrialization elsewhere in the world make it unlikely that the United States can depend indefinitely on other areas for its raw material needs. The effects of United States population growth on availability and costs of raw materials are discussed in the "Paley Report" (1952), which predicted accentuation of water shortages and rising costs of forest products, ferrous and nonferrous metals, fossil fuels, and some foods, especially meat.[14]

Frederick Osborn believes that the present "favored child" condition of this country obscures a long-term threat from advancing population size:

> The United States still has a relatively low ratio of population to land area and natural resources. It has a tremendous and growing industrial plant. It is conditioned to rapid technological change. For some time to come these factors will modify or offset the handicaps imposed by the growth of population. It is understandable that economists do not foresee any lowering of present levels of living during the next twenty-five years, even if growth should continue at the present high rate. The United States appears able to support a population of from 250 million to 300 million toward which, barring unexpected catastrophe, it is headed in the next twenty-five to fifty years. With that larger base the future may look more threatening.[15]

On the other hand, the Paley Commission contended that "the reason Malthusian doom is so overdue is that Malthusian calculations have never given sufficient weight to the extraordinary ingenuity of mankind in extricating himself from situations before they become wholly and finally intolerable.[16] This comment, it may be hoped, applies not only to the United States but to all of human society.

Conclusion

This return to Malthus, supplemented by an optimism Malthus himself appears not to have felt, seems a fitting note on which to end a book

---

[13] Samuel H. Ordway, "Possible Limits of Raw-Material Consumption," in William L. Thomas, Jr. (ed.), *Man's Role in Changing the Face of the Earth*, University of Chicago Press, Chicago, 1956, pp. 989-990.

[14] U. S. President's Materials Policy Commission, *Resources for Freedom*, Government Printing Office, Washington, 5 vols., 1952.

[15] Frederick Osborn, *Population: An International Dilemma*, The Population Council, New York, 1958, pp. 75-76.

[16] President's Materials Policy Commission, *Resources for Freedom, op. cit.*, Vol. I, p. 169.

on trends in population size, character, and distribution, their causes and consequences, and the associated problems and benefits. In surveying the history and prospects of various national and regional populations, the three pervasive variables of birth, death, and migration are seen again and again to be the cornerstones of all demographic structures.

As the world spins, its people change; and in distinction to most of man's experience, at the present moment the population is increasing at a rate so rapid as to be extremely difficult to handle, scientific ingenuity notwithstanding. Still, our collective fate is in our own hands, and men seem likely to be here for many centuries to come, attaining quantities and qualities that offer the prospect of permitting most persons reasonable comfort and enjoyment of their lengthening lives.

✖ *Glossary*

BASIC DATA

1. *Population:* number of people residing in an area at a given time (often at the middle of the year).

2. *Complete enumeration or census:* counting (often also obtaining information about) every inhabitant.

3. *Sample:* part of the population (generally taken to represent the whole).

4. *Registration:* recording of births, deaths, sickness, marriages, divorces, moves, and other demographic phenomena.

5. *Continuous personal register:* maintenance of individual data card containing demographic information, for every inhabitant.

6. *Cohort:* group of people (usually 100,000) born at the same time.

7. *Estimate:* approximation of past, present, or future data not accurately known.

8. *Projection:* type of estimate made by formal deduction from certain stated assumptions.

AGE AND SEX

1. *Age:* years lived as of last birthday.

2. *Sex ratio:* number of males per 100 females.

3. *Population pyramid:* diagram comparing the proportions of males (on left) and females (on right) at every age level.

4. *Stable population or life table population:* group having constant age-specific birth and death rates and therefore an unchanging age-sex distribution and a population pyramid of fixed shape.

5. *Stationary population:* group having constant and equal birth and death rates, no migration, and a fixed total size.

6. *Life table:* life history of a group of people, showing such information as the probability of surviving each age period.

7. *Complete life table:* based on one-year intervals (one-month intervals for first year).

8. *Abridged life table:* based on five-year intervals.

9. *Current or synthetic life table:* uses present age-specific mortality rates, creating a hypothetical cohort.

10. *Generation or cohort life table:* follows an actual cohort throughout their lives.

11. *Neonate:* child less than one month old.

12. *Infant:* child less than one year old.

13. *Aged:* older than 60 or 65 years.

14. *Childbearing ages:* 15-44, 15-49, 20-44, or 20-49.

MORTALITY AND LONGEVITY

1. *Crude death rate:* total deaths occurring per year per 1,000 population.

2. *Corrected death rate:* numerator corrected for underregistration.

3. *Age-specific death rate:* number of deaths per year at a given age (and sex) per 1,000 people in that age (and sex) category.

4. *Standardized or adjusted death rate:* specific rates applied to some standard population (England, 1901; USA, 1940; etc.).

5. *Intrinsic or true or life table death rate:* 1,000 times reciprocal of expectation of life at birth as computed from a life table.

6. *Stillbirth ratio:* number of stillbirths divided by the sum of stillbirths and live births.

7. *Maternal mortality rate:* number of deaths of women in childbirth per year per 1,000 maternities.

8. *Infant death rate:* number of deaths of infants divided by the number of live births.

9. *Death rate by cause:* number dying from given cause per year per 100,000 population.

10. *Fatality rate:* number dying from a disease per 100 having the disease.

11. *Prevalence rate:* number having a disease per 100,000 population.

12. *Incidence rate:* number of new cases of a disease per year per 100,000 population.

13. *Expectation of life:* number of years lived by all members of a cohort after a given age divided by number of people in cohort at given age.

14. *Mean duration of life:* expectation of life at birth.

15. *Median length of life or probable lifetime:* age by which half of the original members of a cohort have died.

16. *Life span:* maximum possible length of life.

MARRIAGE AND FAMILY

1. *Nuclear family:* usually the head of household, spouse, and unmarried children living together.

2. *Extended family:* group of related persons living together, often embracing more than two generations.

3. *Household:* group of persons (not necessarily related) sharing living quarters.

4. *Dwelling unit:* housing unit having its own entrance and cooking facilities.

5. *Crude marriage rate:* number of marriages per year per 1,000 population.

6. *Standardized marriage rate:* age- and sex-specific marriage rates applied to standard population.

7. *Divorce rate:* number of divorces and legal separations per year per 1,000 population.

8. *Divorce ratio:* number of divorces and legal separations per year per 100 existing marriages or per 100 marriages that year.

9. *Net nuptiality:* double decrement table taking account of attrition both through change of marital status and through death.

REPRODUCTION

1. *Fecundity:* biological potential for reproduction.

2. *Sterility:* complete inability to reproduce (temporary or permanent).

3. *Subfecundity:* substantial impairment in capacity to reproduce.

4. *Parity:* number of live children a woman has borne.

5. *Abortion:* death of a previable fetus (that is, one not capable of independent life).

6. *Stillbirth:* death of a viable fetus (20 or more weeks old).

7. *Reproductive wastage:* loss of life from fertilization of ovum to fifth year of age.

8. *Perinatal mortality:* stillbirths plus neonatal deaths.

9. *Crude birth rate:* total births per year per 1,000 population.

10. *Corrected birth rate:* numerator corrected for underregistration.

11. *Age-specific birth rate:* number of births per year to women of given age per 1,000 women of that age.

12. *Standardized or adjusted birth rate:* specific rates applied to some standard age distribution.

13. *Intrinsic or true or life table birth rate:* births per 1,000 population per year that would occur given age-specific birth rates and life table age-sex distribution.

14. *General fertility ratio:* number of births per year per 1,000 women of childbearing ages.

15. *Effective fertility ratio or child-woman ratio:* number of children under age 5 per 100 women in childbearing ages.

16. *Legitimate age-specific birth rate:* number of legitimate births for a given age group of married women per 1,000 married women in that age group.

GROWTH AND REPLACEMENT

1. *Crude rate of natural increase:* crude birth rate minus crude death rate.

2. *Standardized rate of natural increase:* standardized birth rate minus standardized death rate.

3. *True or intrinsic or life table rate of natural increase:* true birth rate minus true death rate.

4. *Size of completed family:* number of surviving children in a family whose mother has completed the childbearing period.

5. *Number of children ever born:* same as 4 above, but not affected by mortality of children.

6. *Total fertility rate:* average number of births to women living through childbearing ages under constant age-specific birth rates.

7. *Gross reproduction rate:* complicated measure of replacement of one generation of girls by their daughters, but with no allowance for mortality.

8. *Net reproduction rate:* complicated measure of replacement of one generation of girls by their daughters, taking account of mortality.

9. *Index of net reproduction or replacement index:* effective fertility ratio of actual population of both sexes divided by effective fertility ratio of stationary population of both sexes.

MIGRATION

1. *Mover:* person who changes his place of residence.

2. *Migrant:* person whose change of residence takes him into a different politico-geographic unit.

3. *Commuter:* person who journeys regularly between work and home (not a migrant).

4. *Seasonal migrant:* person who moves temporarily at certain seasons of the year.

5. *Displaced person:* person who is compelled to migrate, usually by a public authority.

6. *Refugee:* person who migrates of his own volition but in response to powerful pressure to leave.

7. *In-migration:* entry into a politico-geographic unit (called immigration if the unit involved is a country).

8. *Out-migration:* exit from a politico-geographic unit (called emigration if the unit involved is a country).

9. *Net migration or balance of migration:* difference (positive or negative) between in- and out-migration.

10. *Gross migration or volume of migration or turnover:* sum of in- and out-migration.

11. *Internal migration:* movement between two politico-geographic areas totally within one country.

12. *Efficiency of migration:* ratio of net migration to gross migration.

13. *Quota:* maximum number of immigrants of a given type legally permitted to enter a country (often based on nationality).

14. *Population transfer:* large-scale displacement of people.

✖ *Recommended Readings*

Samuel Johnson observed that the best way to learn about something is to write a book about it. Similarly, the best way for a student to study a subject is to write a term paper. What James Boswell recorded in his *Life of Dr. Johnson* in 1775 is equally true today: "I cannot see that lectures can do so much good as reading the books from which the lectures are taken." And ten years after graduation that paper and those books are often the only parts of the course that are remembered. This is especially true in cases where the paper involves guided reflection rather than being merely an accumulation of what Alfred North Whitehead called "inert knowledge."

The following books are recommended for supplementary reading and the writing of papers. These volumes are chosen for inclusion on four bases: their quality, recency, relevance, and the need for variety. The order of listing within each topic reflects the anticipated degree of usefulness to most students, except for the "Description" topics, where the ordering is geographic and chronological. Works of especial utility are identified by asterisks. Articles in periodicals have been kept to a minimum in the interest of brevity and also because many of the better ones are reprinted in the books of readings listed below. Other pertinent articles and books can be traced by footnote citations, locatable through the indexes of authors and subjects.

This bibliography is not merely a topically ordered reproduction of references cited in the text; in fact, these suggested readings were prepared independently of the footnotes. Rather, this list is a compilation of works designed to help a student who, through necessity or curiosity, feels a need to know what books to consult to learn more about a designated subject. The information supplied should suffice to enable him to find the books in the library or to order them through a local bookstore; anyone wishing to write the publishers may find additional bibliographic details through the index or standard library reference volumes.

GENERAL SURVEYS

*United Nations, *The Determinants and Consequences of Population Trends*, 1953.

*Thompson, Warren S., *Population Problems*, 1953.

*Petersen, William, *Population*, 1961.

*Hauser, Philip M., and O. D. Duncan (eds.), *The Study of Population*, 1959.

* Spengler, J. J., and O. D. Duncan (eds.), *Demographic Analysis*, 1956.

International Union for the Scientific Study of Population, *International Population Conference*, 1959.

Wrong, Dennis H., *Population*, 1959.

Landis, Paul H., and Paul K. Hatt, *Population Problems*, 1954.

Hawley, Amos H., *Human Ecology*, 1950.

George, Pierre, *Questions de géographie de la population*, 1959.

Landry, Adolphe, *Traité de démographie*, 1945.

Sauvy, Alfred, *Théorie générale de la population*, 2 vols., 1952 and 1954.

National Bureau of Economic Research, *Demographic and Economic Change in Developed Countries*, 1960.

Political and Economic Planning, *World Population and Resources*, 1955.

Hauser, Philip M., *Population Perspectives*, 1961.

Hertzler, Joyce O., *The Crisis in World Population*, 1956.

Malthus, Thomas R., Julian Huxley, and Frederick Osborn, *Three Essays on Population*, 1960.

Spengler, J. J., and O. D. Duncan (eds.), *Population Theory and Policy*, 1956.

Hauser, Philip M. (ed), *The Population Dilemma*, 1963.

Carr-Saunders, Alexander Morris, *World Population*, 1936.

Smith, T. Lynn, *Fundamentals of Population Study*, 1960.

Cragg, J. B., and N. W. Pirie (eds.), *The Numbers of Man and Animals*, 1955.

George, Pierre, *Introduction à étude géographique de la population du monde*, 1951.

Lotka, Alfred J., *Théorie analytique des associations biologiques*, 1939.

Phelps, Harold A., and David Henderson, *Population in Its Human Aspects*, 1958.

Halbwachs, Maurice, *Population and Society*, 1960 (*Morphologie sociale*, 1938).

Bates, Marston, *The Prevalence of People*, 1955.

RESEARCH METHODS

Barclay, George W., *Techniques of Population Analysis,* 1958.

McArthur, Norma, *Introducing Population Statistics,* 1959.

Spiegelman, Mortimer, *Introduction to Demography,* 1955.

Jaffe, Abram J., *Handbook of Statistical Methods for Demographers,* 1951.

Cox, Peter R., *Demography,* 1959.

Milbank Memorial Fund, *Emerging Techniques in Population Research,* 1963.

United Nations, *Handbook of Population Census Methods,* 3 vols., 1959.

United Nations, *Handbook of Vital Statistics Methods,* 1955.

Cold Spring Harbor Symposia on Quantitative Biology, *Population Studies: Animal Ecology and Demography,* Vol. XXII, 1957.

Greville, Thomas N. E., *United States Life Tables and Actuarial Tables: 1939–41, 1946.*

Wolfenden, Hugh H., *Population Statistics and Their Compilation,* 1954.

Gibbs, Jack P. (ed.), *Urban Research Methods,* 1961.

Greenwood, Major, *Medical Statistics from Graunt to Farr,* 1948.

Wright, Carroll D., *The History and Growth of the United States Census,* 1900.

Stolnitz, George J., *Life Tables from Limited Data,* 1956.

Gutman, Robert, *Birth and Death Registration in Massachusetts: 1639–1900,* 1959.

SAMPLING AND GRAPHS

*Hansen, Morris H., William N. Hurwitz, and William G. Madow, *Sample Survey Methods and Theories,* 2 vols., 1953.

Hagood, Margaret Jarman, *Statistics for Sociologists,* 1941.

Parten, Mildred B., *Survey Polls and Samples,* 1950.

Monkhouse, F. J., and H. R. Wilkinson, *Maps and Diagrams,* 1952.

*Selltiz, Claire, Marie Jahoda, Morton Deutsch, and Stuart W. Cook, *Research Methods in Social Relations,* 1959.

Raisz, Erwin, *General Cartography,* 1948.

Schmid, Calvin F., *Handbook of Graphic Presentation,* 1954.

Yates, Frank, *Sampling Methods for Censuses and Surveys,* 1953.

*Feller, William, *An Introduction to Probability Theory and Its Applications,* 1957.

Duncan, Otis Dudley, Ray P. Cuzzort, and Beverly Duncan, *Statistical Geography,* 1961.

THEORY

*Malthus, Thomas R., *An Essay on the Principle of Population*, 1798, 1826.

Gonnard, René, *Histoire des doctrines de la population*, 1923.

Penrose, E. F., *Population Theories and Their Application*, 1934.

Eversley, D. E. C., *Social Theories of Fertility and the Malthusian Debate*, 1959.

Stangeland, Charles E., *Pre-Malthusian Doctrines of Population*, 1904.

Pearl, Raymond, *The Biology of Population Growth*, 1925.

Smith, Kenneth, *The Malthusian Controversy*, 1951.

Coontz, Sydney H., *Population Theories and the Economic Interpretation*, 1957.

Leibenstein, Harvey, A *Theory of Economic-Demographic Development*, 1954.

Glass, David V. (ed.), *Introduction to Malthus*, 1953.

Spengler, Joseph J., *French Precursors of Malthus*, 1942.

Knibbs, George Handley, *The Mathematical Theory of Population*, 1917.

Bonar, J., *Theories of Population from Raleigh to Arthur Young*, 1931.

Meek, Ronald L. (ed.), *Marx and Engels on Malthus*, 1954.

MORTALITY AND MORBIDITY

*Dublin, Louis I., Alfred J. Lotka, and Mortimer Spiegelman, *Length of Life*, 1949.

*Zinsser, Hans, *Rats, Lice and History*, 1935.

Milbank Memorial Fund, *Trends and Differentials in Mortality*, 1956.

Dublin, Louis I., *The Facts of Life from Birth to Death*, 1951.

Linder, Forrest E., and Robert D. Grove, *Vital Statistics Rates in the United States: 1900–1940*, 1943.

Benjamin, Bernard, *Elements of Vital Statistics*, 1959.

Dublin, Louis I., and Alfred J. Lotka, *The Money Value of a Man*, 1946.

United Nations, *Fetal, Infant, and Early Childhood Mortality*, 2 vols., 1954.

Ramos, Alberto Guerreiro, *Sociología de la Mortalidad Infantil*, 1955.

Rivers, W. H. R. (ed.), *Essays on the Depopulation of Melanesia*, 1922.

FERTILITY AND REPLACEMENT

*Grabill, Wilson H., Clyde V. Kiser, and P. K. Whelpton, *The Fertility of American Women*, 1958.

Milbank Memorial Fund, *Thirty Years of Research in Human Fertility*, 1959.

*Kinsey, Alfred C., Wardell B. Pomeroy, Clyde E. Martin, and Paul H. Gebhard, *Sexual Behavior in the Human Female*, 1953.

Ford, Clellan S., and Frank A. Beach, *Patterns of Sexual Behavior*, 1951.

Gupta, Ajit Das, Ranjan Kumar Som, Murari Majumdar, and Samarendranath Mitra, *Couple Fertility*, 1955.

Edin, Karl A., and Edward P. Hutchinson, *Studies in Differential Fertility in Sweden*, 1935.

Whelpton, Pascal K., *Cohort Fertility*, 1953.

Lewinsohn, Richard, *A History of Sexual Customs*, 1958.

Glass, David V., and E. Grebenik, *The Trend and Pattern of Fertility in Great Britain*, 2 vols., 1954.

Eaton, Joseph W., and Albert J. Mayer, *Man's Capacity to Reproduce*, 1954.

Lorimer, Frank B. (ed.), *Culture and Human Fertility*, 1955.

Henry, Louis, *Fécondité des mariages*, 1952.

BIRTH CONTROL

*Freedman, Ronald, P. K. Whelpton, and Arthur A. Campbell, *Family Planning, Sterility, and Population Growth*, 1959.

Westoff, Charles F., Robert G. Potter, Jr., and Philip C. Sagi, *The Third Child*, 1963.

Kiser, Clyde V. (ed.), *Research in Family Planning*, 1962.

Westoff, Charles F., Robert G. Potter, Jr., Philip C. Sagi, and Elliot G. Mishler, *Family Growth in Metropolitan America*, 1961.

Whelpton, P. K., and Clyde V. Kiser, *Social and Psychological Factors Affecting Fertility*, 5 vols., 1943–1958.

Gebhard, Paul H., Wardell B. Pomeroy, Clyde E. Martin, and Cornelia V. Christenson, *Pregnancy, Birth, and Abortion*, 1958.

Lewis-Fanning, E., *An Enquiry on Family Limitation and Its Influence on Human Fertility During the Past Fifty Years*, 1949.

Henshaw, Paul S., *Adaptive Human Fertility*, 1955.

Meier, Richard L., *Modern Science and the Human Fertility Problem*, 1959.

Stycos, J. Mayone, *Family and Fertility in Puerto Rico*, 1955.

Hatt, Paul K., *Backgrounds of Human Fertility in Puerto Rico*, 1952.

Rainwater, Lee, *And the Poor Get Children*, 1960.

Himes, Norman E., *Medical History of Contraception*, 1936.

Guttmacher, Alan F., *Babies by Choice or by Chance*, 1959.

Sulloway, Alvah W., *Birth Control and Catholic Doctrine*, 1959.

Calderone, Mary Steichen (ed.), *Abortion in the United States*, 1958.

INTERNAL MIGRATION

Milbank Memorial Fund, *Selected Studies of Migration Since World War II*, 1958.

Thomas, Dorothy Swaine, *The Salvage*, 1952.

Rossi, Peter H., *Why Families Move*, 1955.

Bogue, Donald J., Henry S. Shyrock Jr., Siegfried A. Hoermann, and Margaret Jarman Hagood, *Subregional Migration in the United States: 1935–40*, 2 vols., 1955 and 1957.

Lee, Everett S., Ann Ratner Miller, Carol P. Brainerd, Richard A. Easterlin, and Simon Kuznets, *Population Redistribution and Economic Growth, United States: 1870–1950*, 2 vols., 1957 and 1960.

Hannerberg, David, Torsten Hagerstrand, and Bruno Odeving, *Migration in Sweden*, 1957.

Gist, Noel P., C. T. Pihlblad, and Cecil L. Gregory, *Selective Factors in Migration and Occupation*, 1943.

Goldstein, Sidney, *Patterns of Mobility: 1910–1950*, 1958.

Thomas, Dorothy Swaine, *Research Memorandum on Migration Differentials*, 1938.

Malzberg, Benjamin, and Everett S. Lee, *Migration and Mental Disease*, 1956.

INTERNATIONAL MIGRATION

*Taft, Donald R., and Richard Robbins, *International Migrations*, 1955.

International Labour Office, *International Migration: 1945–1957*, 1959.

Isaac, Julius, *Economics of Migration*, 1947.

Borrie, W. D., *The Cultural Integration of Immigrants*, 1959.

Handlin, Oscar, *The Uprooted*, 1951.

Hutchinson, Edward P., *Immigrants and Their Children: 1850–1950*, 1955.

Kuznets, Simon, and Ernest Rubin, *Immigration and the Foreign Born*, 1954.

Petersen, William, *Planned Migration*, 1955.

Divine, Robert A., *American Immigration Policy: 1924–1952*, 1957.

Handlin, Oscar (ed.), *Immigration as a Factor in American History*, 1959.

Hansen, Marcus Lee, *The Atlantic Migration: 1607–1860*, 1941.

UNESCO, *Cultural Assimilation of Immigrants*, 1950.

Sicron, Moshe, *Immigration into Israel: 1948–1952*, 1957.

Zubrzycki, Jerzy, *Immigrants in Australia*, 1960.

Thomas, Brinley, *Migration and Economic Growth*, 1954.

Carrier, N. H., and J. A. Jeffery, *External Migration*, 1953.

Borrie, W. D., *Italians and Germans in Australia*, 1954.

URBANIZATION

*Mumford, Lewis, *The Culture of Cities*, 1938.

*Hatt, Paul K., and Albert J. Reiss, Jr. (eds.), *Cities and Society,* 1957.

Mumford, Lewis, *The City in History*, 1961.
Bogue, Donald J. (ed.), *Needed Urban and Metropolitan Research*, 1953.
Mayer, Harold M., and Clyde F. Kohn (eds.), *Readings in Urban Geography*, 1959.
Bogue, Donald J., *Population Growth in Standard Metropolitan Areas: 1900–1950*, 1954.
Gallion, Arthur B., and Simon Eisner, *The Urban Pattern*, 1963.
Duncan, O. D., and A. J. Reiss, Jr., *Social Characteristics of Urban and Rural Communities: 1950*, 1956.
Woodbury, Coleman (ed.), *The Future of Cities and Urban Redevelopment*, 2 vols., 1953.
International Urban Research, *The World's Metropolitan Areas*, 1959.
Pirenne, Henri, *Medieval Cities*, 1925.
Bogue, Donald J., and Dorothy L. Harris, *Comparative Population and Urban Research via Multiple Regression and Covariance Analysis*, 1954.
Hauser, Philip M. (ed.), *Urbanization in Asia and the Far East*, 1957.

REGIONALISM

*Dickinson, Robert E., *City Region and Regionalism*, 1947.
*Bogue, Donald J., and Calvin L. Beale, *Economic Areas of the United States*, 1961.
Odum, Howard W., and Harry E. Moore, *American Regionalism*, 1938.
Bogue, Donald J., *The Structure of the Metropolitan Community*, 1950.
Duncan, O. D., William R. Scott, Stanley Lieberson, Beverly Davis Duncan, and Hal H. Winsborough, *Metropolis and Region*, 1960.
National Resources Committee, *Regional Factors in National Planning and Development*, 1935.
Tricart, Jacques, *Cours de géographie humaine*, 2 vols., 1949 and 1951.
McKenzie, Roderick D., *The Metropolitan Community*, 1933.
Losch, August, *The Economics of Location*, 1954.
Jensen, Merrill (ed.), *Regionalism in America*, 1952.
Isard, Walter, *Methods of Regional Analysis*, 1960.

ESTIMATES AND PREDICTION

*United Nations, *The Future Growth of World Population*, 1958.
Notestein, Frank W., Irene B. Taeuber, Dudley Kirk, Ansley J. Coale, and Louise K. Kiser, *The Future Population of Europe and the Soviet Union*, 1944.
Calvert, G. N., *The Future Population of New Zealand*, 1945.
Jaffe, A. J., and R. O. Carleton, *Occupational Mobility in the United States: 1930–1960*, 1954.

Whelpton, P. K., *Forecasts of the Population of the United States: 1947–1975*, 1947.
United Nations, *Methods of Estimating Population*, 3 vols., 1952–1956.
United Nations, *Future Population Estimates by Sex and Age: 1950–1980*, 4 vols., 1954–1959.

FOOD SUPPLY

*Woytinsky, Wladimir S., and Emma S. Woytinsky, *World Population and Production*, 1953.
Meier, Richard L., *Science and Economic Development*, 1956.
American Philosophical Society, *Proceedings*, Vol. XCV, No. 1, 1951.
U. S. Department of Agriculture, *Climate and Man*, 1941.
Bennett, M. K., *The World's Food*, 1954.
Russell, John E., *World Population and World Food Supplies*, 1954.
Simoons, Frederick J., *Eat Not This Flesh*, 1961.

RESOURCE UTILIZATION

Hatt, Paul K. (ed.), *World Population and Future Resources*, 1952.
Osborn, Fairfield, *Our Plundered Planet*, 1948.
Vogt, William, *Road to Survival*, 1948.
Hirshleifer, Jack, James C. DeHaven, and Jerome W. Milliman, *Water Supply*, 1960.
Mumford, Lewis, *Technics and Civilization*, 1934.
Osborn, Fairfield, *The Limits of the Earth*, 1953.
Huntington, Ellsworth, *Principles of Human Geography*, 1940.
Cottrell, Fred, *Energy and Society*, 1955.
Francis, Roy G. (ed.), *The Population Ahead*, 1958.
Brown, Harrison, *The Challenge of Man's Future*, 1954.
Sax, Karl, *Standing Room Only*, 1960.
Vogt, William, *People!*, 1960.

QUALITY AND EUGENICS

United Nations, *Report on the World Social Situation*, 1957.
Osborn, Frederick, *Preface to Eugenics*, 1951.
Stern, Curt, *Principles of Human Genetics*, 1950.
Li, Ching Chun, *Population Genetics*, 1955.
Boyd, William C., *Genetics and the Races of Man*, 1950.
Cook, Robert C., *Human Fertility*, 1951.

NATIONAL POLICY

*Eldridge, Hope T., *Population Policies*, 1954.
Hauser, Philip M. (ed.), *Population and World Politics*, 1958.

Duke University School of Law, "Population Control," *Law and Contemporray Problems*, Summer 1960.

Sauvy, Alfred, *Fertility and Survival*, 1961 (*De Malthus à Mao Tsé-Toung*, 1958).

Hill, Reuben, J. Mayone Stycos, and Kurt W. Back, *The Family and Population Control*, 1959.

United Nations, *Survey of Legislation on Marriage, Divorce, and Related Topics Relevant to Population*, 1956.

Glass, David V., *Population Policies and Movements in Europe*, 1940.

National Resources Committee, *The Problems of a Changing Population*, 1938.

Thompson, Warren S., *Plenty of People*, 1948.

Vadakin, James C., *Family Allowances*, 1958.

Bowen, Ian, *Population*, 1954.

Myrdal, Alva, *Nation and Family*, 1941.

CHARACTERISTICS AND COMPOSITION

UNESCO, *World Illiteracy at Mid-Century*, 1957.

Sheldon, Henry D., *The Older Population of the United States*, 1958.

Glick, Paul C., *American Families*, 1957.

Jacobson, Paul H., *American Marriage and Divorce*, 1959.

Wayland, Sloan, and Edmund de S. Brunner, *The Educational Characteristics of the American People*, 1958.

Durand, John, *The Labor Force in the United States: 1890–1960*, 1948.

Jaffe, Abram J., and Charles D. Stewart, *Manpower Resources and Utilization*, 1950.

Wolfle, Dael, *America's Resources of Specialized Talent*, 1954.

Lee, Rose Hum, *The Chinese in the United States of America*, 1960.

Duncan, O. D., and Beverly Duncan, *The Negro Population of Chicago*, 1957.

Bancroft, Gertrude, *The American Labor Force*, 1958.

Miller, Herman P., *Income of the American People*, 1955.

Burgess, Ernest W. (ed.), *Aging in Western Societies*, 1960.

Tibbitts, Clark (ed.), *Handbook of Social Gerontology*, 1960.

DESCRIPTION: AMERICAS

*Bogue, Donald J., *The Population of the United States*, 1959.

*Taeuber, Conrad, and Irene B. Taeuber, *The Changing Population of the United States*, 1958.

Vance, Rupert B., *All These People*, 1945.

Thompson, Warren S., *Growth and Changes in California's Population*, 1955.

Lind, Andrew W., *Hawaii's People*, 1955.

Roberts, George W., *The Population of Jamaica*, 1957.

Smith, T. Lynn, *Brazil*, 1946.

Davis, Kingsley (ed.), "A Crowding Hemisphere: Population Change in the Americas," *Annals of the American Academy of Political and Social Science*, March 1958.

DESCRIPTION: EUROPE

*Kirk, Dudley, *Europe's Population in the Interwar Years*, 1946.

Royal Commission on Population, *Report*, 1949.

Hubback, Eva M., *The Population of Britain*, 1947.

*Thomas, Dorothy Swaine, *Social and Economic Aspects of Swedish Population Movements: 1750–1933*, 1941.

Huber, M., H. Bunle, and F. Boverat, *La population de la France*, 1954.

Mayer, Kurt B., *The Population of Switzerland*, 1952.

Myers, Paul F., and W. Parker Mauldin, *Population of the Federal Republic of Germany and West Berlin*, 1952.

Moore, Wilbert E., *Economic Demography of Eastern and Southern Europe*, 1945.

DESCRIPTION: OTHER AREAS

Beaujeu-Garnier, Jacqueline, *Géographie de la population*, 2 vols., 1956 and 1958.

Milbank Memorial Fund, *Population Trends in Eastern Europe, the USSR, and Mainland China*, 1960.

Lorimer, Frank B., *The Population of the Soviet Union*, 1946.

*Davis, Kingsley, *The Population of India and Pakistan*, 1951.

Coale, Ansley J., and Edgar M. Hoover, *Population Growth and Economic Development in Low-Income Countries*, 1958.

Sarkar, N. K., *The Demography of Ceylon*, 1957.

*Taeuber, Irene B., *The Population of Japan*, 1958.

Chen, Ta, *Population in Modern China*, 1946.

Barclay, George W., *Colonial Development and Population in Taiwan*, 1954.

Smith, T. E., *Population Growth in Malaya*, 1952.

Thompson, Warren S., *Population and Progress in the Far East*, 1959.

Barbour, Kenneth M., and R. M. Prothero (eds.), *Essays on African Population*, 1961.

Kuczynski, Robert R., *Demographic Survey of the British Colonial Empire*, 3 vols., 1948–1953.

DESCRIPTION: HISTORICAL

Reinhard, Marcel R., and André Armengaud, *Histoire générale de la population mondiale*, 1961.

Krzywicki, Ludwik, *Primitive Society and Its Vital Statistics*, 1934.

Beloch, K. Julius, *Die Bevölkerung der griechisch-romischen Welt*, 1886.

Gomme, A. W., *The Population of Athens in the Fifth and Fourth Centuries B.C.*, 1933.

Russell, Josiah Cox, *Late Ancient and Medieval Population*, 1958.

Russell, Josiah Cox, *British Medieval Population*, 1948.

Ho, Ping-Ti, *Studies on the Population of China: 1368–1953*, 1959.

U. S. Bureau of the Census, *Historical Statistics of the United States: Colonial Times to 1957*, 1960.

Borah, Woodrow, and S. F. Cook, *The Population of Central Mexico in 1548*, 1960.

Sutherland, S. H., *Population Distribution in Colonial America*, 1936.

Spengler, Joseph J., *France Faces Depopulation*, 1938.

Connell, K. H., *The Population of Ireland: 1750–1845*, 1950.

Chevalier, L., *La formation de la population parisienne au xixe siècle*, 1950.

DEMOGRAPHIC JOURNALS

Population Index, Population Association of America, Princeton (since 1935).

Demography, Population Association of America, Chicago (since 1964).

Population Studies, London School of Economics, London (since 1947).

Population, Institut National d'Études Démographiques, Paris (since 1946).

Milbank Quarterly, Milbank Memorial Fund, New York (since 1923).

Population Review, Indian Institute for Population Studies, Madras (since 1957).

Population Bulletin, Population Reference Bureau, Washington (since 1945).

Statistical Bulletin, Metropolitan Life Insurance Co., New York (since 1920).

Le Démographe, International Union for the Scientific Study of Population, Washington (since 1955).

RELATED PERIODICALS

Annals of the American Academy of Political and Social Science, Philadelphia.

Human Biology, Wayne University, Detroit.

Eugenics Quarterly, American Eugenics Society, New York.

Eugenics Review, Eugenics Society, London.

Progress in Health Services, Health Information Foundation, Chicago.

Journal of the American Statistical Association, Chicago.

Journal of the Royal Statistical Society, London.
Geographical Review, New York.
*American Sociological Review, American Sociological Association.
American Journal of Sociology, University of Chicago.
Journal of Regional Science, University of Pennsylvania.
Social Forces, University of North Carolina.
Sociometry, American Sociological Association.
Economic Development and Cultural Change, University of Chicago.
Journal of Heredity, American Genetic Association.
Law and Contemporary Problems, Duke University.

SERIALS AND REPORTS

*U. S. Bureau of the Census, *Current Population Reports* and other publications.
*U. S. National Center for Health Statistics, *Vital and Health Statistics* and other publications.
U. S. Immigration and Naturalization Service, *Annual Report* and *I & N Reporter*.
*United Nations, *Population Bulletin* and *Population Studies*.
Scripps Foundation, *Studies in Population Distribution*.
Milbank Memorial Fund, *Proceedings* of Annual Conferences.
Population Council, *Studies in Family Planning*.
Official publications of many countries, states, and cities.
Reports by metropolitan and county utilities and large private corporations.

BIBLIOGRAPHIES AND COMPENDIA

Population Index, Princeton (since 1935).
Sociological Abstracts, New York (since 1953).
*United Nations, *Demographic Yearbook* (since 1948).
Eldridge, Hope T., *The Materials of Demography*, 1959.
Glass, David V. (ed.), *The University Teaching of Social Sciences: Demography*, 1957.
United Nations, *Multilingual Demographic Dictionary*, 1958.
UNESCO, *International Repertory of Institutions Conducting Population Studies*, 1959.
Zelinsky, Wilbur, *A Bibliographic Guide to Population Geography*, 1962.
United Nations, *Analytical Bibliography of International Migration Statistics: 1925–1950*, 1955.
Chasteland, Jean-Claude, *Démographie*. 1961.

Index of Names

✖ Index of Subjects

RALPH THOMLINSON is Chairman of the Department and Professor of Sociology at California State College at Los Angeles. Before coming to California State, he taught at the University of Wisconsin (1953–56) and at Denison University (1956–59). Professor Thomlinson's areas of specialization are population, statistics, research methods, and urban sociology. He has served as a city planner and researcher for the Metropolitan Life Insurance Company and the Bureau of Applied Social Research, and is the author of *Sociological Concepts and Research*. Professor Thomlinson received a B.A. from Oberlin and an M.A. from Yale, and was awarded his Ph.D. by Columbia University.